Contents

4. Materials and methods (cntd)

5. Greening the home

6. Greening commercial

7. Outdoors

8. Inspiration and help

9. Appendicies and index

Printed on Revive silk paper and board which contain 50% FSC certified and 50% recycled fibre.
Printed by Cambrian Printers, an FSC accredited company (TT-COC-2200): 01970 627111
www.cambrian-printers.co.uk

All web links in this book were checked and live as at August 2008.

Welcome to your future. Your future is green building!

Welcome to Volume 1 of the fourth edition of the Green Building Bible. As in previous editions, my aim has been to ensure that we compile a comprehensive snapshot of the 'green building' movement in the UK. With the help of many other willing and dedicated green building professionals and enthusiasts, I am confident this has been achieved with this edition. I am therefore confident that this book will serve well as your first point of reference in your trip towards greening your living and working spaces.

We have to learn how to live sustainably and we have to learn quickly. We have to remodel our living environments in such a way as to drastically reduce our burden on the planet. As each year passes by, not only do the opportunities to make a difference decrease but the repair task will actually get harder. However, every cloud has a silver lining. If fossil fuels continue to get more expensive then it will help focus the minds of those among us that weigh every decision they make against financial paybacks. Alternative energy generation methods such as PV and windpower will increasingly look more cost-effective. It could soon even become prudent to grow your own fruit and vegetables, generate your own electricity or cut your own logs for the fire.

There are no easy answers and many different paths ahead, but in this book (and its companion, Volume 2) you will find encouraging, practical and immediately useful hands-on information from both long-term green building professionals and enthusiastic newcomers to the movement. The fundamentals chapter will quickly introduce you to the main issues and what needs to be achieved. The 'trends and direction' chapter brings you a snapshot of the deep green and the mainstream green agendas - yes, to confuse you, they are different! Following these chapters the book goes on into the details of each particular subject one by one.

This is a big book and we have covered just about every subject area in some detail to help get you up to speed. However, to be sure you are not left wanting, we have included many references and suggestions for further reading and contacts, either at the end of each story, or in the appendices at the back of the book. We have tried to leave no stone unturned in this edition. If it is not in here then it is not green building!

Have you got Volume 2? If not, then I suggest that you get a copy. It goes beyond the introductions and gives you, in an easy to understand format, the science behind low energy and green building. The book includes detailed examinations and explanations of siting, building form, fabric, renewable technologies, environmental factors, lighting strategies, heating and cooling systems, energy management, monitoring and lots more.

Finally I would like to extend a personal thank you, to all those who have contributed to, and supported, the production of this fourth edition. You know who you all are!

Keith Hall

Keith Hall - publishing editor - keith@greenbuildingpress.co.uk

This edition would not have been possible without the dedicated commitment of two people - my wife Sally and my close friend Jerry Clark, who have both worked with their usual deep dedication and commitment, far beyond the call of duty, in order to keep to my tight deadlines. Also grateful thanks to my son Keith Jnr, for his tolerance of my mood-swings during the busy and stressful time creating this edition.

Finally, I dedicate this issue to the future in the hope that we can learn from our errors of the past.

Almost 60 authors!

There are profiles and contact details of all the authors that contributed to this book on page 462.

1 Primary goals

We need green buildings

Sustainability and quality of life are highly influenced by the buildings in which we live and work. At their best, buildings can be inspiring, efficient structures which facilitate health and creativity, and enable us to live in harmony with one another and the planet. **John Shore** opens Chapter 1 ...

Future building design should aim to cause the minimum possible harm to both users and the environment. This philosophy should be incorporated throughout the design, construction, use, repair and eventual end of life recycling of the building. Despite green and sustainable construction becoming increasingly popular, this comprehensive, cradle to cradle philosophy, is still not common currency.

Perhaps the first rule of a green building philosophy should be to avoid the desire to replace or abandon existing buildings as unsuitable without proper consideration. Secondly, adaptability and loose-fit are an essential prerequisite. For example, for any building to be called truly sustainable, it needs to be designed to be able to service the needs of many generations of diverse users. An adaptable building will be a loved building. Buildings also need to be part of a sustainable community infrastructure to really deliver their full potential.

Green building, as a concept, is straightforward and makes perfect sense. It means making thoughtful design choices and using ecological materials in ways that create quality, long-lasting environments with minimum damage to the planet. Natural ambient resources (sunshine, light, wind and rain) can and should be used for services - energy - heating - cooling - water etc.

Imaginative and enlightened building and community design is essential if we are to achieve this. Planning policy needs to adapt to our needs for wider, super-insulated walls, equal access to sunshine, decent sized gardens, green spaces and trees, space to work from home, a softer infrastructure and less need to travel.

We need to radically rethink our contemporary housing policy which is still based on simplistic, polarized thinking and out-dated concepts. Unsustainable and badly conceived development builds impoverished communities and long-term, usually negative social costs. People need supportive environments that are worth caring for.

Green buildings can provide us with an easy way to help combat climate change. New buildings can be designed to be zero-heat and zero-carbon in use. With the application of external wall and warm-roof insulation, most existing buildings need not be replaced and can make a significant contribution. For more energy-dependent buildings, efficient wood log, chip or pellet stoves can be used.

Cities and urban areas will need to be greened - less buildings and more nature, more localised fresh food production. Rural areas could benefit from sensitive development, so they become less isolated and more sustainable. Independently serviced (autonomous) buildings and neighbourhoods can reduce the need for travel and our demand for imported energy and expensive infrastructures.

Building to a green agenda now has widespread support and there is an increasing range of products and techniques to hand. Whether you are drawn to use timber from sustainable sources, straw bale or earth, lime-based renders, plasters and paint - or want to harvest the rain, sun and wind - you will find a good range of products and people who can help you.

Green buildings will soon become the new vernacular form, providing we are not afraid to design with integrity and use materials with a new honesty. Simple, economical forms require less materials, energy and maintenance. The ever-increasing centralised bureaucracy surrounding the building industry should be resisted and reversed, so as to encourage local solutions and greater diversity. High standards in construction are increasingly essential, but building regulation should not stifle innovation or make buildings unaffordable. Enabling affordable land release for self-build would be an ideal way to develop green building skills and lively, sustainable communities, while helping avoid the soul-destroying scourge of identi-kit houses. For green buildings to make a real difference, they must be practical and affordable. Cost-efficiency must be a pre-requisite for sustainability, because income generation always has environmental consequences. Green designs should not be overly complex or costly. If it's not affordable it's not sustain-

This zero carbon home in London is proof that even individual buildings in a city location can be designed and fitted out to be a positive contribution to the energy supply/demand mix.

Photo courtesy of Will Anderson
www.treehouseclapham.org.uk

able. We should design and build with integrity and responsibility. For instance, highly complex multiple-layer walls, or a wall or roof of south-facing double glazing may not be the most efficient or most sustainable building form. The technologies needed to make a building autonomous have always been tempting, but unless they are cost-effective, simple and reliable they may not deliver the intended benefit.

Unfortunately, many ordinary buildings have recently been badged as green or ecological without any real justification. This just causes confusion and sidetracks society from the goals that are most important. Simple, efficient buildings that enable us to reduce our ecological footprint are so much more important than being seen to look green.

Get the design right!

Always look for the natural, simple, efficient and elegant solution, rather than the complex, high-tech, design-victim approach so often seen on TV. Carefully designed, easy to build, robust buildings that are healthy to live in and perform well year after year, without causing harm to the planet, are urgently needed. We must rise to the challenge of climate change - but without having to resort to building with unecological materials! A building is not just a machine or a lock-up for our possessions, but something we intimately live with, care for and love. The key aspects to consider for a green building are listed below:

Reduce or eliminate

- site intervention, and unnecessary infrastructure; roads, street lighting etc.
- material and resource wastage
- toxic or highly processed materials and processes (paints, preservatives and components).
- heating systems that rely on fossil fuels
- electromagnetic fields from cabling.

Incorporate

- long life – low maintenance, robust and adaptable design, which fits in with, and harmonises with, the local topography and climate.
- ecological foundations and substructure
- super-insulation and thermal capacity
- vapour-diffusive structural elements and good airtightness
- natural materials and products
- energy conservation measures and renewable energy harvesting systems
- natural (passive) heating, lighting and cooling.

With the above in mind, be clear about your design strategy. A south-facing passive solar building will require a different approach to an east-west facing building. Houses which achieve a generalised U-value of 0.1 to 0.15 are often described as zero-heat, which means they do not require a conventional heating system. But even when combined with passive solar space heating they will still usually require small amounts of heating for short periods. The creation of a zero-heat house will require a thickness of 235-300mm of (air-based) insulation in the walls, 300-400mm in the roof and 200-250mm in the floor, depending on the properties of the other elements used. Any subsequent savings can be invested in a solar hot water system.

Good natural lighting and solar space heating can be achieved without massive areas of glass, which has high embodied energy. Glazing areas should be sized appropriately for the orientation, construction and type of building, together with the provision of adequate shading and ventilation to avoid summer overheating. Double glazing with a 1.5 U-value (frame+glass) is now more common and can be supplemented with low energy blinds. Insist on the use of non-conductive glazing spacers (such as Superspacer) and pay special attention to airtightness, the quality of seals, materials and fittings used for doors and windows.

Ventilation is an increasingly challenging area of design. We need passive systems that can provide adequate fresh air in winter, without uncontrolled heat loss in varying weather conditions, but can also provide summer cooling during heat waves. Why use fans, electronics, filters and pipes if there is a less resource-gobbling, natural solution?

New insulation materials that are denser than normal, such as T&G woodfibre boards, can perform a number of roles, insulating and reducing thermal bridging, delaying summer heat flow and supporting external render. To be effective, insulation must intimately fit without gaps. Expensive and easily damaged membranes can often be eliminated if care is taken to correctly build a vapour resistance gradient across the wall or roof. Ensure that internal materials and finishes are robust to provide thermal capacitance and also eliminate the need for wasteful renovation.

Water use can be reduced in a number of ways, but the simplest is by fitting aerating taps, showers and low flush toilets. Installing professionally engineered dry (composting) toilets may be a better water saving measure than installing a rainwater harvesting system to flush water closets, while also delivering infrastructure savings. More efficient use of hot water also means less water vapour to eliminate. For electrical and other services keep wiring simple and pipework compact and reduce or eliminate unnecessary pumps, boilers and techno-gizmos. Design to allow the easy reuse of materials in the future - buildings do not have to be irreversible.

Buildings have an unhealthy appetite for energy, and energy consumption is increasing, despite the introduction of more efficient technologies. Green buildings have the potential to become energy producers rather than just energy consumers. The key to making these systems cost-effective is to use them as part of an integrated design where they eliminate the need for conventional energy systems. There is still massive potential for the further development of energy-efficient appliances and for improving the way we live and work, which can reduce our energy use.

Solar and wind energy can be utilised at many sites and we should make better use of these independent, renewable resources. Using renewable energy makes us more dependent on climate and reduces our vulnerability to scarce, imported and increasingly costly fossil fuels. Driving down energy demand makes it much easier for a building to become self-sufficient by using ambient energy sources. The increasing demand for green electricity makes it essential and urgent that we harvest more renewable energy for export to the national grid. Solar water heating is one of the most cost-effective and reliable renewable energy systems at present. Photovoltaic (PV) electricity is looking ever-more competitive as electricity prices follow other fuels in an upward spiral. Easily mounted on the roof and walls of buildings, PVs are increasingly used to pump solar hot water systems and to feed appliances in buildings (often eliminating transformers) or for export to the electricity grid or for battery charging during times of excess.

Small-scale (but not building mounted) wind turbines still cost less than PVs and can work both day and night, but for best results they need to be mounted on tall towers away from trees or buildings. Quieter, slow-speed turbines are becoming available and some can be building-mounted (with great care!). However, be cautious and realistic, because urban wind-speeds are normally very low and turbulent, and some manufacturers are making unrealistic performance claims. There are even some turbines of questionable design and quality. Wind turbines of a suitable size can also be used to provide heat or pump water without the need for battery storage. If well designed and maintained, a wind turbine system can have a virtually unlimited life.

For both healthy living and quality of life, we need to green not just our homes, but also our places of work and our surroundings. We also need to drastically reduce our need for travel and change the way we work to enable more flexibility and the use of local, natural resources. And we urgently need to stop endlessly talking about it and actually do it now – because tomorrow may be too late. For a society that can develop spacecraft, micro-computers and mobile telephones this should not be too great a challenge? ☯

Reduce consumption

John Sauven, executive director at Greenpeace UK, wonders whether we can make do with less and still prosper.

The founder of Italy's Slow Food Movement, Carlo Petrini, recently criticised some environmentalists for their approach to changing peoples' behaviour. 'Our Western culture is rooted in Puritanism', he said. 'Environmental activists set out to win souls for their ideology with the same religious conviction as Calvinists. The path to a healthier planet would be forged through moderation and abstinence. That's a mistake. Who could be motivated that way?'

He has a point. Expecting the global environment to be protected by a kind of mass appeal to thrift is highly unlikely to work. On the other hand, it is clear that our increasing appetite for material things is primarily responsible for key environmental problems, from deforestation to climate change. It is also clear that the global economy in its current form, encourages, indeed depends upon, stoking that appetite further and further.

Increased material consumption is the lifeblood of the global economy – yet in promoting it we are making a healthy economy symbiotic with an unhealthy biosphere. Former World Bank economist, Herman Daly, puts it well: 'The most basic thing to understand about our global economic system is that it's a subsystem. The larger system is the biosphere, and the subsystem is the economy. The problem, of course, is that our subsystem, the economy, is geared for growth; it's all set up to grow, to expand. Whereas the parent system doesn't grow; it remains the same size. So as the economy grows, it displaces, it encroaches upon the biosphere, and this is the fundamental cost of economic growth.'

Simple maths indicates that this cannot go on forever – and all the evidence shows that huge damage has already been done to the Earth's natural systems, and that more will be forthcoming if we cannot retool our economy to fit within that parent system. When the United Nations conducted an exhaustive audit of the planet's health in 2005, even some environmentalists were surprised by the stark conclusions. 'Over the past 50 years', it reported, 'humans have changed ecosystems more rapidly and extensively than in any comparable period of time in human history... this has resulted in a substantial and largely irreversible loss in the diversity of life on Earth.' Among the casualties they reported were 20% of the world's coral reefs, 50% of wetland ecosystems, 30% of the world's mangroves, 70% of the planet's fish stocks - overall, 60% of the ecosystems of the entire planet 'degraded' by human activity in just five decades.

How do we square this circle? How to sustain a healthy economy without destroying the basis for it? One recent answer has been the explosion in popularity of 'green consumerism.' Some businesses, and indeed some environmentalists, have seen in this the path to planetary salvation. People increasingly express themselves through consumption, the argument runs: if that consumption is sustainable, everyone is a winner. It is an alluring argument, and certainly buying 'green' products is better than buying destructive ones. But we need to question the notion that we can avert, for example, climate change by shopping, when the cumulative, worldwide effect of our material consumption remains enormous and hazardous.

Furthermore, green consumerism can create as many problems as it solves. Take the recent craze for biofuels. The idea of replacing fossil fuel in cars, which contributes to climate change, with fuels made from crop plants, which don't cause climate change, sounds like the ultimate example of green consumption – until you look further. From the USA to Indonesia, land that would previously have been used to feed people is being used to feed vehicles instead. And vast areas of irreplaceable tropical forest are being felled and burned; replaced with palm oil plantations, a primary biofuel source. As Greenpeace detailed in a recent report, such biofuels do not even reduce the climate impact of the fossil fuels they replace: in some cases, once the burning of forests and peatlands and the energy used to clear land for crops is taken into account, biofuels are worse for the climate than oil.

Such examples demonstrate that green consumerism is not enough. We need to recognise that the causes of our environmental problems are deep and systemic. They are about how we organise ourselves as a society, how we use and price resources, how we relate to the natural world as both producers and consumers. For this reason, solutions need to be deep and systemic too. Relying on individuals or consumers to power the change that is needed, in the necessary timeframe, is never going to be enough. Change needs to be led by the powerful actors in society, especially in business and government. They need to become part of the solution.

That solution is going to require two things. Firstly, that we consume smarter, more efficiently and with far less – if any – waste. And secondly, that we consume less. Less is a hard word for us to hear. We live in a society which tells us that more is always better – that less means poverty, privation and suffering. But there is no reason why reducing our consumption needs to lead, as many critics of the environmental movement like to claim, to poverty, a denial of 'choice' to developing countries or a 'hair shirt' mentality in the rich world.

Instead, we need to look at how society can use the tools available in both government and business to tackle the hugely destructive and wasteful way we currently use resources, from oil to plastics and from wood to steel. This requires a paradigm shift in governmental action, structural change, and long-term thinking by companies. As Albert Einstein put it, 'we can't solve problems by using the same kind of thinking we used when we created them.'

The challenge here for government is to put in place strict and well-enforced environmental regulations that encourage both consumers and businesses to clean up their act. Working with the market will be crucial, as will unlocking innovation and new technologies. Government also needs to ensure that its words match its deeds: talking about tackling climate change whilst building new runways and coal fired power stations, for example, convinces no one.

Meanwhile, a revolution in business practice is needed – one which some companies are already leading. Today, business aims at maximising returns for shareholders – which in turn tends to mean maximizing consumption of resources. We need to turn every business into an environmental industry: a lean, efficient, green organisation. This means applying new principles to every stage of the company's work: make more with less; design out waste; begin to decarbonise the energy supply. The ultimate aim should be clean production: zero carbon, zero waste, zero deforestation, efficient use of resources both in manufacture and use. Working together, government and business could achieve this, creating new opportunities and new sectors of the economy as they do so. Greenpeace will support the process all the way.

Perhaps at the end of the day, this debate about consumption is also a debate about our values. What do we want as a society? What are our guiding principles? Is the pursuit of economic growth the highest goal we have? Do we really regard the bounty and beauty of the natural world simply as a 'resource' to be turned into money? If not, we need to change things – and quickly, because time, for many of the world's ecosystems, is literally running out.

The French futurist, Gaston Berger, once said that the purpose of looking to the future is to disturb the present. It is only by being disturbed that we stand a better chance of shaping the future rather than being its victims. It is advice we would now do well to heed.

Climate change and peak oil

Professor Susan Roaf reminds us that the four greatest challenges that society faces are climate change, peak oil, resource depletion and pollution.

In 1988 the United Nations Environment Programme (UNEP) and the World Meteorological Organization (WMO) established the Intergovernmental Panel on Climate Change (IPCC)[1] to build scientific consensus around the facts and inform and educate policy makers on global warming. Since 1990 the panel has published numerous reports on how the growing accumulation of human-made greenhouse gases in the atmosphere is 'enhancing' the greenhouse effect, and how humanity can, and must, respond to climate change. In 1992, at the Earth Summit in Rio de Janeiro, the United Nations Framework Convention on Climate Change (UNFCCC)[2] was adopted. The treaty called for industrialized countries to take the first steps to prevent 'dangerous anthropogenic interference' with the climate by voluntarily reducing their emissions to 1990 levels by the year 2000. These voluntary measures have not proved effective, despite the fact that the Kyoto Treaty was ratified on 16th February 2005.

Climate change

The 4th report of the IPCC in 2007 is unequivocal about the rate and scale of global warming and the increasingly urgent need for swingeing 90% reduction targets over this century to stabilise climate change. The best model to date for doing this equitably, by apportioning everyone equal shares of emissions by 2100, is called 'contraction and convergence', and is proposed by the Global Commons Institute[3]. To keep climates stable scientists reckon we must reduce CO_2 levels in the atmosphere to below 450ppm (parts per million) but we are already at 385ppm and rising at around 2-3ppm each year. James Hansen of NASA now says we may have to return to 350ppm to avoid climate catastrophe by the end of the century[4].

Peak oil

Since the beginning of the industrial revolution we have relied on cheap coal, oil and gas to power our industry, transport and lifestyles. Unfortunately we have reached the end of cheap fossil fuels, and as the global consumption soars, global supplies are declining rapidly further driving up energy prices and hastening economic decline[5]. Britain will have largely run out of its own supplies by 2020 and then, being situated at the end of European supply lines, be increasingly dependant on fossil fuels from less stable regions of the world.

Resource depletion

The systems of the planet itself are beginning to buckle under the challenge of providing more resources for more people in a changing climate that threatens not only our vital fresh water reserves but also the plant and animal species on which we are mutually dependant for survival. There is currently concern that the greatest individual ecosystem of them all, the Amazon Basin, is on the brink of being turned into a desert[6]. As the ecological footprint of human beings goes up, the number of other species declines dramatically.

Pollution

And as the sheer scale of our plundering and processing of the earth's resources accelerates so does the scale of its pollution. The vast range of pollutants we generate contaminate the earth, air and water. Most food is grown using fertilisers, products are made by industrial processes and there are emissions from transport[7]. Today, nearly one-third of the World's population lives with chronic shortages of water, with chronic impacts on human health, agriculture and economic development. More than 1 billion people lack access to safe

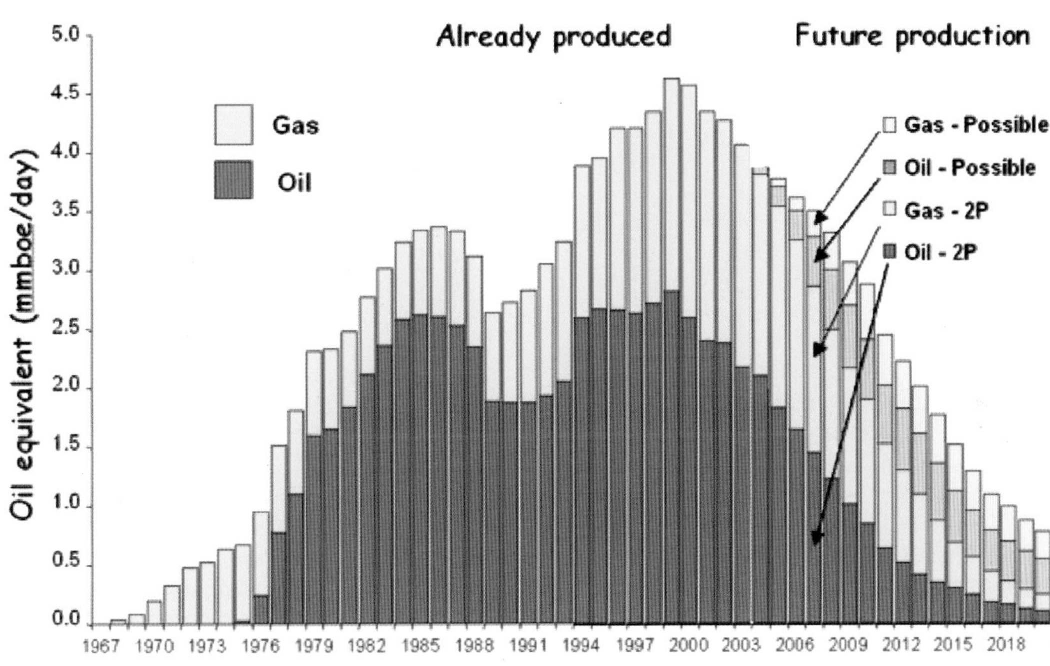

Produced and predicted oil and gas reserves for the UK.
Source: UK Department of Trade and Industry, via ***www.peakoil.net***

drinking water, more than 2 billion adequate sanitation. Some 6,000 children die every day from water related diseases. By 2025, nearly two-thirds of the World's population will experience some form of water-related stress[8].

The world is changing fast: extreme weather, scorching summers, catastrophic floods and soaring gas, electricity and petrol costs ring alarm bells for all of us. The discussions we had a decade ago of 'sustainability' have now become peppered with concerns about the more urgent issue of 'survivability '. We know what the problems are, we have the technologies and the understanding of what changes are necessary, but all we seem to lack is the will to implement the already prepared action plans for change.

References

1. *See:* ***www.ipcc.ch*** *An excellent recent book is 'The Weather Makers' by T Flannery, (2005), published by Allen Lane at Penguin Books.*
2. *For a full state of play on the climate conventions see:* ***http://unfccc.int/2860.php***
3. ***www.gci.org.uk/contconv/cc.html***
4. *The co-authored papers by James Hansen target atmospheric CO_2: supporting material (arXiv:0804.1135) and target atmospheric CO_2: 'Where should humanity aim?' (arXiv:0804.1126) are posted on* ***http://arxiv.org*** *the Cornell University research publication site.*
5. *See:* ***www.energywatchgroup.org/fileadmin/global/pdf/EWG_Oilreport_10-2007.pdf***
6. *F. Pearce (2006). 'The Last Generation', Eden Books, Transworld.*
7. *See:* ***http://en.wikipedia.org/wiki/Pollution***
8. *See:* ***http://en.wikipedia.org/wiki/Clean_water***

Build an eco-society

Professor **Sue Roaf** outlines how we can all play a part in building an eco-society, and at the same time a more 'sustainable' lifestyle for ourselves.

We have about eight years in which to build an 'eco-society' that is capable of putting the planet, the global common good and 'survival' at the top of its agenda. If we are to survive with our society and planet intact our challenge now is to build a society that values the good of the 'global commons', one able to drastically reduce consumption and greenhouse gas emissions, to adapt to survive the impacts of extreme weather without fossil fuels, to meet our needs from sustainable resources and minimise the pollution we inflict on the planet.

What would such a society look like?[1]. There would be a shared understanding of the values of an eco-society. An eco-society should, for instance, act as a protector, not destroyer, of the environment. It would be built on the fundamental values of equality, responsibility, respect for human dignity and our fellow species. It would recognise the importance of happiness, well being, quality of life, joy, health and beauty. The only way to build such values into our lives would be through the medium of thriving communities that work together to improve the lot of the individuals within them, based on altruistic actions, openness, truth and democratic politics. There would inevitably also have to be clear leadership and enforced adherence to strategies that limit the impacts of that society to levels that do not cause social or ecological devastation and that afford individuals within that society a fair earth share of the available resources. There would have to be rules. A new economic system would have to be built to support this society, one not dependant on the need for continual economic growth driven largely by the exploitation of the planet's resources[2].

Resources would have to be highly valued, both finite and infinite, by an eco-society where economy, with a small 'e', is paramount. It would be efficient, resourceful, innovative, capable of optimising system 'yields', calculating system capacities and allocating resources fairly. Resources would have to be efficiently shared, reused and re-cycled; renewable materials and energy chosen in preference to finite resources and waste minimised, with users employing conservation strategies in closed resource loops where possible. Non-toxic and non-polluting materials and processes are used where possible in a value-driven, sufficiency-oriented and native economy.

Buildings in an eco-society would enhance nature, the environment and the community and connect them. Buildings would be constructed to have minimal impacts on the eco-sphere and be designed to promote peace. They would generate their own energy, use local materials and be designed to provide shelter and comfort, even when the infra-structures of societies break down. They would keep people safe in the event of extreme weather events, and be robust and resilient enough to minimise the vulnerability of their occupants at difficult times. In America there is already a movement towards 'passive survival' buildings in which people could survive when centralised systems fail and the climate becomes even more extreme[3].

Citizens within an eco-society would be not only educated and self-aware of their own local impacts, but would also understand about how their actions impact on the rest of the world. They would thus be well 'connected' to others, and also more self-dependent than many today, who may find it difficult to cope with less money and energy. Eco-citizens will need to work to understand and minimise the impacts of their own life styles[4] and the impacts of the 21st century on them, understanding the dangers of debt in an unstable economy that may go into free-fall at anytime for reasons of oil depletion or climate chaos. Eco-societies promote communal activities singing, dancing, art, carbon-awareness with shared endeavour and enjoyment. Such citizens work together to build ideas, understanding and consensus in a secure and self-aware local, regional and global society.

This sounds like a very tall order but the extraordinary thing is – it is happening. Around Britain a huge number of different eco-communities are being formed. At one end there are villages like carbon neutral Ashton Hayes[5] and the increasing number of other CRed, carbon reduction communities[6]. Low carbon Wolvercote[7] in Oxford is one such village where the added benefits of an increasingly strong community spirit, built around the climate change agenda, were demonstrated when the village all but flooded in the summer of 2007 and everyone pulled together to ensure the most vulnerable were safe. Strong communities are resilient communities.

Perhaps the fastest growing of these movements is that of the 'transition towns', where a community works together to look peak oil and climate change 'squarely in the eye' and address this BIG question: 'for all those aspects of life that this community needs in order to sustain itself and thrive, how do we significantly increase resilience (to mitigate the effects of peak oil) and drastically reduce carbon emissions (to mitigate the effects of climate change)?' The transition town philosophy also recognises two crucial points[8]:

- the need to use the scale of creativity, ingenuity and adaptability employed on the way up the fossil fuel energy supply slope, to manage the descent down the other side
- the need to collectively plan and act early enough to create a way of living that is significantly more connected, more vibrant and more in touch with the environment than the oil-addicted treadmill that we find ourselves on today.

Communities as far apart as Totnes[9], Lampeter[10] and Stroud[11] have all risen to the clarion call of the movement, and with some remarkable results. In Stroud working groups have been set up in the town, dealing with a wide range of issues including energy, buildings and water, food, lifestyle and livelihoods, etc in what amounts to almost an alternative council for the town, working bottom-up, using the strengths of the few to build and grow resilience for the many. And these are just the first wave of the great change that will likely characterize the decades ahead.

I believe that the Green Building Bible has been at the forefront of the movement towards a more sustainable eco-society, and we hope that what you read in it helps you to build a stronger, safer world for your family and the community you live in. ☯

Sue Roaf, S., D. Crichton and F. Nicol published a book containing a fuller account of the issues outlined in this article. Adapting Buildings and Cities for Climate Change, Architectural Press, Oxford.

References

1. The section on 'Building an Eco-society' resulted from discussions at the 2006 summer retreat of the Society of Buildings Science Educators in the USA in Pingree Park in the Colorado Rockies in July 2006: **www.sbse.org**

2. See: **www.neweconomics.org**

3. See: **www.buildinggreen.com/press/passive-surviv-ability.cfm**

4. See: **www.bestfootforward.com/footprintlife.htm** *for a general carbon lifestyle calculator. For information on how to environmentally rate resources for buildings see many of the specialist sites on Google and also the chapter on materials in: Roaf, S., A. Horsley and R.Gupta (2004). 'Closing the Loop, Benchmarks for Sustainable Buildings', RIBA Enterprises, London. For low impact ecohousing see: S Roaf, M. Fuentes and S. Thomas (2007). 'Ecohouse 2: A Design Guide', Architectural Press, Oxford.*

5. See: **www.goingcarbonneutral.co.uk**

6. See: **www.cred-uk.org/index.aspx**

7. See: **http://climatex.org/wolvercote**

8.See: **www.transitiontowns.org**

9. See: **http://totnes.transitionnetwork.org** *and 'The Transition Handbook' by R Hopkins.*

10. See: **http://transitionculture.org**

11. See: **www.transitionstroud.org**

Decentralise our power

Localised energy provision needs to be a central component of any eco-society. Decentralising our power supplies would put people, companies and local communities in control of their energy destiny and democratise our energy future. **Leonie Greene** explains how we can do it ...

Architects, local authority officers, estate managers, farmers and builders are just some of the professions unlikely to avoid the pending sea change in how we generate and share energy. The outdated centralised system that dominates the UK poses a serious threat to our energy security. Greenpeace set out the case for a fundmental change of approach in its 2003 report Decentralising Power; An Energy Revolution for the 21st Century. The report explained that the centralised power system is the embodiment of technological inertia, performing little better today than it did in the 1970s. Almost two-thirds of the primary energy used to generate electricity is wasted in the UK's centralised electricity system (see below), mostly lost as heat through cooling stacks to the atmosphere, and in volumes that actually exceed the entire UK built environment thermal energy needs for space and water heating. And that's before the electricity is even exported to our staggeringly energy inefficient homes. In the face of climate change, this is indefensible – particularly since the knowledge and technologies to address this have been with us for decades. The current shocks to our global energy market, described in 2008 by Gordon Brown as greater than those of the 1970s, means we can expect renewed political vigour in pursuing a more secure and sustainable model of energy generation and supply.

In 'Decentralising Power'[1], Greenpeace argued for an end to this wastage and the now outmoded centralised power model and called for the delivery of an integrated energy system fit for the challenges of the 21st century. Since then, while the need to accelerate the deploy-

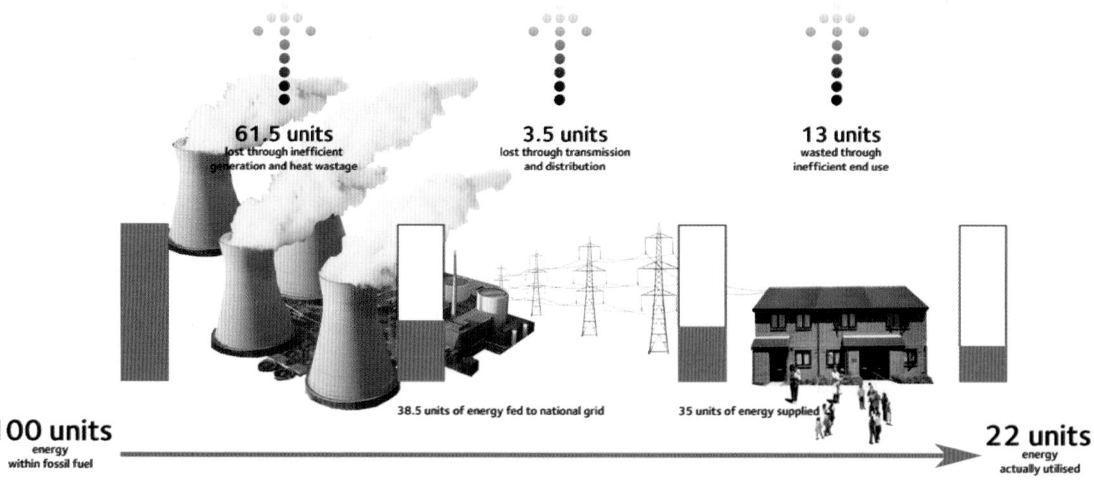

Centralised energy infrastructures waste more than two thirds of the energy available from fossil fuels. This accounts for more than 20% of the UK's CO_2 emissions. Diagram courtesy of Greenpeace.

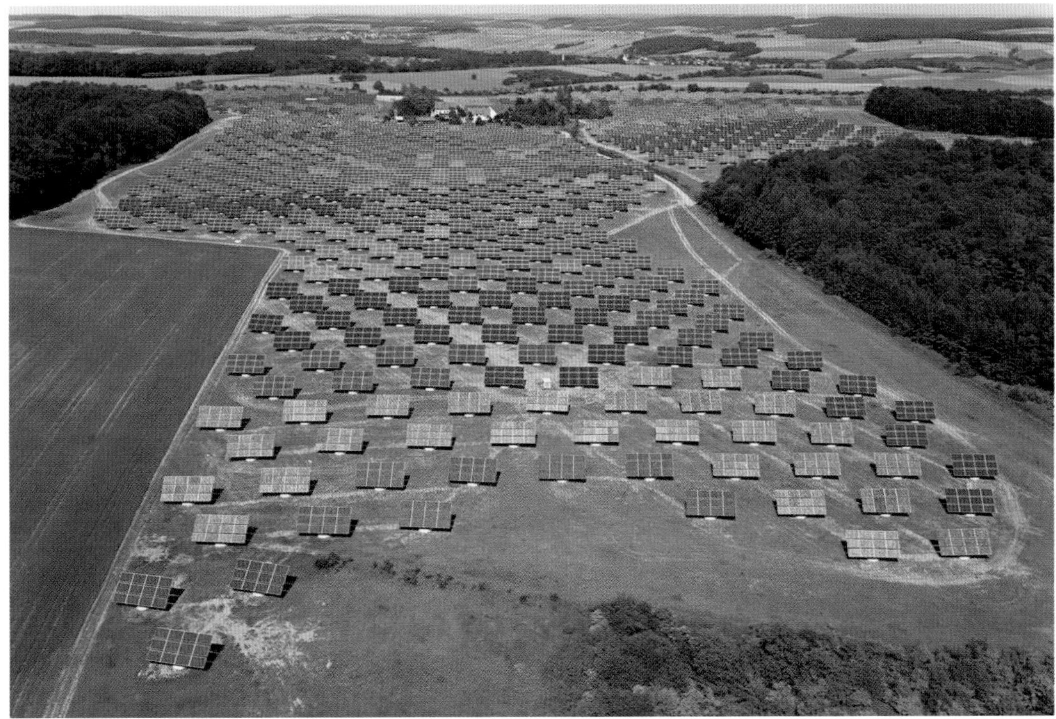

These solar fields at Eralsee in Germany demonstrate the commitment that other European countries are putting into the need for decentralised renewable energy sources. Photo: © paul-langrock.de

ment of large-scale renewables is essential to meet new EU renewables targets, it has also become widely accepted that a sustainable system also means the expansion of decentralised energy (DE). DE presents an opportunity to deliver on all four key energy policy goals set out in the 2003 Energy White Paper, namely:

- improving security of supply
- tackling fuel poverty
- enhancing competition
- reducing carbon emissions.

DE is not a difficult concept. It is simply energy generated at or near the point of use. It can be heat and/or power from multiple generation methods of many differing capacities. With this in mind, the link with buildings, particularly green buildings, is obvious. Intermittent renewable technologies like wind and solar, can be coupled with other non-intermittent DE technologies, such as biogas or biomass CHP and tri-generation, or hydrogen fuel cells to develop localised - human scale generation systems, with the potential to dramatically reduce the contribution our energy system makes to climate change. The stability and effectiveness of this approach has been demonstrated in practice by the Institute for Solar Energy Systems (ISET) at the University of Kassel. In its ongoing experiment, called the KombiKraftwerk ('combined power plant'), 36 decentralised biogas plants are linked with wind, solar and hydropower installations. The project supplies electricity continuously regardless of weather conditions and in accordance with fluctuations in demand.

DE technologies suggested in the Greenpeace report include those you would expect; photovoltaics, biogas and biomass CHP and tri-generation and geothermal, wind, wave, tidal and small-scale hydroelectric power, dedicated heating technologies like ground source and air source heat pumps, solar thermal and biomass heating. However, the report also advocated natural gas CHP (or tri-generation) as a bridging technology. Through developing CHP closer to areas of high density heat demand (namely urban centres of factories) care can be taken to ensure that fossil fuels are used as efficienty as possible by ensuring waste heat can be put to good use, rather than lost to the atmosphere, Localised CHP and tri-generation plants have proven to be able to achieve efficiencies of over 90% and can offer a complementary energy profile to more intermittent renewable technologies.

There is also evidence that, in the medium term, a DE pathway may not actually be more expensive. For instance, there are many economic benefits to DE, like reduced skills training costs and reduced lead-in times to plant construction. Amory Lovins, in his book 'Small is Profitable'[12], lists over 200 economic benefits of DE but one of the most striking is that it obviates the need for massive future investment in hugely expensive, high-voltage transmission and distribution networks. The International Energy Agency estimates that the EU will invest some $1.35 trillion in electricity infrastructure to 2030, nearly half of which ($648 billion) will be spent on transmission and distribution networks. DE technologies simply do not require such expensive centralised infrastructure, since their energy sources are, by definition, close to users. They also offer the potential to engineer a highly dispersed and varied system which is more resistant to outages caused by faults, weather or even any (perceived) terrorist threat.

Power failures are not only stressful and potentially dangerous, but expensive. For example, they cost the US economy a staggering $80 billion a year. Moreover, the vulnerability of centralised systems is set to increase as a result of the impact of climate change, and our dependence on energy imports. Anyone living in Gloucestershire in 2007 will be well aware of just how close they were to mass evacuation if the local substation on the banks of the River Severn had been flooded. Gloucester suffered blackouts for many weeks, along with food and water shortages. It is alarming that our infrastructure was so ill equipped to cope with a weather event such as this – the kind of weather event climate scientists tell us will increase.

Just decentralising our electricity supplies alone will not cure all our ills. We need to couple this with vigorous demand reduction (energy efficiency). However, demand reduction measures and DE have a natural synergy; DE technologies can help drive energy efficiency at the point of use. When energy consumers choose to also become producers, they have an incentive to reduce their own energy demand to minimise their capital outlay on a generator and, in some cases, (e.g. biomass boiler) to reduce the running costs of generation equipment. The introduction of smart metering will allow for the reward of any renewable energy generated (see about the 'renewable enrgy tariff' further on) and will also give householders the information they need to change their levels and patterns of energy consumption.

Energy efficiency purists often bemoan the fixation with 'sexy' renewables like PV, but their undeniable appeal needs to be celebrated, embraced and harnessed in parallel with demand reduction. The silver glint of PV or a wind turbine in motion down the street brings home the reality of the renewables' revolution. Action by the built environment professionals, to bring renewables into the mainstream of their work, will help win hearts and minds and buy-in to the climate agenda as people increasingly encounter local low-carbon generation on their doorsteps, understand energy better and develop a sense of responsibility for their own energy footprint.

DE democratises energy. It offers a means to turn lip service into reality. Opening up the marketplace to DE will mean that local government would be able to actively participate in the reduction of CO_2 emissions in its catchment area – through the delivery of community DE schemes. Local political champions can emerge

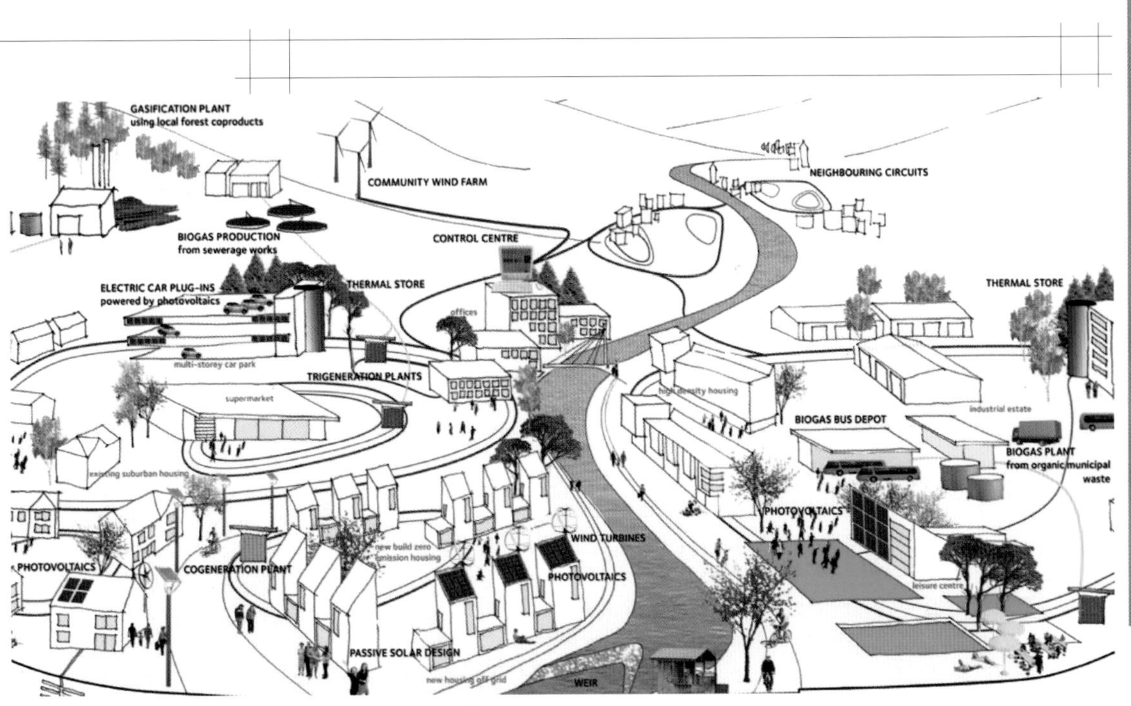

Above: a vision of a decentralised society where buildings and businesses generate and exchange energy on a localised grid network. All types of renewable energy sources can be incorporated, with dedicated co-generation and tri-generation plants acting as backup when wind and solar power is not available. Storage can also take place as hydrogen for powering fuel cells. Image courtesy of Greenpeace.

and put central government's less than impressive performance on renewables to shame. Crucially, devolving and democratising energy decision-making promises to curb the influence of hugely powerful, vested interest that currently have so much sway over policy.

DE is highly flexible; it allows solutions to be tailored to unique localities and budgets without first needing investment in over-specified, phenomenally expensive infrastructure. That is a vital consideration in developing countries where DE allows for piecemeal development of low-carbon energy infrastructure as skills and resources allow. Western governments face a considerable challenge to demonstrate, not just promote, a far more sustainable energy model than they themselves have achieved thus far.

Despite ticking all the boxes for the UK's stated energy policy goals, barriers to DE remain immense. Market liberalisation rests on the unspoken presumption that expensive centralised infrastructure should be taken as given in the UK electricity markets, where meaningful competition thrives only at the wholesale level. What that means from the consumer perspective is the only real choice is between different providers of centralised power. The regulatory regime acts as a ring-fence around the business as usual model. Far from supporting technological advances and market innovation, the UK model serves to entrench an outdated system, because it perpetuates and rewards the characteristics of old technologies. Smaller scale DE is effectively excluded from a market place into which its model simply doesn't fit. Under a DE scenario, a million consumers of energy are also a million potential suppliers. A whole new regulatory and market regime is therefore needed, that is responsive to the needs of the small and innovative.

The lack of any such framework is painfully predictable, given the bizarre misalignment between the electricity regulator Ofgem's remit and the government's repeated rhetorical commitment to a sustainable energy system. Ofgem's primary remit is still to protect short-

Below: the vision in action at Bo01 at Malmo, Sweden. Solar thermal and PV systems are mounted on many of the buildings and a nearby offshore wind turbine links into the local grid.

term consumer interests - no one needs a crystal ball to predict the outcome. The government's failure to correct this misalignment, in turn, surely reveals its fear of implementing the radical changes needed in the energy sector to put us squarely on a low-carbon trajectory. Government's readiness to embrace the Kingsnorth application for a new coal-fired plant gave the starkest illustration of the gap between rhetoric and reality.

Readers may be familiar with the oft-referred[3] local low-carbon network set up by Woking Borough Council. Woking overcame many of the barriers to DE through the use of private electricity wires. These are relatively cheap to lay – particularly in a new build situation. Yet, it is only very recently that the regulator has sought to tackle the regulatory barriers to the use of private wires. Increasingly local authorities and regional governments are seeking to take control of the impacts of their energy footprint. Kirklees is another notable example with its huge installed PV capacity and it hands out free insulation to households.

Since the publication of Decentralising Power, and following sustained argument by Greenpeace and many other groups - notably the UK Sustainable Development Commission on the role of Ofgem, things are changing. The Conservative Party has taken DE up as its policy. Ofgem has initiated a major review into the regulation of networks, recognising that the regulation of Distribution Network Operators (who manage local systems) may have to change 'profoundly' to ensure they are incentivised to connect and manage the flow of DE energy. They are also undertaking a consultation specifically on DE. Furthermore, the detailed 'industry codes' that govern the system, are under review as it has now been recognised that currently the codes can work against renewables and DE.

The new EU renewables' target which aims to deliver 20% of Europe's energy from renewable sources by 2020, is extremely challenging for the UK and will require the accelerated take-up of every renewable technology available. It is the arrival of this target, together with growing political interest in the plight of DE, that has turned the current Energy Bill into something of an unexpected battle for the government. The Renewable Energy Association (REA), together with Friends of the Earth and allies, including the Home Builders' Federation and the National Farmers' Union have been lobbying for a 'renewable energy tariff', to tackle the exclusion of smaller renewables from the marketplace. Like the highly successful German system, the tariff would reward all smaller scale renewable generators with a simple fixed payment for every kWh of power or heat they produce. Unlike the renewable obligations, which has proved unattractive to many small generators and those outside the energy industry, the tariff is easy to understand and the certainty of revenue it provides installs confidence in potential investors.

Such was the extent of support for the measure in the Commons that 38 Labour MPs voted against the government and in favour of the measure, meaning the tariff prompted the biggest rebellion of Gordon Brown's leadership to date. In the Lords there is strong advocacy on all side for the measure and a likely chance of its reinstatement under the current Energy Bill. If successful the tariff clause would mean from 2009 we could see a proliferation of local renewable energy schemes. It would also assist the 'zero carbon homes' agenda, as the dramatic slump in the house building sector means greater financial support will be needed. At the same time there was also much political interest in the remit of Ofgem. Again, Lords from all parties are advocating strongly for an overhaul of regulation to ensure it supports, rather than hinders, renewables and DE.

There are strong reasons to be hopeful that since Greenpeace set out its DE vision in 2004, a UK framework to enable its realization is drawing closer. Further developments for DE since then include the Code for Sustainable Homes and the new Planning Statement on Climate Change, which broadly incentivises local DE schemes – although battles have been fought on whether the detail will deliver what is intended. Yet we cannot afford to assume that enough can be done in time. UK CO_2 emissions are still on the rise, with hope of government meeting its CO_2 reduction targets fading fast as the UK spirals into recession and a wholly predictable energy crisis. Furthermore, the science has moved on - avoiding 'dangerous' levels of climate change would involve a revolution in our energy systems on a totally unprecedented scale – even the International Energy Agency is sounding the alarm that radical action is needed immediately. We must hope that the record-breaking cost of oil will now focus the world's political minds on delivering the essential energy revolution. But we must do more than hope. Climate change is simply too important to be left to politicians and industry insiders but how can the people hope to grasp the nettle of the energy crisis when all the cards are being held by players outside the UK? DE can put power into the hands of people to act. And action is what is needed.

So from a vision in 2004, DE is now a very live political issue. Buildings' professionals have a particularly important role to play in ensuring we get the measures we need to turn DE into a reality and fast. It is vital that those outside the traditional energy industry recognize their potential importance in delivering solutions to climate change and demand of the powers that be they need to play the fullest part. We must take power into our own hands. ☯

References

1. 'Decentralising Power: An Energy Revolution For The 21st Century' (10mb - 74 pages) ***www.greenpeace.org.uk/files/pdfs/migrated/MultimediaFiles/Live/FullReport/7154.pdf***

2. Small is Profitable, A Lovins et.al. ISBN 1881071073 Earthscan.

3. Most recently: Green Building magazine, vol 17, no 4.

Further information

For more information on the Renewable Energy Tariff campaign please contact Friends of the Earth: ***www.foe.co.uk*** *or the Renewable Energy Association (REA):* ***www.r-e-a.net***

Interestingly, the publication (editing, page layout etc) of the Green Building Bible is done entirely using decentralised, (not-grid-connected) renewable energy.

This story was first published in Building for a Future magazine in 2004 but has been substantially updated by the original author to reflect developments since then.

Don't demolish - renovate

The government's 'brownfield' strategy has actually drastically increased the trend for bulldozing many useful and very serviceable buildings. **Adrian Birch** wonders where it will end?

A renovated building will have a number of advantages over a new build. For instance, the initial embodied energy expended in construction will be largely retained and less waste will be generated. Normally less energy is consumed in the process of renovation than would in replacement. The process of renovation would also normally be quicker than redevelopment, reducing site overhead costs and interest charges, and permitting earlier occupation and, in the case of commercial buildings, earlier income flow.

Planning permission and listed building consent may not be necessary, and where permission is required, the planners may be more sympathetic towards extension. Planning policies may be restrictive for new-build, which would need to conform to current policies on plot ratio, parking provision, height etc. Where a building is occupied, certain works can be done with tenants remaining in place and disruption to tenants can be minimised if the work is properly planned, with noisy operations being carried out during reasonable hours. Overall, this can be cost-effective for both owner and occupier.

There are several levels of renovation possible. These may include fabric repairs and consequential making good. Upgrading of common parts - toilets, lift, reception. Aside from the common desire to sweep aside and start afresh, and the misplaced encouragement of the government for building on brownfield land[1], the replacement of existing buildings may seem the best option if the building requires major repairs, underpinning etc, or contain asbestos or other 'deleterious materials'. Other problems may be that existing mains services are inadequate, such as drainage systems but buildings, especially robust ones, are highly adaptable and, from an ecological perspective, all possible renovation avenues should be examined before demolition is considered.

Do a feasibility study before demolition

Before financial commitment is entered into, a feasibility study should be prepared by a suitably experienced person or organisation and should, ideally, encompass all or most of the following if possible:

- cause of obsolesence
- change of use
- design and use constraints

Buildings get demolished for a variety of reasons.

Excuse	***Reason***
Unsound structure	*Physical deterioration of the structure and fabric*
Not fit for purpose	*The original purpose no longer exists*
Obsolete	*Does not perform as well as modern alternatives*
Location	*Often as a result of infrastructure changes*
Economics	*When occupation is not the cheapest alternative*
Socially and legally	*As a result of changes in legislation*

Only when this and other financial information has been collated can risk be assessed. Further detailed investigation of the structure and fabric may be necessary. The feasibility study should attempt to demonstrate a comparative analysis of the renovation or redevelopment options, when time and other factors are included.

Obsolescence

It is important to identify the original causes of obsolescence at the outset, to ensure that the renovated building does not perpetuate the original shortcomings. If a building is to be retained and renovated, it may be necessary to look at a change of use as the only way to overcome obsolescence.

Change of use

30 years ago there was a trend to convert elegant town houses to office use. Today the trend is reversed. With the ongoing demand for new housing, offices in secondary locations may be more valuable if converted to residential use. The corresponding growth in higher education has also created a demand for student housing and it is no coincidence that, in many university cities, redundant offices have been converted to student accommodation. Increased inward tourism has also generated demand for budget hotels in many cities. Again redundant offices may be suitable for such a change of use, where strong demand exists.

The planners should be consulted early

Below: this building was successfully renovated to high ecological and energy efficiency standards.

in the process to determine their views on a change of use before following this route. There are particular issues regarding fire resistance, compartmentation and means of escape in case of fire, that must be addressed, as well as matters such as car parking, amenity space, availability of food shops etc. When assessing offices for renovation or redevelopment the change of use option must not be ignored.

Design constraints

Apart from major defects to the structure or fabric, one of the main constraints upon renovating existing office buildings is the floor to ceiling height. In 60s and 70s buildings the height was usually less than 3 metres, with concrete downstand beams reducing the effective height to no more than 2.7 metres. It is virtually impossible to fit traditional ducted ventilation and air conditioning systems at ceiling level, and provide an adequate raised access floor, whilst maintaining a floor to ceiling height of 2.6 metres in the occupied zone.

Some renovation schemes incorporate ducts externally or have extended floors outwards to permit ducts to be incorporated at the building's perimeter. Alternatively, localised heat pumps or fan-coil systems (fan assisted heat exchangers) can be used, relying on heated and chilled water to serve ceiling or wall-mounted cassettes to temper and recirculate the air in a space. An alternative is to use the raised access floor as a huge duct or plenum, with floor-mounted fan coils.

All these traditional approaches require heavy investment in fans, ducts and chiller plant. Where buildings can be naturally ventilated, this has to be the best option. Many renovated buildings are 'mixed mode' buildings where mechanical ventilation is used to assist the natural ventilation as required. This is cost-effective in winter if heat reclaim systems are incorporated. These do not have to be complex and many 'through the wall' fans can incorporate heat reclaim devices. Summer cooling can be a problem, but 'packaged' air conditioning systems should be avoided as they consume excessive amounts of electricity. However, they may be justifiable where there are isolated areas of internal heat gain, such as office equipment spaces.

Environmental assessment tools

An initial comparative analysis can be undertaken using software produced by the BRE (**www.bre.co.uk**). This is free to use and provides ecopoints for each strategy adopted. It is relatively simple to use and will give a relatively simple printout. For other tools see the Green Building Bible, Volume 2.

The BRE Environmental Assessment Method, (BREEAM) has been in use for 14 years and provides a more sophisticated approach. This applies to new and renovated buildings, as well as empty offices and is divided into two main sections: 'design and procurement', and 'management and operation' (**www.breeam.org**). This provides designers with a more detailed checklist. The design will be externally assessed and, if receiving an 'excellent' rating, a renovated building may compete more favourably with a new building. It is difficult to obtain accurate information on how many projects are assessed in this way. It was designed by BRE to help market energy efficient buildings, but has yet to be universally adopted by developers and owner-occupiers. All government projects are assessed, and it may be that all non-domestic buildings exceeding 1000m^2 will require such assessment as part of the new EC Directive.

References

1. The National Brownfield Land Strrategy: ***www.englishpartnerships.co.uk/brownfieldstrategy.htm***

Further reading

'Creative re-use of buildings', two volume set by D Latham.

'The Survey and Repair of Traditional Buildings – a sustainable approach' by R Oxley.

'McKays Building Construction' is invaluable for tradtional building techniques. This classic (originally 3 volumes)has been re-published in one book.

The above books are published by Donhead: 01747 828422 ***www.donhead.com***

Regular discussion on the appropriate maintenance and repair of old buildings goes on at the Green Building Forum, which is a free internet resource: ***www.greenbuildingforum.co.uk***

Renovate with care

"The contribution of the existing building stock is immensely important and we need to better understand our traditional buildings before we attack them with modern materials and techniques", says **Richard Oxley** ...

If we are to make any real progress in the reduction of carbon emissions from the existing building stock, all improvements must be carefully thought through. Real and effective improvements can only be made when you have an understanding of the building that you wish to improve. The first step to take, is to recognise the age and construction of your building. For example there are significant differences between older and modern buildings, such as the materials and methods of construction, which affect how the buildings perform.

Currently around 20% of the existing building stock in England and Wales pre-dates 1919. Most of these will be of a solid wall construction, of which it is estimated one million are listed buildings or situated in conservation areas (where modification or improvement may need permission). With older buildings the history of alteration and changes in the materials of repair will influence the methods that will best be employed when considering improving the thermal performance of the building.

These older buildings, with solid walls, will have been built with permeable fabric (stone, earth and brick) that both absorbs, and desorbs (through evaporation) moisture - a breathing building.. This is in contrast with many modern buildings, that are constructed with impermeable materials, designed to exclude moisture, for example physical barriers, cavity walls and damp proof courses. The significant difference in the performance between traditional and modern buildings makes it crucial that the materials and methods of construction and the intended performance of a building, together with the way in which the construction, and intended performance may have been modified over time, are identified and understood.

Damp certainly influences the manner in which improvements should be made. The presence of high levels of damp in a wall lowers the thermal resistance of masonry and increases the risk of decay, as damp conditions provide an environment where rot and wood boring insects can thrive. The introduction of impermeable materials and barriers, such as cement plasters and vapour checks, will change the performance of the building and likely introduce new problems.

In a building where the traditional performance has been detrimentally changed, the levels of damp can no longer be 'controlled'. The ability of moisture to readily evaporate has been removed. The well-meaning, but damaging repair with impermeable materials, introduces an environment where damp and decay causes problems for the condition of the building, the health of the occupants, or exerts a negative influence on the environment.

A failure to identify and distinguish between old and new, creates a dichotomy for older buildings, where improvements that rely on modern materials can cause physical damage and / or accelerate rates of decay. This can lead to the loss of irreplaceable fabric, where there is an adverse change in the traditional breathing performance.

Special value and special interest

As a society we have identified a group of buildings as being culturally important, as deserving statutory protection to assist in their preservation. Within the UK these buildings are protected by their status as listed buildings or by their situation in conservation areas. Does this formal recognition make the other older buildings, mentioned earlier, more vulnerable to inappropriate and damaging work, than the minority that are protected?

Older buildings can have a 'value' that modern buildings will not have yet attained. This 'value' can be described as the special interest of a building. Each individual building will have its own particular qualities that contribute to this interest; these may be attributable to any one, or a combination of age, type, method of construction, style of the building, together with any association with famous people, events or designing architect.

Any damage to, or loss of, fabric will only act to devalue or detract from the interest of a building, with the loss of a building diluting the character and appeal of its surrounding environment. It is not just the economic value, or the level of embodied energy, but the fact that in many instances, fabric lost can never be replicated in the same manner or to the same standard, no matter how much we try. It will never be authentic. The workmanship, skill and knowledge of the craftsmen who constructed and repaired those buildings needs to be included in any assessment of the value of traditional buildings. Although difficult to quantify, it is an essential part of what makes old buildings special; it is an integral part of their cultural embodied value.

The investment of embodied energy of the building fabric, and the cultural embodied value of the knowledge and information contained within these buildings, provide us with a tangible link with our past. A link that, in most cases, is highly functional and that can continue in beneficial use, if allowed to perform as intended and is improved, repaired and maintained in a sympathetic manner.

Many traditional buildings can provide excellent role models for new buildings that strive to be sustainable in their design and construction. Attitudes to how buildings should function are coming full-circle. The benefits of 'breathing' buildings are no longer exclusive to traditional buildings. 'Breathability' is now a high profile benefit upon which many new materials and systems are marketed; for example the renaissance in lime-based mortars, limecrete, hemp and earth building and the extensive use of vapour permeable roof membranes.

Adopting an informed approach

Acknowledging the difference and value that older buildings offer suggests that we need to approach their 'upgrading' in a philosophical and rational manner, to fully consider the implications of one's decisions before acting. The case for preservation, rather than restoration, was developed during the nineteenth century, with John Ruskin's 'Seven Lamps of Architecture' laying much of the foundations of the philosophy that is in use today, both in building and environmental conservation. William Morris developed Ruskin's theme of sustainability to arrive at the tenet that we are only trustees for future generations. Certainly, tastes and values change over time, as do the pressures for change. For this reason great care is needed to avoid the loss or dilution of authenticity, physical loss or accelerated decay, as this could prejudice the functional use and enjoyment of buildings by future generations, who may come to place a greater value on them, whether for their architectural or historic merit, or because they contain resources that are no longer available.

How to - or rather - how not to!

If you do not understand the building you are working with, and which materials are compatible, then your efforts could cause more problems than they will solve. For example, the impact that a simple repair, using inappropriate materials, can have on the performance and condition of a traditional building can be illustrated where a lime-based mortar is raked out and re-pointed with an impervious cement mortar (see photo above right). Simple everyday responses like this can expose a building to irreparable damage. Not only can serviceable fabric and evidence of previous finishes be lost but also the appearance and presentation can be changed, as well as the long-term performance of the building – which will eventually affect its structural condition and the rates of decay that will be suffered.

This photo shows frost damage to the bricks from the use of hard cement mortar pointing which has caused water to be retained in the wall.

The very real need to introduce insulation is a recent phenomenon that was initially driven by fuel prices in the 1970s, and now measures to mitigate global warming. The energy performance of the existing building stock has, with justification, been targeted for vast improvement. The potential conflict between energy conservation policies and the conservation of the historic environment is of concern and there needs to be a balance to prevent either being overtly compromised.

Introducing insulation and increasing air-tightness levels to traditional buildings, in particular to the levels required to make the savings needed, has not yet been proven over time. We do not yet know the long-term implications of introducing insulation to buildings that were constructed and designed without insulation or airtightness in mind. The real dangers of introducing inappropriate materials to solid walled buildings have not yet been fully appreciated by those advocating the external insulation of solid walled buildings with systems that use cement-based renders. The use of a cement-based render will impair the ability of solid walls to breathe, and increase the levels of damp within the wall and put timbers in contact with the wall at increased risk of decay. There are similar issues with the introduction of internal insulation, which needs considerable care and attention to detail if it is to be effective and does not create new threats to the condition of the building.

Conclusion

It is imperative that improvements made to the existing building stock, to improve their energy efficiency, are based upon an understanding of the buildings in question, if previous mistakes in the management of these buildings are not to be repeated. To mitigate the risks associated with the introduction of insulation and increased air-tightness to buildings we must learn from past mistakes and not introduce improvements that will shorten the service life of the building. The lessons learnt by those in the field of building conservation have to be heeded and solutions need to be devised that are appropriate for the traditional construction and that also improve the thermal performance of these buildings.

Many traditional buildings that survive today have only done so because they have adapted and changed over time, to meet the demands and requirements of subsequent owners and users. This flexibility has allowed existing resources to continue in use, without creating the demand for much further investment in materials. These qualities are the very virtues of sustainability. We have a duty to pass these buildings on in a serviceable condition by making real and effective improvements.

Further reading

'The Need for Old Buildings to Breathe' by P Hughes, Information Sheet 4, The Society for the Protection of Ancient Buildings (SPAB), Spring, 1986.

'Seven lamps of Architecture' by J Ruskin, most recently published in 1998 by Kessinger Publishing ISBN: 076610716.

'The Survey and Repair of Traditional Buildings – a sustainable approach' by R Oxley and published by Donhead Publishing: ***www.donhead.com***

The English Heritage website provides information to help those who own or manage houses built of traditional construction understand more about the potential impacts of climate change and ways to save energy: ***www.climatechangeandyourhome.org.uk***

Design for good health

Designing buildings to be healthy environments appears to be quite far down the scale of importance for most architects and builders. **Chris Morgan** wonders why ...

Why we fail to design healthy buildings is strange for three reasons. Firstly, pollution is conceived largely in terms of 'out there'. Many people believe that pollution is a problem of the outside world in the wider environment but there is little grasp or even a desire to grasp the effect that indoor pollution is having on us, personally.

Second, whilst awareness of health and of healthy lifestyles is quite advanced in our culture; gyms, vitamin pills, organic food and alternative therapies, all attest to a broad appreciation that our health is not all it might be, and yet the places where we spend the vast majority of our time, homes and workplaces seem to escape any critical analysis beyond the most immediately apparent.

Third, there have been scares. Most people now know that asbestos is dangerous, like lead in paints and pipes, and the media have picked up on concerns about electricity pylons, chemical treatments for rot and others. But like most things, these are considered isolated cases, and few recognise that we live in a generally harmful built environment. The rise in awareness of 'sick building syndrome' has made some headway in this regard, but to most people it is still not an issue.

And yet those who investigate the subject are shocked to discover the extent to which we have exposed ourselves to a wide range of untested combinations of known carcinogens, mutagens and other harmful elements, and in such close proximity to ourselves and our loved ones.

There is some resistance to such investigations. Manufacturers are understandably reticent about any possible health risks associated with their products, and it is notoriously difficult to make clear links between symptoms and the plethora of possible causes. However, a great deal is now understood about what is likely to be both good and bad for health, and it is possible to design and build homes and workplaces which are broadly free from pollutants and actively beneficial in supporting the health and comfort of occupants.

What are the pollutants in our buildings?

Many pollutants have nothing to do with the building. Smoking is a significant pollutant, as are the many external fumes and particulates which can come in through open windows and air entry systems: agricultural spray drift, car and industrial process exhaust fumes, dust and pollen. Then there is electromagnetic radiation from pylons and cables, and even radon from the ground itself in some places. Clearly there is a limit to what can be done to avoid these pollutant sources, but in some cases, the addition of 'buffer' spaces filled with plants and water, acting as conditioners for the incoming air can help.

Airborne risks

Some years ago, research in Denmark showed that the biggest source of pollutants in offices was not occupants, not smoking, not even the off-gassing of materials, but the air intake ducting, machinery and process itself. In other words, the equipment specifically installed to keep the air clean and healthy was the single biggest polluter. In most UK homes this should not be an issue, but it is relevant and worth further investigation wherever there is a forced air supply - something to watch out for as more homes get mechanical ventilation systems fitted.

Electricity

The radiation effects of electrical equipment and cabling are much debated, but the links between electrical fields and electro-magnetic fields (commonly known as EMFs) and health are becoming harder to ignore, particularly where high voltage is involved. Electric fields are produced whenever there is a voltage (for example, in an electrical appliance and the cable to it, even if it is switched off), while electro-magnetic fields are only produced when current is flowing – the appliance is switched on. Both fields reduce in strength with distance away from the source, so the most common advice is simply to keep a distance, for example, between the plug, cable and electric alarm clock from your head while sleeping (see boxout).

Electrical fields are quite easy to shield through the use of metal trunking or sheathing, but electro-magnetic fields are harder to avoid. The UK standard ring mains around buildings and rooms is one source of the relatively high magnetic field in a room and one way of avoiding this is to produce a 'radial' or 'spur type' wiring arrangement, but this can lead to more costly wiring installations. The UK is a long way behind other countries in recognising the risks attributed to electro-pollution. The main problem with ring mains is that they complete a loop and therefore create a large magnetic field inside each ring or cross rooms.

Fumes

Some of the most lethal pollutants are from incomplete combustion fumes from boilers and stoves, leaky flues, old chimneys where the masonry has deteriorated or flues where there can be backdraft in the wrong wind conditions. Needless to say, these should be checked regularly as a priority.

Paints and coatings

Decorating our buildings can be bad for the health of the decorator and longer term bad for the health of the occupants. Paint stripper, and most old paint is of real concern, and conventional paints and varnishes etc. are some of the worst offenders for environmental pollution in their manufacture, and in terms of their effect

Electrical and magnetic fields explained

Electric fields

Plugging an appliance into an electrical outlet creates electric fields in the air surrounding the cable and the appliance. The higher the voltage, the stronger the field produced. Since the voltage can exist even when no current is flowing, the appliance does not have to be turned on for an electric field to exist in the room surrounding it.
Electric fields around the wire to an appliance only cease to exist when the appliance is unplugged or switched off at the wall. They will still exist around the cable behind the wall.

- Electric fields arise from voltage.
- Their strength is measured in volts per metre (V/m).
- An electric field can be present even when a device is switched off.
- Field strength decreases with distance from the source.
- Most building materials shield electric fields to some extent.

Magnetic fields

Magnetic fields are created only when the electric current flows. Magnetic fields and electric fields then exist together in the room environment. The greater the current, the stronger the magnetic field. High voltages are used for the transmission and distribution of electricity, whereas relatively low voltages are used in the home. The voltages used by power transmission equipment vary little from day to day, currents through a transmission line vary with power consumption.

- Magnetic fields arise from current flows.
- Their strength is measured in amperes per meter (A/m). Commonly, EMF investigators use a related measure, flux density (in microtesla (µT) or millitesla (mT) instead.
- Magnetic fields exist as soon as a device is switched on and current flows.
- Field strength decreases with distance from the source.
- Magnetic fields are not shielded by most common building elements or materials.

Source: World Health Organisation (WHO):
www.who.int/peh-emf/about/WhatisEMF/en
Another useful document that discusses the risks of emfs can be found at:
www.cancer.gov/cancertopics/factsheet/risk/magnetic-fields

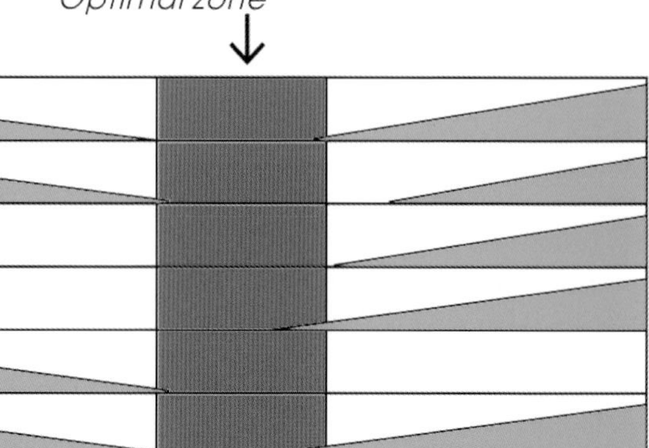

Relative humidity plays a major role in the health quality of any building. As the chart shows, most harmful agents avoid environments where relative humidity is between 40-60%. Too dry is little better than too humid!

on the health of occupants. The main concern is from the solvent fumes (as the paint dries). Even water soluble paints have some volatile organic substances and may need to be avoided by chemically sensitive people - certainly, advice would be to test a small area before using any paints. Natural, non-toxic paints are available and while some are more expensive, switching to these is one of the simplest ways of reducing pollution and safeguarding your health. Remember that painted or varnished surfaces occupy a very large area of our buildings.

Furniture and decor

A great deal of furniture and fittings contain toxic chemicals not only internally, but in the coatings which are applied to make them stain-free, fire-proof, 'low maintenance' and so on. Chemicals, such as formaldehyde, benzene and phenols are found in plywood and particle boards (chipboard and 'mdf'), plastics, resins, glues, adhesives, synthetic textiles, flooring such as laminates, vinyl, insulation, carpets, curtains and furniture. Many of these chemicals 'offgas' slowly over months and even years, and their effect can be traced in all areas of the body, particularly the nervous system.

Avoidance of furniture made from composite materials and large amounts of furnishings is the simple solution, so it makes sense to keep to furniture and furnishings which are as close to natural as you can find – linoleum not vinyl, real timber not chipboard, screwed not glued, oiled or waxed not varnished and so on. Common sense – and a dash of scepticism – can take you a long way in this regard.

Timber preservatives

One of the most insidious pollutants is the chemical treatment of timber, for example, in the roof rafters, or sometimes all over in the case of some timber frame buildings. Even in old properties, such treatment is rarely necessary. Merely for 'peace of mind', your property could be made thoroughly toxic to you, as well as the insects or fungi that are targeted. It is possible to avoid all chemical treatment of timber if the building is designed properly, and still ensure durability.

Humidity

The need to moderate humidity in buildings goes far beyond the risks associated with damp and mould, to well understood aspects of human health. Humans need a fairly balanced relative humidity of roughly between 40% and 65% (see boxout top right), outside these, there are very close correlations with increased health risks, as clearly shown in the chart above).

Central heating - is it healthy?

Most central heating not only warms the home but actually dries it out. This is good if the building had high relative humidity (RH) before the heating was turned on but bad if the building was already dry enough. Dry enough would be a RH of about 50-60%. This is just about as low as our bodies enjoy to stay healthy. Below this our mucus membranes can dry out and symptoms such as coughing, asthma, eczema and itching can begin to develop (see chart left). However if the background RH of an unheated house is naturally over 70% then any heating will work to reduce this and probably only to a level of between 55-65%. This would be perfect but we do not live in a perfect world and the background RH will actually vary depending on which part of the building you test. Just as over-dry buildings are bad for us, then so too are over-moist ones. At RH over 75% moulds and bacteria could develop and where the background moisture content is persistent, damp walls etc. then this, coupled with artificial heating can cause an explosion in bacterial or fungal populations. In short, heat + humidity = breeding ground for bugs. From this it becomes clear that a sensible heating level, somewhere between 18 and 20°C on most central heating thermostats, would lower the risk of over-drying of the room air and keep temperatures slightly below those where bacteria and mould might proliferate (the same advice applies to cold or flu viruses).

Air conditioning could theoretically help to moderate humidity but, like chemical preservatives, this comes with a possible health risk attached. It is possible - and preferable - to moderate humidity passively through the use of the building fabric and materials which naturally 'absorb' and 'desorb' (retain and release) moisture. Materials that can do this without risk of deterioration are known as 'hygroscopic' and can perform a valuable role in the design of healthy buildings. Clay is by far the most effective material for achieving this, but other natural materials like timber, lime and sheep's wool also work, as long as they are not coated with or contained within impervious materials.

Water

Increasingly, the water that comes into our homes is likely to contain, not only beneficial minerals and other 'impurities', but also a great number of potentially harmful pollutants such as nitrates, metals, synthetic (and some volatile) organic compounds, radon and controversial additives like chlorine and fluoride. For those concerned, various types of water filtration system are available, each tending to deal better with some and not other pollutants.

Creating healthy conditions

So for new designs, avoid the specification of timber preservatives, chemical paints and complex fit-outs. Also design electrical cable runs to be as far away as possible from busy 'people areas' and try to keep all cabling together in a single route to avoid creating an 'electromagnetic web'. In existing homes or refurb projects, once you have followed the preceding advice about pollution, the next step is to try to create the ideal conditions for comfort. Even without any pollutants, it is possible (and quite common) to design things so badly that the health of occupants will be at risk. The green building designer's job is to do the opposite.

Radiant and convected heat

In convection heating, air is heated when it comes into contact with hot surfaces. People feel warmer because of the higher air temperature. Some convection heaters use a fan to draw the cool air in. Conventional radiators are convection heaters whereby air is drawn from below the radiator, warmed and the heated air rises and creates a warming current.

In radiant heating, surfaces (including people's skin and clothing) are heated by warmth radiated from a warm surface or object. Radiant heat emitters cause a small amount of convection, but it is not the primary means of heating. The feel of the sun on your skin is the best example of radiant heating at work. Radiant heat emitters can be run at lower temperatures.

Heating

The health effects of heating are the least appreciated aspect of healthy building design. A great deal is known about the thermal efficiency of heating appliances, particularly amongst the environmental design community, but what about from the point of view of human health? In my opinion, the only healthy heating system is a radiant heating system. Let me explain. Human thermal comfort is far more than having a thermostat set at 20°C. The most comfortable thermal environment for humans will be created when the surfaces in the room (walls and floor) are a little warmer than the air, when the air is relatively still (not too many draughts, or convective currents) and there is sufficient thermal and moisture mass in the building fabric to moderate both temperature and humidity swings.

The conditions described above are almost impossible to create with any convective (warm air) system, and these systems may have a number of other disadvantages, which negatively affect the health of occupants, such as dust scorching on over-hot radiators. A low temperature radiant heating system, ideally at floor or wall level, not in the ceiling, is best.

Ventilation

Fresh air is needed to replenish the oxygen we use when breathing, and to exhaust the carbon dioxide we produce. The required ventilation rates in the building regulations have developed in order to account for other aspects too. Air extract is needed to cope with pollutants and odours produced by people, materials and services. Extract is also needed to deal with (excessive) humidity and is good for clearing out micro-organisms and day to-day pollution.

In a building with few pollutants and near perfect humidity levels, the need for ventilation is much reduced. Such high levels of building quality (usually passivhaus standards) are not recognised by the UK regulations yet, but the argument has been successfully submitted in Norway to reduce ventilation levels without health risk to occupants, and to save energy, both in servicing, and in heat loss.

This brings us to another consideration of ventilation; that in extracting air, we are usually extracting warmth, hence the rise in the use of heat exchange extract fans. Given the increase in fabric insulation levels, the percentage of heat loss through ventilation has increased and so these fans perform a valuable function. However, they are 'covert' convection heating systems and, again from a health point of view, might warrant further investigation.

Passive ventilation, vents that open automatically when there are high humidity levels, would be another way to deal with varying levels of humidity, though bear in mind that these do not control heat loss in any way.

Lighting

Too much artificial lighting has an ill effect on health. Natural light varies and in so doing keeps people connected to the natural passing of time, which is increasingly valuable as we now spend so much time indoors. If we design buildings with rooms that have windows in more than one wall, it will help us keep our natural balance, equilibrium and will help to enhance these changing patterns of daylight.

Bright, light surface finishes will reduce the need for artificial lighting, and when designing lighting layouts, it is worth ensuring that task lighting or mood lighting are considered separately. This can be more energy efficient and likely to be more pleasant to use and control. Lighting with poor flicker should be avoided. Daylight bulbs can be helpful to overcome the lack of daylight where this is unavoidable.

Noise

Excessive noise is obviously to be avoided, but low level background noise, often associated with machinery, and noise from sources that cannot be controlled, are considered to have the greatest potential to stress people and cause health problems. Many noises can be attenuated, but not all, and in many cases this can conflict with other requirements, such as the need for fresh air, so design strategies where noise is likely to be an issue, need to be considered early.

Plants

Plants can use the carbon dioxide we breathe out, and in return give off oxygen that we can use. Fresh air is largely 'fresh' because of the activities of plants in the wider environment, so it should not be surprising that by putting plants inside our buildings we might benefit. Beyond the carbon/oxygen balance, it has been found that some plants have an extraordinary capacity to absorb some of the pollutant gases which we produce in our modern lifestyles, so their use will have benefits, especially in office environments. Plants (and the earth in which they tend to be planted) can also help to moderate humidity, so should have a more important place in our homes, beyond 'looking nice'.

Conclusion

Prioritising issues is important as it is easy to lose perspective. Everyone will have their own list, but consider the following as a starter:

- we spend a lot of time asleep, in one place. Sleep is the body's time for recuperation on a number of levels. If you can only make one place 'healthy', make it the bedroom
- children, whose bodies are developing quite differently from adults, are at much greater risk from the effects of toxins. They also spend more time closer to the floor than adults, so pay particular attention to floors and children's bedrooms
- arguably the worst offender for health in many people's homes can be the unassuming wall to wall carpet, not only because of the materials and treatments it contains, but its capacity to store dirt and harbour dust mites and their faeces. Beyond steam cleaning, if you are experiencing health problems and suspect carpet, replace with wooden floors, linoleum, tiling or similar. Smaller rugs which can be washed do not tend to pose the same risk
- the great majority of applications of chemicals for protection against infestation, rot, mould and so on are unnecessary. If you have a problem, consider contacting a specialist (not one trying to sell you a chemical treatment) who will probably be able to assess the situation independently and offer remedial solutions, such as better ventilation, better drainage and so on, without the need for chemicals.

Finally, a word or two on perspective. The famous poet, Wendell Berry wrote that "*No place can be considered healthy until all places are healthy*". This serves to remind us of the interconnectedness of these things, and of the fallacy of describing a house as 'healthy', particularly when you cannot control the way in which a building will be used.

Studying buildings and health can turn you into a sort of building-related-hypochondriac. One cough and you begin to eye the skirting boards suspiciously, whereas there may just be a virus going around at school. If you live an otherwise healthy life, it is likely that you will survive your home and workplace, but as with most things, why take the risk, when there is a much more comfortable and healthy way to live?

Pollutants in the air are absorbed through microscopic openings in leaves called stomata.
Water vapour is emitted into the atmosphere from plant leaves through a process called transpiration.
Convection currents set up by leaf transpiration transport pollutants to the root zone.
Root microbes (e.g., Pseudomonas sp.) biodegrade the pollutants into structures that can be used as a source of food for the microbes and the plant.

Image Copyright Bill Wolverton, 1996. Eco-Friendly Houseplants, published by Seven Dials.

Further reading

'Ecology of Building Materials' by B Berge.

'The Whole House Book' by C Harris and P Borer.

'The Natural Plaster Book' by C Rose Guelberth and D Chiras.

'The Toxic Consumer; how to reduce your exposure to everyday toxic chemicals' by K Ashton & E Green.

'Using Natural Finishes' by A Weismann and K Bryce.

The above books are available from Green Shop Books: ***www.greenshop.co.uk***

Design for adaptability

Just like human beings, buildings need to be allowed to develop over time, to mature, grow and evolve; otherwise they often deteriorate and become obsolete. If they become obsolete then we need to ensure they can be reused. **Mark Gorgolewski** reports ...

In his very interesting book 'How Buildings Learn', Stewart Brand[1] talks about buildings that age honestly and elegantly over time. But to create such buildings we need to accept them as evolving entities, whose design and construction phase is just the start of a long process of evolution over their life. Yet this is alien to the current ways in which many buildings are designed and procured.

Design for adaptability

For most buildings, it is impossible to consider, or even to know, at the design stage, all the different potential activities and uses that they may be used for over an extended life. The modernist idea of form following function becomes redundant when we accept that a building may have many changing functions over its operational life, and that, even if it is used for the same purpose, such as an office building, for example, the nature of office work changes at such a pace that the building is likely to accommodate a variety of different activities over its life. All we have to do is think of the changing nature of work over recent years to see how the demands on buildings are changing.

Shifting business practices, new technologies, and new management processes mean that buildings quickly become obsolete. Employers want working environments that are closed and private one day, then open and collaborative the next. Spaces that cannot accommodate this frustrate occupants and hamper business objectives. Adaptable interior workspaces are essential for companies likely to face uncertainty and change as markets shift.

So how should building designers respond to this challenge? First of all we must get away from the glossy journal notion of buildings as style icons. So many buildings are photographed and reported in journals at the time they are completed, often before they are furnished and unoccupied. They are presented and analysed as abstract forms which are assumed to be at their best the moment they are completed, rather than functional and useful objects which develop, change and improve over time. There is little consideration of how well they actually work. Although recent interest in building performance, including 'probe' studies[2], increase interest in how buildings operate. Nevertheless there is little consideration by designers or critics of how well buildings work over time, and it is rare for an architectural magazine or journal to go back and look at how a prominent building is performing long-term.

Right from the start of the design process, there is a need to consider how buildings will perform and change over time. This inevitably requires that buildings can adapt and change over their life to meet new demands on their spaces, structures and systems. "*If a building doesn't support change and reuse, you have only an illusion of sustainability. You may have excellent building orientation and other energy-saving systems, but the building must also be able to be flexible to meet a change in curriculum.*" Croxton (2003)[3].

Buildings are complex assemblies of many

Before and after photos of the Sustainability Centre in Hampshire, where an ex MOD building received a much needed eco-facelift and new lease of life.

Photos by Tony Cohen.

different resources, with a large investment of materials, labour, and energy. A building which allows its parts to change with time will place a lighter load on natural resources, and provide better value to future generations. Buildings that are not adaptable, are destined to become lost resources more quickly. Adaptability takes advantage of the embodied energy of the components, as less processing or transport is required if a building's life is extended.

A building is more adaptable when it can be easily modified, extended, and strengthened to allow a new or changed use. So how can a designer help to achieve this? A method termed 'open building'[4] suggests an approach to the design of buildings that recognises that the contemporary built environment must allow for both stability and change. The open building approach includes the idea that the built environment is in constant transformation and that change must be recognised and understood. It recognises that the built environment is the product of an ongoing, never ending design process that includes many participants, including users / inhabitants making design decisions as well as professionals.

Key principles for adaptable buildings

- Minimize the number of internal structural components (columns and load bearing walls) and optimise structural grids to allow for possible changing uses of space. Use simple structural grids with clear support lines.
- Allow some redundancy so that additions and changes to the building can be accommodated. Over-designed structural capacity may be appropriate to allow alternative uses and the option of extending the structure. Ensure that floor loads used in design reflect foreseeable changes in occupancy patterns.
- Separate structure from cladding where possible to allow independent alteration and replacement.
- Allow for good vertical circulation by lifts and stairs, and for service routing.
- Separate services into clearly accessible locations to allow easy change and upgrade. Raised floors can also permit easy upgrade of services. Integrate heating and electrical systems so they can easily be upgraded or replaced. These systems generally require far more regular replacement than other components of the building. Some over-provision of flexibility in service routing allows for future upgrade.
- Design with a building depth to allow for daylighting of the main spaces, and for a variety of different ways to divide up the spaces.
- Provide a 'loose fit' to allow some redundancy to accommodate future additions/changes.
- Integrate finishes so they can be easily upgraded and replaced, without making access to other components difficult.
- Keep designs simple to help with future change; independent systems allow changes where necessary. Strong inter-dependence reduces the scope for change.
- Provide sufficient space for machinery needed for dismantling, renovation, and addition.
- Avoid complex composite materials that are difficult to separate. This includes some treatments and finishes applied on site.
- Incorporate each component so that it can easily be removed and recycled when obsolete. Use demountable internal partitions.
- Consider drainage carefully as this often limits changes to building plan.

Open building suggests that buildings should be separated into the 'base building', which consists of the more permanent parts, and 'fit-out' that changes more often. To achieve this, the connections between technical systems must allow easy replacement of one system, with another performing the same function. This approach allows the designer to consider strategies for both long term and short term change.

Early in the design process, the design team should try to identify what type of changes may take place and how these could be accommodated in the building. Through this process alternatives should be discussed and a range of possibilities developed that will help achieve adaptability. The possibilities will vary for each project.

Adaptable buildings should incorporate, at the design and construction stage, the ability to make future changes easily and with minimum expense to meet the evolving needs of occupants. It means designing a building to allow its different parts to change, each in its own timescale. Incorporating adaptability into a building during initial construction can save time, money, and inconvenience when changes are needed or desired later in the life of a building, and can significantly extend its life.

Design for deconstruction

Even adaptabilty has its limits and eventually even adaptable buildings will become obsolete. But that should not be the end of the life of the materials and components in the building. Designers can make it far easier for buildings and building componets to be reusable if they consider this at the design stage. Designers should keep in mind how the environmental and financial value of a building can be maximised at the end of its useful life and how it may be taken apart with the least damage to its useful components. In this way the supply of reclaimed components for reuse can be increased. "*Disassembly technology is the antithesis to the technology that put the building together in the first place. Simply by reverse running the process of construction (back to the manufacturer if needs be) and looking at the building and its constituent parts we may have far reaching consequences for the transition point of building demolition.*" (Wyatt & Gilleard 1994)[5].

Other industries are beginning to rethink how products are put together so that they can increase the usefulness and value of components at the end of their life. EU legislation is putting the responsibility for disposal of products at the end of their useful life on the producer - "*Reversible joints, upgradeable components, and materials that can be separated are all now being incorporated into the next generation of appliances. For example, Xerox, the photocopier supplier, has adopted the DfD (design for dismantling) approach. At the end of a photocopier's life or when it is superseded, it is taken back and 'asset stripped'. This basic disassembly frees many of the existing elements enabling them to form the basis of the new model.*" (Fletcher, et al 1990)[6].

Car manufacturers have been encouraged by legislation and competition to consider the end of life disposal of their products. Cars are now being designed to enable recovery of components on 'unassembly lines' and for easier replacement and reuse of worn parts. These companies have begun to realise that simpler designs, and assembly processed using less materials and components, in some cases leads to cost savings and the cars are more suitable for disassembly. Although the nature of construction, and the timescales involved are very different to most other industries, similar approaches may soon be extended to the construction sector, requiring producers of goods to take them back at the end of their life for reuse, recycling or disposal. Such a policy is likely to lead to more interest in buildings that are designed to be deconstructed.

Traditional demolition practices are generally destructive and usually result in damage to components, which are then only suitable for waste or recycling, but not for reuse.
As the economic value and the demand for reclaimed components increases, while the cost of disposal to landfill also goes up, demoli-

Components should be assembled using removable fixings, so deconstruction for extension, remodelling or replacement can be carried out without the need to destroy the components. This allows them to be available for future reuse. Such a strategy could also make access to hidden components more accessible should repairs need to be carried out.

Photo courtesy of Gaia Group

tion practices may gradually change towards deconstruction. This provides more opportunity for components to be extracted undamaged, suitable for reuse, with little or no reprocessing.

The lifetime of components in a building varies considerably, ranging from thirty years to several hundred years for the main structure, to perhaps only a few years for internal fit out. Often building obsolescence is reached because some components have reached the end of their useful life and they are difficult to replace, even though other components may still have many years of useful life.

Key principles for deconstruction

- Consider the actual process of deconstruction at the design stage and provide a deconstruction plan for the building.
- Ensure that accurate as-built drawings and records of all changes over the life of the building are kept in a building log book.
- Consider a building as a series of layers related to different life-spans of components
- Use durable components that can be reused again after removal.
- Ensure that individual components can be readily removed when necessary and maintained or replaced.
- Use simple structural grids with clear support lines
- Limit the number of parts, number of tasks, number of tools, and the time or degree of difficulty of the deconstruction tasks to reduce cost and time involved.
- Where possible use prefabricated components that are assembled on site and can be disassembled for reuse/recycling.
- Use appropriate fasteners and connections. Consider connections that can be reversed and avoid irreversible processes; reversible mechanical fixings such as bolts or screws can usually be removed, adhesives and nails are more difficult.
- Where possible use dry construction processes, which are more readily dismantled than wet construction processes.
- Integrate services with care so that they can be easily identified and removed.
- Provide sufficient space and capacity to accommodate machinery needed for dismantling.
- Consider who might be doing the reclaiming - the manufacturer or a third party? Do they need information or instructions such as disassembly or refurbishment plans or specifications for the qualities of the materials?

Deconstruction is the process of taking a building apart into its components in such a way that they can be more readily reused or recycled. It minimises the destructive aspects of the process of removing buildings, preserving components and materials, not wasting them. Designing for deconstruction means considering, at the design stage, how a building can be taken apart. Many temporary and relocatable buildings and structures around the world are already assembled using reversible processes. The same idea can be applied to new construction. Designers can increase the potential for deconstruction considerably by considering the building as a kit of parts that can be assembled in layers, so that each component can be removed at the end of its useful life.

In his book, Brand proposed a conceptual framework for layering a building, depending on the life expectancy and use of the components (see table on following page). Layers that have a shorter lifespan should be positioned to be easily accessible without impacting the longer lasting layers. The distinct composition of these layers creates relationships between building components, allowing for independent serviceability and an increase in deconstruction potential. Much waste can be avoided during maintenance and demolition by minimising the impact of one layer on another.

The serviceable life of the structural layer will usually be longer than the life of most of the other layers in the building, often 100 years or more. In a layered design, components such as internal finishes, mechanical equipment, cladding, and even fireproofing can be readily removed from the structure and sent for reuse or recycling. In this way the useful life of the structure can be extended. In addition, stripping back the layers at the end of the life of the building means the various components can be more easily reused.

The critical factor is for designers to consider the interface between the layers to allow easy removal of the shorter lived layers without damage to the longer lasting layers allowing components to be replaced in the building during its useful life. This means looking at the building systems and technologies used to ensure they can be readily and economically separated. The design team needs to think through, at the concept stage, the likely lifetime changes to building components.

Potential problems during refurbishment and eventual dismantling should be anticipated. For example, allowing site access for machinery and suitable floor loads to take demolition plant and deconstruction loads. Another key issue is the availability of relevant documentation and information about the building at the time of deconstruction is needed for safe and effective deconstruction. To help with this, the design team can provide a disassembly plan. Demolition is the reverse of construction, and the design team should consider this process and prepare a strategy for the dismantling of the building, similar to that developed for many temporary, relocatable buildings. Also, a log book, that is kept during the life of a building, can include information on the design of the original building, specifications of materials and components used in construction, details of refurbishment work carried out during the life of the building, and information relevant to dismantling, which would enable materials to be readily extracted for reuse and their specifications to be followed through their different life phases. ☯

Site	*Geographic setting of building*	*Period*
Structure	*The load-bearing elements including foundations*	*30 to 300 years*
Skin	*The exterior surfaces providing the weather protecting layer*	*20 years*
Services	*The working guts of the building – HVAC, electrical, plumbing, sprinklers, etc.*	*7 - 15 years*
Space plan	*The interior layout – internal partitions, doors, etc.*	*3 – 30 years*
Stuff	*Furniture, equipment, personal positions of occupants*	*Daily*

Hierarchical layering of building systems (from Brand, 1994).

References

1. 'How Buildings Work' by S Brand (1994) New York: Viking.

2. ***www.usablebuildings.co.uk***

3. Croxton, (2003) Architectural Record, Aug 2003, pg 147.

4. ***http://open-building.org***

5. D Wyatt & J Gilleard 1994, 'Deconstruction: an environmental response for construction sustainability. Sustainable Construction', Proceedings the First International Conference of CIB TG16, Tampa, Florida.

6. S L Fletcher, O Popovic & R Plank. 2000, 'Designing for future reuse and recycling', in the proceedings of "Deconstruction – closing the loop", Building Research Establishment, Garston, UK.

Further reading

For more information about design for deconstruction see the publication from the Scottish Ecological Design Association: ***www.seda2.org/dfd/index.htm***

'The Un-private House' by R. Terrence. (1999). New York: Museum of Modern Art.

Eco-minimalism - less is more

If we are serious about making our buildings green, then it is crucial that we don't get carried away by the trends and the fads. A green building needs to be economic to run, simple to maintain and gimmick-free. **Howard Liddell** tells us how we can achieve this goal...

If we are to move forward from the pilot projects of individual eco-houses, mini eco-villages, green expos and now eco-towns - towards mainstreaming ecological design as an integral part of building for the 21st century, then it is crucial that it is accessible, economic, genuinely environmentally-sound, gimmick-free and not stigmatised as a style.

It is almost easier to persuade newcomers to green building than the old diehards that the 'technical fix' icons of the green movement (wind turbines, photovoltaics, heat pumps etc) may not all be as green as they seem. This is especially true when set against a strategy of good housekeeping (thrift) and energy conservation. The fact that a building can be genuinely green without being self-conscious, or having to look radically different, is also very attractive to a large number of people.

The misconception that green buildings will cost more to build is almost impossible to shift. I have personally been involved in designing and building green buildings for over 30 years without the benefit of being offered bigger budgets (or fees), and my contention is that those who ask for more money for building green are missing the point. Being green is about less not more! Thankfully, my own and work by others have proven this point time and again.

For example, an airtight and super-insulated building will need very little, if any heating or fuel storage, therefore saving all the running and maintenance costs that involves. The financial savings from this 'designing-out of technology' can pay for increased building fabric quality - a straight trade off with no extra up-front costs.

Another example would be for dealing with humidity. Hygroscopic materials, which are readily water absorptive and evaporative, (e.g. clay plaster and untreated timber) are up to 9 times more effective at dealing with indoor humidity (safe absorb and release) levels than mechanical ventilation. Therefore, with careful considered design, the building user gets a building that is self-regulating and healthy. The financial savings from not needing fans, ducts, grilles and filters easily pays for the specification of slightly more expensive components and wall finishes.

The 'green' house - with bells and whistles

About 30 years ago I was asked to be involved in a Granada TV programme called 'House for the Future'. An early example of reality TV - It took a typical family and got them to self-build their low energy home by converting an old brick barn. The barn was gutted and wrapped up tight on the outside with 250mm of insulation. Whilst this was self-sufficient enough for the worst of winters, it was a little too straightforward for a series identified for 13 programmes. So new technology got layered on week by week.

By the end of the series, the house had passive and active solar collectors, a rock store, a heat pump, heat recovery, a wind turbine and so on and so forth until it ended up looking like a Christmas tree. Monitoring one year later revealed that the heat recovery from the kitchen was sufficient to warm the whole house year-round. The solar thermal roof array (only

2% of the heating) and heat pump were virtually redundant, the rock store short-circuited (air in to air out by the shortest route). From here on I was a convert to the concept of doing more with less.

Defining eco-minimalism

The term 'eco-minimalism' as I see it, incorporates a combination of simple common sense with a sharp, uncluttered design. It is rooted in the 'passive design' approach (which is discussed in greater detail elsewhere in this book and in Volume 2). Passive design requires a degree of scientific understanding, coupled with lashings of common sense. A desire to understand how buildings work will lead to knowledge of how to design them. The alternative - resorting to off-the-shelf, one-size-fits-all technology, is a recipe for disappointment.

Eco-minimalism is purely and simply an approach, a philosophy if you like, it is not a style. Indeed, whilst my practice may have a preference for a modern designs, eco-buildings can actually be built in virtually any style.

If the badge fits - wear it!

In many (but not all) circumstances a good number of the so-called 'eco-technologies' can be shown to have somewhat suspect green credentials. Most obvious among them are heat pumps, wind turbines, solar panels, rainwater harvesting, turf roofs and even latterly

Heat pump experiences

In a swimming pool project, many years ago, I had the sobering experience of having a heat pump switched off after only one month, in favour of simply using mains gas because it was significantly cheaper to run the building that way. No mystery, the CoP (coefficient of performance) of the heat pump was 3:1 and the tariff difference between gas and electricity was nearly 5:1. I was moved to look into this a little further, only to discover that in using the carbon intensive UK grid (as distinct from, say, the Norwegian hydro power dominated grid) even the carbon impact of the heat pump was worse. The illustration below explains the logic which has changed little since then.

If a heat pump is to be used (most are electrically powered) then electricity is needed: this starts with power station losses of nearly 60% in the conversion of gas to power. There are then the grid losses (8%), and eventually this very high grade energy source powers the heat pump, which then delivers a lower grade energy output at efficiencies - claimed initially to be capable of about 4:1 but usually delivered at around 3:1 or less. All that effort and expense to achieving virtually the same net output than if the same primary fuel was delivered to the home and fed straight into a high efficiency boiler.

In terms of the swimming pool project the heat pump was not the only example of redundant technology in the building. It turned out that other specifications were surplus to requirements, including the heat recovery unit and two boilers. In fact the outcome of a recent review - 10 years on - has demonstrated that around 33% of the capital cost dedicated to the technical services could have been reduced to 25%, without any effect whatsoever on the building's efficiency. In subsequent buildings we have been able to reduce this to as little 10%, and in a recent school brief, capped the technical element to 15% of capital cost, and had the consultants sign up to this as part of their contract, they eventually delivered 13%.

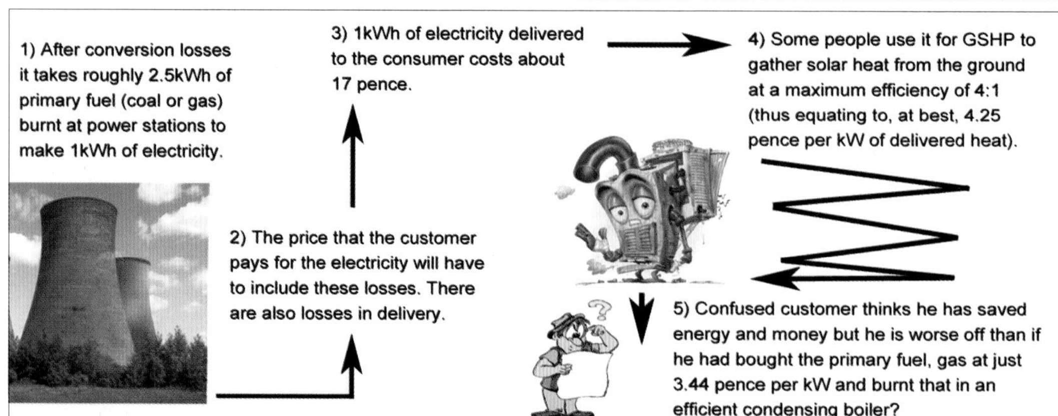

1) After conversion losses it takes roughly 2.5kWh of primary fuel (coal or gas) burnt at power stations to make 1kWh of electricity.
2) The price that the customer pays for the electricity will have to include these losses. There are also losses in delivery.
3) 1kWh of electricity delivered to the consumer costs about 17 pence.
4) Some people use it for GSHP to gather solar heat from the ground at a maximum efficiency of 4:1 (thus equating to, at best, 4.25 pence per kW of delivered heat).
5) Confused customer thinks he has saved energy and money but he is worse off than if he had bought the primary fuel, gas at just 3.44 pence per kW and burnt that in an efficient condensing boiler?

This diagram above shows two ways of using gas as a fuel. We could run a power station to create electricity which, in turn, would be sent to your home to run a ground source heat pump (GSHP). Alternatively we could use the gas directly in the home to run an easily maintained, efficient gas boiler. Prices for comparison are taken from John Willoughby's Domestic Fuel price Guide No 33 which can be found on page 461.

conservatories. All these need to be put under strict scrutiny as to their suitability before they are specified or used. When the numbers are crunched, the costs and benefits evaluated and the eco-footprint identified, for a specific project, they are either appropriate or not; indeed every project is unique to either the site, client or climatic context - and often all three.

If a heat pump is the answer *what was the question?*

There will be circumstances where micro photovoltaic/wind power combo's make cash and carbon sense. However, my practice has had new clients start talking about heat pumps and reed beds etc, even before mentioning what kind of building they want - they put their green-gadget shopping list ahead of their intended function for the building. Photovoltaics are experiencing a temporary trough right now but heat pumps are back in vogue. The technical jargonists have raised their game, they don't want any old heat pump, it has to be a 'ground source' heat pump (GSHP) or, for the nouveau-techies, a 'geothermal' heat pump, which trips off the tongue with the enthusiasm of one who has discovered the philosopher's stone.

As with photovoltaics, technically advanced solutions, like heat pumps (which are very expensive bits of kit), must be made to stack up (short and long term) against the likes of biofuels and wind power. The economic questions, such as the issue of payback periods and annual degradations in equipment efficiency, must be properly addressed.

The elements rule

It can be useful to categorise a building project into the four elements; fire, air, earth and water as our buildings incorporate all of these and all have an effect on health and wellbeing whilst being interlinked. The discussion in each category below seeks to draw out the relative advantages of an eco-minimalist (good housekeeping) approach but is certainly not exhaustive.

Fire

The fire element is energy. The first rule for a building's energy strategy should be to reduce, or even remove, the need for energy consumption as far as is reasonably possible, before looking into the supply side.

Part of an energy efficiency approach would also include the viability of group buildings in terraces, rather than having them in detached form (often a social challenge) and perhaps considering community scale CHP (combined heat and power) - the Achilles heel of which is the summer hot water surplus (unless there is a hospital or swimming pool in the vicinity, with a constant 365 day, hot water need).

Air

The air element is both the indoor and outdoor environment - outdoors, shelter belts and planting which will give energy savings in preventing wind chill losses on the conservation side, and maybe wind power, on the supply side.

As Albert Einstein said "things need to be as simple as possible but no simpler." This philosophy need not be a hamstring to good building design but a useful tool. If we consider the pressing need to make our buildings less of a burden on the planet early enough in the design we can find and incorporate real, sustainable energy and material saving solutions without the need for bolt-on technologies.

Photo courtesy of Gaia Architects.

A recent trend has been to bring the outdoors indoors and vice-versa. This is a disastrous trend for the environment. For example, conservatories were taken out of the planning and building control regulation arena, supposedly to encourage the free use of solar gain and reduce wind chill (argued as a buffer zone). This wishful thinking, however, has been totally undermined by the fact that 90% of conservatories have been found to have heating systems installed in them. In terms of indoor climate issues, the air element includes; designing for airtight construction and the concomitant need to deal with moisture movement and relative humidity - a link to the water element, and also the benign materials' specification - the earth element.

Earth

The earth element is also indoors/outdoors. Externally so much can be done to deal with the impact of building in a more natural way than has become the norm. The cities of Berlin and Malmö have adopted a 50% rule, whereby every square metre of built footprint has to have an equivalent amount of bio-diverse rich landscape (soft surfaces and water).

The earth element also covers more design specific material choices, and a couple of eco-clichés need addressing here. The first is 'local materials'. For example in Glasgow, the city council manufactures its own uPVC windows - so these are claimed to be 'local', a statement that is defended adamantly on grounds of local employment provision but other aspects of the windows are conveniently overlooked - issues about the base material (embodied toxicity) etc. which certainly is not local.

The second eco-cliché relates to the generally held assumption that a material like wood is inherently 'good'. Apart from the oft-aired issues around where the timber comes from (source), it is also clear that a vast majority of wood used in the construction industry has been treated by the time it reaches the builder - usually with something like CCA (copper chrome & arsenic), permethrin or a toxic stain. In fact many wood based materials used in buildings are a bit of a toxic time-bomb. The industry is awash with products that are formaldehyde rich from the glues used in them; MDF, OSB, chipboard, plywood, blockboard, laminated beams etc. Therefore, just specifying 'timber', is no real guarantee of purity or is it inherently environmentally sound? I don't want to belittle the great efforts that are put in to check and certify the origin of many exotic timbers as we hear almost daily about 'stolen' rainforest timber from Greenpeace and others, but we do need to be fully aware that there are other issues.

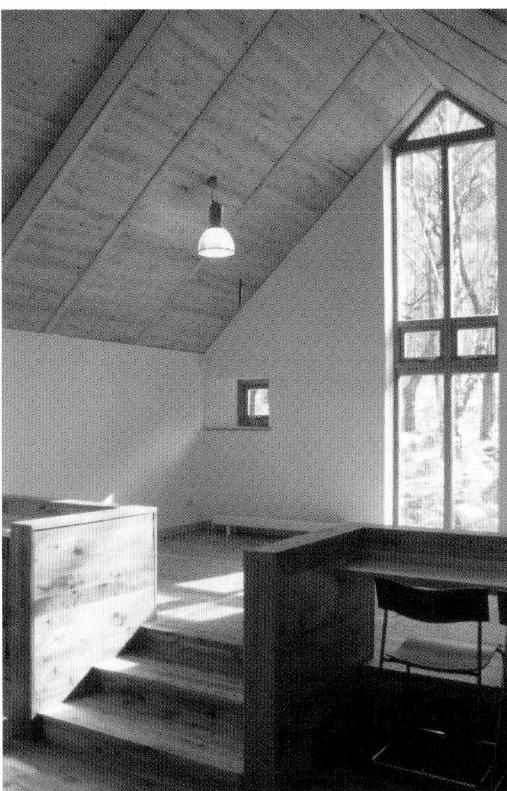

Eco-minimalism has connections to holistic ways of living. Anyone that is truly concerned with caring for the environment will be aware that less is more and that the planet is unable to support our ever hungry, fickle and highly consumerist society. Solutions for our buildings are similar to solutions for living lightly. Less has actually been proven to be more fulfilling.

The above photo is of a building that embraces this philosophy. Local wood and natural surfaces and finishes compliment the bright and lively space.

Photo courtesy of Gaia Architects.

Water

The water element speaks for itself. As we seek to exploit and recycle water - rainwater, greywater and even blackwater, the costs of alternatives to the mains water and the sewage infrastructure become increasingly financially onerous and sometimes even perhaps questionable environmentally and socially. Yet again, using less in the first place - 'eco-minimalism' makes sense. We can install water saving appliances and fittings (spray taps, low-flush WCs and waterless urinals, 'A' rated appliances etc).

I am totally mystified as to why anyone would wish to engage in installing a reed-bed system in an urban area where there are sewers. Of the water collection and reuse options, grey water irrigation to the garden seems the most effective and least risky strategy in terms of both health and finance, better than attempting to recycle it.

However it is in dealing with water in another sense - as moisture and humidity in buildings - that we see the time-old traditional contest between builders and the elements. Whether it be coming out of the sky, up from the ground or from moisture rich indoor activity, it is a battleground as old as buildings themselves. Whilst the concept of thermal mass is now well understood by designers, however the concept of moisture mass is still not understood. We continue to seal up our buildings in the interests of energy conservation, we also seal in the moisture created in bathrooms and kitchens as well as the perspiration from active pursuits and overnight sleep. This has led to exponential growth in the mechanical ventilation industry - which is actually not nearly as effective in removing moisture as hygroscopic materials. Running such artifical ventilation systems causes energy consumption to rocket. We are rushing headlong towards being a society dependant on air conditioning. It is just like pressing on a balloon - press down in one spot to solve a problem and it just pops up in another area as a new problem.

We need to stop putting surface water into pipes and deal with it at source. Sustainable urban drainage (SUDs) schemes have been one of the most economically viable, as well as positive amenity strategies of recent years. SUDs are a win-win deal and offer flood resistant landscaping as an integral part of the development budget, whilst also responding to biodiversity in a fantastically positive way - encouraging diversity in not just flora but also fauna (birds and butterflies etc).

Conclusion

Eco-minimalism is a holistic approach to the whole environmental agenda. But as long as we continue to only address single issues in their conceptual silos, and fail to tackle problems holistically, then we will go round in circles looking for tecno-fixes.

For those who have an uninformed view of what the sustainable building agenda is, or should be, the solutions continue to be unreliable and, as such, ineffective - or worse creating an equally large, or even larger problem, elsewhere. On the other hand, those who come to realise that the challenge is more complex and interlinked but have taken some time (and thought) in their search for solutions, often find them complicated and daunting with a long list of interventions, which they have also assumed will come with a high price tag. But after presenting the eco-minimalist approach to a wide range of people, from architects and builders through to clients and the general public, it has become clear that most find this perception complex but convincing and therefore easier to embrace and more accessible than the quick fit and bolt on technology that is becoming so popular at the moment. ☯

Howard Liddell first wrote about eco-minimalism in 2002 with co-author Nick Grant, long before the wider public acceptance of the green agenda. The motivation at the time was that they had simultaneously become tired of the clichés in eco-building design - trotted out almost unthinkingly as technical fixes, add-on solutions whether they stood up to rigorous scrutiny or not. Howard is author of 'Eco-minimalism – the antidote to eco-bling' published in July 2008 by RIBA Publications.

Design for airtightness

Expensive, heated air is constantly escaping from our buildings, giving rise to uncomfortable draughts, high energy bills and speeding up climate change. **Paul Jennings** tells us how to stop this...

Regardless of how much or what type of insulation you put into your building, if you fail to ensure that the fabric is airtight – i.e. free of uncontrollable draughts – your energy-saving expectations will never be fully realised. As insulation levels continue to be increased, an ever greater proportion of energy losses from our homes will occur through air leakage (see chart below).

Draughts are uncontrolled air movement and they make us uncomfortable. The wind blowing on our buildings can force cold air in via gaps around windows and doors and through a wide range of other gaps and cracks. Also the stack effect of warm air rising in our buildings creates suction which, if there are gaps at high level, pulls cold air in elsewhere or even through the same gaps. Yet we always need ventilation to provide a healthy living environment but such uncontrolled air movement (draughts) is not the answer. Ventilation needs to be controlled and deliberately induced, using openable windows, trickle vents, heat extract fans etc. Most UK buildings have too much air leakage when it is windy and not enough ventilation on calm, still days. Remember, draughts are bad; ventilation is good.

Ventilation is the controlled replacement of degraded indoor air with external air and all buildings need ventilation. We need ventilation to breathe, and we need ventilation to get rid of indoor pollutants – cooking and other smells, but particularly water vapour. Minimising the buildup of moisture helps prevent condensation and mould growth, and discourages dust mites. Relative humidity of between 50% and 65% will provide the most comfortable and healthy living environment. If you have open flued appliances, such as wood-burning stoves, we need more ventilation for safety, and if people smoke we need lots more ventilation.

As well as allowing costly warm air to escape, air leakage degrades the effectiveness of insulation by as much as two-thirds and also allows potentially damaging moisture to enter the structural fabric of the building. The slogan 'build-tight, ventilate-right' has been used among green building professionals for several years to encourage us to improve our buildings

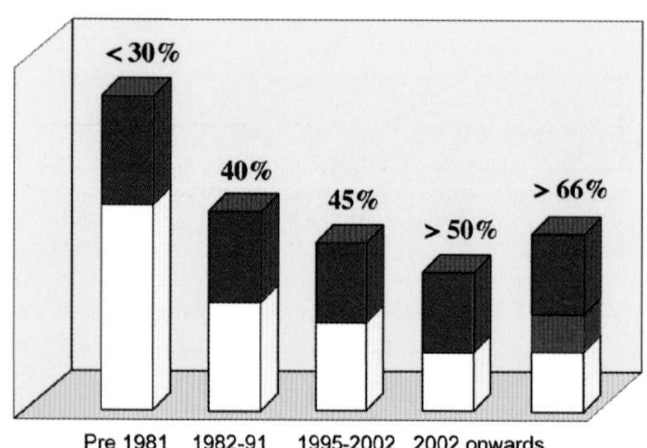

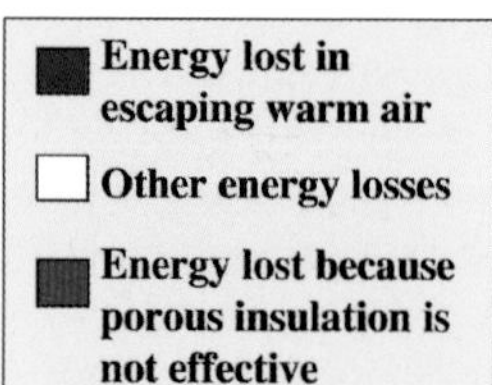

Figure 1. Illustrating how air leakage has been a growing proportion of heat losses in buildings as insulation levels increase.

and reduce the shameful waste of heat that draughts cause. It has been suggested that it is impossible to build a building too airtight, although it is clearly possible to fail to design sufficient and appropriate ventilation.

As insulation levels installed in UK buildings have risen, particularly in recent years, then the waste of energy through escaping warm air has become more significant. Figure 1 illustrates how the percentage of energy lost through air leakage has increased in line with increasing insulation levels to the point where it can account for more than half of all energy losses in buildings constructed to building regulation standards.

Despite increasing requirements for airtightness testing under the England & Wales Building Regulations, and now the Scottish Building Standards, the requirement for better quality buildings to meet stricter airtightness targets is not yet widely appreciated by the UK construction industry. Business as usual will not suffice. Most UK builders have still not yet grasped the nettle and learnt how to construct and finish airtight dwellings and other buildings. Sample air leakage testing of dwellings is mandatory under the revised Part L of the Building Regulations (April 2006), and eco-builders, aiming to achieve substantially lower carbon emissions than the relatively lax building regulations targets, should have testing to verify that they have achieved their target air permeability values and resulting calculated carbon emissions. Suitable targets for eco-builders are an air permeability of 3.0 air changes per hour (ach) (compared with the Building Regulations maximum of 10.0ach) in naturally ventilated dwellings, and 0.75ach in dwellings with MVHR systems. These correspond to the AECB's silver and gold (CarbonLite) standards respectively. The passivhaus target is an even more onerous 0.6ach.

How testing is carried out

A 'blower door', also known as a 'door fan', is the principle tool used for measuring airtightness and identifying leakage in dwellings and other new or existing buildings. It consists of one or more calibrated fans that are mounted in an open doorway, using an adjustable door panel system. A series of steady-state pressure differences are then applied using the fan.

Once steady state conditions have been achieved, the airflow measured through the fan equals the sum of the air leaking through all the different gaps, cracks and openings in the envelope of the building or volume under test, adjusted for temperature difference. By measuring the corresponding imposed pressure differentials, the leakage characteristics of the volume being tested can be established. Door fan testing is used to:

- provide an acceptance test for new dwellings, offices or other buildings
- identify leakage sites, provide quality control on remedial sealing works, if required
- check the performance of ventilation, extraction or mechanical ventilation and heat recovery (MVHR) systems
- establish ventilation rates in existing properties, for example to investigate the cause of condensation problems.

Test results published by BRE clearly show that improved airtightness in our buildings is essential – UK offices are around 2 to 4 times leakier than equivalent buildings in Scandinavia or North America, whilst industrial buildings are found to be more than 4 times as leaky. In housing, recent experience of testing supposedly airtight timber framed houses encountered many of the same problems found when testing the TRADA low energy house at Energy World in Milton Keynes nearly two decades ago!

The leakage sites to be found in dwellings and other buildings can be subdivided into two types: structural leakage and services leakage (see illustration on page 52).

Structural leakage sites occur at joints in the building fabric and around window and door openings. Loft hatches and access openings (usually non-domestic) also fall within this category. There may also be leakage through cracks in masonry walls – poor perpends

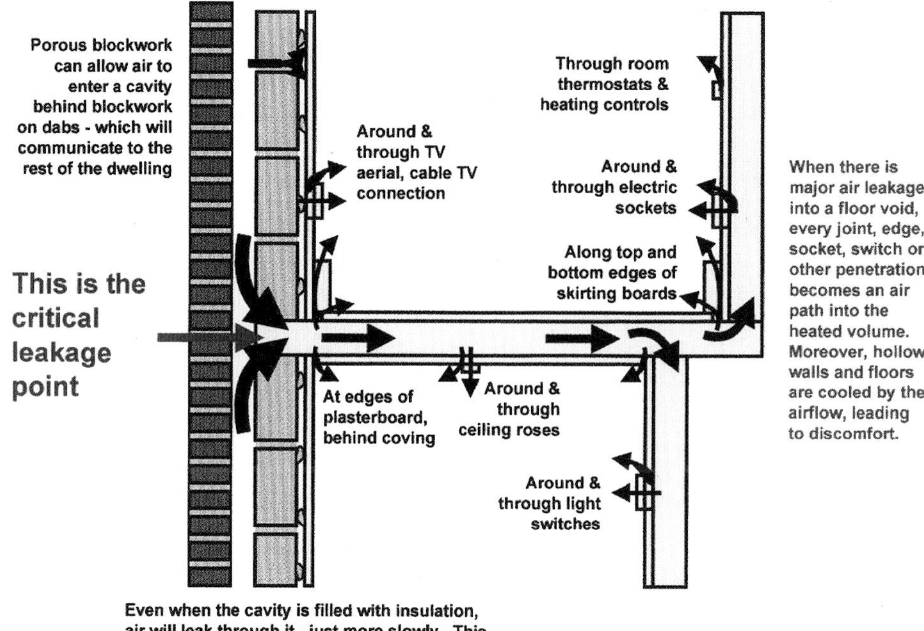
Porous blockwork can allow air to enter a cavity behind blockwork on dabs - which will communicate to the rest of the dwelling
This is the critical leakage point
Around & through TV aerial, cable TV connection
Through room thermostats & heating controls
Around & through electric sockets
Along top and bottom edges of skirting boards
When there is major air leakage into a floor void, every joint, edge, socket, switch or other penetration becomes an air path into the heated volume. Moreover, hollow walls and floors are cooled by the airflow, leading to discomfort.
At edges of plasterboard, behind coving
Around & through ceiling roses
Around & through light switches
Even when the cavity is filled with insulation, air will leak through it - just more slowly. This will also reduce the effectiveness of the insulation - by up to 2/3rds

Figure 2. The critical leakage points in upper floors where joists penetrate walls.

(vertical mortar joints) in blockwork inner leafs being the most common cause – and some diffusion through materials. These are the hardest to retrofix. Good detailing at the design stage is therefore essential. Builders also need appropriate training, so they understand how to build airtight buildings to achieve a good test result. Service leakages occur where pipes and cables pass into the building. These can be sewerage pipes, water pipes and heating pipes. As well as electricity cables there may also be television aerials and cable television connections. The worst problems tend to occur when these two types of leakage problems interact (see Figure 2).

Once there is a failure of the airtight barrier where a hollow intermediate floor is supported from the external wall, a connection exists from a cavity in the external wall (which may be filled with insulation) through hollow internal partition walls to pretty much the whole of the building. Hollow floors and walls are inevitably used to run services – and just as inevitably tend not to be sealed where the services run from one element into another. The result is that electricity sockets and switches, light fittings (especially spotlights), television aerial and cable television connections, heating and plumbing pipes, waste pipes and soil stacks all become points at which air will leak into the dwelling. Even such minor items as room thermostats and heating controllers will permit air leakage around or through them. Moreover, if one such leakage site is sealed, most of the air will still escape at another site, since they tend to connect and to have a similar resistance to the movement of air through them. Whilst it may be possible to laboriously seal all these sites and thereby cut the air leakage significantly, cold air will still get into hollow floors and walls, cooling internal surfaces and giving rise to discomfort.

Another major source of problems is the boxing-in of services, particularly water and waste pipework and soil stacks and also riser shafts in non-domestic buildings. Once services are out of sight, it is all too easy for sealing works to be overlooked and forgotten, even if they were specified in the first place. There is no culture of airtight construction on UK sites, and until this is achieved, detailed planning and preparation, rigorous site supervision and air leakage testing will be essential to achieve satisfactory buildings. In fact, air leakage testing provides an effective, rapid and reasonably priced method to check the quality of buildings.

Designing for airtightness

Legislation

In England and Wales the relevant regulation on airtightness is contained within Approved Documents L1A for dwellings and L2A for non-domestic buildings (2006). The requirements are much more onerous in England & Wales than in Scotland, with essentially all non-domestic buildings requiring testing and samples of each dwelling type on a site that has more than 2 units requiring testing. There is a general requirement to avoid excessive air leakage, although the normal maximum air permeability of 10 m³/hr/m² @ 50 pascals (Pa) should be considered a disastrous result for an eco-builder. Further tightening of the regulations are expected in 2010.

In the new Scottish Building Standards, the relevant section is 6.2.5 for both domestic and non-domestic buildings. In the domestic version, designers are directed to Building Research Establishment (BRE) Report 262 – "Thermal insulation, avoiding risks" 2002 edition, and in the non-domestic version, to the BRE document BR 448: Airtightness in Commercial and Public Buildings, but it is stated explicitly that "within the Building (Scotland) Regulations 2004 there is no requirement, mandatory or otherwise to test buildings".

Changes in practice in England & Wales, following the 2006 Building Regulations revisions, have led to almost all non-domestic buildings requiring testing, frequently because a lower air permeability target than the maximum of 10 is set as part of measures to reduce carbon emissions below the target value.

Measurement

A range of units for measuring airtightness have been used in the past and this can complicate matters. However, one method only - "air permeability" - is the measure used in European Standards, the new editions of the various UK Building regulations and in CIBSE's TM23 Testing methodology and has been used throughout this document. The air permeability is defined as the volume flow in cubic metres of air per hour per square metre of the total building surface area (including the floor) at 50Pa pressure differential, expressed in m³/hr/m² @ 50Pa.

The main difference between the air permeability and previous practice in the UK is the inclusion of the non-exposed ground floor in the calculation of the 'total surface area' of the building. The difference between the new measurements and older ones tend only to be marked therefore where there are large volumes and ground floor areas.

Of the range of measurements used previously, the 'average air leakage rate (or index)' is similar to the 'air permeability' except that non-exposed floors are excluded from the measurement. Another common expression is the 'air changes per hour at 50Pa (ach@ 50Pa). This is a useful measurement in houses (but only houses) because, when divided by twenty, it gives an approximate value of the natural infiltration rate of the house under normal atmospheric conditions, which can then be used to help size heating and ventilating plant etc. The measurement units ACH @ 50 Pa are used by both the German passivhaus and the Canadian super-E schemes in their acceptance criteria.

Yet another measurement is the 'equivalent leakage area' (ELA) at 50, 10 and/or 4Pa. This figure gives a representation of the sum of all of the individual cracks, gaps and openings as a single orifice and helps to visualise the scale of the leakage problem. The main problem of changing the measurement technique is the ability to compare data.

Targets

As can be seen from the table below, the target of 10m³/hr/m² at 50Pa. is relatively easily achieved compared to the good and best practice noted in the 2000 document by CIBSE, TM23. This is the test methodology still referenced by the Scottish Building Standards, but superseded in England and Wales by the ATTMA (Air Tightness Testing & Measurement Association) Technical Standard 1. See ***www.attma.org*** *for more information*

The table below is extracted with permission from SEDA ***www.seda2.org/dfa/ch2.htm#3***

Resources

Volume, 10 No. 3 of Building for a Future magazine covered the subject of airtightness in-depth, including a number of case studies. It can be viewed free of charge at: ***http://www.buildingforafuture.co.uk/winter00/index.php*** *as a downloadable pdf file.*

This the name of probably the most useful resource on the internet covering this subject. ***www.seda2.org/dfa***

Building type	**Air permeability (m³/hr/m² at 50Pa)**	
	Good practice	Best practice
Dwellings	10.0	5.0
Dwellings (with balanced mech. vent.)	5.0	3.0
Offices (naturally ventilated)	7.0	3.5
Offices (with balanced mech. vent.)	3.5	2.0
Superstores	3.0	1.5
Offices (low energy)	3.5	2.0
Industrial	10.0	2.0
Museum and archival storage	1.7	1.25
Cold storage	0.8	0.4

Air leakage standards, based on CIBSE TM23 2000 (upper five), BSRIA Specification 10/98 and BRE BR448, 2002 (lower four).

Structural air leakage (white numbered arrows)

1. A frequent and often very significant leakage site where cracks and gaps around the ends of floor joists (or hangers) connect with the floor void and thence with studwork partition walls and/or with gaps behind plasterboard on dabs.

2. Cracks and gaps beneath inner window sills and around window frames. Often connect to a cavity in the wall, or may be direct to outside.

3. Leakage through windows where draughtproofing is missing or ineffective, or through hollow window frames (usually uPVC), where a continuous leakage path exists. Can include leakage through supposedly sealed double-glazed units.

4. Leakage through doors – particularly double doors - where draughtproofing is missing or ineffective.

5. Cracks and gaps beneath doors, typically through unsealed joints between the doorframe and the edge of the ground floor.

6. Cracks along the top and bottom edges of skirting boards, connecting with gaps around the edges of suspended floors.

7. Leakage between sections of suspended floors, usually timber.

8. Gaps around loft hatches. Can be particularly bad with lightweight, modern hatches.

9. Leakage paths through the eaves of a building, connecting into roof rooms directly or via unsealed service voids.

10. Major leakage frequently found around rooflights, normally where a wooden frame is not sealed to the roof timbers.

11. Another common leakage path through the eaves of a building, which connects into the top of upper rooms, through gaps behind plasterboard on dabs or hollow studwork walls.

12. Leakage through a porous masonry inner leaf. Often through poor-quality mortar joints at perpends between blocks, but can also occur directly through blockwork. Frequently connects to gaps behind drylining.

Services air leakage (red numbered arrows)

13. Gaps in the inner wall where gas or electricity supplies from external meter boxes enter the building.

14. Leakage around ceiling roses and pull-switches, where unsealed cabling passes through to a roof space or cold intermediate floor. Also leakage around electrical sockets and switches mounted in hollow studwork walls that connect to a floor void or roof space.

15. Cracks and gaps around boiler flues.

16. Gaps where water and heating pipes penetrate into hollow floor voids and partition walls, frequently boxed in or hidden by kitchen or airing cupboards.

17. Gaps around waste pipes where they pass into hollow floor voids and partition walls, again often hidden by boxing.

18. Around waste pipes where they pass through the innermost layer of a wall, usually out of sight behind kitchen cupboards or beneath a bath.

19. Gaps around heating pipes into floor voids, which in turn may connect to a cavity in the external wall.

20. Gaps around and often through spotlights recessed in ceilings.

21. Around waste pipes, gas and water supplies, cables – electricity, telephone & television – which penetrate the lower floor.

22. A large hole can often be found around the top of the soil stack where it passes into a roof space.

23. Leakage through MVHR systems. More frequently, gaps around distribution or extract ductwork where it connects to a terminal mounted in a ceiling. Can also be major leaks around and through subfloor warm air heating ducts.

24. Cracks and gaps, sometimes large holes, around any or all water and heating pipes where they pass into a loft.

25. Around and through wall-mounted extract fans, also ducted vents from cooker hoods, tumble dryers and fans in internal bathrooms or other rooms.

Common air leakage routes in our buildings

There are two types of air leakage in buildings. Via the structure and via the service entry points

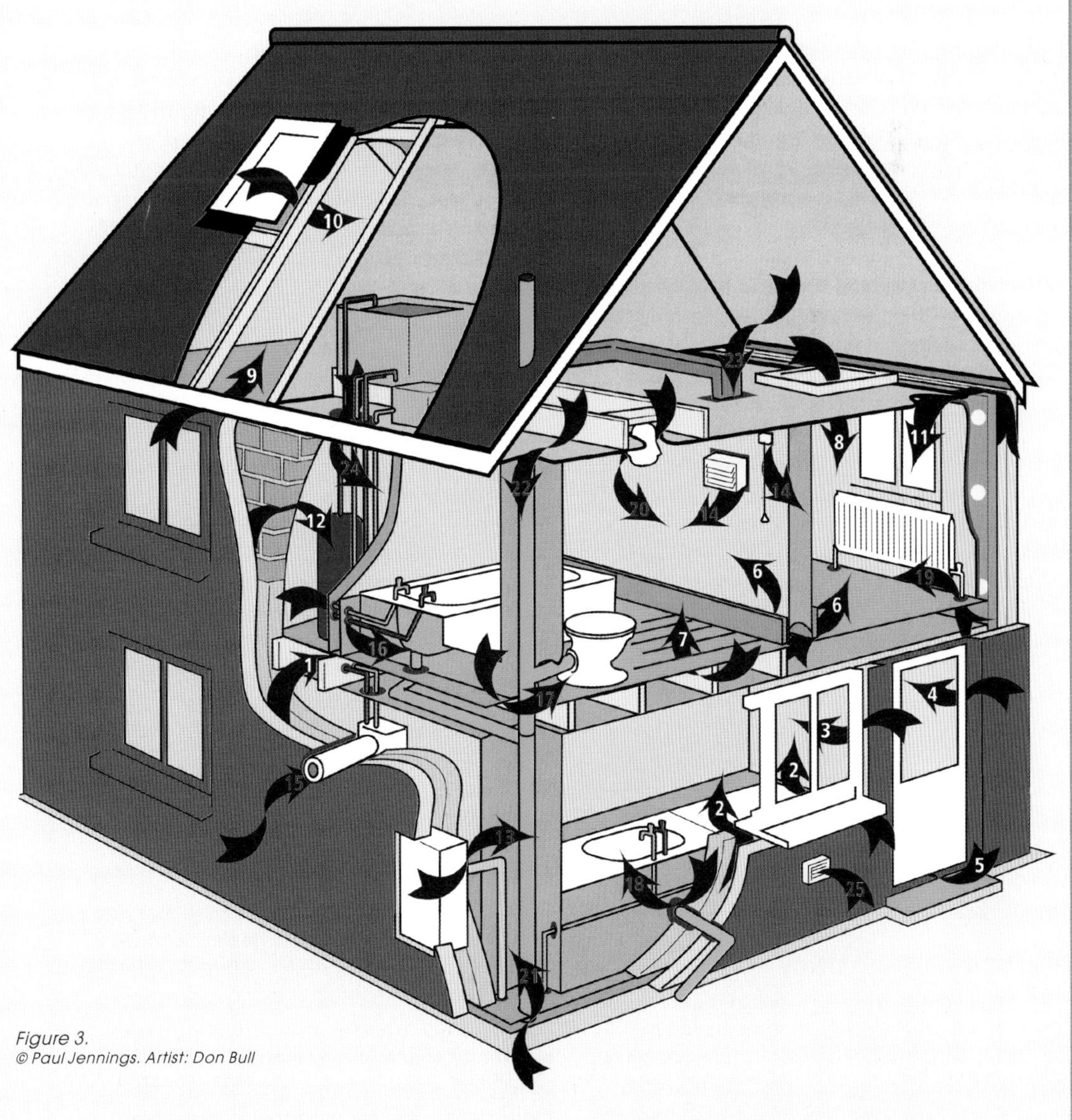

Figure 3.
© Paul Jennings. Artist: Don Bull

Design for passive heating

Exploiting beneficial heat from the sun within buildings may be a rather obvious priority for environmentally conscious building designers. However, it is one that is often misunderstood or inadequately applied. **Stephen Lowndes** examines passive solar design ...

An appreciation of how best to manipulate natural energy resources is fundamental to successful green building design. Here we examine the key concepts behind the effective use of daylight, sunlight and solar heating potential which should be embraced early in the design stage of a project.

Buildings that exploit the sun's heat and light to the best of their advantage can benefit from significant savings in energy and ultimately CO_2 emissions. It is important to understand that all the rules that underlie the successful application of passive solar building design are intrinsically linked. Orientation, window design and shading strategies, thermal mass and building envelope are all influenced by, and supportive of, each other. A badly orientated building, for example, affects the performance of each of the other rules, requiring their re-optimisation to compensate. Similarly a building with optimised orientation, but limited thermal mass may require other enhancements to help maintain comfortable temperatures during the extremes in winter and summer. In the UK we have to design to accommodate the excesses of cold and hot weather patterns, and this will always dictate how far the designer is able to pursue each particular aspect of what has collectively become called passive solar design.

What is passive solar energy?

Most people have, at one time or another, stood next to a brick wall on a warm summer's day and felt the radiating heat. You are feeling some of the radiant energy that the masonry has absorbed from the sun. The health benefits of radiant heat were discussed at length in the story, 'Design for good health', earlier in this chapter. Radiant energy is felt more directly next to a window, the epitome being the heat one can experience, even on a cold, bright winter's day, within a greenhouse. A greenhouse is, of course, designed to maximise the capture of the sun's radiant energy and is an example of a building designed to optimise solar energy in terms of heat and light. Buildings that are constructed to take advantage of solar radiation are known as 'passive solar buildings'.

Such buildings are designed specifically to exploit this 'free' energy, making use of the sun's heat, especially in the winter, for warmth. However the very same natural process can be employed in the summer to mitigate the extremes of heat experienced in that season. As a bonus, buildings designed to maximise beneficial solar heating will usually maximise daylight utilisation, although this is not always the case and the use of solar heat and daylight are not necessarily mutually inclusive. The energy utilised by the building is passive by definition, since the building has not generated the energy itself or exclusively by artificial means, rather it is effectively capturing, transferring and usually storing the energy from the sun.

You may be forgiven for thinking that the climate in the UK would not make passive solar design worthwhile. However, studies undertaken in this country do show that even conventionally designed housing, with primary glazed elevations specifically orientated towards the south, will achieve annual energy savings of the order of 3%-4%[1] and that if conventional housing layouts are planned so that most principle rooms face south, further annual energy savings of 1%-2% should be possible[2]. These savings relate to applying the first basic rule of passive solar design - orientation - to our building design brief, and usually without incurring any additional construction costs.

Specifically designed passive solar housing schemes have demonstrated annual energy savings in excess of 8% - 10%[3]. Any additional monetary costs for implementing passive solar design over and above conventional build cost can be negligible, depending on the extent of the design solutions adopted and the nature of the project. These solutions will revolve primarily around the parameters of building orientation, shading, window design, thermal mass, ventilation and air-tightness.

Rule 1 - orientation

Imagine the ultimate passive solar house which is constructed upon a large revolving turntable. It slowly rotates so that the primary occupied rooms are continually facing the sun throughout the day during the winter, and in the summer the house rotates so that these areas are continually in the shade. Unfortunately such a fantastic proposition is impractical to those other than the super-rich and likely to be somewhat disorientating for its occupants, as well as needing additional energy to revolve the building! This shows, however, that passive solar buildings need to be designed so that rooms occupied for most of the day are exposed to optimum sun for winter warmth and daylight, as well as receiving benefit from any seasonably available shade during the summer.

The maximum incident solar radiation on a vertical wall occurs for an orientation facing due south, typically 5kWh/m^2 in January, which drops to about 2kWh/m^2 if the wall faces due north[4]. Fixed room orientations up to 30° east of south, result in exposure to the sun in the morning, whereas orientation up to 30° towards the west of south achieves maximum exposure in the afternoon[5]. This diurnal variance in optimum solar exposure tends to dictate the layout of passive solar buildings. As a result it is usually recommended that living rooms and major bedrooms in dwellings achieve an exposure within 45° of south[6]. Accurate design parameters for this aspect are discussed fully in Chapter 6 of Volume 2.

Rule 2 - shading

Passive solar buildings need to take optimum advantage of the different sun altitudes throughout the year. In the winter, the sun's altitude is low, which may mean adjacent buildings obscure beneficial direct solar radiation. Ideally, the building would be positioned clear of the obstructions. The reverse is true in the summer, when an adjacent obstruction is beneficial, providing shade at the start or end of the day. There are a number of ways to solve this dichotomy. For example planting deciduous trees on southerly aspects, enabling solar penetration in the winter months when the tree's branches are bereft of foliage but giving shade in the summer from a renewed green canopy.

External summer shading measures can be employed in the design, such as large overhanging roof eaves or deep window reveals or shading attachments can be added to the building, such as brise solail, although care should be exercised to ensure shading measures do not exclude too much daylight. These structures could also potentially provide other useful functions, such as use as a balcony, doubling up as an external light shelf to help reflect more daylight into the building or reducing reliance on artificial lighting. Internally located blinds are less effective in terms of reducing summer heat gain and can reduce the effectiveness of any natural ventilation through the window that they are covering.

Rule 3 - thermal mass

Modern methods of construction (MMC) and a desire to build more and more of our buildings offsite is beginning to favour the use of lightweight materials. Yet the ability of thermally massive materials to store or release solar heat, when used as part of a building's structure for subsequent beneficial release later in the day, is recognised as a fundamental principle of passive solar building design. However, in the UK it is rarely exploited properly.

Buildings that make wise use of thermal mass tend to take longer to heat up from cold, but retain their heat for longer once warmed. However, buildings that have a lot of thermal mass badly installed can find that heat losses are exacerbated and the best examples of high mass, thermally poor buildings are old solid walled cottages and farmhouses that are cold all winter and cold all summer.

However, thermal mass, when understood properly can enable occupants to take advantage of all available solar heat received in the day, re-radiated slowly during the colder evenings, when there is greatest need for heat. In the summer, thermal mass also acts as a buffer, with the same thermal storage properties helping to attenuate any peak solar gain to the space, thus minimising the risk of overheating. The physical properties of a material govern its ability to store heat. This is known as its specific heat capacity. Materials such as softwood have a heat capacity of about 760kJ/m^{3}K and brick 1360kJ/m^{3}K (see table in following chapter). Brick has a lower heat capacity and hence lower thermal mass than dense concrete with a heat capacity of 2300kJ/m^{3}K[7]. (*Note: specific heat capacity is the amount of energy (kJ) required to raise the temperature of a given material by 1°C.*)

For any thermal mass to be effective it needs to be exposed to the occupied space and not completely shrouded with lightweight finishes. Placing an insulating layer or an air cavity in front of a heavy weight material isolates the mass from the internal environment and will reduce the material's ability to exchange heat with the surroundings (see Figure 1). A compromise between acceptable finishes, poor acoustic environment (often a problem with excessive hard surface exposure) and adequate thermal coupling with the building mass, needs to be struck. *Thermal mass is discussed in much greater depth in the next article.*

Rule 4 - windows and buffer zones

To minimise the requirement for space heating, passive solar designs usually incorporate

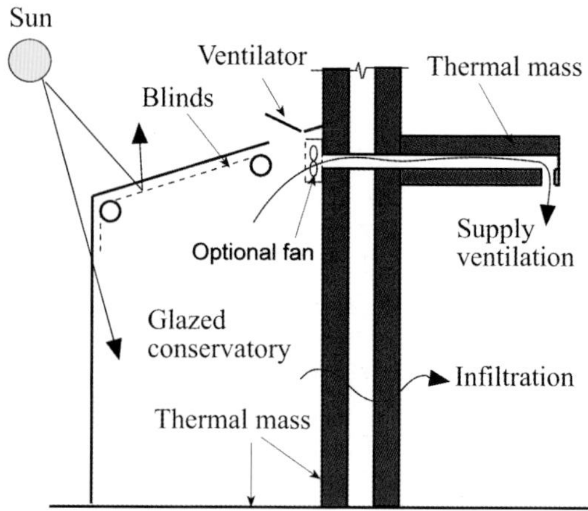

Figure 1. South facing glazing, thermal mass and a small amount of passive or mechanical ventilation can gather radiant energy from the sun and transfer it to other parts of a building. *Diagram courtesy of Richard Nicholls.*

reduced glazing areas on the north, east and west elevations in comparison to the south (where glazing areas may actually be increased). The associated reduced winter heat losses on these elevations is usually greater than any solar gain the windows may have given, even when low emissivity double or triple glazing is utilised. Increasing the southerly aspect of the glazing and by using low E double or triple glazing will usually provide a net winter day-time heat gain over night-time losses in most parts of the UK[8].

Further enhancements can be gained by unheated conservatories, atria, entrance lobbies and porches, to provide a cushion or barrier between the core building and the external environment. These are called buffer zones and act as the first line of defence against the elements. In the context of passive solar design, a south facing conservatory can also make use of solar radiation to increase the temperature relative to the outside. This means that the conductive heat losses through the separating wall from the occupied space, and the heat loss due to natural infiltration, is reduced because of the reduced temperature difference between the inside occupied space and that of the buffer zone.

A judgement on how big south facing windows need to be to maximise beneficial utilisation of daylight will be a function of the amount of visible or unobstructed sky potentially available; the room depth; room height and internal finish of the room walls. Formally, the measure of acceptable daylight within a room can be expressed in terms of a daylight factor. In theoretical terms this is (simplistically) the ratio of internal daylight level to external daylight level within a room, expressed as a percentage. It is possible to calculate this using formula found in most building science text books and obtain an optimum glazing area for a particular room design. Typically, living rooms should achieve minimum daylight factors of 1%, kitchens 2% and bedrooms 0.5%[9].

In practical terms good design, that aims to encourage maximum daylight penetration within a room, should be pursued wherever possible:

- consider roof lights - about twice as effective as the equivalent area of window within a vertical wall (although they may lose more heat)
- allow windows that open into conservatories and atria to be larger than normal - the heat loss is reduced by the buffer zone effect
- incorporate splayed window reveals, light-shelves and light coloured internal finishes to ceilings and walls - all help to provide increased reflective surface areas and bounce light further into a room
- provide dual aspect windows - maximise light source throughout the day, depths greater than six metres are difficult to light from one glazed elevation.

Rule 5 - airtightness and ventilation

As discussed by Paul Jennings in the previous article, there should be an emphasis on well sealed buildings that minimise uncontrolled infiltration of air. This can be achieved by careful design and well monitored site practice - avoiding ill fitting windows and doors and poor building details. However, the drive towards airtightness raises awareness of the importance of ensuring that the building users get the right amount of controlled ventilation for a comfortable and healthy environment. Passive solar design can be exploited to provide naturally powered ventilation using controllable ventilated cavities or trombe walls. In a trombe wall, an air cavity separates an internal wall from a series of glazed panels. Outside ventilation air enters the cavity at low level. Solar radiation heats both the air within the cavity, as well as the mass of the wall, which conducts heat to the adjacent space. The buoyant, heated air is displaced to the top of the cavity by cooler incoming outside air of greater density. The heated air at the top of the cavity flows into the adjacent internal space providing ventilation. Attention to detail would be essential but the method provides a natural alternative to powered fans and/or heat exchange units.

Don't forget the regulations

All new and modified buildings constructed in the UK must comply with the current Part L of the Building Regulations (Part J in Scotland). Passive solar buildings should easily be able to show compliance based upon the new 'carbon index' method of compliance, providing that the energy (therefore carbon) saving design strategies can be demonstrated to the satisfaction of the building control officer, since Part L now specifically takes into account schemes that incorporate passive solar heating.

In the case of dwellings, SAP ratings (often required by local authorities and housing associations to give an indication of the energy efficiency of an individual house design) have the potential to be improved when passive solar design techniques are correctly adopted.

References

1, 2, 3 Energy Efficiency Best Practice Report 27, 'Passive solar estate layout', p2, table 1, BRECSU, Building Research Establishment, Watford.

4, 5, 6 'Energy and Environment in Architecture a Technical Design Guide' by N Baker, K Steemers, (2000), pp20-24, and 36-37, E & F N Spon.

7 Good Practice Guide 79, 2001, 'Energy efficiency in new housing – a guide to achieving best practice', p8, BRECSU, Building Research Establishment, Watford.

8 Energy Efficiency Best Practice Report 27, 'Passive solar estate layout', p9, BRECSU, Building Research Establishment, Watford.

*9 'The Whole House Book' by P Borer, C Harris (1998), p37-38, (latest edition available from **www.greenbuildingpress.co.uk**).*

Consider the thermal capacity

If we design our buildings to admit solar energy then we should ensure that elements of the fabric are able to absorb and release this free heat at appropriate times to provide user comfort and help save on energy bills. **Jerry Clark** and **Keith Hall** report ...

What levels of thermal mass should we aim to use in our buildings and what might be the most effective strategy? This article is based on a study carried out by energy consultant, John Willoughby, and first published in Building for a Future magazine[1] that attempted to answer this question.

The physical property that describes the ability of a material to absorb heat is the specific heat, that is the heat required to raise the temperature of 1kg of material by 1°C. In buildings, however, a more relevant unit is the heat capacity, which describes the heat needed to raise a cubic metre of material by 1°C. The table (right) shows the specific heat of a small range of building materials.

Let's categorise thermal mass in a building into three types - primary, secondary and tertiary. Primary thermal mass is the small area of the interior which is warmed by direct sunlight. Secondary thermal mass is gains from from cooking, lights, appliances, furniture etc. Thermal mass in adjacent rooms, with no direct sunlight, is tertiary .

The way thermal mass works is often misunderstood. To be effective the mass needs to be well connected or 'coupled' with the space it is serving (the room). Spreading the mass thinly around all of the surfaces is much more effective than having just one very heavyweight wall, for instance. Thus the effectiveness depends on the mass and the area coupled to the space[2]. Fitted carpets, soft furnishings and even wall-hangings will all be effective at reducing the efficiency of any available heat transfer to the thermal mass.

Research has suggested that during a normal diurnal cycle, 90% of the recoverable heat flow is limited to a depth of about 50mm in dense concrete, and 50% to the first 25mm. Thus for thermal storage over a 24 hour time-span, there is very little to be gained from very thick masses of concrete or masonry[3]. From this one could conclude that just the provision of a double thickness of plasterboard in a light-weight building could go a long way towards providing reasonable thermal mass.

Overheating and cooling down

Most of us have experienced the effect that thermal mass can have upon a building and our comfort. If you have ever walked into an old stone cottage on a hot summer's afternoon you will have felt the influence that the 'mass' of the building has in reducing the temperature. In modern houses, which are better insulated and built of lighter weight materials, the effect is less pronounced, other than in north facing rooms that are closed off. Lightweight (timber-framed) houses can be much more prone to overheating than heavyweight structures, such as stone cottages.

There follows a simple example of the predicted effect of thermal mass on controlling temperatures on a hot August day, modelled on a timber frame (lightweight) and a masonry (heavyweight) home using the admittance method[4]. Let's consider a 15m^2, unoccupied living room with 3m^2 of south facing glazing and 1.4m^2 of glazing facing north. If the modelled house is built with standard timber frame walls, timber floors and stud partitions, peak temperatures in the room could reach over 30°C, whereas in a masonry house they are likely to only reach just over 27°C. The average temperatures in the two models are much the same - around 25°C, but the swing about the mean is 2.3°C in the heavyweight house and 5.6°C in the lightweight one. If the south facing window in the model is replaced by patio doors, the situation is even more extreme. Temperatures in the masonry house are predicted to reach 29°C, whereas the timber frame house is likely to peak at over 34°C.

Further studies

A 1997 simulation study[5] investigated the difference in energy use between heavy and lightweight designs. Five sites around the UK were chosen, ranging from Plymouth in the south, to Aberdeen in the north, and the difference in energy use between the two types of construction was never greater than 5%. The lightweight buildings fared better than the heavy when heating was intermittent, due to the lesser mass of material, which needed warming before the occupants could feel the benefit. However, it was apparent that the heavyweight buildings performed better at balancing out diurnal temperature swings in the summer, although the heavyweight buildings heated up more slowly during the day, their effect in a prolonged heatwave was to cool down more slowly at the end of the period. During a cold spell though, a modern, well insulated building, is unlikely to cool down so rapidly that heating is needed during the non-occupied part of the day, even if the building does not contain significant thermal mass.

Interest has grown, over the past 20 years or so, in the use of passive solar energy as discussed in the previous article. This has placed the spotlight firmly on the role of thermal mass as a means of storing the surplus heat generated during the day. In all but extreme situations, the storage period desired was that of day to night, or possibly to the following early morning. It is possible to calculate the theoretical volume of thermal mass required in relation to the proposed area of south facing glazing.

For instance, the Pennylands housing devel-

Material	Density (kg/m^3)	Conductivity (W/mK)	Specific heat (J/kgK)	Heat capacity (kJ/m^3K)
Mineral fibre	25	0.04	750	20
Carpet	190	0.06	1360	260
Fibreboard	300	0.06	1000	300
Timber	630	0.13	1200	760
Lightweight aircrete concrete block	600	0.16	1000	600
Plasterboard	950	0.16	840	800
Brick	1700	0.62	800	1360
Medium density concrete block	1400	0.51	1000	1400
Stone	2180	1.5	720	1570
Dense concrete block	2300	1.63	1000	2300
Water	1000	1.9	4200	4200

Specific heat of several common building materials. It can be seen from the table that generally heat capacity increases with density. Also the thermal conductivity does the same - i.e. the denser materials conduct heat faster. This may sound obvious but often people confuse insulation and thermal mass. An old stone cottage will have a very high thermal mass but the wall U-value may be as high as $2W/m^2K$. This means that, without insulation, the cottage walls will act as excellent conductors to remove the internal heat from the dwelling during winter. Source: John Willoughby.

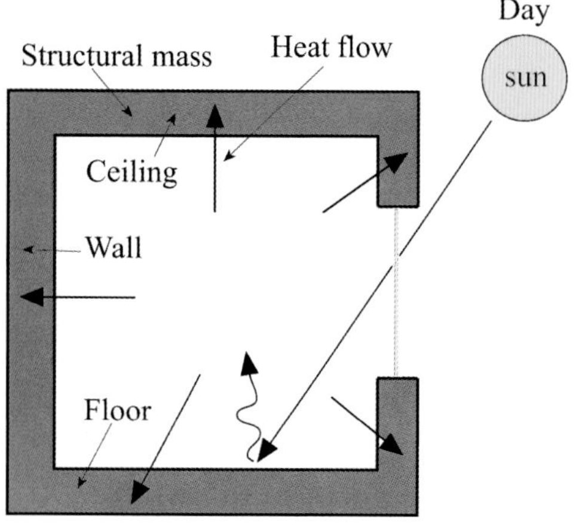

To be effective, thermal mass needs to be coupled with the space receiving the heat and preferably evenly spread. Research[3] has suggested that 90% of the recoverable heat flow is limited to a depth of about 50mm in dense concrete, and 50% of this to the first 25mm. *Diagram courtesy of Richard Nicholls*

opment in Milton Keynes was one of the earliest passive solar schemes in the UK, consisting of around 180 houses, with large, south facing windows and an unusually large provision of thermal mass, including dense concrete inner partitions and concrete ground and first floors. These buildings were extensively monitored for energy consumption. It soon became apparent that the 100mm of rockwool insulation, in the cavity walls had a far greater effect on reducing fuel consumption than did the thermal mass.

Human behaviour was seen as a drawback to the passive solar and thermal mass storage design on this project because the large windows led to a perceived lack of privacy for the occupants, resulting in profligate use of net curtains, thereby reducing the potential solar gain. Additionally, the British love affair with fitted carpets, considerably reduced the effectiveness of the thermal mass.

More recently a number of Scandinavian style, lightweight 'super-insulated' houses have been built, using prefabricated timber designs with no particular attempt made to collect solar energy, but these houses have been shown to have a lower fuel consumption than passive solar designed buildings. This is mainly because in a well designed highly insulated building, over half of the winter heating requirements can be met by incidental gains: from people, cooking, solar radiation, lights and appliances.

Many scientific papers on the 'lightweight versus heavyweight' subject have since been published. Unfortunately studies are often funded by vested interest groups on one side or the other. However, the balance of evidence suggests that the benefit of thermal mass in storing solar energy becomes a dis-benefit in intermittently heated buildings.

Winter energy consumption

The ability of thermal mass to absorb heat and smooth out swings in internal temperature in the summer, can also be important in reducing heating use in winter, but this applies only to well insulated buildings. In well insulated buildings with a large area of south facing glazing, the provision of adequate (but not too much) thermal mass could supply around half of the winter heating needs from solar gain. However, depending on the amount of mass included, the need for auxiliary heating is likely to be greater than that of a well insulated lightweight design.

In poorly insulated houses, thermal mass is almost certainly going to be a dis-benefit in winter, as in the example of the old stone cottage. Extra energy will be needed to heat up the mass, which then cools down rapidly. The thermal mass becomes a heat thief.

Other issues

Air conditioning

A recent worrying trend is the increasing use of domestic air conditioning to combat high summertime temperatures. Not only is air conditioning expensive to run, it is also a significant source of carbon dioxide emissions. In addition the refrigerant gases often contribute to the depletion of the ozone layer. So, from this it is possible to deduce that thermal mass could have an important role to play in combating the extravagant and unnecessary use of domestic air conditioning by helping to slow and reduce diurnal temperature swings. However, attention to window design and size of roof overhang, along with increased levels of insulation, could go a long way towards reducing the temperature swings in lightweight buildings.

Airtightness

The main point to make is that good insulation alone will not be enough to keep houses comfortable if they leak air like a sieve. Thus, the aim is to build an airtight shell, regardless of whether the construction is heavy or light. Most of the work on airtightness was done in Scandinavia and Canada where lightweight buildings predominate, airtightness being achieved with liberal use of sealants and membranes. Airtightness in heavy buildings relies more on wet plastering of walls and ceilings, along with good seals around windows and doors. The weak point in traditional cavity wall construction is where the intermediate floor joists penetrate the inner blockwork of external cavity walls. Modern design suggests that joist hangers should be used. Bespoke joist shoes (sometimes called boots) have been launched on the market in an attempt to address this serious heat loss route, but it is still too early to decide if these products are achieving the desired goal.

Attention to detail, regarding the sealing of the inner skin of outside walls, is of great importance in preventing interstitial condensation, which could pose a greater long term risk in lightweight constructions.

Conclusion

Energy consumption of buildings, it would seem, is only weakly influenced by thermal mass though it can play an important part in limiting the diurnal swing in temperature. Therefore, provided that solar and casual heat gains can be limited to moderate values, sufficient mass can be provided easily in all but ultra lightweight constructions and is best applied across the living spaces rather than in a single large mass centrally. To be effective though, thermal mass must be coupled to the space in which the gains are expected, either by radiant or convective heat flow paths. Highly insulative internal finishes (e.g carpets) will almost completely negate the beneficial effects of thermal mass.

Moderate amounts of thermal mass, when combined with high standards of envelope insulation, will offer a long cooling time constant and give occupancy comfort. However, since all buildings are, to some degree, intermittently heated, the better solar utilisation of the heavyweight buildings is compensated by the quick warm-up time of well-designed lightweight ones. Very heavyweight buildings will perform better than lighter buildings during heat waves - the build up of heat will be slower, but will remain longer. However, to benefit from night ventilation buildings must have thermal mass coupled with the cooling air, and also coupled with the occupied space.

It can be concluded then that, in terms of comfort and energy use, there is not a huge difference between heavy and lightweight buildings. The occupants of heavy buildings may benefit from reduced temperature swings, but this is at the expense of slightly higher energy consumption. However, there are other issues which require consideration when making a reasoned choice. The most important of these is the lower embodied energy in lightweight structures. The foundations can be less substantial and many of the major components can be short term, renewable crops (i.e. timber products).

Many thanks to John Willoughby BSc, MPhil, CEng, MCIBSE for the original study from which this article is built.

References

1. First published in Building for a Future (now Green Building) magazine. ***www.buildingforafuture.co.uk***

2. 'Energy and Environment in Non-domestic Buildings - a technical design guide' by N V Baker. Cambridge Architectural Research Ltd.

3. 'Environmental Performance and the Role of Structure and Materials' by N Baker. The Martin Centre for Architectural and Urban Studies, University of Cambridge.

4. Guide Book 'Environmental Design'. (CIBSE) Chapter 5 Thermal Response and Plant Sizing'.

5. 'Should it be Wood?' by P Smithdale (1997). Thesis submitted for MSc to University of East London.

Thermal mass is discussed at much greater length in the Green Building Bible, Volume 2.

Avoid electrical heating

Many people are mislead by the idea that if they buy their electricity from companies offering 'green' tariffs, they can continue using the same quantities, or even more electricity, under the illusion that they are no longer harming the planet. **Cath Hassell** and **David Olivier** dispel a few myths ...

Electric heating systems have been enjoying a growth in popularity in recent years, especially in the new homes' market. This is due to a number of reasons:

- the privatisation of the power supply companies
- good marketing strategies by these new, highly competitive businesses
- simpler installation and lower cost for the housebuilder or installer.

However, for the consumer there is:

- less controllability
- higher running costs
- fewer options for keeping warm in a mains electricity power failure
- the prospect of rising electricity prices
- the difficulty of changing to another fuel in the future.

The above points aside, the fact is that there is not currently enough green electricity to satisfy demand. So, even if you are paying a green tariff, 95% of the electricity you are consuming now is, in reality, either nuclear or fossil fuel generated.

Increasing energy use is the problem

Since 1990 energy use in the domestic sector has risen by a staggering 19% and now accounts for 30% of all energy consumption in the UK. Once we have insulated our buildings to the maximum levels possible, we should then look to use the lowest carbon fuel source for our heating and other energy needs. See the domestic fuel price guide in the Appendix at the back of this book for a comparison of the $C0_2$ pollution of various fuels.

Obviously, we have to use electricity for lights and most appliances, so we should choose the most energy-efficient options. However, there are better environmental choices than electricity for heating, hot water and cooking in our homes. These include gas, and LPG for cooking as well as heating, oil, wood pellets or chips and solar power for hot water. Most of these are discussed at length elsewhere in this book and in Volume 2.

Electricity generation is the most significant source of emissions of greenhouse gases in the UK, as well as a source of air pollutants. Given the current generating mix for UK electricity, 0.55kg of CO_2 is produced for every kWh of electricity delivered (DEFRA figures). Therefore, any increase in electricity demand will lead to an increase in CO_2 emissions, as more inefficient coal fired power stations are brought back on-line to meet increased demand. Of the current electrical generating mix, only 5% comes from renewables (the government target for 2007 was 7%). Yet 20% of the UK's electricity is consumed on just lighting our buildings and streets. Not until 2020 (and that is if the government's target of 20% is met) will renewables cover merely the lighting demand.

No spare capacity

All the renewable electricity produced in the UK is eagerly purchased by electricity suppliers under a renewables obligations' scheme. This will remain in place until 2010, thus ensuring a growing market and encouraging more investment in new renewables' generating capacity. Due to the great demand for 'green' electricity there is none spare. Therefore, our collective aim should be to 'reduce' our consumption of electricity, not to generate 'extra' demand. If we install electric central heating, then we shall be increasing demand and this demand can, at present, only be met from fossil fuel generation with its associated greenhouse gas emissions. There is also great concern that our increasing use of electricity has lead to the government favouring new nuclear power stations being built as the UK desperately tries to reduce the rising CO_2 emissions. Some building specifiers use the argument that by specifying electric heating they are future proofing against the time that supplies of natural gas runs out. However, if the supply of natural gas does run out, it would be simple enough to change from a gas boiler to another fuel.

The facts speak for themselves

It is interesting to note that in a dwelling built to the new 2006 Part L amendments of the Building Regulations, the hot water energy consumption could well be greater than the heating load. For example: a family of four, heating their hot water using a gas condensing boiler, would produce 1 tonne of CO_2, while heating the same hot water using electricity, would produce 2 tonnes. That extra tonne could not be offset by improving the insulation standards of the dwelling beyond the statutory requirements.

Another example: in a block of flats, over 1 tonne of extra CO_2 would be produced per 60m^2 floor area per year if electric space heating is specified instead of a condensing gas boiler. (These are emissions from a flat built to the 2002 Part L standard with an 'A' rated gas condensing boiler). We can more than double this penalty if a 90m^2 rural semi-detached house is fitted with electric heating instead of a condensing LPG boiler, because the heating demand of the house is much larger than the small flat.

Denmark has restrictions on the use of electric space heating in permanent dwellings. 60% of Denmark is now supplied by district heating, fed by CHP plants and industrial waste heat. The heat mains extends to detached houses in suburbs and even some nearby villages; there are no complaints from homeowners about lack of control but there are positive comments about the convenience of receiving mains hot water and heating compared to maintaining an individual boiler.

Conclusion

Electricity use for purposes other than those where there are no alternatives, (lights and appliances), cannot be justified, even by those signed up to 'green tariffs'. The likelihood of there being an abundance of renewable generated electricity is so far off that it is not worth considering as a serious heating energy source.

In a district heating situation, the idea of future proofing is incompatible with electric resistance heating. A building heated by electrical resistance could not participate easily in a community heating scheme. For example, Southampton's city centre is now heated this way - this would not have been an easy option if the hotels, hospitals, council offices etc, had originally had electric heating. District heating schemes commonly use industrial waste heat, waste heat from a CHP plant or seasonally-stored solar heat (developed par excellence in Sweden and Germany and now scheduled to supply 50% of Denmark's heat in the long term). Genuine future proofing would be to specify versatile heating systems that can use any type of fuel, not to lock owners or tenants into a blind alley with buildings heated by electric resistance wires. Electric resistance space and water heating is not environmentally sustainable.

We both buy our electricity from a 'renewable' supplier and urge readers of this article to do the same; it is important to show support for renewable electricity. However, neither of us use electricity for space or water heating and of course we have energy-efficient lights and appliances. ☯

In a cruel twist, the new Code for Sustainable Homes seems to be inadvertantly encouraging more, not less, elctricity use for heating of new homes Code level 3 and 4. See critique at: ***www.goodhomes.org.uk/downloads/news/101.pdf***

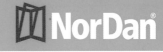

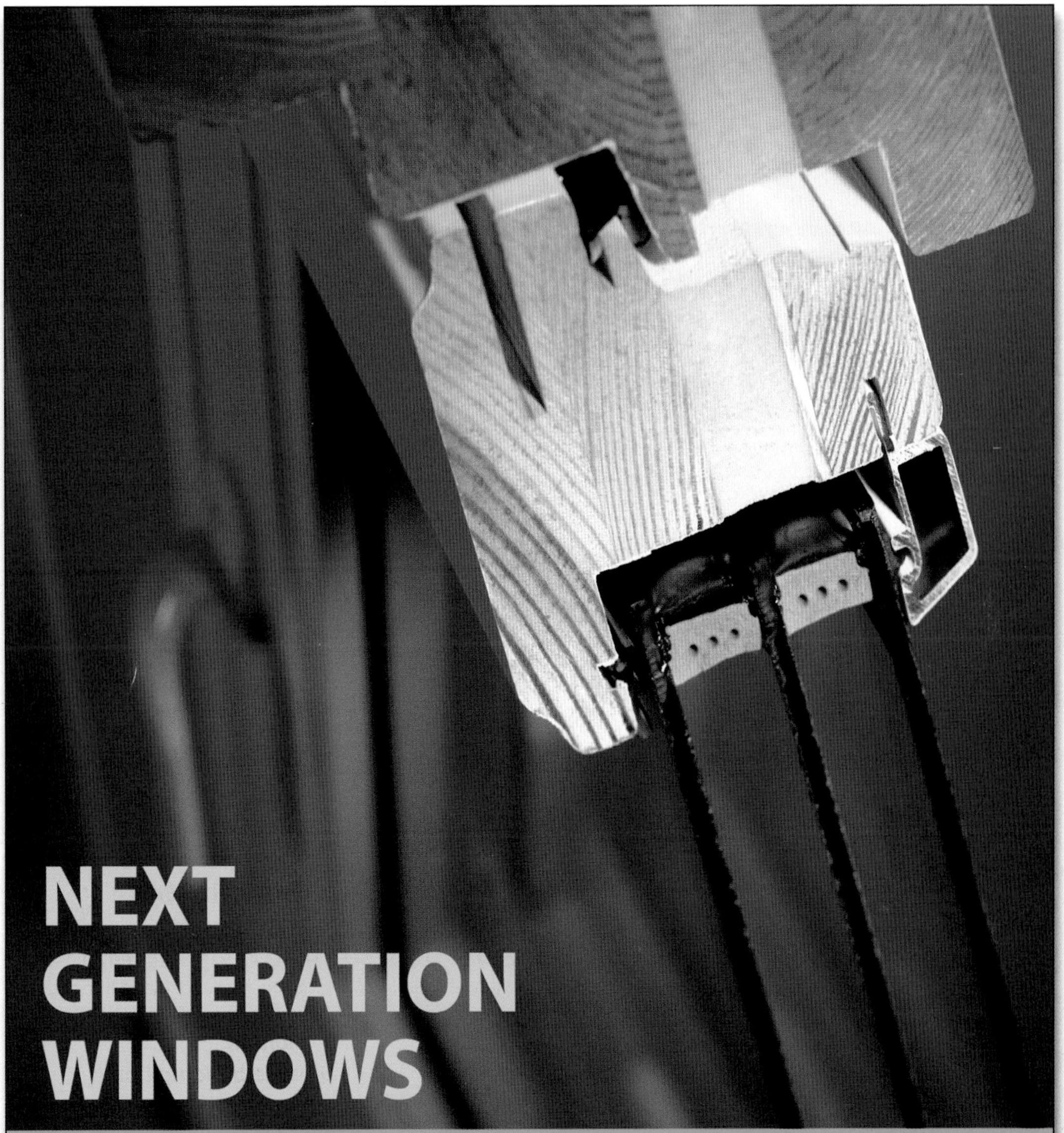
NEXT
GENERATION
WINDOWS

2 Trends and direction

Architecture review

Things are moving along fast in both the green building sector and the mainstream. But is this industry's new-found interest in environmental care doomed to flounder on the rocks of recession. **Oliver Lowenstein** looks at what has been happening since 2007 ...

Driven by the sudden mass conversion – in words at least – of the mainstream to the environmental cause, the green building community has watched on with a certain degree of astonishment at the sea change that has been occurring in the industry.

Whereas in 2006 the industry at large was just trying to get it's head around the latest changes to Part L of the Buildings Regulations, (and many are still struggling) the momentum for further greening of our buildings has really ratcheted up a number of notches, if only virtual. Government announcements, regulatory frameworks, and professional bodies have all come thick and fast. The primary reason for these changes has been a much more widespread recognition of the importance of green issues, expressed culturally in the green 'spike' across the general public, and politically in the government's belated recognition that the building status quo, energy and carbon emissions-wise, could not hold if they were to get serious about their EU and international emission reduction obligations of 60% by 2050.

If these commitments were driven by global warming fears, since then there's been the dramatic rise in oil and energy prices, bringing home to many the interconnected nature of the crisis. The government's attempts to push through legally binding change has underwritten the plethora of new initiatives and targets which, just a few years ago, many would have said, were unthinkable. From the setting up of the UK Green Building Council in February 2007, the remarkable (though probably unachievable) aspiration/goal of achieving zero-carbon in all domestic new build by 2016, the Code for Sustainable Homes (CSH) was launched in April 2008, through to the announcements on eco-towns, sustainability becoming a core agenda within the Building Schools for the Future (BSF) programme in 2007, and new news seemingly by the week. The impression that the country's building industry is in the midst of a serious step-change has been hard to avoid. All this is requiring new thinking and new approaches for many in the 30,000 strong architectural community in the UK.

Of course, grand pronouncements, targets and committees are a very different thing to what actually happens on the ground, but as White-Design's, Craig White says, '*there has been a transformation in the engagement of the issues,*' adding that *'while the challenge remains the same, during the last two years a tipping point has been reached and, rather than pushing horizontally, the momentum is now downward, spreading, fast moving and very fluid'.* White notes that the commercial world is 'hoovering up the agenda' with the corporate sector 'engaging at an amazing pace.' He cites his practice's contribution to Marks & Spencer's hundred-point energy reduction plan as evidence of corporate receptivity as an example; the contribution resulted in an additional thirty-two points being added, says White, to the supermarket's list. In practical terms this is playing out with the use of glulam, rather than steel, in some of Marks & Spencer new supermarkets. Vindication, White believes, in the argument led by Greenpeace and other NGO's of engaging, rather than sniping at the corporate world. '*It doesn't work to kick against the commercial sector*,' he believes. This is the optimistic and benign perspective on the corporate culture's commitment to environmental thinking, and White also acknowledges that his optimism is tempered by an, at times, and in his phrase, 'deep scepticism' as to how effective such change will actually be.

Certainly across what could be described as the traditional sustainable architecture community you get a spectrum of optimistic through pessimistic voices about the transformational step change, along with a ready awareness that this changing agenda is happening right under the community's feet. One repeated concern is how, with the arrival of both larger construction industry players and their mainstream architectural partners, the reliance on the technical fix, on gadgetry and yet further iterations of the tick box mentality is increasing beyond anything hitherto imaginable. Often the blame for this state of affairs is related to public-private partnerships which have come to dominate public building since New Labour came to power. As Architype West's director, Jonathan Hines, notes, cost-competiveness, *"is as tight as ever if not more so,"* and while there is now the added pressure of doing so within the new sustainable regulation what goes out of the window is design quality in favour of the easiest-to-deal with route, invariably arrived at through pursuing the technical fix option.

The design quality issue has been raised by the Commission for Architecture and the Built Environment (CABE), in its Sustainable Design, Climate Change and the Built Environment briefing. The briefing highlights the technical fix

White-Design's, Knowle West Media Centre in Bristol, which the practice claims is the largest modular straw panel structure in the south west of England.

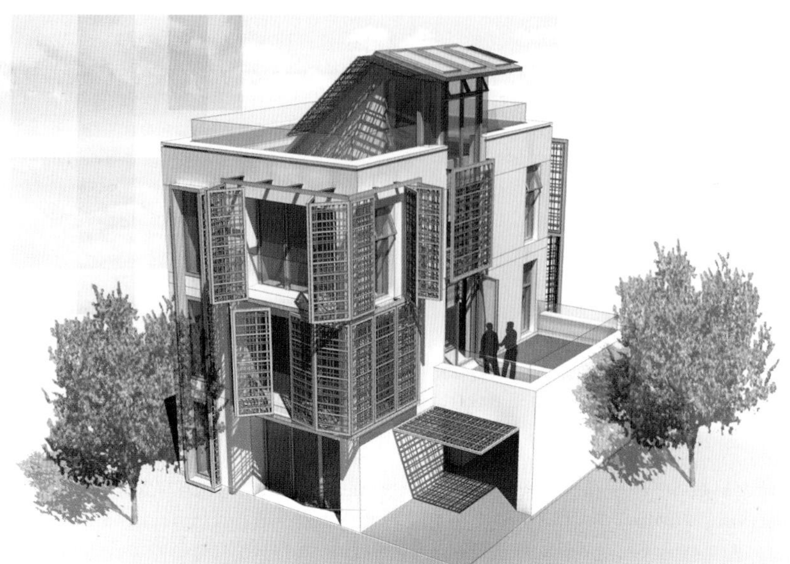

White-Design has extended its ModCell modular straw bale system into a concept carbon neutral house, aptly titled 'BaleHaus'.

mentality endemic at the architectural end of the debate. Calling for wholesale changes which move significantly beyond this prevalent green gadgetry mindset, the briefing, which looked at 700 projects, pointed to how very few of these began to genuinely grapple with sustainability issues, beyond the technical add-on level. This isn't news in itself, although the fact that CABE are publishing reports, which are getting discussed in the architectural and broadsheet media, can be construed as signals of change underway. Similarly, anyone from the committed deeper green wing of architecture may not have been surprised at the take-off achieved by greener trade fairs, such as Ecobuild, which in 2008 doubled in size with the big corporate players muscling in, if not fully taking over.

What was also evident is that the sector, architecturally as much as in construction terms, is dividing along almost ideological lines, with the mainstream arguing how much more energy efficient steel, concrete, and the business-as-usual materials base are becoming, and the architectural community quite happy to buy into this rebadging of old products.

The lower-tech, greener end of the construction materials and resources' market, often naturally sourced and therefore renewable, stayed largely stuck at the fringes, if making gradual but continued inroads into pockets of the market. It may be early days in terms of how relaxed bodies such as the new UK Green Building Council, are at this status quo situation given their road map to achieving carbon neutrality, but so far it seems unlikely that the sector can cope with considering anything much more more radical, such as the Centre for Alternative Technology's (CAT) Zero Carbon Britain ***www.cat.org.uk***, with its strong emphasis on a convergence and contraction strategy.

Arguably the core development for those interested in the prospects of an architecture more significantly informed by and built from the lower tech, naturally sourced end of the materials' palette has been the take-off in timber, discussed in greater length later in this chapter. Wood now seems to be an accepted and respected material, even if on occasion it is for the partial or complete purposes of fancy facades that come with a strong hint of greenwash. This said, today there is both architectural receptivity and new-found credibility attached to wood. No longer shunned, this is indeed a time for timber. The return of wood has, it seems, eased the door somewhat open for interest in the other natural materials, primarily earth and straw. While it is hard to claim that anything comparable to the initial momentum of timber is now beginning with either of these other natural materials, the complete and total barriers to their use does seem to be beginning to break down.

Just over ten years after CAT opened its rammed earth 'AtEIC' resource centre, the bastion of all things alternative energy, it is now three-quarters through one of the most ambitious rammed earth projects so far attempted in Britain. The WISE graduate school building, designed by the pairing of two of the old hands from the sustainable architecture scene, Pat Borer and David Lea, this time round, is also using hempcrete/lime hybrid materials. Further south-west in North Cornwall a project sponsored by the Duchy of Cornwall, is apparently going ahead with an all cob secondary school on the outskirts of Newquay. At the other end of the architectural spectrum, the Building Design Partnership (BDP) is also involved in a rammed earth build.

As regards popularising straw bale, White-Design has applied its ModCell system (modular straw bale box panels) to a number of buildings, including the York Eco-Depot and the most recent build, Knowle West Media Centre in Bristol, which the practice claims is the largest modular straw bale structure in the south west. White-Design have extended the ModCell into its concept carbon neutral house aptly titled 'BaleHaus' which was unveiled in 2008.

In parallel to this, Arco2 recently launched 'EcoFab'. A non load-bearing straw bale panel system. Arco2's, Martin Penk, talks of having developed EcoFab from scratch, without supporting funding from third parties, saying *"Our system has evolved from our previous on-site framed straw bale school buildings and involves the production of all basic elements, including roof and floors in modular panels or cassettes using timber products, straw and reclaimed lambs wool."* Arco2 has undertaken two projects with the system so far, one being an extension to Bosvigo's primary school in Cornwall. Penk believes EcoFab and ModCell are the only modular straw bale panelling systems currently available, although acknowledging that the wider the range, the broader the building solutions, which suggests he expects others to follow.

It's in timber however where the growth in renewable, natural and non-toxic materials is most clearly evident. At BRE's Offsite expo, showcasing zero energy homes last June, the majority featured were as high in wood usage as they were low in their zero energy affordable solutions. With Gordon Brown taking over as the country's new prime minister in May 2007, the focus on an early policy commitment of upping the annual rate of house building by 25%, from 180,000 to 240,000 per annum, with an end goal of three million new homes by 2020 was likely a developer's dream come true. But what came next sent shockwaves through the industry - the demand that all domestic new build would come with statuary requirement to be zero carbon by 2016. Taken together the policies opened up new possibilities for wood. If there continued to be considerable genuflections about how realistic and achievable the target is, the same target propelled the series of affordable zero energy prototypes demonstrated by the volume housing builders at BRE's Offsite expo.

EcoFab from Arco2 brings modular straw bale to housing in Cornwall.

Below and right: the Stewert Milne and Kingspan offerings at the BRE's Off-site expo in 2007 showcased their take on what zero carbon homes might look like.

A significant proportion of these, including Stewart Milne, Kingspan and Osborne, displayed their eco-concerned demonstration liveable wares, using wood as a central part of their representative designs, and it seems a fair anticipation that if the three million housing target maintains momentum, a significant element to meeting the zero energy dimension will be done by using wood. That said, with the economy in serious difficulties and all three of the largest volume builders, Barratts, Taylor-Wimpey and Persimmon hitting rough economic waters, reaching anything like the annual numbers the government is wanting seems unlikely; a recent report stating the volume-build sector would be hard pushed to complete an estimated 80,000 domestic homes in 2008.

Similar economic, though also social, question marks also hang over the final ten eco-towns which the government originally announced in 2007. What finally comes of this may provide some new development in greening medium and high-rise domestic building, including with the structural use of timber. This could be along the lines of Architype's five storey post and beam student housing for Swansea University, or the structural application of massive wood as seen in London architect's, Waugh Thistelton's nine storey tower bloc, Murray Grove Stadthaus in north London, the highest in Europe (see photos on page 82). Once the ten final sites are announced over the next months, and with a head of critical steam gathering about their rationale, architectural, design and master-planning questions ought all to be coming to the fore as to nature and quality. We will have to wait and see how green the eventual eco-towns will actually turn out to be. Bioregional's link up with developer Quintain, in Middlehaven and various other sites across the country, may provide one answer, and is also another instance of how developers are beginning to see the commercial attraction of sustainable development.

Alongside Bioregional's trademarked OnePlanetLiving and partnership link-ups with Crest Nicholson, and the World Wildlife Fund, it seems comprehendible that Bioregional-Quintain is calling itself the first large-scale sustainable developer in the UK. The first three projects, the Middlehaven site in Middlesborough, the zero energy Gallions Park in the Thames Gateway and One Planet Living in Brighton will make or – maybe damage - Bioregional-Quintain's reputation. A major north-eastern regeneration initiative, Middlesborough's scheme, has brought in young and fashionable practices not immediately associated with sustainability; Alsops, FAT and Studio Egret West, while at Gallions Park and Brighton, architecturally, Feilden Clegg Bradley Studio are running things. Along with various other big claims these eco-district projects will show how well Bioregional's OnePlanetLiving concept works in practice. With BedZED's now exhaustive public exposure has come the less welcome publicity that it hasn't quite lived up to its zero carbon claims, with some of the kit not working as efficiently as was hoped. And with the mainstream media now much more attuned to sustainability building issues, the success or otherwise of the Bioregional Quintain project will surely be watched closely, with failings – real or perceived – highlighted in the national press.

If there's uncertainty as to how and whether the new eco-towns, eco-districts and the greening of volume building can be, for architects there are, or should be, questions regarding the architectural quality of this whole sector. The same charges regarding design quality, which so concern CABE, are being spoken of with respect of the eco-towns plans and the volume market generally. Vicky Richardson, editor of design magazine Blueprint, while no close friend of the sustainable architectural community, has a point when, in a recent opinion piece, she blasted the lack of design ambition across the current British 'eco-town' and housing architecture landscape.

Alongside the acknowledged standards in finishing, detailing and other quality of build issues, anecdotally often underlined as 'just as bad as ever,' the actual architectural quality can make one apprehensive about what will come out of this unprecedented opportunity for integrating sustainability into the built environment. The temptation for contractors to cut economic corners, to value-engineer and to maximise speed over quality of build, all contribute to such concerns. For some a turn to the more rigorous detailing and design qualities found over many parts of the Nordic and German speaking countries, and particularly within the passivhaus movement, are exemplars to be applauded and pursued. This, however, may be changing. If British architects have been slow to notice the passivhaus movement, news is finally beginning to disseminate; Architype, for instance, sees it as a significant contribution and in London, Bere Architects' principal, Jonathan Bere, has been proselytising on behalf of passivhaus.

The wasted opportunity theme also nags away close to the heart of the debate of Building Schools for the Future (BSF). The £45 billion, largest school building programme in fifty years which, although stalled, seems to be beginning to deliver schools across the early county-wide waves of its fifteen year timetable. CABE have again produced a report, highlighting the continuing overall low design standard of new schools coming on stream. Some new school building may be meeting the challenge of being well-designed, educationally functional and effective, as well as highly sustainable projects; dRMM's Kingsdale sports' and music hall (2007) stands out in this respect and there is movement in the system – Devon County Council, for instance, is working on a passive secondary school in Bideford. But CABE's 2006 briefing, Assessing Secondary School Design Quality - where half of 120 or so schools built in the previous five years were judged to be of poor quality – has since been followed up with further warnings and another report, this time on embedding design champions into the design process. Yet with the DfCSF announcing that all schools would also be required to be zero-carbon by 2016, this seems only a part of the uphill challenge facing the whole BSF project.

With BSF continuing to encounter difficulties, and with the perception that it is early days for whether the volume builders are up to meeting the zero carbon 2016 deadline, that apprehension is in the air isn't surprising. Superceding these uncertainties, is the economic turmoil brought on by both the credit crunch and the rapid rise in oil and energy costs. There's also the question of what happens to public sector investment with the resurgent Tory party, were it to win the next election? What consequences would these have on the boom in sustainable architectural culture, a boom which has been on the back of New Labour's good economic times? How emphatically would a triumphant new Conservative government, who has flourished by adding greenery to the heart of its re-invention, really push the sustainable agenda in building culture? Whoever wins the next election, the oil and energy issues, so central to the raison d'etre of sustainable building, are hardly going to go away.

Energy prices are already having divergent and multilayered effects; building in the country is slowing down at the latest count to an estimated 80,000 domestic homes a year, even if in energy terms this is arguably a good thing. But if the economic downturn continues, the lack of investment may well squeeze out some sustainability choices until and unless the economic benefits of carbon neutral and low energy building are right in front of client's eyes, rather than an added cost with only abstract future advantages.

The next few years may be the critical period in defining the nature of the transition to fully-fledged sustainability within British architectural culture. The extent to which both much more holistic and organic approaches will be taken up by both the mainstream architectural, as well as the wider building culture, could well be determined during this period. Some in the industry may hope that with the likes of CABE and the UK Green Building Council engaging in the field, issues such as addressing architects reliance on technical-fix solutions, in contrast to more rounded approaches, will get the exposure to influence changes in professional mindsets as well as how architectural students learn within the country's architecture schools.

Sustainable architecture's one-time community and alternative identity and belief-system may be long gone, yet up to a point it may still be able to influence this debate, providing examples and showing the benefits of different approaches for a technically-minded industry. Parts of the same architectural community are, these days, also very much at home within the arena of big industry public-private partnerships, and exert a degree of influence on the current emerging sustainability in building ethos. At times the ethos, in its beliefs and commitments, can appear pretty interchangeable and hardly different to that which it once appeared to define itself against.

You might ask, do all our homes, schools, communities and other building types being built, beyond their aspirations to carbon neutrality, point to anything fundamentally different in the future of a culture? Or did a certain John Lydon, once of the Sex Pistols, get it right when he screamed, "your future dream is a shopping scheme?" Lydon is now himself a developer in California. Too crude, probably, an anti-vision of the future. Yet the West's consumer mindset, its cult of money and materialism, is not, on the whole, territory architects venture into. Partially, surely, because architects are all too implicated in this tricky, uneasy territory. And also, it seems, because of its overlap with politics and power of a different, all too human kind. Might it mean that while much of the architectural world is at the first, early stages of its sustainability journey, for others crowded out by the new arrivals, the journey may well be close to ending? ☯

Green legislation review

Since the last edition of the Green Building Bible there has been a steady flow of legislation and consultation documents. **Michael Smith** reports ...

Since the publication of the planning for a sustainable future consultation, there has been a regular flow of construction related legislation. This supports the 'approved documents', clarifies European Directives, while some is entirely independent. This brief review will begin with documents affecting the Building Regulations and then work outwards.

Changes attached to the Building Regulations

The Code for Sustainable Homes (CSH) was introduced to improve the overall sustainability of new homes by setting a single national standard within which the home building industry can design and construct homes. It offers a tool for developers to differentiate themselves within the market, while giving homebuyers better information about the environmental impact of their new home and its potential running costs. The CSH was also accompanied by a technical guide, which sets out the requirements for the code and the process by which a code assessment is reached, while making this as simple, transparent and rigorous as possible: **www.communities.gov.uk/publications/planningandbuilding/codeguide**
and
www.communities.gov.uk/publications/planningandbuilding/codeguidesummary

Direct amendments to the regulations

The Building (Amendment) Regulations (SI 2008/671), and the Building and Approved Inspectors (Amendment) Regulations (SI 2007/3384) - both of which amend the Building Regulations 2000, the latter also affecting the Building (approved inspectors etc.) Regulations 2000. While these changes are not entirely green, they do have an effect on all site work. **www.opsi.gov.uk/si/si2008/uksi_20080671_en_1**
and
www.opsi.gov.uk/si/si2007/uksi_20073384_en_1

Legislation not attached to the Building Regulations

There are several sustainability issues that have been highlighted in legislation during the last year. Due to the confines of space only a brief summary of each is below;

The Home Information Pack (No. 2) Regulations (SI 2007/1667) - prescribe the documents to be included in home information packs and the circumstances in which they are included. They provide for exceptions and enforcement and make further provision in relation to home condition reports. The 'No.2' refers to the issue of the Home Information Pack (Revocation) Regulations (SI 2007/1525), which revoked the Home Information Pack Regulations (SI 2006/1503) and (SI 2007/992), with effect from 31st May 2007. **www.opsi.gov.uk/si/si2007/uksi_20071667_en_1**

Site Waste management plans regulations (SI 2008/314) - require any person intending to carry out a construction project, with an estimated cost greater than £300,000, to prepare a waste management plan. The plan must be updated in accordance with the regulations, which are enforced by the Environment Agency and the local authority. **www.opsi.gov.uk/si/si2008/uksi_20080314_en_2**

Environmental Permitting (England and Wales) Regulations (SI 2007/3538) - replace the system of waste management licensing in Part II of the Environmental Protection Act 1990

(Ch. 43) and the Waste Management Licensing Regulations (SI 1994/1056), with a new system of environmental permits in England and Wales. **www.opsi.gov.uk/si/si2007/uksi_20073538_en_1**

Energy Performance of Buildings (Certificates and Inspections) (England and Wales) Regulations (SI 2007/991) - implement articles 7, 9 and 10 of European Directive 2002/91/EC, which lays down requirements for the production of energy performance certificates when buildings are constructed, sold or rented out, display of certificates in large public buildings, and regular inspections of air-conditioning systems. **www.opsi.gov.uk/si/si2007/uksi_20070991_en_1**

Town and Country Planning (General Permitted Development) (Amendment) (England) Order (SI 2008/675) - amends Part 2 of Schedule 2 to the Town and Country Planning (General Permitted Development) Order 1995, inserting a new Part 40 to the Schedule. It provides permitted development rights for the installation of specified types of microgeneration equipment, including solar PV and solar thermal equipment on or within the curtilage of dwelling houses, subject to certain criteria. **www.opsi.gov.uk/si/si2008/uksi_20080675_en_1**

Stamp Duty Land Tax (Zero-Carbon Homes Relief) Regulations (SI 2007/3437) - provide relief from stamp duty land tax on the first acquisition of a dwelling, which is a 'zero carbon' home in accordance with sections 58B and 58C of the Finance Act 2003 (Ch. 14). **www.opsi.gov.uk/si/si2007/uksi_20073437_en_1**

The Sustainable Communities Act 2007 (Ch.23) - intends to make provisions for local authorities to submit plans in connection with promoting the sustainability of local communities and to specify the indicators by which the sustainability of local communities may be measured. **www.opsi.gov.uk/acts/acts2007/ukpga_20070023_en_1**

Ecodesign for Energy-Using Products Regulations (SI 2007/2037) - implements requirements of European Directive 2005/32/EC establishing a framework for the setting of ecodesign requirements for energy-using products (see right). **www.opsi.gov.uk/si/si2007/uksi_20072037_en_1**

Renewable Transport Fuel Obligations Order (SI 2007/3072) - implements Chapter 5 of Part 2 of the Energy Act 2004 (Ch. 20), and imposes on transport fuel suppliers, in the UK, an obligation to produce evidence that a certain amount of renewable transport fuel has been supplied. **www.opsi.gov.uk/si/si2007/uksi_20073072_en_1**

Communities Department

The Communities Department has produced several important documents, but of special note with regard to green issues are the Code for Sustainable Homes (mentioned earlier), and the supplement to PPS 1. **www.communities.gov.uk/publications/planningandbuilding/codesustainabilitystandards**

Planning and Climate Change - Supplement to Planning Policy Statement 1, PPS 1 - sets out how planning, in providing for the new homes, jobs and infrastructure, should help shape places with lower carbon emissions and resilience to the climate change now accepted as inevitable. The supplement to PPS1 sets out how planning should contribute to reducing emissions and take into account the unavoidable consequences. **www.communities.gov.uk/publications/planningandbuilding/ppsclimatechange**

The future

Judging by recent head of state meetings in Tokyo (summer 2008) (a world drop of 50% in carbon emissions is needed) there could be a whole lot more sustainable legislation, especially in light of the current economic and oil and gas crisis. However, watch out for the backlash, the construction industry is being hurt from all sides and suffering badly; it won't be long before it can no longer cope with the pressure.

The implementation of the **Energy-using Products Directive (EuP) (2005/32/EC)**, expected to occur over the 2 year period 2009-2011, will signal changes in the way many energy-using products are designed and specified. Inter governmental agreements, under the EuP, might actually reduce the number of products on the market or could mean industry having to give energy ratings for complete systems; some industry commentators and organisations are in favour of this, though exactly what shape the EuP is likely to take is not yet clear. The European Commission believes that the EuP can reduce Europe's energy consumption by about 10%; however, a study by the International Energy Agency (IEA) on energy savings, has attributed around 30% of all energy saved to product standards of the type envisaged in the EuP.

The framework for the implementation of the EuP provides a basis for establishing minimum eco-design requirements for energy using products. The aim of the directive is to reduce the environmental impact of these products, contributing to sustainable development while also ensuring the free movement of products within the European Union.

The market transformation programme (MTP) entrusted with ensuring the UK marketplace offers products in line with national sustainable policies, has segregated and targeted 19 product groups, ranging from laptops to commercial boilers to street lighting, which are likely to be affected by the introduction of the EuP directive. Since the EuP was published in July 2005, the MTP has been organising product analysis to see where energy savings can be designed in.

Manufacturers, consultants and EU groups are now beginning to set the criteria their products must begin to meet by the end of 2009. Final details of UK criteria will be decided by the MTP, DEFRA and the Department for Business, Enterprise and Regulatory Reform (BERR). However, to get there, a series of consultations and proposals, based on production possibilities and technical performance, must be gone through. The EU, though, insists that there is a clear intention for the EuP to avoid in-depth legislation on design. Rather, it hopes to encourage voluntary action by manufacturers to eco-design their products.

Implementation of the EuP into UK law could be through amendments to the Building Regulations or, as a last resort, Brussels could issue a European Regulation, which would then have to be implemented, without national consultations or debates. The links below showcase the implementing measures and latest news on how the various groups are likely to be introduced, as well as current events relating to the EuP directive itself.

Boilers and combi-boilers (gas/oil/electric)
www.ecoboiler.org
Water heaters (gas/oil/electric)
www.ecohotwater.org
Personal computers (desktops and laptops)
www.ecocomputer.org
Imaging equipment: copiers, faxes, printers, scanners,
www.ecoimaging.org
Consumer electronics
www.ecotelevision.org
Standby and off-mode losses of EuPs
www.ecostandby.org
Battery chargers and external power supplies
www.ecocharger.org
Office lighting - public (street) lighting
www.eup4light.net
Residential room appliances (air conditioning etc)
www.ecoaircon.eu
Electric motors 1-150kW, water pumps, circulators in buildings, ventilation fans (non-residential)
www.ecomotors.org
Commercial refrigerators and freezers, including chillers, display cabinets and vending machines
www.ecofreezercom.org
Domestic refrigerators and freezers
www.ecocold-domestic.org
Domestic dishwashers and washing machines.
www.ecowet-domestic.org
Domestic lighting (Part 1) and domestic lighting (Part 2)
www.eup4light.net
Complex set top boxes
www.ecocomplexstb.org
Solid fuel small combustion installations
www.ecosolidfuel.org
Vacuum cleaners
www.ecovacuum.org
Laundry dryers
www.ecodryers.org

Wood in architecture

Designing with, and specifying of timber has been increasing dramatically across many projects compared to just a few years ago. **Oliver Lowenstein** discusses the progress and the drivers for this renaissance ...

The intervening period since the third edition of this book has been marked by the emergence of sustainability as a serious part of the building industry's mindset. When looking at how these changes are influencing the fortunes of different building materials, the ensemble of regulatory, economic, cultural, and industry changes have probably seen their most striking effect as regards the use of wood across the architectural community. So much so, that people openly talk of the present moment as the, or at least a, time for timber. Time and again I've found many talking of 'everything's changed'. This may be a mite too dramatic, but a point to begin with is that the situation is radically different, and the cautious hope of two years ago has been replaced with an open acknowledgement that timber as a material of choice has returned to favour among architects, and is no longer cold-shouldered by a profession which, until recently, perceived it to be provincial and non-modern.

All this said, timber – in terms of the sustainable architecture debate, rather than its use in the volume market – is still a small part of the materials' mix across building types in Britain, rather than up there on anything like equal footing with modern materials; i.e. concrete, steel, brick and glass. And what of course is, to use the inglorious oil-inflected phrasing, 'driving' timbers resurgence, is the mix of referents noted above. To top it all, timber won an audience vote at Ecobuild 2008 in a battle of the most sustainable materials' choice and thus became the recipient of much attention, with the industry scrambling to figure out how it could deliver buildings within the brave new carbon rulebook of our government's CSH dreams.

If then, zero-carbon is the first 'plank', which has underpinned the changes in this twenty-four month period, the second has to be the green 'moment' or green 'spike', which has engulfed the cultural mood in Britain. This has been good news for timber. With a modicum of hindsight it's becoming clearer that the big push for quasi-iconic timber showcases in the first five years of the new decade, such as the National Assembly for Wales building (right) was timely in feeding through into this greening of the general public's senses.

That such timber showcases have been more evident in England and Wales than in Scotland, has been explained by Ivor Davies at the Edinburgh's Centre for Timber Engineering, as due to wood in construction being an already established, rather than 'new exotic' building material north of the border, compared to the south. Be that as it may, there seems to be a slowing of large scale timber showcases on the level of Eden Project's 'core' building, the Savill Gardens' gridshell, or the Welsh Parliament building in Cardiff (right), but an increase in use within the educational and health sectors and privately funded projects.

A third obvious factor in favour of wood is economics. Not so long ago part of the reasoning as to why so few timber projects were getting anywhere; was that they were just so costly and expensive. Today using timber is competitive. Nowadays, buildings of wood can be delivered much more competitively against the other main materials. This is, in part, due to continual commodity and material price hikes in steel and, to a lesser extent concrete, with the former often unavailable at prices which British specifiers could afford, increasingly outbid by

The National Assembly for Wales building in Cardiff, completed and opened after years of extended wrangling. The Assembly building employs natural passive heating and cooling, an earth heat exchange system and a wood fired boiler.

Photo courtesy of Redshift Photography

their counterparts in China and India. That was a year ago. A year on oil has moved to the front of the page, its unstopable rise in cost, now beginning to give shudders even in the mainstream. For peak-oil proclaimers this is only the beginning. In such a climate, with transportation costs soaring – Baltic and middle European timber is being seen in a new light. Even if timber prices are rising, Europe though may be the kind of local sourcing that some readers of Green Building Bible consider as genuinely local, and therefore sustainable enough.

However, for those working in the mainstream, getting timber from middle Europe - Austria or Southern Germany to London and the South East, a journey of around 1000 miles, is not really much farther than Scottish stands, were it to even exist in commercial quantities. Also, timber prices, in Scotland of larch and Douglas fir doubled in 2007-2008. A moving target at the moment given how oil and energy prices have only recently been concentrating people's minds.

At the moment, school buildings, are the most common recipients for the latest timber system designs. BDP (Building Design Partnership) won RIBA's 2007 Schools award with their Marlowe Academy in Ramsgate, which features a Gordon Cowley engineered glulaminated gridshell canopy over its main hall/circulation area. The practice has a long list of schools on its books. By contrast RMJM's ECOspace for Lauder College, Fife used green timber throughout its new extension area, aiming to highlight local Scottish timber, though ironically, due to lack of local availability, they had to procure some of the greenwood from Normandy, highlighting, for some, the supply problem of indigenous Scottish woods.

Down in Bristol, White-Design architects and Architype are producing a steady stream of wood based educational buildings. Architype's focus is on post and beam, with a new three storey school, Green Park Special School in Wolverhampton, as well as a long string of primary and other early years schools and family provision centres for Lewisham, South East London, most of which use timber. At the smaller end of the scale there are various small practices using wood in schools such as Phinn Manassah's Penzance Haymoor secondary school's new hall, which was the only timber-build to get through the Sorrell Foundation's Charity, JoinedUpDesign, schools' project. These are only a few representative examples, and what this fly-through list doesn't state is how widespread wood in school specification is at the moment.

Timber is also making inroads into the commercial sector. Tesco have apparently commissioned BDP for its first glue laminated supermarket canopy, for better or worse. There are reports of other retailers with similar eco-makeover plans. This is, of course, seriously mainstream and can be taken as evidence of how timber is now seen as the carbon neutral alternative. Is this just going with the flow, greenwash or for that matter just one more nail in the coffin of any meaningful sustainable architectural movement as harbinger for another kind of future? Arguably more significant are the signs of timber as part of a new paradigm in office building environments. Here, as in Page & Park's new Scottish Loch Lomond and Trossach's National Park Authority Head-Quarters in Balloch (below) on the edge of Loch Lomond. The building, which uses native Douglas fir in its post and beam system, is the largest greenwood build in Britain. David Page, one of the practice's directors talks of the building as significant for the 'embryonic' Scottish timber industry, but at £5 million Loch Lomond's an expensive building and whether there will be further developments may well depend on whether there is spare money in the Scottish government's pockets to continue these sorts of exercises. In the larger scale of things, the integration of wood's tactility and warmth, indeed its material and expressive qualities, is a hopeful signal about the way the British countries is thinking about its working culture, although whether it will be taken up by the commercial sector again remains to be seen.

Aside from Loch Lomond, White-Design is replaying its Velux Loughborough showroom office in Midlothian, and glulam turns up in

Page & Park's new Scottish Loch Lomond and Trossach's National Park Authority head-quarters in Balloch on the edge of Loch Lomond. The building, which uses native Douglas fir in its post and beam system, is the largest greenwood structure in Britain.

many of the smaller eco-industrial parks found on the outskirts of towns across the country. Some of the immediate aspirations of the both the greenwood and timber frame community, making inroads into different segments of the mainstream, may rest on whether Loch Lomond will translate into a longer term success story, in terms of new and further research, and in the bigger clients commissioning new buildings. Another very recent high visibility Scottish showcase is the Culloden visitor centre, on the site of the famous historical battle a few miles from Inverness. The build dramatically applies larch cladding, making a case for how this Scottish tree can be used effectively. It may be premature of Page to talk up this embryonic native industry, while in the next breath speaking out of turn about imported massive wood beginning to be used in Scottish projects. The hope must be that both will flourish, with massive wood turning into a home-grown sector, along with projects such as Loch Lomond providing inspirational springboards for a thorough re-evaluation of greenwood's value, both in Scotland and in the south.

Below: the industrial scale music room and sports' hall. Phase 2 of Kingsdale School's redevelopment. Both buildings are constructed from prefabricated timber panels allowing for speedy site erection.
Photos: courtesy of KLH.

Even as there are new, inspiring examples of timber frame arriving, the most dramatic change in the timberbuild scene is the rush in uptake of engineered woods over the last two years. Across the engineered woods' sector, laminated wood has, according to Liam Dewer, director at Eurban, more than doubled in the last year in tonnage being imported. If this has grown from a low, if already existing, base, the arrival of cross-laminated panelling systems has grown exponentially from almost non-existent beginnings three or four years ago, to, again, a doubling in orders in the last twelve months on 2006. While cross-laminated timber has been used for over twenty years on the continent, the sudden conversion of many architects, and rapid uptake of cross-laminated timbers to sustainability agendas seems to be linked to the realisation that a planar rather than merely linear wood material can replicate aspects of the qualities of reinforced concrete.

Highest profile so far is dRMM's Kingsdale Schools sports' and drama hall (below) in south-London. The practice has used the Austrian company, KLH's cross-laminated panels expres-

sively, leaving exposed all the walls, a design approach which has rarely been part of the continental design ethos. Kingsdale is being followed by the visitors' centre at the Edinburgh Botanic Gardens, designed by by Edward Cullinan Architects, and Sherrart Pringle Richards new Coventry, Herbert Art Gallery arcade (opening 2008), where the panels being used have been curved, the product this time coming from the other main operator in the UK, FinnForest Merk. Perhaps the biggest current news, however, is the KLH system being applied to the tallest timber high-rise so far built in Europe, Waugh Thistleton's nine-storey, Stadthaus, in Hoxton, North London. This building is engineered by Techniker – who has done the maths for a 14 storey as well, and says it works – opening the gates to timber mid-rise across the urban fabric, potentially drawing down such dense urban domestic builds into carbon neutral and positive numbers.

Whether this will happen is perhaps moot; the developers of Stadthaus, Telford, is hardly a paragon of green building, with over 300 projects on site this year alone, and none of these containing anything like this level of built-in sustainability. It is also, apparently, less enthusiastic in repeating a wood build of this kind. KLH meanwhile has moved on, with its largest timber order for another secondary school, this time the St John Fisher secondary school in Peterborough, designed by Gotch Saunders Surridge, currently on site in the midlands. Eurban also have the St Agnes primary school project in Manchester on their books, using up to 16,000 logs, which once processed will finally result in the materials required for the build.

What happens next is almost as interesting as where things have arrived at. With the credit crunch, the inexorable hike in oil prices and the downturn across the Western world in economic fortunes, how will the next two years play for wood use across the building sector? If depression brings less building, one consequence may be less carbon emissions, the stay-in-bed theory of saving the world. Architectural practices are already noting a lessening of orders from the private sector. With Gordon Brown and the Labour party on the ropes, there could

The KLH timber panel system is being used to build the nine-storey 'Stadthaus' in Hoxton, North London. This is the tallest timber high-rise building yet built in Europe, designed by Waugh Thistleton architects.
Photos courtesy of Will Pryce.

well be quite a big question mark as to what will happen to Brown's flagship £45 billion Building Schools for the Future programme, along with the general public building investment if the Tories return to power, presumably towards the end of the next two years.

Oil hikes, and a general increasing awareness of sustainability within the population at large, ought to work in timber's favour though, especially since more in the architectural community and particularly those at the younger end of the profession, seem to be increasingly tuned into the material's various possibilities. Signs of this are summer schools and wood workshops currently emerging. The young Bath practice, Mitchell Taylor Workshop, has been organising special timber summer schools in Gloucester for interested young architects; note that these only first started up in 2006. Also the Architectural Association, which now owns Hooke Park, may finally be getting something together down in Dorset, which would open up this ahead-of-the-times wood-world centre. Also the Centre for Contemporary Arts and the Natural World (CCANW) at Haldon Forest, Exeter, Devon is finishing its two year Wood Culture programme and are running architecturally related, wood courses, as is the Flimwell Woodland Enterprise Centre in East Sussex. In terms of wood culture, Flimwell, continues to teeter on turning into something rather unique, carrying on the mantle left by John Makepeace at Hooke Park, as a showcase for how indigenous, low-grade English hardwoods; particularly chestnut, as well as Douglas fir and larch, can be re-engineered for specialist use in buildings currently being built or on the drawing boards at the centre.

The specialist manufacturers of these, In-Wood, have increased their output significantly, although the share of hardwood engineered timber, compared to softwood, remains minimal, at perhaps 3%. The argument here is whether these local adapted hardwoods can service more than only a local and specialist market and move into any larger segment of the timber market. If they do so, they will be fulfilling one of the core sustainability issues that has taken root at a popular level across other areas, i.e. buying locally, either food or other products, the kind of vision that animates the often interwoven permaculture and transition town movements. This suggests the possibility of a two-track timber culture, one that is working and services the architectural and building wing of corporate culture, which is increasingly seeing timber as a more credible, acceptable material than before. And a second, grassroots take-up of timber, interwoven into the larger re-awakened and new energies that the green moment has engendered. How far each of these actually grow will unfold during the next two years. ☯

The Woodland Enterprise Centre at Flimwell, East Sussex, where Woodland Enterprises Ltd has championed the rebirth and re-introduction of local timber use by developing new ways of using local timbers.
Inset: Shorne Wood Country Park in Kent.
Both projects are built with sweet chestnut in the cruck frame method.

Code for Sustainable Homes

Our built environment accounts for over half of our carbon dioxide emissions. We now have the Code for Sustainable Homes (CSH) to help designers and builders of new homes in the UK. But will it help or hinder? **Keith Hall** reports ...

In April 2008 the government launched the Code for Sustainable Homes (CSH), calling it a 'step-change in sustainable home building practice'. The scheme that it replaced, and that it is modelled on (EcoHomes) failed to capture the imagination of the very conservative house building industry outside token projects that were blessed with government funding or control through either English Partnerships or the Housing Corporation and housing associations.

Unlike EcoHomes though, the CSH feels much more like a mandatory, rather than an optional code. It has been introduced following lots of chest beating by high ranking politicians. Interestingly, the mainstream housing industry did actually sit up and take notice, as did the Construction Products Association. In fact they did a lot more than that, they got involved with its development. Why? Well, mainly because at the political level, a lot of carrots were dangled around and, although we have begun thundering towards a recession, at the time of its introduction we were at the pinnacle of a housing boom, with massive demand for homes and a lot of potential new housing sites hanging in the balance.

The government used this almost unprecedented demand to throw down the challenge. Permission would be given for new sites as the carrot (new eco towns), but adoption of the CSH is the stick. Essentially, the feeling was that any volume builder, who could prove to be singing from the 'zero carbon home' song sheet, could expect to be favoured with easier planning permission. It sounded good for the shareholders, good news for home buyers and good news for the environment. But is it?

Well the answer has to be a guarded 'yes' because it has captured the imagination of many mainstream developers and the industry as a whole. However, on the downside, since the launch of the CSH we have seen unprecedented levels of greenwashing. The most striking example is that many, very ordinary building products are being re-branded green, purely based on the assumption that they could be used in projects built to the CSH standards. No Code level is mentioned but let's not forget that Code level 1 is barely better than current Building Regulations! Another example is industry trade groups[1] claiming that all their members are now zero carbon but merely on the back of carbon offsetting! Are they now CSH compliant?

The true definition of 'zero carbon' has yet to be properly defined and big players in the industry have recently discovered that they may have bitten off more than they can chew by going along with the government's rallying cry of 'zero carbon by 2016' (in Wales by 2011). This is an impossible goal and doomed to failure from the beginning, but we need to watch this space over the next couple of years for a further re-definition and a probable watering down of what 'zero carbon' actually means. For the time being though see the boxout (far right) for the present definition. One concern is that it will get diluted in its requirements but not in name. For instance, there is a proposal on the table suggesting that builders who are unable to meet the zero carbon target by that time will be allowed to pay a fee. A fine, if you like, which, it is touted, will be used for carbon offsetting elsewhere. Therefore, one word of warning before we go on, what you read here may well not be what will actually be required in 2016.

	Date					
Who it affects	**2008**	**2010**	**2013**	**2014**	**2015**	**2016**
English Partnerships funded projects	*Code level 3*	*Proposed code level 4*			*Proposed code level 6*	
Housing Corporation funded projects	*2008-2012 Code level 3*		*2013-2015 Code level 4*			*Likely to require code level 6*
Everyone else via Building Regulations	*Assessment mandatory for all dwellings*	*25% carbon improvement **	*44% carbon improvement**			*Proposed zero carbon homes*

Table 1. Expected rollout programme for CSH in England.

** below 2006 Building Regulations baseline.*

Another, more subtle and perhaps overlooked, aspect of zero carbon is that, if aiming for level 6, builders (site owners) are having to enter the power generation business at a hopelessly uneconomic scale, which somewhat ignores the efficiencies of the renewables obligation certificate system (ROCs). At present it seems that on-site renewables will be eligible for tradable ROCs, which effectively renders them part of the national renewable generation grid, and despite being on-site, adding nothing, or very little, to the national total. Feed in tariffs (that have proven so successful in other European countries) to encourage more on-site generation, may well have been a better route towards 'zero carbon' than ROC's, certainly at this small scale where plant costs are high and returns are low.

Zero carbon is not the only problem facing anyone wanting to achieve Code level 6. When you get to that level other difficult requirements also kick in, some of which are step-changes, such as increasingly stringent water use restrictions (more on this later). But at Code level 6 the Lifetime Home standard becomes mandatory[2]

The SAP (standard assessment procedure) software that forms the basis of the Part L of the current Building Regulations also underpins the energy category of the CSH. This has come under much criticism and is due to be updated in 2009 when, hopefully, all the anomolies will be corrected and the procedure brought up to date. For a fuller description of SAP see page 92.

Background to the CSH

The CSH was developed, at least in part, in response to the European Parliament's Directive 2002/91/EC on the energy perform-

The 'zero carbon' home

(as defined in the Code)

A 'zero carbon' home is where net carbon emissions resulting from ALL energy used in the dwelling is zero. This includes the energy consumed in the operation of the space heating/cooling and hot-water systems, ventilation, all internal lighting, cooking and all electrical appliances. The calculation can take account of contributions from renewable/low carbon installations on/in the dwelling, or provided by an energy services company (ESCO) on/offsite, provided it directly supplies the dwelling. Alternatively it is acceptable to include, in the estimate of carbon emissions, the contribution from 'accredited external renewables'. For a true zero carbon home, it will also be necessary to ensure that the fabric of the building significantly exceeds the standards currently required by Part L of the Building Regulations 2000 (as amended). The 'heat loss parameter' (covering the walls, windows, air tightness and other elements of the building design) must be no more than 0.8W/m^{2}K.

CSH uses the SAP (standard assesment procedure) computation which takes into account energy consumed through heating, lighting and hot water provision. Homes will have to reach zero carbon for these factors using the SAP computation. Heat and power for this element must be generated either in the home, or on the development, or through other local community arrangements, (including district heat and power) and must be renewable (i.e. non-fossil fuel) energy. A zero carbon home is also required to have zero carbon emissions from use of appliances in the homes (on average over a year). SAP does not contain any provision for energy consumption of appliances but will be updated to do so in due course. Until SAP is updated the 'appliances' element of the qualification will be that each home must provide an amount of renewable electricity equal to a specified amount of kWh per metre squared of floor space, in addition to that required to meet zero carbon in the SAP 2005 to approximate to the average appliance energy consumption. This additional power must be renewable power, produced either within the area of the building and its grounds, elsewhere in the development or beyond, as long as the developer has entered into arrangements to ensure that the renewable generation is additional to existing plans. The amount of such additional power can be reduced by any surplus from the arrangements to meet zero carbon on heating, hot water and lighting.

Extracted from the CSH Technical Guide 2008.

Award level	*Minimum points required*
Code level 1 (★)	*36*
Code level 2 (★★)	*48*
Code level 3 (★★★)	*57*
Code level 4 (★★★★)	*68*
Code level 5 (★★★★★)	*84*
Code level 6 (★★★★★★)	*90*

Table 2. The CSH award levels, the percentage points required for achieving each level.

On-site low and 'zero carbon' generators

(as defined by the Code)

At the time of publishing, the following technologies may be considered for achieving zero carbon homes, as defined by CSH:

Solar:
- solar hot water
- photovoltaics

Water:
- small scale hydro power

Wind:
- wind turbines

Biomass:
- biomass single room heaters/stoves
- biomass boilers
- biomass community heating schemes where the majority of heating comes from biomass

Combined heat and power (CHP) and micro CHP for use with the following fuels:
- natural gas
- biomass
- sewerage gas and other biogases

Community heating:
- can include utilising waste heat from processes such as large scale power generation where the majority of heating comes from waste heat.

Accredited external (off-site) renewables

(as defined by the Code)

Renewable energy schemes located offsite may be accredited renewables (as defined by the Energy Act 2004). These will be 'renewable energy guarantee of origin' (REGO) certified. They have to be new installed generation capacity, designed to meet the loads of the dwelling being assessed (i.e. not just units of carbon), and are additional to capacity already required under the renewables' obligation

Adapted from the CSH Technical Guide 2008

ance of buildings, itself a response to Kyoto. In 2006 the government announced the 10-year timetable towards a target that all new homes from 2016 must be built to 'zero carbon standards'. This would be achieved through a step by step tightening of the Building Regulations, see Table 1. Since April 2007 the developer of any new home in England could choose to be assessed against the Code, (technical guidance is now available[3]).

On the 16 November 2007 the government confirmed that it would be proceeding with the implementation of mandatory ratings against the Code for all new homes, following responses to the consultation on making a rating mandatory. From May 2008 all homes built in England need to be rated to the CSH. The Code is a voluntary scheme for private builders but, from May 2008, every house has to have a Code rating. At face value this appears to be self contradicting. The key is the difference between the rating and the assessment of a building. It is possible for no assessment to take place, and if so, the building would be awarded a nil rating, even if it would perform well under the Code criteria.

The CSH builds heavily on EcoHomes 2006, and actually uses much of the format as well as content. This is because the Building Research Establishment (BRE), who established EcoHomes, has been heavily involved. Many have wondered why EcoHomes was not actually updated instead of introducing what seems to be a totally new standard. The CSH uses a one to six star rating-system (see Table 2), with one star being the entry level, which has been set above the current building regulations requirements. Here are the key differences from EcoHomes:

- minimum standards for energy/CO_2 at all levels (see Table 3)
- uses different measurement method for CO_2 (% reduction on TER (target emission's rate)) rather than $kgCO_2/m^3$
- different weightings for points to EcoHomes
- materials' section relies heavily on the Green Guide from the BRE
- points previously awarded under EcoHomes

for public transport and amenity have been dropped
- the addition of surface water run-off and waste as new categories
- the removal of a location-dependent category (transport). It is thought that the reasoning behind this was that the planning system will soon be able to deal with this aspect
- minimum standards, water efficiency at all levels (see Table 4).

Code level	Minimum percentage reduction in dwelling emission rate (DER) over target emission rate (TER)
Level 1	10
Level 2	18
Level 3	25
Level 4	44
Level 5	100
Level 6	'zero carbon' home, (as defined in box out on page 85)

Table 3. Carbon dioxide (CO_2) emissions resulting from operational energy consumption and calculated using SAP 2005)

Source: Code for Sustainable Homes Technical Guide[3]

Code level	Maximum potable water consumption in litres per person per day
Level 1	120
Level 2	110
Level 3	105
Level 4	90
Level 5	80
Level 6	80

Table 4. Potable water consumption (from WCs, showers and baths, taps and appliances, calculated using the CSH water calculator).

Source: Code for Sustainable Homes Technical Guide[3]

Although the CSH replaced EcoHomes for new housing built in England from April 1st 2007, EcoHomes 2006 continues to be required for all Housing Corporation funded housing in Scotland and Wales, as well as refurbished housing in England (EcoHomes XB).

BRE, who developed the CSH on behalf of the government, has also been appointed to act as the registration, quality assurance and certification body under contract and is co-ordinating the training of assessors to the new standards and it is hoped that take-up and enthusiasm among the house building fraternity matches that of the government.

As said earlier, there is concern among stakeholders that not all homes will be able to be built to Code level 6, as it is currently defined. Already two reports have called on the government to better define its zero carbon aspirations. In August 2007 the Renewables Advisory Board (RAB) published a report entitled 'The Role of On-site Energy Generation in Delivering Zero Carbon Homes'. Using a computer model developed by professional consultants, Element Energy, they simulated the choices that developers would have to make when attempting to build 'zero carbon homes'. Using the RAB assumptions the model predicted that 11.6% of dwellings constructed will be unable to meet the current requirements.

Given that the government has set stretching targets for the number of dwellings that need to be delivered, as well as the standards at which they must be delivered, a zero carbon definition that stops homes being delivered is clearly not desirable. And in November 2007, the Callcutt review recommended that 'The government should set out, as soon as possible and no later than the end of 2008, exactly how zero carbon performance is to be defined, and how far the use of renewable energy is to be taken into account in the assessment of performance. The assessment rules should differentiate between local and remote renewable generation, and should allow for the different circumstances of different sites.'

Regardless of the above, the rest of this article will look into the composition of the Code, but not the fine detail. We will examine how it has been assembled, with the view to further in-depth analysis of categories and

	1	2	3	4	5	6
	Category	**Explanation**	* See Table 6 ** See Table 7	**Credits**	**Mandatory**	**Maximum**
Mandatory categories (must achieve the minimum credits in these categories)	1. Energy/CO_2	The most testing category with rising minimum DER standards of improvement over TER* at each Code level for Ene1 (see also Table 4 far right). Credits can be gained up to the maximum using heat loss parameter (HLP) of the building fabric, Other credits are awarded for internal lighting, drying space, specification of ecolabelled white goods, locally-provided low or zero-carbon energy technologies, cycle storage and the potential for a home office.	Ene 1: Dwelling emission rate (DER) *	15	Yes	29
			Ene 2: Building fabric	2	No	
			Ene 3: Internal lighting	2	No	
			Ene 4: Drying space	1	No	
			Ene 5: Energy labelled white goods	2	No	
			Ene 6: External lighting	2	No	
			Ene 7: Zero/low carbon technologies **	2	No	
			Ene 8: Cycle storage	2	No	
			Ene 9: Home office	1	No	
	2. Water	Rising minimum standard (and credits) for internal water use at each code level – as well as points being awarded for rainwater collection.	Wat 1: Indoor water use	5	Yes	6
			Wat 2: Exterior water use	1	No	
	3. Materials	The minimum standard here is set at code entry of BRE Green Guide 2006 D-rating for at least three of: roof structure and finishes, external walls, upper floor, internal walls, windows and doors – and additional points for responsible sourcing of materials (both basic and finishing elements).	Mat 1: Environmental impact of materials	15	Yes	24
			Mat 2: Responsible sourcing of materials - basic building elements	6	Yes	
			Mat 3: Responsible sourcing of materials - finishing elements	3	No	
	4. Surface water run-off	Compliance to the minimum standards here does not earn credits. However, credits up to the maximum for this category can be earned for SUDs schemes and location according to flood risk zone.	Sur 1: Management of surface water runoff from developments	2	Yes	4
			Sur 2: Flood risk	2	Yes	
	5. Waste	With mandatory requirements for household waste storage – and additional credits (2) for household recycling facilities, construction waste management and provision of composting facilities.	Was 1: Storage on non recyclable waste and recyclable household waste	4	Yes	7
			Was 2: Construction site waste management	2	Yes	
			Was 3: Composting	1	No	
Optional categories	6. Pollution	Credits are available for global warming potential (GWP) of insulants, and NOx emissions from space heating / hot water systems.	Pol 1: Global warming potential (GWP)	1	No	4
			Pol 2: No_x emissions	3	No	
	7. Health and wellbeing	Credits can be gained for extra provision of daylighting and sound insulation standards, the provision of private space and meeting lifetime homes standards.	Hea 1: Daylighting	3	No	12
			Hea 2: Sound insulation	4	No	
			Hea 3: Private space	1	No	
			Hea 4: Lifetime homes	4	No	
	8. Management (man)	Credits available for provision of a home-user guide, various construction site impacts, and compliance with the Considerate Constructors' Scheme and 'Secured by Design' standards.	Man 1: Home user guide	3	No	9
			Man 2: Considerate constructor scheme	2	No	
			Man 3: Construction site impacts	2	No	
			Man 4: Security	2	No	
	9. Ecology (eco)	Credits available for ecological value of the site (and change in ecological value), ecological protection and enhancement, and overall building footprint.	Eco 1: Ecological value	1	No	9
			Eco 2: Ecological enhancement	1	No	
			Eco 3: Protection of ecological features	1	No	
			Eco 4: Change in ecological value	4	No	
			Eco 5 Building footprint	2	No	

Table 5. At a glance description, credits and weightings of the 9 categories that make up the Code for Sustainable Homes . For guidance only, it shows the whole process of categorisation, credits, weighting values and minimum expectations at each of the six code levels.

7	8						
	Maximum weighting (points) available						
Credits get converted to weightings using the weightings value	**Minimum (%) weighting required to achieve each level**						
1.26	1.2	3.5	5.8	9.4	16.4	18.8	36.5
1.50	1.5	1.5	4.5	4.5	7.5	7.5	9
0.30	0.2	0.2	0.2	0.2	0.2	0.2	7.2
0.55	2.2	2.2	2.2	2.2	2.2	2.2	2.2
0.91	0	0	0	0	0	0	6.3
0.70	0.7	0.7	0.7	0.7	0.7	0.7	2.8
1.17	1.1	1.1	1.1	1.1	1.1	1.1	14
1.11	2.2	2.2	2.2	2.2	2.2	2.2	10
1.33	1.3	1.3	1.3	1.3	1.3	1.3	12
Code level	**1**	**2**	**3**	**4**	**5**	**6**	**Total 100%**
Points needed at each level	**36**	**48**	**57**	**68**	**84**	**90**	

% Improvement (reduction) of DER over TER	*Mandatory at*	*Credits*
> 10%	*Level 1*	*1*
> 14%		*2*
> 18%	*Level 2*	*3*
> 22%		*4*
> 25 %	*Level 3*	*5*
> 31%		*6*
> 37%		*7*
> 44%	*Level 4*	*8*
> 52%		*9*
> 60%		*10*
> 69%		*11*
> 79%		*12*
> 89%		*13*
100%	*Level 5*	*14*
'Zero carbon home' (see boxout on page 85 for definition)	*Level 6*	*15*

Table 6. Credits are awarded in the energy/CO_2 category. These are based on the percentage improvement in the dwelling emission rate (DER), (estimated carbon dioxide emissions in kg per m^2 per annum arising from energy use for heating, hot water and lighting for the actual dwelling), over the target emission rate (TER) (the maximum emission rate permitted by Building Regulations), for the dwelling where DER and TER are as defined in AD L1A 2006 edition of the Building Regulations. Note that to reach level 6 (zero carbon) there are additional requirements. Additional calculation sheets are required to include the appliances and cooking element. Each home must provide an amount of renewable electricity equal to a specified amount of kWh per m^2 of floor space in addition to that required to meet zero carbon in SAP 2005, in order to offset the CO_2 due to appliances and cooking.

Ene 7. Zero/low carbon technologies	***Credits***
Where energy is supplied from local renewable or low carbon energy sources funded under the Low Carbon Buildings' Programme (or similar), or is designed and installed in a manner endorsed by a feasibility study prepared by an independent energy specialist	
AND	
There is a 10% reduction in carbon emissions as a result of this method of supply.	*1*
OR	
There is a 15% reduction in carbon emissions as a result of this method of supply.	*2*

Table 7. The controversial 'Ene 7' component of category 1 expects on or near-site zero carbon generation for all energy needs of projects that are targeting Code level 6.

sub-categories in later stories or future Green Building Press publications. However, at the moment the lower levels of the Code are essentially dead-weight and not really worth aiming for if you are serious about creating real green buildings and wish to take the government's aspirations for zero carbon homes by 2016 seriously. Certainly, all of the demonstration homes built to date, and the first few real projects that have been completed and assessed to the CSH, have been aiming high - levels 5 and 6.

Details of the Code

The Code itself comprises nine categories, with tradeable points in each, so that developers can choose categories that offer the strongest sustainablilty agenda for any particular site. The award levels of the Code (built from the combination of scores from the nine categories) is in 6 levels, with level 1 being the lowest.

Table 5 on the previous spread shows how each category plays a part in earning points towards building a total score to conclude, at a given code level, with the minimum and maximum attainable points (%) for each category. It is worth remembering, at this stage, that each level of the CSH is awarded on the basis of achieving BOTH a set of 'mandatory' minimum standards and a minimum overall score. Many of the credits within the method are tradable against measures in other categories, so a developer/designer can make choices on the most appropriate (and achievable) issues/solutions for a given site. This gives a degree of flexibility in achieving the Code.

Trying to get a handle on how all the credits, weightings (%) and, finally, points all come together to give an overall score, is a little like rocket science, but a short explanation, with some help from the Code's technical guide (2008), will help us to understand the system of scoring. First, take a look at Table 5 in particular make a note of the numbers in the top row as they relate to the example below. Within each category, credits are awarded for achieving specified degrees of performance (column 4). The weighting factors (column 8) show the contribution made by each category to the total performance recognised and rewarded by the Code. The total available contribution is expressed as 100%. The weighting of each category is expressed as a fraction of this, such that the sum of all the category contributions equals 100%.

Simple worked example

As an example, the maximum 29 credits available in category 1, energy and CO_2 emissions, contribute a possible 36.5% of the total available points. But each particular level of the Code has a minimum that has to be achieved, so if you want to achieve Code level 3, then you need to earn enough credits from the issues in that category (Ene 1 to Ene 9) to convert using the weighting value (column 7) into a minimum of 5.8%. From Table 4 we can see that Code level 3 has a minimum DER over TER requirement at this level (see Table 4) so 5 credits will need to be earned from the energy saving measures in the structure. This alone would be enough to meet the minimum as 5 x 1.26 = 6.3. However, in practice it is very likely to be coupled with any number of the non-mandatory sub-categories in that category (column 3) to get your score up higher. This higher score can then be traded against less easily achieved aspects in other categories. Another example, the four credits available for pollution can contribute up to 2.8% of the total available score.

What is the weighting value?

By dividing the weighting factor by the number of credits for each category, we arrive at an approximate weighted value for each credit. For instance the energy/CO_2 category, 36.4% contribution (column 8) to the total, divided by the 29 possible credits available (column 6), means that each credit in this category is worth about 1.26. The same formula applies to each of the other categories. It is very important to note that weightings apply at the category level only and not for individual credits to avoid rounding errors. It is worth keeping in mind that achieving a high performance in one category can sometimes result in a lower level of performance for another. For instance, if biomass is used to meet heating demand, credits will be available for performance in respect of energy supplied from a renewable source, but credits cannot be gained for low NO_x emission. It is therefore impossible to achieve a total percentage points score of 100.

Keep in mind that categories 1-5 are mandatory, where the minimum credits have to be met for every level of the Code. Of the mandatory categories, energy and water are the only ones that carry points. These can be added to the tradable points achieved in all the other categories to achieve a total number of points. This can then be used to determine the Code level that has been achieved.

In the water category there are increasingly stringent mandatory minimum water consumption requirements for each level of the Code and nobody seems to know what the best and most workable solution is, to achieve the higher level requirements. Overall, the methology behind this category seems to have been developed with the best intentions, then tweaked during the hasty preparation of the Code but due to vagaries of different types of properties or family sizes the water category is proving to be one of the greatest bones of contention in the CSH. For example, unless there is some amendment to the requirements, developers are likely to fit flow restrictors that could easily be tampered with after occupation and install rainwater harvesting systems which can be used to offset the consumption of water using appliances such as toilets, outside taps etc.

In the materials category (Mat 1), there is a mandatory requirement, with no credits to achieve a Green Guide rating of between A+ and D for at least three of the following five elements of the building envelope:·

- roof
- external walls
- internal walls (including separating walls)
- upper and ground floors (including separating floors)
- windows

Is it time to get into the CSH?

If you have decided that now is the time to knuckle down and tackle CSH sooner rather than later, then you first need to decide what level of the CSH you want to target. Zero carbon (level 6) will not be a requirement in England until 2016 and remember that all energy use must come from renewable sources on or adjacent to the site, so it is quite a big task at the moment but not impossible for the innovative. Code level 5 has already been achieved by one or two real projects but at the time of publishing Code level 6 has only been achieved at the CSH demonstration houses at the BRE's Watford site (though a number of Code level 6 projects were at the late planning stages and about to go on site).

Perhaps the first thing you should do is visit the BRE's Green Guide website (**www.thegreenguide.org.uk**), which will help you get aquainted with the A+ to E rating system based on embodied environmental impacts of construction elements that has been adopted by the BRE for the structural and non structural elements of buildings, which the materials' category of the CSH relies upon so heavily. It is probably worth pointing out here that there is much criticism, particularly from the natural building product sector, regarding the methodology used for the ratings in the Green Guide.

There is no easy way of achieving the higher levels of the CSH without lots of research and dedication to the goal. Many offsite system manufacturers, using modern methods of construction (MMC), are working overtime to come up with off-the-shelf solutions to achieving the higher levels. Whatever route is chosen will need practical airtightness training for those involved in the on-site assembly to ensure what is designed is actually built.

Here is a brief introduction on how to go about registering a project, choosing a code level and getting the whole site approved. The assessment has to be done before any work on site begins, so it is not possible to retrospectively gain the CSH certification. The whole process is audited so that random checks can be carried out on any project for quality control. The process includes the following;

- first choose your assessor for the CSH from

the register at **www.communities.gov.uk**
- next, your assesor will register your site with the BRE. Registration lasts for five years
- your dwellings will be registered as types, and each type will need to be assessed as 'code dwelling types'. Points are then assessed on 'site wide issues' and for 'dwelling type issues' and on a house by house basis, so for homes that have solar panels on, for instance, orientation could be an issue and some could score badly if they faced east or west
- the CSH assessment will be carried out in two stages; the first being at the design stage - at this point each code dwelling type is given an 'interim' code certificate. The second stage is after completion of the building phase, when each dwelling is given a 'final' code certificate.

It is difficult to assess the cost of the CSH assessment procedure itself but suffice to say there will be a number of hidden costs. As well as the actual cost of certification, there will probably be a need to employ specialist consultants to advise on acoustic, ecology and sustainablilty issues to say the least. Regarding the physical cost of upgrading a range of housing types to meet various levels of the CSH, English Partnerships and the Housing Corporation comissioned a report which may be worth reading[4].

Conclusion

Having read this, hopefully you will now have a basic understanding of how the CSH ticks. As you read on through this book (and Volume 2 if you have a copy) it will become clear how the issues covered relate back to the basic assumptions in the CSH. Whilst we will not attempt, in this edition, to walk you through every particular aspect of every subject and its relationship to the CSH, when we do mention it, you should be able to cross-reference back to Table 5 to refresh your memory of how things fit into place. What should have become rather clear from this discussion is that the CSH is not a building standard, but an award scheme which, if everything goes to plan for the government, will soon be a basic requirement. Because it is not a building standard perhaps those aspiring to achieve the higher echelons of the CSH should now seriously look towards building standards that can offer robust and repeatable results that will ensure that homes built following the standards will pass the required level of the CSH. Later in this book we will briefly examine the currently available standards.

Standard assessment procedure (SAP)

The 'standard assessment procedure' (SAP) is a compulsory assessment that must be carried out on all new buildings, or converted buildings that have undergone a change of material use. This was made compulsory under the amendments made to the Building Regulations Part 1, which came into place in April 2002. SAP 2005 is used as the government's standard assessment procedure in order to show compliance with Part L of the Building Regulations. It replaces the older SAP 2001 standards.

SAP is used to give a building a rating from 0 to 120, based on the annual energy costs of the building. The procedure also outputs a carbon index, which is a measure from 0-10.0. This is expressed as a 'national home energy rating' - a certificate can be issued to this effect giving a simple indication of the home's energy needs for space heating and hot water.

The outputs of the SAP procedure are:

- a measure of the energy consumption per unit floor area of the building.
- a SAP rating (energy cost rating)
- environmental impact rating
- DER (dwellings emission rate) which is the rate at which a building produces CO_2

The SAP procedure looks at the amount of energy that is needed for space heating and water heating. This is just one of its limitations – it does not take into account electrical loads and many other factors.
How SAP ratings compare to the A-G scale:
A. 92 or more
B. 81 to 91
C. 69 to 80
D. 55 to 68
E. 39 to 54
F. 21 to 38
G. 1 to 20
To give a general overview, most of the existing UK housing stock would come out with an average SAP rating of between 40 and 50.

The SAP specification can be downloaded from: **http://projects.bre.co.uk/sap2005/pdf/SAP2005.pdf**

This story is intended only as an introduction to the CSH. It does not go into depth regarding the flaws identified in the energy and water categories, for example. Some believe it is just about ticking boxes and there is criticism about the lack of transparency and accountability - should a mandatory code be managed by a private body, such as the BRE? It is evident when looking at the CSH, and how it works in detail, that a whole new sector is being created, with all the added bureaucracy, costs and environmental impact this entails. One does begin to wonder why it was necessary to develop it as a separate entity. Most of the measures that CSH brings to the table might better have been gradually introduced into the existing Building Regulations structure. And ... a final word, use your own judgment when you view green claims from product manufacturers that their products are 'zero carbon' or 'CSH ready'! ☯

With thanks to the following people for reading and commenting on the content of this article: John Garbutt, Peter Armfield, Sally Hall, Jerry Clark, Neil May, Nick Grant, Chris Herring, Mike George, Alan Clarke, David Olivier, Andy Simmonds and Liz Reason.

References

1. 'Carbon Copy' newsletter in which the Mastic Asphalt Council (MAC) announced carbon zero status for the whole of the mastic asphalt industry. This was achieved by merely adding a small levy to the cost of all materials to pay for carbon offsetting!

2. The Lifetime Homes checklist: ***www.lifetimehomes.org.uk/codeassessors***

3. 'The Code for Sustainable Homes Technical Guide' 2008 is free to download from : ***www.communities.gov.uk/publications/planningandbuilding/codeguide***

4. 'A Cost Review of the Code for Sustainable Homes' February 2007: ***www.cyrilsweett.com/pdfs/Code%20for%20sustainable%20homes%20cost%20analysis.pdf***

Notes and further reading

For commercial buildings, BREEAM will continue as the 'industry standard' for the time being. A new update was released in May and comes into force in August.

Free software: Stroma, the multi-displine accreditation scheme, has made its Code for Sustainable Homes (CSH) software free to anyone and everyone that wants it - accredited or not! ***www.stroma-ats.co.uk/form2.htm***

The Energy Saving Trust has published three documents to support those wishing to achieve Code levels 3 and above (CE290,291,292). They can be downloaded from the EST website: ***www.energysavingtrust.org.uk/housingbuildings/publications***

Published critiques of the CSH

'Levels 3 and 4 Technical comment': ***www.goodhomes.org.uk/downloads/news/101.pdf***

'A critique of the CSH water Efficiency Requirements': (GHA internal document).

Claimed to be the first Code level 5 social housing development in the UK, these homes in South Nutfield, Surrey, built by developer, Osborne, on behalf of the Raven Housing Trust, achieve a 100% reduction of carbon emissions over 2006 Building Regulation standards. The homes were built using structural insulated panel (SIPS).

Countdown to zero carbon

John Garbutt takes a look at what regulated emissions' targets may be in 2010 and 2013 before hitting the 2016 deadline, what kind of measures will work, and asks whether zero carbon is really the way to go ...

As the planet is hotting up, so is the pressure on the construction industry to build 'zero carbon' buildings. But however desirable it may be to achieve this target, it also has to be practicable. This task will get even harder as we nosedive towards a recession. The Code for Sustainable Homes (CSH) is the key policy instrument in achieving this goal, a position endorsed by the incorporation of its carbon dioxide emissions' targets with the proposals for the next three revisions of Approved Document L1A (ADL1A). But what exactly will it mean in terms of the practical elemental standards to which we build?

First of all it is important to take stock of the Approved Document L1A requirements that came into force in 2006 and to consider whether we have successfully taken this initial step. This is important as it forms the baseline for both the Code and future editions of the Approved Document. If there was a Code level 0, then 2006 ADL1A carbon emissions' standards would equate to the standard of Code level 0.

The complexities of changing from a simple elemental method of calculating compliance, to looking at the carbon emissions of the whole building, that were introduced in the 2006 Approved Document, appear to have had the effect of both stimulating innovation and, at times, stifling common sense. In the first place there are concerns that not all buildings, supposedly being built in compliance with the 2006 Approved Documents L (ADL) are actually meeting the required standards, let alone the far more demanding ones that are being bandied about for 2010 ADL1A and beyond.

Meanwhile debate also continues over the extent and role that sources of renewable energy can realistically play in this vital mission to reduce greenhouse gases. Anomalies, such as the current greater carbon emissions' allowance for buildings operating a heat pump (which permits an astonishing 48% more carbon output than buildings without) are blatant absurdities that it is to be hoped will not appear in future revisions. Because of this loophole, it is possible to build a building in compliance with the 2006 ADL1A that emits more carbon than it would have done if it were built to the old 2002 Approved Documents. Although there is no question that renewable energy is a crucial factor in reducing carbon dioxide emissions from the generation of heat and power, the conservation of energy and the provision of energy from renewable sources are not the same thing, and it is important that we do not focus all of our attention on the latter at the expense of the former.

For example, the change to an overall CO_2 emissions' target within the Approved Documents L was driven by Article 3 of the European Energy Performance of Buildings' Directive (EPBD). The EPBD also entails assessing a building's energy performance, giving it an 'asset rating' (AR) based on designed performance and an 'operational rating' (OR) based on actual performance and issuing an 'energy performance certificate' (EPC) rating that performance. Every time a building is let or sold the OR comes under review and the revised EPC forms part of the legal process.

Any deterioration in performance will become apparent and could ultimately affect the value of the property. The whole ethos of the Directive is therefore focussed on delivering real, long term and visible reductions in emissions.

Now it may seem very tempting to simply take the basic envelope, design in airtightness to, say 5m³/hr/m² instead of 10 at 50 Pa, and then add in some state of the art photovoltaics or solar thermal systems. However, there are potentially grave problems with taking this route, especially in the context of the aims outlined above.

The question you have to ask yourself is whether you can be confident that elements, such as site installed renewable energy sources will perform as specified, or even still present ten or twenty years down the line? There is a chance that they won't, as their continued contribution will be dependent on the building owner being prepared to maintain or replace potentially expensive equipment and systems. One simple fact remains: the most fundamental and effective way to save energy, and therefore cut CO_2 emissions, is to have a highly thermally efficient building envelope in the first place.

The recommended starting point for designers to achieve compliance with the current 2006 Approved Documents L comprises U-values of 0.27, 0.22 and 0.16 W/m²K for walls, floors and all roofs respectively. So how straightforward is it for the industry to meet these standards now?

When considering cavity walls, for example: 0.27W/m²K is a significant jump from the 0.35W/m²K that is the current required performance standard. The mainstream building industry does not like wall constructions wider than 300mm, and if you look at a traditional wall detail, 100mm block internally with 100mm brick externally leaves just 100mm of cavity for the insulation. Needless to say, filling the complete void with insulation may not be a robust solution (dependant on exposure and the technical ability of site staff) because of the risk of potential rain penetration, so that would leave us with just 50mm for partial fill insulation, if we were to stick with the industry's preference for a 300mm overall wall thickness. This can be achieved, but only with products at the top of the range of thermal performance.

In light of EPCs (see page 107), and if we are truly to achieve meaningful cuts in CO_2 emissions, it is also vital that the insulation should continue to perform at the specified level throughout the lifetime of the building. Air and moisture infiltration and compression can all seriously affect how well some insulants perform, and this too needs to be taken into consideration.

Perhaps one of the most important steps along the road to genuine progress is the proposed adoption of carbon dioxide emissions' target from the Code for Sustainable Homes (CSH) for the next 3 changes to Approved Document L1A (ADL1A): at level 3 for the 2010 revision, level 4 for 2013 and level 6 or zero carbon for 2016. Although achieving the CSH standards is voluntary for the private sector at present, the requirement for builders to adopt the standards required to achieve level 3 for houses built with public money or on public land at this stage, is excellent preparation for the regulatory requirements to come.

Bearing in mind the issues raised above, with regard to the 2006 editions of the ADLs, even using the highest performing insulants, the industry is going to have to move away from traditional practice and get creative with space. The recommended starting points for designers to achieve compliance with the next two changes to the ADL are shown in the table below:

Table 1. Recommended starting point U-values.

Element	2006 Approved Document L1A	CSH level 3 (W/m²K)	CSH level 4 (W/m²K)
Floor	0.22	0.13	0.10
Wall	0.27	0.18	0.15
Roof	0.16	0.13	0.10

Source: Kingspan Insulation, 2008.

So far, so good: these U-values are certainly challenging, especially within the constraints of traditional construction methods, but with a bit of creative thinking and the use of efficient insulation materials they are achievable. For instance, they may mean a move away from cavity walls to monolithic walls with an insulated render or cladding system. The real stumbling block lies with the final jump to Code level 6 or zero-carbon homes, which has been adopted for ADL1A, and there are a number of real concerns surrounding this.

Firstly there is the question of practical feasibility. The construction industry has, so far, failed to consistently deliver air-leakage rates of $7m^3/m^2/hr$ or less using traditional building technologies. If high levels of airtightness are achieved there is then the necessity to provide adequate ventilation to maintain a healthy home.

Balanced whole house, mechanical ventilation with heat recovery (MVHR) appears to be the best solution for this, as at least the energy recovery will go some way to offset the capital cost by lifetime energy savings. But all of this costs hard cash and the system itself requires energy to run, so the optimum size of unit must be specified or else the whole procedure is self defeating as it could create more carbon dioxide than it saves.

Secondly, an even greater obstacle is that of meeting the requirements for renewable energy – low and zero carbon technology only works cost effectively in the right situations, so a blanket policy, regardless of the size or location of a development, simply will not be economically feasible or make the necessary carbon savings.

There is also some considerable debate about the desirability of some of these homes, and fears that the whole culture change associated with low carbon living will be unpalatable to the many prospective occupants who prefer features such as large, opening windows and central heating.

Finally, it has been proven that low or zero carbon construction is possible, but the realities of repeating this on a large scale are often overlooked. Trying to build the sheer quantity of new homes needed may be an obstacle to achieving the very high levels of specification involved in zero-carbon homes – both from the point of view of time, cost and manpower.

Since the industry is not being wholly successful in achieving compliance with the current requirements of ADL, how then can the leap to zero carbon dioxide emissions possibly be achieved? Well, the simple answer is that it may not be possible, although a certain amount of tweaking of the definition of zero carbon will undoubtedly make it appear more feasible.

For example, currently a proposal is on the table to allow developers to pay a levy in lieu of achieving zero carbon dioxide emissions in 2016 for small developments. The revenue would be ploughed back into saving the carbon dioxide elsewhere ... preferably into energy efficiency upgrades of existing buildings, thus tackling fuel poverty and improving standards for the majority of people, not just the few.

According to the Housing Forum there are around 26 million existing homes, so even if the government managed to hit their 240,000 new homes a year target, and even if all of those new homes were 'zero carbon' from the word go, it would be over a hundred years before the number of new, energy efficient buildings had a greater impact on carbon emissions than the existing stock. Isn't it time we took control of where we can make the biggest difference, instead of placing impossible demands on the mainstream new build sector, and focused our energy and resources on creative refurbishment solutions every bit as avidly as we have sought to build zero-carbon show homes?

When it was being prepared, it was hoped that the CSH would encourage better practice in house building. But it is a big leap from the requirements of Approved Document L1A to meeting the broader and tougher aspects of the Code, particularly from level 4 upwards. So what incentives are there for developers to build better than they have to?

Perhaps the biggest spur of all will be the arrival of the Planning and Energy Bill, put forward by Michael Fallon and likely to be given Royal Assent even as this article is being written. The Bill will empower local planning authorities in England and Wales to impose requirements for carbon dioxide emissions, energy use or energy efficiency in local plans, over and above those that are set out in regulations as long as they are couched in terms of regulations, policies or guidelines made by the appropriate national authority – e.g. they could demand the carbon dioxide emissions' target of a specific code level well ahead of that level being mandatory nationally.

This provides local authorities with a golden opportunity to shape future developments, to encourage environmentally sustainable construction and to allow the private sector to get to grips with the higher standards ahead of regulatory control, whilst discouraging LA's from hanging their hat on tokenistic policies like the Merton Rule.

Why should the Merton Rule type requirements be maligned? The answer is simple – requiring a minimum percentage of power generation on a development from renewables as a stand-alone measure to cut carbon is not very well thought through, either from a practical or a financial point of view.

For example, it is reported that standard micro wind turbines just don't work effectively in urban environments, where air flows are very turbulent, and results are patchy.

The jury is out on heat pumps, their payback periods may not be seen as reasonable and they can require a substantial amount of space, which simply may not be available in an urban development. Micro generation may not be economically feasible for small scale projects. These costly and unreliable aspects of renewable energy are the biggest potential barriers to achieving zero carbon construction. Therefore, to make renewables mandatory without first and foremost focusing on maximising energy efficiency could be entirely counter-productive on the road to carbon salvation.

Table 2: The CSH minimum standards.

Code Level	Carbon dioxide emissions (percentage better than Approved Document L1A* 2006)	Water (litres per person per day)	Discretionary credits required
1	10	120	33.2
2	18	120	42.7
3	25	105	46.2
4	44	105	53.4
5	100**	80	58.9
6	A 'zero carbon' home***	80	63.6

Notes

** Building Regulations: Approved Document L1A (2006).*

***Zero emissions of carbon dioxide from heating, hot water, ventilation and lighting.*

**** Zero net emissions of carbon dioxide from all energy use in the home.*

In summary, I think it is going to be an interesting journey to zero carbon dioxide emissions, regardless of whether you are doing it voluntarily as a discretionary adopter of the Code, or as a mandatory requirement because of public sector housing requirements or the Approved Document. My guess is that we will get there, but probably not by 2016. There are likely to be a number of fudges introduced to mask this industry's inabilities, and not without a lot of painful change within the industry. Perhaps the recession will be useful. Hard times always seem to breed innovation and improvements in efficiency.

Critique of the CSH

Many green building experts are questioning some of the aspects of the CSH. Others are wondering whether we should be aiming for 'zero carbon' at all. **Neil May** of the Good Homes Alliance (GHA) comments...

Conceived primarily to cut the carbon dioxide emissions and reduce the overall environmental impact of our new homes, the Code for Sustainable Homes (CSH) has sparked widespread debate throughout the house building industry. As has been pointed out in earlier stories in this chapter, the CSH was introduced initially as a voluntary standard for new homes and is an ambitious, and in many ways admirable standard, that aims to bring not only environmental advantages, but also lower running costs for our buildings and improved human health and wellbeing.

Though covering a great deal of issues, arguably, it is the energy reduction aspirations and the quest for zero carbon that are the real driving forces behind the CSH and it is this aspect that is generating the majority of the dialogue.

Right from the outset, the CSH has presented the industry with many challenges. The very definition of 'zero carbon', and its suitability as the end goal, has been a point of contention. The Stamp Duty Land Tax version required all energy to be generated on, as opposed to off-site, and this has now been adopted by the CSH.

However, I believe that the premise that all energy should be generated on-site is flawed and should not be a requirement for the highest levels of low carbon homes. On large scale developments some form of CHP may be appropriate, but generally the extra money and manpower needed to achieve Code level 6 makes the development uneconomical, environmentally dubious and unrealistic.

Although the Good Homes Alliance (GHA) is keen to rise to the challenge of achieving substantial carbon reductions, it currently deems that aiming for zero carbon is not the best use of resources for UK builders. Instead, we should be concentrating on reaching high standards of airtightness and thermal insulation, with additional measures to reduce hot water use, which can result in as much as a 70% reduction in carbon emissions compared to the average building stock. If we focus on this goal, resources can be released to address the sustainability of the existing housing stock. This is preferable to installing expensive micro-renewables, which contribute little to overall carbon reductions and involve significant levels of maintenance.

Meeting the zero carbon challenge for all new homes by 2016 will be a huge task. With such a small percentage of low carbon homes built in the UK to date, the knowledge and skills are not yet in place and it is difficult to achieve in practice what should be possible in theory. The UK must undergo a complete culture change in terms of building practices, materials used, contracting and financing.

Setting the zero carbon issue aside, recent analysis of the CSH, sponsored by eco developer Kingerlee Homes, led to the identification of several technical glitches which reduce its effectiveness.

A loophole makes it easier for developers to achieve levels 3 and 4 with cheaper electric heating than with more carbon efficient gas heating. This is because the 'fuel factor' used in Building Regulations and the CSH to calculate the target emissions rate (TER), from which you are then required to make your percentage reductions to achieve the different Code levels, allows much higher carbon emissions if you use electric heating. This is a rule put in place to provide relief to dwellings, such as blocks of flats where a gas service to each flat is impractical. Starting from a higher base makes reductions easier, particularly when using a high carbon fuel like electricity.

At Building Regulations' levels therefore, electrically heated properties have to achieve a shell at least as thermally efficient as if they were gas heated. Conversely at Code levels 3 and above, developers installing electric heating can reach the same Code levels as those using gas with a less efficient building envelope. As the cost and difficulty of retrofitting energy efficient thermal shells is very great, the UK will lose a great opportunity if we allow this practice to continue in new buildings. It will also lead to greater carbon emissions than Building Regulation's level buildings using gas.

The evidence also suggests that it is easier to comply with Building Regulations and achieve Code levels 1 to 4 if the building is bigger with a less efficient form. Due to the percentage reduction scale, small and efficient building forms are penalised, driving developers to increase the inefficiency of the building envelope. Furthermore, large houses will meet high Code levels more easily than smaller affordable developments and this goes against the expectation of high Code standards in social housing.

All this said, the GHA remains strong advocates of the CSH and wants to help to rectify any temporary glitches. GHA's own solution has been to introduce its own standard, to be known as level 3++, that its members are required to reach. This is CSH level 3 with two additional requirements. The first is a fixed maximum carbon and energy target per m^2 per year, set according to building type to ensure absolute energy and carbon reductions in new dwellings. The second is post occupation monitoring of new homes for at least two years to compare the design objectives with the actual property performance. Monitoring is essential if we are to learn from our current practice and make substantial improvements to the sustainability of our housing stock.

Monitoring and learning from feedback are essential, not only to ensure that designed energy standards are met in reality, but also to avoid the very real risk of unintended consequences, such as risk to human health, less robust buildings and financial waste. To avoid risk to human health, for example, developers must take the potential for trapped moisture into consideration when increasing insulation and airtightness levels. High humidity levels allow dust mites and also moulds and bacteria to thrive, causing and exacerbating cases of asthma and other respiratory and auto-immune diseases.

These conditions can also lead to moulds and other decay mechanisms which damage the building fabric and in particular organic parts of the building, such as timber. The need for super insulation and air tightness has considerably raised the stakes in regard to building health, putting the long term performance and durability of the building into jeopardy if it is not designed, constructed and maintained correctly.

It is therefore essential that buildings are monitored to identify problems early on, and that industry takes on board the changes in design and construction practice necessary to avoid these problems. This means training at all levels, proper feed back from existing projects, and a change in site organisation and building systems.

It is not currently mandatory for new homes to be designed and built to the CSH standards. However, all new homes have had to have a certificate to confirm that they have been rated against the CSH since 1 May 2008. Properties will either receive a Code certificate with a star rating at levels 1 to 6, or a nil rated certificate if the developer has taken the decision to build to normal Building Regulations. At the moment, pushing for all new dwellings to comply would probably be a little premature. First the CSH needs to be adjusted to ensure it is a useful and trusted mechanism for achieving carbon reduction in new housing. It should also be said that legislation will not be effective without sufficient resources being put into monitoring, learning and training.

The CSH is a key piece of legislation that, although not yet perfect, could be hugely instrumental in helping to reduce the carbon emissions and energy usage of our new housing stock, as well as placing emphasis on the need for sustainability in the broader sense. Its greatest achievement to date has been in provoking meaningful discussion throughout the house building industry.

The big question is whether this industry can make the changes in its culture and operations which are necessary to deliver sustainability in reality and in the broadest sense, and not just on paper. ☯

Members of the Good Homes Alliance are already building to high environmental standards but the higher levels of the CSH may be asking too much, too soon for even the most dedicated green home builders.

Heading towards passivhaus?

The term 'passivhaus' refers to specific construction standards for buildings which, if followed, offer excellent comfort levels in both winter and summer. **Sally Hall** explains why this standard, regardless of the CSH, is likely to catch on in the UK...

The 'passivhaus' (passive house) system, originated in Europe and is considered by many to be the world's leading design standard in energy efficient construction. Passivhaus design essentially relies on airtightness and superior thermal insulation, coupled with mechanical ventilation. This combination offers a controllable environment. If the design guidance from the Passivhaus Institute is followed correctly, then the house should achieve heating savings of at least 80% when compared to current building standards.

In Europe over 4,000 dwellings, with a wide variety of designs, have been built according to passivhaus principles but very few have been built in the UK. The passivhaus standards are currently being promoted and marketed in the UK by the AECB (the sustainable building assocation) under its CarbonLite Programme (CLP) (see following story) and, to a lesser extent, by the Building Research Establishment (BRE).

To quote the Passivhaus Institute, 'passive houses are buildings in which the space heat requirement is reduced by means of passive measures to the point at which there is no longer any need for a conventional heating system; an air supply system essentially suffices to circulate the heat that is generated'. This heat is only generated by people living in the building, equipment such as lights, TV's etc. and, of course, passive solar energy from the sun. The same air supply system will expel excess heat when necessary, and or return heat from waste air via a heat exchanger to the incoming fresh air. The standard measuring stick for a passive house energy consumption is 15kWh per square metre of floor area of the building per annum (this would essentially be the running cost of the air handling unit).

Passive houses are essentially solar houses. The main glazing should be south facing in order to maximise the passive solar benefits and windows should be carefully dimensioned to provide the necessary daylight and solar gain when available. Incoming solar energy should provide roughly a third of the house's heat needs. Triple-glazed and super-insulated windows allow in more solar energy (heat) than they lose. The building envelope design must be exceptionally good, eliminating all thermal bridges and air leakages. In addition, insulation must reach certain minimum requirements. A dwelling built to passivhaus standards would therefore need to include:

- very high levels of insulation, with minimal thermal bridging
- good solar access
- energy efficient windows
- excellent levels of airtighness (below 1 air change per hour)
- a whole house mechanical ventilation system, with highly efficient heat recovery.

Putting the theory into practice

Building to the passivhaus standard means careful design and the optimisation of two key components:

- the building envelope
- the windows.

These key components can be designed and insulated to a level where their combined efficiency negates the need for a conventional heating system. Just imagine, a warm, welcoming home, but without a traditional heating

Birth of the passivhaus

Dr. Wolfgang Feist founded the Passivhaus Institute in 1996 in order to further the propagation of highly efficient house buildings. It also functions as a certification institute, testing the various technologies inherent to passive houses.

The passivhaus concept actually evolved from a converstion with Professor Bo Adamson of Lund University (Sweden) in 1988. Their motivation was to find a solution that was at the same time comfortable, energy efficient and cost effective. The low energy prices at the time (late eighties, early nineties) meant that the saved energy costs could never cover the additional investments required. Therefore, the key idea was to reduce the energy demand so much that the necessary HVAC technology would be dramatically simplified. This results in a reduction of the investment costs.

Comfort was a main motivator, for the simple fact that people do not wish to live in uncomfortable houses. Cost effectiveness was also an important factor; no one wants to pay more. Finally, energy efficiency was obviously important to the concept, even if the majority of the people haven't accepted or understood this yet. However, now that the energy prices have so clearly increased, and threaten to go even higher, it is gradually becoming clear why we must use energy more efficiently. The fact that energy resource scarcity can be a source of conflicts is also clear. In addition a reduction in our use of fossil fuels as a source of energy is important if we want to limit 'global warming'.

The development of the passive house standard was based upon a variety of experiences and theories. There was already the experience of the successful construction of low energy houses (publications from Adamson in Sweden, Feist in Germany). These houses were used to validate the calculation and simulation methods. They simulated the first houses completely on the computer before building them. There was also an extensive pre-construction research project, financed by the Hessian Ministry of the Economy.

Although few people claim to have yet built a true passive house in Britain, the 'BedZED' houses by the architect Bill Dunster are, in principle, passive houses – even if he doesn't name them as such. The passive house is not protected, everybody can build passive houses, it's a group designation people can use freely.

The construction of passive houses has expanded very gradually after the first pilot buildings: Darmstadt in 1991, Stuttgart in 1993, Naumburg, Wiesbaden, and Cologne in 1997, the first houses in Austria in 2000, Sweden in 2001. First projects in Italy (southern Tyrol) in 2002, the first house in the US in 2003, Ireland in 2005,

The knowledge and experience gathered so far must be passed on, and the know-how must be learned. The expansion, therefore, requires a certain period of time – largely because almost everyone is convinced that such a building, a) simply cannot function, b) probably leads to 'frozen' inhabitants, and c) when a + b don't occur, it's all certainly far too expensive. This was also the general opinion in Germany, until proved the opposite. Interestingly, this is experienced everywhere. It requires a lot of stamina in order to render such an innovation reality.

Further reading and internet links

CEPHEUS: Living Comfort without Heating. Ed. Helmut Krapmeier, Eckart Droessler. Vienna: Springer, 2001

CEPHEUS-Project Information No. 36: Final Technical Report. Dr. Wolfgang Feist et al. Hannover: enercity, 2001

Passive House Institute (a selection of pages in English): **www.passiv.de**

'Wohnen & Arbeiten' (a few pages in English): **www.passivhaus-vauban.de**

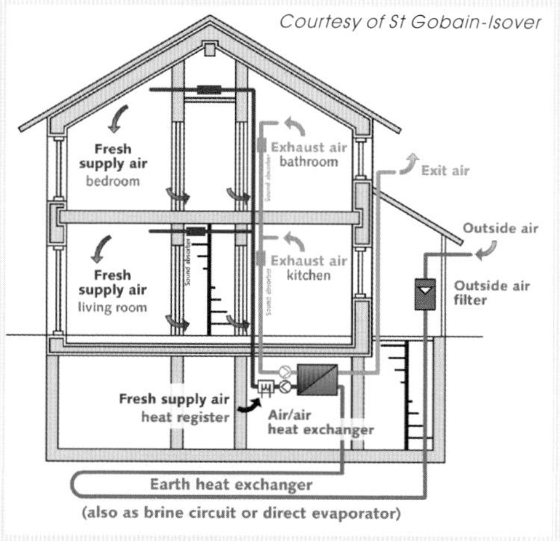

system yet still remaining comfortable throughout the year. However, at times of extreme weather, some small additional heating may be required and this could come from a wood burning stove or simple heater.

Any new building can be built to the passivhaus standard and theoretically any construction method could be adapted, Meeting passivhaus standards therefore need not signal a change of character of our buildings but it is clear that some house types would be easier to adapt than others. The key is to get the detailing right and the on-site staff involved in the knowledge of airtight construction and other necessary techniques. Then, to ensure that it has been achieved, the building must be pressure tested on completion and perhaps every few years after that during occupancy.

With improvements as outlined above, the installation of a heat recovery system for the management of ventilation air completes the system. This automatic ventilation system should provide a continuous, but precisely regulated, supply of fresh air, warmed by a high efficiency heat exchanger transferring heat captured from the extracted indoor air (usually coming from the kitchen and bathrooms). These airflows are not mixed. The extra costs of

FACTOR 10+ passivhaus homes

* Future-oriented living without wasting energy
* Light-flooded rooms
* Ecologically sensible construction using wood and concrete
* In the Velox Factor 10+ House, regional raw materials are turned into local building materials
* Scientifically simulated thermal properties
* Lowest possible material input - perfectly ecological
* The energy needed to produce heat insulation is already saved in half a heating period
* The massive structure creates a balanced room climate, even without shading the façade facing south
* LEK = 24 (thermal leakage) LEKeq = 4
* HWB = 8kWh/m^{2}a (energy needed for heating a building)

This page shows example buildings from a company that builds only passivhaus homes, Velox Factor 10+ houses.
Builder: Dieter Tscharf: ***tscharfd@aon.at***

detailing and building to passivhaus standards can be partly offset by the fact that an oil, gas or electrical heating system is no longer necessary. This gives two savings: the installation and maintenance cost of the equipment no longer needed and the reduced fuel costs over the lifetime of the building.

The Passive House Planning Package

The Passive House Planning Package (PHPP) is a tool for passive houses, developed and used for the first time in 1998. It is a clearly structured design tool that can be used by designers and builders constructing to passivhaus standards. A spreadsheet-based design tool, it is used to calculate the complete energy balance of a building and allows the building designer to accurately determine the building's heat losses caused by transmission and ventilation. It also allows for careful consideration of solar and internal heat gains so they can be allowed for, or offset, in the final calculations. The fact that such gains are not always achieved at times when they are needed is accounted for by setting them off against the losses. The 'difference' between losses and useful gains results in the building's 'demand' for heating energy that will be required.

In order to obtain correct results, it is important to distinguish between significant and insignificant factors. This includes, for example, the thermal output of inhabitants and household appliances, or the solar radiation available inside a house. For this purpose, the PHPP contains standard values which have proved successful in comparison with other measurements. Apart from establishing the buildings' heat balance, the PHPP also deals with other project-specific issues that come up in the course of planning. Among others, this includes the heat extract ventilation system, the energy demand for the household electricity, domestic hot water etc. The PHPP includes tools for:

- calculating U-values
- calculating energy balances
- designing comfort ventilation
- calculating the heat load (no heat load climate data contained yet for locations outside Germany)
- evaluating summer comfort calculations
- other useful tools for the reliable design of passive houses.

The package (which can be purchased from **www.carbonlite.org.uk**) includes worksheets for heating energy balances (heating period or monthly techniques), heat distribution and supply, electricity demand and primary energy demand. The package is continually updated and new design modules have been added over the years, e.g. calculation of window parameters, shading, heating load and summer performance. The PHPP is continuously re-evaluated and refined, based on measurements. As part of accompanying scientific research studies, more than 300 projects have so far been compared with calculation results. The PHPP energy balance module was shown to be able to describe the thermal building characteristics of passive houses surprisingly accurately. This applies particularly to the new technique for calculating the heating load, which was developed specifically for passivehaus.

The AECB has undertaken a comparison of SAP with PHPP and the analysis has produced some interesting results.[1] A key element of the work is to compare the results of calculated heat loss by both programmes against the performance of major elements of the building.

Reference

1. Green Building magazine, Summer 2008, Vol 18 No 1 and ***www.aecb.net***

Web links

The AECB's CarbonLite programme: ***www.carbonlite.org.uk*** *(the PHPP can be purchased from this site).*

PassivhausUK: ***www.passivhaus.org.uk***

Promotion of passive houses in Europe: ***www.europeanpassivehouses.org***

International Conference on Passive Houses: ***www.passivhaustagung.de***

Further reading

Green Building magazine, Summer 2008, Vol 18 No 1.

'Details for Passive Houses, a catalogue of ecologically rated constructions' (2nd edition) ISBN: 9783 2112 97636.

'Built for the Future - the Isover Multi-comfort house' available from isoverpr@saint-gobain.com

Green building standards

We already have the Building Regulations, now we have the Code for Sustainable Homes but how will other 'green building' standards interact with these? **Keith Hall** reports ...

Planning issues aside, the Building Regulations are supposedly the final word on what we can and cannot build. However, over the past 15 years or so they have become largely descriptive, rather than prescriptive with the 'deemed to satisfy' concession enabling the building designer or developer to interpret the requirements and make proposals which the Building Regulations' officers can then accept or reject. Since 2002 the regulations have relied on the Standard Assessment Procedure (SAP) for the energy and CO_2 calculation aspects, yet it is widely accepted that SAP has loopholes (some of which have already been discussed in this chapter) that have been abused. The Building Regulations are likely to come to rely more on such 'bolt-ons', and now we have another, the Code for Sustainable Homes (CSH), with all the bureacracy this entails (experts, consultants, assessors, etc). What we are ending up with is a prolonged and high cost paper trail rather than clearly defined, prescriptive document that anyone can study and design buildings to comply with.

We should all know by now why SAP and the CSH are there - to combat climate change, but it is the way they are being incorporated which is causing the problems. The CSH is still new and although it is built on the EcoHomes scheme it has not yet been tested properly. Even though the mainstream building industry were making the right noises about it in 2007, there is a growing sense of dread surrounding its integration by 2016, so there is a risk it could flounder, especially in a poor economic climate. There are also many highly skilled green building practitioners in the UK (usually formed into groups such as the AECB and latterly the Good Homes Alliance) that have long known what is needed and they are beginning to concur that the CSH, as it is, may not be the answer we need. Both have introduced their own standards. However, in the light of how the CSH has been introduced, one does wonder who is likely to use these 'other' standards if they are not made a mandatory requirement or at least referred to in the Building Regulations.

Talking of other standards, I believe that buildings should be constructed around the well developed passivhaus standard. Thankfully the AECB has already come to this conclusion and is modelling its standard, the CarbonLite Programme, on the European passivhaus standard. Passivhaus is as much a philosophy as a 'standard', which is why it has worked so well in Europe. Its main focus has been on energy usage and efficiency and less so on the wider 'sustainability' issues. For those with a sense of concern for the wider ecology of our planet, a narrow focus on energy efficiency alone will probably be seen as a negative point but it would be relatively easy, for example, to develop it further to include such issues.

The Energy Saving Trust (EST) had its own standard which, like passivhaus, was energy focused, but the EST has withdrawn this in favour of concentrating on the promotion of the CSH as it believes that the CSH has fully replaced all the high standards that were part of the EST offerings.

AECB CarbonLite Programme (CLP)

The AECB has been promoting eco building for nearly 20 years and saw a need to develop robust methodologies for saving energy. This resulted in design guidance being produced and the launching of the AECB's CarbonLite programme, which is backed up with comprehensive and practical training opportunities. The standards within the programme are not compulsory for its members and any designer or builder can apply to use the scheme. Liz Reason, Carbonlite programme director, told me that *"CLP is a transparent energy standard, related to CO_2 emissions, so it can be used as the energy performance element of the CSH that will more certainly deliver on the targets."* The CLP has three levels, as described below.

CarbonLite Silver

This a low-cost, low-risk and easily achieved introduction to high performance building. The silver standard is aimed at those wishing to create high-performance buildings using widely available technology at little or no extra cost. It is estimated that this low-risk option will reduce overall CO_2 emissions by 70%, compared to the UK average for buildings of each type - a highly significant result given the relative ease and low cost with which this standard can be met. Individual self-builders and large-scale residential and non-residential developers could make a valuable contribution to low-carbon building by meeting this standard.

CarbonLite Passivhaus

This is Europe's best-known standard, and uses proven technology to minimise risk as well as emissions. The passivhaus standard takes full advantage of existing energy-efficient technology, without entailing the perceived risk associated with radical innovation. A considerable improvement on normal UK building practices, it is estimated that the passivhaus standard would reduce overall CO_2 emissions by approximately 80%, compared to the UK average for buildings of each type. Some imported products are required to meet this international best practice standard, but most of the products are already available through agents based in the UK.

CarbonLite Gold

Gold is the highest of the AECB's standards, setting the lowest limits on CO_2 emissions and overall primary energy use. The AECB estimates that the gold standard would reduce overall CO_2 emissions by 95%, compared to the UK average for buildings of each type, since this standard is almost identical to the passivhaus standard in terms of thermal efficiency, but sets even lower limits on CO_2 emissions and overall primary energy use. As well as a requirement for energy-efficient electrical appliances, this standard demands a greater emphasis on electricity-producing renewables to offset power used for lighting, appliances and ventilation. Building costs would be higher than those associated with normal properties, though careful design and planning, coupled with growing expertise and experience, could help reduce these additional costs in future developments. Again, specialist technology would need to be imported but is already catered for by UK agents.

Good Homes Alliance CSH 3++

The Good Homes Alliance (GHA) believes it is vital that we have appropriate standards and guidelines in place to ensure that building is truly sustainable, robust and healthy. The GHA has identified several shortfalls and gaps in the CSH, so it has implemented its own additional standard (benchmark), Level 3++, which has been designed to sit alongside the Code and is compulsory for all developer members of the GHA. The new benchmark requires GHA members to build 100% of their properties to level 3 of the Code, as well as achieving a further two criteria for at least 50% of their new homes. This structure provides an initial realistic lead-in time and compliance target and will be subject to reassessment.

The first 'plus', which makes up the additional criteria of Level 3++, is a fixed maximum carbon and energy target per m^2 per year, compared to the average in the existing stock in 2003. This target is set according to building type and ensures absolute energy and carbon reductions in new dwellings of 70%.

An absolute carbon and energy target is not present in the CSH as the Code uses a 'fuel factor' to calculate the target emissions rate (TER), from which developers are then required to make percentage reductions. The 'fuel factor' varies for different types of fuel and therefore the reductions also differ.

The second condition of Level 3++ requires developers to commit to post occupation monitoring of their new homes for a minimum of two years post construction. In order for this process to prove successful, the GHA will work closely with its members to ensure they have the necessary support and that the monitoring process is meaningful. The membership requirement states that data collection must cover the whole development, including all dwelling types. In addition, the monitoring plan must demonstrate a clear mechanism to learn from problems in performance and to rectify these in future developments.

Level 3++ is intended to act as a statement about the GHA's determination to reduce environmental impact in reality and not just on paper. It is a way of showing commitment to sustainable building and of learning from our developments in order that experience can be fed back into design practice and the future development of the standard. Most importantly, the GHA's standard is to be seen as part of a process of improvement that they say will be revised every two years to further improve the overall environmental and social impact of GHA homes.

With the technical build standard in place, the GHA believes that the next step is to explore and develop standards for the health, social and community aspects of good homes. The ultimate objective is to see these factors included in future drives for performance improvement in the UK house building sector by leading the way with its own membership requirement which is currently being considered.

Further information:

www.carbonlite.org.uk
www.passivhaus.org.uk
www.goodhomes.org.uk

EPCs and HIPS

In 2003 the EU published the Energy Performance of Buildings Directive (EPBD) to increase energy efficiency in buildings. The Directive requires a reduction of CO_2 emissions in buildings. One of the most significant requirements of EPBD is the need to provide energy performance certificates (EPCs) for new and existing residential and non-residential buildings whenever they are constructed, sold or rented. The certificate gives an overall energy rating expressed as letters 'A' - 'G' on a colour-coded coded bar-chart scale, with A' being the most energy efficient rating. The rating system is based on the CO_2 emissions calculated using BRE SBEM or other accredited, computer software. The average rating is currently 'D' so there is a lot of scope for improvement. Valid for 10 years (provided there are no changes to layout or structure), the certification will also recommend potential cost-effective improvements that can be made to improve the energy performance. It rates the standard of the building fabric, building services' equipment and controls. Buildings over $1000m^2$ will be required to display a slightly different energy certificate to enable the public to see how the building is performing in use.

EPCs are one of the compulsory requirements for inclusion in the Home Information Packs (HIPs). All owners, at their own cost, must now produce a HIP when selling any property. This brings together valuable information at the start of the conveyancing process. From January 2009 the compulsory documents that must be included are;

* a home information pack index
* an energy performance certificate
* a sale statement
* standard searches
* evidence of title
* additional information for leasehold and common hold sales, where appropriate.
* a newly built home must have a certificate (or interim certificate) showing the rating that the home has received in respect of the Code for Sustainable Homes, or a nil-rated certificate showing that the home has only been designed to meet current Building Regulations.

HIPs can be compiled on a DIY basis, using a solicitor, estate agent or specialist HIP provider. Even some supermarkets have indicated they will be providers. The regulations are being enforced by trading standards officers, who will investigate any complaints.

Useful information

www.homeinformationpacks.gov.uk
Association of Home Information Pack Providers
www.hipassociation.co.uk/home.aspx

Progress in straw bale building

There are some 4 million tons of surplus straw being baled in the UK each and every year. This is sufficient to build 250,000 homes a year. **Rachel Shiamh** reports on how trends in traditional straw bale building could help see that happen ...

During the past twenty years, straw bale building has begun to show its integrity across the world in countries such as USA, Canada, Australia and New Zealand. Its recognition has only really grown over the past ten years in Europe and now, here in the UK over the past five years it has reached the public through growing media interest. It has begun to touch the mainstream as an example of one of the best solutions for low impact and sustainable building practices. My own straw bale home, Penwhilwr, the UK's first two storey load bearing straw bale house, won the 2008 Grand Designs 'eco house of the year award', by public vote, and has gone even further in raising the profile of this fast developing building technique and craft.

Yet even since building my home in Pembrokeshire techniques and methods have advanced and been improved in order to develop more efficient, quicker and economical ways of straw bale building. There are four million tons of straw a year surplus to requirements in the UK now. This is sufficient to build 250,000 homes a year. Amazonails, a West Yorkshire based not for profit, social enterprise, is the UK's leading straw bale designer, consultancy and trainer, with over 100 straw bale buildings completed in Britain. This enterprise has, as others too around Europe, developed many of its own techniques, which are different to those employed in the USA. A prime example is the use of more environmentally friendly coppiced hazel and clay and lime plasters, instead of steel, cement and gypsum. It has also developed low-impact foundations for straw buildings and put them through the Building Control process.

Foundations

Rammed earth tyres is one more 'modern' option for straw bale foundations. As an example of a low impact, environmentally friendly building technique, it is hard to better the use of recycled car tyres as a foundation material. If not exposed to ultra violet light via sunlight, their estimated life expectancy is about 30,000 years! Significantly longer than environmentally high impact concrete.

There are four known straw bale buildings in the UK that have planning permission and building approval for rammed earth tyre foundations. One, a load bearing one storey, was given approval for; 'foundations... of recycled car tyres, with side walls, packed solid by clay and rubble, the central core being filled with free-draining gravel. The tyres themselves being made from waterproof material, act as a damp proof membrane.'

For a load bearing eco centre building in Richmondshire, the county council asked for several load bearing tests to be carried out on site, and approved the method using well compacted stone as the ramming material. The tyres are coated in ultra violet reflecting paint to ensure durability. Tests on such load bearing tyre foundations have shown, surprisingly, that they were actually stronger than concrete.

Straw bale building methods

Straw is being utilised in a number of innovative ways for new building design, as has already been touched upon in 'Architecture review' earlier in this chapter. However, I want to concentrate on reporting on developments in the more traditional straw bale building methods, and these have not stood still. In the

Above: the Ecology Building Society meeting room. It is attached, via a walkway, to the Society's new headquarters at Keighley in West Yorkshire. This loadbearing design, straw building, was built by volunteers.

Left: Penwhilwr, the straw bale home of the author.

past few years, Amazonails has been developing a lightweight compressive frame method. The two common methods for traditional straw bale building, therefore, are load bearing and infill or timber frame.

Load bearing means that the building is constructed from a brick like construction of straw bales without a frame, with the bales themselves taking the weight of the roof. The bale walls are pinned to the foundations and to each other, with coppiced hazel and have a wooden roof plate on top which spreads the floor and roof loads across the width of the wall. The roof plate is fastened to the foundations and bale walls with hazel and strapping. The roof is constructed, in the usual manner, on top of the roof plate. There is then a settlement and compression of the straw of about 70-100mm.

The one challenge that Penwhilwr, the load-bearing straw bale house had, and indeed all load bearing straw bale houses can face during their construction in our British climate, is the protection of the bales from inclement weather. Since the bales must not get wet, there can be much time spent tussling with large tarpaulins, especially with a two storey house.

Infill or timber frame straw bale building requires a wooden framework, with a roof already built on top. The bales then are used as an infill insulation between or around the posts. So Amazonails have come up with the lightweight compressive frame design in order to retain both the benefits of the load bearing style straw bale house, but enabling the roof to be constructed before the straw bale walls are built. This therefore gives protection against the weather throughout the wall raising process. It uses a timber framework, which is so lightweight that it could not stand up alone, and which requires temporary bracing and props to give it stability until the straw is in place. The straw is an essential part of the structural integrity of the building, more so than the timber, and it works together with the timber to carry the load of the floors and the roof.

Timber posts are located at corners and either side of the window and door openings. These are designed so that the timber wall plate at first floor and/or roof level can be slotted down into the posts, or screwed down with threaded rod once the straw is in place, allowing for compression on the bales. Compression of the straw bale infill walls is essential for stability. To increase stability, the bales can be pinned externally, and the pins are secured onto the base and wall plate of the framework once all the settlement of the walls has completed. It is constructed in such a way that the wall plate and roof are held approximately 100mm above the finished straw bale wall height, whilst the wall is being built. Once the bracing and props are removed, the roof is allowed then to come down, which causes compression of the straw beneath it. The roof weight can be encouraged to compress the walls faster by strapping it down to the foundations and mechanically compressing the walls using ratchet straps.

Advantages of this method are mainly that the roof can be constructed before the straw is put in place, which provides much safer weather protection. The framework and posts can be constructed off site. This framework construction vastly reduces the amount of timber used in comparison to the traditional post and beam method. However, in comparison to the load bearing method; it is more costly and complicated to construct and greater technical ability is required to make the structure stable whilst straw is being placed.

One successful example of the above method is the large two storey house; the first self built straw bale house in Italy, 'La Boa'. Another example is the building for Sworders Ltd, a fine-art auctioneers based in Essex, who wanted a sustainable building for their own offices and show premises. As well as straw bale walls, this building will have rainwater catchment, solar water heating, bio-mass space heating and lime rendered walls. It is the largest straw bale building in the UK so far, being 1022m^2. It opens the doors for straw bale commercial retail buildings.

Amazonails is also working with North

This project in Italy ,called La-Boa, is built using the infill timber frame method. This relies on a wooden structural frame-work, which supports the roof and the bales are added after the roof is complete.

Kesteven District Council in Lincolnshire, with a view to building straw bale council houses. Amazonails is also designing affordable housing for housing associations and local authorities, as well as working with mainstream contractors to install straw bales, using course participants in on-site training courses.

Stretching across Europe, there are similar projects developing the straw bale building technique. This was evident at the 2007 ESBG (European Straw bale Building Gathering) in Germany. Countries from around Europe gathered to take part in conferences, courses and skill sharing. The Straw bale Building Training Group was set up with a view to create high quality training courses in straw bale building, with a core of trainers across Europe and where different modules can be taken in one or more countries. It is intended for this training to be available by 2009.

There is also a regulation group set up to aim to have a European wide set of building regulations for straw bale building. This is being steered by Jakub Wihan of Amazonails. At present, in Germany, regulations do not allow the building of habitable loadbearing straw bale houses. There are also regulations existing around Europe that could be improved in order to accommodate the lighter load and footprint that straw bale building offers.

It is an exciting time for the growth and development of straw bale building in the UK and around Europe. Whether it be on the smaller eco hut it the garden to the state of the art straw bale house, or corporate building, a common thread that runs through this industry and craft, is the community of cooperation and learning that lends itself so well to straw bale building and design. ☯

Further reading

'Designs of Straw Bale Buildings' by B King.

'Building with Straw Bales' by B Jones.

'The Last Straw': a quarterly magazine and website with links to worldwide tests: ***www.thelaststraw.org***

There is a more detailed story about straw bale building in Chapter 5.

Straw bale panels

Just as those who started growing food organically about thirty years ago were regarded as cranks, so were straw bale builders - up until recently that is. Now straw bale building is 'cool and clever' says **Tom MacKeown**!

At the time of writing, a two storey straw bale house, Penwhilwr, has just won the Eco-Build category in Grand Designs Live, the Channel 4 programme (see previous story). What's more, the profile of straw for use in buildings was further raised by Kevin McCloud's inclusion of a straw bale wall in his concept house at the Grand Designs' Exhibition. At last straw bale has come of age – the age where it can grow out of the dark green and hairy image that has surrounded it, into the main stream of the construction industry. These two very different examples demonstrate the versatility of straw.

For years the benefits of straw have been trumpeted. Finally the rest of the world has heard the tune. It is cool to use straw! There are now well over a hundred straw buildings in UK, including some that have planning consent!

However, it must be stated that there is still some reluctance to use straw in larger scale projects. It is just too irregular, with each bale being slightly different. Straw is highly susceptible to damage from water; the risks of rain in our climate are too great for most, and finally there are not that many straw bale builders around! But there is another way!

Straw bale panels.

A wooden frame (in this case an engineered laminated timber frame) encases a number of bales to form a section of wall. The bales are compressed in the frame and the faces are rendered or plastered, as appropriate, before delivery to site. The panels are weather resistant when delivered. A small team can then install the panels in a relatively short time so that exposure to the elements is kept to an absolute minimum.

Finished panels (those shown in the photos in this article) are 490mm thick, so thicker than a 'conventional' brick and block wall. But a conventional brick and block wall, with mineral wool to give the same thermal insulation, would have to be even thicker (533mm).

How 'green' is a straw panel?

Straw is an agricultural by-product. Much of it is just chopped up and left on the fields to rot. It is plentiful – there is a new crop every year! It is local – almost all of UK has access to straw within a few miles. Similarly the timber used in the manufacture of the frame is made from off-cuts from the timber industry. In order to lower the carbon footprint, the panels are made as near as possible to the site and the source of the straw (farm). Local labour and local skills all help to make the footprint as small as possible.

A straw bale panel is thought to be carbon negative: a 3 x 3 metre panel has almost 600 kg of carbon dioxide sequestered in the fabric; as the crop has grown, carbon dioxide is absorbed into the growing plant, much of which is carried in the straw.

Straw bale panels have a very good ratio of mass, in the form of lime plaster, to super insulation of straw. This means that there is a heat lag of 8 hours, which is ideal for most purposes. A straw bale panel has a U-value of 0.13, or about three times better than current building regulations require. A straw panel house can help to deliver a zero heat dwelling, saving both carbon emissions and money!

Straw bale panels are expected to last a minimum of 75 years, though they should last considerably longer. Manufacturers offer a 50

The two photographs above show the various stages of straw bale panel manufacture. Interestingly, the manufacturers buy local straw and rent farm units close to the building site where the panels are required. They are thus fabricated locally and sent to site with a render basecoat already applied (see also below).

year warranty. They are completely reusable and/or recyclable. Lime renders can be reused, straw can be composted, any metal fittings can be recycled. The finished panels weigh up to 1.7 tonnes, so a crane, or other suitable lifting equipment, is required on site to handle them.

Once the straw is protected by the lime render, it is highly unlikely to rot. Straw begins to decompose at moisture levels above 25%. Straw panels are designed to be breathable and this ensures that the moisture content remains below 20%, which in turn, prevents any rot from occurring. Whereas loose straw may offer an attractive home for rodents, tightly baled straw does not. In addition, the straw is encased in a timber frame and is covered by lime plaster or render, which will deter any infestation.

The panels are surprisingly fire resistant too. In order to burn, the straw must be exposed to a sufficient supply of oxygen. Once the panels are protected by their render and/or plaster coats, they are almost airless, thus offering very good fire protection. Tests indicate a fire rating of up to 2 hours.

Uses for straw bale panels

Such panels have been used in the construction of several buildings in recent years. The most well-known is the 'EcoDepot' in York. This is the largest building of its type in Europe. Designed by 'White Design' the EcoDepot is built of straw panel, made by AgriFibre Technologies. Known as ModCell, the panels were manufactured off-site in a 'mobile factory' at Easingwold near York. They were transported to site and erected into position complete with their surface appli-

cation of lime-rendering and rain-screen, thus minimizing the risk of damage from exposure to the elements. Other projects successfully using the ModCell system include the Knowle West Media Centre in Bristol, the Torfaen EcoBuilding in Wales the UWE Studios at the University of England in Bristol.

The predicted benefits include a massive 76% reduction in energy requirements to heat the new depot. The EcoDepot also features rainwater harvesting and grey-water recycling. Electricity generated on site will provide 12% of current use – a figure set to increase as the EcoDepot could use even less energy, thus further enhancing the sustainability of the project.

Other projects are already using this technology and are discussed at more length in the 'Architectural trends' story, earlier in this chapter.

To sum up then, the main advantages of timber-straw panels are:

- off-site manufacture to ensure speed of erection on-site (see picture below)
- a very low carbon footprint with local resource and labour use.
- no waste on site and 'known' repeatable performance characteristics
- full sustainability, even on large projects
- a plentiful supply of material: a new crop is harvested every year!
- affordable housing can mean just that, not only to the pocket, but also more importantly, to the environment.

Useful links

www.agriboard.com

www.arco2.co.uk

www.white-design.co.uk

www.york.gov.uk/council/Council_departments/buildings/ecodepot

www.modcell.co.uk

www.agrifibretechnologies.com

Photo courtesy of White-Design

Taking construction off-site

Off-site construction OSC is promoted as one of the modern methods of construction (MMC), through government funded initiatives such as 'Constructing Excellence in the Built Environment'. **Paola Sassi** reports ...

Off-site construction (OSC), involves the partial or complete manufacture of buildings in factories and it has received increasing attention as can be seen in a number of the stories preceding this one. Certainly, as the last story confirmed, OSC need not preclude the increased use of natural materials and a number of innovative architectural, construction and engineering practices are bringing new, ecological systems to the market.

OSC is applicable to all building types, from housing to hospitals, and is seen as having the potential for speeding construction, improving build quality, increasing productivity and therefore profitability and addressing the ever important construction skills' shortage issues.

The uptake of OSC and MMC has been slow, with only 10% of house builders in 2004 using MMC. Figures published in 2005 indicate that around 2.1% of all construction and 3.6% of all new build spending in the construction industry goes towards OSC[1]. The reasons for the initial slow uptake was due to a lack of understanding, of the systems, an absence of agreed product and process standards, a perception of OSC being high cost, and, not least, the association to its historic precedents of prefabrication with its reputation for poor quality building and poor design.

In respect of housing, there have also been incidences where mortgage applications for OSC housing have been turned down by mortgage lenders. This reluctance to embrace OSC in this sector was a missed business opportunity according to Dennis Lenard, Chief Executive of Constructing Excellence in the Built Environment, (formed by a merger of the DTI funded Constructing Excellence and supply chain body Be). Lenard believes OSC can offer a number of business advantages by potentially reducing construction time by 30%, freeing the construction process from weather constraints and contributing to achieving a higher quality build. A useful asset in these times with a recessed housing market and credit limitations.

There are also some environmental benefits associated with the use of OSC. Working in a controlled and weather tight environment improves working conditions and reduces health and safety risks. Pollution and waste production can be controlled and minimised more easily. Water can be recycled in a factory situation. The higher quality of finishes not only affects aesthetics, but can also improve building performance by, for example, creating more airtight structures. The reduced period on site reduces the local impacts, such as noise and dust.

Claims that OSC is inherently more energy efficient are, however, simply incorrect. OSC is about the building process and while some OSC technologies facilitate the achievement of highly energy efficient structures, others do not. Furthermore some forms of OSC have high embodied energy, and some of the lightweight construction systems may, in a future of elevated average temperatures, fail to provide comfortable environments by passive means.

Cost

A current analysis[2] of the housing stock published in 2007 identified a deficit of 373,000 social housing units in the UK. The government's targets[3] for 200,000 new homes by the year 2016 are underpinned by the belief that the best way to tackle the shortage of affordable housing is to increase the housing stock.

Addressing this issue is a priority for sustainable development and OSC is thought to be well-placed to help with alleviating this deficit. Yet the National Audit Office issued a report in 2005 that stated that while MMC can produce four times as many homes as traditional building technologies, using the same amount of on-site labour, it also acknowledged that MMC are still more expensive than traditional ones.

A greater uptake of OSC would bring prices down, but for now its contribution to affordable housing is still unclear. There are, however, examples of cost-effective OSC. PCKO designed and coordinated the procurement of eight flats for key workers within a four storey block in Barling Court, London for Hyde Housing. The volumetric steel framed system, (main picture far right) which has a 60 year lifespan, was manufactured in Poland. The volumetric units have been designed so they can be disassembled and relocated elsewhere. The installation of the modules took only four days and at £1260/m^2 it is equivalent to a 12% reduction on traditional construction methods and 20-30% reduction on other prefabricated methods.

Below: Kingspan was not slow off the mark in launching its range of Tek houses a few years ago. Kingspan has secured a strong position in offsite manufacture, with a wide range of homes that homeowners can choose from a catalogue.

Off-site construction has been used by eco-builders for some time, but the mainstream industry has been slow to catch on. Above: URBANe, in 2004, erected a highly energy efficient eco-home to a watertight stage in just 24 hours, using a system called 'Tradis'.

Transport

A number of European and even Canadian companies are marketing high quality prefabricated housing systems in the UK. Some systems are highly insulated and incorporate PVs and solar hot water panels. However, for an overall assessment of the full sustainability of using OSC, the question of the embodied transport-related energy needs to to be asked. Even when not imported from abroad, OSC may also involve double transport, i.e. from the material manufacturer to the OSC manufacturer and from there to the site.

OSC in the future

The infrastructure to support OSC is increasing with initiatives such as LPS2020 (Loss Prevention Standard for Innovative Dwellings) addressing the Council of Mortgage Lenders' and the Association of Building Insurers' concerns regarding the longevity, buildability and performance of OSC. Increased uptake of OSC should reduce costs, in particular, if standardisation of prefabricated modules is encouraged. Standardisation is, however,

Barling Court housing development, by PCKO for Hyde Housing, was built on a site that was made available for a limited amount of time and was therefore designed to be re-locatable to a new site in future. The development constitutes 5 rows of volumetric elements, stacked one on top of the other, four storeys high. All finishes and services were installed in the factory and the balconies were installed on site.

The Knowle West Media Centre, which is made up of straw bale panels. These were built off-site nearby and taken to finished for erection. The OSC builders choose a nearby location to undertake the prefabrication of the panels and include the use of locally harvested straw bales.

associated with concerns from the architectural community believing that it equates to loss of design freedom and individuality. Architects, Cartwright Pickard, have tried to address this issue by developing Optima Homes in collaboration with Pace Timber. Their aim was to provide a system that would allow architects to design almost any housing form for up to five storey apartments, but would benefit from standard components. If this truly succeeds then one of the barriers to adopting OSC is removed.

If standardisation does take off, then it would be of paramount importance that energy efficiency standards are set at suitably high levels from the start. Setting up manufacturing facilities and supply chains, involves significant effort and investment and manufacturers would understandably be reluctant to upgrade these in the near future. Government pressure should be for OSC to be synonymous with the AECB's Silver and Gold standard, not just compliance with Building Regulations.

Finally it is worth keeping in mind that new build occupies, particularly within the housing industry, only a part of the building industry. As reported in Hyde Housing Association's 'The Hyde Commission: Principles and Practice' (2004): the fact is that 50-60% of construction in the housing sector is remedial work. Will we in future see OSC applied to this area in greater volume?

References

1. *Pan, W., Gibb, A., Dainty A. (2005), Modern Methods of Construction in Housebuilding. Perspectives and Practices of Leading UK Housebuilders, Loughborough University.*

2. *Hills, J (2007), Ends and Means: The Future Roles of Social Housing In England, CASE report 34, London: ESRC Research Centre for Analysis of Social Exclusion.*

3. *ODPM: Housing, Planning, Local Government and the Regions Committee (2006) Affordability and the Supply of Housing, Third Report of Session 2005–06, Volume I London: The Stationery Office Limited.*

Further information

'Off-Site Fabrication: Prefabrication, Pre-assembly and Modularization' by A G F Gibb , Caithness: Whittles Publishing (1999).

'Off site construction: an introduction, Good Building Guide' (leaflet), Building Research Establishment, Watford: 2003.

'Off-site produced housing: a briefing guide for housing associations' by M Gorgolewski (SCI), M Milner (TRADA), K Ross (BRE), Building Research Establishment, Watford (2002).

IP 16/01 - Information Paper 16/01 is in three parts: Parts 1 and 2 describe two case studies and Part 3 summarises the research into best practice in flexible and modular residential construction.

'Prefabricated housing in the UK: a case study - Murray Grove, Hackney' by C Bågenholm, A Yates and I McAllister, Building Research Establishment, Watford (2001).

'Prefabricated housing in the UK, a case study: CASPAR II, Leeds' by C Bågenholm, A Yates and I McAllister , Building Research Establishment, Watford (2001).

Design and Modern Methods of Construction, CABE, 2004, funded by Housing Corporation and can be downloaded at ***www.housingcorp.gov.uk/server/show/conWeb-Doc.3306***

Useful websites

www.buildoffsite.com

Constructing Excellence ***www.constructingexcellence.org.uk***

The Concrete Centre ***www.concretecentre.com/mmc***

Timber Frame Association ***www.timber-frame.org/index.php?page=129o***

Hanson's ecohome: claimed as near zero carbon, which was on display at BRE's 2007 offsite exhibition.

Avoid stolen timber

Because of massive global demand for this resource, timber is targeted by criminals on a huge scale. **Sally Hall** investigates what is being done to help ensure that all of our supplies are legal and sustainable.

The Earth was once covered in ancient forests. Home to around two-thirds of all plant and animal species found on land, as well as millions of people who depend on them for their survival, they still form some of the most diverse ecosystems known to science and are vitally important to the health of our planet, especially when it comes to regulating the climate. But ancient forests around the world are still under threat with a staggering 80% already destroyed or degraded, and half of that has been in the last 30 years. Illegal and destructive logging, industrial-scale farming and, increasingly, climate change all threaten the remaining tracts of forest that have stood for thousands of years. Countless species face extinction and entire communities are being displaced. If current rates of deforestation continue, some of the last areas of ancient forest could be lost within our lifetimes.

Organisations such as Greenpeace and the Environmental Investigation Agency are campaigning hard for genuinely sustainable timber, but they continue to discover trails of illegal logging, and 'stolen' timber remains a major factor driving deforestation. For example, the rapid growth of Vietnam's wood processing industry is threatening some of the last intact forests of the region. The country has tried to conserve its own remaining forests but its hugely expanding furniture industry has led to corruption and much evidence that 'stolen timber' persistently turns up as garden furniture in the UK, imported by suppliers who are either unaware or unconcerned about the origin or impact.

The largest consumer of wood products is still the United States. However, it has recently become the first country to ban the import and sale of illegal timber[1]. It is hoped that the UK and elsewhere will introduce similar legislation to combat such deforestation. The process has started in the UK with Barry Gardiner MP, the prime minister's special envoy for forests, introducing a new bill in April 2008.

If this becomes law anyone caught knowingly selling illegal timber in the UK could face up to 5 years in prison and a £100,000 fine. "*The UK is the fourth largest consumer market of imported timber, yet only a fraction of it can be said with any degree of certainly to have been legally sourced.*" Gardiner told parliament, "*Critically this bill will protect UK businesses and workers that currently have to compete on an uneven playing field that pits honest merchants against rogue traders*".

References

1. In May 2008 the long standing wildlife trafficking statute, the Lacey Act, was amended to include timber, wood products and other plants.

Web links

www.greenpeace.org.uk/forests

www.eia-international.org

Watch out for greenwash

Protecting the environment is in vogue and perhaps not a moment too soon. However, the downside is that we are now seeing many of the same old building products being re-badged and promoted as green. **Keith Hall** reports ...

The top priority for any business is to stay in business. Nowadays being seen to be green is the way to stay ahead of the competition. If the product is not green, then just imply it is! Our own construction industry seems to be storming ahead in the 'green stakes'. This sudden interest appears to be fuelled mainly by government and local authority interest/ demands, rather than by builders or architects having suddenly seen the light. Is this a bad thing? Well not really, especially if all was as it seemed. The reality is, however, that just about every builder and specifier is now being bombarded with the latest eco-buzzwords (eg. 'sustainable', 'environmentally friendly', and the current favourite 'zero' or 'low carbon'). There is no escape, these phrases are being used in all the trade magazines. In some cases their use is justified but in many it is not and there are an increasing number of adverts and, more insidiously, editorial, that can only be described as misleading. Evidence of greenwash is very easy to find.

The problem is, can the average person make the distinction between what is true and what is not? Housebuilders are the latest soft targets. Renowned for their nonchalance towards the concept of sustainability, they are now having to face up to the idea of all their homes being 'zero carbon' by 2016 (or 2012 if they are in Wales!). The government doesn't even know how this will be achieved yet! However, if we are to believe all the adverts and thinly veiled stories we read, the construction products sector already has it sewn up for us.

In the first six months of 2007, the Advertising Standards Authority received 268 complaints regarding 200 so called 'green' adverts. The number of complaints has continued to grow as green advertising has become more commonplace.

Most editorial that is presented in the building trade press (especially the free ones) is advertising led. The text is more often than not written by PR agents employed by the company that make the products the story is about. As an editor myself, I know how these stories come about. They are written predominantly by journalistic staff, who probably have little knowledge about sustainability or construction, but the story is wrapped up and presented as knowledgeable prose with all the right power words. As for the adverts, few of the environmental claims made, if properly challenged, would stand up to scrutiny.

If you've got it, why not flaunt it?

Can we blame businesses for just trying to do their bit, biting the eco-bullet, taking it on-board at board level and wanting to tell their customers about their enlightenment? There is a saying; 'nobody preaches like the recently converted'. But believe me, this is dangerous ground and there are no easy answers. The recently converted are welcome but their enthusiasm can get ahead of them. As the larger companies get in on the act, with their huge advertising budgets, a lot of damage can, and is being caused. Especially if they overstep the mark and deliberately or inadvertently mislead readers by making claims that may be seriously flawed. Whilst they may argue that their focus is firmly on demonstrating environmental concern and action, it is clear to those of us that have been studying this subject for many years, that little can have changed in so short a time.

What I am seeing, and many others agree, is the same old products just being re-branded and re-packaged in a new suit of clothes. For example, should electric resistance heating (it has been around for 50 years at least) really be promoted as an ecological option when the generation of electricity from the national grid is clearly one of the largest contributors of greenhouse gases and uses about 3.5 times the amount of fuel per kW of heat produced? And then we have the companies that are claiming their products are eco because they pay for 'carbon offsetting'. Should the funding of low carbon projects in the third world act as an antidote to the carbon the product manufacturer has created and thus give them the right to claim that their entire product range is zero carbon? In my opinion this is all greenwash. Greenwash is insidious and it is everywhere, in magazines, on the web, at exhibitions and events, on the TV and radio. Publishers and programme makers are the main propagators. Greenwash fills precious pages or airtime. It would seem that it doesn't really matter to some publishers what is said as long as the space is filled and the pages look right.

Top greenwash claims

No 1 greenwash has to be carbon offsetting. It continues unabated and is one of the fastest growing sectors, earning billions globally, despite suffering bad press. Even the government is worried and is establishing a set of standards to help regulate the practice. It has been attacked for its lack of transparency and inconsistencies. To businesses, and increasingly to a punch drunk public keen to appease any feelings of guilt, offsetting is the fantastic, 'do little but say a lot' option that allows anyone to just throw cash at the problem, whilst carrying on as normal. Once traded, the 'offset' business is free to make all sorts of claims to suit their target audience and the geographical distance involved is usually so vast that customers could never check what has really been done. The benefits, if there are any at all, of carbon offsetting projects have always proven difficult, if not impossible to verify. Many in the environmental movement agree that it is just a stalling tactic allowing a 'business as usual' with no real commitment.

No 2 in the greenwash stakes is green tariff electricity. Again, an opportunity to fix it with cash. In fact, businesses that are prepared to shop around will often find that they can become 'greener than green', and make financial savings, just by switching energy provider. In fact, recently submitted evidence to the Department for Business, Enterprise and Regulatory Reform (BERR) from the Association for Environment Conscious Building (AECB) stated that "In recent years the proportion of electricity from renewables has not actually met the legal minimum percentage set by government. In 2007 the legal mandate was 7% but the actual amount produced was 5%." So, there is just not enough genuinely renewable electricity available, regardless of how many companies sign up. Number 3 greenwash in this industry at the moment seems to be the very latest - 'CSH ready' or 'zero carbon' . Both claims are intending to imply that the product, process or business is, in some way, going to achieve for the user instant accreditation to the Code for Sustainable Homes.

In 2008 the Mastic Asphalt industry proclaimed in its newsletter[1] that the whole mastic asphalt sector was 'zero carbon'! It had merely utilised 1, 2 and 3 in a combined 'triple whammy'!

Beware of misleading tradenames

Whilst written claims of greenness need to be proven if challenged, a tradename or trademark that implies greenness need not be! For example, there are several instances of the word 'organic' being used in this way. The latest is for a PVC profile that has recently been launched. Organic PVC, I ask you!

Greenwashing also has a government twist

Interestingly, our government has also been criticised for greenwashing. For instance, in 2003 Tony Blair was accused of attempting a 'greenwash' of the government's environmental record as he launched a white paper on energy provision[2]. And again in 2007 investigative journalist, George Monbiot, went to the trouble of commissioning a team of environmental scientists from the University College, London, to conduct a peer-reviewed audit of the government's planned greenhouse gas reductions as he was concerned about greenwash. *"Our audit reveals that the government's assessment of its own policies is wildly optimistic. Instead of a 29-31% cut by 2020, it is on course to deliver a reduction of between 12% and 17%. At this rate the UK will not meet its 2020 milestone until 2050. This result suggests that the government's claim to be 'leading the world on tackling climate change' is simply another product of the Downing Street spin machine."* [3]

Green labels - do they help or hinder?

Can green labels help? At the current time they are more likely to add extra confusion. This is because there are no firm rules or restrictions on the use (or abuse) of labels to promote products. In the late eighties, the government became concerned about the plethora of green labels being produced without suitable supporting data and I was under the impression that the use of self generated eco labels had been outlawed. But it has not, and readers need to understand that any company can (and they are doing) invent an eco-label of their own, with standards and compliance criteria to suit their own taste.

The government's Department for Environment, Food and Rural Affairs (DEFRA) offers advice on how companies can make claims about their products and there is a 'green claims code'[4] which sets out a standard of information which the public may expect to see. It also suggests what those who are offended by claims can do to try to get them corrected via the 'Control of Misleading Advertisement Regulations 1998'[5]. The green claims code mentioned above, though, has no statutory force, but it has been supported by two government departments and is supported by Trading Standards and some industry bodies, so it is reasonable for regulatory or formal self-regulatory authorities (the courts on trades descriptions and the Advertising Standards Authority[7] on media advertising) to take it into account.

The government has introduced the European ecolabelling scheme[6]. The Ecolabel is only awarded to goods and services which meet strict criteria limiting the impacts of consumer products on the environment. The criteria applies to every stage of the product's life, from manufacture through to disposal, and covers every impact which is relevant to a specific type of product, such as the natural resources, energy, water and chemicals used in manufacturing, through to recycling. Products with the Ecolabel are independently certified. However, the Ecolabel is currently a voluntary scheme backed by the EU and run by DEFRA in the UK. Very few products (no building products) have applied to use the Ecolabel in the UK.

What about accreditation type labels?

These are similar to standards and tend to be sector-wide or created by group agreement. Known accreditation schemes that are relevant to the construction industry are listed below.

BRE Environmental Profiles[8] provide a life-cycle assessment of construction products in a standardised way that is open to scrutiny. However, the scheme is expensive and take up has been low.

Heating boilers are assessed against the **SEDBUK** label (seasonal efficiency of domestic boilers in the UK). The rating enables compari-

Heat pumps. Are they just hot air?

An example of where there is widespread confusion is heat pumps and electric heating in general. Regarding heat pumps, the government is not helping. On its Department for Business, Enterprise and Regulatory Reform (BERR) website (where the 'Low Carbon Building programme' (LCBP) grants are dished out) it states of ground source heat pumps, "For every unit of electricity used to pump the heat, 3-4 units of heat are produced. As well as ground source heat pumps, air source and water source heat pumps are also available"[12]. However, according to submitted evidence to the Department for Business, Enterprise and Regulatory Reform (BERR) from the AECB, (the sustainable building association) 'There should be a thorough review of the design and installation errors in LCBP-supported heat pumps. These have reportedly led to widespread CoPs of less than 2.5' !

There is a growing band of professionals and campaigners that think that heat pump technology has wrongly been classified as a 'renewable technology' as heat pumps require electricity, a top level fuel, and there is not enough data available yet to justify the high CoP (co-efficient of performance) claims that some companies are making. The AECB has called for the removal of the renewable's name-tag from the technology: present labelling of electric heat pumps as 'renewable energy' is highly misleading. Coefficients of performance from plant that has been monitored are not as high as the manufacturers state, with as much CO_2 being emitted as a result of the electricity being used to run them, as is being 'saved' by using the heat pump as a heat source. A highly efficient gas, LPG or oil boiler would usually emit less CO_2. It is open to further challenge but we hope that the government will abandon this wording as soon as possible."

The AECB goes on to point out that, "Belief that heat pumps are a form of 'renewable energy' has already caused some people who live in towns to install a heating system which costs three to four times more to install and emits more CO_2 than the gas boiler it replaces. A serious mis-allocation of resources has been subsidised from public funds".

Heat pumps are not the only technology or product sector creating concern regarding misleading claims. The small scale wind turbines sector had a good year of unwarranted promotion, supported by naive ministers and seized upon by the copy hungry press before claims about under-performance and other issues were brought to the public's attention.

son to be made between the energy efficiency of different boilers, according to the familiar A to G scale, with A as the most efficient and G the least[13].

The BFRC (The British Fenestration Rating Council) Window Energy Rating, is a voluntary scheme in which the whole window (the frame and glass) is assessed according to its efficiency at retaining heat, using A to G bands where A is the most efficient[14].

FSC is the trademark of the Forest Stewardship Council. The FSC is an international organization that has brought together the forestry industry and the environmental movement to find a standardised methodology for monitoring the harvesting, converting, shipping and end-use of timber and timber products. It would seem that the FSC scheme is the only globally recognized standard for forest management. Governments can specify FSC certification in their procurement policies without breeching World Trade Organisation (WTO) rules.

PEFC is another forestry timber certification scheme run by the Programme for the Endorsement of Forest Certification. It is an independent organisation and, like the FSC, provides assurance that timber and paper products that have passed through its chain of custody scheme, have been independently audited as coming from sustainably managed forests.

However, due to the remote nature of logging and the world demand for timber neither of the above forestry schemes are without their critics. There are plenty of websites that suggest that the certification of some timber supplies by multinationals is just a greenwash smokescreen for some of their other, less palatable practices[9, 10, 11]. In fact, in response to criticism, the FSC has drafted an anti-greenwash policy to help counter such accusations.

Let's not proliferate false claims!

The builders and specifiers among us need to take care in our choices and recommendations. Our customers are becoming ever more adept at spotting misleading claims. It is not going to get easier either. There are already plenty of other codes, standards and legal commitments to meet - now we have to add protecting the environment to the list. We need all the help we can get in providing what the customer wants - a sustainable building, but, if we were to just trust what we read, who will get the blame when the cat gets out of the bag! An interesting point that has probably yet to be tested in a contract, but tested it will be, eventually. Certainly from a professional perspective, the accreditation schemes, such as those mentioned above, represent a promise that can be verified by independent inspection and so should offer the best reassurance of what is offered actually being delivered.

So what can we do?

It is rarely acknowledged, but very few manufactured products have yet proven to be totally harmless to the environment. Claims such as 'greener' are deemed acceptable if advertisers can prove that the product gives an overall improvement in environmental terms when compared to a similar, competing product. All facts should be accurate; claims should not be exaggerated and should be backed up by documentary evidence if the customer requests clarification.

We know that greenwash is rife, so we need to redouble our resolve to ensure that our own hopes and aspirations for a really greener world are being fulfilled. We should:

- check all claims carefully before committing to specifying or buying products that are labelled as green
- be prepared to spend some time personally checking and asking for proof to back up claims that are made. Contact the head office of the manufacturer making the claim. Ask for an explanation of the claim and how it can be shown to comply with the 'Green Claims Code'
- if you believe that a green claim is simply untrue, or even after explanations from manufacturer or the retailer you believe that a claim may be misleading, it is best to take this up with your local authority

trading standards department (contacts can be found in your local telephone directory). In Northern Ireland, enforcement responsibilities rest with the Trading Standards Service of the Department of Enterprise

- complaints about a claim in a radio or TV advertisement can be made to the Radio Authority or the Independent Television Commission
- complaints about adverts can be made by letter or by completion of a simple form on-line to the ASA (Advertising Standards Authority). Adjudications are posted up on its website weekly[7]. If complaints are upheld the business is expected to take appropriate action immediately but if problems persist the Office of Fair Trading (OFT)[15] and Offcom can become involved.

It is the ASA that sets most of the rules with regard to environmental claims in advertising but they are reactive rather than pro-active. The ASA is an independent body set up and funded by the advertising industry to police the rules laid down in the advertising codes. The ASA can regulate the content of advertisements, sales promotions and direct marketing in the UK. As you might expect, a quick search of the ASA website reveals an increasing number of complaints relating to the use of false environmental claims. Most of the complaints are upheld, yet the practice of greenwashing continues seemingly unabated. The prize of increased sales is obviously worth the small risk of a rap on the knuckles. The burden to provide proof falls on the advertiser to justify the claims they make, if and when challenged. Unless a complaint is made, a business can and is likely to continue to make misleading claims until challenged, so it is vital that as many people as possible become vigilant and examine advertisements and their environmental claims carefully.

Conclusion

Out of all this it is clear that there is no easy answer that will allow specifiers and users to be absolutely sure that their choice has been the best for the planet. In-fact, rather than getting easier to source the most appropriate green products, we are being drowned in a tidal wave of conflicting information. Sadly, for the foreseeable future, there will be no substitute for personal research. On the plus side the internet has made what once would have been lengthy phone calls and library visits a thing of the past. We now have a worldwide library of information at our fingertips. Use it! It only takes a few minutes, on a search engine such as Google, to bring up a host of facts and opinions on any given topic. It is a valuable weapon to have in your arsenal.

With thanks to Sally Hall for the initial research on this story

References

1. *Carbon Copy, newsletter of the Mastic Asphalt Council published summer 2008 'Mastic Asphalt, One industry - zero carbon'.*
2. ***www.guardian.co.uk/environment/2003/feb/24/energy.greenpolitics***
3. ***www.guardian.co.uk/politics/2007/mar/05/media.greenpolitics** Guardian online: 'Wiping Out Greenwash': **www.guardian.co.uk/media/2007/nov/19/mondaymediasection.climatechange***
4. ***www.defra.gov.uk/environment/consumerprod/gcc/index.htm***
5. ***www.opsi.gov.uk/SI/si1988/Uksi_19880915_en_1.htm***
6. ***http://ec.europa.eu/environment/ecolabel/whats_eco/greenstore_en.htm***
7. ***www.asa.org.uk/asa***
8. ***www.bre.co.uk/page.jsp?id=53***
9. ***www.pefcwatch.org***
10. ***www.wrm.org.uy/countries/Uruguay/book.html***
11. ***www.illegal-logging.info/item_single.php?item=news&item_id=2411&approach_id=1***
12. ***www.berr.gov.uk/energy/sources/heat/page43671.html***
13. ***www.boilers.org.uk***
14. ***www.bfrc.org***
15. ***www.oft.gov.uk***

Useful information

*Ethical Consumer magazine's online scoring system for products: **www.ethiscore.org***

*Ethical Trading Initiative: **www.ethicaltrade.org***

*Carbon offsetting: **www.foe.co.uk/resource/briefing_notes/carbon_offsetting.pdf***

*Ethical Marketing Group: **www.ethical-marketing.co.uk***

*Ecolabelling: **www.defra.gov.uk/environment/consumerprod/ecolabel***

*'Consumer Protection from Unfair Trading Regulations': **www.berr.gov.uk/consumers/index.html***

www.futerra.co.uk/services/greenwash-guide

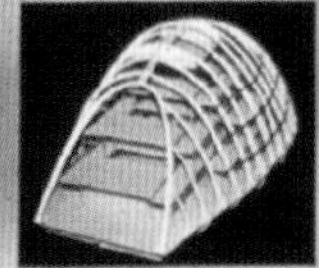
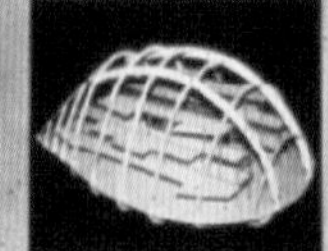
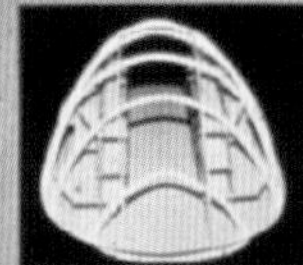

Buildings during their construction and subsequent operation consume vast amounts of natural resources. They account for half of the UK's primary energy consumption. They demand quarrying and exploitation of forests and other natural resources to supply the materials from which they are made. In use building emissions add to global warming, damage the ozone layer and create waste disposal problems.

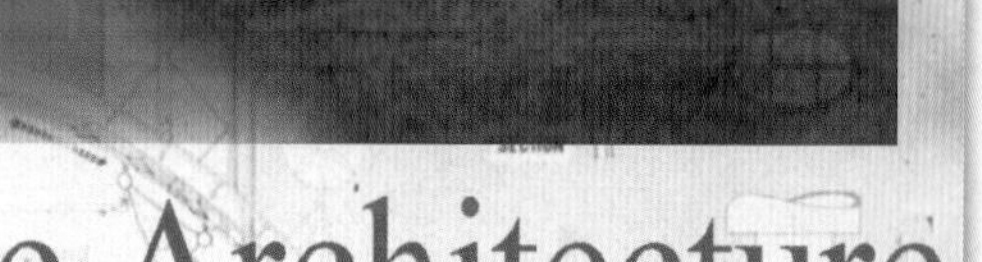

MSc. Sustainable Architecture

One year full time - two years part time

The internal environment has been linked with ill health ranging from chronic illness caused by discomfort to life threatening illness due to the collection and concentration of pathogens and carcinogens. This course considers the tools available to alleviate these environmental and health problems such as; design methods, technologies (alternative and high tech) and legslation.

The subjects covered include: low energy design, research, management and academic methods, theglobal environment, health and contemporary sustainable architecture. The major component is a final research project or design thesis.

The course is aimed primarily at graduates in a discipline associated with the built environment (architecture, civil engineering, planning, building services etc.) but other disciplines will be considered.

This course offers graduates and practitioners the opportunity to expand their skills in an area of great concern both to clients and the public as a whole.

For further details contact:

Richard Nicholls
Tel 01484 472652, email R.Nicholls@hud.ac.uk
Department of Architecture, Huddersfield University
Queensgate, Huddersfield, HD1 3DH

living space sciences

UNIVERSITY OF EXETER

3 Power, heating and water

Energy should be human scale

Green energy is energy that comes from clean, renewable, sources such as the sun, wind, water and biomass etc. **Sue Roaf** introduces clean green energy ...

The term renewable describes sources of energy that are driven by the sun and moon, and the resulting climate and weather systems they create on the planet (wind, rain, wave etc). The two main influences on localised climate are latitude and the location of a site in relation to large land and water masses. Weather is driven by a multitude of influences, and the regional and local micro-climates of a given site are shaped by its location in relation to the local and regional geomorphology. The available energy from the sun, wind, waves and water will result from the climate and weather of a site, while the biomass energy sources are additionally influenced by man's management of the land and water. Geothermal and ground source energy is also available from heat in the Earth's crust (latent sunshine) or the mantle.

All renewable energy sources arise from regularly repeating natural processes, in contrast to the very finite nature of fossil fuel reserves that took millenia to lay down. Fossil fuels; coal, gas and oil, are largely at or past their 'peak' of production, forcing the higher and higher oil and gas prices that we have been seeing throughout 2008. Hopefully this will provide a stronger impetus for a rapid move to renewable energy use[1]. Interestingly, and frighteningly, the built environment uses up to 50% of all energy produced on the earth.

Nuclear power and energy from waste incineration are often claimed to be 'green' power, but neither are anywhere near carbon neutral supplies due to the high energy costs of maintaining such large and dangerous power stations and the resultant waste arisings, and highly polluting processes.

Not all green energy is green!

So called green energy purchased from green energy suppliers cannot be technically counted as such because the carbon emission reductions of the suppliers have typically already been included in the supplier's quotas and cannot then be double counted into the customer's carbon quotas. What is important for a site is what its potential energy yield is from the different sources of energy.

Every location or building will have a different range of opportunities for the harvesting of green energy. For wind, the continental location of a site is important, as coastal sites typically have far higher windspeeds than inland locations. *This subject is discussed at length in Chapters 1 and 5 of Volume 2 of the Green Building Bible.*

It is vital that wind turbines are not shaded by adjacent buildings, land obstacles or trees. The temperature of any ground source heat available to a building will depend not only on latitude, but also on the location of the system. Ground temperatures on the north side of a hill, for instance, can be many degrees lower than those on its sunny side. Geothermal heat from deep boreholes would fluctuate less as it does not depend so much on latent solar

This page and next: various views of community renewables installed on and around homes and offices in Kirklees, as part of a drive to make the region less dependant on grid power.

energy than does ground source, which is typically harvested from about 1 metre below the surface. Solar energy is considered the best renewable source for urban locations, as PV systems are noise free, unobtrusive and can be fitted to almost any building roof or facade, with minimal infrastructure remodelling, although the higher levels of air pollution found over cities may lower the overall yield.

Latitude also plays a major role in the potential yield of a solar array, be it active for heating or PVs for electricity, as will the terrain and weather around a building. The angle of a roof on which the panels are located, and the building orientation, help in optimising the potential yield of the systems[2], as does its location in relation to adjacent structures or trees that may shade it from the sun. The careful planning and design of renewable energy systems is vital. For instance, there is no use designing micro-hydro systems for a river that dries up in summer droughts.

A major characteristic of any weather driven renewable energy system is that it is impossible to predict the weather. The supply of wind, water or sun are intermittent, and so are their resulting energy supplies. The UK system of energy supply is dominated by a monolithic 'national grid' supplying either gas, or electricity, generated from coal, hydro, gas or oil fuelled power stations. The grid is hugely inefficient, with only around 36% of the original energy used being actually delivered to our building due to losses in the generating plant (averaging 57%) and the distribution network (around 7%).

Electricity blackouts are becoming more common around the world as grids buckle under the strain of excessive demand, and the cut back on generation capacity, imposed by privatised energy companies driven by the need for shareholder profits. 20th century society became dependant, for its ordinary functioning, on a constant, and high quality, supply of electricity that is totally reliable (without interruptions); with a high power quality (relating to frequency and voltage stability, waveform abnormalities etc.) and a structure that is rapidly repairable. This type of supply will be increasingly difficult to produce and we are becoming more concerned with issues of the security of supply and the environmental impacts of the supply in light of the climate change[3] and peak oil challenges. In this emerging '21st century' market, micro-grids, supplying embedded generation, are a very attractive social, environmental and commercial proposition.

Embedded generation (also known as distributed embedded or dispersed generation) is electricity generation connected to a local distribution network, rather than the high voltage national transmission network, or grid. Distributed generators are mostly (though not exclusively) those who are generating power from environmentally friendly, renewable energy sources, (including small hydro, wind and solar power) or from combined heat and power (CHP) plants.

The nature of national grid networks today play into the hands of multinationals at the expense of smaller generators who find it difficult and expensive to connect to networks that were not designed to accommodate them. The output from a single PV house into the grid is little more than noise on the line, but when the whole street has solar hot water systems and PV arrays, then the solar contribution to powering houses down the street becomes significant, especially if the householders are out all day at work during the week but at home during the weekend.

Matching the load profiles to the electricity supply will be a real challenge, as a range of very 'frisky' energy sources cutting in and out of the supply, causes difficulties and is still the subject of extensive research. There are many innovations being introduced and tested in Europe where other countries are much further along the renewable energy route.

In order to solve the supply and quality issues associated with distributed micro-grids, much work is currently being done in the UK, but while this goes on we should not rest on our laurels, as there is no reason why in the coming years we should not move back to the old 20th century systems of the local 'municipal grid'. Perhaps in the 21st century, as we adapt to live with the rapidly changing climate, and to kick our addiction to dwindling fossil fuels, we will increasingly move to community owned and controlled grids, to supply our energy from a cocktail of embedded, clean, renewable energy generators, many of which may be located in or around our own homes. ☯

References and further reading

1. For more information on the peak oil and gas issues see: ***www.peakoil.net*** *and* ***www.energycrisis.com*** *and for books see:* ***www.eci.ox.ac.uk/***

2. ***www.macslab.com/optsolar.html***

3. For extensive and authoritative information on climate change and its impacts see: ***www.ukcip.org.uk*** *and* ***www.ipcc.ch***

A good place to start researching your own local renewable energy needs and potential is the website of the Centre for Alternative Technology - a pioneer in this field, providing information, education, courses and consultancy: 01654 705989 ***www.cat.org.uk****; or email:* ***info@cat.org.uk***

There are some excellent scenarios of what future climates might look like at ***www.ukcip.org.uk*** *.*

The Environment Agency has detailed information on the seasonal flows and trends of all the rivers in the UK. For those who want to design for future climates, see the excellent design weather guide produced by CIBSE: ***www.cibse.org/index.cfm?go=publications.view&PubID=317&L1=164*** ***www.lboro.ac.uk/crest/education-modulespecs.html****.*

Grants

Low Carbon Building Programme grant scheme covering wind, hydro, solar PV and more. Grants for householders, small businesses, community schemes, and larger projects: 0800 915 7722 ***www.lowcarbon-buildings.org.uk***

Scottish Householders and Community Renewable: 0800 138 8858 ***www.est.org.uk/schri***

Energy Saving Trust: You may be eligible for additional local grants: 0800 512 012 ***www.est.org.uk/myhome***

Related organisations

British Photovoltaic Association, information about permissions and approvals (G83/1) needed for grid connected systems: 01908 442291 ***www.greenenergy.org.uk***

British Wind Energy Association promote wind power. Web site includes advice on siting a turbine and connecting it to the grid: 020 7689 1960 ***www.bwea.com***

British Solar Trade Association: 01908 442290 ***www.greenenergy.org.uk/sta***

OFGEM (Office of Gas and Electricity Markets) regulates renewable obligation certificates (ROCs): 020 7901 7000 ***www.ofgem.gov.uk***

Green energy suppliers

There are a few companies who both supply and buy back electricity from renewable sources. Two such companies are:

Ecotricity: 0800 0326 100 ***www.ecotricity.co.uk***

Good Energy: 0845 456 1640 ***www.good-energy.co.uk***

Understanding energy use

Richard Nicholls looks at patterns of energy use in buildings and the cost implications of our choices ...

Each type of building will have a different pattern of energy consumption throughout each day and throughout the year. However, for the purpose of this discussion, we will split buildings into two broad categories so we can discuss energy reduction strategies. These are:

- domestic (houses)
- non-domestic (commercial property).

Predicting the energy used by a building is complicated because of the wide range of factors that affect its energy consumption. These include;

Building type. Buildings enclose a wide range of human activity. For example, they can be places of education, work, entertainment or living. Within each building type there are variations, for example, dwellings may be flats, terraced houses or detached homes. The prime difference here is the physical size of the building, specifically areas and volumes.

Building fabric. One role of the building fabric is to protect the occupants from the discomfort of the external environment whilst letting in those elements that are beneficial, such as fresh air and daylight. Thermal insulation, thermal mass, air tightness, and quality of workmanship all have an effect on energy consumption. See Green Building Bible, Volume 2 for a more full discussion of these issues.

Building services. It is the primary building services, space and water heating systems, cooling systems and lighting systems that use energy to create comfort in buildings. It follows that the type, capacity, efficiency and method of control of these services will all have a significant effect on the amount of energy used by a building.

Load on the services. The principle factor, making the operation of energy consuming services necessary, is the variation in external climate. This could be too hot, requiring cooling, or too cold, requiring heating. The amount of sunlight may fluctuate, varying how much solar energy is deposited in the building. It may also be too dark requiring the use of artificial lighting.

Human behaviour. When humans interact with the building services they can modify the amount of energy used by them. The extent of the interaction varies between building types. For example in the home there is every opportunity to turn heating and lighting on or off as required. No two sets of occupants are alike. One person may be energy aware and use energy frugally, another may be profligate with the energy and use it wastefully. In other buildings there is little opportunity for modifying energy using systems for example when working in an office the services are often controlled centrally, with no accessible manual controls.

The effect of all the above is to create a continuous variation in the amount of energy used by buildings. It is necessary, therefore, to consider statistical indicators of energy consumption to get an idea of the amounts of energy being consumed. The coarsest method of considering energy use in buildings is to consider two broad categories of building; domestic buildings (dwellings) and non-domestic buildings. This is a broad grouping of many different types of building within each category but is often used when describing UK energy use. For example, government statistics reveal that of the 761.7TWh of energy used

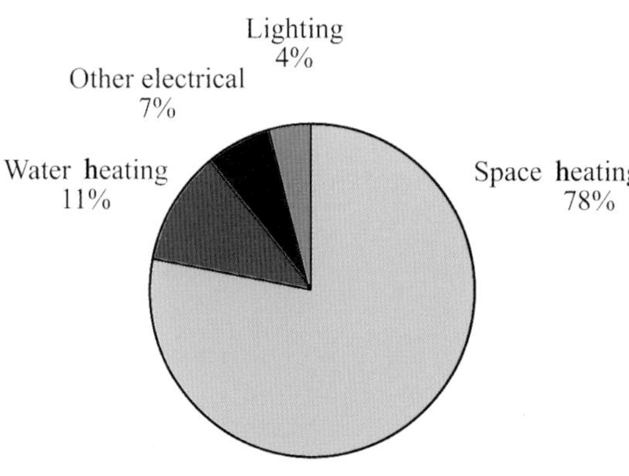

Figure 1. Breakdown of domestic energy consumption.

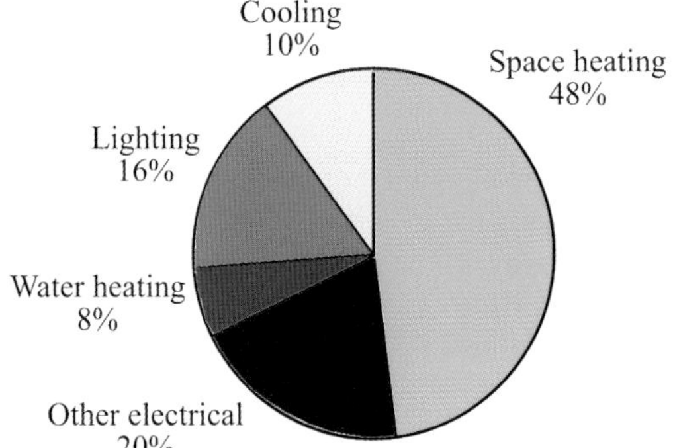

Figure 2. Breakdown of air conditioned office energ consumption.

each year in buildings, roughly 70% (530.3TWh) is used in housing and 30% (231.4TWh) is used in the services' sector (non-domestic buildings - note the services sector also includes a small amount for agriculture)[1].

Figures 1 and 2 show that space heating energy consumption is by far the largest contribution to the total energy consumed in both the domestic building and air conditioned office[2], comprising 78% and 48% of the total respectively. By comparing the two charts it can be seen that the proportion of the total energy used for space heating diminishes as the building complexity increases from domestic to non-domestic. This change can be attributed largely to the working environment of the non-domestic building, which requires increased electricity consumption to provide higher standards of lighting and thermal comfort. In particular there is additional electricity consumption by the air conditioning chillers and fans.

The pie charts have been drawn the same size to illustrate where the energy goes and to allow a comparison between the different building types. The area does not represent the amount of energy used. If the area did represent quantities of energy used (per m^2), the mechanically ventilated and air conditioned office chart would have a much bigger area than that for the domestic building. This is because the total energy consumption in any building depends on a range of factors including:

- the localised climate
- installed services
- the insulative quality of the building fabric
- the behaviour of the occupants
- the overall size of the buildings.

To consider energy use in buildings in more detail it is necessary to look at average values for a number of similar buildings over the course of a year. To be able to make a comparison between two types of building it is necessary to normalise the energy consumption. It is usual to divide the total amount of energy used over the year by the building's treated floor area. This gives energy consumption in kilowatt hours per square metre per year ($kWh/m^2/y$). For our two building types, typical energy consumptions are:

Type	*kWh/m²/y*
Domestic	150
Air conditioned office	460

The aim of low energy design is to reduce these values as much as possible. An interim target consumption can be set based on good practice values that have been found by looking at energy efficient buildings. The target good practice energy consumptions on this basis are:

Type	*kWh/m²/y*
Domestic	88
Air conditioned office	260

It is clear then that space heating uses the lion's

share of our energy and, as building complexity increases, then so it is likely that overall energy consumption will increase too. We have also shown that a number of measurable factors influence total energy consumption and that these are often not appliances but behaviour. The figures above show that a low energy building design can reduce energy costs by around 50% without any real behaviour changes needed. If these measures were coupled with behaviour changes (the way we use energy) then further savings would be found. Concern over climate change has begun to motivate people to think more carefully about how they use and manage buildings. Aside from the need to reduce CO_2 emissions and stave off global warming, there are other reasons why it is important to reduce the amount of energy consumed by our buildings but the reason that engages most people's attention is cutting costs, especially as fuel costs are rising so fast at the moment.

Cutting fuel costs

Different forms of energy have different costs per unit (1kWh) of energy. Table 1 shows the typical cost to a domestic consumer of different forms of energy and also the cost relative to gas. Actual prices will vary depending on market fluctuations, supplier and quantities purchased. From this simple analysis it can be seen that coal is the cheapest form of fuel, followed by oil then gas. Electricity is significantly more expensive per unit of energy than the primary fossil fuels.

Fuel type	Price p/kWh	Cost relative to gas
Gas	2.71	1.00
Oil	5.63	2.08
Coal	2.10	0.77
Electricity	14.7	5.42

Table 1. Cost of 1kWh of various fossil fuels relative to gas (taken at its lowest possible price).
Source John Willoughby's domestic fuel price guide April 08, *see page 460.*

This is because the unit cost of any source of energy depends on both the extraction costs and any processing costs. Electricity might seem to be an ideal fuel. Of every 100kWh of electrical energy used by a heating appliance, 100kWh of thermal energy is released. In other words at the point of use it is 100% efficient. However, we must not forget that electricity is generated primarily from fossil fuels in power stations, therefore is a product of further process.

Figure 3 shows the energy flows in a typical power station. It can be seen that of every 100 kilowatt hours of energy input to the power station, in the form of fossil fuels, approximately 57% is lost jointly as hot flue gases and as steam in the cooling towers and a further 7% is lost during electrical transmission (heating up of wires whilst overcoming resistance). This results in a conversion efficiency which varies between 31.5 and 36% depending on operating conditions. This wasteful method of production makes electricity costs high in relation to other fuels, such as gas that is extracted, at some cost, from the North Sea (and further afield), but with little further processing.

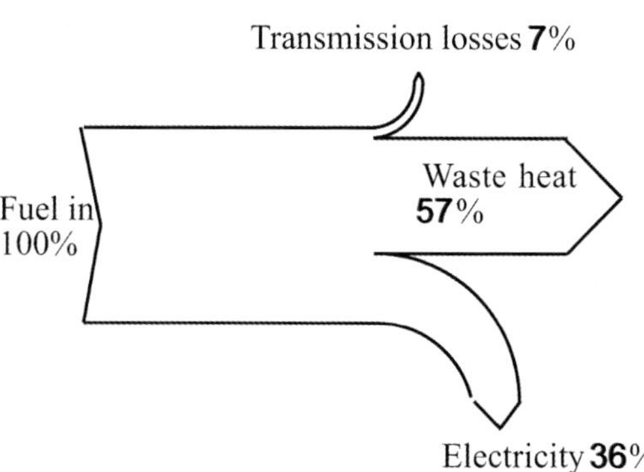

Figure 3. Energy flows in a typical power station.

The generation of electricity represents a scandalous waste of energy that should really be captured and used for heating purposes. In the UK many fossil fuel power stations are just too large and sited near coal fields and away from large urban areas where the waste heat could be more readily used in a district heating scheme. Smaller, decentralised generation schemes make much better use of the waste heat energy arising from electricity generation by using it in local buildings or processes (see Chapter 1 and the section on combined heat and power in Green Building Bible, Volume 2 for more discussion about this). Local generation also eliminates much of the transmission losses.

Green tariff electricity

It is possible to purchase electricity that has been generated from renewable sources such as windfarms and hydropower. This is known as green electricity because its generation releases no carbon dioxide or other products of combustion into the atmosphere.

In reality, the electricity you take from the grid may be from a nuclear or fossil fuel power station. However, the utilities are required to prove that they are buying and supplying the same amount of renewable electricity to the grid as is supplied to customers on green electricity tariffs. A new EU green electrical markets' directive will require electricity suppliers to hold a renewable energy guarantee of origin (REGO) certificate to validate their sources. Green electricity can cost the same as standard tariffs, or slightly more, but the excess is often collected in a fund for 'green' initiatives. The websites of suppliers will give individual costs and schemes. A list of green tariffs is available on the Energy Watch website **www.energywatch.org.uk**.

Fuel price competition

The relative unit energy costs shown in Table 1 are for domestic customers. Commercial users of energy are able to negotiate a contract price for fuels from competitive suppliers due to the large quantities they consume. This tends to make unit costs lower, although there may be a complex arrangement of additional standing charges associated with patterns of energy demand throughout the year. Fuel price competition is now available to domestic customers also and there are a number of price comparison websites available to do a crude comparison of costs based on previous consumption. One of the problems with lower fuel costs is that it is known to encourage greater consumption of energy. On the other hand higher prices are a disincentive to use fuel.

Energy conservation investments

The decision on whether or not to include an energy saving feature in a building is usually made by calculating and assessing a rate of return on the investment. The most basic way of calculating this is to use the simple payback period. This is the number of years required to recoup the initial capital cost from the value of energy savings made. The payback period is calculated from the formula:

$$\text{Payback period (y)} = \frac{\text{Capital cost of energy saving feature (£)}}{\text{Value of energy savings per year (£/y)}}$$

Industry usually requires a payback period of less than 3 years for expenditure on energy saving features to be seen as worthwhile. From the payback formula it can be seen that the payback period will decrease if the capital cost of the equipment decreases or the value of saved fuel increases. The biggest change in these two factors, over recent years, has been in fuel costs. Most recently these have increased due to global competition for diminishing supplies of energy. This has been especially noticeable in domestic gas and electricity prices, which have risen considerably. The recent increases in fuel prices have two effects. Firstly, as energy costs rise people tend to use less, secondly, it shortens the payback period of energy saving investments. Both factors eventually contribute to a reduction in energy consumption.

References

*1. Department for Business Enterprise and Regulatory Reform. UK Energy in Brief July 2007. page 13.National Statistics Publication (available to download from **www.berr.gov.uk**).*

2. Energy Consumption Guide 19: Energy use in Offices 1998.

Heating our homes without fossil fuels

With conventional grid-supplied electricity and natural gas prices currently on the rise, maybe the time has now arrived for serious consideration of the alternatives. But **Stephen Lowndes** wonders just how easy is it to adopt non-fossil fuelled heating within our building projects?

Thankfully, the choice of alternative ways to heat your building using non-fossil fuels is growing, whether you are considering a cosy log burner in your renovated country retreat or a wood pellet boiler to run your office heating system. The first thing to do is make an assessment of your heating load or get a heating engineer to do it for you – the amount of heat you need to maintain your building at a comfortable temperature, during the coldest period of the year, is going to play the biggest role in deciding what you can reasonably expect to achieve.

The priority should be to minimise the heating load as far as possible, in order to conserve fuel and optimise financial payback. Good standards of thermal insulation, glazing specification, air-tightness and ventilation should be adopted. Whilst this may be easier to implement for new build projects, the importance of upgrading existing buildings should be integral to any change or upgrade of a space heating system. Other issues relating to heating controls are also important and will depend very much on the actual system used to heat the building.

Fuel choice

The choice of fuel will be influenced by a number of considerations. All fuels need to be able to satisfy an end-user's requirement in terms of environmental impact, affordable cost, availability, whether specialised equipment or facilities are needed, whether it is 'user friendly' and whether it needs to meet both heating and cooking needs.

Solid fuel

Non-fossil solid fuels include hard and soft wood and timber derivatives, such as processed timber bricks. Pellets and chips may also be classed as a solid fuel, although due to their own specialist development over recent years these fuels are considered separately. Basic non-fossil solid fuel is predominately derived from logs, timber processing and forestry thinnings, commonly used for small scale applications, such as firewood in individual homes. The ability to burn a solid fuel like wood may be very limited if you live in an area classed as a smoke free zone. Under the Clean Air Act, you may have to apply to your local authority for an 'exemption licence', to burn any type of wood fuel. However, there are now many wood burners that burn efficiently enough to be used in a smokeless zone. Ensure you check with the supplier.

Logs

If you are lucky enough to live near to forest or woodland you may find you are close to a conveniently sourced supply of timber. Of course permission to cut trees, unless they are on your own land, cannot be assumed and even when trees are on your own property, there may be local covenants and restrictions in place preventing you from doing so. To put this into perspective, the amount of timber a typical home, operating entirely on solid fuel timber for all space heating, hot water and cooking needs is likely to be in excess of five tonnes a year. If you have plenty of land, the option to grow and harvest timber on a coppicing basis might be an alternative. This sort of enterprise, even on a small scale, planting densely, high-yielding varieties such as willow or poplar, is likely to require at least 1 hectare for self-sufficiency[1].

Wood fuel must be available to burn in as dry a state as possible. You should avoid burning green, damp and unseasoned wood on the grounds, not only of reduced combustion efficiency, but because it can also cause a harmful build up of resinous deposits in the chimney, preventing it from functioning safely. Any building that incorporates solid fuel heating using timber will therefore require spatial allocation to ensure dry storage of the wood fuel.

Photo courtesy of Jerry Clark.

Logs and other wood fuels need to be as dry as possible. Wet wood releases tars and pollutants to the atmosphere, increases the risk of chimney fires and reduces efficiency drastically. Dry wood from sustainable sources (reforested or coppiced), is hard to beat as an ecological fuel and can create local employment.

Small-scale domestic solid fuel is usually burnt within wood-burners, which heat the space they are in directly. Their primary means of control is governed by manual adjustment of combustion air intake by the user. The wood burner, which could be a cooking range located in the kitchen, or a box stove in the living room, may be connected to a hot water storage vessel for domestic hot water use and can also incorporate a pumped hot water circuit to remote radiators to heat the rest of the house. Prices range from around £350 for a 3kW single room stove to several thousand pounds for a solid fuel boiler. Flues may utilise existing chimneys, although, depending upon their condition, internal liners may be required. New flues are usually stainless steel and are required to comply with UK Building Regulations Part J (Part F in Scotland).

Wood chips

Chipped wood is commonly available from timber processing and tree surgery waste. Timber can be chipped on site using machines, where it should also be possible to dry the chippings. Until quite recently wood chip heating was predominantly restricted to large-scale, non-domestic applications. In recent years smaller wood chip boilers have become commercially available, down to about 25kW output, making them suitable for large domestic or small-scale commercial use. A wood chip boiler can connect to conventional pumped hot water heating circuits and hot water storage cylinders.

Modern woodchip boilers keep a small core of the fire-bed continuously alight, allowing the boiler to respond to periodic drops in heating load. Unlike conventional gas fired boilers, they cannot respond instantaneously to changes in heating demand. To accommodate periods when there is no heat demand, a heat accumulator is recommended, to store the heat produced during peak burn for use later, either for space heating or domestic hot water.

A dry storage facility for the wood chip fuel is necessary and this needs to be adjacent to the boiler location so that the chips can be fed automatically to the boiler. Combustion efficiency will be dependant upon moisture content. Wood chips are typically supplied pre-dried at 20-25% moisture content. It may be possible to obtain chips with higher moisture content at a lower price than drier fuel, but it is difficult to dry-out in bulk before use on a small-scale and the lower calorific value could make, what seemed like a bargain at the time, a false economy.

Wood pellets

Wood pellets are a type of reconstituted wood-fuel and originate from the by-products of the timber processing industry, utilising sawdust and shavings extruded into small cylindrical pellets. They are of consistent quality and size, have a low moisture content (5 to 10%), are relatively clean to use and produce less smoke and ash, compared with un-refined forms of wood fuel.

Pellets can be used in a wide range of stove and boiler equipment, making it a convenient choice for heating domestic properties and small buildings. Wood pellets are usually gravity or screw fed into the appliance automatically, at a rate that is varied, depending upon the desired heat output from the appliance. Larger wood pellet boiler models are usually installed within designated boiler rooms or utility spaces and are screw fed from covered fuel stores located outside of the building. As with all solid wood fuel the pellets must be kept dry.

Prices start at around £1000 for an 8kW (maximum) pellet burner that has a combined hopper feed. Grant funding is available under the UK Low Carbon Buildings' programme. As a private householder you may be eligible for a grant to cover a good proportion of an installation and if you are undertaking a community project up to 50% of capital and installation costs (up to a maximum limit) may be available. These grants are unlikely to be awarded to DIY installations, as the funding is meant to encourage development of an accredited installer network.

Although supply sources are improving, wood pellet fuel can be difficult to source and is one of the reasons why pellets can be a more expensive fuel when compared with wood chip or seasoned logs. Price will also be dependant upon whether you buy in bulk or in bags. Recent comparisons[2] placed bulk purchased wood pellets and seasoned logs cheaper than natural gas. Of course natural gas prices are currently on the rise, so the comparison is heading more in favour of wood fuels.

Solar heating

Up until now we have concentrated upon heating that involves the direct or indirect combustion of bio fuels. Using the sun's energy directly, in the form of solar heat, to heat buildings and hot water is a way of offsetting the fossil fuel that would have otherwise been used by conventional heating plant. Even with our UK climate, the application of passive solar design within our buildings can be worthwhile, helping to minimise space heating load and making the installation of solar panels effective at contributing to reduced operation of boilers to service hot water demand. Passive solar design is discussed in detail elsewhere in this publication, so a brief look at solar hot water heating is covered here.

Solar hot water heating is an established technology and whilst ideally optimised when drawing up plans for a new build project, systems can also be incorporated fairly easily into existing buildings and often without the need to throw away your existing hot water installation. Solar panels are able to utilise the sun's heat, even on cloudy days, with a typical system capable of providing enough heat to satisfy up to 50% of the average annual household hot water demand.

There are various types of solar panel, ranging in efficiency from fairly basic flat plate designs that are often available as DIY kits and comprise black aluminium fins fixed to a copper piping grid, enclosed in a thermally insulated box with a glazed top facing the sky. More efficient and more expensive designs consist of factory made arrays of evacuated tubes, each enclosing a heat pipe, connected to a water manifold. Hot water is either circulated via thermosyphon effect or pumped through a solar panel and used to indirectly heat water in a hot water storage cylinder. Usually the solar heated water is stored separately from the hot water generated by a conventional boiler and connected so that the solar hot water pre-heats the conventional cylinder, reducing the need for the boiler to operate. Solar panels are usually roof mounted, although they don't have to be and thermosyphon systems require the panel to be below the hot water storage cylinder, making roof mounting impossible on some buildings. For optimum effect panels should be located on an aspect within 45 degrees of south. A typical solar hot water system employed on a house would require about 4m^2 of roof space for the panel.

Domestic scale solar hot water systems currently cost in the region of £2500 to £4000 to supply and install, and with typical annual savings on conventional hot water heating bills of well over £50, financial paybacks are therefore long[3]. As mentioned earlier, it maybe that your project is eligible for funding under the Low Carbon Buildings' programme.

Electric heating from renewables

You may be considering the use of electricity, generated from a renewable non fossil fuel source. The ability to plug in electric heaters anywhere within your building might appear an attractive and convenient form of heating, but how can you ensure the electricity used is fossil fuel free? Well, the only sure way is to ensure you generate enough electrical power on site to service all your electrical consumption for space heating and hot water, but for most of us that is just too big a load at the moment. In most cases it is unlikely that you could achieve 100% self sufficiency in electricity for heating lighting and cooking, even when incorporating a mixed bag of renewable generation, including photovoltaic and wind power (known as a hybrid system). If you have no intention of generating any of your own power at all you will of course be totally reliant on the national grid to power your heating.

The use of grid supplied electricity that is sourced solely and directly from a renewable basis is not feasible at the present time. This is because the national grid is a UK wide network of power distribution taken from a number of different generation sources, of which renewables account for only a tiny proportion in comparison to coal, gas and nuclear (see previous story for details). Your commitment to purchase electricity using a green tariff scheme may, on the face of it, be a way of ensuring you contribute to investment in renewable power on the basis of the amount of electrical power that you use. But not all is at it seems on the face of it. There is only one power company in the UK that guarantees 100% investment in new renewables generation - most others are just trading in existing output.

Conclusion

The reality is, that for most homes aiming to totally avoid the use of fossil fuels for heating, this is only going to be possible if you have a really thermally efficient new building which encompasses the principles of passive solar design. Those with existing buildings which are well insulated could install a biomass system, such as logs or wood pellets backed up with solar hot water generation.

References

1. *'The Whole House Book' by P Borer, C Harris (1998) (new edition available from* ***www.greenbuildingpress.co.uk****)*

2. *Published by John Willoughby, see page 460.*

3. *Energy Saving Trust:* ***www.est.org.uk***

Sources of further information

Information on all aspects of wood heating can be obtained from the Renewable Energy Association); ***www.r-e-a.net***

The government website for grant funding information for biofuel heating and building integrated renewable projects is ***www.lowcarbonbuildings.org.uk/home***

Fuel cells and micro-CHP

The next few years could see significant changes in the way we heat and power our buildings. **Kevin Boniface** introduces us to the technologies that could become more commonplace - fuel cells and Stirling engines.

Fuel cells

Fuel cell technology draws on the fundamental principle of combining hydrogen and oxygen to produce electricity, heat and (usually as a waste product) water. In comparison to combustion, fuel cells use an electrochemical process to generate energy which leads to an inherently clean, quiet (and arguably the most important) very efficient fuel conversion process.

Fuel cells can be connected to the grid to provide supplementary power, or can operate independently to provide electricity where on-site generation is the only practical and economically feasible option. Although commonly referred to in texts as a 'renewable energy technology', fuel cells can only be truly classified as a renewable source of energy if the electricity used (in producing the hydrogen fuel) is, itself, generated by a renewable energy source, such as a photovoltaic array or a wind turbine.

Fuel cells are similar to batteries, but they do not run down or require recharging – provided that hydrogen fuel is available. The diagram right shows the basic operating principle of a fuel cell. A fuel cell consists of two electrodes separated by an electrolyte. Generally hydrogen gas is fed to the anode and oxygen enters the fuel cell at the cathode. A catalyst is then used to split the hydrogen into protons and electrons, with the protons able to pass through the electrolyte. The electrons however, have to take the long way round, which creates an electrical current, before they return to the cathode. They then reunite with the hydrogen and oxygen to form a molecule of water.

Unlike most combustion based generation systems, there are no moving parts, although as with other types of battery, the electrical output is quite low per individual cell, typically about 0.7-0.8 volts. For this reason, fuel cells adopt a similar structure to batteries. In that they utilise multiple cells connected together in series to produce a useful working voltage.

Applications

Although the fuel cell was invented by Sir Charles Grove in 1839, serious development work only started in the 1950s. Fuel cells are

Simplified fuel cell operating principle.

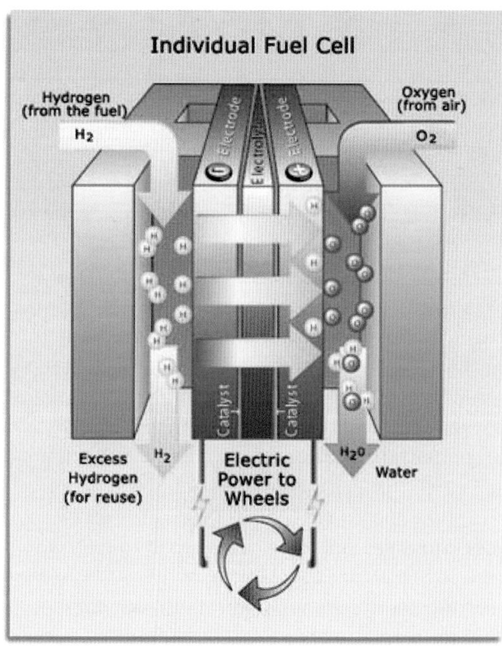

essentially a family of technologies and there are several types in existence today for a range of applications[1].

Future developments

Fuel cells do offer huge potential for high efficiency power generation in homes. It was estimated by 'Fuel Cell Today' in 2003 that about 1900 small stationary units had been developed and operated around the world. Many of these were in the USA, but the percentage of units installed in Japan and Europe has increased dramatically. Although certain types of fuel cell are commercially available, more research and development is needed, particularly on the technology itself and infrastructure issues, before more widespread uptake can occur in domestic applications.

A major application for fuel cells in the future could be in powering micro-CHP units. Stirling engine technology is more advanced and likely to lead the domestic market for micro-CHP initially, but the high fuel efficiencies possible with fuel cells make it an attractive technology for micro-CHP. For more information on fuel cells and their developments in the UK, see the Fuel Cell Network[2]. There is also a fuel cells club that was formed to bring together commercial stakeholders to accelerate the development of fuel cell technology in the UK[3].

Stirling engine micro-CHP

The Stirling heat engine was originally invented by Robert Stirling in 1816 and uses the behaviour of a 'working' gas in terms of pressure, temperature and volume and how these properties vary, with increases and decreases in temperature. Stirling engines have the potential to be much more efficient than conventional combustion engines, and could be run by anything that provides a source of heat, including solar energy and biomass.

The engine works by repeatedly heating and cooling a sealed amount of gas (typically air, hydrogen or helium). This is achieved by transferring the gas from a 'hot' heat exchanger, comprising a chamber and external heat source, to a 'cold' heat exchanger, which has heat sink attached for cooling. As the gas is heated its pressure also increases and this acts on a piston to produce movement. When the gas is then cooled, less work needs to be done by the piston to recompress the gas on the piston's return stroke, meaning there is a net power gain. In its simplest form, the gas simply flows cyclically between the hot and cold chambers.

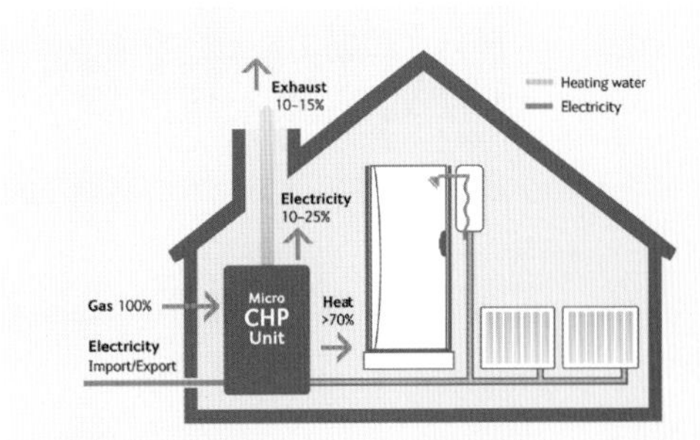

A typical micro-CHP unit system layout. Source: Whispergen.

Applications

Stirling engine technology has been used in a variety of different applications and of different scales. Currently they are only used in specialised applications such as in submarines, as power generators for yachts, and wherever conventional engines would be too noisy. A successful mass-market application for Stirling engines has not yet been found, however micro-CHP could provide the opportunity for Stirling engines to be a household name.

References

1. The various types of fuel cell technologies and their application are discussed in detail on page 145 in Volume 2 of the Green Building Bible, Fourth Edition.

2 **www3.imperial.ac.uk/fuelcells**

3. **www.fuelcellsuk.org**

Further information

Dave Elliott discusses the results of early trials of Stirling engine micro-CHP 'Micro-CHP still a way off', in the following story.

Baxi has developed a unit called the Ecogen, a Stirling engine micro-CHP unit which is claimed will be available from 2009. More info can be found at: **www.baxi.co.uk/products/baxiecogen.htm**

Micro-CHP still a way off

A lot of very different technologies are bundled together under the micropower banner, but not all technologies are equal. **Dave Elliott** assesses this emerging field ...

Micro-wind and domestic scale solar PV may have their detractors, given that they are expensive, PV in particular, and you may get more carbon reductions from other types of larger investment (e.g large scale wind farms), but once they are installed, they are at least carbon free supply technologies. By contrast micro-combined heat and power units use natural gas to power a Stirling engine or fuel cell, and that means there are direct carbon emissions. In theory, since they generate electricity and heat, they should be more efficient than say a conventional gas boiler, so micro-CHP should produce less emissions. However, in summer, when you don't need heat, you will not generate much electricity, so the overall energy efficiency will be reduced. Detractors say the electricity conversion efficiency averaged over the year can be as low as 11%, and translated into carbon emission avoidance that may mean you might do better with a gas condensing boiler - which would also be cheaper. But as yet only a few hundred micro-CHP systems have been installed for testing, so we are only now beginning to have an idea of what their actually performance is like over time.

Nevertheless, as was mentioned in Building for a Future magazine[1], the Carbon Trust reported preliminary results from practical consumer trials, and they did not look very good[2]. Whereas some earlier modeling work had predicted up to 40% emission savings, the trials have found that, in practice, over the full year, some of the units have only averaged 18% reductions and in some case much less. Indeed, in some cases the units yield 18% lower reductions than achieved by conventional systems. The Trust says that 'more trials are needed, since only a relatively few units were available for test, but even so the emerging trial data indicates there is unlikely to be a significant carbon emissions reduction opportunity from wide deployment of the technology at this stage in its evolution. From the results of the trial to date, carbon savings are in the range of plus or minus 18%. The reasons behind this are being investigated, but appear to relate to the interaction of the devices with the heating system, building and occupancy'. It adds that, 'if this trend continues for the full trial, there will be a material risk of an increase in emissions if micro-CHP is deployed at scale without regard to the different performance characteristics of specific technologies and the circumstances of their installation, maintenance and use.'

Part of the problem is that the technology is still at a relatively early stage of development. In its initial publicity, the British Gas (Centrica) offshoot, Microgen, claimed its micro-CHP unit would have an overall efficiency of 90% or more, and could typically lead to a 25% annual reduction in CO_2 emissions from homes. However, subsequently it was announced that, 'following a comprehensive review' of the programme, it was decided that the company would need to '*invest more time on product design and reliability testing before launching the Microgen system*' and '*together with confirming energy savings and CO_2 performance was of paramount importance to the success of Microgen and micro-CHP generally*'. Further stringent field-tests were undertaken in 2005. This inevitably delayed the commissioning of volume production. It was hoped that the commercial launch date would be spring 2007. The hope was that, as the technology and experience with using it improves, higher performance would be achieved.

Certainly, a review of micro power technology produced in November 2005, for the Energy Saving Trust (EST)[3], was upbeat about the longer term prospects of micro-CHP. It says that by 2050, micogeneration, including micro-CHP, solar PV, micro wind, heat pumps and micro-biomass, if widely adopted by consumers, could potentially provide at least 25% of UK electricity and around 220GWh of heat per annum, with micro-CHP dominating. This assumes regulatory incentives, subsidies and proper payment for any excess power exported to the electricity grid (i.e. net metering or as the EST report calls it 'energy export equivalence'). On this basis, the EST report finds that by 2050, overall, micro-generation could reduce UK emissions by 14.5% (based on 2005 levels). It sees Stirling engine micro-CHP as being one of the likely leaders, particularly in larger houses. It puts its likely breakthrough date, when costs become competitive with conventional sources, as 2010. By 2050, it says that, assuming proper support, 8 million domestic units could be installed, supplying 40% of domestic heating and 6% of UK electricity, but, interestingly, only cutting UK emissions by 1.9%. Fuel cell micro CHP will, it says, develop a bit more slowly, with a cost breakthrough date of 2017. By 2050 there could be 8GW(e)[4] in place, supplying 9% of UK electricity and cutting emissions by 3% per annum. Micro wind has a cost breakthrough date of 2015 and by 2050 there could be 15GW(e) in place, supplying 4% of UK electricity and cutting emissions by 6%. Cost effectiveness of solar PV is not predicted to occur until 2030. However, a technology breakthrough could reduce capital costs and bring this forward towards 2020. PV solar could also be supplying 4% by 2050 - cutting emissions by 3%. The prospects for solar water heating and micro biomass, however, are not seen as very good (perhaps 6TWh pa and 4.5TWh pa respectively by 2050). Finally, micro hydro supplies are forecast to be 100MW(e) by 2050.

Well there is some way to go before we can expect anything like that. The EST report noted that there are currently under 100,000 micro-generation units in the UK, mostly solar water heaters installed pre-2000, and that micro-CHP was only just beginning to enter the market - there were around 950 micro-CHP units in place. The big issue is whether this will grow and from the results so far, that is far from clear.

In mid 2007 Centrica decided to abandon the Microgen project, but subsequently supported a new option, the gas-fired fuel cell micro-CHP system developed by a company called Ceres. Centrica still believes that micro-CHP could take 30% of the domestic boiler market by 2015.

With the government's target of having all new-build houses 'zero carbon' by 2016, that may not be so unrealistic - amongst other things, it depends on what happens with the other micro renewables. The prospects for PV are looking better, but micro wind has suffered some adverse assessments, with a BRE study in Nov 2007 suggesting that devices in most urban locations 'are unlikely to pay back either their carbon emissions or the home owner's costs for installation and maintenance'.

A report by the government's Renewables Advisory Board in early 2008, argued that an accelerated programme of technical and market development would be needed if micro renewables are to be able to meet the zero carbon requirements[5]. Whether that will happen remains to be seen - not everyone is convinced that the zero carbon target can be met by 2016, just by using efficiency improvements and on-site renewables.

References

1. Vol. 15, No. 4 (Spring 2006): ***www.buildingforafuture.co.uk***

2. For the Carbon Trust Trials preliminary report see: ***www.thecarbontrust.co.uk/carbontrust/about/publications/181105_01.pdf***

3. For a summary of the report to EST see: ***http://www.energysavingtrust.org.uk/uploads/documents/aboutest/Microgeneration%20in%20the%20UK%20-%20final%20report%20REVISED_executive%20summary1.pdf***

4. (e) denotes electricity production

Note: 1MW = 1000kW
1GW = 1000MW
1TW = 1000GW

5. ***www.renewables-advisory-board.org.uk/vBulletin/showthread.php?t=136***

Biomass industry review

Can biomass play an important part in reversing the UK's impact on climate change? **Gideon Richards** investigates ...

Biomass is a term bandied around liberally by the government, the renewable energy sector and electricity generators, but what is it exactly and what contribution can biomass continue to make to green building? Biomass is defined in the Oxford Concise English Dictionary as 'organic matter used as a fuel, especially in a power station for the generation of electricity'. This description must have been provided by the government, who still find it difficult to appreciate the true benefits that biomass heat can bring to solving energy security and demand.

In more human scale terms, biomass is known as woody material, supplied either as virgin material, such as logs and woodchips or a by-product from the wood processing and manufacturing industry recently in the form of pellets. Wood pellet fuel is almost always produced from residues (wood waste) from some other process. However, we are starting to see other feedstocks being introduced to the market, like straw, grain, miscanthus (elephant grass), and there is even talk about using rape meal, the by-product of the pressed rape from the rapeseed oil pressing.

Over the last 3 years the UK has seen an emergence of modern, highly efficient, controllable boilers using woodfuel. These have come in a number of designs, using various fuel forms. However, it is noticeable that predominantly, most of the technology comes from abroad – Austria, Germany, Denmark and Italy. There are now UK suppliers emerging, most would be better recognised for their fossil fuel appliances, however, some others are dedicated to biomass. This emergence has come about from a number of fronts:

- the prices for fossil fuels have jumped to record highs and there appears to be no

Fuels from organic matter explained

Don't get them confused

Bioenergy is a term used to encompass a whole range of fuels made from growing material which can be replenished in human timescales. For the sake of clarity, we include below a short (though not exhaustive) list of the key sub-categories with a short explanation of each. However, only biomass is discussed in the main article. It should also be noted that more and more, people are realizing that there could be serious environmental and food security issues involved in biofuel production. (www.foe.co.uk/campaigns/biodiversity)

Biomass (also called solid biofuel) is organic material, which has stored solar energy in plants from sunlight via the process of photosynthesis. Biomass fuels include agricultural wastes, crop residues, wood, woody wastes and organic wastes etc. When biomass is discussed it is usually in the context of solid matter that has only been processed to reduce in size to fit into combustion equipment, i.e. sawn logs, chipped or pelletised.

Biogas converts solid biomass into a more convenient gaseous form. This process is made possible in a device called a gasifier. A gasifier system comprises a reactor, where the combustible gas is generated and the gas is made available for power generation/thermal application after the required cleaning and cooling process. Anyone that has listened to the Radio Four programme, 'The Archers' will have heard about the bio-digester (also known as an anerobic digester) that has been planned and which will use mainly farm wastes, slurry and waste crops (and produce gas for burning), but could also be used for local organic waste matter from the local authority.

Biofuels is a generic term used to describe liquid fuel which is derived from refined agriculturally grown oil rich plants such as rape, linseed etc. Bioethanol, which is made from sugar cane, is a form of fermented biomass and is commonly in use in South America in place of regular transport fuel. Biodiesel is made from vegetable oil. It can be used in any diesel engine with or without modifications, as necessary, to the vehicle. It is a renewable, non-toxic, bio-degradable, and domestic fuel with a similar engine performance as diesel fuel, but does not require petroleum. The very greenest form of biodiesel is made using waste cooking oil from fish and chip shops but the potential for widespread use is very limited.

change in this trend for the foreseeable future

- in 2007 the UK government, along with our European partners, signed up to a binding 20% of all energy to come from renewable sources. For the UK this equates to a probable 15% target, approximately ten times what we currently have (2008) (this has a direct impact on large and small-scale usage)
- the co-firing market has stimulated the development of supply chains
- the renewable obligation certificates (ROCs) have supported the co-firing and electrical generation markets for a number of years now. This has created a demand for larger volume consumers of woodfuel (and other biomass) which, in turn, has created economies of scale to create an economic value for the fuels
- the EU and UK Emissions' Trading Scheme (ETS) provides a mechanism for biomass to be valued as an offset in carbon reduction targets.

Most of the above points are relevant to large scale use. For the domestic and smaller appliance user, other than staggering rises in the cost of heating fuel, the points may seem remote and of little consequence. However, in their way, these points have been an instrumental part of creating the stimulus within the market and will continue to do so. But even at the small and domestic scale:

- there are grants to help offset the differential in cost between fossil fuel burning appliances and biomass boilers
- there is more choice of stoves and boilers in the UK
- wood fuel continues to become more readily available and the distribution networks are starting to develop around clusters, enabling economies of scale to stabilize and reduce the price of the fuel in comparison to individuals ordering on their own
- climate change is focusing people's attention and biomass is a CO_2 neutral way of heating a building without making an impact on the planet
- the market structure is becoming such that biomass supply is seen as less of a risk.

There is much discussion about fiscal heat and electrical mechanisms, which will promote the use of heat and small scale (domestic) on-site electrical generation. We now have a number of government strategies that recognise heat as a major contributor to the UK's reduction in CO_2, such as, the Biomass Strategy, Woodfuel Strategy for England and, much more recently, the UK's Renewable Energy Strategy.

One major influencing factor in many areas, and particularly the London boroughs, has been the so called 'Merton Rule', which requires new buildings over 1000m^2 to generate 10% of their energy from on-site renewable energy sources, (either electricity or heat or a combination of the two). Also, the government's insistence that all homes in England should be zero carbon by 2016, with 100% of energy (again heating and electricity) being generated on or near site is

Below: These wood pellet silos ensure that boilers running on the fuel have an adequate supply, so that fully automated running of a commercial scale biomass heating system is ensured and there is no extra work than would be required for any other type of boiler.

another mind concentrating factor for developers and interest in small scale biomass systems has rocketed.

Regional spatial strategies (RSS) and local development frameworks (LDF) will be a growing feature of planning policy over the coming years as the policies come into force. Being statutory policies will mean that there is a requirement to deliver the on-site generation (based on the Merton rule). Planning will not be refused unless there is a very good reason why it can't be done.

For many developers, biomass is the simplest, cheapest answer to meet the above requirements. Additional to these, the European Commission published the EU biomass action plan in December 2005, which focuses on the development of biofuels for transport and biomass for heating. The UK has also had a government backed task force, looking at how we can utilise biomass (Biomass Task Force report to government - Oct 2005)[1] and a subsequent response from the government on the task force's recommendations (June '06)[2].

As a direct result of the Biomass Task Force report and the new Climate Change and Sustainable Energy Bill, 2006, the government's response was to review, and start developing a mechanism for, a heat obligation of some form. This is important as 89% of energy used in domestic buildings, and between 56% of energy used in commercial buildings, is currently for heating and hot water and a heat obligation mechanism could well provide a major renaissance in community heating schemes.

The increasing requirements of the domestic building regulations (Part L) to reduce CO_2 levels by a further 25% in 2010, 45% in 2013 and 100% in 2016 (for new-build see the CSH stories in the previous chapter) and hopefully considerable reductions CO_2 requirements from existing dwelling too, along with a target for all new commercial buildings to be zero carbon by 2019, the race appears to be on in many quarters to work out how these challenges can be achieved. It is clear that biomass will have to play an ever-increasing role in the renewable energy mix

Technology

The technology used to heat buildings with biomass has moved on a pace from the open fires, roomheaters, solid fuel stoves and cooking appliances of the past, but these old fashioned appliances still exist in the marketplace. However, increasingly the requirements for more efficient and cost effective heating systems are putting the squeeze on them are likely to continue to do so, due in part to the new Part L of the Building Regulations on the conservation of fuel and power and the requirement, from 2007 that mandatory 'home information packs' (HIP'S) will require the seller to declare energy performance information.

Appliances fall broadly into four categories:

Space heaters, which heat the room the appliance sits in, although there are systems that allow hot air to be circulated by ducting to other rooms.

Space heaters with back boilers, stoves and cooking appliances, which do a combination of space and hot water heating. These can run a small radiator heating system, but some are limited in output. The output efficiencies vary greatly dependant on the type of appliance being used.

Boiler systems, these can be from 2kW for very well insulated buildings, through to large multiple boiler systems. Some use heat stores and accumulator tanks, to buffer the heat loads. Boilers are usually highly efficient, with many of them being highly automated, to a degree where they automatically de-ash, can clean the heat exchanger tubes, provide heat metering and auto switching on and off. As interest in energy efficiency and fuel choices increases, we are now seeing more schemes using, what would normally be considered as individual dwelling size boilers being installed as small community network boilers. It is also likely that, as the requirements for higher levels of the Code for Sustainable Homes are targeted/

required, that this trend will continue.

CHP plant, which has been developed at various sizes and various combinations, almost exclusively for community or small industrial scale. Such systems at present require a constant heat load to make the economics stack up; which is often the difficult part. Wood fuel often also only makes up a portion of a range of fuels in such plant which can be co-generation (biomass and gas) or tri-generation (biomass, gas and a third fuel). It is the intention of the government that all multi-use schemes should consider CHP as a first option. Although the UK has a chequered past regarding the installation of district heating schemes (now often called community heating schemes), such biomass fuelled schemes are used all over Europe very effectively.

With the increasing requirements for builders to squeeze more properties onto a plot of land, there is a great opportunity to use biomass community heating schemes, which maximize the useable space and hence the saleable floor area in the individual buildings. It will also reduce the energy requirements of the buildings, through matching the energy demand better with one appliance, instead of having larger than actually required gas boilers for each building to cover every eventuality. In turn this will reduce the carbon footprint for the development by requiring less energy and finally cost the end-user less money, as they decouple from spiralling grid energy prices.

Interestingly, the direct replacement for oil fired boilers is being carefully considered by the oil heating industry as a good way of decarbonising their industry, without having to make too many changes.

Fuel

As the technology develops, the one question that always arises is that of the fuel availability. While there has and, in some circumstances, there still is, an issue with getting fuels of the appropriate quality and volume, this is changing substantially, month on month, in the UK.

The three currently available forms of fuel being used are logs, woodchips and wood pellets. All have had issues with regards to quality in the past. However, end-users are becoming more competent at specifying the quality required, including implementation of new European standards to support the trading and use of the fuels. There are also a number of good reference documents which deal with biomass fuel quality[3].

As with all wood fuels, logs will burn clean and give little pollution if stored and dried for a suitable length of time prior to combustion.

The UK government, in its response to the Biomass Task Force (BTF) report, announced that it will adopt the European standards for wood fuel. With this endorsement, it is important that end-users, fuel producers and the equipment manufacturers and installers, use fuels to the standards, and that there is an understanding of what the standards mean. In addition to incorporating the standards, the industry is working on a woodfuel certification scheme, which should help provide confidence to users of the fuel.

Sustainability and air quality concerns

In the last twelve months much has been said about the use of biomass fuels, particularly in terms of their sustainability (source fuel) and the localised emissions from the combustion of the fuels. It would be remiss of us not to tackle these issues head on. This is a complex set of issues that this article does not have space to fully cover. However, it is fair to say that the true sustainability of biomass is constantly being re-appraised against both European and International standards and that many of the small scale appliances that we have discussed will be fuelled from raw material sourced in the UK. As for emissions from biomass combustion, it should be noted that best available modern high efficiency equipment is already very low in emitting particulates (some ten times lower than equipment only 10-15 years old) and any debate on this subject is only really relevant for urban areas. The current debate about particulate emissions and oxides of nitrogen (NOx) are controvertial and the subject of ongoing discussion between industry and government.

Installers

To solve the problem of rogue installers the 'renewable energy assurance listed' (REAL) scheme[4] was launched in July 2006 to provide a consumer code for companies supplying microgeneration products to end-users. This scheme will be Office of Fair Trade certified, and once again, is designed to provide buyers with the confidence to pick companies which are prepared to provide a quality service and support structure.

In addition to this the UK's microgeneration certification scheme (MCS) has been established over the last few years and is now currently providing standards for both products and installer (including biomass) and quality assurance for consumers. The MCS will also be the minimum requirement for government grants in the future for small scale (<45kW) appliances.

Grants

There are a number of grant schemes available for biomass schemes and equipment. The Low Carbon Building Programme[5] (LCBP) is still running (for all microgeneration technologies). This scheme allows individuals, communities and developers, wanting financial support with their schemes, to apply for a grant. The scheme is split into two streams. In the first phase; stream 1 being for householders and communities, with a £10.5 million pot over the three years, and stream 2 for larger scale developments, with an £18.5 million pot, which will be allocated through a bidding process. The latter scheme is hoped to generate enough volume in the market to bring economies of scale into the renewables industry, thereby reducing equipment costs. The second phase is for £50 million and is being developed to support public sector projects, with a particular emphasis on education.

In addition to the LCBP there is also the Bio-energy Capital Grants scheme, Bio-energy Infrastructure Scheme and regional development agencies have various support structures in place for biomass projects.[6]

Future trends

At this point it would be good to do some crystal ball gazing. How is it anticipated that the industry will develop and what new products will be developed?

These are difficult questions to accurately answer. However, the biomass industry is developing rapidly. If the government continues to support biomass, and fossil fuel prices keep rising, the industry will continue to grow. This growth will start in the public sector, as more and more local authorities incorporate biomass-heating schemes into their own building stock. As this develops and the supply chains strengthen, commercial and domestic users will grow. This can already be seen in councils such as Barnsley MBC who have introduced a biomass policy.

The development of a heat mechanism, in whatever form, is likely to be a stimulus for the heat market, and the biomass industry in particular. However, there is considerable concern from environmental groups that the biomass industry is developed in a sustainable manner, which also takes account of biodiversity.

In terms of the technology, it is likely that biomass microCHPs, biomass condensing boilers, biofuel and potentially micro biogas boilers will be developed and be introduced to the UK market over the next 5 – 10 years. Along with this, heat meters and smart meters will develop for the smaller scale heating appliances to enable them to benefit from energy supply contracts (companies supplying energy). Additionally, to increase the emissions' efficiency of biomass combustion, small scale emissions abatement technologies, such as electrostatic precipitators (ESP), baghouse filters and ceramic filters will come forward and resolve many of the urban emission fears from biomass.

With the introduction of building performance data for the HIPs and tightening of air quality requirements, energy generating appliances will require labels, in much the same way as white goods do (part of the European directive on ecodesign of energy using products). This information would demonstrate the appliance's efficiency and emission levels against the current regulatory levels, and the fuel required for a standard building (whatever that may be).

Conclusions

The biomass industry can contribute considerably to the energy mix in the UK, and play a major part in reducing CO_2 emissions. Biomass is the only renewable energy source that is not intermittent. This gives it an advantage over other renewable energy sources. However, due to the space required for fuel storage, in comparison to other technologies, it may find it hard to take its rightful place for smaller individual domestic properties. That said, the way building developments have been reducing their footprints, the opportunity to provide community heating is growing all the time.

Now with the government committing us to 15% of all our energy to come from renewable sources by 2020, it is likely that this will require approximately 30% of that renewable resource to come from biomass, so the scaling up of the biomass industry is potentially going to be massive.

Current fossil fuel prices, and confidence that fossil fuel prices won't come down, can only be a good thing for the biomass industry. The development of a robust supply chain over the coming years, and homegrown fuels, such as wood pellets, can only help the confidence in the market. Don't be surprised if the next house you buy is heated by a biomass heating system!

References

1. ***http://ec.europa.eu/energy/res/biomass_action_plan/green_electricity_en.htm***

2. ***www.defra.gov.uk/farm/crops/industrial/energy/biomass-taskforce/index.htm***

3. *See Biomass Energy Centre Website:* ***www.forestry.gov.uk/fr/INFD-6P8G8E***

4. *REAL Assurance Scheme:* ***www.realassurance.org.uk***

5. *The Low Carbon Buildings programme:* ***www.est.org.uk/housingbuildings/funding/lowcarbonbuildings***

6. ***www.biomassenergycentre.org.uk***

CHP technology and other biomass appliances are discussed at great length in Chapter 6 of Volume 2 of the Green Building Bible.

DHW heating from solar energy

Solar water heating systems are capable of providing up to 60% of annual domestic hot water requirements in the UK. Dispelling the myth that there is too little sun in the UK for solar to work, **Iain Calderwood** reports ...

The domestic hot water (DHW) requirement in the typical UK home remains constant throughout the year but during the summer months, the operational efficiency of even the most modern boilers will fall off because they have to short cycle on part load just to provide the DHW. To counteract this inefficiency, a well-designed solar water heating system could provide around 90% of the DHW requirement during this period. In the winter, though, it would fall to around 20%, but at that time boilers will be running more often and therefore more efficiently.

Interestingly, for those wanting to install a new solar system, the Town and Country Planning, England, regulations were amended in March 2008 and as from the 6th April 2008 installation of domestic solar panels, solar thermal for DHW or solar photovoltaics (PVs) is permitted, provided the equipment does not protrude more than 200mm beyond the plane of the wall or roof slope when measured from the perpendicular with the external surface. Planning permission is not therefore required in England.

Systems

With suitable specialised components, systems are straightforward to install, reliable and durable. The collectors will work during overcast days, even when there is no direct sunlight, but work best when in direct sunlight. Heat from the sun is transferred to water contained within the collector and circulated to a special solar cylinder, where it can be topped up to a useable temperature, as and when required by a conventional boiler or immersion heater. Collector performance will be optimum when facing due south un-shaded and inclined

between 25-60°C but, in practice, any situation between south-east and south-west will result in only a 10% fall off in efficiency and can be considered acceptable. Even east or west facing elevations will provide around 80% of optimum and should be considered since an oversized collector can be fitted. Some evacuated tube collectors can also be rotated within their manifold by up to 30°C in order to compensate for an unfavourable position. Consideration should also be given to mounting the collectors vertically on a wall or at ground level or flat roofs on purpose built 'A' frames, available directly from most collector suppliers.

Resultant savings in CO_2 emissions will vary according to the fuel being displaced and the hot water demand. A typical 4m^2 flat plate solar collector will save around 1000kg of CO_2 when displacing electricity or 450kg of CO_2 when displacing natural gas.

Before going further it would be wise to note that like any other aspect of green building, we should examine our existing water consumption habits and appliances. There is a good argument for installing low water use appliances at the same time as you install the solar DHW system to ensure that none of the hot water that is made from the solar energy is wasted.

Types of collectors

Many thousands of solar water heating systems have been installed in the UK since the 1970's and while the majority of early systems continue to perform well, a new generation of commercially produced solar water heating systems and controls continue to be refined. Solar thermal collectors for DHW are typically found in two types. Buyers of systems should ensure that anyone offering them a system includes collectors that are certified to BS EN 12975.

Flat plate collectors (photo top left), containing a specially treated absorber plate to maximise solar gain. The collector is glazed with either solar glass or plastic and is highly insulated to minimise heat loss. Collectors are available for both roof integration and above roof fixing. The one shown here is roof integrated.

Evacuated tube collectors (photo left) in which the absorber plate is enclosed in an evacuated glass tube. These collectors can operate at higher temperatures due to the vacuum insulation and are usually more expensive.

The solar primary circuit

The most common types of solar primary circuit are either the traditional fully filled and pressurised type (shown below), containing a special solar heat transfer fluid to provide frost protection. The other type is drainback, in which the solar collector is filled only when the solar primary pump is running and contains only water.

Hot water storage

Hot water stores are best designed to encourage heat from the solar collectors to work effectively in combination with input from a conventional heating system, such as a boiler or immersion heater. A well-designed store will ensure that water is pre-heated prior to reaching the boiler heat exchanger. The most common way of achieving this is to use a dual coil type of cylinder and this is the most common system throughout the UK and mainland Europe (see diagram below).

Though you should be guided by your chosen installer, when you are considering what

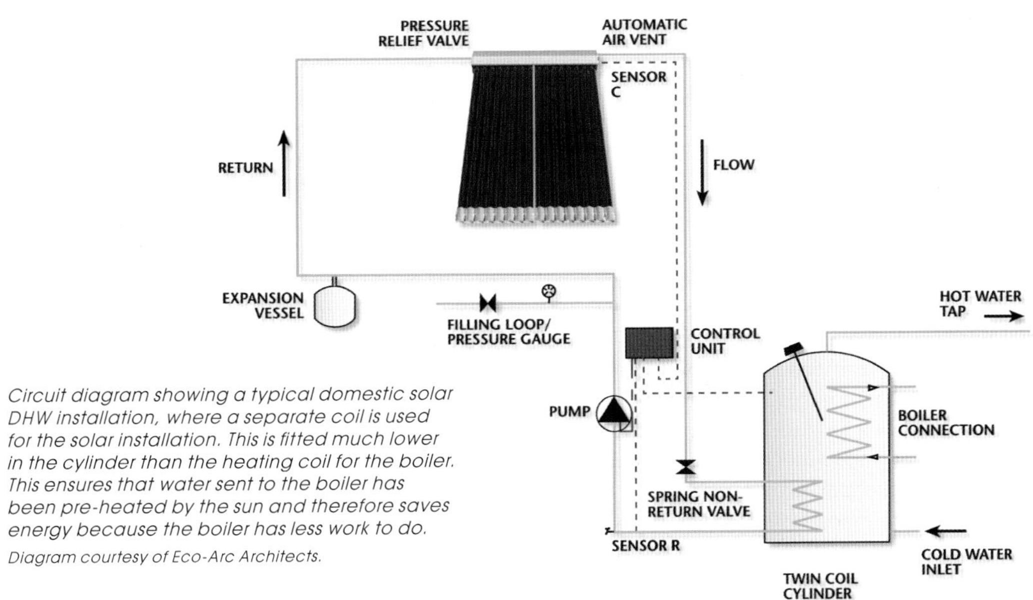

Circuit diagram showing a typical domestic solar DHW installation, where a separate coil is used for the solar installation. This is fitted much lower in the cylinder than the heating coil for the boiler. This ensures that water sent to the boiler has been pre-heated by the sun and therefore saves energy because the boiler has less work to do.

Diagram courtesy of Eco-Arc Architects.

size hot water cylinder to install you should take into account the types faucets and number of uses that the system will be required to supply. Bear in mind that high performance showers often operate at up to 3-bar pressure and require a large volume of water. Care must be taken, when designing this type of installation, to ensure that there is sufficient volume for the occupants requirements to be heated by the boiler, whenever there is insufficient solar gain to heat the contents – typically a minimum of 120 litres. Additionally there should be sufficient volume below the boiler coil to enable the solar system to perform efficiently whenever the boiler is firing. Typical storage ratios are around 50-60 litres of stored water per square metre of flat plate collector installed or 80-100 litres per square metre in the case of very high performance evacuated tube collectors.

Ideally cylinders should be designed to ensure stratification, indeed some manufacturers have gone to great lengths to design cylinders that automatically compare temperatures. However, in order to maximise the efficiency of the solar system, a height to diameter ratio of 2.5 or 3.1 should be allowed. The heat exchanger should be located as low as possible and have a large surface area (0.2m^2 minimum per square metre of collector) in order to maximise solar contribution at times of low solar radiation. Solar collectors can be connected to traditional open vented cylinders, mains pressure cylinders or thermal stores, although the performance of the latter is likely to be lower due to the lack of water movement and the need to maintain higher temperatures.

Controllers and other equipment

Unlike a conventional heating system, the temperature, in the solar primary circuit, will vary continuously. The sun cannot simply be switched off and high efficiency solar collectors can easily reach temperatures in excess of 200°C. Careful control of the solar system is therefore essential in order to prevent overheating and to ensure that water previously heated by fossil fuels is not pumped back round the solar circuit to warm the sky.

A differential temperature controller will ensure optimum performance from most types of solar water heating system. The controller measures temperature in the solar collector and compares this with the temperature in the lower part of the cylinder. When the controller senses that the collector is hotter than the store, the circulating pump is energised and heat transferred. When the temperature difference falls, the controller switches the pump off. In most controllers, the switch on and switch off differential is adjustable, enabling the installer to programme the unit to match the operating characteristics of the individual systems and types of solar collector.

Water must be distributed at a safe temperature. If the temperature is too low, then there is a risk of legionella. Most controllers incorporate a thermostat, controlling a second relay, in order to switch on a boiler, although many installers prefer to use a traditional cylinder thermostat. If the water temperature is too high, then there is a risk of scalding and potential lime scale deposition (in hard water areas). All controllers should have an adjustable 'top limit' thermostat. Many controllers have the capability to indicate faults. For example, sensor defects, reverse circulation, (the collector heats up at night) or too high temperature differential (indicating that the pump is not running when it should).

Heat meters

Heat meters can provide a heat quantity measurement enabling more precise monitoring of the performance of the solar system. The location of the cylinder sensors is critical. In a cylinder with an internal coil type heat exchanger, the lower sensor should be no lower than the mid point between the flow and return connections. Ideally sensors should be fitted into pockets to give a good contact with the stored water. ☯

Stratifying cylinders are available from The Green Shop:
www.greenshop.co.uk
Grants are available for solar installations:
www.est.org.uk/housingbuildings/funding

Space heating from solar energy

Designing for passive solar heating was discussed in Chapter 1, but here **Chris Laughton** discusses how solar heated water can be used to heat not just domestic hot water but provide space heating in well insulated buildings ...

The use of the sun to provide space heating, even during our darkest winter days, will soon become a fast growing sector for the UK solar industry. Why has it not ben utilised already? Well, when we need our space heating most, (the winter), the sun is at its lowest in the sky, frequently hiding behind storm clouds - if not invisible for days on end. Never-the-less, with some forward planning, it is possible for an active solar system to contribute nearly 20% to the annual space heating of a well-insulated new home. Perhaps with passive solar design incorporated too, this figure could be much greater. In either case, be prepared for a significant re-designing of your home. Serious solar powered space heating is no simple task and even with massively increasing fossil fuel prices cannot be justified by cost-effectiveness alone. However, fully committed enthusiasts should read on.

For those lucky enough to be building from scratch, the first strategy is to orientate the roof and living spaces towards the south during the design process. It's the lower sun paths of spring and autumn we are most interested in for solar space heating, so watch out for the long shadows of hills and don't forget the trees may not have dropped their leaves at that time (Volume 2 of the Green Building Bible goes into great detail about designing for sun angle, and also includes sun path diagrams).

The portion of winter that solar heating can target is the 'shoulders', early and late in the season. Deep winter has too little sun to be harvested and during the summer we don't

Many homes in mainland Europe are of low energy design and take advantage of solar power for space heating. This building has fully integrated solar thermal (DHW) and solar PV panels.

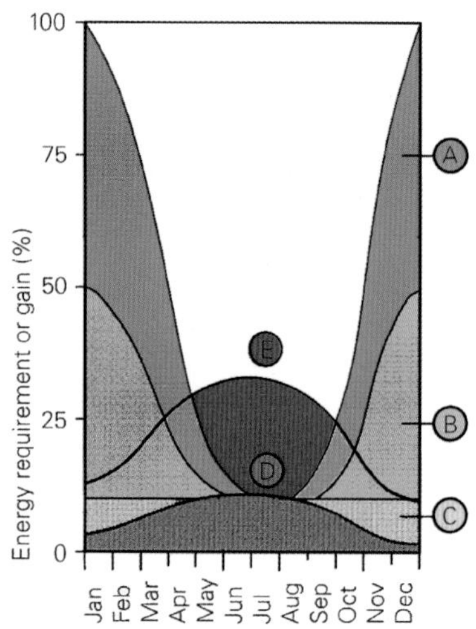

Left: diagrammatic profile showing how the contribution of space heating can rise, as a percentage of the total heating needs, as buildings become more energy efficient.

need much space heating. But on those bright, sunny days between autumn and spring, useful gains can be made.

As with all forms of solar thermal energy, storage is the key to success. An active solar system for the average home should be designed with around 8m^2 of collector, accompanied by no less than 750 litres of water storage (this will also allow for some domestic supply too). This forms the backbone of what has come to be termed 'a solar combi-system', common in Sweden and Austria. In these countries, expect to find a store of this size in the cellar or a bespoke lean-to outhouse.

The other vital featue of a solar space heating system is a wet underfloor heating circuit, designed to flow at temperatures well below 50°C, ideally nearer to 30°C. This aspect allows the use of low temperature solar heat that has been collected and stored in the tank, but is too cold to use for domestic hot water (DHW). Providing the dwelling is extremely well insulated and wind tight, the regular circulation of modest amounts of low temperature stored solar heat will provide a welcome background heat. With the use of timers and pumps, this heat is fully controllable.

Passive solar heating, without the use of pumps, is often discussed but rarely put into practice in the UK. There is potential to make greater use of darkened 'thermal mass' (masonry, concrete or water) to store heat when it is sunny to moderate the temperatures of living space and this was discussed at length in Chapter 1. Unfortunately the results of poorly executed passive solar design is often overheating, glare and a lack of privacy or security. Worse still, the risks of a net annual loss of heat, through increased sized glazing, leading to increased fuel bills to counteract heat losses through the glass at night. It is worth noting that underfloor heating and passive heating, when combined/adjacent, make poor companions, since stored passive heating is difficult to control.

The 100% solar space heated house is starting to become a little more than a pipe dream, given the recent trend in warmer winters, providing we combine the heating system with high insulation standards, airtightness and heat recovery ventilation systems. Passive houses, as they are called, rely on people's body metabolism, and waste heat that is generated from electrical appliance's, to keep the house warm. Despite the best laid plans, however, many yet built in the UK resort to occasional roomheaters (maybe a woodburner) to achieve full comfort throughout the year.

Pursuing a high solar fraction for space heating can lead to a dilemma on sizing appliances for the shortfall. For what may only be a few kW to find on the coldest nights, it barely makes sense fitting a gas or oil boiler when it will be hardly used. Woodburners and mobile electric heaters are often chosen first, either for their smaller footprint, less capital cost, less maintenance or for their ambience.

It can't be emphasized enough that if the dwelling is not first extremely well insulated and airtight, then solar space heating will turn out to be a very expensive pursuit. In all cases, the provision of domestic hot water heating should be the first priority for the solar system, since it is most cost effective to transfer heat to the cold water entering the DHW tank from the mains. Thereafter, heated water is transferred to the cool return of the under-floor space heating before being heated further by other sources

The physical area of solar collector necessary, for reasonable space heating contribution, significantly exceeds the size of a system designed just for solar domestic hot water by at least 3 times. Therefore, unless care is given to the system design, this could lead to overheating problems in the summer. Most modern sealed system solar heating designs can cope with over-sizing of collectors, without necessarily losing fluid from boiling in the summer when the house is perhaps empty. For design guidance allow up to 3.0m^2 of solar collector area for each 10m^2 of floor area.

Orientation can help us to avoid summer overheating and gather maximum winter available sunshine. Pitching them up steeply will naturally shade out the high summer sun but they will remain well targeted for the low winter sun. Commercially available software simulation programmes, such as TSOL[1], can help to simplify the design of solar space heating systems. A wide range of equipment can easily be compared, along with sizes to achieve a balanced solution.

As for collector and storage fluids, water in bespoke insulated steel or concrete tanks (called accumulators) is normally the first choice for the storage of solar heat, as it is cheap and readily available. Heat, once collected, can also be stored in swimming pools, insulated 'ponds' or similar underground reservoirs. Rocks or other masonry can also hold heat, although here the inability to pump heat out quickly is a disadvantage. System designers should plan for heat storage over several days, and indeed this is necessary for solar space heating to work well. However, 'inter-seasonal' storage has been used on larger projects but is much more difficult to do, and to do well.

As a guide, each square metre of collector should give 350kWh per annum if sufficient storage is provided. Even the best insulated houses are likely to require about 7000kWh of heat, and the average home has a net space heating load of around 13,000kWh, after considering useful free heat from passive solar, cooking and metabolic gains.

Below: the community on the island of Samsø in Denmark was keen on a total eco-approach, right down to the way in which the buildings are used and heated. The photo belows shows their community scale solar heating system.
Photo courtesy of Arketima and Samsø Energy Academy.

Commercial scale solar heating

Solar heating can be successfully used in commercial properties. For assistance with process heat, hot water preparation and even space heating. The successful integration of solar heating systems into buildings where we work is significantly affected by how the building is being or going to be used. For those buildings that contain a lot a glass, such as some office blocks, the sun's energy can even cause a net energy loss, due to the electrical cooling loads necessary during summer from air conditioning. Compared to domestic properties, commercial properties need greater care at the system design, generally to ensure that there is no conflict with other technologies and that the installed equipment is robust enough to survive working environments. The techniques for solar pre-heating of hot water and space heating are similar to residential properties. However, process heat requires special attention.

Some of the largest solar collector areas in the world are located on hospital roofs, indicating the huge hot water demand of medical laundries and canteens. Combined with hotels and care homes, such buildings provide a consistent hot water load ideal for solar pre-heating, and often containing existing floor space for the location of vital solar storage cylinders. Such buildings also require much greater attention to the risk of bacterial poisoning, that a poor quality design can magnify.

With the right equipment, such as plate exchangers, solar pre-heating need not increase bacterial risks beyond that of any typical hot water heater. Scalding risks can also be eliminated with accurate thermostatic pump control, now routine equipment in high quality systems. Compared to domestic properties, far greater liability falls on the solar system designer and owner in respect of the law. Written risk assessments are an essential start of compliance to such regulations as COSHH (Control of Substances Hazardous to Health regulations). Commercially available software simulation packages become invaluable in pre-empting temperatures around a system, which can then be used in such assessments.

Schools have an unfortunate habit of breaking up when the sun is at its best! Unless there is an on-site school canteen to provide a steady after-lunch hot water demand of hand dish washing, a disappointing utilisation factor can result. Club houses for field sports also have a poor overall efficiency as the hot water demand for canteens and baths tends to occur

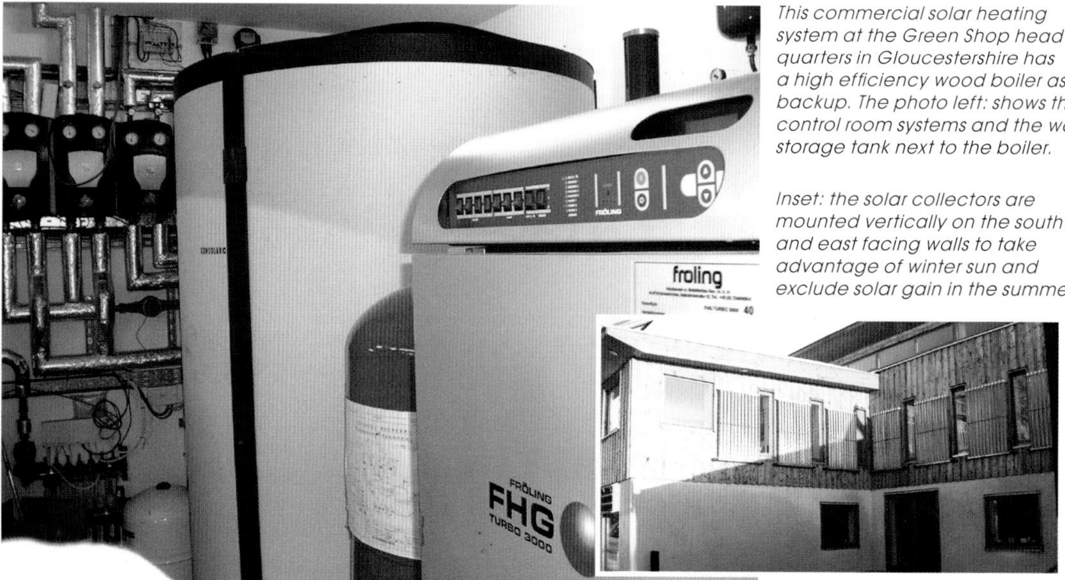

This commercial solar heating system at the Green Shop headquarters in Gloucestershire has a high efficiency wood boiler as backup. The photo left: shows the control room systems and the water storage tank next to the boiler.

Inset: the solar collectors are mounted vertically on the south and east facing walls to take advantage of winter sun and exclude solar gain in the summer.

in peaks at weekends and often during the winter. Furthermore, the hot water appliances are rarely centralised, making a single solar system, serving the whole building, difficult to integrate. Nevertheless, using a well insulated store, solar can be allowed to build up during the week and significantly reduce energy demand at the weekend when the sports events tend to be held. Summer sports clubs, such as cricket or tennis, would work well, being in harmony with the solar high season.

Process heat, such as that used in car washes or food preparation, provides excellent solar efficiencies, since the daytime cold water passing into the hot water system use is high and readily accepts solar pre-heating. In these cases, the normally vital storage of solar heat becomes less important, as the heat can be used almost as it is produced. As usual, a back-up heat source provides the shortfall, whenever the solar is not available. Dairies require very hot water for sterilisation both early in the morning and in the late afternoon. To contribute to both times requires good storage volumes to hold over through the night. Agricultural buildings typically have lightweight roofs that provide a challenge for structural fixings, but in rural areas, the cost of bottled gas or peak electricity, often makes the solar capital cost seem more attractive.

Camping and caravan sites, particularly those with swimming pools, provide an excellent accord with the seasonal increase of solar energy. However, finding space for extra solar storage vessels is difficult in already cramped plant rooms. Municipal pool plant room areas are often more generous but can contain heat recovery apparatus that makes solar integration difficult. Flat roofs, that often accompany swimming pool enclosures, provide difficult structural issues with wind and snow loading in some exposed regions during winter, although evacuated tube type collectors provide a simple way to lay the collector flat with minimal visual impact. Tube collectors can also be used to great architectural effect on balustrades, awnings and vertical facades on all buildings. The ability to rotate the absorber within the tube mounting permits this flexibility.

For any commercial concern, feasibility starts with assessing the heat demand that could usefully accept pre-heated solar input. Look for cold feeds and cool returns on available circuits and check that 'downstream' top-up heating appliances will accept pre-heating and thermostatically respond to it. A significant number of appliances are not compatible with pre-heating, including most dishwashers, many new washing machines, combination boilers and even electric point-of-use heaters. Adequate thermostatic control and heat resistance of materials are necessary for safe and efficient performance. In new builds, careful specification of compatible appliances and short-run distribution of DHW can help make best use of solar.

Grant aid for businesses remains possible through the government's Enhanced Capital Allowance (ECA) scheme **www.eca.gov.uk** where a list of the more stringently tested solar collectors can be found. Significant capital funding can sometimes be found with local schemes in regenerative areas or with educational concerns. Progress towards procurement of solar energy through results purchasing (no sun = no pay !) is advancing for larger commercial systems, where results can be guaranteed over the long term and payment is made on a per kWh basis. Here, the contractor uses remote monitoring of the solar plant using the internet or other methods, with responsibility for performance falling to them and not the building owner.

Further reading

Solar Heating Design and Installation guide ISBN 978-1-903287-84-2 .

Low or zero carbon sources – a strategic guide - Department of Communities and Local Government .

Solar Thermal Systems – Successful planning and implementation - James & James.

IEA Task 24 Solar Procurement, IEA Task 26 combisystems Stiftung Warentest April 2003– Solaranlglen.

Planning and Installing solar thermal systems - James & James.

References:

1. TSOL: ***www.solardesign.co.uk***

Space heating from logs

With no-one able to confidently predict when the prices of heating and cooking fuels will stabilise, perhaps it is time to re-consider our reliance on fossil fuels? **Keith Hall** puts a case for the local fuelwood option ...

We can no longer rely on gas supplies from the North sea, from now on most of the UKs gas and other major fossil fuel supplies will come from abroad, eastern Europe and farther afield, and we are at the end of a very thirsty pipeline. We have been over-complacent about our fuel supplies. Now is the time to take a serious re-examination of the fuel that we choose to heat our homes.

If you planned to heat your home with a gas or oil condensing boiler, it may be prudent to think again! If you have been thinking of a heat pump running on electricity, then think again. There is a more economical, eco-friendly and healthier option that will also offer some security of supply, particularly if you have access to woodland. When my family and I first moved to our farm in west Wales we made a conscious decision to avoid the use of fossil fuels in the heating of the farmhouse and nearby farmyard buildings. Twelve years later I am thinking that this was a very wise and farsighted decision. We installed a 50kW log burning boiler and have not looked back since.

Why burn wood?

With only about 10% of the UK covered in woodland, and most of that is coniferous, you might imagine that there is not enough firewood to go around. This would be true if the whole country switched to wood burning overnight but this is not going to happen. What we are seeing is a gradual re-afforestation of the UK as we learn to 'value' and re-assess our native woodlands, rather than plunder those of far-off lands.

The resources that we need to nurture are those that are sustainable. It all has to be balanced of course. There has always been a need to grow food, but now we are seeing that there is a need to grow fuel too. Most native woodlands in the UK have been neglected over the past 50 years and these woodlands therefore offer us the potential of a currently under-managed resource. In the past land-owners with woodland or potential woodland sites have been reluctant to plant or maintain woodland because there has not been a 'market' for the wood. We are beginning to see a change in attitude and the woodland cover of the UK has risen over the last two decades by about 2%, from roughly 9% to 11% now, and is still increasing.

Historically, native UK woodland would have been managed for construction timber, firewood, coppice crafts: charcoal, fencing, hurdles etc. Many of these uses have all but died out, other than as novelty craft revival interests. Most construction timber is imported but if more of us were to burn wood to heat our homes, offices and factories it would offer encouragement to owners of native woodlands to invest more time in growing high quality construction and joinery timbers. Firewood is usually harvested from the thinnings during the growth of quality timber and side branches during timber harvesting.

Contrary to popular belief, neglected temperate woodland is not as good for wildlife as managed woodland, so re-introducing sustainable management techniques, such as coppicing, will actually encourage more diverse and dynamic flora and fauna.

Burning wood actually helps the environment

It is now widely agreed that, when burnt efficiently and sustainably (from re-forested areas), wood gives off far less pollution than fossil fuelled appliances. Efficiently burned wood only releases the same amount of carbon dioxide (CO_2) as the wood has locked up during its growth (even less if the timber originates from coppiced woodland, as the roots remain in the ground to grow again, therefore acting as a real carbon sink). Comparisons of CO_2 output from various fuels[1] indicate that wood is the best option, either logs, chips or pellets (see following table).

Fuel	*kg CO_2/kWh*
Wood pellets and logs	*0.03*
Gas	*0.19*
Oil	*0.27*
Coal	*0.27*
Electricity	*0.42*

CO_2 pollution from various fuels.

Burning wood is healthy

Almost every day we hear of new techno-gadgets promoted to make our lives easier and more satisfying. But the reality is that, far from making us more satisfied with life, they just separate us further from the natural environment, making us lazier. As a result our waists expand and obesity is fast becoming the UK's biggest killer.

Most of us are very separated from the need to provide ourselves with basic food, shelter and warmth. This alienation may cause a negative imbalance in our lives. Putting in at least a little physical effort towards making our homes warm and comfortable reconnects us, both mentally and physically, with the natural environment, and you do not have to live in the countryside to experience it. Even with the best, most energy efficient and mechanised equipment, wood burning offers a measure of laborious input.

With the right attitude from the outset, wood cutting, collection, converting, stacking and burning is one of the most satisfying, enjoyable and health promoting tasks that you could undertake. It's real satisfaction too, every log stacked in the shed becomes an investment - not only financially, as we all tend to measure things these days, but as an investment in your own personal health and well-being.

The sustainable heating fuel

Prices for oil and gas, though rising, are still too low considering the damage their extraction and use has on the environment. Demand is beginning to outstrip supply. Improvements in energy efficiency are barely keeping pace with global demand. On the other hand, wood when used for heating, has everything going for it - the sustainable cycle for wood is well within human life-scales.

Whenever you mention wood burning to anyone they immediately think of a focal stove in the living room. Few people know of the technically advanced systems that are now available from long established European manufacturers. Whilst the UK turned its back on wood burning decades ago, other countries, particularly Scandinavia and Denmark, pursued and invested heavily into refining the technology that we have available today.

The cost of an efficient wood heating system

The capital cost of a woodburning boiler system will vary, depending on the sophistication of the equipment chosen (for sophistication, read mechanisation, not efficiency - efficiency is essential in all systems) and the fuel choice (logs, pellets or wood chips). As a very rough guide you could expect to pay the following + VAT costs for a fully installed system in an average sized, detached home using a 15-30kW boiler:

- logs £7-11,000
- wood-pellets and chip £9-19,000

The Low Carbon Buildings Programme grant scheme[1] is now available for domestic wood fired boilers up to a boiler size of 30kW. For industrial sized applications there is the 'enhanced capital allowance' scheme, which allows 100% capital allowances' tax relief for the first year on investments in energy saving equipment listed on the 'energy technology list'[2].

As far as efficiency is concerned, all of the systems compare well with the best condensing gas or oil boilers. As for running costs, the comparison between the various wood fuel option are: logs £65 -£85 per tonne; pellets £148-235 per tonne[3]. Prices include VAT and delivery. Wood chips would fall somewhere in between. Wood fuel efficiency is highly dependant on the moisture content of the wood fuel used. Pellets have a guaranteed moisture content from the manufacturer that is below 12% .

Logs, with a good storage regime, can easily be brought down to 15-20% (well within high efficiency levels) in two to three years, so a minimum of two year's storage should be allowed for. Wood-chips are the most difficult to dry and, unless mechanical turning equipment for drying and large storage areas are available, then they might not be a good choice. Of course if you are lucky enough to own your own woodland, then your ideal system choice would be logs. If you have plenty of space but want more mechanisation and less manual labour, choose wood-chips.

The modern log boiler

I chose a high efficiency, log burning boiler rather than a pellet or wood-chip (even though I have a chipper) for two reasons. Firstly, the price of log burning boilers are, at present, significantly cheaper than pellet boilers, due mainly to the more straightforward technology involved. Secondly, I have more than ample supplies of timber at the farm and enjoy managing my own woodlands. I might have considered a pellet boiler if machines were available to make pellets from your own timber (a long way off yet).

There is only one efficient method of burning wood. It has to be done fast, and at very high temperature. A water jacket around the combustion chamber is a definite drawback as it cools the temperature of the fire. So how have manufacturers overcome this problem? Well, in my boiler, the water jacket is behind the chamber, rather than around it (see picture). It is in a pre-chimney where gasses leaving the combustion chamber are sucked by an inbuilt fan, at temperatures around 900°C, through a collection of water filled baffles (heat exchanger).

This is where the heat is effectively transferred to the water without having any cooling effect on the combustion process at all. This arrangement allows the boiler to operate at an efficiency of 89-91%, which in reality is probably better than most condensing gas boilers perform. The real work of the boiler takes place in a ceramic flame tunnel (ceramic is one of the only materials able to withstand such high temperatures) directly below where the wood is loaded and this combustion takes place at full output with an appropriate mixture of primary and secondary air.

Right: high efficiency down-draught boilers can be more efficient than the best condensing gas boilers and only need firing once per day, or even two days when an accumulator tank is used (far right).

Once lit the boiler needs no further adjustment and switches itself off at the end of a burn. My boiler is rated at 50kW, which means that when running it will output 50kW of heat per hour. A full load of ash species timber will burn for up to 4 hours, therefore creating towards 200kW hours of heat as hot water which is stored in a well-insulated accumulator tank (large water vessel) sized appropriately for the boiler - in my instance 2600 litres. The accumulator tank serves as a large battery, which reduces firing times. In my case, depending on the weather, I usually fire up once every two days in the spring and autumn and each day during the winter.

Accumulator tanks

Accumulator tanks are now quite widely available. At the time of my installation, I converted an old oil tank with a view to replacing it sometime in the future when there is more choice and lower prices. Most of the suppliers of log boilers should be able to offer something. **www.greenbuildingforum.co.uk** has regular discussions on the availability and installation issues of log boilers, tanks and associated subject matter.

During recent research I found that accumulator tanks are now readily available in the UK and most wood boiler distributors will also hold stocks of such tanks. For anyone not wanting to use an accumulator tank, due to space limitations etc, most boiler suppliers produce log burning boilers that have advanced modulating controls which allow the boiler to be coupled with a much smaller accumulator tank. These are known as 'lambda controlled'. However, the boiler costs are far higher, the refuelling would be more frequent and the efficiency does drop, (though not by much if you believe the literature). Pellet and woodchip boilers use a hopper and or auger systems that are automated, therefore they have less need for accumulators. Personally I like the accumulator concept as it allows me to run the boiler at times when it is most suitable and most safe, i.e. when I am around. They also allow the system to perform much like any other heating system - very nearly fully automated.

Conclusion

I see woodburning as the future. No doubt systems will continue to become even more sophisticated and there is little doubt in my mind that pellet fuelled appliances will ultimately find the lion's share of the market as they will appeal to users that want minimal input into the running of the system. Pellets are now more widely available, although at present most are imported from Europe. UK produced pellets are slowly becoming available. However, if you choose a log burning boiler you can rest assured that you will have chosen perhaps the most environmentally friendly system possible - whilst at the same time contributing towards the reforesting of the UK. ☯

References

1. **www.lowcarbonbuildings.org.uk/micro/biomass**
2. **www.eca.gov.uk/etl**
3. *The 'John Willoughby Domestic Fuel Price Guide' April 08, see page 460.*

Left: a typical accumulator tank for a large domestic wood boiler. They are now widely available in the UK.
Photo courtesy of Peter de la Haye Engineering.

Space heating with heat pumps

Heat pumps have fast become a darling of the mainstream building industry. Rightly or wrongly, they are included in the 'low carbon technology' list. **Kevin Boniface** discusses them ...

Heat pumps use the time proven refrigeration cycle (that we all have in our refrigerators and freezers) to transfer heat from a source (such as the ground, the ambient air or water) through a heat distribution circuit to an internal space. A working fluid (or refrigerant) is driven around a circuit, comprising an evaporator, compressor, condenser and an expansion valve. The heat source transfers heat to liquid refrigerant, which causes it to evaporate. The refrigerant is now at a low temperature and pressure; it then enters the compressor, where the temperature and pressure are increased, as a result of work done by the compressor.

The refrigerant gas enters the condenser, where the heat absorbed by the refrigerant in the evaporator, is released to be used in the building, via a low temperature distribution system, such as underfloor heating or low temperature radiators. The refrigerant, which is still in the form of a gas but reduced in pressure and temperature, is throttled back further in the expansion valve before the cycle starts again.

Heat pumps will consume electricity, since it is required by the compressor. However, for every one unit of electricity used, somewhere between 2 and 4 units of heat energy is produced (commonly described as the 'coefficient of performance' - CoP). The total amount of heat energy delivered to the building is equal to the energy input through the compressor, plus the energy extracted from the heat source. The diagram below shows the basic operating

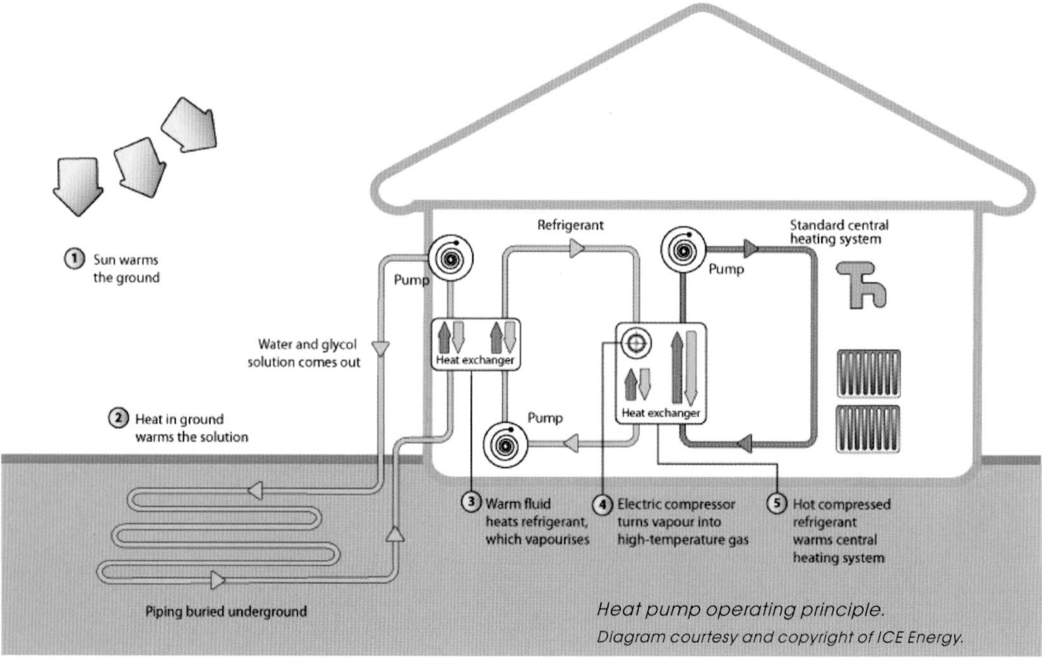
1 Sun warms the ground
Pump
Refrigerant
Pump
Standard central heating system
Water and glycol solution comes out
Heat exchanger
Heat exchanger
2 Heat in ground warms the solution
Pump
3 Warm fluid heats refrigerant, which vapourises
4 Electric compressor turns vapour into high-temperature gas
5 Hot compressed refrigerant warms central heating system
Piping buried underground

Heat pump operating principle.
Diagram courtesy and copyright of ICE Energy.

principle of a heat pump, using the ground as a heat source.

The technology in heat pumps is essentially the same, whether the heat source is from the ground, the air or water. However, as there is an inherent difference in temperature stability between these sources, the overall efficiency will tend to vary.

Heat pump systems will be at their most cost-effective in applications where high levels of insulation have already been installed and mains gas is not available. Although it is possible for a heat pump to produce hot water at up to 55°C (depending on the heat source and heat pump type), the CoP will increase as the required water temperature reduces. In other words, if a distribution system can be designed to effectively heat a dwelling using water heated to only 35-40°C, then the CoP will be significantly better than a similar system that is required to heat water to 55°C.

GSHP (ground source heat pumps) - with a ground source system, the earth absorbs a large proportion of the incident solar radiation, which in the UK helps to ensure that the ground stays at a relatively stable 11-12°C all year round. Air-source systems, however, cannot offer the same year round efficiencies, since the ambient air temperature is far more variable. This means that efficiency tends to drop off, just when there is a demand for heat.

ASHP (air source heat pumps) - for air source heat pumps, there are obvious space benefits, since the unit sits outside the building, and most other infrastructure works will be internal. A ground collector, however, will require a substantial amount of space, since they will either use a vertical borehole or horizontal trench, depending upon the land available, local ground conditions and excavation costs.

WSHP (water source heat pumps) - this is the least common of the heat pumps but spring-water body (lake or pond) sourced systems potentially offer the best CoP. However a viable water source will only be available for a small proportion of potential applications.

Future developments

Heat pumps are much more widespread in domestic applications across Europe and in North America, but are gaining in popularity in the UK. Although often queried by some as a true renewable energy technology (since they require electricity to run), they may offer reductions in running costs and carbon emissions in comparison to heating systems using conventional electrical heating systems. If heat pump installations were run using on-site renewables, such as PV, wind or hydro to supply power for the compressor and circulating pump, this would make them a truly renewable source of energy.

For more detailed information on heat pumps, their suitability to different environments and their costs, download a copy of 'Domestic Ground Source Heat Pumps: design and installation of closed loop systems' (CE82) from the Energy Saving Trust: ***www.est.org.uk.***

There are many discussions regarding the pros and cons of heat pump technology on the Green Building Forum: ***www.greenbuildingforum.co.uk***

Don't confuse GSHP with geothermal energy

Readers should remember not to confuse ground source heat pumps (GSHP) technology with geothermal energy.

GSHP captures latent solar energy that was probably stored in the ground through the previous summer season. Pipes for GSHP are only buried about 1 metre below the surface and therefore careful design calculations are needed to ensure that the system will not try to extract too much heat.

Geothermal energy, on the other hand, is heat from within the earth which is thought to have been trapped since the earth was created. This 'earth' heat is stored at a much greater depth in the ground, which is captured usually by pumping water down one long bore-hole and back up to the surface through an adjacent one. This method allows hot rocks to transfer heat to the water by simple conduction, which is then used to heat to buildings. Where temperatures of geothermal are not high, such as in the UK, a heat pump system may well be used in conjunction with the geothermal to boost the energy.

Electricity from solar energy

When people talk about putting 'solar panels' on their roofs, many assume these are for producing hot water. This is not always the case, as solar panels for generating electricity are becoming increasingly popular. **Gavin Harper** introduces us to solar photovoltaics ...

Solar photovoltaic cells (PVs) offer a clean way to produce electricity for use in our buildings. Whilst the benefits of owning your own solar PV array are not immediately apparent, when you begin to think about the rapidly rising costs of electricity and other fuels and the safeguard they can offer against rising energy costs, the prospect of being sent a cheque by your energy supplier, and the knowledge that the energy you are generating is clean, green and carbon free, you begin to realise what an asset they are to any home. In this article, we are going to be exploring what is entailed if you wish to generate electricity, using solar power, for your home.

Whilst a solar cell will produce the largest amount of power on a clear, bright sunny day, even on comparatively dull days, a solar array will still be providing cheap, green electricity. The amount of power a solar cell produces is proportionate to the amount of light that it receives. The more light, the more power. For this reason, you want to try, as far as possible, to minimise any obstructions and large objects which might overshadow your solar panels, siting them in an area where they have a clear view of the sun. Ideally, we want to face our cells due south to receive the most light throughout the year. However, any angle within 45 degrees of due south will produce satisfactory results. Similarly, cells which are placed on a pitch between 20 and 50 degrees will yield best results. PVs do not necessarily need bright sunlight to work – of course the amount of power produced is governed by the availability of light, but even on overcast days some power will be produced.

Types of collectors

There are a couple of ways of integrating solar PV collectors. You can integrate them into the fabric of the building or they can simply be 'bolted on' to a suitable roof.

Framed panels are the most common and least expensive, at the moment, especially in refurbishment situations are the bolt-on type (see photo below).

Solar slates, on the other hand, perform the same waterproofing function as an ordinary roof tile but create electricity at the same time (see pictures top right and bottom right). In a new build, for instance, or where a roof needs to be replaced. One might assume that it saves costs by eliminating the need to buy a separate set of tiles or slates but be warned, unless really

Below: council houses at Kirklees were upgraded by the local authority to include solar PVs. Right: a house at Fordingbridge where solar PV slates have been integrated with regular roof tile to ensure a smooth roof profile.

The picture above shows the fixing method for solar slates. They are installed in a similar manner to normal roofing slates.

expensive handmade slates were going to be used, this method is likely be a more expensive solution than fixing ordinary roof slates with conventional framed panels over the top. However, visually, it does look better. Some solar slates use a base tile, so the solar part of the slate can be clipped into the base tile after completion of the roof and other associated building work.

Traditional roofing tile manufacturers, such as Redland, Marley and others, now offer a range of roof integrated PV tiles – these are designed to integrate with their own brand tiles. Solar tiles and the latest framed panels come pre-wired with simple waterproof connectors that can be joined together in the chosen configuration (depending on the voltage chosen etc.) and connected to the existing electrical system via batteries (in off-grid systems) and an inverter for bringing the electricity up to grid voltage. There are a wide range of inverters available for most configurations and for those who want to export any surplus that is generated.

System sizing

Before you attempt to size the PV array that you need, it is first better to carry out a careful assessment of the present or expected energy consumption of the building and its occupants. Then look for ways to reduce this consumption to an absolute minimum. This will pay dividends and is the most cost effective aspect of the whole process. The less energy that you need to generate the better. This will help ensure that there are no disappointments once the system is up and running.

The amount of electricity produced by a given solar PV array is directly proportional to its surface area and, of course, the amount of direct sunlight or bright daylight that shines upon it. Therefore it is important not to choose a roof or suitable surface that is shaded by trees or other buildings at any extended part of the day, or the installation will fail to live up to expectations. When installing any device onto a roof, whether its a new roof or retrofitting onto an existing one, loading needs to be checked carefully to ensure the structure of the roof is adequate to support any system. Always obtain the correct weights for the system that you are using, but as an example, the Marley solar tile weighs 40kg per square metre.

For commercial buildings, there are a wide range of solar claddings which can be used to generate electricity, whilst simultaneously protecting the building fabric from the elements.

Solar panels produce direct current electricity – this is the sort of electricity we would get from a battery. Electrons flow round the circuit in one direction. They also produce electricity at relatively low voltage. By contrast, our mains electricity supply is alternating current. This means that electrons flow back and forth through the circuit – and they do so at much higher voltages. This means that there must be an intermediate step between the solar PVs and mains electricity wiring - an inverter. An inverter takes the low voltage direct current, and using solid state electronics, turns the low voltage DC into high voltage AC, at a frequency that is appropriate for the mains supply, which in the UK is 50 hertz. The inverter is sized appropriately for the solar installation. It is important to note that although the voltage increases, no electricity is 'made' – as a result of the voltage increasing, the current available decreases, so whilst the PV array might be producing high current DC, the output of the inverter is AC at a lower current.

If the installation is connected to the grid, a new metering system will need to be installed, which can take account of electricity going back into the grid. Think, if you like, that when electricity is fed back into the grid, your meter needle 'spins backwards' - this is a good way of visualising the balance between electricity coming to and from your home. In reality, with peak and off peak tariffs, the metering arrangement is a little more complicated, but essentially, the detail is all the same - the electricity you feed into the grid is subtracted from that which you use from the grid.

On-grid?

Most houses in the UK are within easy reach of a grid connection. This is very convenient as it allows us to use the 'national grid' as a giant battery. Energy can be 'sold' to the grid at times when the building produces a surplus which is not being used by the occupants. When the solar arrays do not provide enough power for the buildings requirements, power can be 'bought back' from the grid.

If you are going to connect to the grid, you will need to seek the appropriate permissions from the local distribution network operator (DNO). If you are having your PVs professionally installed, your installer should take care of this for you. You will be paid a different rate for 'exported' electricity, depending on your supplier. As the amount paid varies so widely, it could be worth changing supplier to take advantage of better prices for your exported electricity. Again, your installer should be able to find you the best deal

Off-grid?

New micro technologies are bringing new opportunities for people to gain a more independent lifestyle with the ethos of the late sixties and self-sufficiency. If you want to live in a manner that is wholly self sufficient, then you need not now live in a home with candles and gaslamps. You can consider an 'off-the-grid', battery system solution for storage.

This involves storing the electrical energy in batteries. Lead acid batteries are currently the most pragmatic way of storing electricity. However, in the next couple of decades there might be interesting opportunities opened up by hydrogen fuel cells, which would allow storage of power as hydrogen gas. However, for widespread adoption, this is not currently practical. One word of advice though - solar PVs alone cannot really be relied upon in the UK climate to provide a comprehensive supply. Those that have successfully transferred to an offgrid system, such as the publisher of this book, Green Building Press, has installed a system, which combines a number of technologies: (multiple PV arrays, two wind turbines, a pico-hydro and biomass for heating). This is known as a hybrid system.

Of course sometimes these systems can produce more energy than needed, even for charging large batteries. In this case, when the national grid is not being used, you can store the electricity in what is known as a 'dump load', such as water or directly to electrical resistance heaters for heating the building.

One concern that many people have is that

over the life cycle of a solar cell, it will produce less energy than was used producing the PV. This is not the case. The carbon payback period of PVs is controvertial and highly dependant on location and exposure.

For installation, you will also need to consider access to the roof. Scaffolding and mobile towers are expensive – and if these are required, they must be added to the cost of the installation when calculating payback periods.

Similarly, people often ask about the financial payback of photovoltaic systems. This will obviously be dependent on the cost of the installation and whether there were any factors which 'pushed up' the cost of the installation. In Volume 2 of the Green Building Bible it states that when using a normal charge controller, with reasonable solar access, a solar PV installation could give a financial payback of 23 years, on a commercial building, and over 35 years, on a domestic building, (due to economies of scale). Of course, these figures are not set in stone. As energy becomes more expensive and suppliers start to introduce feed-in-tariffs, solar PV power will start to look more attractive. Most solar module manufacturers guarantee that their cells will produce energy for around 25 years.

Planning issues

Planning permission is generally one of the first concerns that people voice (next to cost). Planning permission is not required in the majority of cases, although check with your local authority.

The amendment in April 2008 to the General Permitted Development Order (GPDO) allows for the installation of solar PV or solar thermal equipment on the wall or roof of a dwelling-house or a building within its curtilage, so long as the equipment does not protrude more than 200 millimetres. Stand alone solar PV or solar thermal will be permitted if its height does not exceed four metres above ground level and it is more than five metres from the boundary. There are restrictions that apply to solar in conservation areas, in World Heritage Sites and to listed buildings, so in these cases check with your local authority.

Grant information

Photovoltaics were previously funded by the major photovoltaic demonstration programme. However, this has been replaced with the Low Carbon Buildings Programme. There are two streams; stream 1 is for smaller projects and stream 2 is for larger micro generation projects. Most domestic solar installations will fall into the first stream, whilst larger commercial installations will fall into the second.

Monitoring data from a couple of small PV arrays and regular discussions regarding off and on-grid living can be found on the Green Building Forum: ***www.greenbuildingforum.co.uk***

Social housing in Scotland.

Photo courtesy of Solar Century.

Electricity from wind power

The UK is blessed with the best wind energy resource in Europe, yet, despite the efforts of a number of pioneering individuals and companies, our use of wind power lags far behind other EU countries. **John Shore** thinks we should give wind power a chance to prove itself ...

In the past, large windmills (often made mainly of timber) were commonplace throughout the UK and provided an essential local energy source. Later, the familiar wind-pumps provided water supplies and before the widespread introduction of grid electricity, small stand-alone wind turbines were used to provide lighting. Today, although wind technology has made some major advances, we currently only have perhaps a few thousand small turbines (to which this article mainly refers) and most of these are recreational (yachts and caravans), with perhaps a thousand or so domestic-sized machines installed for eco and off-grid houses. The use of medium-sized turbines for horticulture and industry has hardly begun.

Domestic-scale wind turbines can be beautiful, highly efficient, and can have a very long working life. In the USA, turbines dating from the 1900s are still bought, sold and are fully repairable. A carefully designed eco-house can power its basic needs from a 500 watt or 1kW turbine, depending on household numbers and lifestyle.

What is available

Small wind turbines can be classified in the following main categories:

- low or high voltage turbines, which directly provide electricity for heat, drive a suitable motor or pump water, perhaps from a borehole (no batteries required)
- low-voltage (12, 24, 36 or 48V) turbines, which charge batteries and power low-voltage lights, appliances etc. without inversion to higher voltage
- low-voltage turbines, which charge batteries which, in turn, is inverted to power 240V lights, appliances, pump water etc. via an inverter
- high-voltage (115 or 230V) turbines, which feed into the mains electricity grid, usually via a special inverter, (no electricity is available during grid failure, unless a charger/battery/inverter is also added).

Despite the current optimism and media hype about roof-top, micro, grid-connect turbines, we should not assume that low-voltage turbines have had their day. Not only are batteries recyclable, but alternative power storage methods are being developed. We may yet live to see a whole new range of low-voltage domestic products, especially designed to work efficiently with low voltage renewable energy!

One small turbine, the AIR wind module was one of the first small turbines intended to be mounted onto buildings. The design concept was for a powerful, low-cost, modular unit which could be installed in a row and make use of the enhanced wind flow that a large flat or gently curved roof can provide. The design was so popular that 70,000 were supplied world-wide in the first 10 years, and the latest version offers a programmed cubic power curve, automatic shut-down in gusty winds, or beyond 500W output, and built-in voltage regulation. However, high blade speed and noise are two aspects of this particular model which could be improved.

Where should turbines be located?

I have worked with wind energy for over 30 years as a researcher, designer, manufacturer and supplier and I passionately wish to see small wind turbines used on, as well as around, buildings. Since many of our customers install their turbines on yachts, and often sleep in a cabin underneath, there is no reason why suitable turbines should not be mounted on buildings and we have already supplied building-mounted turbines in this country and abroad. But be realistic - a roof-mounted turbine will generate significantly less power, and operate for less hours than a turbine sited on a high mast, with a windy, open aspect (see below).

Turbines are usually mounted on steel tube masts, ideally hinged near the ground to enable the turbine to be safely lowered for inspection and maintenance. Batteries and inverters can be housed near the mast, so only low-cost, high-voltage wiring is run to the point of use. To obtain good performance the turbine should be sited 10m above any obstruction within 150m. Building-mounted turbines should be mounted on a steel or aluminium stub mast, which attaches to the building structure through twin rubber noise and vibration isolation mountings.

Community and domestic scale wind turbines, when given the correct provision of space and aspect, can contribute to a renewable energy future.

The ability to operate safely in high winds is paramount. While larger turbines usually incorporate a furling mechanism, some small turbines have little or no protection. Some new companies are selling inadequately engineered designs and are also making performance claims which are impossible to achieve. Be very wary of vertical-axis turbines, which have a long track record of failure. Take independent advice from experienced consultants before specifying or buying!

Turbines should not be mounted on chimneys (for obvious structural reasons) and building insurance will also be an issue. Because a smooth, steady air flow is rarely found close to buildings (or trees), a careful assessment should be made as to whether the turbine/s will produce enough power to be a sustainable concept. Roof-mounted turbines do have potential, especially on larger buildings, but a completely new design approach and type of turbine may be required to deliver safety and cost-effectiveness.

Guide costs and outputs

- A 1.1m (swept area) 400W turbine costs £700 excluding installation (this would provide about 200W at 11m/s with a peak output of 500W at 13.5m/s).
- A 2.7m (swept area) 1.0kW grid-connect turbine/inverter system will cost around £3,300.
- A 3.5m (swept area), 2.5kW grid-connect system, will cost about £5,500.

All prices above exclude VAT, installation or any savings from grants.

Average urban wind speeds are quite low and while a 1kW wind turbine might deliver only 750kWh/year on a domestic urban roof - assuming 3.85m/s (metres per second) average windspeed, the same turbine should easily exceed 3000kWh/year in an open rural area. Resource assessment is an essential indicator of project viability, and to match demand to seasonal variation it is important to gather 'monthly' average data for the site before proceeding with an installation. For comparison, a 1kWp (7.72m^2) grid-connect, roof-mounted

PV array would cost around £5,000 and deliver around 750kWh/year. PV can provide power in summer when winds may be light - wind can provide power in dull winter weather when heat and lighting loads are greater.

Grants

The present system of grants for wind energy equipment is not entirely a good idea, as it stifles the DIY approach which has been so popular with wind power enthusiasts, and many reputable dealers do not have the resources needed to support installation teams. £1,000 per kW of electrical output (up to £2,500 maximum per household) and limited to 30% of the installed cost, is only available if installation is carried out by a very limited number of accredited contractors, who will often need to charge for travel, labour and maybe even accommodation. Because the level of grant relates to the rated power specified by the manufacturer and not to a standardised wind speed or to actual energy production, some turbines get more grant than their output justifies.

The future

New designs for building-integrated wind turbines are being developed, some as ridge-mounted arrays and others hidden from view in ducts which enhance wind flow and power production. For safety and public confidence turbines will need to operate at much slower rotational speeds and with lower noise levels than most currently available turbines. Minimum weight, combined with high strength, low installed costs, zero maintenance and fail-safe operation in high winds, will be prerequisites for any successful roof-mounted product.

Fossil-fuel energy will have to be targeted for essential uses in the near future, so using the ambient energy around buildings for power generation is bound to increase.

Further reading

'See Green Building Bible, Volume 2', for an in-depth analysis of the potential output from 1 - 2m diameter wind turbines.

See BFF magazine, Vol 15, No 3. for more opinions of potential outputs from roof mounted turbines: ***www.buildingforafuture.co.uk//winter05/index.php***

There ia a useful website that discusses turbine siting, expected outputs, wind speeds etc: ***www.windpower.org/en/tour***

British Wind Energy Association: ***www.bwea.com***

These turbines at the University of Sheffield site are quite exposed and have reasonably average wind speeds (5.3 m/s). The two turbines selected, (WES 30MkI from Wind Energy Solutions BV), with a nominal rating of 250kW, will provide sufficient energy (around 600,000 kWh per year) to achieve carbon neutrality for the adjacent buildings. During periods of low power demand, when the buildings are empty, the turbines will feed any excess electricity generated back to the grid.

Healthy heating systems

With space heating being a major drain on fossil fuels, many will be looking for more efficient ways of keeping warm. This is an opportunity, says **Chris Morgan,** to also examine what effect central heating is having on your health.

With the increasingly airtight and super-efficient eco-homes of the future we need to think of the whole building and how we plan to heat it. We may no longer need the cumbersome and space wasting central heating systems that began to be so popular in the seventies and eighties. They are probably not healthy anyway.

Let's take a step back and think of our biological heritage. The two heat sources with which we have evolved for millennia are the sun, and fire. Both deliver light, and heat in the form of infra-red radiation. In terms of our evolutionary make-up, it is probably fair to say we react well to a source of radiating heat, warm surfaces, cool air and probably a little air movement. It is no surprise, therefore, to read that our biological needs for thermal comfort go far beyond the number '20°C' on a dial, and in fact are influenced by a complex matrix of:

- surrounding surface temperatures
- surrounding air temperatures
- air movement
- moisture in the air and objects nearby
- and the type of heat emitter.

In addition we know that certain parts of our body are more susceptible to heat loss (or gain) than the rest. We know that a cool head (speaking in strictly thermal terms!) aids concentration, while cold feet are particularly uncomfortable, and that in general, we require a cool head and warm feet (and to a lesser extent hands) to be comfortable and function well.

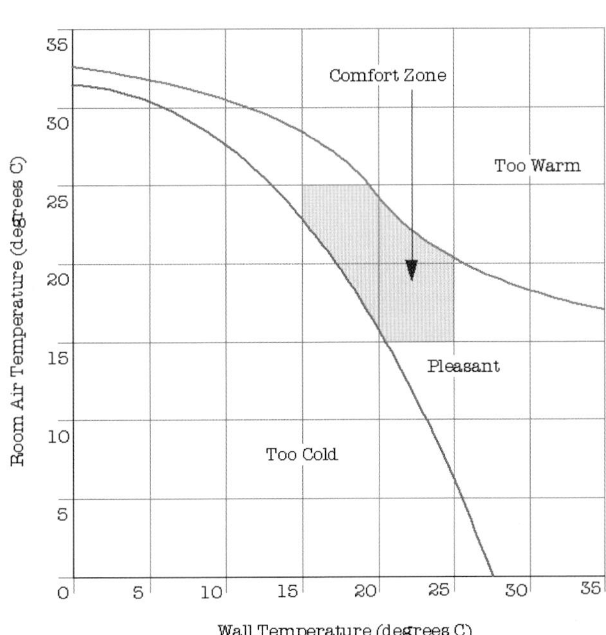

All of these aspects and more need to be considered when deciding on the heating regime of a building and its occupants, bearing in mind too that occupants' needs change with the days, the seasons, with age, and from person to person.

So what would a healthy heating system be like?

Warm surface temperatures

This is possibly the most important aspect of thermal comfort, yet it hardly registers in discussions about heating. We gain and lose a significant percentage of our heat through radiation heat exchange. What we need are surfaces which are a few degrees warmer than the ambient air temperature. Within certain tolerances (see diagram on previous page) the warmer the surfaces, the cooler the air can be whilst still maintaining comfort. The subsequent potential to save energy through lower air temperatures, whilst improving health, has yet to be fully appreciated in the eco-building community.

The way to achieve warm surfaces, generally, is to use radiant heating, either from a point source, like a stove or fireplace, or from a large surface area, as in underfloor heating. This tends to heat the surfaces and the objects in a room without heating the air in between – just like the sun. Some heating of air takes place of course, but it is minimal (see diagram).

Air temperature

Air temperature dominates our common understanding of temperature, yet it is only one constituent part, and unfortunately, the most problematic. In trying to keep warm, many people simply increase the air temperature, which in addition to being only partly successful, tends to exacerbate health problems.

Excessively warm air temperatures reduce concentration and performance, increase pulse rates, skin moisture and likelihood of fatigue. Warm air heating and air conditioning systems have also been associated with common colds, dried mucous membranes, headaches, irritability and weakened circulation. Cool air, on the other hand, tends to have the opposite effect, and aids deeper breathing which is particularly important when sleeping.

Warm air is lighter than cold air so rises and collects below ceilings. This can be very helpful in summer where high level windows and vents readily exhaust warm air and aid comfort, but in winter, it means that most of the warmth is where people aren't! This means more heat has to be generated to 'swell' the warmth down to where people are operating (or move the warm air down using fans), which leads to excessive heat input and, significantly, excessive warmth to the head, whilst feet remain too cold. This is exactly the wrong way around for human comfort and health.

Since we have to maintain fresh air levels at all times, ventilation is critical, but in exhausting air for freshness, we are also exhausting heat. Heat exchange ventilators are now common, but it remains the case that by heating the one thing that we need to get rid of, we are to an extent making a rod for our own backs. With warm air heating, lobbies become crucial to stop heat escaping each time we come in or go out, and if windows or trickle vents are left open, we are simply heating the sky. When the building fabric itself is warm and the air is cool, as it should be, such draughts are much less of a worry.

So all in all, warm air heating makes for a sorry tale, and since all heating systems will heat the air to some extent, it is unavoidable. Clearly though, we can seek to minimise this, whilst optimising the benefits of cooler air in the process.

Air movement

Moving air, however warm, will tend to cool the body by evaporation. Thus there is something strangely counter-productive of first heating, and then moving something which by moving it, serves to cool things!

What is needed for health is a small degree of air movement. Think of a warm day and a light breeze and the truth of this is apparent. Too little air movement and we cannot get rid of our moisture (sweat) or odours through evaporation, respiration is impaired, we get warm and tired; too much air movement of course and we will get cold. Bear in mind however that occupants sitting for long periods will appreciate less air movement while those working manually will need more. Air movement is also related to the airtightness of the building and to the ventilation strategy.

Excessive air movement tends to lift and circulate dust which creates further health problems. In forced air systems, the movement of air also creates friction in the ducts and positive ions in the process. In (overly) simple terms positive ions are relatively bad for respiratory health, whilst negative ions are relatively good. Think of yourself by the side of a mountain stream with fresh, gurgling running water for an image of an environment with higher negative ions and you can get a sense of this. Positive ionisation of the air also creates problems for the respiratory system.

Humidity levels

Whilst humidity levels do not directly affect the heating regime, the interactions between air, temperature and moisture levels are subtle and complex. Low humidity levels, for example, will increase respiratory problems associated with higher air temperatures, greater air movement, dust scorching and circulation, electrostatic charges and positive ionisation, while higher humidity levels will mitigate against them. On the other hand high humidity levels are associated with condensation and mould, which themselves lead to other health problems. In general, relative humidity levels should remain between 40 and 60%. This is harder to achieve with warm air heating, since the heating of the air itself dries out the air.

Kachelofens and other massive masonry stoves are close to ideal for healthy heating systems.
Photo courtesy of Samsø Energy Academy.

Heating options at a glance?

Underfloor heating, and wall heating (almost unheard of in the UK until recently, but more common in Europe) are close to being ideal. Kachelofens and other massive masonry stoves are also close to ideal. Forced warm air heating is really to be avoided. Systems, such as radiators and electric convectors, are effectively, warm air systems and are probably not ideal.

Open fires are wonderful, but so wasteful of fuel that they need to be seen as mood heating, rather than a main source of heat these days. Individual room stoves are often alright because they emit heat largely through radiation.

Ceiling radiant heaters (like you see in churches and village halls), are often useful in large open spaces, but creating hot heads is never a good idea. Ceiling panel heating is to be avoided.

It is important to stress, that, quite apart from the times when the ideal approach isn't possible, there will always be circumstances where the above advice does not apply!

Heat emitter surface temperature

Fires and hot surfaces on stoves and radiators etc. have the effect of scorching dust, which is unhelpful for health, but more significantly they stir up air movement creating convection currents which then move all that scorched dust around.

Low surface temperature emitters which reduce this problem, have become more common, largely due to quite separate health and safety concerns surrounding children and other vulnerable people burning themselves. However, radiation is more effective with a higher temperature, so to achieve the same heat input, these heat emitters need to be larger to make up for the lower temperatures, which can sometimes be a problem.

Temperature gradients

I have already mentioned the problem of hot heads and cold feet created by warm air systems. But since most systems contain a large percentage of convection (air) heating, temperature gradients are common. Radiators, for example, hopelessly mis-named, produce more of their heat output through convection than radiation. Place your hand beside, and then above a radiator to see for yourself.

Fans can be used to disturb the heat pockets which develop at ceiling levels, but again these have the effect of moving the air and thus cooling occupants at the same time. Reducing temperature gradients can only really be done at the design stage. One of the major advantages of underfloor heating is that heat is delivered in arguably the best place – the floor – and at low temperatures which reduce the air movement such that you strategically reduce stratification.

Temperature monotony

Most of us are familiar with the welcome cooling effect of moving into a cold stone building on a hot day, or of entering a warm room after a snowball fight! Passing between areas of different temperature is invigorating. Conversely, experience suggests that having all rooms the same temperature has a deadening effect on the body as an organism. It is important therefore to zone areas of the building with this in mind; some rooms warmer and some cooler.

Controls

Heating systems which cannot easily be controlled can be both wasteful and uncomfortable in equal measure. Controllability (along with low installation costs) was often the rallying cry of the warm air heating brigade, and it is true that, in general, air heating is easier to control than radiant heating, especially the large surface, thermally massive systems (like underfloor heating) which in most other respects are preferable. In practice though, controllability is not just about the controls of the heating system itself, but about the way the system interacts with the thermal mass of the house (or lack of it) and the lifestyle of the occupants. Care needs to be taken at the design stage.

Conclusion

Hopefully it is clear that a healthy heating system is relatively easy to create if you use mostly radiant heating, whilst it is relatively difficult to create using convective, or air heating. You are looking then, for a system which creates warm surfaces, but relatively cool air, but a system where the heat emitter itself is not too hot. You are looking for a system which does not create excessive air movement, avoids excessive gradients but allows for different temperatures in different rooms. It needs to be quiet and easy to control, working well with the ventilation system and with the control of humidity.

The issue is likely to become more compelling as we seal up our homes and begin to see heat from exhaust ventilation as the main heat losses in very low energy homes. Such heat exchange makes perfect sense in energy efficiency terms, but it is really just convective heating and as such needs to be looked at cautiously for those concerned about health.

Heat can also be stored passively, along with moisture. My own view of the future of low energy housing is that it is the capacity of buildings to absorb and desorb heat and moisture ('thermal mass' and 'moisture mass') which is the key to super-efficient energy use, rather than warm air heat exchange technology. It is the buildings themselves, a holistic approach and the laws of nature, rather than applied technology that will help us out.

As we make our homes more airtight, the quality of the air and the warmth becomes more important still. Energy efficiency and healthy buildings can be mutually exclusive, but with good design they can also be mutually supportive. Let's get this right for our own, as well as our planet's health! ☯

Resources

Information on radiant heating: ***www.constructionresources.com/products/services/radiantheating.asp*** *which describes the 'Variotherm' range of radiant heating products.*

'Natural Heating' magazine BBE No.21, winter 1995. Available from Building Biology and Ecology Institute of New Zealand at: ***www.ecoprojects.co.nz***

Venolia, Carol, 'Healing Environments', Celestial Arts 1988 USA.

Underfloor heating

Underfloor heating is fast becoming the norm rather than the exception in UK homes. Is it because it is a space saver and allows us more freedom or is it the perfect green home heating system asks **Olwyn Pritchard**?

There is something magical about that warm glow underfoot. What are the advantages of this form of heat delivery over conventional radiators? This article analyses why this system of heating has become so popular.

Firstly, the only underfloor heating systems that should be of interest to green builders are those that pass water through coiled pipes, running under or in the floor. As far as we are concerned, electrical underfloor heating has drawbacks that make it highly undesirable from an environmental viewpoint; issues such as electrical and magnetic fields (EMF's) and the high CO_2 emissions associated with using main's electricity.

Background to heating

The idea of any heating is to warm a living space during times when outside temperatures are falling enough to force the internal room temperatures to drop. This will occur in just about every building but there will be vast differences in the rapidity of the change, depending on a good number of variables; structure type, insulation levels, airtightness, heating settings, furnishings etc.

Depending on the above, the reaction time of the heating can have a great effect on the energy that is consumed and, of course, on the comfort level of the occupants. A lightweight building will be more responsive to changes in temperature than a heavyweight building. This cuts both ways - more responsive could mean that the building is equally as responsive to falling outside temperatures as it may be to internal rising temperatures (from the heating). A heavyweight building will be slower to respond and our direct experience is that a heavyweight building gradually reacts to the seasonal changes, rather than day to night fluctuations. These are just a couple of the considerations to bear in mind when considering the heat delivery method for your building.

Types of wet underfloor heating

There are basically two types of wet underfloor heating - 'heat store' or 'fast delivery'.

Heat store underfloor heating systems comprise pipes laid within a relatively thick concrete or limecrete slab, which would be insulated below and around the perimeter; slower to heat up but also slower to cool. The speed of cooling will, of course, be influenced by the temperatures and airtightness of the room.

Fast delivery underfloor heating is via pipes laid on top of insulation - either in a thin screed or in specially formed insulation, containing trenches for the pipes to sit in beneath a thin screed or timber flooring.

Logic would suggest that the former would be most suitable for a heavyweight building and the latter for lightweight buildings that need a faster response. However, there is no reason why they cannot be mixed and many lightweight buildings would actually benefit from the addition of a 'heat store' floor.

Floors v/s radiators as heat emitters

Heating a space sufficiently to maintain a comfortable body temperature, without lowering the humidity so much as to cause discomfort, can best be achieved by a large area of radiant surface, with the mean radiant temperature just a few degrees higher than the air temperature. If the radiant surface is large, such as a floor, for example, then the temperature required to effect change can be lower.

Both radiators and underfloor heating are radiant heat emitters but to very differing degrees. In fact radiators only emit about 15-20% of their heat by radiation, the rest is achieved by convection. Because conventional radiators are generally quite small in comparison to the room, to work effectively, they need to deliver hot water at temperatures above 60° C. This creates localised hot spots, and the convected air thus created by the radiator always rises to the ceiling, flows across the top of the room and down the other side as it cools. Cool air will then be drawn towards the radiator at floor level and begin again. As an aside, the convection current will also carry dust and will lower the humidity of the air - both of which can cause problems for allergy sufferers. That said, radiators, properly sized, can deliver heat very quickly.

Underfloor heating (and in-wall heating) on the other hand is a large gently radiating surface, which needs to be only a few degrees warmer than the air in the room (using water temperatures between 45-55°C). Because of this, the differential between the floor and the room temperature is usually so small that convection is avoided, and because radiant heat energy works like sunlight, the heat from the floor warms the occupants directly as well as the air. It is accepted that comfortable conditions can be achieved using much lower water temperatures (thus saving energy), without drying the air, and with no localised hot or cool spots in the room (read the previous story to discover the health benefits of this).

From a 'green' point of view, underfloor heating is desirable, not only because it uses fuel more efficiently, but because it does not dry out the air too much by moving it around unnecessarily. This will offer health benefits to people with sensitive respiratory systems. Evidence also suggests that where underfloor heating is used, occupiers will tolerate lower temperatures, because the warmth is more 'natural'. This again offers opportunities for good energy saving. Our own experiences suggest that 18-20°C is acceptable.

Heat sources for underfloor heating

Underfloor heating systems can be operated using a variety of heat sources. Any kind of fuel can be used to warm the water, including condensing boilers. However, using a small heat store may be the best way to integrate such a boiler, as to operate at full efficiency condensing boilers need to have a high differential between the feed and return flows.

A number of green projects have taken advantage of underfloor heating due to the low flow temperatures needed. In fact they are ideal for connecting to alternative heat sources, such as solar panels, a heat recovery system, ground source heat pumps (but please not grid connected), or a wood or other biomass stove (e.g. straw, wood chips or pellets). Such systems can also be used in combination.

Underfloor heating systems are generally no more expensive to install than a comparable radiator system. A further advantage of this form of heating is the low maintenance required. Once the pipework, a (continuous winding loop - usually one large loop per room (advise max 75 metres long), is installed, there is little to go wrong and the in-floor part of the system could last the life of the building.

Underfloor heating need not be limited to ground floors. It can also be installed between joists in upper floors, either attached to the sides of floor joists or on top of specially fitted insulation. A point to beware of though in any 'joisted' floor installation, be it ground floor or upper floor. Such floors tend to be draughty and some clever design strategy will therefore be needed for the system to perform efficiently in these circumstances.

Floor coverings

Virtually any kind of floor covering can be used with underfloor heating. On a solid or screeded floor, tiles, stone or slate are probably the best, as they transmit the heat effectively and are unaffected by changes in temperature or humidity, but take care on thickness - the thicker the slate, then the farther down the heating pipes will be, which could affect the heating-up times. Wood floors are fine – so long as the wood is perfectly dry before it is laid, or warping can occur. Many people opt for laminated wood flooring as it is thought to be more stable than real wood boards but there may be other environmental issues to consider, such as adhesives or origin of the species used within the laminations. Carpet, being somewhat insulating, is the least desirable. It will require the system to run at a slightly higher temperature, and could, with the added warmth of the heated floor, provide an improved breeding ground for dust mites, etc. Sheet floorcoverings, such as linoleum, rubber or, dare we say, vinyl, should first be checked out with the manufacturers before use.

A 'heat store' floor of concrete and slate

a case study by Keith Hall

I installed a heat store floor system across two-thirds of the ground floor area of my renovated farmhouse. The floors have three circuits, and hot water is supplied from a 2600 litre heat store, fed by a high efficiency wood fired boiler. The water is delivered through a mixing port, which ensures that the water temperature delivered to the floor is no higher than 50°C. This is achieved by mixing the returning water (bottom of heat store) with the flow water from the top of the store (which can be as high as 95°C as the wood boiler operates at very high temperatures for maximum efficiency).

The floor comprises of 150mm of polystyrene insulation below 125mm concrete into which the heating pipes are embedded (see diagram below). The finished surface is 7mm thick reclaimed roofing slates bedded on a 25mm cement screed. To the untrained eye it appears that thick slate slabs have been used. Essentially the pipes were kept in loops and in the (vertical) centre of the slab by attaching them to reinforcing mesh while the concrete was poured.

The system generally works well, except for two design faults which have had to be 'chalked up to experience'. The first is that very little perimeter insulation was installed between the edge of the floor and the thick stone walls. My reasoning at the time, now thought to be badly flawed, was that heat leaking from the floor to the walls (old stone and rubble) would help to keep them dry in the absence of any kind of damp proof course. However, through a number of other measures, and the fact that the house is built in a reasonably free draining shale, the walls are essentially dry now but the edges of the floors are always cold. On future projects I would definitely return the polystyrene up to just below the slate surface. Another mistake was in having one overly long run of pipework. The three circuits were installed: 50m, 75m and 100m . The problem is that the 100m circuit required far more pumping pressure than the two shorter ones. I have therefore had to install a second pump on the 100m circuit with a zone valve connected to a thermostat which shuts off the shorter circuits when the areas served by them are up to temperature. This allows the longer circuit to benefit from the full pressure. This has worked well as a solution but could have been avoided. In future I would limit circuits to a maximum of 75m.

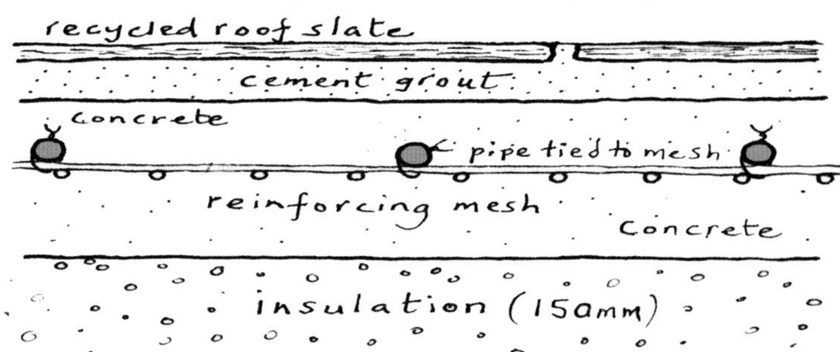

Water and appliances

Opportunities for saving water start with a change in our attitude to water use. Here **Stephen Lawndes** and **Keith Hall** review water saving techniques that can be incorporated into our homes and buildings ...

The water flowing out of our taps has undergone complex and energy intensive processing to clean it ready for drinking and pump it from the reservoir or rivers to our buildings. We take water for granted but we would soon miss it if it stopped flowing. Drinking, washing, cooking, bathing and showering, flushing toilets and watering gardens all rely on a constant, never-ending supply. Offices and community buildings, consume vast quantities of water for large scale catering, swimming pools and manufacturing processes. Here we will take a brief and introductory look at what opportunities there are to provide fittings, components and other measures that help reduce water consumption.

First of all it might be interesting to take a look at what the Code for Sustainable Homes (CSH) will be expecting new homes to achieve in energy saving over the next few years. The table below outlines the expectations and as was discussed in some detail in chapter two, the CSH requirements will be introduced over the next few years with Code level 6 becoming a mandatory requirement in 2016. However, it should be noted that the detail of the water saving category of CSH is proving to be very controversial and may well change between now and that date.

Code level	***Maximum potable water consumption in litres, per person, per day***
Level 1	*120*
Level 2	*120*
Level 3	*105*
Level 4	*105*
Level 5	*80*
Level 6	*80*

Potable water consumption for new homes will need to be reduced in gradual steps by 2016 if the Code for Sustainable Homes continues to be implemented.

Source: Code for Sustainable Homes Technical Guide

But back to the here and now. What can the rest of us do that already have a home and want to implement water saving right away. Water bills are not getting cheaper and droughts are not the only thing that interrupts water supplies. Leakages, floods and sheer demand means that the water main is under severe pressure to cope. Let's take a quick look at the regular fittings and appliances to see where some saving can be made.

Taps

Taps left running can waste enormous amounts of water. When the opportunity arises to install replacements, spray-head taps should be used. Spray head taps are particularly suited to wash hand basins and can save up to 50% of water, compared to conventional taps. These work by slowing the flow of the water by passing the it through a very fine mesh nozzle which adds air to the stream so it appears to be a full flow. They are elegant and very successful.

Where taps are not due for replacement, an adjustable flow restrictor can be fitted near to taps so that a lower flow rate can be set. This could be adjusted to ensure the best compromise and could give similar savings to the spray-head taps, if implemented with care. Because the water regulations now require all outlets to incorporate an isolating valve of some type, fitting a small flow regulating service valve, rather than a standard isolating valve would kill two birds with one stone.

Water saving shower head with flow regulator.

Regulated aerators are available to retro-fit on to many existing taps or shower heads (see above). These work well and can offer good water savings if there is adequate water pressure.

Baths, perhaps due to fashion or a desire for more comfort tend to be getting larger rather than smaller. The CSH is addressing this issue for new homes but smaller baths may not be a measure that people will tolerate and many in the industry believe that most small baths builders install to meet the CSH will be ripped out within the first year. Not exactly the environmental saving envisaged! There is no easy answer to sizes of baths that people should have or the number of times they are used. Suffice to say that water pricing and education may be the only real solution here short of draconinan measures.

Hot water supply

Although we have discussed taps and their use with hot water, there are some more particular issues relating to hot water outlets and distribution pipe work which will affect efforts to conserve water. For instance, the thermal insulation of all of the hot and cold water distribution pipes should not be overlooked. As hot and cold water pipes are usually run together, the mains cold water may be warmed up by the adjacent un-insulated hot water pipe and vice versa. Apart from the obvious heat lost from any un-insulated hot water pipe, users will also waste water by running the cold water for prolonged periods when they try to get a cool drink. There will also be condensation on the outside of the pipe if insulation is ignored.

On the hot water side it is worth looking (when maintenance opportunities arise) for ways of reducing lengths of pipe runs. 'Dead-legs', i.e. lengths of pipe work with un-circulated hot water, should be kept to an absolute minimum, so that hot water is readily available at all draw-offs. Some argue the case for a hot water circuit and these are discussed more fully in Volume 2 of the Green Building Bible. As previously mentioned, if dead legs on the hot water system are too long, a great deal of water will be wasted before the hot water appears at the tap.

Toilets

Flushing toilets is usually the principal consumer of water within most buildings. Since conventional WCs utilise drinking quality water and generate sewerage for processing, it is in the interests of those who wish to reduce water consumption to seriously consider ways in which use can be moderated. Dual flush toilets[1] can offer great savings against even the most modern low flush loos, so the replacement of older existing units, during refurbishment

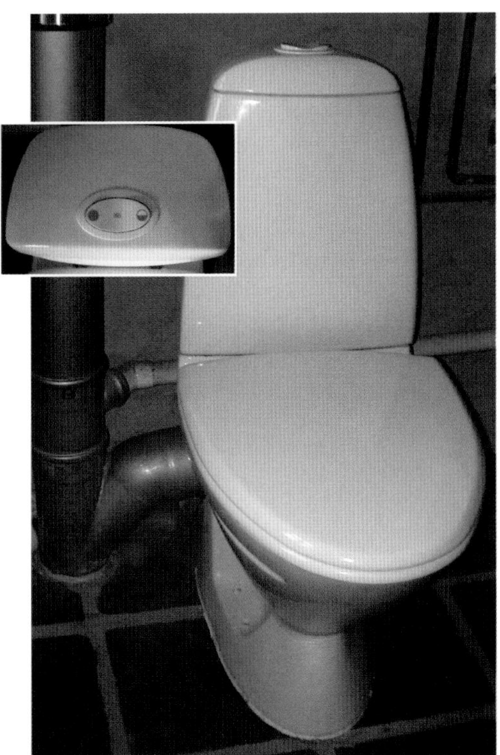

The ifo Cera dual flush loo flushes just 2 or 4 litres.

projects, is usually worthwhile. It is possible to install WCs with ultra low flush capacity, utilising a four and two litre dual flush. If your loo flushes 9 litres (80% of houses still use this size cistern) then there are retrofit systems available [2]. Once fitted, the average household of 2.4 people could save 27,000 litres per year, which equates to a saving of around £50 per annum and rising.

Composting toilets

Composting or waterless toilets compost the waste into a form that can be safely used as fertiliser. Human waste contains nitrogen as well as magnesium, sulphur, phosphorus, potassium and other trace elements that are, in the form of compost, beneficial for plants and help condition soil. Rather than flushing the waste away with water the user throws in a handful of 'soak' (sawdust or shredded cardboard). A chamber under the composting toilet receives the waste and the soak and facilitates the composting process. Composting chambers range in size from a large box located within the toilet area, to a chamber under the floor. In most cases more space needs to be allocated for a composting toilet compared to a conventional WC and access must be provided for final removal of the compost and for interim turning and raking. Because human faeces contain pathogens, care needs to be exercised and contact with waste in its raw state avoided. Of course there needs to be a ready use for the compost. Without a garden you might need to rely on your friends to take your compost away!

Urinals

Water flush urinals are commonly installed in public toilets and in toilets within commercial premises. Where urinals are installed, automatic flush controls should be installed as a minimum. With the older type of automatic flush, the urinal stalls are only flushed if the automatic flush valve senses a change in water pressure. Newer devices enable flushing if movement in front of the urinal is sensed, using an infra-red detector. Although automatic flush control valves reduce water consumption, if you really want to save water in a urinal installation you might consider turning the water off to the stalls altogether. Waterless urinals, in essence, are just that – a urinal bowl without the flush. However, they need to incorporate a syphonic trap, or an outlet in the urinal waste with a perfume impregnated pad, designed to reduce the smell of urine.

Urine-separating flush toilets are a variation on the waterless urinal and ordinary loo. Aimed at the domestic application these toilets separate solid and liquid waste at source. They usually work on the principle of accepting liquid waste at the front of the toilet bowl and solid waste at the rear. Because the solids and liquids are separated in the toilet bowl, the former can be flushed in the conventional manner, while the latter requires no water to flush away.

Showers

Although taking a shower normally uses much less water than a soak in the bath, there is still scope to ensure that the water utilised by a shower is no more than it needs to be. The problem here, though, is that a low flow rate from a shower does not give a very invigorating experience. So whilst flow restrictors can be installed, their effect is likely to be at the expense of shower performance. The use of thermostatic shower mixer valves, with a fixed maximum flow and mains pressure atomising shower heads, can help maintain acceptable performance, even with low water flows. The available water pressure head plays an important part in water flow delivery. Direct mains fed outlets will almost always receive a higher flow pressure, compared to tank fed outlets, unless you live in an area of low mains water pressure. The available pressure at outlets, such as showers and taps fed from loft tanks, rather than direct from the mains, is dependant upon how high the storage tank is above the outlet. The higher the tank, the greater the pressure head and therefore the strength of flow of water from the outlet.

White goods

If you are fitting in new appliances, such as washing machines and dishwashers, you should be looking at 'A' or 'AA' rated units. In the case of washing machines and dish washers this label means that the appliance should be a low consumer of water, compared with a 'B' or 'C' rated machine. It is not always the case that an 'A' rated machine is more expensive to purchase over a lower rated appliance and of course it always pays to shop around.

It is possible to purchase hand operated 'pressure wash' devices, that are claimed to use only a very small amount of water and do not run on electricity[3]. Hot water is poured into and sealed in an airtight washer drum. The heat from the water causes the air in the drum to expand, which builds pressure, driving soap and water into the clothing. Hand operation is required to agitate the clothes within the drum and effect cleaning. However, whether in reality, these sorts of devices use significantly less water to achieve the same result as a conventional 'A' rated machine, is difficult to conclude without reliable data (but of course they will use less electricity).

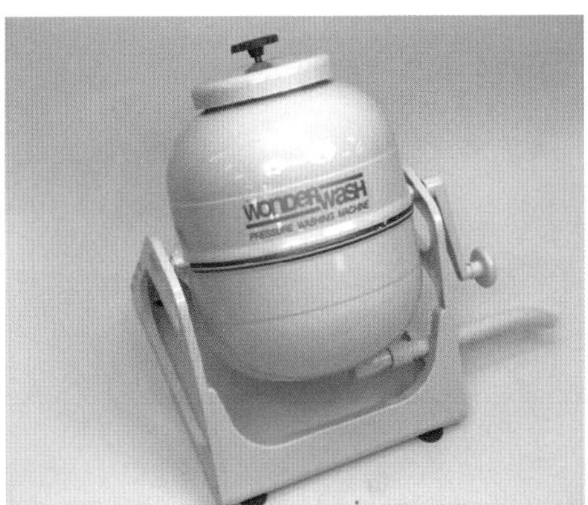

For those who want to keep fit, save water and elctricity, the Wonder Wash is hand operated pressure washing machine. Just turn the handle!

Rainwater harvesting

Rainwater harvesting is a new way of obtaining water for some uses around the home or building. If a rainwater harvesting system is installed carefully it could certainly reduce demand on mains water and provide some measure of security in the event of mains failure. However, in all but the most complex of systems, it can only really supply toilet flushing and perhaps car washing. This subject is discussed more fully later in this book

Conclusion

This article has introduced and discussed some of the technologies and systems that could be incorporated into a project with the aim of saving water. Many of these solutions are likely to require the involvement of experienced professionals (a plumber at least) in order to implement them successfully. At the other end of the scale there are comparatively simple solutions, such as the installation of water saving taps and retrofit components that are possible for a competent DIY'er to undertake and will go a good way to reducing consumption in a reliable and cost effective manner. The way in which the building is used will ultimately have the biggest influence on the water consumption and occupiers need to be encouraged to adopt responsible usage patterns, so that water use can be optimised. With the cost of our water predicted to soar in the near future and the introduction of water meters on both existing and new buildings, there has never been a better time to take control of your water use.

References

1. A good example of a high quality, dual flush lavatory in the UK is the Ifô Cera range which is available from: ***www.rainharvesting.co.uk*** *or* ***www.greenbuildingstore.co.uk***

2. One example of a retrofit WC flow limiter would be from a company called Interflush who make a Water Council approved product (also on Water Technolgy List for Enhanced Capital Allowance) that can be simply installed in most common WCs: ***www.interflush.co.uk***

3. Hand operated washing machine. Available in UK from Mailspeed Marine: ***www.mailspeedmarine.com/ProductDetails/mcs/productID/101375***

Further reading

'Sewage Solutions; answering the call of nature' by N Grant, M Moodie and C Weedon. This book deals with all aspects of non-mains sustainable sewage treatment.

'Lifting the Lid; an ecological approach to toilet systems' by P Harper and L Halestrap is probably the classic book on waterless toilets!

'The Humanure Handbook' by J Jenkins

'The Toilet Papers' by Sim Von der Ryn

The above books are available from Green Shop: 01452 770629 ***www.greenshop.co.uk***

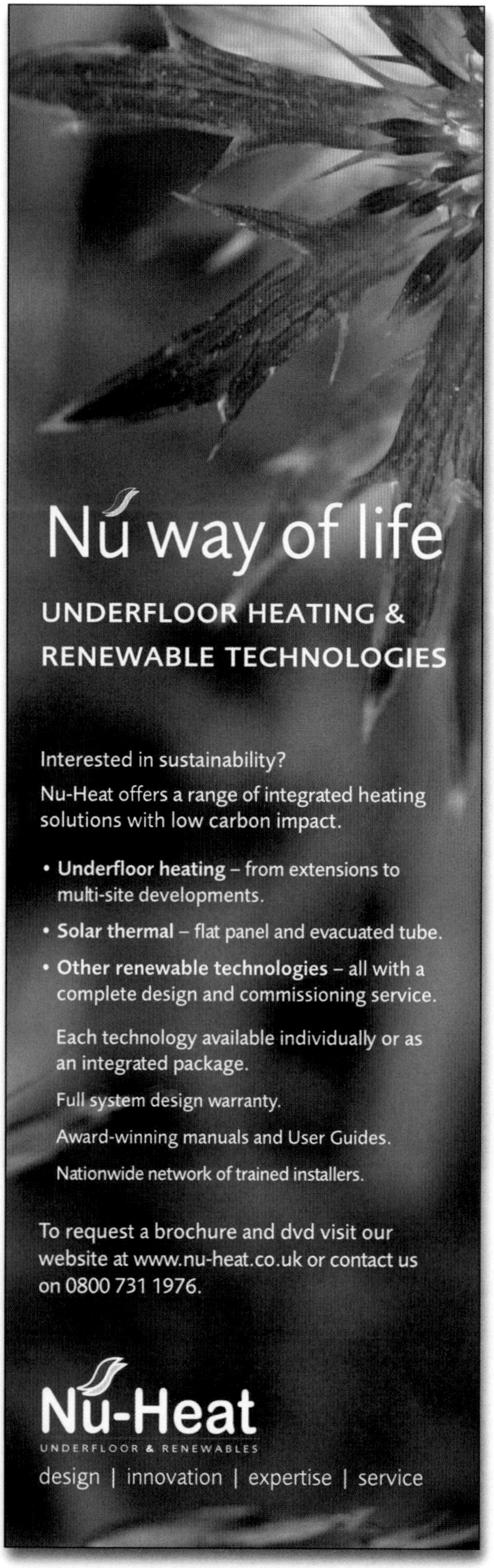

West Wales Renewable Energy
Electricity from the Sun and Wind
Photovoltaic panels from BP Solar
Small and medium wind generators
Full installation service
Workshop and demonstration site
Advice to DIY installers
ATA Member
Clear Skies and EST accredited
Phone: 01974 298851
Fax: 01974 298060
Mobile: 07977 057723
Email: charles@solawind.demon.co.uk

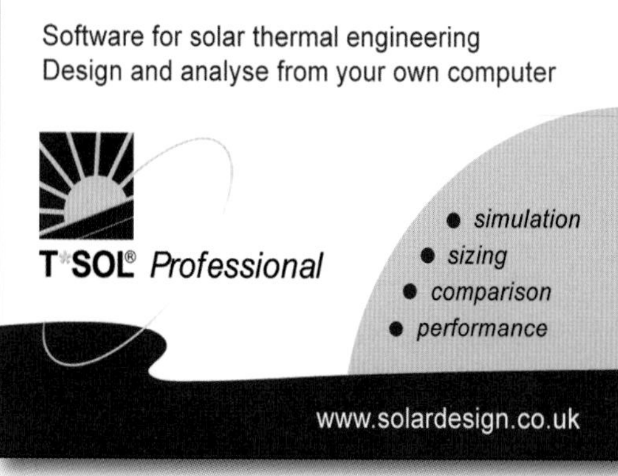
Software for solar thermal engineering
Design and analyse from your own computer
T*SOL® Professional
simulation
sizing
comparison
performance
www.solardesign.co.uk

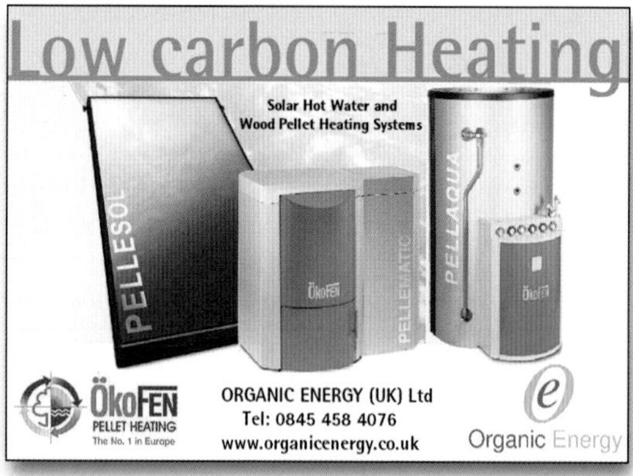
Low carbon Heating
Solar Hot Water and Wood Pellet Heating Systems
PELLESOL
PELLEMATIC
PELLAQUA
ÖkoFEN
PELLET HEATING
ORGANIC ENERGY (UK) Ltd
Tel: 0845 458 4076
www.organicenergy.co.uk
Organic Energy

ME Mech Services
Plumbing & Heating, Solar Thermal systems
Wood Fired central heating
East Midlands & South Yorkshire
01522 520146
memech@btinternet.com
Matthew Elkin, 41 Cross o'Cliff Hill, Lincoln, LN5 8PR

Euroheat
The Stove Company
Green with Envy
Not only do Euroheat have a range of wood stoves that are undeniably beautiful,
with a maximum efficiency of 84%, they are also an ecologically desirable investment
Traditional
Harmony
INSPIRATIONAL
Inserts
CONTEMPORARY
Hwam
Stanford
full range of
exclusive
accessories
now
available
Euroheat
The Stove Company
Euroheat
Unit 2, Court Farm Business Park, Bishops Frome,
Worcestershire WR6 5AY
AUTOMATED BROCHURE REQUEST LINE 01885 491156
TO SPEAK TO ONE OF OUR ADVISORS 01885 491112
www.euroheat.co.uk info@euroheat.co.uk

4 Materials and methods

General material selection

Mark Gorgolewski introduces this chapter with a look at some basic selection principles that we can apply to materials for our projects ...

Many building materials use large amounts of energy and produce toxic wastes during manufacture. Some are not healthy to use or to live with, and many are difficult to dispose of safely, as well as having adverse effects on the environment when land-filled or incinerated. All of these issues need to be considered at the earliest opportunity when designing our buildings. The choice of materials and components for improved environmental specification is complex, and requires the balancing of many issues which often conflict.

It is important to consider the environmental impact of a material over its full lifetime; manufacture, construction, operation, maintenance, demolition, and disposal. And in each phase it is important to take into account the energy used, resources consumed, waste generated, potential for reuse or recycling, health impacts and pollution emissions generated. In addition, materials need to be durable and perform well throughout their life to limit the environmental impact of their maintenance and replacement.

General guidelines

It is not easy or practical to rank materials, as their environmental impact will be linked to the purpose they will used for in the building, and how they are to be integrated. However, environmental performance is one of the main aspects that we should consider when choosing materials for a project. The following are a set of general guidelines that can be used.

Minimise waste - try to minimise the volume of materials used and avoid wasteful specification. Using less material can reduce the overall environmental impact of the building. Planning the building around standard sizes of elements, such as plasterboard and timber, can reduce off-cuts on site. Minimise waste through co-ordinated design and site practices. Most waste occurs through poor co-ordination of components during design and badly organised site procedures. Consider how to co-ordinate dimensions to reduce material use, perhaps through a design grid, and be sure to employ accurate material ordering and site procedures for storage and handling.

A significant amount of site waste is from discarded packaging or over-ordering. A site strategy is required to maximise recycling of packaging waste, in particular pallets, other timber, cardboard, plastic containers and sheets and polypropylene bags. There will often be conflicts and trade-offs between the various principles at stake and a decision about each material or component will have to be made on a point by point basis. The specifier must use their judgment to make an appropriate choice for each particular case and keep the client informed. The good news is that this is all a learning process and once instilled into the thought process it becomes second nature.

Use natural or local materials - as materials closer to their natural state will tend to have had less processing, which often means less energy use, less waste and less pollution. Local materials can reduce the need for transport and benefits the local economy and community. However, it is important to consider other factors and ensure that the materials have not been moved around the country for processing, before being returned to their starting point for delivery to site. Look for local, reused components. Local materials also minimise road transport. About 30% of UK road freight is due to movement of construction materials, which contributes significantly to climate change and local environmental problems. Any project should set out a strategy for minimising the impact of transport through; using locally sourced materials wherever possible, batching deliveries to site to ensure full loads are used, wherever possible using local labour on site, providing shared transport for labour to site and providing transport links to the building during the in use phase.

Even natural materials need to be harvested in a sustainable way or the environment will be degraded. Timber has a vital role to play in green building, yet the timber industry is still having a huge effect on the environment. If sourced from outside the UK then all wood components used should be timber certified by the FSC (Forestry Stewardship Council) or the PEFC (Programme for the Endorsement of Forest Certification).

Choose durable materials - replacement of a component during the life of a building adds life-cycle environmental impact. Durable components that have a long-life are often beneficial as they avoid replacement and maintenance.

Maintenance of non-durable materials, such as painting, and even cleaning, can be very environmentally damaging over the life of the building as it occurs regularly for many years, and once the building is complete the designer usually has little control over this. It is therefore beneficial to minimise the need for regular maintenance, such as painting and replacement of floor coverings, by using appropriate materials. Surfaces, such as polished concrete floors and masonry internal finishes, can minimize the need for replacement. Natural materials (see later) have durability if they are kept near their natural state in the building. For instance it is not wise to paint timber as it prevents it from breathing and can trap moisture leading to rot and deterioration. Research by the Timber Research and Development Association (TRADA) found that un-finished windows of appropriately durable species of timber proved to be far more durable than painted windows.

Materials that may seem durable often are not. For instance, PVC guttering suffers from fast UV degradation and constant shrinking and expansion from heating by the sun causes early failure of the seals leading to leakage and regular replacement. Windows that are sold as 'non-maintenance' should really be called 'non-maintainable' because the description really means - when a component part breaks, the whole window needs to be thrown away and replaced.

Use materials from renewable sources - to avoid depleting stocks of non-renewable materials, it is often preferable to use renewable materials. These are materials that will re-grow or regenerate at a rate which at least replaces what is taken, or harvested. Recycled or reclaimed materials can be considered to be a renewable resource even if they are made from fossil fuels. Their use and eventual re-recycling can save on primary non-renewable resources. Reuse of components can be very beneficial as this avoids waste and reduces new manufacture. Research suggests that this strategy can lead to significant greenhouse gas savings. However, for some critical components, such as glazing, it may be more appropriate to use the latest high performance systems. A word of warning though. In some cases, the energy used in transport and reprocessing of recycled materials can be high, and negate the benefits that were originally desired.

Appropriate design and construction practices can help components to be easily extracted at the end of their useful life, without being damaged, in such a way that they can be reused or recycled. This means careful consideration of connections and junctions between materials to make them reversible, and the use of mechanical fixings, such as screws and bolts, that can be undone.

Source from ethical manufacturers - some manufacturers have developed materials and products that are aimed at reducing environmental and/or ethical impact. Others have ISO 14001 environmental management systems in place to control their environmental impact. These manufacturers deserve support, but conversely, beware of green-wash. Some manufacturers or suppliers happily provide environmental data and take environmental control of their processes seriously and will be able to provide appropriate environmental information on their products in their literature. However, again beware of green-wash, as some manufacturers may make very general or unsubstantiated environmental claims.

Avoid toxic components and finishes - this is a complex area and general guidance is difficult. However, where they are necessary, low emission or preferably natural paints should be used. Mineral based paints are good for mineral surfaces, such as renders and plasters externally, and have shown great durability. Breathable wood-stains, based on natural oils and waxes can be used if unfinished timber cannot be accommodated, but be aware that regular maintenance will be required once applied.

Avoid hazardous materials - such as lead. Also, avoid materials that are significant sources of VOCs (volatile organic compounds) in the indoor environment should be avoided. These include many synthetic carpets and man made fibres, vinyl flooring and wall covering materials and many adhesives and sealants. Solvents are used in timber treatment, many paints (even water based ones), and polyurethane coatings for timber. Many wood based boards contain formaldehyde, such as chipboard, melamine faced chipboard (kitchen units), plywood, MDF and OSB (though OSB has the lowest content of all).

Conclusion

Often, the above strategies may conflict with each other and the specifier needs to make judgments about what is most appropriate. A local material may not be the most appropriate for reasons such as the availability of a better performing material from further away. Or a recycled material may be available but only from a long distance. An example of such conflicts is bamboo flooring, which is a fast growing renewable timber product, but is imported from China, and may be subject to questions regarding the growing and harvesting and certainly the transport issues. It is therefore important to look at the bigger picture and then make informed choices. If a more scientific approach is needed, life cycle assessment methods could be used to compare environmental impacts.

Further information

GreenPro, the on-line eco-building product database at ***www.newbuilder.co.uk*** *contains listings of over 1000 building products available in the UK that have ecological merits.*

'Green Building Handbook' by T Woolley, S Kimmins, P Harrison & R Harrison

'Ecology of Building Materials' by Bjorn Berge available from ***www.greenbuildingpress.co.uk***

'BRE Green Guide to Specification' - available from the Building Research Establishment: ***www.bre.co.uk***

'Handbook of Sustainable Building' by D Anink, C. Boonstra & J Mak, James and James, 1996.

Greenpeace web site for PVC alternatives: ***http://archive.greenpeace.org/~toxics/pvcdatabase***

'Environmental handbook for building and civil engineering projects', Vol 1 and 2, from CIRIA: ***www.ciria.org.uk***

List of EU eco-label products including some construction products: ***www.eco-label.com***

London Hazards Centre for information about emissions from paints and other products: ***www.lhc.org.uk***

Forestry Stewardship Council: ***www.fsc-uk.org***

Programme for the Endorsement of Forest Certification: ***www.pefc.org***

UK Woodland Assurance Scheme: ***www.forestry.gov.uk***

Certified Forest Products Council: ***www.certifiedwood.org***

Healthy Flooring Network: ***www.healthyflooring.org***

ISO 14001: ***www.iso14000.com***

'Natural Building - a guide to materials and techniques' by T Woolley available from: ***www.greenshop.co.uk.***

Choosing materials

John Shore tells us that if we are careful in our choice of materials and processes we can minimise the ecological impact during construction and in long term use of the building ...

The purpose of green building design is to aim to achieve a sustainable balance between human needs and environmental protection. This balance is not just a scientific matter - following your intuition is equally valuable and essential. Recent history shows us that many of the fantastic innovations and inventions once considered as wonderful and life-enhancing have often proved to do more harm than good.

In green building, the philosophy of 'less is more' really does apply. We need to create healthy environments and this can only really be achieved with materials that are simple and close to nature.

Making weighted decisions

We all have very individual likes and dislikes about how we should live and the same applies to buildings and the homes that we want to live in. Some are drawn to living closer to nature and like building with biodegradable materials, while others are much more risk-averse and argue fervently for products that seem to offer long-lasting properties, such as concrete and foam-plastic insulation. However, the 'long lasting' adage is not always properly applied to the long lasting materials. Through careful design we can avoid the need for many of the less eco-friendly materials, without compromising longevity or durability.

The popularity of green building among the general public has begun to encourage a stampede of false claims about many conventional building products. For instance, many manufacturers argue that 'green' equates to just energy saving. They draw a veil over the environmental and social costs of materials extraction, processing, toxicity issues and the manner of production, or the costs of sales and distribution. Therefore care needs to be taken, since similar products from different sources may vary greatly in their environmental properties and impacts.

While it is often true that the embodied-energy of a material may be insignificant, compared to the energy-saving potential a material offers over the lifetime of a building, we should always aim to find and use materials which deliver on all aspects of environmental sustainability.

In order to lighten the burden we place on the environment, we can create buildings mainly from renewable, 'biological' materials, which rely on the income, rather than the capital resources of the planet. Thankfully, we now have a wide range of green materials so we can use glass, metals and plastics more efficiently, where greener alternatives do not yet exist. Non-PVC pipes and cables are available. Kitchens can be made from real wood or pine-board and do not have to be full of energy consuming appliances. And if we claim to be green, do we really need to fill our floors and walls with a spaghetti of plastic pipes and electrical cables?

To help us draw a clear distinction between natural and processed building materials, it is useful to pidgeonhole materials into five main groupings:

- short term renewable origin (timber, wool, straw etc)
- extracted or mined (earth, sand and gravel)
- extracted and further processed (lime, cement, plaster, slate, stone, brick)
- extracted and highly processed (steel, glass and plastics)

- recycled or reclaimed (reused timber, brick, aggregate, steel, glass, insulation).

Many green designers and builders prefer to work mainly with renewable, extracted and recycled materials and, by doing so, help the building industry evolve and develop along a more natural path.

Material properties

We can use materials' properties and performance characteristics to help us in our choices. For instance if we are looking for an insulation, then the thermal performance characteristics may be one of the first things we would like to find out (see Table1). Following this we should look into the suitability of the range of insulations that we found within the performance band, for use in (a) the type of structure we are designing and (b) the environment in which we intend to use it.

Having now narrowed this down, we could then take a look at the embodied energy of our chosen product or material (see Table 2) but please be aware of the enormous range in some of the values shown in the tables. For instance, if we were looking into windows – aluminium (commonly used as a spacer in insulated glazing units) has a thermal conductivity of 198W/mK, while the silicone used in superspacer is just 0.158W/mK!

No product will be perfect in every respect. The building designer has to consider an incredibly wide range of information and possibilities and then try to select the best solution. Do local materials really exist and in the quantities required? Would their use be appropriate for a low-energy, green building? Is quarrying or mining ecological, desirable and sustainable, even if it is local? What is true though, about localisation, if we were all requesting (with supporting knowledge) materials with the high environmental credentials, we would then be encouraging the development of new green businesses and lifestyles.

Natural materials

Timber frame, recycled paper insulation, straw

Table 1. Thermal conductivity of materials.
For guidance only.

Material (highest to lowest)	W/mK
Copper	380.000
Aluminium	198.000
Steel	48.300
Granite	3.810
Limestone	1.530
Dense brickwork	1.470
Dense concrete	1.440
Sand/cement render	1.410
Very packed damp soil	1.400
Sandstone	1.295
Bricks (engineering)	1.150
Dry soil	1.140
Clay bricks (compressed, unfired)	0.950
Brickwork and tile hanging	0.840
Loose soil	0.700
Water	0.580
Adobe	0.520
Glass	0.500
Glaster (recycled ground glass in lime plaster)	0.378
Earth blocks	0.340
Thermalite blocks	0.140-0.190
Plaster board	0.180
Recycled wood-fibre and gypsum plasterboard	0.176
Hardwood	0.160
Superspacer (warm-edge glazing spacer)	0.158
Clay board (alternative to plasterboard)	0.140
Softwood / plywood	0.120 - 0.138
Oil tempered hardboard	0.120
Chipboard	0.108
Stellac wood / ThermoWood	0.100
Thermoplan multi-cellular clay blocks	0.100-0.120
Straw bales (dry)	0.080-0.100
Strawboard	0.098
Woodwool slab (light)	0.082
Soil stony (normal)	0.052
Sawdust	0.051
Bitvent 15 sheathing board	0.050
Foamed glass insulation	0.036-0.046
Diffutherm T&G wood-fibre boards	0.044
Cork	0.043
Fibre-glass insulation	0.040
IsoNat hemp/recycled cotton insulation	0.039
Hemp and recycled cotton insulation	0.039
Thermafleece sheeps-wool insulation	0.039
Inno-Therm (recycled cotton) insulation	0.038
Warmcel 500 wall insulation	0.036
Warmcel roof insulation	0.035
Mineral wool insulation	0.032
Rigid polystyrene insulation	0.029-0.036
Rigid polyurethane foam insulation	0.022-0.028
Rigid phenolic foam insulation	0.021-0.024

Table 2. Primary embodied energy of materials.
For guidance only.

Material (highest to lowest)	(approx) kWh/m³
Lead	157,414
Copper	133,000
Steel (iron ore) blast furnace	63,000-80,000
Aluminium	55,868
Plastics	47,000
Steel (recycled) electric arc furnace	29,669
Glass	23,000
Fibre cement slates	12,783
Cement	2,860
Aluminium (recycled)	2,793-3,910
Clay tiles	1,520
Bricks (non flettons)	1,462
Plastic insulation	1,125
Gypsum plaster / plasterboard	900
Autoclaved bricks	800
Concrete 2 : 4	800
Imported softwood	754
Foamed glass insulation	751
Concrete Tiles	630
Concrete 1 : 3 : 6	600
Lightweight clinker blocks	600
Local slate	540
Local stone tiles	450
Sand cement render	400
Bricks (fletton)	440
Mineral fibre insulation	230
Home grown green oak	220
Crushed granite	150
Cellulose (recycled paper) insulation	133
Home grown softwood (air dried)	110
Sand and gravel	45
Sheeps wool insulation	30

Sources: Centre for Alternative Technology; Environmental Science Handbook; Pittsburgh Corning; Timber Trade Federation; CIRIA; GreenPro.

bale and earth, all are close to natural and all are becoming popular materials for green building. Each brings its own strengths and weaknesses – no one method or material offers the only solution for all situations. We may need to combine a mixed range of materials in order to create successful buildings. A straw bale wall, with external timber cladding and internal earth plastering, might be a logical strategy. Vapour-diffusive materials, which transport moisture from the interior to the outside air, are increasingly popular.

Timber (from sustainable sources) is versatile as a beautiful, structural, easy to work material which may be locally available. New vapour-diffusive membranes enable us to build timber frame buildings with high levels of airtightness and greatly reduced heat loss. Very simple and affordable walls can be made using timber studs, clad externally with rendered wood-fibre board to reduce thermal bridging, such as shown below. The possibilities are endless and as you read through this book the options and opportunities will become clearer.

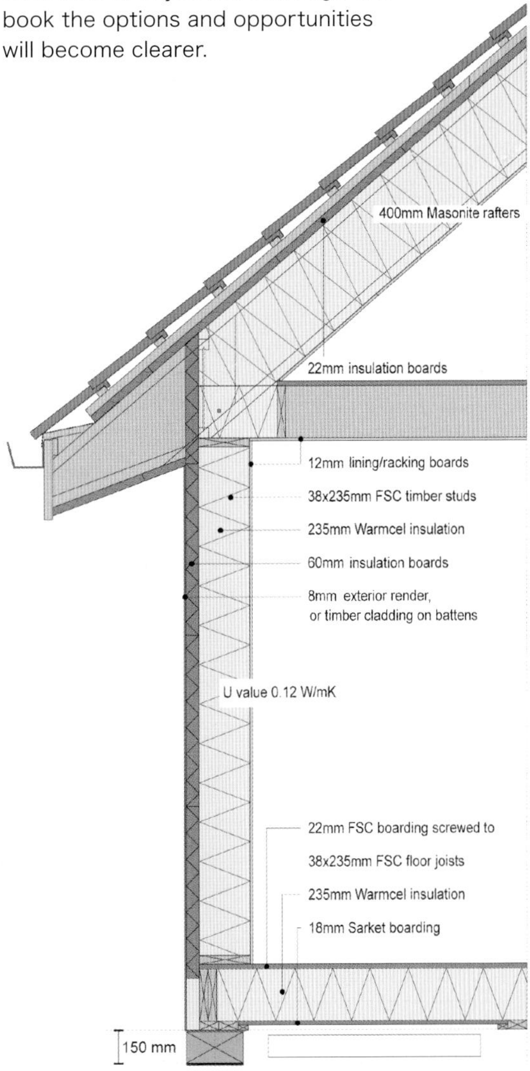

Design details of a lightweight, thermally efficient, timber framed building.
Image courtesy of John Shore, Ecologic Design.

Thermal Mass

There are various schools of thought on how much thermal mass to include in a building. All buildings have some level of mass, regardless of the general make-up, as all materials have some thermal capacity which will take up heat (see table right). This article considers how much thought or 'weighting' the building designer should give to this aspect and how decisions should be based on thermal mass impact on the style of building or the choice of materials? The answer to this question is, of course, there are many factors influencing the design, and thermal mass is another new one of many. Passive solar design as discussed in the previous chapter will be somewhat dependant on thermal mass to be effective and other influences will include the site, the local climate, and the uses the building has to fulfil.

Heavyweight buildings

Interestingly, studies of heavy-weight buildings have revealed the need for constant background heating to provide thermal comfort. Since mass has to be heated, it soon becomes clear that too much mass can be as much a problem as too little. Also, the usefulness of solid materials as a thermal buffer reduces with thickness and is highly influenced by surface area. Hot thermal mass will not cool a building but can contribute to overheating. As Table 3 shows, the materials commonly specified for thermal mass have poor thermal capacity.

Lightweight buildings

It is worth noting that many people already live in buildings that have minimal thermal mass (timber framed buildings) and provided that these were designed and built with appropriate sized glazed areas, shading and sufficient insulation, they are not likely to experience summer overheating. However, the potential technical problems of reliably keeping our buildings cool in a future global-warming scenario should not be underestimated or idly cast aside as unimportant. For those wanting to ensure some amount of thermal mass it is worth remembering that a relatively small amount of water could provide a simple solution to the provision of thermal storage in lightweight, super-insulated buildings. Water is more than twice as efficient as dense concrete, while being ecological, non-hazardous and available at zero cost. Glaster (recycled ground glass encapsulated in lime plaster) has thermal storage potential for ceilings, walls and floors. Ceilings are ideally placed to act as a heat-exchange medium, whereas floors and walls are often rendered ineffective by furniture and insulating coverings.

Phase-change materials (PCM)[1] are now becoming available as a type of plasterboard for use on ceilings and walls. These could be used to increase the thermal capacity of new and existing lightweight buildings. There is also potential for the further development of PCM using plant-derived oils and waxes.

References

1. Green Building magazine Vol 17, No3: ***www.greenbuildingmagazine.co.uk***

Table 3. Thermal capacity of a range of materials
For guidance only.

Material	*Wh/m³ K
Phase change material (PCM)**	5,000
Glass	1,250
Water	1,158
Cast iron	1,104
Lead	1,040
Steel	1,014
Slate	653
Stone	450 - 650
Dense concrete blocks	483
Sasmox gypsum-wood board	458
Alluvial clay - 40% sand	457
Plaster on render	440
Quarry tiles	418
Brickwork	374
Earth	356
Lightweight concrete blocks	336
Gypsum plaster	314
Dry oak, beech or ash	252
Woodwool slabs	250
Wood chipboard	224
Gypsum plasterboard	219
Softwood flooring	217
Aerated concrete blocks	140
Tradical hemp-lime wall infill	157

*The heat (watts per hour) needed to raise the temperature of one cubic metre of material by 1° C.

** Gypsum plaster with encapsulated PCM (room temperature swing 22° C to 27° C).

Reclaimed and waste materials

Are there opportunities for establishing closed loops for the flow of materials in construction? **Mark Gorgolewski** considers the options ...

The concept of waste does not really exist in nature. All material is used in some way; the residual products from one species are utilised by another. Yet the way we design and construct our buildings creates a huge amount of waste and uses large amounts of non-renewable, primary materials, which are extracted with great environmental damage.

In an ideal industrial ecosystem, resources are not depleted any more than those in a biological ecosystem; a piece of steel could potentially show up one year in a drink can, the next year in an automobile and 10 years later in the structural frame of a building, 'Manufacturing processes in an industrial ecosystem simply transform circulating stocks of materials from one shape to another; the circulating stock decreases when some material is unavoidably lost, and it increases to meet the needs of a growing population. Such recycling still requires the expenditure of energy and the unavoidable generation of wastes and harmful by-products, but at much lower levels than are typical today'[1].

Currently, standard construction and demolition practices focus on the fastest, easiest and most economical way to get the job done. When this is combined with a lack of clear information and guidance for designers and owners about the implications of specifying reclaimed components and recycled materials, it creates barriers to a more ecologically sound use of resources. To move significantly towards an ecosystem based approach, there needs to be changes to the way things are done in the construction industry and, in particular, the availability of reclaimed components and recycled materials needs to increase. We should employ construction methods that will make disassembly of buildings easier, so that components used today can become valuable resources for the next generation of buildings.

There are four ways of reusing previously used materials or components in a project:

1. Reuse an existing structure on the site and possibly add to it or extend it. It may be possible to use this approach, often called 'adaptive reuse', in many urban developments. It is now relatively common, for example, with heritage structures, as they are seen to have cultural value, but is also appropriate for many existing buildings.

2. Move most, or all, of an existing building to a new location. Relocation sometimes occurs for pre-engineered buildings, such as industrial buildings and warehouses, and occasionally for other building types. Temporary buildings offer lessons for designing to allow future relocation.

Typical demolition practices are destructive, and do not take care to extract valuable components for reuse.

3. Reuse individual components extracted from the demolition of one project in a new building. This form of reuse is commonly known as 'component reuse'. Thus, structural components, such as beams, columns or non-structural components, such as cladding panels, bricks or staircases, are taken from one project and used in another. This is not yet common, other than for heritage components. It is important to consider, at the design stage, how a building will be deconstructed to make it more feasible that components are reused.

4. Traditional recycling approach of using materials that have a high recycled content. For example, most metals have a significant recycled content, and other materials, such as mineral wool insulation, are increasing their recycled content.

Reuse is different from recycling, (where a material is fed back through the manufacturing process). From an environmental, and economic, point of view, reuse of buildings or reclaimed components (1 to 3 above) are usually more beneficial strategies than recycling of materials. Reuse of components or whole buildings, generally requires little reprocessing, so greater environmental benefits often result, compared to recycling. Reuse is not possible for materials such as in-situ poured concrete, as this is broken up during the demolition process, but can be crushed for use as aggregate - down-cycling. Components, which can be deconstructed undamaged, can be reused. However, when reusing components, designers and contractors need to be more flexible in their approach. Designers who have attempted such an approach say that 'using reclaimed materials adds a whole new level of complexity to the project'[2]. Reclaimed components may not be readily available off the shelf, and may be difficult to source. One of the principal problems with reuse is to co-ordinate demand with supply, and this can affect the whole design and construction process 'reclaimed materials do not show up at the right time, in the right amount or the right dimension'[3].

These open web steel joists were salvaged from an old building for use in a new project.

Photos courtesy of Bioregional: www.bioregional-reclaimed.com

Designers need to recognize that there are some significant differences to the design process, if reuse of construction components is a goal of a project. With a traditional approach to design, the construction components are specified and sized to suit the performance requirements of the architect's proposals, usually using standard sizes and other established performance criteria. But reclaimed components do not generally come 'off the shelf' and sometimes their specification needs to be established. Rather, they are identified on demolition sites by salvage contractors. Thus, when proceeding to construction, the required size or type of component may not be readily available. This may necessitate a redesign to suit available salvaged components, or choosing whichever oversized components are readily available.

Certain key factors have emerged from pioneering projects that have focused on reuse. These include:

- it is important to have the commitment of the entire design team at the early stage of the process
- projects need clear goals with commitment of all the design team and client
- the 'integrated design process' facilitates a great likelihood of successfully using

reclaimed and salvaged materials and components

- sourcing salvaged materials requires designers to foster new relationships with organizations they may not traditionally be in touch with
- responsibility for identifying salvaged materials needs to be clearly established - who will source the particular components?
- procedures for grading salvaged components need to be established and any regulatory issues identified
- cost savings are possible in material costs, but some of these are offset by additional labour costs
- there can be additional design costs. This can be due to redesign to suit when sourcing reused components
- projects with the highest savings usually focus on reuse of the existing building already on site.

Ideally the specific reused components need to be identified at an early stage in the design process, perhaps when traditionally a contractor may not yet be involved. The standard design stages, as outlined in the RIBA plan of work, (and other similar manuals in other countries) will need to be adapted with new tasks included that focus on what needs to be achieved, and at which stages, to facilitate successful component reuse. The starting point for a new design may, in the future, be an inventory of the available materials from salvage. For structural design, the size and length of the available members will then determine the spans and spacing possible in the new structure, so that structural efficiency can be maximised from the available components. This requires that the available components are identified early in the design process, and that these are purchased or reserved to prevent the salvage contractor from selling them elsewhere.

One problem is that few, if any, salvage contractors will guarantee the availability of specific materials or products for the duration of the design and tender period, that may last years. This has severe cash flow implications and management consequences as the client may be required to dedicate resources to the purchase of components early in the design phase, when a contractor has not yet been appointed.

The design team may be required to take on considerable additional research at the front end of the project to identify, locate, inspect and choose appropriate components: 'Creating a workable structure for a new building using salvaged materials can be the single biggest challenge for architects. Many other materials and products are straightforward to use, but may be more difficult to source. .....Procuring all the materials in advance of tender requires money up front and a great deal of research, but enables tender documents to be complete, and contractors to view the materials before submitting a bid' [4].

If components cannot be pre-purchased it is essential to design in flexibility, particularly into the structural design, so that it is possible to use alternative options and adjust the design depending on the availability of components later in the process. This requires appropriate contractual procedures to be used, since the final materials may not be specified at the time of tendering. It is helpful for engineers and architects to develop working relationships with salvage and demolition contractors so they can easily find available salvaged materials, thus improving their choices when these components are required. Alternatively, it may be possible to purchase a suitable building already condemned for demolition, that contains appropriate components, and reuse as many of these as possible in the new project. ☯

References

1. *Frosch, Robert A. and Gallopoulos, Nicholas E. 1989, Strategies for Manufacturing, Scientific American. 189(3) pp152.*

2. *Chapman, L. & Simmonds, C., Mountain Equipment Co-op Ottawa Store, CBIP-C2000 Case Study, NRCan: Ottawa, 2000.*

3. *SCI, Environmental and economic assessment of a steel frame building using recycled and reused materials, Steel Construction Institute Publication P305, Ascot: UK, 2000.*

4. *Taggart, J., Salvaged materials in new buildings, Canadian Architect, 46(1), pp. 32-33, 2001.*

Reclaim and reuse

A reclaimed brick is one which has been cleaned and can be reused, a recycled brick is one which has been crushed and destroyed for hardcore. **Thornton Kay** reports...

For every 12 bricks that are reclaimed, a gallon of petrol is saved. A recycled brick loses the embodied energy of the brick forever, and it also loses the additional fossil fuel energy needed to crush the brick. Clearly it makes more sense to reclaim old bricks than to down-cycle and crush them (it is in fact 400 times more energy efficient to clean an old brick than to crush it), and this principle applies to most old building material. The UK produces 3.5 billion new bricks a year and destroys around the same number from demolition. Around 150 million are saved for reuse. The rest are mainly crushed for no apparent benefit, the most beneficial use being to create farm tracks and engineer landfill sites. The UK taxpayer subsidises crushing through cash grants. No such help is offered to reclaimers.

In energy terms reclaiming an old brick saves the energy needed to manufacture a new comparable brick of around 4kWh (less for Flettons) and costs 0.009kWh to reclaim (9Wh of human energy compared to 2Wh of fossil fuel to crush an old brick). So using 10,000 old bricks, instead of new bricks to build a house saves around 40,000kWh.

Despite the apparent environmental recklessness of destruction, England is perhaps the western world's most efficient brick reclaimer, with around 5% of the English brick supply market being reclaimed. As an example, this compares to Germany and Denmark with an estimated less than 0.5% reclaimed, many of which are imports from countries such as Poland and Belgium. Sourcing domestic

Reclaimed bricks, as shown here at the Salvo Fair 2008 on the stand of Herts Architectural Salvage. Salvo reckons that over 3 billion new bricks are made in the UK each year, and over 3 billion old ones are demolished and crushed (boxout), with only 150 million being saved for reuse.

reclaimed bricks has become harder in the UK because demolition contractors have now all moved into crushing bricks rather than saving them. Salvo runs an international website for reclaimed materials and has gradually seen supply lines increasing. In 2007 inter-continental brick reclamation was seen for the first time, with reclaimed bricks being offered to the UK market from Brazil and China. Although this might seem irrational, and it is certainly not being recommended by Salvo, a brick can travel 800 miles by truck or 40,000 miles by ship before its embodied energy asset is exhausted. Obviously we should be reclaiming bricks available locally first.

All material arising from demolition and refurbishment can either be reclaimed for reuse, or recycled by being used as a feedstock for a process which creates a new material and destroys the old material. Or it can be destroyed in a waste to energy process which could be incineration or landfill, with or without methane energy recovery. Since 1990 there has been a well-established waste hierarchy which the UK government has weakly encouraged (but not enforced) of reduce, reuse, recycle, waste to energy, disposal, in that order of priority.

Industry has lobbied hard in Brussels to prevent the adoption of the waste hierarchy because it would reduce market share through reduction and reuse, and could increase costs imposed by producer responsibility for recycling, waste to energy and disposal. The European Commission appeared happy to accept the industrial lobbyists' views and were proposing to give a partial hierarchy of reduce, recovery, and disposal the status of a guiding principle. This would have placed reuse equal to waste to energy or recycling, and the guiding principle would not have been mandatory. However, in June 2008 the MEPs overruled the bureaucrats and the European Parliament passed the new EU Waste Framework Directive, which includes the complete waste hierarchy, with the status of a priority order. This means that in future, in law in the UK, reuse will be given priority over recycling.

Large building projects must now operate site waste management plans, but these do not require the waste hierarchy to be implemented at present. However, these plans will have to incorporate the waste hierarchy and prioritise reuse in future. This should mean that the reuse and the supply of reclaimed materials should increase.

It is likely that the type of materials that are reclaimed in future and the way they are used, will change. For example, the traditional pallet of cleaned, reclaimed handmade or wirecut bricks taken from a 100 year old building, where the bricks were bedded in soft lime mortar, may be replaced by a pile of metre square diamond cut hard portland cement brick panels pre-assembled offsite. Innovative reuse in a modest way has been around for a while, especially in the DIY sector. For example the editor of this book is not the only person to have successfully used old roof slates as a flooring material in Wales.

Mainstream construction has historically been a poor supplier and reuser of reclaimed materials. The UK market for core construction products is around £35 billion a year and the total sales of salvaged materials is around £350 million a year giving the reuse sector around 1% of the total market share. In 1991 Salvo recommended that a target of 5% by value should be set for reuse of reclaimed building materials in all building and landscape projects. This figure is still a realistic goal but will be harder to achieve now than then, due to the shift in technology. In 1990 most 100 year old products were not fundamentally different in function to their modern counterparts, and they were often considerably more durable, and so could be easily reused. Nowadays 30 year old products from demolition struggle to find a reuse function, competing against ever more complex and sophisticated products designed to comply with increasingly complex regulations, and with increasingly diminished durability. But reuse is always a possibility for the most unpromising material. For example, Salvo suggested that the acres of exposed aggregate panelling on the facades of the huge old government environment offices in Marsham Street in London could be used as paving for the pedestrian areas outside the Millennium dome. The suggestion was not taken up.

Reclaimed materials are not well liked by mainstream construction professionals due to factors such as: lack of standards of supply, lack of availability, prices too high, liability and professional indemnity issues, embodied and acquired toxicity or contamination, requirement for on site storage space, higher wastage rates, contractor uncertainty, more time needed for sourcing, non-conformity with modern regulations, and testing needed.

Should the professional designer abandon their reuse hopes? Emphatically not. Reuse in mainstream construction is almost always client-led. Designers seldom initiate reuse of reclaimed materials. Reuse happens as a result of positive attitudes and decisions by the client, often overriding the opinions of their design, technical and building team. This is why more than 90% of the market for reclaimed materials is outside mainstream construction to private customers, DIYers, small up-market developers, fashion shopfitting, and hotel and pub refurbishment.

The Code for Sustainable Homes (CSH) measures sustainability against a number of categories of design to give an overall percentage rating which is converted to a star rating system (see Chapter 2 for an in-depth explanation of the CSH).

Materials can gain up to 24 credits representing 7.2% of the total points. The split is:

- environmental impact of materials: 15 credits
- responsible sourcing of materials - basic building elements: 6 credits
  finishing elements: 3 credits

Waste management can gain up to 7 credits representing 6.4% of the total points:

- storage of non-recyclable waste and recyclable household waste: 4 credits
- construction site waste management: 2 credits
- composting: 1 credit
- compliance with the 'considerate constructors' scheme', or one similar (*which includes the criterion that 80% of the site timber is reclaimed, re-used or responsibly sourced*); 2 credits

Reuse needs to be confirmed at design stage and post-construction stage using trade information, written statements, purchase orders and receipts. Same site salvage (always the environmental best option) can be self-certified and will straddle both the materials supply and waste management credits.

From April 2008 all projects with a value exceeding £300,000 are required by law to have a site waste management plan (SWMP), they are also required for lower value building projects under the CSH. SWMPs have a presumption in favour of reuse over recycling, but no compulsion, and no additional credits are obtained for reusing bricks, rather than crushing them for hardcore. The aim of this part of the CSH seems to be more about reducing waste of new materials through their reuse onsite, which is really not reuse since those materials were never used in the first place, but it could be recycling as in the example of bricks above.

In December 2007 reclaimed building materials were included in the BRE's Green Guide for the first time, namely:

- reclaimed bricks for internal use
- reclaimed wood flooring
- reclaimed clay roof tiles and reclaimed roof slates.

Reclaimed bricks, for internal use, achieve an A+ rating, the highest possible in the Green Guide which underpins the CSH. The Green Guide web site shows how the environmental impact is assessed (see chart right). In other words, reclaimed bricks come out very good and achieve the highest rating in the CSH.

Oddly though, the same rating has been given to bricks laid in portland cement mortar, although this would be deemed not so eco-friendly by Salvo (and many others) because the resulting wall is likely to be harder to dismantle and salvage the bricks for reuse at the end of the building's life. Another oddity is that design for deconstruction does not feature in the CSH.

Of course, futureproofing buildings and their materials, is a very difficult task. Who knows how long a building will last, or what technologies may exist to cleanly dismantle it at the end of its life, or whether the reclaimed bricks would be reused anyway? Incidentally, the same A+ rating also applies to new materials, such as aircrete blockwork with paint finish and, curiously, the massively high embodied energy new 100mm glass blockwork. The worst walling product, at E rating, is precast concrete panel (non-load bearing, 150mm) with plasterboard and paint.

Reclaimed floorboards, as part of the element of structure of a floor, receive an A+ rating, with a presumption that floorboards made from reclaimed wood are also A+ rated, but this should be checked with the assessor first.

Reclaimed clay roof tiles and slates are also A+ rated, as part of the element of roof structure. Salvo would like to see concrete roof tiles, and possibly other reclaimed roof coverings also included, but at present these have been left out, possibly by omission rather than design, although it may be worth asking an assessor to include any reclaimed roofing as A+ rated.

The Green Guide writers and committees did not include any reclamation specialists, so omissions and anomalous misdescriptions will be corrected in future revisions of the CSH. The production of the CSH and the Green Guide has been a scientific and political tour de force by the BRE. There were problems prising trade-sensitive information out of construction materials' manufacturers who all wanted their products ranked highest. Salvo has long lobbied for more attention to the value of reclaimed materials within the BREEAM standards and latterly in the CSH.

Finally, the best salvage is always local to your building project but, as explained earlier, most reclaimed materials can travel long distances before their embodied energy is 'used up' by the transport energy needed to get them to your site. Salvage yards are a very good source of reclaimed materials, and **www.salvoweb.com** lists these so you should find one local to you.

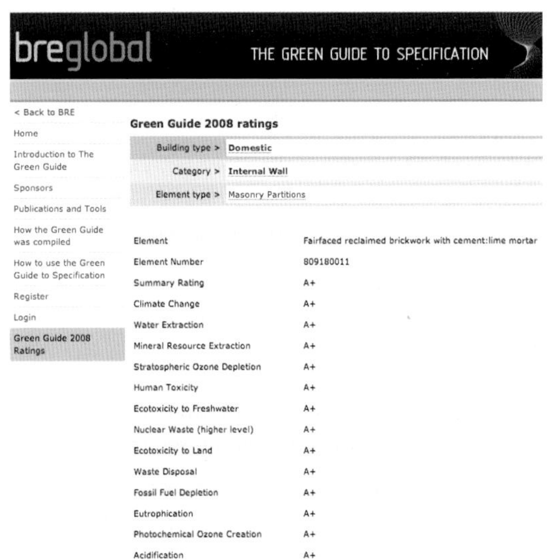
breglobal THE GREEN GUIDE TO SPECIFICATION

< Back to BRE
Home
Introduction to The Green Guide
Sponsors
Publications and Tools
How the Green Guide was compiled
How to use the Green Guide to Specification
Register
Login
Green Guide 2008 Ratings

Green Guide 2008 ratings

Building type >	**Domestic**
Category >	**Internal Wall**
Element type >	Masonry Partitions

Element	Fairfaced reclaimed brickwork with cement:lime mortar
Element Number	809180011
Summary Rating	A+
Climate Change	A+
Water Extraction	A+
Mineral Resource Extraction	A+
Stratospheric Ozone Depletion	A+
Human Toxicity	A+
Ecotoxicity to Freshwater	A+
Nuclear Waste (higher level)	A+
Ecotoxicity to Land	A+
Waste Disposal	A+
Fossil Fuel Depletion	A+
Eutrophication	A+
Photochemical Ozone Creation	A+
Acidification	A+

Chart taken from the BRE's latest Green Guide.
www.thegreenguide.org.uk

Salvo runs a code of practice for reclamation dealers. It also operates an annual salvage fair at Knebworth, undertook the first demolition audit and can act as consultant for building projects, particularly where same site salvage is being considered. It has also produced a handy guide to reclaimed materials, from the top-of-the-market architectural antiques through to reclaimed building materials and demolition salvage. It is available free at:
www.salvo-fair.com/2004/sn242sm45q1.pdf

Cement and alternatives

Cement is a very useful material but its manufacture is responsible for massive CO_2 pollution and when applied wrongly it can cause damage to buildings.
Rob Scot McLeod examines our addiction to cement ...

Cement is a major industrial commodity that is manufactured commercially in over 120 countries[1]. Mixed with aggregates and water it forms concrete, which is used for a wide range of practical applications. Interestingly, even in countries where wood is in good supply and is the vernacular style, concrete now features heavily in the construction of buildings.

In fact twice as much concrete is used in construction around the world as the total of all other building materials[2]. Despite its relatively low embodied energy, this scale of cement use is alarming given that cement production is responsible for 7-10% of total CO_2 emissions worldwide[3,4]. This places cement as the third biggest greenhouse gas culprit after the transportation and energy generation sectors[4]. With the cement industry growing at a rate of about 5% per year[5], increasingly severe CO_2 reduction measures will be required to keep cement emissions in line with levels set by the Kyoto Protocol[6].

There is no doubt that carbon taxes and other legislative measures to reduce carbon emission levels will provide the cement industry with an economic catalyst for change. But whilst such environmental weighting drives up the production costs for carbon emitters to the benefit of their non-emitting (or less emitting) competitors; there remains a practical need to find solutions to the problem.

With many industries it is obvious how we can make them greener or less polluting; buildings can be better designed or retro-insulated and vehicle engines can be made to run more efficiently or use alternative fuels. Cement manufacture, however, is a well-established process and any improvements are likely to be incremental as old plant is upgraded.

So what CO_2 reduction options are available to the cement industry, and how can we establish whether these improvements are substantial enough to meet this sectors' share of the Kyoto CO_2 targets both now and in the future? Although there are several different types of cement, portland cement (PC) is the most widely used, and for simplicity I will refer to PC and cement interchangeably.

Cement production emissions

In 1994 Professor Joseph Davidovits of Caen University was the first to document the climate change implications associated with high levels of PC production. According to Davidovits a worldwide freeze of CO_2 emissions at 1990 levels, as agreed under the Kyoto Protocol, is not compatible with the high cement demands of developing countries[4]. China and Japan are increasing cement production by 5% per year and Korea and Thailand by approximately 16%.

On average global cement production is rising by 5% per year. At this rate world cement production would reach 3,500 million tonnes by 2020, a figure which represents a threefold increase on 1990 levels[7]. Assuming this prediction is correct, then only by implementing replacements that emit one third or less of the CO_2 produced by current cement manufacturing can we keep to this target in twelve years time. Redirecting the building industry away from its reliance on cement and steel will take time and in the interim there is an urgent need to promote lower CO_2 cement replacements.

Essentially there are three ways to reduce the CO_2 emissions from cement manufacture. Perhaps the most obvious is to scale down production, but this concept would not be popular with manufacturers or developing nations currently expanding their infrastructure. Therefore, we are left with two options: to reduce emissions within the existing industry; and to replace cement with viable alternatives, where possible.

Alternatives in the cement industry

There are a number of cement and concrete making initiatives that are tackling CO_2 emissions, both in the manufacturing of the product, the end use, and via the waste stream.

Industrial wastes: the proportion of 'pure' cement in a cement based mixture can be reduced by replacing some of it with other pozzolanic material (i.e. material which has the ability to act as a cement like binder). Industrial wastes, including fly ash slag, a by-product of the coal power industry, silica fume and rice husk ash, all have the combined benefit of being pozzuolana that would otherwise be destined for landfill.

Whilst every tonne of pozzuolana effectively saves a tonne of cement, there are often engineering constraints limiting the percentage of cement that can be replaced. In the past these limits have typically been in the range of 10 -15%[4] but more recently structures containing high volume fly ash at 50 - 60% replacement levels have been built[8].

Autoclaved aerated concrete (aircrete): quicklime is mixed with cement, sand (or pulverised fuel ash - PFA), water and aluminium powder to form a slurry which rises and sets to form lightweight structural blocks. These blocks are then heated in a pressurised autoclave to give them strength. Aircrete blocks have excellent thermal and acoustic properties, and are suitable for load bearing walls in low and medium rise buildings. Typically the cement component of an aircrete block is approximately 20% by dry weight[9], which is comparable with a conventional aggregate block. Since aircrete blocks are less than half the density of conventional medium density blocks, less than half the cement is required for an equivalent built volume. Autoclaves operate at relatively low temperatures and use far less energy than traditional brick kilns.

CaO^- and MgO^- waste stream carbon sequestration: this is a method of using waste products from the cement industry to re-absorb CO_2 directly from the ambient air. Waste stream sequestration is estimated to cost in the region of \$8 US/tonne of CO_2 absorbed[10]. This figure represents a small fraction of the price that the Intergovernmental Panel on Climate Change places on the value of carbon credit, whose bottom estimate is \$55 US/tonne of CO_2[11]. Given that mandatory carbon taxes may soon be on the agenda, waste stream sequestration could become a financially viable alternative for the cement industry.

Alternatives to cement

There are few alternatives available in the UK that can be used as a cement replacement, but careful research should be carried out by anyone planning to use them before direct replacement is considered. The most obvious replacement is probably lime in one form or another.

Lime and limecrete: before delving into the intricacies of lime it is important to remember that lime is essentially formed in the same way as cement. By converting limestone to quicklime, the raw product from which all calcium based lime is made, carbon dioxide is released. Burning fossil fuels to provide the heat for this reaction also releases CO_2, although temperatures required by lime kilns are lower than cement kilns, thereby producing less CO_2. Interestingly, cement is, in fact, composed predominantly of lime, the lime content of portland cement being around 63.5%[1]. There are two forms of lime commonly referred to. These are hydraulic and non-hydraulic lime. Hydraulic lime mortars are formed by burning and slaking chalky limestone which contains a high silica content allowing stronger bond formations than non-hydraulic mortars. The more hydraulic a lime is, the more cement like its properties are. However, it is the traditional non-hydraulic lime putties, known for their permeable and flexible characteristics, that have a greater ability to re-absorb CO_2 by carbonation during their prolonged setting process.

Hardening by carbonation occurs when calcium hydroxide, in an aqueous state, breaks down to bond with dissolved carbon dioxide, forming calcium carbonate with water as a by product. Some non-hydraulic limes are capable of re-absorbing nearly all of the CO_2 released in their chemical formation, but this figure does not account for the CO_2 released by the kiln which can be on a par with PC[12]. In practice carbonation occurs gradually over a long period of time and is often only partially achieved. John Harrison (the founder of TecEco[13]) attributes this situation to the use of aggregates that are too fine to permit water and gas vapours to pass freely through the material. Limecrete can be made by mixing lime with a suitable aggregate or for insulation purposes, e.g. Leca[14].

Geopolymeric cements: this type of cement has its origins in the original Roman cements first used over 2000 years ago. Geopolymeric cements are formed in a different manner to PC and lime and do not involve the release of bound CO_2. The raw materials for geopolymeric cements are aluminium and silicon rich materials that are activated by alkali compounds. This silicate based chemistry can be achieved at relatively low temperatures, with the added benefit of requiring far less capital investment in manufacturing plant and equipment. The net result is a product that sets in a matter of hours, with CO_2 emissions that are 80% - 90% less than PC[4].

Earth: locally sourced alternative materials, utilising earth, have been in use all over the world since man first began building shelters. One good example of how effective earth can be is the work undertaken by Tom Morton and ARC Architects which uses earth bricks and mortars. Other earth building systems have been well documented in Green Building magazine (formerly Building for a Future magazine). Cob, adobe and rammed earth will all have major parts to play in reducing cement/concrete use in the future. Another localised example might be that of termite mounds, which are widespread throughout the African savannah and are often destroyed by farmers[15]. If an environmental impact assessment could establish that their use as a local cement substitute was relatively benign, then significant financial and CO_2 savings could result. This low tech approach demonstrates that this global problem can be tackled locally and on many levels.

Conclusion

In summing up, we must remember that to prevent rapid climate change, it is necessary to reduce net CO_2 emissions drastically. Based on current consumption rates there will be a 3-fold increase in cement manufacturing CO_2 emissions between 1990 levels and 2020[7]. Using the Kyoto Protocol's 'first commitment period' CO_2 reduction target of 5.2% below 1990 levels as our initial base line target, we will need to cut our cement CO_2 outputs by two thirds plus 5.2%, i.e. 73% by 2020[7]. Subsequent Kyoto commitments set even greater reduction targets.

Cement type	Manufacturing temperature	% Energy consumption	% Net CO_2 emissions
Portland cement	1450-1500° C	100	100
PC + PFA(15) †	1450-1500° C	85 (-15%)	85
Non hydraulic (lime putty)	1350° C	100	50
Hydraulic lime (NHL2)	<1000° C	50 (-50%)	40

Comparison of relative energy consumption and net CO_2 emissions for cement against available alternatives, assuming portland cement = 100. † PFA (15) and PFA (50) refer to pulverised fuel ash at 15% and 50% PC replacement levels respectively.

Geopolymeric cements and earth (for low rise buildings) are the only products/materials reviewed here that are clearly capable of achieving CO_2 reductions of this magnitude, whist still maintaining some of the beneficial characteristics of portland cement. This is because all of the other products use either a large percentage of PC, or rely on a similar calcination process to cement, which releases large quantities of CO_2 by virtue of the chemical reaction and furnace heat required.

Other products outside a UK context

Eco-cement, and other magnesium based cement alternatives, have the potential to be fired at much lower temperatures than PC (possibly utilising waste heat) and are potentially stronger and less dense than calcium based cements.

However, at the time of publishing, there were no new eco cements coming onto the UK market. Products like Canadian EcoSmart concrete have already demonstrated that, by using high volume fly ash, CO_2 emissions can be halved whilst creating cement that is both structurally superior to PC and cheaper to produce. Carbon taxes, mandates, assessment ratings and other incentives that drive all cement manufacturers and building specifiers to adopt such practices are urgently needed.

Comment from the cement industry

In response to this article, Martin Casey, Director of External Affairs at the British Cement Association (BCA) pointed out that he disagrees with the figure of 7-10% as the global CO_2 contribution of the cement industry. The cement industry has always stated that the figure is 5%.

Casey also made the point that magnesium is not available in the UK, meaning that for the cement industry to use this technology it would need to be imported, increasing embodied energy. A fair comment.

Casey also said that the BCA represents the British cement industry, while the article is global and that he could not comment on what was beyond the boundaries of the BCA, other than to say that all the developing nations are using the most efficient methods possible to produce cement and have invested heavily in plant upgrades to this end.

His final point was that the BCA has an overt sustainability policy, and has published a performance report detailing how the industry is addressing corporate responsibility and sets out plans for delivering real environmental benefits. This can be found at ***www.cementindustry.co.uk***

References

1. *IUCC. (1993) Why Cement Making Produces CO_2, Information Unit on Climate Change:* **www.patentstorm.us/patents/6908507.html**

2. *Sustainable Settlement in South Africa (2002) Climate Change:* **www.sustainablesettlement.co.Za/issues/climate.html**

3. *Godfrey, P (2000) TecEco Magnesium Cement Project:* **www.tececo.com/technologies.tececo_cements.php**

4. *Fauldi,J. (2004) Concrete - A Burning Issue World Changing, November 2004:* **www.worldchanging.com**

5. *Davidovits, J. (2004) Up to 80% reduction of CO_2 Greenhouse Gas Emissions during Cement Manufacture. Geopolymer Institute:* **www.geopolymer.org/library**

6. *European Commission. (2004) Kyoto Protocol. European Union @ United Nations:* **www.europa-eu-un.org**

7. *Davidovits, J. (1994) Global Warming Impact on the Cement and Aggregates Industry. World Resource Review, 6 (2) 263-78:* **www.geopolymer.org/library**

8. *EcoSmart Canada (2004):* **www.ecosmart.com/commercial/about/panel.asp**

9. *Spong, C. (2005) Durox Topblock Technical. Telephone interview, April 9.*

10. *Stolaroff, K et al. (2004) Using CaO and MgO Rich Industrial Waste Streams for Carbon Sequestration. Energy and Conservation Management 46 (5) 687-99:* **www.sciencedirect.com/science**

11. *IPCC. (2001) Climate Change 2001: Mitigation. Intergovernmental Panel on Climate Change Third Assessment Report:* **www.grida.no/climate/ipcc_tar/wg3/index.htm**

12. *St Astier (2001):* **www.stastier.co.uk/index.htm?articles/mortars.htm~rbottom**

13. *Harrison, J (2005). Carbonating and Hydraulic Mortars:* **www.tececo.com**

14. **www.limecrete.org.uk**

15. *Olusola, K et al (2005). Studies on Termite Hill and Lime as Partial Replacement for Cement in Plastering. Building and Environment, 33 (11):* **www.sciencedirect.com/science**

Insulation considerations

Insulation is a fundamental component of any energy efficient and sustainable building. The type of insulation and its thickness needs to be considered. **John Garbutt** gives his views on the most environmentally sustainable options.

Most now agree that the 'energy saving potential' of insulation, measured over the lifetime of a building, should be the dominant factor in its specification. In fact, the lifetime differences between various insulation products are small. The most important factor of all is to ensure that the insulation is correctly installed.

Over the past few years choosing an eco-friendly insulation material was quite simple. All you needed to do was select one that did not use CFC or HCFC[1] blowing agents in its manufacture. However, with the successful phase-out of ozone destroying gasses by EU law (based on the Montreal Protocol)[1] it became a less clear-cut decision.

So how can we choose the most environmentally sustainable insulation to use in our buildings? Many might argue that 'natural is best' but others counter with 'natural cannot promise durability'. It is true that some insulation applications are accessible enough for us to replace them occasionally throughout the lifetime of the building if we so wish but, likewise, some application decisions are 'whole building life' choices. Let's take a look at some of the environmental issues that may apply to building insulation.

Embodied impact – does it matter?

For a number of years now, insulation materials, among many others, have been compared on the basis of embodied energy (the energy used to build the construction elements). However, if energy saving is high on your agenda, I believe that it is the balance of the embodied energy against the 'in-use' energy consumption over the lifetime of a building that is more important. Indeed, due to the fact that insulation, by its very nature, is there to save energy, it has become widely accepted that the embodied energy of any insulation material is insignificant compared with the energy saved by it over the lifetime of the building in which it is installed.

Having said that, we should not be complacent. The above statement will only hold true whilst we continue to design buildings with quite high levels of energy consumption. All this will change when (if) our buildings have low or zero heating/ CO_2 emission requirements. This can only be achieved by using insulation wisely at appropriate thicknesses and by detailing our buildings properly to ensure airtightness. Only when our buildings get to low or zero heating levels will the embodied energy of the insulation choice become significant enough to worry about.

One measure of embodied impact is the rating system used in the BRE's Green Guide to Building Specification[2]. This publication rates

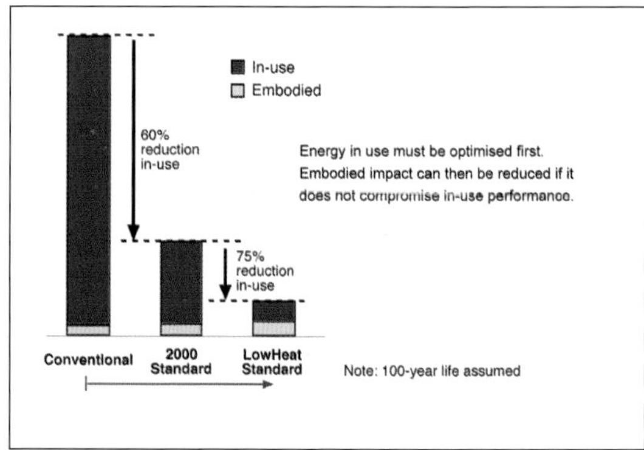

How in-use energy is far more significant than embodied energy.
Source: XCO2 conisbee

products from A+ to E on a basket of environmental impacts, including embodied energy. These ratings are based on generic life cycle assessment (LCA) data. You will find that almost all insulation materials, for which data is given, get the top ratings of A+ or A. The common exceptions are cellular glass, extruded polystyrene and high-density (128 kg/m^3 and higher) rock mineral fibre; this is a clear reflection of the fact that the embodied impact of insulation materials is relatively insignificant. However, it does illustrate that it is important to consider the density of the insulation material, as more dense insulants may have a low embodied impact per kilogram, but not per m^3 or m^2.

Interestingly when the impacts for insulation are combined with the impacts of other materials that make up, say, a wall or a roof, the different ratings of insulation products become largely irrelevant as they are masked by the impacts of the other materials in the construction. A fact which illustrates my earlier point. In the guide. it is perfectly possible for a wall insulated, with extruded polystyrene, to get an overall A+ rating, even if the insulation itself does not, (some might argue that this is a failure of the rating system used). It is equally possible for a wall insulated with an A rated insulation material to get an overall E rating because it is the rating for the whole construction that counts as far as the Green Guide data is concerned. Accurate and unbiased embodied energy / embodied impact figures for insulation materials are difficult to find, other than in BRE's life cycle analysis (LCA), and therefore should be treated with care.

In-use performance

It is widely accepted that reducing "in use" energy consumption of buildings is the key to their environmental sustainability. Therefore, the major parameter on which to compare insulation materials must be their ability to deliver their specified thermal performance over the lifetime of a building. This is one of the key themes of an independently produced report on the sustainability of insulation materials, funded by BING (the European trade association for manufacturers of rigid urethane insulation products)[3], which brought to bear the concept of risk factors. These are all factors which could detrimentally affect the thermal performance of individual insulation materials, sometimes in very different ways, and hence the environmental sustainability of buildings. These risk factors may include the impacts of:

- liquid water or water vapour
- air-infiltration
- compression or settling.

On the whole it will be poor sitework that will allow these risk factors to come into play. On-site installation practices are notoriously uncontrollable and all materials will perform badly if installed without due care and attention. However, for some insulation materials the problem may stem from what is claimed for the product in the first place.

Adherence to common rules for thermal performance claims should be checked. The EU Construction Products Directive has created a set of harmonised product standards for insulation which demand that the thermal performance of all products is quoted in a comparable way that takes account of ageing and statistical variation. It is called the Lambda 90:90 method. All major UK insulation manufacturers have adopted this approach to quoting thermal performance. It is worth noting that the introduction of the harmonised product standards added about 10% to the thermal conductivity of the insulation products that are covered (i.e. made them 10% worse). However, at the present time there are a number of smaller scale products for which there is no harmonised standard available and therefore no consistent method that takes account of statistical variation. No doubt these will be brought into the fold soon but, until then, inconsistency will reign. One particular case in point is that of multi-foil insulation[4].

Once the global issues have been considered it is then time to consider less pressing, but still important, issues such as recycled content, local sourcing, disposability etc. The key to the environmental sustainability of any product is a balance of all these issues. Taking just one issue and over-focussing on it could be counter-productive.

Recycled content of products is going through something of a revolution in the UK construction industry. The Government has funded a body called The Waste & Resources Action Program (WRAP) to promote materials that have a recycled content. It gives very specific rules as to what counts as recycled content and what does not. These rules follow the definition cited in the ISO standard on Environmental Labels and Declarations[5].

Some insulation already contains recycled content. However, when examining the recycled content of insulation materials please bear in mind that recycled content is the proportion, by mass, of recycled material in the product. Only pre-consumer and post-consumer materials should be considered as recycled content.[6] This means that surplus material, cut from the edges of products during their manufacture and shredded and added back in at the start of the process don't count.

Another, often overlooked aspect of the performance of insulation materials is their performance with respect to fire. This is quite a complicated area but, roughly speaking, there are two facets to consider: reaction to fire and fire resistance. Reaction to fire is measured by the 'Class 0' type rating system enshrined in Approved Document B to the Building Regulations in England & Wales or the risk categories shown in the Technical Handbooks in Scotland. These ratings can be achieved by reference to the new Euroclass system for reaction to fire or by the tried and tested BS 476 Parts 6 and 7.

There is a debate in the insulation industry, at present, as to which route is best. What has caused this confusion is the fact that the new Euroclass rating system for reaction to fire is irrelevant when applied to 'naked' insulation products, as the system was developed for wall and ceiling linings and insulation is rarely used as such. The reaction to fire test has slightly more value when used for products tested 'in-application', since insulation products are then tested mounted as they would be in practice, for example behind plasterboard.

Proponents of the Euroclass system suggest that 'naked' products lie around building sites all the time and that the products are exposed when, say, holes are cut in walls, but I cannot understand how testing a product as a wall or ceiling lining can relate to packs of products lying on the ground. Regardless, the test still gives no indication of a product's ability to resist fire. It is this crucial distinction that can make all the difference to the ability of a building to withstand a fire and maintain structural integrity long enough to enable occupants to leave safely, and allow emergency services more time to get the blaze under control and salvage the building. Mistakenly choosing a material based on its reaction to fire, without taking into account its resistance to fire, may therefore at best be costly, and could at worst prove fatal.

The crux of the issue is that some materials have excellent fire resistance qualities but relatively poor reaction to fire ratings, whereas others have the best reaction to fire ratings but relatively poor fire resistance properties.

What about the Code for Sustainable Homes?

There are a number of different insulation materials that, if installed correctly, can meet the low energy requirements of the higher levels of the Code for Sustainable Homes (CSH) - introduced in Chapter 2. For example, the thickness of insulation required, and whether this impinges on useable space, needs to be considered.

But having excellent levels of insulation is not enough – it is vital to also consider the overall impact of the materials used, and their effectiveness over the lifetime of the building. In the past the environmental sustainability of insulation materials has been compared on the basis of embodied energy. However, this may not deliver a true picture of environmental impact and it is now recognised that a much wider range of issues needs to be considered, not just embodied energy.

LCA techniques provide a good, holistic tool to achieve this, but it is also important to look at the whole construction and not just one component of it. The CSH has endorsed this approach by awarding credits based on the BRE Green Guide ratings for the roof, external walls, internal walls, floor and windows of a house construction, which are themselves based on LCA analysis. If all 5 elements achieve an A rating then just 2.7 credits are awarded, if they all get an A+ then a maximum 4.5 credits can be awarded.

It is also important to recognise that it is operational energy use that creates the vast majority of environmental impact, and this too has been reflected in the CSH in the balance of credits allowed for reduced CO_2 emissions versus those allowed for materials: 17.6 and 4.5 discretionary credits respectively. However, there is one vital aspect of environmentally sustainable buildings which is not addressed by the CSH, and that is the point that the longevity of the standards of operational performance is critical.

For example, the performance of some insulants, such as rock mineral fibre, can deteriorate rapidly if exposed to water penetration, moving air penetration or compression. This may increase operational energy use and hence compromise the environmental sustainability of the finished building to an alarming degree. Other insulation materials, such as rigid phenolic and rigid urethane insulation, are not vulnerable to any of these problems. The question of longevity is particularly important in the light of the requirement for energy performance certificates for all houses. These certificates are an important part of the resale or let process, tracking the energy performance of homes over time.

So when it comes to achieving the best standards, and meeting some of the key objectives behind the CSH whilst still delivering reliable long term performance, there are three important considerations: in the first place, work to the lowest possible U–value regardless of insulation type, design out the risk of the chosen insulant not performing as specified, and, if you can't, choose an insulant that is at low risk of failure.

In this way the industry knows that it can deliver housing that meets the increasingly tough criteria for carbon dioxide emissions, without having to rely on expensive technology or worry about site restrictions. In other words, a smart solution that keeps the numbers of new projects and higher standards within the realm of both the achievable and the realistic. ☯

References

1. *All insulation materials (in the UK) are now free from CFCs and HCFCs and have been since Jan 1, 2004. As the issue of CFC and HCFC use is now historic, no mention is made here of these blowing agents.*

2. ***www.thegreenguide.org.uk***

3. ***www.bing.org***

4. *See my 'Resource guide to the properties of most commonly available building insulation materials' on page 283 of the 4th edition of Volume 2 of the Green Building Bible for a full technical review of these and other insulation products.*

5. *BS EN ISO 14021: 2001. Environmental labels and declarations – self declared environmental claims (Type II environmental labelling). BSI. London. 2001.*

6. *Pre-consumer waste is material diverted from the waste stream during a manufacturing process. Excluded is re-utilisation of materials such as re-work, re-grind or scrap generated in a process and capable of being reclaimed within the same process that generated it. Post-consumer waste is material generated by households or by commercial, industrial and institutional facilities in their role as end-users of the product, which can no longer be used for its intended purpose. This includes returns of material from the distribution chain.*

Natural insulation

Generally, the type of insulation used is determined by its thermal properties and not by its wider environmental impact. However, for those of us that want to be more selective, **Dave Barton** summarises the 'natural' insulation materials that are currently available to us ...

We are all becoming keen to see energy use in buildings reduced, to help protect the environment and help us save money on ever-rising fuel bills. To this end, the government has embarked upon a number of programmes to encourage us to put increased levels of insulation in buildings, many of which have already been or will be discussed in this book. In most cases, the type of insulation used is determined by its thermal properties, its costs and availability. But what about the whole story? How is the insulation made and what about the raw materials that it is made from?

With most businesses in most sectors promoting their own products on 'selected' environmental credentials, it can be very confusing for the specifier to figure out which claims to believe and which to dismiss. And even though the 'alternative' 'green building' market is beginning to mature, there is still a lack of independent, credible research available to help specifiers and householders make cut and dry decisions that they can be sure will have true environmental benefits. The insulation sector is no different. However, as a guide, when choosing or specifying insulation, perhaps we should be giving consideration to the following aspects, alongside cost, thermal properties and efficacy as a building component:

- the embodied energy of the insulation (energy consumed within its processing and transportation)
- the raw material that it is made from
- possible toxicity and any related health issues in manufacture, installation and for the occupants
- ability to be recycled.

The type of insulation used is an important consideration, alongside that of the level of insulation fitted to a building. The right specification of insulation could be a significant part of reducing the overall environmental impact of a building (remember, the environment is more than just an energy issue). The current major players in the insulation market, mineral and glass wool, do not contain any chemicals and are quite inert, but they have quite high embodied energy and some create dust problems during handling and the waste from them can be difficult to dispose of.

The UK construction industry tends to be rather conservative and slow to respond to 'new' materials. Not all natural insulation materials have yet been assessed to BBA or BSI standards but without such approval they are unlikely to be taken up by the market at large.

Some products are still relatively new to the market and consequently there is limited experience in the industry regarding specification and installation, limited availability and accessibility and generally a price premium (though this is claimed to be falling). On the plus side, the 'naturalness' of such insulants can be great components for use in a 'breathing' construction which is the preferred way of designing buildings used by many 'green' architects.

Although natural materials can breath (i.e. absorb and release moisture without any adverse effect, they are not water resistant like some of the plastic insulants and are therefore mainly limited to specific applications, e.g. lofts, timber frame walls, internal walls. They are not suitable for use as a cavity wall insulation.

Innovative use of cork in cavity walls for the AtEIC (autonomous environmental information centre) building at the Centre for Alternative Technology at Machynlleth. The cavity wall structure is compressed earth blocks with corkboard cavity fill insulation. A fact sheet on the whole building is available from CAT 01654 705980 and a building diary, featuring the project, can be found at ***www.cat.org.uk***

One exception to this rule might be cork. The Centre for Alternative Technology (CAT) used cork for the AtEIC building, (see photo above).

The choice?

There are a growing number of renewable insulation materials already on, or coming on to the market at the moment. The better known ones are sheep's wool, cellulose and flax but these are currently only available at a few niche outlets, compared to the major insulants, but their use is becoming more widespread and accepted, which should lead to them becoming easier to obtain in the future.

There are several types of natural/renewable insulation, as summarised below.

Cellulose fibre is made from post and pre-consumer waste paper and is available in boards of various thicknesses or loose fill in bags for loft applications. It can also be wet sprayed within timber frame construction. Cellulose is particularly suited for use in ventilated or breathing constructions. Of the renewable insulation materials available, it is also the cheapest and DIY is an option in some applications.

Sheep's wool insulation is made from either new or recycled wool, some of which comes from sheep that have not been dipped in any pesticides. The insulation comes in rolls and batts of different sizes and thicknesses. Due to its hygroscopic properties, it is ideal for use in breathable roofs and timber framed walls as it allows water vapour to move through the structure. No special tools are required in its application. It can be cut with a sharp pair of scissors or a knife. A major benefit of sheep's wool (as with the plant products below) is its ability to absorb (and release) more than one third of its own weight in moisture, without impairing the insulating properties of the fibres. This means it can control condensation in the insulated cavity and helps to cool the building in summer and warm it in winter. Wool insulation has low embodied energy and is completely biodegradable.

Flax is mainly used in the production of linseed oil but a few companies are exploiting its fibres for insulation. Flax insulation is made from the short fibres from the flax plant, currently from flax grown in Austria and Germany. Flax can be grown in the UK and is most suited to growing in Wales and the south west of England. Flax insulation is available in rolls or batts in a range of thicknesses and lengths. It can be used in pitched roofs between and over ceiling joists, in suspended floors and in timber or steel frame walls.

Hemp is thought to have great potential as an insulation product. Hemp fibre is increasingly being used in the automotive industry as a superior product to synthetic materials, typically for interior panels. It is also used for making prestige paper, horse bedding and garden matting. Hemp is a fibre crop, well adapted for cultivation in the UK, and in fact can grow in many countries throughout the world and in a range of climates. Currently the largest European producer is France.

Cork has been available for some time as an insulation product and as wall and floor tiles. However, the insulation board is still not widely available at builders' merchant type outlets although it can be obtained from more specialised companies. Cork comes from the cork oak tree grown mainly in Portugal as well as Northern Africa and Spain. Cork forest management does not require pesticides, fertilizers or irrigation and the cork produced is both renewable and recyclable. Cork insulation comes in boards of varying thicknesses, which are generally used as insulation for warm roofs (i.e. on the rafters not the joists) and in timber frames. They can be used in dormer cheeks as well.

Cotton insulation is not suitable for growing in the UK and all cotton used in this country is imported. Cotton grows in warm, humid climates and tends to need large amounts of pesticide, fertilizer and water. Using 'new' cotton for a renewable insulation does not therefore make much environmental sense. However, products are now available from recycled fibres mixed with wool and polyester. There are now at least three companies in the UK supplying insulation from waste cotton.

Wood insulation boards are a range of boards made from pulped wood waste (usually softwood) from sawmills. The insulation is made by first pulping the wood shavings or chippings and soaking in water before compressing to various densities and at various thicknesses. This method of manufacture has been very successful and a very wide range of insulation boards are now available.

The future for natural insulation

Cost, certification and construction design still remain the main barriers to the more widespread uptake of natural insulation. Although a survey carried out for the research paper behind this article found that respondents felt that a 10% to 30% price premium over 'normal' insulation would be attractive to the general market (premiums in the research were found to range from 0% to 500%).

The technical specifications of many of the products examined was found to be impressive, even though there is still limited (not widespread) experience of their application in the UK. Of course, they need to be specified correctly to optimise the overall thermal properties of the building and are more suited, on the whole, for breathing buildings (or breathable elements of a building).

Further information

Further details can be found in 'Renewable Insulation Materials, A guide' published by Impetus Consulting. This contains:

- *information on thermal conductivity, density, U-values and energy consumption in manufacture*
- *feedback from users of the different materials*
- *a product use comparison table and*
- *examples of stockists.*

The report from which this information is extracted was created with some funding from the Pilkington Energy Efficiency Trust. This culminated in the production of a guide to using these materials. The key points from this research are summarised in this article:

www.impetusconsult.co.uk/what.htm

Sheep's wool is so natural you could sleep under it!

Photo courtesy of Thermafleece.

Windows and glazing

Timber window manufacturers have focused hard on their products and have been rethinking, redesigning and reconsidering. **Keith Hall** reports on an industry reborn ...

Consumers might be forgiven for thinking twice before choosing timber windows. They certainly earned themselves a bad reputation in the sixties and seventies and this reputation for poor quality in workmanship and material opened the door for, first aluminium windows and then later, uPVC. Thankfully, the quality of timber windows has increased greatly but dispelling the perception that timber windows need intensive maintenance regimes that could carry hidden costs is not so easy to fix. Lately, not just the materials and workmanship have changed, the industry has learned from its rivals and introduced modern production and finishing techniques, including offsite pre-finishing and quality assurance schemes.

From an environmental perspective, drivers such as the Environmental Protection (Prescribed Processes and Substances) Regulations of 1991, have led to a shift by the industry to using 'safer', preservative treatments and coatings, with some going even further and producing 'eco' windows specifically for this sector of the market. Manufacturers have also paid heed to performance expectations, adopting an 'holistic' approach to the specification of all materials used, and giving due attention to better component design.

Thermally decoupled 'passivhaus' standard windows are now available from a few suppliers in the UK. Photo courtesy of Green Building Store.

Now, window manufacturers build into the design a very wide range of factors. For instance, which timber species should be used, chosen on the basis of its durability, dimensional stability and above all its sustainability and environmental impact, with many now offering Forest Stewardship Council or Pan European Forestry Council certification as standard across their range. Certainly, at the 'green building' end of the timber window spectrum there have been some great advances in the UK with at least two new facilities starting production of high quality, high environmental standard and super efficient ranges.

The wood coatings' sector has also responded to environmental concerns (and legislation changes of course) by reducing solvent content and developing high-solids' coatings and improved water-borne formulations, with lower dirt retention characteristics. However, the expectation of higher performance and sustainability carries with it its own demands. Pre-finishing of external joinery has many advantages which offer the end user a very high quality product. But in order for the end user to benefit from that quality, there needs to be a parallel responsibility by the whole construction industry (the builder in particular) to handle and use this pre-finished joinery in a manner which reflects its value.

There are ways of ensuring that the products (windows and doors) are given adequate protection until the point of hand-over. This may require the adoption of such practices as installing windows into openings built around pre-fabricated formers. One of the most recent developments in the industry has been the introduction of energy performance certification, similar to that given to domestic appliances (see below).

It is clear that the joinery and wood coating industries are responding positively to change through a process of integration and closer co-operation. It is only by further extending this approach, working with the installers, going beyond the manufacturing operation into the building process, and above all, meeting and addressing the requirements and concerns of the consumer, that timber windows will secure their rightful place back on our buildings.

Energy Window

Energy Windows Ltd.
XYZ 68/abc

A
B
C
D
E
F
G

C

Energy Index (kWh/m²/year) -15
(Energy Index certified by BFRC and based on UK standard window. The actual energy consumption for a specific application will depend on the building, the local climate and the indoor temperature)

The climate zone is: UK

Thermal Transmittance (U_{window}) 1.5 W/m².K
Solar Factor (g_{window}) 0.41 W/m².K
Effective Air Leakage (L_{factor}) 0.02 W/m².K

Reg. No.: XXX
www.bfrc.org

This label is not a statutory requirement. It is a voluntary label provided as a customer service to allow consumers to make informed decisions on the energy performance of competing products.

Passivhaus windows

A development for the UK has been the introduction of windows manufactured to the German passivhaus standard. Not only do these incorporate the most advanced triple glazing, with typical glazing U-values of around 0.6W/m²K, but to meet the stringent comfort criteria of the the passivhaus standard, solid timber frames are not sufficient. As a result various innovations incorporating thermal breaks in the timber frames have been developed. A number of ranges are now available in the UK, mostly manufactured in Europe, and some certified by the Passivhaus Institut as complying with its requirements. Arguably these represent the limit of thermal performance available with currently available glazing and frame technologies. They will be required for those designing to the passivhaus standard, as well as offering solutions for those working to higher levels of the Code for Sustainable Homes.

Turning to glazing, on new homes, double glazing is just about standard now but many existing properties still need to be upgraded. With our increasing love of large glazed areas, it may well pay to consider enhanced double glazing, or even triple glazing, if we want to keep those wide open views but avoid large heating bills, and minimise carbon emissions. Whilst double-glazing can reduce heat loss through windows by up to 50%, our love of large glazed areas is undermining these reductions. The technology for high and ultra-high performance glazing is well established, and the uptake is improving all the time but until newer advanced

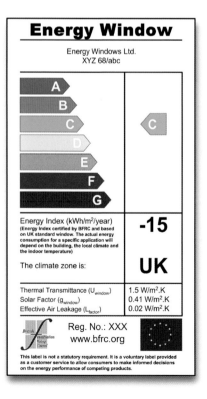

Average U-values	*W/m²K*
Single glazing	*5.4*
Double glazing with 12mm air gap	*2.6*
*Double glazing with hard low-e coating**	*1.8*
Double glazing with hard low-e and argon gas	*1.5*
Double glazing with soft low-e and argon gas	*1.2*
*Triple glazing (including 2 x soft low E, argon fill)**[8]*	*0.5 - 0.7*

Average U-values of a range of glazing types.
** minimum Building Regulations requirement.*
*** typical passivhaus standard window.*

technologies, like vacuum glazing, become commercially viable, which is likely to be some years yet (see Volume 2 for a description), there is not huge scope for improvement on the current best practice.

An air gap between the glass of 16mm and 20mm is considered to be the optimum, and the difference between the two is negligible. Below 16mm the direct heat transference between the panes reduces the effectiveness and over 20mm air convection between the panes that has a similar effect. The basic standard for sealed unit double glazing, as required by the Building Regulations, would be a 28mm thick unit combination as such: standard float glass / 20mm air gap / hard coat Low E. This would have a U-value typically of about 1.8W/m^{2}K.

Low-e coatings

Low-e (low emissivity) coatings are a microscopically thin metal oxide or semiconductor film applied on one or more surfaces of the glass, usually on a face between the panes of a double glazed or triple glazed unit. Double glazing, using low-e coated glass, gives energy conservation properties equivalent to standard triple glazing. The coating is usually applied on the outer face of the inside pane (or outer face of both inner panes in triple glazing), facing the air cavity. These coatings work by reflecting long wavelength heat generated within the room (radiators and heating appliances), back into the building, whilst at the same time allowing short wavelength, solar energy (from daylight and sunshine) into the room. The incoming short wavelength solar energy is re-radiated by internal building surfaces at longer wavelengths, which are then re-reflected by the coating back into the room.

Comparing low-e glazing

Hard coat - also known as pyrolytic coating, this coating is applied at high temperatures and is sprayed onto the glass surface during the float glass process.

Advantages:

- the coating is durable, which allows for ease of handling and tempering
- can be tempered after coating application
- can be used in single glazing applications
- utilizes passive solar heat gain.

Disadvantages:

- higher U-values, compared to soft coat, low-e, products
- higher solar heat gain coefficient, compared to soft coat, low-e, products
- hard coat glass also has the possibility of a slight haze, which can be visible at certain angles.

Tradenames:

K glass is made by Pilkington.[6]

NOTE: Pilkington do supply a type of soft coat low E glass known as Optitherm but in the UK most of their Low-E supply is in the form of Pilkington K Glass.

Soft coat - also known as 'sputter coating', this is applied in multiple layers of optically transparent silver, sandwiched between layers of metal oxide in a vacuum chamber. This process provides the highest level of performance and a nearly invisible coating.

Advantages:

- high visible light transmission with optical clarity - minimal color haze
- ultra-low emissivities, giving optimum winter U-values
- up to 70% less UV transmission, compared with standard clear glazing.

Disadvantages:

- soft coat low-e must be used in a double glazed unit; the soft coating is sensitive to handling
- most soft coat, low-e, products require tempering the glass prior to the coating application
- edge removal of the coating is required to ensure a proper seal in an insulated unit
- more expensive than hard coat, low-e, glass.

Tradenames:

Saint-Gobain (Planitherm Total)[5]
Pilkington (Optitherm)[6]
Interpane (Iplus)[7]

Low-e coated glass looks identical to ordinary clear glass, as the coating is almost invisible. Its effect on light transmission and reflection is hardly noticeable. It can be used everywhere, from the largest office block application to domestic conservatories, windows and doors and whilst designed for double glazing, it can also be used as the inner pane in secondary glazing, although hard coat low-e would be recommended for this application as it is tougher and more resistant to scratches (see boxout above for more details). The advantages include the following;

- improved insulation
- reduced heating bills
- reduced carbon dioxide emissions
- reduced condensation

- reduced cold spots and down draughts
- takes advantage of the sun's heat.

Gas fills and glazing bars

Argon and other gasses

Instead of air; argon, krypton or xenon gas can be injected between the panes. These gasses have better insulation properties than air and contribute to much better overall insulation (see table). For instance, with an argon fill the U-value would be reduced by over 30%. The gasses only displace a proportion of the air in the unit and it is generally accepted that the double glazed unit should achieve a 90% fill gas-to-air concentration. This concentration will gradually reduce with age, at a rate estimated from 0.5 to 1% per year. Units filled with argon do not degrade significantly until they reach 75% concentration, which adds up to about a 20 year performance durability, after which the unit will perform the same as an air filled unit (this may vary depending on the type of spacer bar used).

Not all double glazing manufacturers are yet able to offer double glazing with a gas filling. Contact the GGF[1] for details of those that can. Other gasses, such as krypton and xenon, can be used but they are harder to source and more costly. Chris Herring, of the Green Building Store[2] who sell a range of exceptionally high specification windows said "Given optimal cavities, argon filled units give virtually the same performance as those filled with the denser and much more expensive gases Krypton and Xenon. Their advantage is that they enable the cavity of the glazing unit to be reduced without affecting performance. Given the expense, their use is best limited to retrofit units which are required to fit narrow glazing situations. High performance argon filled triple glazed units, for example 4-18-4-18-4 with two soft coat low E coatings can achieve almost 0.5 W/m^2K centre pane value".

Spacer bars

Advanced technology spacer bars are now becoming an essential part of any double glazed unit that intends to achieve seriously low U-values. There are now a number of different types available with the foam rubber 'Superspacer' from Edgetech IG[3] being the most common. Herring said "I am not convinced there is much to choose between the advanced spacer bars, they all seem to perform well, with pretty marginal differences. The important thing is to get away from metallic spacers to true warm edge spacers. Our Ecoplus range of windows use the Superspacer, which we have found to be perhaps the spacer with the widest take-up in the UK. However our Ecoclad range normally use Swisspacer or Thermix[4], which are more widely available in Eastern Europe where they are manufactured.".

Whichever of these advanced spacer bars you choose it will significantly reduce the heat loss around the edges of the units. Most people will have witnessed the condensation that forms around the edges of double glazed units, well the advanced spacers significantly reduce or eliminate this (condensation on glazing may vary with a number of environmental factors as well as technical factors to do with the composition of the unit). However, the most significant savings using these types of spacer bar will be achieved on windows where small (Georgian) type glazing units are used due to the edge to area ratio. However, their use on all sizes of double glazing units will enhance the energy saving potential of the window. Warm edge spacers can also reduce sound too – up to 2 decibels (according to Edgetech) compared to aluminium spacer bars. ☯

References

1. *The Glass and Glazing Federation:* ***www.ggf.org.uk***
2. *Green Building Store:* ***www.greenbuildingstore.co.uk***
3. *Edgetech:* ***ukenquiries@edgetechig.com***
4. *Ensinger:* ***www.thermix.de***
5. *St Gobain:* ***www.saint-gobain.co.uk***
6. *Pilkington:* ***www.pilkington.com***
7. *Interpane:* ***www.interpane.de***
8. *For triple glazing the coating is usually applied to faces 2 and 5, i.e. outer face of inner pane and inner face of outer pane.*

Further reading

There is an in-depth feature about windows (including passivhaus windows and design criteria) on page 57 in Volume 2 of the Green Building Bible.

Natural paints and stains

For over 30 years, a handful of natural paint producers have maintained a small presence within the wider paint industry. This niche market is growing, **Lynn Edwards** explains ...

The synthetic chemical paint industry only really took off during the relative affluence and consumer boom following the 2nd World War. These paints and finishes, that are so easily available in the mainstream, like many other modern consumer products, have relied on fossil fuels as the raw ingredients for many of their components – binders, solvents (volatile organic compounds - VOCs), pigments and additives. However, these resources are unsustainable and no longer as abundant and cheap as they used to be. The manufacturing process, extracting and refining them, uses huge amounts of energy. Their production often results in toxic waste and there has been concern, for some time now, about the health effects of using synthetic chemical products. Thankfully, in the EU, there are increasing regulations restricting solvents and other harmful chemicals.

Manufacturers and suppliers are driven to provide paints and finishes well suited to their primary purpose: to protect precious building materials from external elements such as rain, UV light, and atmospheric pollution. Vapour permeable products, that allow the building to 'breathe', also prevent damage to the building fabric. Interior surfaces may also need protection from general wear and tear. Some of the natural paint producers have just hung on in there - continuing to make the traditional finishes; limewash, milk-paints, linseed oil and natural waxes - finishes that have been used to protect and decorate our homes for centuries.

Why use eco-finishes?

The motivation for ecological paint manufacture and use are the same as for any area of green building:

- minimisation of pollution to the air, water, earth and to our bodies and those of other creatures - during the whole lifecycle of the product
- reducing or eliminating carbon emissions from intensive energy use
- reducing our dependence on fossil fuels as raw materials
- intelligent and responsible use of natural resources: whether renewable, or abundant.

Over half of UK landfill waste is thought to consist of construction materials. The more 'lightly' a building material is finished, or the easier it is to remove or re-coat the finish, the easier it is to reclaim and reuse building materials following demolition. Eco-paint manufacturers avoid the use of certain surfactants, and phthalates, which are thought to be hormone disruptors. They make minimal use of preservatives and biocides – choosing those that they feel are less harmful to human health. They also avoid the use of other VOCs such as toxic co-solvents and plasticisers. Residual monomers are another type of irritating, and potentially toxic, VOC. They are responsible for the familiar, fresh paint smell that follows the use of many conventional emulsions. Some eco-paint manufacturers say that they use high quality synthetic binders, which result in a minimum level of un-reacted monomer off-gassing following their use.

Planning a low impact decoration job

Buying from ecopaint suppliers is a positive start. But there is more you can do to make your painting and decorating greener. First, keep decoration to a minimum, where possible. If you are starting from scratch (in a new building perhaps), you could choose building materials and design details that need no decorative finish or extra protection from the elements. For instance, windows and doors which are made from durable UK grown oak or sweet chestnut can be left unfinished and they will last indefinitely and look wonderful. As the wood ages it takes on a silvery sheen, which is nature's own protection.

If you are going to decorate, choose simple finishes, made from renewable or abundant materials that have minimal processing. Natural paints and finishes are available from distributors all over the UK now, and some are actually made in the UK. You can even make your own and some of the books in the 'further reading' section, at the end of this article, contain recipes and instructions. As with any finish, all paints must be suitable for the purpose, properly applied and maintained. In certain circumstances, if durability is the primary concern, it may be more prudent to revert to a finish that has a heavier 'footprint'. Most natural finishes will not need stripping before they are renewed (over-painted). They tend to 'weather' from the surface, rather than suffering from film failure, flaking or peeling. This avoids the use of stripping products and the resultant waste.

Choices

There are plenty of environmentally friendly products to chose from; this article can only be a brief introduction to the subject. A choice can be made according to building type and location, substrate, accessibility and ease of renovation. Budget, plus personal aesthetics and awareness of maintenance cycles will also affect choice.

Exterior walls

Exterior walls are coated to offer the building fabric some protection – from erosion by the weather and environmental pollutants, and to slow the penetration of water. It is worth noting here that it not wise to try to make exterior walls completely waterproof as this will prevent moisture escaping and will act to trap any water that does penetrate past the waterproofing layer. This is one reason why natural finishes are so perfect for exterior decoration, they allow the wall to breathe. In green building terms the choice is generally between two types of mineral coating: limewash or a silicate paint. Both paints rely upon the natural 'chemical bonding' of a coat of stone (either limestone, or quartz) to the wall. Neither limewash nor silicate coatings rely on the formation of a film of paint 'binder' for their stability. Both finishes 'weather' from the surface, and never need stripping off before re-decoration.

Limewash has been in use for thousands of years. It is especially suitable for use on buildings constructed by 'traditional' methods, such as cob, and is the perfect finish for lime render and plaster. Limewash is an extremely simple, inexpensive finish. It consists of lime putty, water, and natural pigments. The lime putty is made from limestone, an abundant material. The 'lime cycle' is a closed, sustainable process. Apart from the quarrying of the limestone, the major environmental cost of producing limewash is the energy needed to 'burn' the limestone in kilns at around 1000°C. At one time there were small limekilns all over the country,

What are VOCs?

VOC stands for volatile organic compound. This title sounds relatively harmless, especially the word, organic which seems to imply that it is from natural sources. Alas the truth is far from this. Organic compounds can be a potentially lethal mixture of benzene, toluene, methylene, chloride, formaldehyde and more. 'Volatile' means they evaporate easily at room temperature. According to the Environmental Protection Agency, exposure to VOCs cause symptoms such as nose and throat discomfort, headaches, breathing difficulties, nausea, asthma attacks, skin irritation and allergies. High levels of exposure may cause damage to the nervous system and there is emerging evidence that VOCs act as carcinogens.

Most synthetic household paint, emulsion, gloss and varnish all contain VOCs. Do any of the above symptoms sound familiar? Are you literally dying to paint your house? With just a little research one may find shocking evidence of how prevalent these toxins are in our day to day life, not only in paint, but also in synthetic furniture stuffing, carpets and even laminate flooring. The government is aware of the health and environmental risks due to exposure to VOCs and is constantly working, alongside EU Directives, to reduce the use of VOCs in industry and manufacturing, which should lead to improvements in air quality and public health.

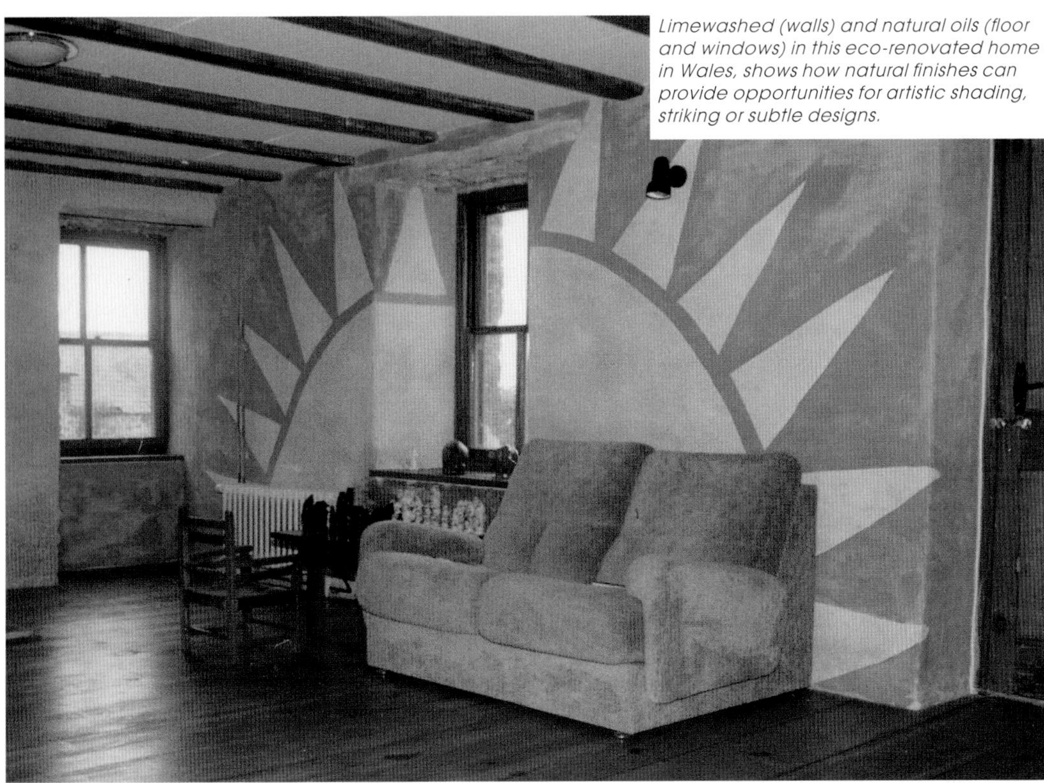

Limewashed (walls) and natural oils (floor and windows) in this eco-renovated home in Wales, shows how natural finishes can provide opportunities for artistic shading, striking or subtle designs.

fired with locally sourced wood, supplying lime for buildings in their immediate locality. Limewash, like lime mortar and render, is a 'breathable' material. This means that it is good for the health of the building itself. Lime is also highly alkaline and therefore antiseptic and anti-fungal. Traditionally, limewash is regularly renewed with simple wetting and overpainting – perhaps once a year. Limewash can also be used for interior walls.

Silicate coatings are exceptionally durable and this is proven as they have been in use for over 125 years. Like limewash, they are made from abundant raw materials: quartz sand and potash, melted together at 1400°C, to make potassium silicate (waterglass). Like limewash, silicate coatings are solvent and biocide free. They are completely odourless and inert, making ideal interior finishes for allergy sufferers. They are also fire retardant and are not susceptible to attack by mould. Silicate coatings are more expensive than limewash, but are particularly hardwearing and weatherproof. They are also resistant to atmospheric pollution, so are very suitable for exterior use in urban environments. Silicate coatings last several times longer than modern synthetic masonry paints, needing maintenance only after around 20–25 years.

Silicone resin paints are sold by a couple of eco-paint suppliers. Although these may be classified as synthetic film forming paints, the film is microscopically open pored and therefore vapour permeable. This is very important for the health of the building, and also improves the durability of the finish, because moisture vapour is not trapped underneath. Silicone resin paints are highly water repellent and weather resistant and have a re-decoration cycle of around 15 years. They are straightforward to apply, and can also be used over sound pre-painted surfaces.

Interior walls

Most wall paints are made white and opaque by using white pigments and fillers. Chalk is one basic type, but in modern paint formulations the most highly valued and commonly used white pigment is titanium dioxide. Titanium dioxide is responsible for most of the energy used to produce wall-paints because, although an abundant natural element, it is not easily accessible and requires a high level of purification. Most eco-paints are additionally coloured with natural earth and mineral pigments, resulting in soft, neutral tints. Some manufacturers also use non-toxic synthetic pigments in order to achieve brighter, deeper shades.

Distempers are rarely used now, having become unfamiliar since the advent of DIY-friendly emulsion paints, but there could be a revival of their use as ecological finishes. Distemper is easily made from water, glue, chalk and natural pigments with, possibly, the addition of some linseed oil. It is a 'reversible' coating, meaning it can be washed off. This increases the potential recycle-ability of building materials but will limit the areas in which it can be used.

Casein paint is made from dried milk curd mixed with an alkali such as lime. Again, these are cheap, renewable or abundant ingredients. Like distempers, many casein paints do not contain titanium dioxide and are naturally free of solvents and other VOCs. Casein, a versatile paint, can be used on woodwork as well as walls and finished with oils, waxes and glazes. An emulsion of casein and linseed oil was one of the first ready mixed wall-paints and casein emulsions are still available from a couple of eco-paint manufacturers. Emulsion paints are a more familiar type of product than casein paint or distemper, and are convenient and easy to apply.

Oil and resin emulsions are emulsion paints for walls that are bound with plant based oils and resins. These raw materials are fairly easily extracted and processed. Any by-products from the manufacturing process are biodegradable. Natural emulsions are available in a range of finishes, suitable for any interior area, including busy public buildings, kitchens and bathrooms.

Because many natural paints are based on traditional recipes, and therefore have naturally muted tones, they work well in helping to create a traditional ambiance, without seeming dull or tardy.

Synthetic resin emulsions are made by some companies that call themselves 'eco' paint manufacturers. They use a synthetic paint binder derived from petrochemicals. What differentiates these products from the main-stream? In these products, the manufacturers will have focused on reducing their use of ingredients such as titanium dioxide, in order to lower the overall environmental impact of their product. They have also made their paints healthier for the end user. It is mainly paint additives, not the binders, which are often the culprits in paint toxicity.

Claypaints are thick, so really effective at both covering and filling. This hygroscopic finish regulates the moisture content and improves the feel of indoor environments. Clay is not a renewable resource, but it is abundantly available. Some claypaints are 'self coloured' by their natural mineral content, so additional pigments, including titanium dioxide are not required.

Exterior woodwork

Exterior woodwork is usually given a 'finish' in order to protect it from damage by weather and ultra-violet (UV) light. Dense timber types like oak, and certain coniferous woods, such as Western red cedar and Douglas fir, are naturally resistant to moisture absorption. Open-pored wood, such as pine, really needs the protection of paint – otherwise it will continually swell up as it gets wet with rain and dew, then shrink again as it dries out in wind and warmth. It is important to protect wooden windows, doors, frames and sills from moisture damage.

Oil finishes are the most simple, low impact option for treating exterior timber. Applying linseed oil is a common choice and is particularly suitable for treating wood. Other plant and animal oils and waxes are also used throughout the world - often whatever is locally available. There are obviously a number of environmental benefits to be had from using these minimally processed renewable ingredients, especially if plants are organically and locally grown. In the case of linseed oil, for example, even the 'waste' product can be used, eg. as an animal feed. The oil penetrates the pores of the wood, helping to keep moisture out, and thereby minimises the natural movement that occurs with timber exposed to the elements. It also aids water repellence. Oil finishes oxidise on contact with the atmosphere and sunlight, so need to be renewed frequently. The maintenance cycle varies according to conditions, but may be every 6 to 18 months. Timber treated with clear finishes will be bleached by sunlight and turn a silvery-grey colour. The surface structure of the wood will also be degraded by UV light, becoming rough and fibrous.

Oil stains work by penetrating the pores of wood. Oil bound stains have the same moisture regulating effect as clear finishes. However, because they contain pigments, transparent stains also give the surface structure of timber some UV protection. Opaque stains give increased protection. As with clear oil finishes, stains gradually oxidise, and the finish needs to be renewed every two to four years.

Oil paint gives the highest level of UV protection. Add chalk and pigment to a 'drying' oil like linseed, and you have a simple traditional oil paint. Linseed paint is one of the best paint systems. It involves a penetrating oil primer that nourishes the wood and forms a good bond with subsequent layers of paint. The whole paint system remains slightly flexible, so the paint is less likely to crack if the timber does move. Cracked paint not only flakes off, it allows moisture ingress and rot. Linseed paint does not fail in this way. As the surface oxidises, it becomes matt and chalky, but the wood remains protected and the paint is easily renovated with a coat of linseed oil after 5 to 7 years. The major drawback with traditional linseed paint is that it must be applied in several thin coats, and each coat can take a long time to dry if atmospheric conditions are not warm and dry. There are other natural oil based paints on the market, some of them are water-soluble.

Alkyd resin paints are made from natural 'semi-drying' oils, such as soya bean oil, refined and combined with synthetic resins. Alkyd resin paints can be used in much the same way as conventional gloss paints and dry much more quickly than traditional oil paints. Solvent free, water-borne alkyd resin paint systems do not penetrate the wood like linseed oil. However, they form tough, durable paint films with good adhesion to the substrate.

Interior woodwork

Interior surfaces are 'finished' to give them protection from wear and tear and to make them easier to clean, or for purely decorative reasons. Much of the following applies equally to natural materials other than wood such as cork, stone, and unglazed tiles. Although the focus here is on floor finishes, the same or similar products can be used on worktops, shelves, furniture etc. Of course, interior woodwork can also be stained or painted.

Floor soap is an extremely natural low impact finish that, being alkaline and frequently renewed, has a mild antibacterial action. A concentrated solution of floor soap in water is scrubbed into bare softwood floorboards, until the pores are saturated. A thin surface layer of dried soap gives light protection to the floor. Regular washing with a dilution of soap cleans and replenishes the finish. Should be thoroughly renewed every 3 – 6 months.

Oil finishes penetrate the pores of wood, replenishing its natural oil content and making it less absorbent of moisture and dirt. The finished effect is extremely natural and very easy to renovate, but offers minimal protection from wear and tear, or staining. Linseed oil is commonly used, together with other plant oils derived from beans, nuts and seeds. Additionally, resins and waxes are often included in oil finishes. These may be sustainably sourced, like colophony (rosin), or they may be derived from coal tar or petroleum, but included for their toughness and resistance to moisture, acids and alcohol.

There are many different types of oil finish on the market. Some are simply neat oil plus driers. Others may also contain plant-derived solvents. Some manufacturers use isoaliphates – solvents derived from natural gas. Solvents have been one of the main suspects in concerns about paint toxicity. All solvents have the potential to affect human health by inhalation of their vapours and through contact with the skin. Solvent free, water based oil finishes are also available.

Casein sealer is another alternative, solvent free and quick drying, way of treating softwood. Floors that are going to be waxed can first be glazed using a casein sealer.

Wax is usually used as a topcoat for floors that have already been oiled. Wax gives more protection from general wear and tear, dirt and liquid spills – although these should be promptly wiped up to avoid watermarks. Wax is vulnerable to abrasion, especially in high traffic areas, and requires regular maintenance. Waxed floors are easy to 'spot repair', but should ideally be totally re-waxed and buffed once or twice each year. Traditionally, the most commonly used type of wax is beeswax. However, plant waxes such as carnauba and candelilla, may also be used. Other waxes, derived from petroleum, may be added for their toughness. Wax finishes come in solid or liquid form, and solvent free products are available. There are some alternative products on the market, also based on a combination of natural oils and waxes, which do not need buffing. These finishes are hardwearing, easy-to-maintain, and very suitable for high-traffic areas.

Varnish is a thicker, more hardwearing and more protective finish than wax. A varnished surface is waterproof, heatproof, stain resistant and easy to clean. However, scratches inevitably occur and these are more difficult to touch up without the finish becoming patchy. Total renovation, although infrequent, may mean re-sanding the whole floor before re-varnishing. Like wax products, natural varnishes may be solvent borne or water borne. ☯

Further reading

'A Handbook for Eco Paints and Finishes', by L Edwards, published by Eco-logic Books in 2008.

'Natural Paint Decorator' by L Edwards & J Lawless, (first published in 2002 as The Natural Paint Book).

The books above are available from: ***www.greenshop.co.uk***

Using natural paints

Pam MacDonald offers guidance to help you choose which methods and materials to use when trying out eco-friendly finishes on your next decorating project ...

Natural paints are available to cover many different kinds of internal and external surfaces and stockists will help you choose the best products for the job and the finish required. Walls need to breathe and be coated with micro-porous finishes that help to alleviate damp and condensation problems and contribute to a healthier living environment. Calculate the exact quantity of paint needed for the job to eliminate waste and disposal, allowing a small extra amount for touching up later. Always read the instructions for use on the container, as some products need to be diluted with water. Note the drying times between coats and be aware that natural finishes need time to harden. The declared ingredients' list will alert you to any potential allergy concerns and here tester pots can be very useful, not only for trying out colour but for noting the way that the product behaves and smells.

Natural paints are now available in a huge range of pre-mixed colours and finishes but mixing your own is another exciting option, using non-toxic earth and mineral powder pigments. These need to be measured and soaked overnight in either oil or water, depending on whether the pigment is to be mixed with an oil or water based product. Stir thoroughly, test for colour and note the quantity needed, then add the mixed colour into the paint. For large quantities use a power mixer or a kitchen whisk for small amounts and wear a mask to prevent inhalation of the fine dust particles.

Natural emulsion often contains titanium dioxide that gives the paint whiteness and opacity, therefore, mixing in pigments will not produce strong colours. Using a low titanium product will produce medium strength colours, whilst powdered casein paint, based on milk protein, lime and chalk, contains no titanium dioxide at all and will achieve the deepest, most intense shades. Alternatively, full tone liquid colours can be used neat or mixed into emulsion to achieve varying depths of colour.

Surface preparation and application

Preparation is the first and most important aspect of decoration. A properly prepared surface will form a solid, reliable base for the finish layers. Walls must be sanded down to remove old flaking paint or plaster and paintwork rubbed down to remove dirt and grease and provide a key for subsequent coats. Layers of paint or varnish can easily be stripped using a safe, effective water-based product. Holes and cracks in walls and wood need to be filled with chemical free fillers, based on natural ingredients like gypsum.

Natural emulsions can be applied by brush, roller or spray and look like and perform in a similar way to conventional products. They are designed to cover old finishes as well as new plasters and can have a washable or wipeable, matt or silk finish. For use as a primary coat on new plaster, most brands can be thinned with water or a specific plaster primer can be used. These paints can take longer to dry, one coat per day is normal, with two coats achieving the best results. Once opened, these paints have a limited shelf life as they contain no chemical fungicides or preservatives.

Clay paints offer a beautiful, durable alternative finish that can be used in kitchens, bathrooms and on timber and masonry. The clay absorbs moisture, regulating the internal humidity of the building and making it ideal where condensation is a problem, though it should not be used on walls in direct contact with water. Casein paint will cover most absorbent surfaces, including wood, and has a lovely soft, matt, chalky finish that is wipeable and breathable, but cannot be used in damp rooms as it will become mouldy. It needs to be applied in thin coats with a brush and appears translucent until it has dried. It is sold as powder that needs to be dispersed in water, mixed and left over periods of time before applying and used up fairly quickly once mixed. Clear or tinted translucent wall glazes can be used over finishes that need added protection or to give greater vibrancy and depth.

Limewash is probably the cheapest of all natural paints. It is made from either slaked or hydraulic lime, it is breathable and durable and can be applied to most surfaces, externally and internally. Limewash can be bought pre-mixed or you can make your own using lime putty diluted with water and coloured with natural pigments. This traditional finish is best used on other lime or absorbent, non-smooth surfaces and should be applied in thin coats and dried out slowly. As lime is caustic, eye and skin protection is essential. Another natural external paint is silicate mineral paint and this was discussed in the previous article.

There are a range of natural paints, stains, oils, varnish and waxes available for coating and protecting timber surfaces that can be either oil/solvent or water based systems. Linseed oil finishes take time to dry but penetrate the wood and replace oils lost through age and weathering, keeping them flexible and reducing the risk of flaking and cracking. They won't disintegrate under ultra-violet light like most modern synthetics, but eventually wear thin with age, thus making the application of a maintenance coat straightforward. Water based systems, used externally are not as durable and need more regular maintenance than a highly pigmented linseed oil paint that is time consuming to apply initially, but can last up to fifteen years.

When using paints or stains on wood it is important to choose a product that will adhere to the surface to be coated. Some can only be applied to bare wood, i.e. coloured stains and glazes, clear primers, oils, varnishes and waxes, and old coatings will need to be removed. However, natural satin/gloss paints will generally cover old paint coatings as long as they are cleaned and sanded first. Paints based on soya alkyds will happily sit on acrylics but don't take shortcuts on coats - undercoats add to the durability of the finish, especially when used externally. Allow plenty of drying time and adjust your decorating schedule accordingly: floor finishes take a long time to harden and need to be treated with caution until then. Water based products, in particular, will raise the grain of the wood and need de-nibbing or light sanding between coats. Whilst oil paints provide an easy flowing, brush-mark free finish, water based coatings can be more difficult to pull out and lay off with the brush, especially those that are quickly touch dry. Here, using a small gloss roller rather than a brush, will make the paint application easier. Paints designed for wood can usually be applied onto metal surfaces, as long as a metal primer is used first.

Clean up and waste disposal

Clearing up at the end of a day's decorating is simple and straightforward. Remove paint from around the edges of containers, as this will dry out and can fall into the paint when the lid is next removed. Never pour paint down the sink. Natural paints that contain biodegradable ingredients can be left to dry out and then be added to the compost heap. Empty containers can be washed out and then reused and any paint not needed for touching up can be kept for intermixing and colouring for use elsewhere later.

Remove as much excess water based paint as possible and wash in soap and water or a gentle cleaner concentrate. Brushes used for oil or solvent based products can be cleaned in thinners containing citrus oils and ethanol. This liquid can be strained after settling out and reused, but must be disposed of at a local waste/re-cycling centre. Linseed soap will do the job without containing any solvent. Using natural paints not only produces a vibrant, breathable and durable finish but rooms can be put back into use straight away without compromising the health of the decorator, the building, or the environment.

Roofing materials

Getting the design of the roof right will give considerable benefits in terms of reduced energy use. But which roofing materials carry the least embodied energy?

Jerry Clark reports ...

Half of all energy use in the UK is in our buildings. Of that total, 90% is consumed while the building is in use, and only 10% is embodied energy, i.e. that consumed in the construction of the building. With this in mind, vast improvements could be made in building structures and insulation levels, to hopefully reduce energy use during occupation by around 75%. If this was achieved then of course, the percentage of embodied energy would become of far greater significance. Roofs are one area where we can look at the embodied energy of a wide range of options with the view to choosing the least energy intensive material or method. Of course whilst doing this, we need to ensure that we do not compromise quality, robustness or durability. Let's take a look at the options available.

Roofing material types

Roof coverings can be manufactured from a wide range of materials. Some of these are described briefly below.

Clay tiles are one of the UK's most traditional materials. The clays (and natural minerals found within) are fired at high temperatures, in excess of 1100°C. This binds and cures the materials into the durable roof tile that adorns many UK homes. The higher the firing temperature, then the longer the life of the tile. On the down-side, of course, the high temperatures involved lead to a high embodied energy, but this embodied energy component is offset by a longer lifespan of the product.

Concrete tiles are made in essentially the same way as any other concrete product, with the proportions of 1:4 portland cement and aggregate. Mixing and chemical curing takes place in highly technical and controlled conditions. From this the manufacturers are now able to offer very long service guarantees – most offering a minimum of 50 years (remember though clay tiles have proven to last many hundreds of years).

Natural slate, as the name suggests, has no man made components other than the skill of the craftsman to 'hew' them from the larger slab. Quality of natural slate can vary, with Welsh slate renowned worldwide as one of the most durable roofing materials ever discovered. Some European slates, though cheaper (due mainly to lower labour costs), have been found to have far less durability due to mineral pockets (usually iron) within the slate seams. These irons eventually rust and expand, causing the slate to crack and decay.

Steel and aluminium has become a popular roof cladding material again. Traditionally steel was used as corrugated sheets, either galvanized or self colour, but latterly colour-coated or with a plasticised coating. More recently we have seen the emergence of fake tiles and slates which are actually sheets of steel, coated with a mineralized surface to mimic the desired appearance. The two main advantages of this type of roofing have been weight, cost and speed of installation. The largest market for these products seems to be roof refurbishment. Steel is produced from mined iron ore, coke and limestone melted together in a high temperature furnace. The coke turns to carbon monoxide, reducing the iron oxide to iron. Between 25 and 40% recycled material is used in the final steel making process.

Bitumen is the residual material produced after removal of all the volatile products from crude oil, such as petrol and diesel. Asphalt is manufactured from bitumen, blended with limestone

Roof type	Embodied energy (MJ/m²)	Weight (kg/m²)	Lifespan (years)	Material abundance	Recyclability
Clay tiles	270 – 430	40 – 60	30 – 100	abundant	good
Concrete tiles	40 – 90	40 – 90	30 – 100	abundant	good
Natural slates	20 – 40	20 – 30	100+	150 (Welsh)	very good
Coated steel	180 – 290	7	30	230	fair
Aluminium (virgin)	550 – 920	<10	100+	260	good
Aluminium (recycled)	30 – 90	<10	100+	abundant	good
Asphalt shingles	285	low	20 – 30	75	poor
Timber shingles	2 – 14	low	50	renewable	fair
Membranes	high	very low	15 – 25	75	poor

Environmental aspects of a range of roofing materials. The figures in the first two columns refer to one square metre of roof cladding material, thus making it easy to compare various materials. Some materials proved too difficult to obtain accurate embodied energy figures.

powder and fine limestone aggregate. Another source is lake asphalt, a naturally occurring material mainly imported from Trinidad. Asphalt tiles make up 75% of the US roofing market, but unfortunately these products have low durability.

Timber shingles are riven or sawn from suitable timber, such as oak or western red cedar.

What about sustainability

One important aspect of the sustainability of roofing materials, which is not highlighted in the above table, is the pollution caused during manufacture and supply of the various materials. The 'embodied energy' column gives a good indication of the relative quantities of carbon dioxide produced during manufacture, but says nothing of all the other more toxic pollutants. It is therefore recommended that materials should be selected to perform the set task while minimising all impacts, including pollution. Direct comparisons of the various pollution risks are difficult to make, but the following gives a rough indication of the kinds of pollutants involved.

Clay tiles - although the embodied energy is high, there are few toxicity issues involved in their manufacture.

Concrete - has a lower embodied energy, but more CO_2 is released (see 'Cement and alternatives' earlier in this chapter).

Steel - production releases dioxins and other localised pollutants during smelting, and the pollutants produced in the manufacture and application of the now common PVC (Plastisol) coating. PVC manufacture involves considerable amounts of chlorine (a nerve gas) and results in the release of further dioxins when the steel is recycled.

Aluminium - is a highly durable and very recyclable material but its main hamstring is the very high energy consumption of the manufacturing process (though high recycling percentages help to keep consumption comparable with steel).

Lead and copper - both have a high degree of corrosion resistance, but their use for large areas of roofing can lead to a degree of contamination in the rainwater runoff. Copper is extracted from sulphide ores and the mining process is associated with pollution of waterways by heavy metals.

Bitumen and asphalt - systems are renowned for their short product life. Due to their being very difficult to recycle, this leads to further use of precious oil reserves, unless an alternative replacement material is used. Both slate and shingles have no pollution implications, apart from that involved in extraction and transport.

Acknowledgements

Some of the information in this article is based on 'A Guide to Sustainable Roofing' published by Redland Roofing Systems.

Green roofs

Green roofs are now becoming very popular in the UK. There are two types, extensive and intensive, and there is quite a difference between the two. **Olwyn Pritchard** and **Peter Acteson-Rook** tell us about them ...

Green roofs are not a new idea, although they haven't been popular (until recently) in Britain since the days of earth walls and sod roofs. They are far more common on the continent, but over the last few years there has be a renaissance in the UK. Partly responsible for the new trend in green roofs is steel manufacturer, Corus, who introduced a profiled steel tray system called Kalzip Nature Roof, suitable for creating simple but effective, thin soil sedum roofs. Buildings boasting this new breed of roof include the House of the Future at Cardiff's St. Fagans Museum, office blocks, supermarkets, railway terminals and some new homes across the UK.

Green roofs offer a number of advantages in terms of the environment generally, and some to the building and user specifically. For instance, in urban areas, green roofs can provide a useful habitat for birds and invertebrates. So much 'waste' land has been redeveloped that there are few habitats to support the insects on which birds depend[1]. Brownfield city developments often result in the destruction of specialised, drought resistant

An extensive green roof used to interesting effect at the BedZED development, near London.

habitats. These can be recreated on roofs and, if recycled, crushed aggregate from the original site is used, this saves on disposal costs. Green roof/brown roof habitats are ideal for insects to breed and as more are installed we could see the return of certain bird species.

The benefits of green roofs

Firstly, the durability of green roofs need not be a concern as one green roof in Switzerland is known to date from 1914. In fact it could be argued that a green roof might actually improve the durability of the building as a whole by protecting the underlying membrane. Another major advantage is its absorbency, the ability to temporarily store water during a storm, with up to 85% of the rain being delay-released, thereby helping to alleviate pressure on storm drainage systems. Green roofs also absorb heat from the sun, which acts to reduce what is known as the 'heat island effect', a phenomenon now common in built-up areas where temperatures can rise quickly on hot summer days. Noise too is much improved by the use of green roofs, and greenery, in general, will act as an acoustic muffler, both inside the building and outside.

Health benefits

Green roofs have proven health benefits for people living nearby. For example, in Germany, the roof of a Bundepost Office in Stuttgart was 'greened' and absenteeism due to sickness among the workers fell dramatically, compared to neighbouring blocks with conventional roofs.

Localised air quality is improved by green roofs. Ozone, a major contributor to air pollution in cities, is exacerbated by 'heat island' conditions, hence, more green roofs equal less ozone pollution. As a bonus the plants on the roof absorb carbon dioxide, and give out oxygen, further improving local air quality.

A Texan study of post-surgery patient recovery in hospitals demonstrated that recovery was quicker if the patients could look out onto green space. Since then architects have been incorporating green roofs into hospital designs more frequently. A few community hospitals in the UK are now being designed with more green-space provision, and the good-practice work on hospital design being developed by the Commission for Architecture and the Built Environment (CABE) is likely to address this[2].

There is a growing body of evidence that visual and physical contact with natural greenery provides a range of benefits to people. These include both mental benefits (such as reduction of stress) and physical benefits (including the provision of cleaner air). Access to green space can bring about direct reductions in a person's heart rate and blood-pressure, and can aid general well-being. Also, widespread installation of green roofs in cities could, by lowering localised temperatures, reduce the number of heat related deaths during the increasing summer hot spells.

Types of green roof

Green roofs are often referred to as 'intensive' or 'extensive'. Either can be flat or with a shallow/medium pitch.

Intensive green roofs usually have a significant depth of growing medium and support grass, small plants, herbs, etc. A roof garden, at the furthest extreme, could have shrubs and small trees. Simple turf roofs are usually referred to as 'intensive', and these are within the construction capabilities of most self-builders. Intensive roofs usually need some maintenance, such as watering in dry weather, mowing, and weeding. The weight of the soil can be a disadvantage and needs to be considered at the design stage, when water retention and snowloading need to be addressed. A turf roof with 150mm of soil can be 2 or 3 times heavier than a slate roof[3].

Extensive green roofs usually have a much thinner soil layer, are lighter, and are usually planted with drought resistant succulents of the sedum species. These are usually grown on a fibrous mat with a thin layer of porous growing medium (called sedum mats). Sedums are used because they are wind, frost and drought resistant and because they absorb water. The sedum mat is rolled out on a specially designed roof, with several manufacturers now offering complete systems. Although these can be expensive, they are a simple solution and have proven to be very popular in recent years. Like intensive roofs, extensive roofs still provide habitat for insects and therefore a feeding ground for birds. Maintenance is minimal and they are not usually suitable for walking about on like intensive roof gardens, but they are a good choice for a large area of commercial or industrial roof.

Brown roofs are another form of 'extensive' system which has been tried out in inner city areas, to mimic industrial wasteland habitat for biodiversity. As more brownfield land is grabbed for development, then groups like the Wildlife Trusts are encouraging developers to consider putting a brown roof on their buildings. Brown roofs can, in some cases, use recycled aggregate from the site on which the building is built. Such roofs can then be left to colonise naturally or be seeded with a wildflower mix that requires poor soil fertility. Materials may include sand, gravel, stones or timbers, all creating a range of habitats. Some seed and small creatures will be imported with the rubble, and recolonisation takes place much more rapidly than with a sterile growing medium. In most cases, no maintenance is needed or even desirable, as old stems provide necessary nesting places for certain wasps and small bees.

In the remainder of this story, ***Peter Acteson-Rook*** *considers the construction and cost implications of extensive green roofs and what they can achieve.*

Intensive green roofs are what one would, in the past, often refer to as a roof garden. Deep soils of 15cm and over, trees, and other features, these roofs are often suitable for human use. Intensive roofs support a diverse range of vegetation, grasses, trees, shrubs, even ponds and hard landscaping.

Extensive green roofs differ in the fact that they are not designed for walking on, and the soil/substrate depth is anything from as little as 1cm up to 15cm. Often monoculture in their growing species, the most commonly used plants being sedums. These sedums are chosen for their durability and the fact they can survive on shallow substrate depths. Mainly from more arid climates, sedums are succulent plants that survive in dry conditions by storing rainwater in their tissues. Nowadays these plants are commercially grown on matting of set sizes so that the plants can be harvested on rolls and taken to site to create instant green roofs of any size.

Sedum matting on a roll showing just how thin some green roofs can be.

Germany is widely accepted as the centre of expertise in modern extensive and intensive green roof installation. This expertise has developed over the past thirty years and Germany boasts the unrivalled estimation that around 10% of all roofs have been 'greened'[14]. This equates to around 8,000 acres of green roofs, way beyond installations anywhere else in the world at present. The technology involved in green roofing systems is expanding rapidly as more and more research is carried out worldwide.

The main environmental advantages of extensive green roofs include:

- storm water management
- reduction in heat island effect in urban areas/cities
- sound proofing
- insulative qualities
- absorption of carbon dioxide

- offers some protection of roofing membrane from the elements
- improved microclimate and biodiversity.

(the above list could also apply to intensive green roofs).

Stormwater management

One of the main manufacturers of green roofing systems suggests that with a low substrate depth of 2 to 4cm, 40% of rainfall will be retained annually in its roofs, leaving the other 60% to run off naturally. Other manufacturers claim retention figures of up to 90% reduction in storm water run off, and they claim that 'the increasing use of extensive green roofs in cities significantly reduces the risk of flooding'.

Even DEFRA, in its publication 'Greening the Gateway, claims up to 70% water retention on green roofs[5]. One of the leading research bodies conducting thorough experimentation in extensive green roofing is Penn State University in Portland, Oregon, USA. It puts the figure more realistically at around 50% of a 2.5cm rainfall event being retained on the roof. It does state that annually, 50-70% of rainfall could be retained. This is a figure backed up in an article by Theodore Eismann in Landscape Architecture magazine, stating the same 50–75% storm water run off reduction on the recently greened 1,300,000 square feet Montgomery Ward Building in Baltimore USA[6]. Most studies and publications are in agreement that there are major advantages in attenuation of storm water in extensive green roofs. In the past rainwater has been channelled off roofs and roads into drains. In storm conditions run off combines with sewage, and has to be released into rivers in order to prevent sewage combining with storm water and being released into the streets. After the August 2004 storm conditions in the southern UK, warnings had to be issued about bathing in the seas after large quantities of storm water and sewage discharged into the Thames. In one 24-hour period, 3 million cubic metres of sewage were discharged into the Thames in London. The discharge carried 10,000 tonnes of screenable solids, including faecal matter[7] which flowed out into the Thames estuary and its bathing beaches, destroying wildlife in the Thames and killing many thousands of fish.

The urban heat island effect

The uban heat island (UHI) effect is the effect that causes air temperatures around heavily built up areas to be 2-10°C warmer than the surrounding countryside or suburbs (see diagram below). It is caused simply by large quantities of thermal mass in cities and towns, where there is a lack of vegetation. Vegetation allows the principle of evapotranspiration (ET) or the sum of evaporation and transpiration from trees and plants. Quite simply vegetation breathes in much the same way as a human breathes. That 'breath' is moisture rich. Research by the US geological survey (USGS) found that up to 10% of the moisture in the atmosphere is transpired from plants[8]. A large oak tree can give off 415 litres of water per day; an acre of cornfield can give off around 11,400-15,100 litres per day, according to the USGS.

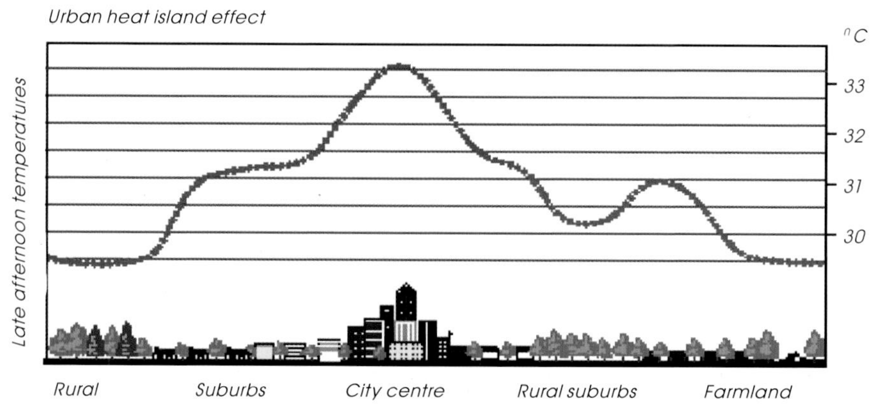

This water is taken up by plant roots and given off by the leaves. Sedum, although a succulent, still gives off this moisture, and although at a much lower quantity as compared to an acre of cornfield, it is still going to be a far more useful surface for roofing than a conventional pitch and felt flat roof system, in relation to reduction of the UHI effect.

One of the contributory factors towards the UHI effect is the increased demand for air conditioning systems in cities and towns. This used to be confined to the warmer climates, but with a succession of hotter summers in the UK, it is more or less standard in the commercial districts, and certainly on the increase in the domestic market. Clearly then, this increased demand for electricity means more power generation and more carbon emissions from our power stations.

Possibly the worst thing about the UHI effect is that the increased heat encourages the increase in air-conditioning units, which, in turn, produce more heat. Air-conditioning units are notoriously inefficient as around 40% of a unit's energy is wasted in the form of heat transfer directly to the outside of the building in the form of heated air into the atmosphere. The warmer a city's atmosphere, the higher the demand for air-conditioning, the more the air-conditioning systems heat the external air, the higher the temperatures will rise, an extremely damaging cycle.

Weight considerations

A typical extensive green roof system has the following components installed and the weights are as stated in the table below.

Product	Use	Weight saturated
Extensive substrate	*Growing medium*	*120kg/m^3*
Sedum blanket	*Vegetation*	*44kg/m^2*
Fleece layer	*Filter layer*	*Nominal*
Reservoir board	*Water storage 10L/m^2*	*10.65kg/m^2*

Most extensive roofs increase the weight by around 70 to 170kg per square metre (when dry), over the weight of a roof constructed from small plain clay tiles.

Product	Weight per m^2
Small clay plain tile	*68-78kg*
Concrete pantile	*46-52kg*
Welsh slate	*17-23kg*

Even with the worst-case scenario of a saturated extensive roof, there are modern lightweight and low cost products strong enough to cope with such a weight, i.e. Masonite 'I beam' as an example for flat roof constructions, as opposed to the standard pitched roof constructions seen in most houses today.

It has conventionally been the case that most extensive green roofs are of flat or lightly pitched construction. Sedum need not be restricted to flat roofs, as modern technologies have been utilised to secure sedum rolls in place on pitched roofs of up to and sometimes over 20 degrees.

One major consideration with green roof construction is the possibility of leakage. With modern methods of joining roofing membranes, they can now be tested for leaks pre-installation, both electronically and by simple flood testing (on a flat roof), before the rest of the roofing layers are built up.

As the industry is in its infancy here in the UK, the costs, at present, are quite high, but the more popular and common green roof installations become, the more likely that costs will begin to fall.

If a green roof is being considered for a conventional flat roof replacement, then there are other considerations in cost savings, as the thicker the substrate level, the better the insulative and cooling qualities. In hot weather the surface of a roof becomes extremely hot, with bitumen flat roofs reaching temperatures in excess of 70°C. This can cause damage to roofing membranes as the constant expansion and contraction from hot day-time to cool night-

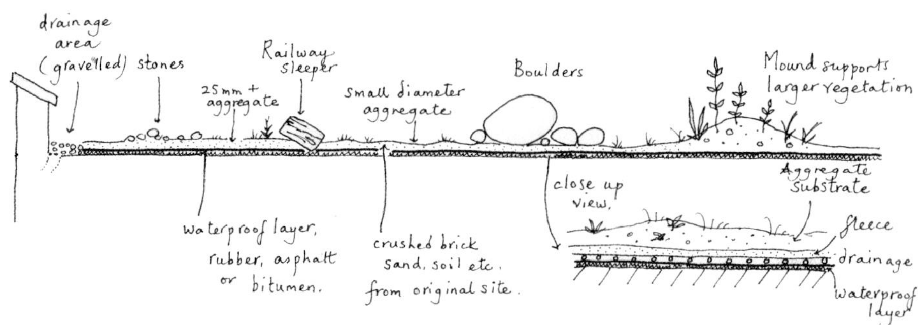

Simple details of green and brown roofs

Drawings by Olwyn Pritchard

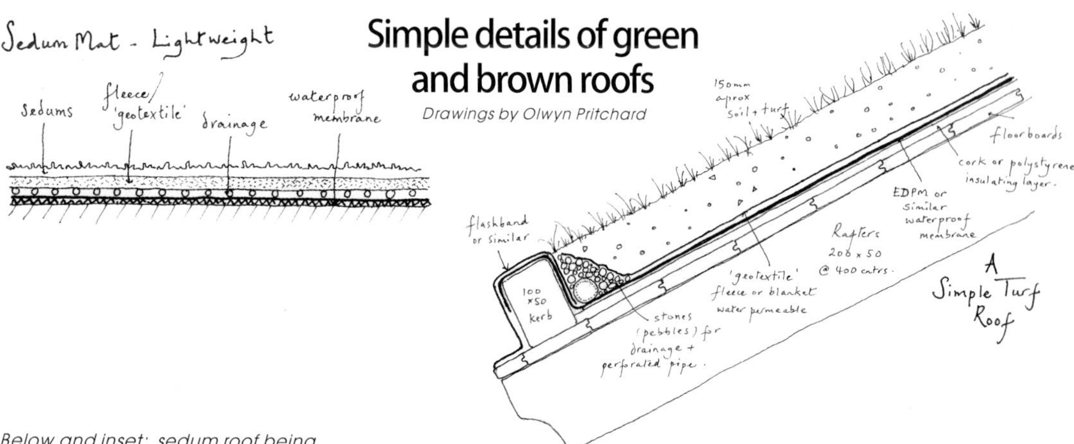

Below and inset: sedum roof being installed in the extensive roof method using the Oldroyd waterproofing system.

Pictures courtesy of Safeguard Oldroyd.

time temperatures causes wear and stresses to the roof. UV damage also occurs and this will reduce the lifespan of a roof. Even with clay tiles or slates, degradation occurs through the effects of freeze, thaw etc.

Placing a layer of vegetation over these membranes, in the form of an extensive green roof, delays the effects of ageing and damage caused by the above. Due to the many and distinct advantages of green roofing it is an extremely viable option to reducing the stresses and strains placed on roof surfaces. Some manufacturers estimate that this would double the life of a roof structure's waterproofing system. In considering costs, although a small gain, the cooling effects and insulation properties of a green roof will contribute to lower energy bills, in respect of either winter heat or summer cooling.

Conclusion

With the call for over a million new houses in the UK in the coming decades, green roofs are a real possibility for a change in the way we deal with the rainwater run off from the surface of our roofs, especially in large-scale developments. Moreover, it could alter the whole way we require and design high-pitched roofs for domestic homes. The many advantages of having a living natural roof surface must surely see this medium increasing in use over the coming years. Extensive sedum roofs could be important in large-scale development in preventing the spread of the urban heat island effect. Integrate sedum roofs with sustainable urban drainage systems, and we may go a long way to helping replenish underground water supplies, by diverting storm-water run off back into the earth, rather than through the easily overloaded sewerage systems.

To sum up then, green roofs offer an alternative to traditional roofing, and are particularly useful where water retention, biodiversity and health benefits are goals.

Note: Early in 2008 the new London Plan came into force and this included the first green roof and green wall policy in the UK. The policy expects all major developments and refurbishments to include green roofs and walls in their plans. ***www.livingroofs.org***

References

1. ***www.blackredstarts.org.uk*** *or* ***www.wildlondon.org.uk***

2. ***www.livingroofs.org***

3. *John Talbot, Findhorn Foundation:* ***www.ecovillagefindhorn.org***

4. ***http://horticulture.psu.edu***

5. *Office of the Deputy Prime Minister, Greening the Gateway Creating sustainable communities, Crown copyright 2004.*

6. *Theodore Eisenman, Sedums over Baltimore, Landscape Architecture Aug 2004 (article).*

7. ***www.guardian.co.uk***

8. *Evapotranspiration and Droughts, USGS, U.S. Global Change Research Program.*

Further reading

'Building Green (A guide to using plants on roofs, walls and pavements)' by Jacklyn Jonston & John Newton, London Ecology Unit.

'Planting Green Roofs and Living Walls', by Nigel Dunnet & Noel Kingsbury (2004), available from the Green Shop, 01452 770629 ***www.greenshop.co.uk***

'Green Roofs Ecological Design and Construction' by Leslie Hoffman et al., Earth Pledge, Schiffer (2005).

'Green Roofs and Facades' by G Grant

'Building Greener', CIRIA guidance document

Useful websites

www.greenroofs.org

www.safeguardeurope.com *(Oldroyd)*

www.enviromat.co.uk

www.greenroof.se

www.greengridroofs.co.uk

www.flaguk.co.uk

www.optigreen.com/start.html

www.kalzip.com

Roofing with thatch

Thatch was the first organic material utilised by early man to provide shelter. It is rarely used now but **Stephen Letch** believes it will become more popular ...

For prehistoric man, thatch kept out the rain, snow and wind. Little thought would have been given to its sustainable and insulation values as it wasn't an issue then - our ancestors would merely toss an extra tree onto their open fire to keep warm. The perception of thatch has, in many respects, not changed through to present day. At worst it's considered a primitive form of roofing and at best a romantic symbol of the past, shrouded in artistic mysticism, seemingly to be preserved only on our old listed buildings for its aesthetic appeal.

It is a matter of debate whether the substitution of slate for thatch, in cottages and small farm-houses, is an advantage. Thatch makes a house warmer in winter, and cooler in summer, than slate. In winter, it prevents the warmth produced by the fires from escaping; and in summer it absorbs few of the sun's rays, allowing little heat to penetrate through it.

Types of thatch

There are four primary raw organic materials that have, or are still used in the UK for thatching purposes. These are water reed (Norfolk reed), heather (ling), combed wheat reed (Devon reed) and long straw (threshed). These last two materials tend to be from the harder wearing wheat crops but could be from rye or oat crops.

Thatching materials are skilfully prepared on the ground and applied to a roof to give, through their individual specifications, very different aesthetics, textures, densities and thickness. Due to these variations in thatch types. we can expect to see slight divergence in their durability and thermal resistance values.

Admirable green credentials

Thatch types do vary with their principle thermal conductivity values, i.e. water reed being 0.09W/mK and long straw being 0.07W/mK. Knowing these values, we can work out the U-values and thermal resistances of each material. Long straw thatching on a new roof frame performs best. Its 450mm thickness specification has an R-value of 6.43, which is equivalent to 150mm of foil backed rigid polyurethane foam insulation. To gain the full benefits of thatch's insulation properties, buildings must be designed to utilize the whole roof space for living quarters, either as a sealed roof

Holiday cottages at Hellevoetsluis, near Rotterdam, Holland.

Traditional cutting of thatch material.

or at least a draft free system, vents circulating warm air back down to the ground floor. As an organic material, thatch breaths. It will slowly absorb moisture to then diffuse/evaporate moisture on its outside surface with the effects of wind and sun. It is still wise to take into consideration the hot/cold break in the roof space at the design stage to avoid excess condensation.

Thatch has virtually no embodied energy. About 25 litres of diesel would be used to harvest and locally transport (30 mile radius) enough of the primary thatching materials to complete an average 100m^2 cottage roof. Manpower energy is the only requirement needed to actually thatch a roof. Long straw/combed wheat reed production is a by-product of our agricultural food industry, which means that embodied energy in crop production is subsidised by the primary grain objective.

Thatch is not carbon neutral, it's more carbon negative! Straw, heather and water reed all take carbon dioxide out of the atmosphere in each growing season and lock it within its biomass. An average thatch would require approximately 4 tonnes of material. Each thatch material has between 40% and 50% of carbon in its make up, which would mean close to 2 tonnes of carbon would be stored within the thatch! Every acre of older tall wheat varieties locks up 1 tonne of carbon in its stems alone each year.

Durability and recycling

With a maintenance programme approximately every 15 years or so (usually ridge attention), a well thatched property, using long straw/Devon reed material, can be expected to have a lifespan of between 30 and 45 years. Water reed and heather thatched properties can last around 50 years. The durability of a thatch can also depend on factors such as quality of materials, skill of the thatcher, pitch, roof design and its position to the elements and sun.

When a thatch has worn down to its fixings, the usual practice is to strip old water reed thatch down to the rafters or, in the case of long straw/Devon reed, strip a top layer(s) of thatch away down to the original rafter fixed coat in preparation for the new thatch. The stripped material, if dry, could be recycled

Roofing material	Manufactured or applied thickness (mm)	Thermal conductivity W/mK	Thermal resistance R-value	Embodied energy KWh/m²	Weight Kg/m²	Lifespan(years) With professional workmanship
Clay tiles	10	1.15	0.017	75-120	40-60	30-100
Concrete tiles	10-20	1.44	0.013	12-26	40-90	30-100
Local slate	5-10	1.90	0.005	6-12	20-30	100+
Local stone tiles	40	1.30	0.023	35	100-150	100+
Timber shingles	10-20	0.13	0.300	0.5-4	40-50	50
Water reed	300	0.09	3.333	1.5	40-45	40-60
Combed wheat reed	300	0.07	4.285	1.5	25-30	30-40
Long straw	450	0.07	6.428	2.25	30-35	30-45
Heather	450	0.09-0.15	?	2.25	50-150	40-70

A comparison of roofing materials against a range of values.

into compressed bales and burnt in a heating system. Alternatively it can be used as a mulch in the garden or composted.

Thatching supports farm diversity. Rural employment would have a great boost if only just a small percentage of the government's target of 300,000 proposed new homes were to be thatched. Inland arable regions would benefit with long straw thatching utilizing cereal by-products. Coastal and estuary areas partially reclaimed by the sea could produce vast stretches of water reed for thatching, instead of importing 80% of thatchers' reed requirements each year from Eastern Europe and China. Small woods could be rejuvenated by regular coppicing of Hazel for thatching fixings.

Risks of thatch fires can be designed out for new build with the use of fire barriers and retardants. It is also important to avoid badly designed chimney flues in conjunction with poor efficiency wood/solid fuel burners.

Netting has been utilised on thatch in the UK for over 100 years, although it did not become the norm until after 1950. It is not a green material and can cause problems. Netting is used to prevent damage to the thatch from birds (particularly sparrows). However, it is the loose, thin stack thatching method that is most prone to this kind of damage. As an experiment the Landmark Trust agreed to leave the netting off (apart from gable ends) a freshly traditionally long straw thatched farmhouse in Norfolk to see what damage the local small sparrow community did to the thatch. Two years on and so far no damage has occurred to the tight thick thatch.

In conclusion, traditional thatching in the UK could become more in demand in the future, if its green sustainable benefits are properly realised as they have been in northern Europe over the past decade. Holland, in particular, has seen tens of thousands of new thatched dwellings built. Many have been built in a very innovative, modern, un-conventional style as the photo on page 238 bears testament.

Further resources

'The Thatchers Craft' stage by stage construction photo's/descriptions: ***www.countryside.gov.uk/LAR/archive/publications/thatchers_craft.asp***

'Thatch and thatching: a guidance note' published by English Heritage: ***www.english-heritage.org.uk/upload/pdf/Thatch_and_thatching.pdf***

Visit East Anglia Master Thatchers Association web-site: ***www.eamta.co.uk*** *for info and specifications.*

An introduction to low impact building

The term 'low impact construction' describes a methodology of construction which seeks to cause minimal disruption to the local and global environment. **Chris Morgan** introduces us to the low impact building arena ...

Much of the discussions in this book so far have been focused around the greening of 'regular' buildings but the next few stories will focus on the 'deep green' end of the green building arena. These building forms often have a quite different approach in their design and the philosophy behind them.

Although the term 'low impact' encompasses a wide range of building techniques, many of the principles, or characteristics of low impact buildings are shared and many can have distinctive characteristics of a region or even country. One characteristic shared by most low impact projects is that they tend to be practised at small scale and usually in rural areas. This often diminishes their perceived value and relevance, so it is worth stressing that there are few technical reasons why most of the construction types discussed here could not be employed on both a large scale, and in urban situations.

It is likely that the small scale and rural aspect to most low impact buildings is one reason why clients and builders feel able to experiment. As a result many of the most valuable innovations and developments, which may pervade more mainstream construction in the future, are probably being tried out even now in sheds, extensions and small homes up and down the country!

Low impact buildings almost always have very low embodied energy in their fabric, where the use of natural materials is often the starting point for clients and designers alike. Because of this, such buildings can, by their structural make-up, be very energy efficient and this is another of their great advantages.

For many who undertake low impact buildings, it is part of a much wider approach to life in general. However, this is not strictly necessary, as the advantages can be appreciated on their own merits. Unfortunately, it is usually only those already disposed toward this sort of thing, and who make the leap of faith which is often required, who are able to experience the advantages.

Plastering a 'low impact 'straw bale wall.

Low impact construction harks back to primeval man, when homes were built from the raw materials that could be found locally. From an ecological perspective this may be one of the best ways forward for mankind. We can employ our ingenuity, resourcefulness and the technical skills that we have learnt over generations, to create beautiful and desirable buildings. Below is one example - the Genesis Centre, which serves as a demonstration project for a range of natural materials.

Photo courtesy of Abey Smallcombe

The myth of maintenance free!

Maintenance has become a dirty word for some, and much talk is made of 'maintenance free' construction and products. However, in cheating the natural cycles of decay, many man-made products invariably contain toxins and alien materials in their composition, which are environmentally damaging and in most cases, can only prolong the inevitable for a certain time. Due to this, the culture of 'regular maintenance' has been abandoned and when something does go wrong, even when only a small part is broken, most 'maintenance free' products are removed, discarded and replaced.

In contrast, an environmental approach – and the approach of all low impact construction – is to accept an element of maintenance and to design this into the process of co-habitation with your building. Maintenance is regular, but simple, and in the process, the building and its elements are able to be kept in good order far longer – and therefore far more cheaply in the long run – than their maintenance-free counterparts.

Types of low impact construction

Low impact buildings can theoretically be constructed from any appropriate material that is found in reasonable abundance in the locality of the site where the building is to be built. Most traditional (vernacular) buildings are low impact due to the fact that our predecessors had few opportunities to transport materials very long distances. For instance, many stone farmhouses across the UK usually boast a small quarry somewhere on the farm. This is where the raw materials for the walls will have come from. Excavated by hand, or with simple machines and transported the short distance to the building site by horse and cart. Nowadays, however, stone is not really classified as low impact, as developers often choose stone from distant quarries and even from distant continents. Not so eco now!

Types of construction that might be included under the term 'low impact' could include:

- earth construction: cob, rammed, adobe and light earth
- hemp
- straw bale and other crops
- timber (though many timber eco-buildings are quite high-tech, the underlying philosophy would still be low impact)
- reused or recycled materials, old tyres for instance, known as earthships.

Materials

Most of the natural materials associated with low impact construction are hygroscopic, which means that they breath - absorbing and releasing moisture, rather than trying to just expel it (which often results in trapped moisture). Clay, in particular, absorbs and desorbs moisture freely and as such can act as a moderator of the humidity in the air, though ventilation

Rammed earth walling at the Centre for Alternative Technology, a low-tech material being employed in a rather high-tech way. Great skill and highly accurate shuttering systems are required for rammed earth. Nice, but highly time consuming and ultimately the most expensive way of employing earth walls in a building.

CAT

remains the key tool for this. This function of balancing the relative humidity in the room is particularly valuable for occupant health, since many of the health problems associated with modern buildings can be exacerbated by extremes of relative humidity.

The same is true regarding heating, and the concept of thermal mass is well understood. With both thermal mass, and moisture mass, some understanding of the issues is required, but it is possible to actually design the internal climate of a building so as to most benefit the health of occupants without the use of moving parts and the associated maintenance problems.

Sourcing materials can be problematic. Simply finding the raw material can be difficult, particularly if you intend to build in an urban area. In addition, materials are rarely standard, nor have any recognised performance criteria (in a conventional sense). This puts the onus onto someone involved in the construction to be sufficiently expert in the field to be confident when it comes to sourcing the right material. In addition there is often no commonly recognised framework for cost, so it can be difficult not only to budget, but to know if you are getting a good deal. And the issue of cost is complicated by transport, storage and by the seasons.

Whilst the material cost of low impact constructions tends to be low (providing excessive transport is avoided), these savings are usually well offset by higher costs associated with labour and time. This often means that the anticipated lower costs of low impact buildings are not realised. Many self builders get involved in building in order to offset some of the labour costs associated with builders and many also run training or volunteer days to draw in labour.

Earth

Cob, rammed earth and adobe - earth construction is still the most widespread construction method used by mankind and one third of humanity still live in earthen buildings. The material even gave its name to the entire planet – or was it the other way around - but in any event it comes with significant pedigree.

Vernacular forms of earth construction survive in many parts of the world and remain instructive on the most efficient way to produce earthen buildings, even today. There are a number of techniques but broadly they can be divided into three. The first involves stacking and compressing earth to form a monolithic wall – examples are 'cob' and rammed earth using shuttering (very specialist), adobe pre-formed and dried into blocks and then laid in the same fashion as normal blocks. These techniques employ earth as the principal load-bearing material. The principal advantage of adobe is that it avoids most of the problems associated with shrinkage, whilst the disadvantage is that it entails double handling. Another alternative is to mix earth with some filler material like straw and apply it to a framework which takes the structural loads. This was more common traditionally where timber supplies were plentiful.

A common disadvantage of all earth construction nowadays is that it can be difficult to attain the thermal insulation values required by the building regulations within the thickness of the wall itself (see pages 249 and 253 for detailed stories).

Light earth - one way around the above problem of poor insulation value is to add an insulating filler to the earth itself. This has been found to help the wall comply with modern

Straw bales being fitted between a timber frame at the Clow Beck Centre, Darlington.

requirements for thermal performance. The main technique employed is by adding straw to the earth before it is applied, usually as an infil to a timber frame structure, as the addition of large quantities of straw reduces the loadbearing properties of the earth (see page 256 for a detailed story).

Crops

Hemp-lime - is similar to the light earth composition. Hemp stalks are mixed with lime to form a solid, non-loadbearing, fairly well insulating mass wall (see page 274 for a detailed story).

Both of the above techniques require drying out times and are relatively labour intensive, though mechanisation can be employed, such as mixing and placing with excavators, though this is a small compromise of the low impact ethos. Most of the earth construction can be self finished or plastered/rendered over. Large roof overhangs are usually employed to help keep off driving rain.

Straw bale - normally involves placing rectangular bales, exactly as bricks are placed, to form a wide, hairy wall which can be either load bearing or infill to a structural frame, and which is normally plastered on both sides with a clay or lime-based render.

Straw bale construction has a number of advantages over earth and insulated earth construction types. It is a dry system and so has none of the (admittedly minor) problems associated with drying out and shrinkage. It is also a very good insulation material which, when combined with the sensible placement of

Above: a simple, but very effective, small scale gridshell roof construction at Pishwanton in Scotland, which was built on site and moved into place by volunteers. Gridshells can use a very small amount of timber to form a substantial span. The gridshell is braced by the over-layers of timber boarding.
www.buildingforafuture.co.uk/winter02/index.php

Below: in stark contrast to the roof left, the huge gridshell roof at the Weald and Downland museum was more akin to army manoeuvres but proves that low impact construction can be engineered to suit mainstream construction and can compete with more energy intensive materials, such as steel.

thermal mass, makes a lot of sense overall in the UK.

Straw buildings are also quite quick to construct, but possibly more involved than the other techniques to adequately finish. There is no doubt, however, that straw bale construction is relatively quick, cheap and easy to do, and increasingly easy to get through the legislative and financial hurdles which often bedevil low impact projects.

Other crops - a number of crop-based materials have found their way into the building material supply chain, though these are mostly imported into the UK. Among these are hemp, flax, and sheeps' wool, all used for insulation, while flax is also used in the manufacture of linoleum. Sisal, coir and jute are used in carpet manufacture, and reeds are becoming a little more common, not only for traditional thatching, but bound and used as backings to plasters and renders.

Thatch for roofs is, of course, one of our oldest surviving methods of providing shelter and is long overdue for a revival. It is made from straw, reed and heather (see story on page 238).

Timber

Timber use is so widespread it is easily overlooked but whilst timber forms the mainstay of much conventional, very high impact construction, it also has the capacity to be an integral part of very low impact construction if used wisely. If sourced from local (at least, not imported) and certified forests, and if used efficiently and without chemical treatment, and if detailed well so as to be durable, timber represents a low impact material choice. Types of timber construction include the following.

Timber frame - a method of building which uses dimensioned timber to build frames that are then raised into place and bolted or screwed together. One, quite well known method of simple timber frame construction, is the Walter Segal method[1], which uses timber very efficiently and is simple enough for self-builders and novices.

Roundpole - as the name suggests, employs poles which can be either direct logs or dimensioned poles (dimensioned poles, however, would take the method out of the low impact construction arena somewhat). The idea of round pole construction reduces the machining of timber, while retaining all of its strength. Log buildings are an example of round pole construction.

Gridshell - enables very efficient use of small amounts of timber, yet can create very large span structures. Gridshells again straddle the low tech/high tech arenas because, for large span buildings, a great deal of structural calculations need to be employed.

Green timber - (using timber that is freshly felled and not dried) - the use of 'green' timber also avoids the energy needed for kiln drying and there are a number of ways in which timber can be used. The most common examples in the UK are green oak frame buildings, such as seen in many of our historic towns and cities.

Traditional stone and brick construction, using lime and clay mortars probably counts as 'lowish' impact as discussed earlier. Brick manufacture can use large quantities of energy but in their favour, stone and brick are extremely durable materials so the 'embodied energy' reduces with age. With this in mind, reclaimed masonry and roof/floor tiles and slates are low impact (providing they are sourced locally). On the downside reclaimed masonry and slates are in great demand and can be very expensive, which tends to negate one of the attractions of low impact construction.

Interestingly there has been use, in some parts of England, of traditional rubble footings employing stone and lime (rather than poured concrete) in what may be termed low impact foundations.

People are becoming more familiar with the use of lime, and increasingly, clay, for mortars and plasters. Perhaps the main advantage of these materials for mortars is that the bricks or blocks can more readily be reused at the end of the building's lifetime, as they clean easily, not like cement mortar which tends to adhere like glue.

Reused and recycled materials

A few constructional techniques have been developed to deal directly with some of the waste arisings from industry. One of the most enduring has been the common tyre. Rammed full of earth and tied together, these have become symbols, especially in the US, of ecological design through the reuse of waste (Earthships). Drinks cans and bottles, short logs and many other unlikely materials have been similarly employed to create walls. The principal of using waste materials is a sound one, and be it tyres or recycled paper insulation, there is no doubt the impact of development is reduced. ☯

References

1. Walter Segal method of timber frame construction see: ***www.segalselfbuild.co.uk***

Further reading

'The Ecology of Building Materials' by B Berge.

'Building with Cob' by A Weismann and K Bryce,

'The Woodland House' by B Law.

'The Natural Plaster Book' by C R Guelberth and Dan Chiras.

'Oak-framed Buildings' by R Newman

The above books are available from ***www.greenbuildingpress.co.uk***

'Using Natural Finishes' by A Weismann and K Bryce.

'The Green Self Build Book' by Jon Broome.

'The Woodland Way' by B Law.

'Low Impact Development: Planning and People in a Sustainable Countryside' by S Fairlie.

'Building Green; a complete guide to alternative methods' by C Snell & T Callahan.

'Building with Hemp' by S Allin.

'The Land,' a magazine helping to empower those dedicated to low impact building: ***www.tlio.org.uk***

'Building with Earth in Scotland, Innovative Design and Sustainability' by B Little & T Morton.

'Earth Construction Handbook, Earth in Modern Construction' by G Minke.

'Rammed Earth; design and construction guidelines' by P Walker, R Keeble, J Martin & V Maniatidis.

'Light Earth Construction' by C Morgan, DTI Research Report 2002: ***www.buildingforafuture.co.uk/winter02/Earth_building.pdf***

'The Straw Bale House' by A & B T Steen.

'Building With Straw Bales: A Practical Guide for the UK and Ireland' by B Jones, Download pdf format ***www.straw balefutures.org.uk***

'Build It With Bales' by M Myrhman & S MacDonald.

'Out of the Woods: Ecological Designs for Timber Frame Houses' by P Borer & C Harris.

Recycled Materials for Housing, Scottish Homes (now Communities Scotland) 1993 by H Liddell: ***www.gaiagroup.org.uk***

Most of the books above are also available from: ***www.greenshop.co.uk***

Below: a breathing wall, timber frame holiday home, on a croft in Scotland. All natural finishes and native timber (except the floors where the client wanted engineered timber over the underfloor heating).

Photo credit: North Woods Construction and Locate Architects.

Permaculture

Sally Hall introduces us to permaculture, a way of living that respects the whole living cycle.

Are all low impact buildings a form of permaculture? Possibly, but not necesarily. Some low impact buildings, and many that will be built in the future, do not encompass or take advantage of local eco-systems that a permaculture approach might suggest. What is permaculture? The term 'permaculture' originated in the 1970's from Australian academic Bill Mollison, and his associate, David Holmgren. They used it to describe "harmonious integration of landscape and people providing their food, shelter, and other material and non-material needs in a sustainable way.

Permaculture is a way of life; a philosophy that anyone can adopt. It has grown to encompass the design of sustainable human habitats – in short it is an ecological approach to providing for all our basic needs (food, building, finance and social structure). It is now practiced as a philosophy (not a religion) world-wide; a design system that is based on working with nature rather than against it and caring for the Earth. It embraces many ideas and skills but is closely modelled on natural ecosystems.

The permaculture vision is based on three ethics; care for the earth, care for people, and living within limits; creating sustainable human habitats by following nature's patterns. It is a complete process of looking at an area holistically and taking matters into our own hands, thinking before we act, making changes in our own lifestyles, rather than demanding that others do it for us. It can deliver productive landscapes and biodiversity with humans as an integral part of the same system. It gives us the fundamental desire to do what we believe to be right, thereby making us feel part of the solution, rather than part of the problem. It uses ideas from traditional building methods and farming practices, as well as modern science and technology, encouraging us to work with what we already have. We can preserve what is best, enhance existing systems and introduce new elements. The resulting solution will therefore differ from one area to another and every project will be unique.

Permaculture is not a set of rules; it is a process of design based around principles found in the natural world, of co-operation and mutually beneficial relationships, and translating these principles into actions. It means thinking about your life or project as a whole system - working out the most effective way to live that involves the least effort and the least damage to others, and looking for ways to make relationships more beneficial.

Permaculture values the home itself as an important energy system. The sun's energy is vital and utilised by passive solar design. It can encompass any of the technologies addressed within this book. A key feature is 'zoning'; placing things appropriately in relation to each other, working on the principle that those things which require frequent attention are placed closest to the home. It is about using time, energy and resources wisely. There are many books on the subjects and regular courses are run throughout the UK.

Permaculture

Permaculture Association Britain: 0845 4581805
www.permaculture.org.uk

Permaculture magazine: 01730 823311
www.permaculture.co.uk

'The Earth Care Manual; A Permaculture Handbook For Britain & Other Temperate Climates' by P Whitfield.

'Permaculture in a Nutshell' by P Whitefield.

'The Earth User's Guide to Permaculture, 2nd edition, a designer's manual' by N B Mollison.

The above books are available from the Green Shop: 01452 770629 ***www.greenshop.co.uk***

Earth building - cob

Cob building is seen by many as a synergy of vernacular building traditions and the modern natural building movement, **Katy Bryce** and **Adam Wiseman** explain why ...

Cob is now being recognised as a fully modern, chic, yet earthy, grounded and accessible building method. It is also no longer confined to being only the chosen method of the 'alternative' self-builder, but is being used in the public realm to create new schools, community centres and modern housing developments. This is because, while not producing a panacea for all building solutions, it has many excellent attributes as one of the most 'green' building materials on the planet.

A new generation is now emerging, of people who are engaged in a global search for alternatives and solutions to the state we find ourselves in; and these solutions are not proving hard to find. Some of these solutions can be seen in the buildings of the past, the structures of the still-existing rural tribes and communities around the world. They are in the very ground beneath our feet, and the grasses blowing in the wind, the sun that warms us, and the hands and feet that we are born with. Sometimes, the simplest solutions can be the hardest to fathom.

Earth building, along with other natural building techniques, is once again being noticed and valued as a practical and life-enhancing solution to the state we find ourselves in. Clay is a healer on all levels. It can heal physical trauma as a receiver of toxins, and can address all levels of society – the academic can analyse it, the scientist and engineer can test it, the poet can lyricise about it, and the child, woman and man can hold it in their hands and build their own home together, to suit their needs, to enjoy for a lifetime.

Imagine a building material that can be dug from or near the site; needs only the addition of locally grown straw, locally sourced aggregate and water; can be mixed with your feet and built with your hands. And when the building is no longer needed, it can fall to the ground, ready to be reused by the next generation of natural builders. This is cob.

Cob is a simple, low-tech material, being composed of the cheap, accessible ingredients of clay sub-soil, straw, aggregate and water. The

Cob mixing can be fun.
Photo ©Harriet Sandilands

materials can generally be sourced on-site or locally, which means that no transport is needed to import foreign materials. These ingredients can be mixed with feet and hands and built onto a stone or brick plinth, using simple tools such as spades, garden forks and wooden mallets

Building with cob is something that is easy to learn, and can be executed by all genders, age groups and levels of ability. All of the materials are 100% biodegradable and recyclable – when the building is no longer needed, or is left to disintegrate, they will simply return to the earth leaving no trace, or can be re-mixed and used to construct a new building

Though earth construction does not provide the best insulation, when constructed as part of a passive solar design, cob can be used to great advantage as a huge heat store. Due to its high thermal mass, when oriented towards the south (in the northern hemisphere) it can absorb the heat from the sun and then release it back into the building when the temperatures decrease at night. It will also provide passive cooling in the hot summer months.

Sourcing the material

Cob is made from the simple soil beneath our feet - but not the topsoil from your garden, which is full of organic matter. It is made from the subsoil layer underneath the topsoil, which may or may not contain in varying proportions, the essential ingredient in cob: clay. The essence of cob building has always been to source the materials as locally as possible, to produce a structure that is literally in and of the immediate environment. Clay subsoils are present in many areas of the UK. Nature gives us clues as to where we may find these clay deposits. Look for areas where water comes to the surface, or where water sits for a long time after a rain storm; also the areas in your garden which are notoriously hard to dig, and where the ground cracks when dry.

The ideal scenario is to source the subsoil from your own back garden or the plot on which you hope to build. If this is not possible, there are many other places where clay can be found locally: old quarries, a neighbour who is digging a pond, a farmer's field (farmers are good people to talk to as they work the land the daily); and our favourite option is to utilise clay subsoil dug up to make way for the foundations of a housing development or road works. This 'waste product' of the building industry is carried off to a landfill and dumped at a cost.

There are many simple tests which can be done to identify the suitability of your subsoil, but the simplest way of identifying the presence of clay is by its colour: from golden browns, oranges, deep reds, pinks, greys and mauve, and also how it feels between your fingers - take a small sample and make it into a paste with water. If it is sticky and smooth there is a good chance it has a high clay content.

How to make a mix

There are many different ways to mix up cob. From the very basic low-tech, low-impact, where the only pieces of equipment you will need are your feet, hands and a tarpaulin, to the more high-tech, high-impact method of using a JCB or tractor as shown below.

To make a good cob mix you must have good ingredients. Your four basic ingredients (see

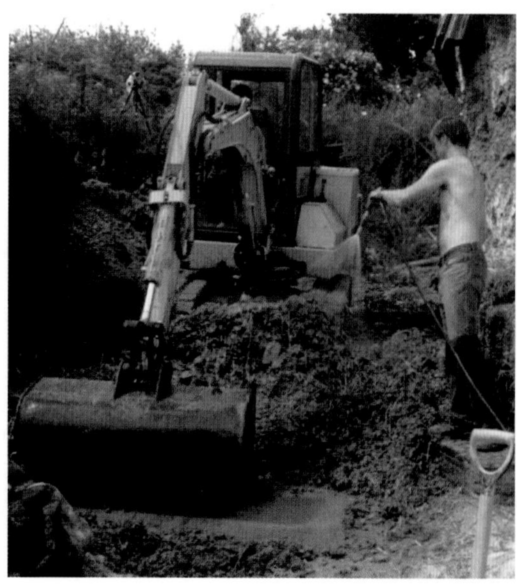

pictures below) are:

- **a suitable clay subsoil** - this acts as a sticky binder to hold the aggregate particles together
- **aggregate/sand** - this stabilizes the clay subsoil, and minimises shrinkage and cracking in the cob
- **fibre** - this gives tensile and sheer strength to the cob wall, and prevents major cracking from taking place once the cob is dry
- **water** - this enables all the dry ingredients to be mixed into a homogenous, sticky batch of cob.

To mix cob on a tarpaulin you simply need a large tarpaulin (laid flat on the ground), onto which proportions of dry clay and aggregate/ sand are placed. The tarpaulin is folded from side to side to mix these together. Water is then added, and the material is stomped on with your feet to mix it all together. The straw is then added in small increments, stomped in, and the tarpaulin rolled back and forth numerous times until all the ingredients are formed into a homogenous cob mix.

Laying

The tools you will need for building with cob are refreshingly simple and low-tech. You can find most of what you need on your body, and after a quick rummage through your garden shed. The two most important tools are your very own hands and feet. Other than that, you will need the following items: a sturdy garden fork for lifting cob up onto the wall, a flat spade for trimming the walls, and a large wooden mallet for compressing the cob from the side.

Cob must always be built onto a stone, brick or block plinth, which is at least 600mm off the ground. This prevents water from seeping into the base of the cob and causing it to disintegrate (see diagram on following page).

A cob wall is built up by compressing forkfulls of cob onto the plinth, which are then trimmed from the side to create a plumb line. The walls are built in a series of 'lifts', or layers,

Clay subsoil and fresh long, strong straw
Aggregate / sand and water

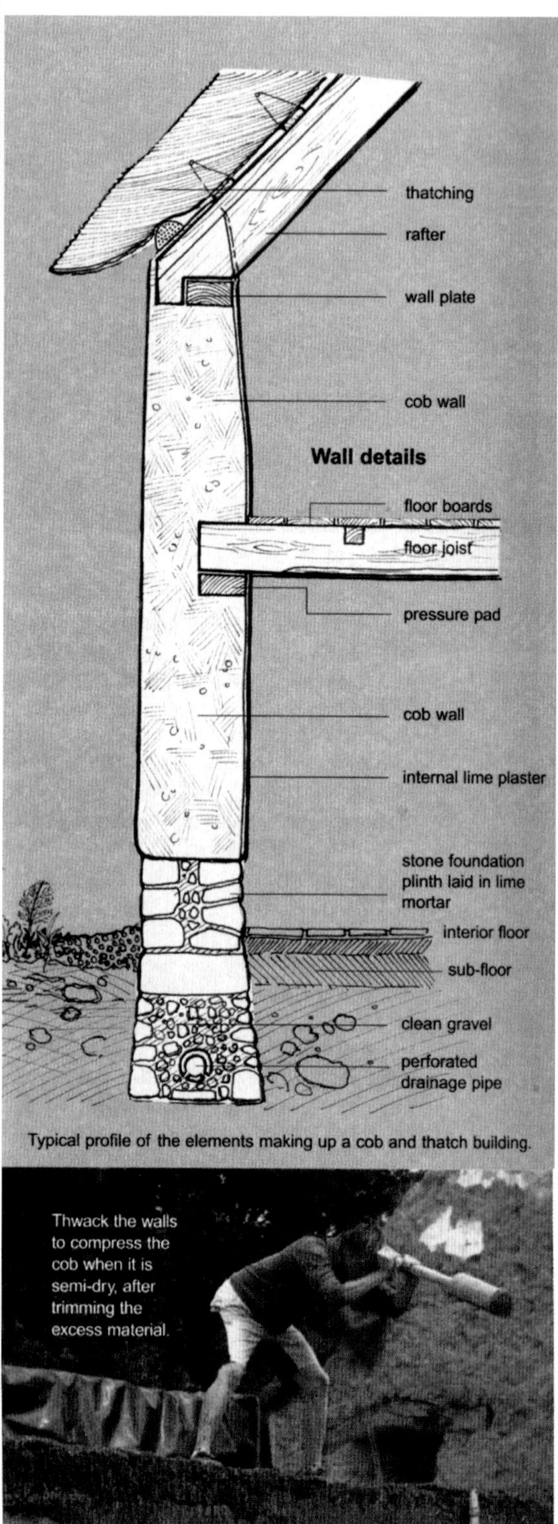

Typical profile of the elements making up a cob and thatch building.

Thwack the walls to compress the cob when it is semi-dry, after trimming the excess material.

which comprise roughly 300-500mm lifts of material built in one session. Building too much in one go will cause the wall to bulge and potentially collapse under the weight of too much wet material. It is necessary to allow the 'lifts' to dry for at least three days in between building sessions. It is essential to keep the walls trimmed as you build up, using a flat spade, so that a straight wall is maintained at all times. The standard thickness for cob walls is 600mm, although walls in Devon are sometimes built up to 900mm thick. Cob is the perfect material for creating organically shaped structures, as it is easy to mould and shape into curvilinear forms.

Suitable finishes for cob walls

Cob walls can be left un-rendered as long as they do not receive driving rain or experience prolonged freezing conditions. A render or plaster, specifically applied to any sort of earthen wall, must serve the purpose of allowing the cob to breathe, and must therefore be made of a porous material. Lime and earth are the preferred materials of choice, as they are soft, breathable and flexible, and will truly enhance the forms and curves inherent in the cob.

The principal breathable finishes that we recommend for cob walls are lime plasters/renders, earth plasters, lime wash, natural breathable paints based on plant materials, also clay paints and casein paints. ☯

The pictures and illustrations for pages 250-252 were taken, extracted with permission, from 'Building with Cob': ISBN 1-903998-72-7. £25.00. Available from the Green Building Press website: ***www.greenbuildingpress.org.uk***

Earth building - rammed earth

John Renwick discusses a sports and arts centre in Lancashire that he designed and built. It incorporates rammed earth walls and in this article he reports on the practical aspects of this type of wall construction ...

Rammed earth building is based on an ancient design system aimed at harmonising the individual with the environment. My company decided to use the technique on a sports hall that we built in Skelmersdale. Here is a summary of how we coped with the technique.

The sub-soil on the site was deemed unsuitable for rammed earth, being mostly heavy and dense clay. After investigating local sources, we selected boulder clay with a more loose structure and a large particle size distribution. Having chosen the clay, we then selected a local coarse sand to mix with it, and this was selected for its ability to mix well with the clay and to provide a strong yellow colour to the finished wall, which would otherwise have been a dull red. After testing various combinations, it was decided to adopt a mixture of 2 parts clay to 1 part coarse sand by volume.

The majority of windows in the sports hall (below) are at a high level, being fixed to the top of the walls under the eaves. The design incorporates only five windows and two doorways in the rammed earth. The decision was made to use arch formers in all but one of these to display the compressive qualities of rammed earth and avoid erosion around the joint under the lintels

Rammed earth wall work sequence

It was recognised, at the outset, that it would be an advantage to build the rammed earth walls under cover. Accordingly, the structure of the main hall, including the roof covering of concrete tiles, was completed before work on the walls was started. The rammed earth walls were built on the south, north and west side of the main hall in that order. The east wall adjoining the lobby was built later in blockwork.

Sports hall for the Maharishi School in Skelmersdale boasting rammed earth walls.

Material handling

The clay for the walls was imported from a quarry near Warrington in 20 ton wagons that were able to tip directly inside the building. In most cases the top of the wagon was literally touching the inside of the roof before the clay would slide off the tipper. It proved to be a big advantage for moisture control to be able to store the clay under cover and on wooden boards. The sand was also delivered in 20 ton loads, but stored outside under a tarpaulin.

Above: tipping of the prepared earth into the shuttering prior to ramming with a hand-held ramming tool.

Mixing

Mixing was always done under cover of the main roof. Initially a paddle-wheel mixer was used, which had the advantage of a large capacity and a grill on top, which stopped large stones in the clay entering the mix. However, it was very expensive to hire so after three walls we reverted to a conventional diesel mixer. This machine required daily cleaning and more careful attention from its user. The first mix of the day was usually discarded because the fine clay fraction would stick to the side of the drum, or else aggregate into smooth balls. Also the stones in the boulder clay, which were more than 75mm across, had to be picked out by hand before mixing.

Soil testing

Initially the 'drop test' was used frequently to establish moisture content. After a few weeks, however, the operatives could reliably estimate moisture content from the consistency and colour of the mix and its behaviour, when handled, if necessary adding water to the drum in very small increments.

The formwork

Forms were made from 2400 x 600mm steel shutters with plywood facings. These were used horizontally and held together by steel straps around the perimeter of each shutter. Vertical make-up channels were fixed at both ends of the forms to give the required length of 2720mm. The concrete columns thus provided the stop-ends. The whole was held in position by scaffolding and bolts running through the columns themselves. Arch formers above the windows and doors were made from plywood. All rammed earth edges were bevelled through the use of timber fillets nailed to the forms.

Moving the mix to the formwork

A wheelbarrow was used to move the batch and tip it next to the wall. The mixture was then shovelled directly between the forms or, for the higher levels, onto a platform. It was then necessary to move the larger stones by hand to the centre of the wall before ramming. If these were left at the sides, then there would be pockets of poor compaction where the stone is up against the form. To combat this we discovered that if the mixture was thrown by shovel against the side of the form, it had the effect of segregating out the large particles, which would rebound into the centre of the wall.

Ramming

The mixture was laid down in 100-150mm layers, which were then compacted to 50-75mm. Two hand-held pneumatic sand rammers were used individually; a low frequency 40kg one with a 175mm diameter head, and a higher freqency 30kg one with a 140mm diameter head. Operatives tended to prefer to use one or the other, but it was always necessary to use the small one in each layer to compact the corners. And it was useful to have two rammers to avoid stopping work when one of them failed.

In general, the wall finish was harder and more durable than we anticipated and both inside and outside faces have an attractive if rustic appearance. There are striking differences in the appearance of the walls on the south, north and west sides that are very visible on the outside faces, differences which are largely due to variations in exposure and quality of workmanship.

The south side was the first wall built and tends to show all the problems, such as evidence of variations in the initial moisture content, poor compaction, roughness from clay sticking to formwork, which were progressively avoided in later construction. The only window opening on this side suffered vertical shrinkage cracks due to late removal of formwork. Despite having the same 900mm eaves overhang as other walls, the south wall is more exposed to sideways rain and direct sunlight. The surface moisture content and colour of the outside face varies enormously, depending on how recent or heavy the rainfall has been. After 7 months, the visible result of weathering is a removal of fines and the appearance of hairline shrinkage cracks in the outer surface of the walls. There has also been a certain amount of spalling of the surface in places where the compaction is poor and where the form tore the face off the rammed earth when it was removed. On the north side, there was no visible weathering and minimal problems were evident due to poor workmanship, other than isolated areas of poor compaction and low moisture content.

The west side is more exposed to rain than the south side but with less sun. All three west wall sections were stabilised with 3-5% cement to counter the anticipated effect of weathering, especially on the door and window reveals. The cement content has reduced cracking and spalling, but not the removal of fines; this effect is more evident on this wall due to heavy sideways rain.

The problems outlined above can be resolved by rendering with hydraulic lime on the outside and plastering on the inside faces. Rendering will, in any case, achieve a better finish and colour, although some external faces will be left without render. The preferred plaster, internally will be clay, which will allow the wall to continue to breathe. ☯

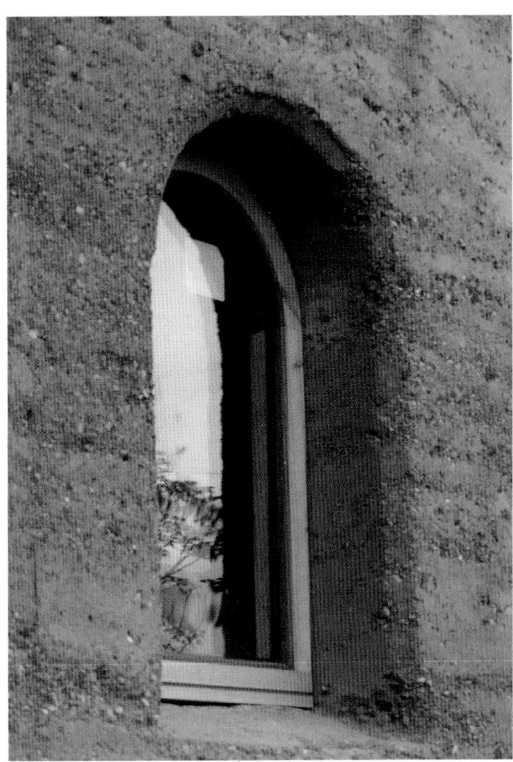

Above: one of the finished windows showing how the natural texture of the wall can give character to the building.

Photos courtesy of Partnership for Natural Building Design

The building featured in this story is a multi-use hall primarily intended for the use of children at the Maharishi School, a small independent school in West Lancashire. This school is unique in that it is a pioneer in the UK of 'consciousness-based education', a system which incorporates the use of transcendental meditation for a few minutes each day, in conjunction with the usual national curriculum. The school is non-selective, yet this innovative approach has yielded remarkable academic results.

Extracted from a story written by John Renwick of Partnership for Natural Building Design and first published in Building for a Future magazine - Volume 10, No 2 Autumn 2000. ***www.buildingforafuture.co.uk***

Earth building - light earth

What do you get if you mix straw or woodchips with clay and water, packed within a formwork that surrounds a timber frame and let it dry to form a solid, insulating wall? You get light earth construction. **Chris Morgan** and **Cameron Scott** researched this method ...

Light earth construction, as practised today, was only recognised in the middle of the 20th Century as a discrete technique and first documented in Germany in the 1930s. It did not develop widely until the 1980s when, along with a number of 'ecological' or 'neo-traditional' techniques, it was promoted and developed by enthusiasts, first in Germany, but later across the world.

Several hundreds of examples have been built across Europe and the US, but it is only in Germany and New Mexico where Light Earth Construction has been recognised within official documentation on building regulations and standards.

Brief construction notes

Light earth is made by mixing clay rich sub-soil with water to form 'slip' to a creamy consistency (see photos below). This is then mixed with fill material, such as straw, woodchip or some other material (usually plant based), to provide the light earth 'mix'. The fill material, particularly straw, must be kept dry before use and be completely covered by the clay slip. Both mixing processes may be manual or mechanical.

A structural frame (usually timber) provides the loadbearing elements of the building. In monolithic construction, either temporary or permanent shuttering is fixed to this framework and the light earth mix is placed between, and lightly compressed or tamped, to form a monolithic mass. This dries to form a solid wall. Care must be taken to ensure that the wall dries as quickly and completely as possible. Walls should be no thicker than 300mm in general.

An alternative to monolithic construction is to use pre-dried clay blocks. Blocks are laid in earth based mortar but otherwise it is the same as any other type of block construction. The use of blocks speeds up construction time on site, reduces the shrinkage that can occur in monolithic construction and enables work to be carried out at almost any time, since drying out is less of an issue. However, block construction

tends to be more expensive, either due to the cost of bought blocks, or the additional time spent in the double handling of materials.

As you might expect, light earth walls are generally, but not exclusively, finished in lime or clay based plasters and renders. Cladding over a ventilation gap is also used externally. Paints, or other surface coatings, must be chosen so as not to adversely affect the vapour permeability of the wall. Services are surface mounted or placed within conduit and fixtures may be fixed directly to the light earth but are more usually fixed to the frame.

Light earth can be used in the renovation of existing buildings. It is often of particular value being fairly insulative but with some thermal capacity and with similar movement characteristics to many traditional materials.

Only a small percentage of the costs associated with light earth are related to materials, the majority is that associated with labour. Thus any labour saving techniques tend to have a considerable effect on the overall cost and programme.

Technical characteristics of light earth

Well designed, constructed and maintained light earth properties will last indefinitely. The only significant risk to the durability of light earth comes from prolonged and excessive wetting, which can lead to decay.

The thermal properties of light earth can be adjusted by design and are intimately linked to its density; the lighter the mix the greater its insulative capacity, while the greater the clay content, the greater its ability to store heat (thermal capacity). In practice light earth is both insulative and thermally massive, which is a valuable and unusual combination offering both energy efficiency and moderated thermal comfort. Density can also be adjusted by the extent of compression of the mix on site, which can make establishing a single density impractical. Most practitioners suggest a range of densities within which they can confidently maintain consistency.

Samples of light earth were tested by Plymouth University Civil Engineering Department for thermal conductivity and capacity as part of the research. These confirmed the validity of the various European tests which have been previously conducted. The results are shown in Figure 1. The lighter mixes can be effectively used in the UK for external walls, being reasonably insulative, but trade-offs may be required under the new regulations.

Light earth construction operates as moisture transfusive construction and so is inherently protected against the risk of interstitial condensation because of the vapour permeability and hygroscopicity of the materials used. In addition, the ability of these materials to absorb moisture allows light earth walls, in conjunction with earth based coatings, to moderate internal humidity levels, with consid-

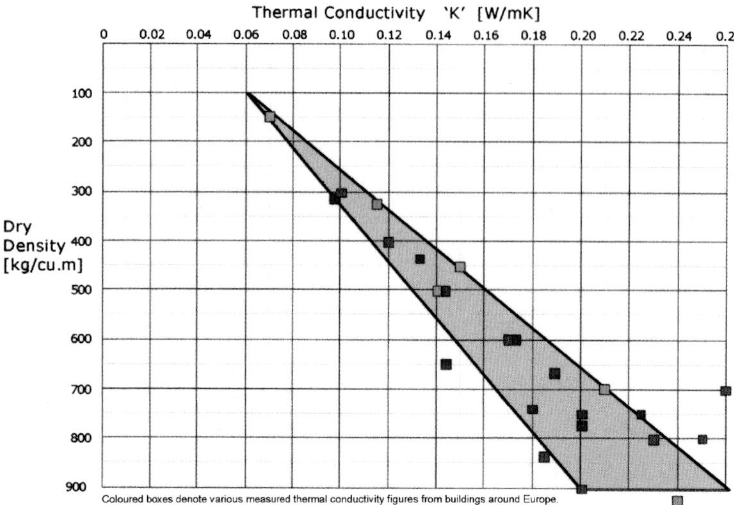

Figure 1. Graph indicating the several test figures for thermal conductivity of light earth against density, from across Europe, showing a fairly consistent pattern.

erable benefits to the health of occupants. Paint or other finishes must be vapour permeable or microporous for this to remain the case.

Acoustic criteria only apply in limited situations but while dense earth performs well in insulating against sound transfer, light earth, having less mass, performs less well. Light earth walls can be designed to perform as required but require cavities in much the same way as timber frame walls.

Light earth is difficult to ignite but officially classed as combustible due to the presence of combustible fill material (unless mineral fill is used). Even without plaster coatings, its resistance to fire is good but the presence of plaster coatings, in use, allows it to be used for all situations under the Building Regulations except those requiring non-combustible materials only. Mineral fill mixes can be used in all situations.

Indicative fire resistance tests were undertaken by Chiltern Fire International on two sample panels. An unplastered straw-clay panel of light earth density 145kg/m^3, less dense than would be normal in a building, lasted 36 minutes in a furnace with temperatures over 1000°C before burning through. A woodchip panel of density 450kg/m^3 lasted 2 hours and didn't burn through at all. Significantly the temperature on the 'cold' side did not raise much throughout the test, see Figure 2.

Even without plasters, the tests showed that combustible materials like straw and woodchip can be effectively protected by the light clay coating. The tests should dispel any residual fears that lenders, insurers, latent defect insurers and valuers have with the technique.

Advantages and comparisons

The ecological advantages of light earth have much in common with straw bale and other earth based construction types; the materials used have very low embodied energy, can usually be sourced locally, are neither themselves toxic nor require additional chemicals or energy to make into something useful and can be safely composted back to the earth after use.

Like the other techniques, the materials are cheap, but the labour required is greater than most conventional construction methods. This shift in the relative costs of labour and materials should allow self-builders, for example, to make considerable overall savings, depending on their accounting system. In addition it is an easy, flexible and safe method of building, requiring less specialised skills and tools. This is another reason why it may appeal to self builders and others not necessarily interested in its 'eco-credentials'.

Like the other methods noted, the finished buildings are potentially very healthy, being both non-toxic, moisture transfusive and capable of balancing the internal climate.

Unlike the other methods, however, light earth can be adjusted in several ways to suit the particular conditions. Most obviously it can be adjusted in density from under 250kg/m^3 (less than straw bale) to 1200kg/m^3, beyond which it is formally no longer 'light' earth and becomes - in terms of density and thermal values etc., much the same as cob, adobe and the others. In this way the technique can respond to varying environmental criteria for different situations, using denser mixes on south facing walls, lighter mixes on north facing, for example.

The materials used can also be substituted. More or less, anything suitable can be coated in clay, set and called 'light earth', though straw and woodchip are by far the most common. Expanded glass or clay beads are used sometimes on the continent. Other materials used have been cherry stones, hemp, wood shavings, sawdust and others.

Light earth construction benefits from the advantages of frame construction, such as speed of construction, the separation of structure and mass freeing design possibilities, and being able to construct the roof early allowing work to continue in the dry. The technique fits into the existing industry preference for, and experience of, timber frame construction so may be more readily adopted than the other radical 'ecological' methods.

An interior view of the light earth building that can be seen under construction in most of the other pictures in this story.

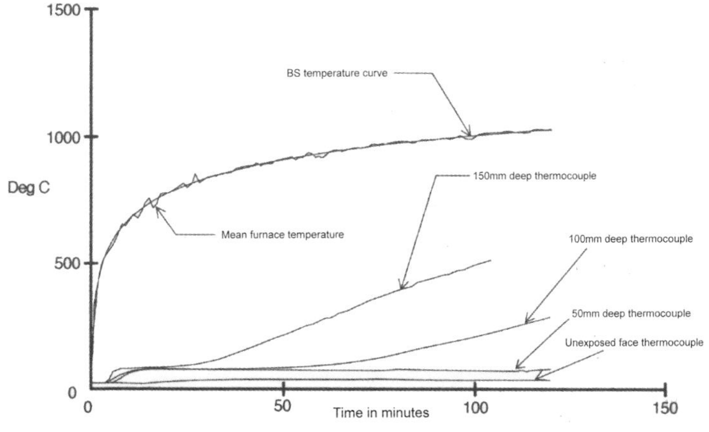

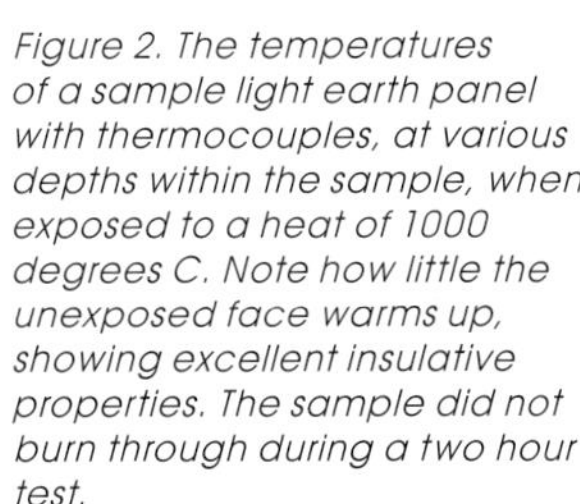

Figure 2. The temperatures of a sample light earth panel with thermocouples, at various depths within the sample, when exposed to a heat of 1000 degrees C. Note how little the unexposed face warms up, showing excellent insulative properties. The sample did not burn through during a two hour test.

Like other earth construction techniques, the thermal capacity of a light earth wall contributes to a moderation of temperature swings, raises the internal surface temperature of the walls, reducing the radiative heat loss of occupants, and improves the thermal comfort of the space overall. The technique has much in common with the French 'Isochanvre' system piloted in the UK by Modece Architects and using hemp and lime. The use of clay, rather than lime, however, is preferable in terms of embodied energy and hygroscopicity of the finished mass.

In comparison with dense earth construction it has been suggested that we should accept the limitations of earth construction and not tamper with what is undeniably a great material. The trouble with this is that it takes no account of the equally undeniable advantage of increased insulation and, moreover, seems to infer that dense earth construction is somehow 'better' than its light earth cousin. Having said that, using dense earth for what it is good at - compression and thermal and moisture mass, and insulating externally with a material designed to insulate well, such as the AtEIC building at CAT, makes a lot of sense. Even so, not every situation is the same and it is always good to have a number of options at your disposal. This is how we wish to promote light earth - not as the solution in all cases, but as a hitherto overlooked but useful option.

Light earth achieves neither the exceptional insulative value and simplicity of straw bale, nor the thermal capacity and freedom from moisture risk as solid earth building. Because of the need to dry out in relatively warm, dry weather it also has a shorter construction season, unless blocks are used. On the other hand, it has some of the insulative value of straw bale, but takes up far less space than thick bale walls, adding floor area and valuable thermal capacity which is otherwise only present in the plaster. Unlike solid earth construction, it can be used for external walls without additional applied insulation. In many ways it combines the advantages and disadvantages of both to produce a method ideally placed to respond to the varying needs of buildings which must last many years serving many masters with different requirements. And this is potentially its greatest strength. If buildings need to last over generations satisfying housing occupants' requirements that we could not anticipate - a thermal/insulative envelope, which does a little of everything, is perhaps better suited than one which does one thing very well but not another.

In practice the lack of thermal mass in straw bale construction can be remedied by thermal mass elsewhere, such as in the floors, and the lack of insulation in dense earth doesn't matter if you don't use it for external walls. We know this, but to reiterate - it's good to have options, especially flexible ones.

Getting planning approval for light earth

Planning departments are not likely to have a specific problem with light earth since it is immaterial to most of their normal considerations. Of the three completed light earth buildings in the UK, only one has needed to be submitted to building control. In this case the officer had three particular concerns; thermal behaviour, vapour permeability/condensation risk, and fire behaviour.

In the case of fire, he accepted that with the use of proven non-combustible coatings either side, surface spread of flame was not a problem. He was provided with German literature regarding the thermal and vapour permeability characteristics of light earth which he accepted, but asked for a condensation risk analysis. This suggested a very slight theoretical risk in very cold spells, but he further accepted that the hygroscopic materials used would render such a theoretical risk negligible in practice.

The subject of this light earth story formed the basis of research carried out by Gaia Architects. This is now completed and can be accessed from Gaia Architects **www.gaiagroup.org**. Mortgage lenders, insurers, latent defects insurers and valuers, among others involved in the technical and financial support of the

construction industry, gave feedback on their view of the technique and all technical obstacles to the eventual uptake and development of light earth have been overcome

The future

Based on observation of European development of light earth, there are three likely ways in which it can develop in the UK. The first is the simple, low-tech way in which self-builders in particular take up the technique because it offers significant material cost savings coupled with useful energy saving and health benefits. The additional labour required is absorbed by the self-builders. The second is through development of mechanical means of mixing and installation, which renders light earth not only economical in materials but in labour too. The technique would then appeal more to larger scale operators who could marry economy with obvious sustainability 'brownie points'. The third - which is already underway - is the introduction and development of light earth products, mainly blocks but also pre-fab panels, boards and such like which simply replace less ecologically benign products. ☯

The photographs in this story show various views of light earth buildings under construction and completed.

All photos courtesy of Chris Morgan.

Earth renders

Earth render will be unfamiliar to many in the UK, but there are pockets of the country that are steeped in the tradition of building with earth. The many surviving ancient buildings are evidence that it is a robust material. Here **Katy Bryce** and **Adam Wiseman** explains ...

Earth renders, (also known as earth plasters or clay plasters) are currently enjoying a revival, from a long history of use in traditional buildings around the world. This resurgence is partly in the form of using home made, locally resourced materials, and partly due to an emergence of ready to use, pre-manufactured earth renders from both the USA and Europe.

Earth renders, prepared at their most basic level, from clayey sub-soil, aggregates and a natural form of fibre, would have been the first method of weatherproofing for primordial structures. This would have been due to the abundance of the necessary materials and the special qualities of the clay, specifically its ability to become plastic and malleable when wet, and hard and water repellent when dry. Earth renders have been used all over the world, in all climates, since shelter building began. In the UK, earth renders were routinely used on internal wall surfaces, alongside lime, up until the end of the nineteenth century. Their regular and common use was due to the local abundance of the materials, and the fact that building lime and good quality aggregates were comparably expensive and sometimes difficult to obtain.

Often they were used as an undercoat, to even out the wall surface before receiving a top coat of lime plaster/render or limewash. Throughout the rest of the world the use of earth in plasters and renders also has a rich history. In both Africa and the Americas the application of earth renders onto earth structures was traditionally women's work. The term 'enjarradora' is the special name given to women in the southwest states of America who carried out these earth plastering techniques. Their methods of application and materials used were highly specific from region to region, and indeed these traditions are still very much alive. In Africa, special relief work and painting carried out in earth plaster onto individual homes, (known as 'litema'), still remains a culturally significant way of decorating their homes and defining their identity within the wider community.

There are many benefits to using earth renders. Earth renders are porous, which means they allow a building structure to breathe, so that it acts like a third skin around the building and its inhabitants. Earth renders also have a thirst for moisture. This means that they can function to regulate levels of relative humidity in the atmosphere. They can absorb and hold moisture vapour within their molecular structure when relative humidity levels are high, and then release it back into the atmosphere when relative humidity levels drop. As well as providing good quality, internal air for the inhabitants, this mechanism also serves to protect the building fabric from moisture.

Due to clay's thirst for moisture, and its ability to hold onto it, it will also help prevent moisture from reaching materials that provide the structure of the building. It will also actively draw moisture away from these materials if they do get wet. For this reason, earth finishes are the perfect option for structures made of the softer, breathable materials such as earth, straw bale and wood. Earth renders are being used in museums and galleries because of these characteristics, to regulate humidity and hence help to protect old and new works of art.

Earth renders, if made without artificial additives, are entirely non-toxic, making them ideal for those with chemical sensitivities. They even have the ability to absorb toxins from other materials and bind odours, such as cigarette smoke, to decrease levels of indoor pollution. Research is also currently being carried out into their ability to screen electromagnetic radiation, such as from computers and mobile phones. On a more subjective and quantifiable level, earth renders generally feel good. They are soft to the eye, and can moderate temperature swings - making walls feel warm in winter and cool in summer. They also work accoustically to soften and round off sound, making them conducive to creating peaceful, calm spaces. Like most materials made from 'natural' ingredients, they demand to be used respectfully and appropriately.

They are often not generally conducive for external use, unless positioned in a very sheltered area, used in a predominantly dry climate, or in conjunction with specific building design details, such as an external wrap around porch. If making up an earth plaster from materials sourced on site and/or locally, the user must be prepared to become their own detective to test and feel their way to a good mix through trial and error. If prepared this way, they can be inexpensive, but labour and time rich. The alternative is to purchase a ready made, pre-manufactuerd earth plaster, which requires only the addition of water. These will provide consistent and excellent results, (as long as all other due considerations are carried out effectively), but can be more costly.

When using locally sourced raw materials, it is very important to be aware that there are wide variations in clay throughout the UK and around the world. For this reason, different craftspeople working with earth renders will sometimes hold different opinions on different recipes and methods of application. Consequently, there is no one formula that can be prescribed for success in all situations. This is perhaps one of the most exciting reasons to embark on using earth renders.

Earth renders are both dynamic and timeless. They can be used to create the most exquisite, contemporary, fine plaster finishes, but are equally at home in rustic, 'organic' and traditional environments. Clay subsoil, the main binder for creating these finishes, far from being just the earth beneath our feet, is an intelligent and chemically complex material. Yet at the same time, it produces a mortar that is easy to handle and safe and simple to use. Capable of being applied in many different situations, the use of earth in buildings could make a very significant contribution to creating structures that are healthy, long lasting, and which tread gently on the planet.

Text and pictures extracted with permission, from 'Using Natural Finishes' ***www.greenbooks.co.uk***

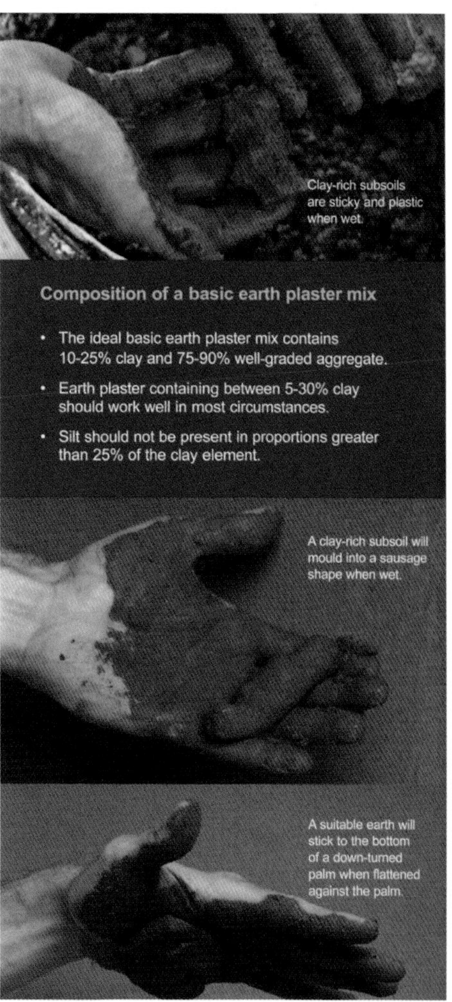

Clay-rich subsoils are sticky and plastic when wet.
Composition of a basic earth plaster mix
• The ideal basic earth plaster mix contains 10-25% clay and 75-90% well-graded aggregate.
• Earth plaster containing between 5-30% clay should work well in most circumstances.
• Silt should not be present in proportions greater than 25% of the clay element.
A clay-rich subsoil will mould into a sausage shape when wet.
A suitable earth will stick to the bottom of a down-turned palm when flattened against the palm.

Earth floors

Natural, traditional, sustainable – or dusty, cold and cracked? Earth floors are found in mud huts in Africa and in cutting edge sustainable construction. Earth is undoubtedly the earliest and simplest material used for the construction of floors. **Paul Jaquin** reports ...

The recent increased popularity of sustainable construction has led to earth floors (rammed earth) being championed by a number of architects and ecobuilders. Martin Rauch has laid rammed earth floors for many earth building projects, notably the Chapel of Reconciliation in Berlin and the Centre for Modern Art in Bregenz, Austria. In Canada earth floors are used in many rammed earth homes, and in the UK earth floors are being used in a number of new projects, usually to complement cob or straw bale construction.

Construction

Laying a rammed earth floor is as simple as any other comparable flooring. The underlying ground must be levelled, and all organic matter removed to prevent any possibility of organic growth through the floor and any voids forming from the decay of organic material. The ground should then be levelled, compacted, and dry before laying of the floor begins. To prevent the possibility of rising damp, a barrier may be placed between the floor and the ground surface (though some practitioners do not believe that a plastic barrier should be used). However, if used, then a regular impermeable material, such as polythene sheeting, can be used to provide this moisture barrier. As you might expect, the membrane must rise up along the base of the wall to meet with the wall damp course, thus ensuring the finished floor is sealed from the ground. Alternatively a vapour permeable geotextile membrane can be used, thus allowing the floor to breathe, and avoiding the problem of moisture being diverted to the base of the walls. However, using a geotextile membrane requires the base layer to act as a moisture barrier.

The sub-floor layer serves a number of purposes, to prevent moisture rising, to help insulate; and to raise the level of the floor as required. For the sub-floor layer to serve as insulation, a product, such as lightweight expanded clay aggregate (LECA), can be used. 230mm of LECA provides the equivalent insulation to 50mm of extruded polystyrene, and importantly, provides an excellent base on which to ram earth. Alternatively, a layer of gravel may be laid, followed by an insulating layer of straw-clay mix or similar. It is possible to include underfloor heating pipes above the base layer, although care should be taken to protect pipes from ramming. Of course a rammed earth floor may also be laid above a standard concrete or limecrete floor, with insulation below the slab.

Finally the earth is laid ready to be rammed (compacted). This involves the laying of fine soil in thin layers, and each well compacted before the next layer is placed. To compact the soil a manual rammer can be used, but pneumatic or electric hammers, such as are used for breaking out concrete but fitted with a flat foot, can get the job done in a much shorter time. If the floor forms part of a new build earth house, then the soil used for the walls can be used, but should be sieved to remove particles larger than around 5mm. Water should be added to the soil to ensure it is not dusty, and is able to be compacted. Joints should be placed to allow shrinkage, and if cracks do form then these should be filled. You can, of course, add different coloured earth or use natural pigments to create designs on the floor, which add immensely to the attractive and earthy feel which a rammed earth floor offers. A protective coating should be applied to finish the floor.

This both protects the floor from scratches and scrapes, and prevents spillages from penetrating. It also prevents dust from rising and allows the floor to be cleaned. Traditionally ox blood and animal dung have been used to seal and stabilise the surface of the floor, but current practice recommends linseed oils or beeswax.

If you are lucky, the subsoil that is removed in preparation to build your building may be suitable for using as an earthen floor. A rammed earth floor is 100% recyclable, and can be simply returned to the ground on demolition of the building. Earthen floors are durable, practical and low maintenance, they can be swept or mopped, and when properly sealed do not create dust. Incorporating heating elements in the body of the floor allows efficient distribution of heat through a building, and the floor itself is able to retain heat, adding to the thermal mass of the building and allowing a pleasant internal temperature to be maintained.

Issues that may arise

There are also a few disadvantages to rammed earth flooring that need to be outlined. Firstly, very few contractors in the UK are aware of, let alone expert in, the construction of rammed earth floors, although with a little experimentation in mix design and ramming technique it is possible to make your own floor. In Canada Meror Krayenhoff, of SIREWall (Stabilised Insulated Rammed Earth), requires clients to acknowledge that the floor may become slightly cracked because of the unpredictable shrinkage of the clay content in the soil. To some, however, this non-structural problem just enhances the leathery appearance and the character of the floor, but to allow shrinkage, and thus reduce cracking, carefully placed control joints can be added. Without sufficient compaction, rammed earth floors are susceptible to scratching and gouging from footwear and furniture. High heels may leave marks in otherwise perfect flooring. Also dust can be a problem if the floor is not properly sealed, but this is easily remedied with the application of a further layer of sealant. Hallways and other high traffic areas of a building may require harder materials, such as stone to be added to the mixture to prevent the floor being significantly eroded, but this can add character and charm. Because it is a malleable material, rammed earth flooring may be neatly joined to any other flooring surface. Rammed earth floors are certainly not as quick and easy to lay as other types of flooring, the process is extremely labour intensive, but the hard work results in a durable and natural floor, which is exactly to your specification.

An earthen floor is the ultimate statement in sustainable construction. With virtually zero embodied energy, and produced exactly to your specification, rammed earth floors are simple to construct and can be built using only materials available on site. The surface exudes a natural and earthy sensation, which adds character and warmth to any room. The low material and construction costs, together with excellent thermal properties means that ecohomes built on a tight budget benefit from both reduced initial construction and lifetime heating costs. Properly constructed and well sealed, rammed earth floors can provide an attractive, high quality flooring option.

Resources

'Building with Cob: a step by step guide' by Wisemann. A and Bryce.K. Available from ***www.greenbuildingpress.co.uk***

'Earthen Architecture: A comprehensive guide' by Houben, H. and Guillaud, H. 1994. Intermediate Technology Development Group: London, UK.

'Rammed Earth'; | Lehm und Architecktur | Terra Cruda e Architettura by Kapfinger, O. and Rauch, M. 2001. Birkhäuser Verlag: Berlin.

'Adobe and Rammed Earth Buildings : Design and Construction Guidelines'; by McHenry, P. G. 1984. The University of Arizona Press: Tucson.

'Building with Earth. A Handbook' by Norton, J. 1997. Intermediate Technology Publications London.

An earth floor can incorporate other materials such as logs, as shown here. Courtesy Rachel Shiamh.

Earthships

Earthships are 'living' green buildings, constructed using earth, waste car tyres, and other recycled materials. They use the planets natural systems to provide utilities - using the sun's energy, wind and rain to provide heat, power and water. **Mischa Hewitt** reports ...

Imagine a building with no utility bills, set free from rising gas and electricity prices and dwindling supplies of water. Earthships enjoy the weather, whatever the weather. If it's raining they catch free water, if it's windy they generate free power and if it's sunny they capture free heat and electricity. Water conservation and energy efficiency measures are at the heart of an earthship and ensure that the rainwater and renewable energy harvested goes as far as possible. Built from recycled and reclaimed materials, Earthships combine many elements of sustainable construction; creating a building with outstanding green credentials. There are now two earthships in the UK and plans for several more.

Earthships embody many elements of sustainable construction and, in essence, are independent buildings that heat, cool and power themselves, harvest their own water and use plants on-site to treat their sewage. They are a style of architecture or 'biotecture', a fusion of architecture and biology that has evolved from 35 years of work by the environmental pioneer Mike Reynolds[1]. In New Mexico, Reynolds has built, and helped others to build, hundreds of Earthships in three autonomous off grid communities called the Greater World, Star and Reach. The whole evolution of the earthship concept has recently been documented in the film, Garbage Warrior[2].

But why are they called earthships? In response Reynolds states, "The typical home has no engine. It's hooked up to a community water system, it's hooked up to a municipal sewage system. So it's dependent. It's not a whole product and that's why we call them earthships and not houses." And this is the key to the earthship approach: reaching out and using the land and resources immediately around them for their construction and day-to-day running, which means that they have a very low environmental impact.

There are currently two earthships in the United Kingdom, one in Fife[3] and the other in Brighton[4]. Earthship Fife is a visitor's centre set by Kinghorn Loch and Earthship Brighton is a community centre in Stanmer Park, Brighton. Both projects can be visited and offer tours and courses. There are regular tours of Earthship Brighton on the first and third Sunday of every month. A recent visitor on a hot summer's day commented "It's an amazing building, not what I expected all. I like the idea that it's nice and bright and warm out there and really cool inside here."

The basic earthship structure

Earthships are 'earth sheltered' timber framed buildings which can be built on any south-facing land, whether flat or a hillside. On a hillside, the site for the earthship is excavated and the soil is piled in front of the building. This is the material that will later be used to fill the tyres, which keeps transportation of heavy materials for the walls down, as only the tyres need bringing to the site. Next the damp-proof membrane and insulation for the thermal wrap are installed and then the tyre work begins. The tyres are effectively used to replace masonry and are rammed a course at a time, up to 10 or 14 courses high. Tyres can also be used for a variety of other structural or non-structural applications, such as the footing for the front two glass faces. Potentially, any wall could be replaced with a rammed tyre wall.

The tyres are lined with cardboard and filled with earth, each tyre taking 2 to 3 wheelbarrows loads. The earth is compacted using a sledgehammer until fully 'inflated' and level. Each tyre takes between 20 to 45 minutes to ram and any type of earth can be used, from chalk to clay, as well as hardcore and other building rubble. The rammed tyres are laid like bricks, and when finished form virtually indestructible steel belted rubber walls. As the tyres are round they lend themselves to building undulating curves and other organic shapes. Between the tyre wall and thermal wrap (insulation) up to 1.5m of earth is compacted to create extra thermal mass and to earth shelter the building[5]. This thermal mass keeps the earthship's temperature stable all year round.

After the tyre work the timber frame part of the building goes up. From here onwards all of the techniques are standard and follow the pattern of a conventional build. Once the front timber frames, roof trusses and structure go up and the windows are fitted, the basic shell is completed and interior decoration can begin. The power and water systems should be installed as early as possible, which means the building site itself can run on rainwater and renewable energy[6].

In total an earthship is likely to take between 4 to 6 months to complete for a team of 5 to 6 builders, a handful of volunteers and a few specialist sub-contractors. The earthship approach readily lends itself to self-build and the Earthship Brighton project has enabled

Earthship Brighton. One of only two earthships in the UK so far. Such buildings are designed to be self sufficient and not dependant on the national grid. That is why they are called earthships.

All photos, courtesy of Mischa Hewitt.

hundreds of people to gain hands-on experience of green building techniques, from tyre ramming, mixing and plastering with adobe, to installing renewable power and rainwater systems. The approach of using volunteers for low skill work is a fantastic way of easily transferring building skills to communities.

Earthship Fife

The Earthship Fife project began in 2000 after Paula Cowie returned from a holiday visiting earthships in Taos, New Mexico. The Sustainable Communities Initiatives was then set up with the aim of transferring the concept to the Scottish climate.

A south facing site on Craigencalt Farm in Kinghorn was found and it was decided that Earthship Fife would form part of the well-established Craigencalt Ecology Centre. After receiving a building warrant, the initial construction phase began in July 2002 with a training programme for 10 trainees provided by experienced earthship builders from America, including Michael Reynolds. During this week the basic structure was completed, with the remaining building work carried out at weekends and on volunteer days until the building was launched in 2004. The earthship is just over 6 x 5m, approx 31 metres square, comprising over 300 tyres, 1500 cans, reclaimed timber and other natural products including sheep's wool insulation, clay membranes and earth plaster.

The conservatory in Brighton Earthship. Passive solar heating through carefully positioned glazing with thermal heat storage in the structure (floor and walls) is the main heating system in earthships.

What would you do with 1000 old tyres and a heap of bottles?

The earthship concept uses a variety of waste materials from reclaimed timber and masonry to recycled glass bottles and used car tyres. The UK throws away 48 million car and van tyres a year. The Landfill Directive that came into full force in July 2006 has completely banned them from landfill[14]. On using tyres Reynolds comments that, "we don't desperately need tyres, but they are growing as fast as trees, if not faster." Rammed tyres are a very versatile building material and can be used in various ways, including foundations for straw bale buildings, and retaining walls. A 130m^2 earthship would typically reuse 1,000 or 10 tonnes of used car tyres.

The Earthship Fife Visitor Centre was launched in August 2004 and in 2005 the Sustainable Communities Initiative won the Vision in Business of the Environment of Scotland Award in the small company category. The thermal dynamics and design of the building have proven that the earthship concept does work in the Scottish climate. During winter the internal temperature has not fallen below 12°C, so very little back up heating has been needed. The whole project is described in detail in the Earthship Toolkit[7].

Earthship Brighton

The Earthship Brighton project began in 2000 with the creation of the Low Carbon Trust. The Low Carbon Trust aims to inspire cultural changes in the design of more conventional buildings and to raise awareness of the connection between buildings, the carbon emissions they produce and the climate change caused through extensive communications work and highly innovative building projects that demonstrate best practice in ecological design and environmental construction.

Earthship Brighton was the Low Carbon Trust's first initiative and will be a community centre for Stanmer Organics, a local organic co-operative, set in a 17-acre site in the beautiful Stanmer Park, near Brighton. It took two years to locate some land, get planning permission, resolve building control issues, raise funds and, with the help of Mike Reynolds, adapt the earthship design to be suitable to the English climate.

Construction began in April 2003 with Reynolds and his crew coming over from New Mexico for a week to build the hut module and train people to deliver the rest of the project. The rest of the tyre walls were constructed over the next couple of months and the shell of the earthship was completed by winter 2003. Due to the experimental nature of the project additional funds were required to complete the build and since 2003 short bursts of focused

The solar collectors on top of Earthship Brighton, which uses four renewable technologies; photovoltaic panels, a wind turbine, solar thermal panels and a wood pellet stove as a backup boiler.

Passive solar design - using the sun for space heating

Up to 60% of the energy used in residential buildings is for space heating. The rammed tyres walls of the earthship are earth sheltered with up to 1.5m of rammed earth as a backfill berm. Behind the earth-shelter is a thermal wrap of rigid insulation, which surrounds the building and makes the thermal mass of rammed tyres and earth act as a storage heater. Just like a stonewall on a hot day, the rammed tyre walls retain heat and release it again when the building cools. The thick walls, coupled with lots of insulation, enable the earthship to maintain a comfortable temperature in any season - the building remains hot in winter and cool in summer. Increasingly a stable in-doors temperature makes a property far more comfortable, given that 9 of the 10 hottest years on record have been in the last decade[15].

The University of Brighton's School of the Built Environment has buried 32 temperature probes in the walls and floor of Earthship Brighton and is currently undertaking a three-year thermographic study of the building's performance[16]. In this climate the addition of a front greenhouse acts as a buffer zone and further increases the thermal stability.

building activity have been facilitated by extra funds being raised.

The power systems were installed in October 2005, including the first wind turbine in Brighton and Hove. In 2006 the last funding needed to complete the project was secured and the building was completed over a 6-week period in the autumn. The water recycling systems were installed and interior fit was completed. Earthship Brighton is now open to the public as a community centre and the project has been documented in a book[8].

Earthship Normandy

The Earthship Normandy project began after visiting the Earthship Community in Taos, New Mexico in October 2005. Kevan and Gillian Trott discovered a small rural building plot on the edge of Ger, a village in Normandy, France and made a planning application or permis de construire to the local French Authorities. The complex French planning application had to receive approval from many layers of French government, but was eventually achieved and work commenced on the site in April 2007.

Trott said: "as someone with environmental concerns, I was won over by the solar principles of the earthship. This is not some wacky housing scheme for hippies - it can be designed to fine specifications or kept very simple. But it certainly provides the best possible housing solution to the problem of over-consumption of energy and disposal of waste."

The initial phase of the project was carried out by Mike Reynolds and the American crew to complete the structural phase of the project and it is anticipated that the building will be finished by summer 2008.

The future for earthships

With the price of utilities escalating, and climate change and resource depletion looming, there has never been a more pressing need for environmentally sound buildings that consume no fossil fuel during their day-to-day running. In response there are various projects across the UK and Europe at various stages of planning. In Scotland there is a scheme to develop an Earthship Visitors centre at Greenhead Moss Community Nature Park in Glasgow[9].

There are also plans to develop an earthship community in Brighton with the council granting planning permission to develop an 'armada' of 16 1, 2 and 3 bedroom earthships, of which 6 would be available as affordable social housing. The project would reuse up to 15,000 tyres and is called the Lizard, as there are rare lizards on the site and lizards work in a similar way to earthships, by orientating themselves to the sun for warmth. The planning department has stated, "the earthship dwellings are distinctive and contrast with the existing built environment in terms of their design and orientation, which aims to maximise solar gain. Each earthship incorporates a wind turbine and photovoltaic panels to produce electricity. The development will not have an adverse impact on the character or appearance of the locality and responds positively to the new agenda for design."

No fossil fuel in day-to-day running

Earthships have no connection to the national grid and no fossil fuel is used for electricity generation or water heating. Earthship Brighton uses four renewable technologies; photovoltaic panels, a wind turbine, solar thermal panels and a wood pellet stove as a backup boiler. Earthship Fife uses some of these as well and has a micro-hydro turbine. The electricity is stored in a battery bank. The biggest energy demand in residential buildings is heat for space heating and as the earthship deals with this through thermal mass, coupled with super-insulation, it is easy to generate any electricity needed from renewable sources.

Collecting and using water at source

Earthships have no connection to the water mains[17]. The roof collects water and channels it through two filters before storing it in underground tanks. The storage capacity tends to be larger than most domestic rainwater harvesting systems, because there is no mains back up for dry periods. As the water collected is consumed, the choice of roofing material needs to be carefully made. The materials used at Earthship Brighton were a Flagon TPO[18] membrane, which has potable water certification, and coated steel[19]. The water then flows to the water organising module, which further filters it to a potable standard by removing any bacteria. Earthship Brighton can harvest over 70k litres of water per year, which coupled with water conservation methods and greywater recycling, is more than enough for the needs of the community centre. With high levels of rainfall in the UK, most buildings are well placed to collect and use rainwater on site and thus have a lower reliance on a centralised water main.

Using plants to treat wastewater - no sewage infrastructure

In an earthship, grey and black water are dealt with separately and all water is treated on site. Grey water is treated with indoor planters or living machines, located next to the south facing windows. The plants thrive in the sunlight and nutrient rich water. They clean the water through natural processes, such as transpiration and oxygenation by roots. All plants work well in the planters, but some hardier species are good to start with including bananas, avocados, geraniums and aloe vera. After being cleaned, the recycled water is then stored in a sump, which is then fed to the toilet cistern for flushing. All black water leaves the earthship to settle in a septic tank before over-flowing to a reed-bed for treatment.

A recent market survey demonstrated how many people like the idea of Earthships and would like to live in one, so the blueprint for the Brighton Marina project could be the first of many in the UK. On mainland Europe where land is cheaper, there are various residential earthship projects already underway, with two in France, one in Ger in Normandy as outlined above[10] and the other in Brittany[11], another project in Spain[12] and one in Sweden[13]. The seeds of the earthship concept have been sown in Europe and are now starting to bear fruit.

References

1. **www.earthship.org**

2. **www.garbagewarrior.com**

3. **www.sci-scotland.org.uk**

4. **www.lowcarbon.co.uk**

5. *Tyre pounding techniques are covered in depth in Earthship Volume 1: How to Build Your Own*

6. *For a more in depth discussion: Earthship Volume 3: Evolution Beyond Economics*

7. *For the Earthship Toolkit:* **www.sci-scotland.org.uk/shop.shtml**

8. *'Building a zero carbon future for homes':* **www.brepress.com** *or* **www.lowcarbon.co.uk/publications**

9. **www.greenheadmoss.org.uk/id14.html**

10. *Normandy Earthship:* **web.mac.com/kevantrott/iWeb/Site/Welcome.html**

11. *Brittany Earthship:* **www.zuluna.com**

12. *Spanish Earthship:* **www.earthship.es/abo_content_detail_p.php/109/Home**

13. *Swedish Earthship:* **www.vaxhuset.se/eng%20index.htm**

14. *For more details:* **www.wrap.org.uk/materials/tyres**

15. **www.met-office.gov.uk/research/hadleycentre/index.html**

16. **www.durabuild.org**

17. *For more information about the Earthship water systems see the book entitled 'Water from the Sky'*

18. **www.flag.it**

19. **www.cagroup.ltd.uk**

Further reading

'The Earthship Toolkit': **www.sci-scotland.org.uk/shop.shtml**

'Earthships; building a zero carbon future for homes' by M Hewitt amd K Telfer.

'Earthship' Volumes 1, 2 and 3 by M Reynolds.

'Water from the Sky' by M Reynolds.

The above books are available from Green Shop Books 01452 770629 **www.greenshop.co.uk**

Lime and lime renders

Lime is often discussed in green circles as one of the most useful and versatile materials of the built environment. However there is plenty of mysticism woven into tales of its use and properties. Here **Katy Bryce** and **Adam Wiseman** discusses the practical applications for lime renders ...

Lime, which is derived from the raw materials limestone, chalk or coral, (all rich in calcium carbonate) has proven itself throughout history and into the present day, to be one of the most versatile, durable and adaptable binding materials. It can be used for a wide variety of construction purposes. It is mixed with sands and aggregates to form both a bedding and pointing mortar for masonry, and as a breathable, flexible internal and external protective finish for most building substrates.

The utilisation of lime today, as an increasingly popular material within the ever-growing eco-build and conservation/restoration sectors, is supported by thousands of years of successful, traditional building works throughout the world. The oldest analysed examples of lime being used in a wall plaster have been found in Jericho in the Jordan Valley and Tel-Ramad in Syria, dating from around 7000 BC. The Greeks and Romans, at the beginning of the first century AD, used lime as their main building binder to construct their vast empires, and as a finish for both their temples and private houses.

During the Medieval Period in England, King John, in 1212, passed a law that all shops along the River Thames were to be plastered and whitewashed with lime, both inside and out, within eight days, after a fire destroyed London Bridge. The lime finish was used because of its fire resistant properties. During the Renaissance Period, the Italians created their famous stuccos out of lime plaster. These were later emulated in other parts of Europe as a finish of the highest order. Lime, throughout history has always been used simultaneously for both the formal, 'high' architecture of the elite, and for the more simple dwellings of the rural populations. Up until the coming of the railways, at the time of the Industrial Revolution, the production of lime was principally a local industry. Each town or village, where there were suitable limestone deposits, would have had their own lime burning kilns.

Many of these remain today, scattered across the country, buried under ivy, or engulfed by the contemporary townscape. Small clues remain if you look closely: road names such as 'Lime Kiln Lane' or 'Kiln Avenue'. Each region produced distinct lime mortars which encapsulated the unique properties of the geological compositions of both the local limestone and the sands and aggregates added. In addition to this, many regions developed their own unique application procedures and styles that reflected the local climate. An example of this would be the rough, open-grained harled finish of Scotland onto a stone substrate, developed to withstand the harsh climatic conditions of the north.

The rough, textured surface improves durability as it enables water to be shed more effectively from the render surface. This can be compared with the flat-trowelled finishes onto wattle and daub panels of the south of England, where the climate was less harsh. Similarly, there have always been distinct differences between the exterior building finishes of the more formal townhouses across the country, where work would have been of a very high quality, multiple-coat system. This produced a very straight, regular finish, often referred to as a 'polite' finish. In contrast to this was the less formal, less time consuming finishing work of rural buildings. This would often comprise fewer coats and would therefore follow the natural undulations of the stone or mud wall beneath.

In 1824, ordinary portland cement (OPC) was developed and patented in England. Despite this, lime still remained in common use throughout England, Scotland, Wales and Ireland up until the end of World War II. At this time there was a need for the rapid construction of new housing, to rehouse those whose homes had been bombed. For this, cement's characteristic speedy setting, strength, and all-weather building capacity, meant that lime, with its more weather dependant setting processes and softer, more flexible nature, virtually fell out of use from the 1950's onwards. Portland cement rapidly became the primary building binder for both new build structures and for repairing historic structures made out of the traditional, softer materials, such as stone, brick, mud, wattle and daub and lath and plaster. This transition was set within an era where there was a dramatic move away from small-scale, local production, and a move towards greater economies of scale through the mass manufacturing of most goods and services.

The use of cement was aggressively marketed as a quick, all-weather, and hence economically superior solution to building, through powerful cement lobbies across the world. The use of cement, instead of lime, on these traditional buildings had, and continues to have, a disastrous effect on the health and overall structural integrity of the building fabric. The two basic premises of why cement does not work well with historic buildings is firstly due to its unforgiving strength. This means that it is unable to accommodate the natural movements of the structure, and hence can crack and allow the ingress of moisture. Secondly, cement has a low permeability (it is unable to allow the free passage of liquid moisture or moisture vapour). Because of this it does not allow the building fabric to breathe, and to relinquish any moisture that gets trapped behind the render/plaster facade. In the 1970's a key group of people began to identify the damage that was manifesting through the use of cement on these old buildings. This instigated the beginnings of a lime revival, primarily concerned with conservation work on historic structures. One key group of people in the UK who identified the benefits of the use of traditional lime finishes, were a team working on the restoration of the west front of Wells Cathedral (Somerset). This was known as the 'great west front project'. Simultaneously, other European countries, from the late 1960's onward, were coming to the same conclusion, as they witnessed their historic building stock begin to suffer the same ill health.

In the late 1960's, Dr. E F Schumacher founded the 'Intermediate Technology Group' (now known as 'One World Action') who further researched and educated worldwide about the use of lime. Out of this organisation came the groundbreaking book, 'Building with Lime: A practical Introduction'[1]. This book has fuelled the way forward for making accessible the techniques and methods for the use of lime in building. From this revived interest in lime, also burgeoned a dedicated group of UK and Irish suppliers of high quality lime products, to provide materials, education and training to the growing number of practitioners utilising this material once more. The lime revival, within the conservation building sector, has brought us to where we are today, with the increasing use of lime not only in traditional buildings, but also within the eco-building sector. Lime performs better than cement in many areas. It produces structurally healthy buildings, and healthier internal living environments. It also enables the use of low energy masonry construction materials such as cob, straw bale and hemp, and is an all round more environmentally friendly material than cement. ☯

References

1. 'Building with Lime: a practical Introduction' by S Holmes and M Wingate (1997).

Further reading

'Using Natural Finishes' by K Bryce and A Wiseman: ***www.greenbooks.co.uk***

Hemp-lime building

Steve Allin, introduces us to this natural and sustainable building material. Hemp buildings breathe, are airtight, lightweight and strong, with good insulating and heat storing properties - impressive green credentials.

France has a long history of industrial hemp production and the evolution of its use in building there was perhaps inevitable. A large number of French architects and builders have developed a broad understanding of how to use natural materials, so being a hemp growing region, hemp was a 'natural candidate'. As a result of many years of use and experiment in France, hemp - as a building product, is now ready to make its entrance into the wider building arena.

The hemp plant (Cannabis sativa L)

One of the earliest plants husbanded by man, hemp materials have seen a revival in interest in the last twenty years, due to world wide demand for commodities produced in a sustainable manner, and the grant aided support within the EU for its production. Hemp could be said to have the highest 'green credentials' of all agricultural crops. Although there are some other plants, such as flax and jute, that provide similar materials of fibres and wood chips, few produce the variety of materials (fibre, wood, and seeds) that have the climatic range or broad scope of uses that can be ascribed to hemp. Few oil crops produce the biomass level attainable with hemp, and if they do, as in the case of sunflowers, there is not the added production of strong fibres.

Many biomass crops only produce combustible materials and do not have the added advantage of being able to provide the energy conscious farmer with an ideal rotation crop. Due to its weed suppressing capabilities, the dense canopy of hemp leaves will reduce the need for other chemical or mechanical treatments, and so it is eminently suited to the organic producer.

The hemp plant, Cannabis sativa L, is a short rotation crop which makes it a highly renewable resource with multiple uses. Photo courtesy of Tradical.

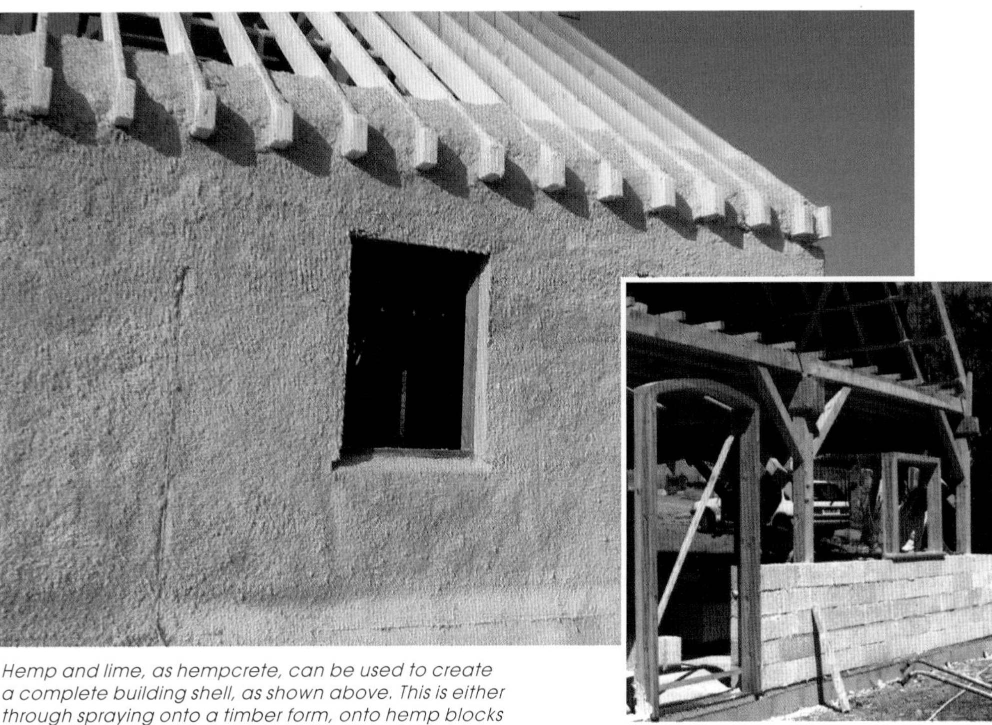

Hemp and lime, as hempcrete, can be used to create a complete building shell, as shown above. This is either through spraying onto a timber form, onto hemp blocks (inset), or from complete shuttering in stages.

Two elements of the hemp plant are used to produce building material, the fibres of the stem (which are used in insulation matting, usually mixed with polypropylene), and the woody core of the stem (which was formerly a waste product), produced in a chip form (called hurds/shives). The 'hurds' have, in the past, been used coated with bitumen or silicates as a dampproof loose fill insulation, but it is the mixing of these chips with cements and limes to form breathing lightweight 'hempcrete'* that has proved to be the most revolutionary.

Hempcrete

Hempcrete* is a term used to describe a mixture of hemp wood chips with lime. The resulting mix has properties that work well across a range of different thermic values; conductivity, capacity and effusity, and in tests, it has been proved that a combination of these values, results in levels of comfort and reduced energy above and beyond what would normally be expected.

Hempcrete has been calculated to be carbon negative to the tune of 108-130kg per m^3 during its life, if we deduct the carbon emissions created from manufacture of the lime binder from the CO_2 sequestered by the hemp crop as it grows. This is not something that can be said for other masonry, or indeed any other building material, except for timber.

Why mix hemp with lime

Lime has more ecological credentials than other binders or cements used in building by comparison of the embodied energy levels. This is certainly one of the reasons why lime is preferred to cement as an ingredient in the hempcrete mix, but more important is the way lime works with moisture mechanically in the structure of the medium. The most common of modern building lime materials is hydrated or white lime sold by builders merchants. This is usually mixed with portland cement to increase plasticity when being applied, and giving flexibility to the structure when set. To be able to

Wet spraying of hemp/lime mix into a modern timber form construction.

mix uniformly with the hemp, the lime has to be in powder form, as opposed to putty. The lime 'community' usually regards this material with scorn, as being inferior to lime putty as it might have started to carbonate by exposure to air in storage. However, I have found, through my use of it with hemp, that provided it is manufactured recently and not stored for too long, it can be used quite successfully with natural hydraulic lime to achieve the initial set, and also on its own as external mortar mixed with only sand and water.

Natural hydraulic lime offers the structural porosity that gives lime its breathability, but can give the added characteristic of setting much faster. So a combination of these attributes is used to produce a binder for the hemp particles. The lime element of hempcrete needs to both bind the hemp wood particles together throughout the mass and allow the moisture to migrate through and out of the resulting structure. The setting time of hempcrete is also important, as it needs to acquire a certain hardness and set to be able to apply the material in an economic and practical timeframe.

Modern uses for hempcrete

Hempcrete provides the ecological house builder or designer with a material that has a wide range of applications. With variations in the proportions of the mix it can be used to insulate roof spaces, between or beneath floors, or to build walls. When mixed with a greater proportion of lime it can also be used as an insulating plastercoat. When used to build walls, it is normally cast around a timber frame.

Post and beam frames are particularly suited to hempcrete use but all types of framing systems are suitable for encasing with this seamless uniform layer of insulating and heat storing material. A lighter weight variation (more hemp, less lime) of hempcrete mix can be cast between the roofing rafters so that a continuous envelope can be achieved (see photo left and previous page). The advantages are that none of the gaps, which may occur when using batts of fibre insulation, are present. It is also possible, in the same way, to produce a thermal and acoustic barrier between floors.

The technique of using hempcrete as ground floor insulation is to many modern architects and engineers, the most unorthodox of uses, as it does not require the inclusion of a damp proof membrane. The only point in the structure that utilises a dpm in hempcrete homes is at the base of the walls, between the timber frame and hempcrete and the foundation of the wall where there is a likelihood of rising damp. In the UK, hempcrete has very definite potential for use in conservation as an infill to the many old oak frame buildings, and as a fireproofing layer beneath thatch roofs. It can also provide the ecologically conscious builder with a natural and simple material. There is still a division in the green building world today, between those that are devising building systems that rely heavily on layers of industrially produced materials and those that wish to utilise natural or traditional materials in a more sophisticated manner. Hemp building would fall into the latter, but once in use can be used by the homeowner as any ordinary dwelling.

Further reading

'Building with Hemp', S Allin: ***www.hempbuilding.com***

**Hempcrete is different to limecrete. Limecrete is a mixture of lime with normal aggregate to make a concrete replacement.*

Straw bale building

In recent years there has been a renewed enthusiasm for this natural, reliable, fun and sustainable way to build. **Rachel Shiamh** explains ...

Straw bale building began over a hundred years ago in Nebraska, USA, just when the baling machine had been invented and farmers were looking for a way to build some cheap, easy and temporary housing. Certainly, at between £1.50 to £2.50 a bale to buy coupled with the knowledge that a bale wall can be raised in less than a week during a group wall raising session (more on this later) - the cost of building a straw bale house is way below the cost of building a conventional masonry house, which brings us to the spirit of straw bale build.

Everyone can participate in straw bale building. As Barbara Jones of Amazonails, a pioneer in straw bale building in Britain and Ireland, reminded a group of us during a workshop whilst building my straw bale house, "*Everyone can help to some degree, if you can make bread or bake a cake, then you know how to mix plaster*" (and there's a lot of that). Everyone, from children, women, to the elderly can contribute their own skills, whether it may be snipping or retying bales, hand plastering the walls, or even making tea (most important). All these contribute in equal ways to the success of the whole project, and to the construction of a well-spirited home.

Straw bale building is an ideal method for most people to have a go at. Here the walls are being built.

A straw bale home is a sustainable one; meaning, that it doesn't take from the earth's resources more than is necessary and can return, to the earth, its organic material if ever taken down. It can have much less impact on the environment than conventional housing. With a typically thick wall of 450mm, the U-value of a straw wall is about two to three times lower than most conventional buildings, being around 0.13, which is a good score in terms of the present building regulations. This also reduces any heating bills considerably. In terms of sound insulation, straw offers good sound-proofing. Also, the acoustics created within a straw bale room offer a warm ambience, a feature which has prompted a wave of music studio building using the method.

The health aspects of a straw bale home are immediately apparent. With a wall coating of lime or clay plaster, not only can the walls breathe, but one has the comfort of knowing that there are no chemicals or toxic glues.

Although straw bale houses can be built and plastered to look like a conventional house, the gift of straw bale design is that it offers so many opportunities to sculpt and curve a structure with an ease and authenticity that brings beauty to an environment, which has all but lost such gentle aesthetics in building.

Straw must be protected from adverse weather conditions. It must therefore have 'a good sized hat and pair of boots'. Whatever the design, it is important that, especially in British climates, the roof has a good 500mm overhang. Also important is that the straw has a good 450mm plinth wall below it to prevent any splashback from rain. Given that, let us look at some of the most common design approaches that can be used:

Straw bales are normally used to bear the weight of the roof, without the use of timber framing for support. This approach, although used in the US, Australia and Canada, has only in more recent years become a more tried and popular method for house building in Europe. The first two storey load bearing straw bale house in Europe was built in Ireland. The first two storey load bearing straw bale house in the UK during 2003-06 in Pembrokeshire.

Earth plastering of straw bale walls at the author's own straw bale home in Cardigan, Wales.

The benefit of this kind of a build is the reduction in the amount of timber used, which saves time and expenditure. It is a recommended approach for self-builders, as the wall raising is a simple process and lessens the need for complex carpentry skills. There is also more flexibility in the design shape; it is easier to create curves and circles and enhance its aesthetic appeal.

Rain on the side of the bales is not a great problem, but if the rain gets in and down the inside of a bale wall, then it cannot dry and will rot and need to be replaced. This can be remedied by using some large, strong tarpaulins to cover over the walls during the build, or if budget permits, by building a temporary roof covering over the site. Another method requires the use of a framework, usually timber, to carry the weight of the roof. The straw bales are then used as an infill material between the framework. This was discussed a little in Chapter 2.

Probably the most well known of this style of straw bale house in the UK is Ben Law's home which was featured on the TV programme, Grand Designs. The benefits of this method are that the framework and roof can be built first, reducing the risk of any straw damage through rain. Disadvantages can be the extra expenditure on carpentry and design, and the requirement of those skills, plus the higher environmental impact.

Detailing for straw bale

Foundations for straw bale houses offer many more choices in both materials and depth, as the overall weight and distribution of the walls is far less than a conventional brick, stone or concrete block house. One example is the recently built straw bale load bearing meeting room building at the Ecology Building Society, West Yorkshire, constructed with the help of Amazonails. Its groundbreaking design is believed to be the first UK building with shallow foundations to be granted building regulations, although historically, it was the practice to have shallower foundations as this minimises ground impact and gives the building the flexibility to move with the earth, rather than being a rigid structure.

Choices of foundations for straw bale buildings can be: local stone, concrete blocks, pier foundations using timber post, blocks or bricks, rammed earth, (or) tyres. Tyres, although not

Below: the author's own straw bale home, under construction, showing footing details.

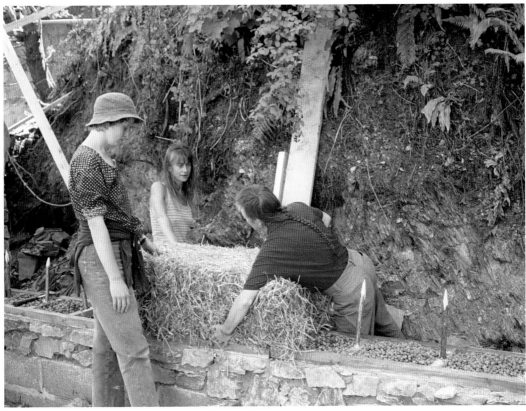

biodegradable, are a waste product and can stand the test of time for thousands of years!

In order to benefit from the high insulation properties of the straw bale walls, it is essential that the plinth walls and the floor are well insulated to avoid any cold bridges into the house.

Roof

It is important to have a good overhang of at least 500mm when using straw bale construction. The roof can be constructed using the same materials as used for most conventional houses. It is important to remember, with load bearing walls, to spread the weight of the roof evenly over the walls to ensure even compression.

Natural slates can be used. We used cedar shingles, which look particularly attractive with straw bale and are sustainable, as is a thatched roof. Shallower roofs can accommodate turf or sedum.

Straw bale walls can be trimmed and shaped before the render coats are applied. This allows the interior surfaces to be worked into interesting shapes, where often alcoves and secret corners are added.

Finishes and services

Once the walls are up, the roof on and, with a load bearing house, the walls compressed (allow about 6 weeks), then it is time for plastering the straw walls. The ideal plaster for a UK climate externally is lime plaster. It breathes and works incredibly well with any moisture in the air. It holds moisture to itself and then releases it back into the atmosphere. This is ideal for a breathable straw wall. In warmer climates, clay is more commonly used as a plaster, with a limewash finish. In the wetter climates, clay can be used inside.

Plumbing and running electric cables in a straw bale house are very similar to a conventional house. However, electric cables should be encased in plastic conduit to protect the walls from any potential heat generated by the cables. Plumbing pipes should also run inside a larger plastic pipe to avoid any potential leakage into the straw.

In conclusion, straw bale building offers a simple and rewarding construction method, whether it is through a self-build project, or with the expertise of the growing teams of skilled 'straw balers' in this country. ☯

Further reading

'Building with Straw Bales' - by B Jones.

'The Beauty of Straw Bale Homes' by A & Bill Steen.

'The Straw Bale House' by A & B Steen.

'The Woodland House' by B Law.

The above titles are available from Green Shop Books, 01452 770629 ***www.greenshop.co.uk***

Building with timber

On one hand timber is the epitome of low impact environmental design, and on the other, thoughtless and indiscriminate use of timber causes some of the worst environmental degradation on the planet. **Chris Morgan** explains how to spot the good from the bad...

Unlike most other building materials and components, timber is a renewable resource, or rather 'potentially renewable'. Sadly, around half of the world's original forests have already been destroyed, largely during the latter half of the 20th century. The timber industry is heavily linked with this forest destruction, even though a large proportion of the clearance is for other purposes, including paper pulp and subsistence agriculture.

Globally, around 1.6 billion cubic metres of timber are harvested annually, and realistic estimates expect this to rise to 2.5 billion cubic metres by 2050. Can this level of extraction be sustained? Well, perhaps surprisingly, current research suggests that with responsible forest management, a major crisis can be averted. In order to be called sustainable, the use of timber on a building should be checked against these four criteria;

- source
- transport
- preservative treatment
- detailing.

Sourcing sustainable timber

A sustainable source is one where the growing, management, harvesting and re-planting of trees is socially, environmentally and economi-

Northwood Construction & Locate architects

cally sustainable. The bottom line is that the forestry work (timber extraction) must be profitable enough to sustain communities, who can afford to stay, raise families, manage and replant appropriately, maintain and even enhance soil conditions, avoid erosion and nutrient loss and generally improve the conditions of the local area. Experience all over the world, and throughout history, suggests that this is not easy to achieve. De-forestation, due to lack of replanting, soil erosion, fires (and firewood collection), conversion to agriculture, lack of management and a host of other reasons, along with subsequent de-population of rural areas, is often the norm.

Certification schemes have been developed to try to account for these many variables because of widespread global concern about the damage being caused, and there is no doubt that great advances, not least in understanding of the issues, have been achieved. None of the schemes claim to be 100% watertight, and there is still a very long way to go.

Independent timber certification

Independent certification is the key to good forest management. Forest Stewardship Council (FSC), is one such organisation that provides a framework for certification standards and auditing that is applied worldwide, another is the Programme for the Endorsement of Forest Certification (PEFC). Most operators who have modified their forest practises to achieve certification have since reaped social and economic benefits.

Studies show that the scale of the challenge of extending certification is manageable given appropriate leadership from industry and the green movement. The biggest producers and users have been identified, and many of these are already making moves in the right direction. There are now many hundreds of companies in the global forest and trade network committed to producing, trading or purchasing forest products certified as sustainably produced. This applies pressure to the remaining, slightly more reticent, companies to clean up their act or lose out as consumers spend elsewhere. If a proportion of the largest companies are brought on board, either producing or using only certified timber, then a critical mass will be created for the uptake of certification.

Sourcing local timber and timber products

In many building projects, timber is normally sourced by the contractor from established connections with builder's merchants and suppliers. More often than not this timber will have come from far off places way outside the UK. However, most contractors will show scepticism when you suggest local timber and will probably be reluctant to deviate from their normal suppliers. Your builder will, of course, be concerned with reliability, durability, cost and so on, so bear in mind there are a number of technical problems to sort out, as well as your ethical and eco concerns! If you do manage to convince him/her, phone a few timber suppliers (see later) to find out what is available locally. It might be worth contacting the Forestry Commission and perhaps estate managers of local landed estates.

With homegrown timber, there will be other issues raised, such as an understanding of the species and durability etc, so one of you (you or your builder) may need to research the subject a bit - there are also fewer universal guarantees to protect you from warped, knotty, late, damp or just plain wrong timber. Remember too that the industry, despite talk of integration and joined up thinking, is not at all joined up yet. You will quickly come to appreciate that, but it will make it all the more rewarding once your wood is safely installed in your project! There does not seem to be a single voice for local timber merchants in England so look at some of the adverts at the end of this chapter or in the yellow pages under 'timber merchants'.

Certification is a process by which an independent third party gives written assurances that a product, process or service conforms to specified requirements. To be effective, forest certification must be based on:

- objective, comprehensive, independent and measurable performance-based standards - both environmental and social
- equal and balanced participation of a broad range of stake holders
- a labelling system that includes a credible chain of custody
- reliable and independent third party assessments, that include annual field audits
- full transparency - to the parties involved and the public. It must also:

- take place at the forest management unit level (and not at country or regional level)
- be cost effective and voluntary
- positively demonstrate commitment from the forest owner/manager towards improving forest management
- be applicable globally and to all sorts of tenure systems, to avoid discrimination and distortion in the market place.

Certified forests now exist in a growing number of countries, including the UK. To be successful the schemes needs support. You can help by insisting that timber and wood products for your projects are certified to either FSC or the PEFC standards.

Transportation of timber

This is an issue largely because of the pollution associated with it, but also because of the failure to realise the potential of revitalising local economies, which is inherent in the worldwide trade in bulk timber. The scale of the pollution associated with transported timber is often under-estimated. There is often more pollution associated with imported timber than there is with other, supposedly 'less green' materials, and so, it makes sense to look at the use of UK sourced timber because only then can it be said, with confidence, that the timber is anything like sustainable. In doing so, a number of other advantages become clear. Using homegrown timber:

- stimulates UK forestry and related rural industries
- creates and/or maintains employment in rural areas, and promotes good woodland management in the UK, which also benefits the local ecology
- has massively lower embodied energy than imported (see table below).

Such considerations rarely show up on 'green building' checklists and assessment schemes, but these aspects are important, and the potential capacity of the construction industry to engage with, and benefit local forest industries, is vast.

There is no doubt that homegrown timber would be the 'greenest' choice for UK projects, but there is a snag... There is no way in which the UK construction industry (let alone the paper, fencing, pallet and other industries) could source all its timber requirements from within the UK. Annually, the UK consumes around 50 million cubic metres of timber. In the same period, it produces only 7.5 million cubic metres of timber. In other words, we produce only 15% of what we consume, and we import the remainder at an annual cost to the nation of around £7 billion (not to mention the environmental cost in CO_2).

This may seem a lost cause, but there are reasons to be positive about the future. First, the amount of timber produced in the UK is set to increase from 7.5 million to 16 million cubic metres by 2020. The challenge is to create a larger market share for this timber in the construction industry. Under 15% of the total wood and wood products consumed in Britain each year come from British woodland. Most of this goes into agriculture and fencing, yet much of it is highly suitable for use in buildings but is simply over-looked by merchants because supplies can be erratic and involve more legwork on their part to ensure throughput.

Timber quality and grade

Most of the timber used in construction (by

Energy embodied in local and imported timber.
Source: Whole House Book.

Material	*KWh/tonne*	*KWh/cu.m*
Timber-local air dried	*200*	*110*
Timber-local green oak	*200*	*220*
Timber-imported softwood	*1,450*	*754*

volume), does not need to be particularly good quality. Studs, joists and rafters, battens and so on, could all be readily sourced from home-grown softwood, though designers may need to alter their practices to account for weaker timber, by specifying lower strength classes, closing up on spacings, increasing section sizes and so on. Choosing to use C16 grade timber at 450mm centres, rather than C24 timber at 600mm centres, for example, is a small price to pay for being able to cut all the pollution associated with importation, and benefit our own forestry industry. Too often, old specification clauses are pasted onto new drawings by architects and engineers. If you are involved on a project and appear bound to use C24 timber, do not be afraid to go back to the architect or engineer and ask if this could be revised to C16 – plus associated changes – to enable local softwood to be used. Sometimes the changes can be simple to make and it will make a huge difference environmentally.

Some have already started to look at initiatives to realise the potential of this extra timber coming on stream, and various investigations are underway, such as high-tec jointing, gluing, de-knotting, heat treatment and so on. These initiatives will doubtless benefit the industry, but there is far greater potential simply by adjusting our expectations and design practice to suit the material we have to hand. One excellent technique, particularly suited to the UK timber supply, is solid wood panel construction. Although pioneered on the continent, one London practice specialises in the technique, but the potential to produce very strong, insulating, structural panels with excellent environmental credentials is huge.

Preservative treatment

The chemical treatment of timber makes it unsustainable for two reasons. First, these chemicals can be harmful to human, as well as other biological life. Second, treatment takes a completely natural, biodegradable material (one of the few available to the modern designer), and turns it into toxic waste, which at the end of its useful life will have to be disposed of at approved sites. The UK has a huge waste

The construction industry is renowned for using vast quantities of variable quality timber, mostly softwood from Europe. The industry also puts toxic chemical preservatives on much more timber than actually needs it.

disposal problem, which is becoming worse, and timber treatment adds to it.

Supporters for the treatment of timber will argue that this is all very unfortunate but sadly unavoidable. Others claim that treatment makes timber more durable – so fewer trees have to be cut down – and people like me ought to be very grateful for it! The answer to both these points is that, with a few exceptions, the treatment of timber is avoidable, and once you know how to avoid it, the continued use of it all around you appears unforgivable. BRE Digest 464, Part 1 gives an indication of the chemicals to be found in all that innocent looking, 'environment friendly' treated timber.

The possible emission of VOCs and formaldehyde should be an important consideration during selection of a building product. Timber studs, frames, and beam supports are usually treated and can contain organic solvents in the timber fibres as preservatives. High VOC emissions can be released from the treated timber and from other coatings.

There are locations and uses where timber is unavoidably at risk and chemical treatment is one answer. Choosing another material which is not liable to decay is also possible, and often preferable. However, the majority of situations can be designed so that timber may be used safely without treatment. There are three main tactics to avoid treatment and these are covered in the next section, which deals with good practice in detailing more generally.

Timber detailing

Good detailing and specification are critical. If the ethically sourced, local and untreated timber that you installed only lasts a few years because of poor detailing, most of the effort (and money) has been wasted, and the whole affair can hardly claim to be sustainable. There are three main tactics worth following to avoid timber treatment and still ensure good durability of timber, all of which need to be considered at the design stage, though of course some of the following is applicable for existing buildings.

The first, and by far the most important, is good design detailing and specification. The second is to design a moisture transfusive structure. The third is species choice. This is in some ways part of the first, but is worth mentioning separately. Good detailing for durability is well covered by organisations such as TRADA, BRE and others. Many specialist publications offer guidance, as well as magazines, trade literature from manufacturers, conference proceedings and other sources of advice. The references list, at the end of this article, gives some of these sources.

The key to good detailing, in general, is to avoid any build-up of moisture, which cannot escape. It doesn't matter too much if timber gets wet, but it matters very much if it stays wet. Stopping it getting wet is normal, but making sure that once wet, it can easily and quickly dry out again, can be more important. One of the most common ways timber stays wet is because it is touching, or within about 4mm of another material. Where this happens capillary action can keep moisture in, and so this sort of detail needs to be avoided, wherever possible. Since timber usually has to be fixed

*This woodland house is built completely from low grade home-grown timber . A book about this house, 'The Woodland House', can be ordered from **www.newbuilder.co.uk/books***

to something, it is clear that different forms of detailing start to emerge.

It is also important to allow for movement of timber, as it responds to varying ambient humidity levels. Grooves can help reduce shrinkage cracks, which externally, at least, can be a significant cause of decay. Leaving at least 6 or 7mm between boards externally, will overcome capillary action (even allowing for board expansion), and sawn faces tend to evaporate moisture more readily than planed finishes, so may be used with advantage on external boards and cladding.

The important thing about timber coatings in external situations is that they are vapour permeable and allow the timber to move without peeling off. Some coatings achieve this by being somewhat elastic. Others, like oil and wax based coatings, do not form a skin in the same way and so are not vulnerable to movement. Light, opaque coatings protect timber better (from UV and thermal movement) than darker and more translucent coatings.

Moisture transfusive construction – well known as the 'breathing wall' is a useful tactic, not only in controlling moisture movement, but in so doing, protecting the timber used from decay. Because moisture in a 'breathing' wall, floor or ceiling will tend toward the outside and safely evaporate, there will be no build-up of moisture which could lead to decay, and so timber studs and so on may be safely left untreated. This is a very important benefit of the technique. While 'breathing construction' is generally considered a good thing to do, the fact that we can then safely use timber untreated is a major benefit for the health of builders and occupants alike.

Lastly, species choice can have a significant effect on the durability of timber elements, and in many cases the cost difference is negligible, since most of the cost is in the machining of

This gridshell building at the Weald and Downland Open Air Museum was built from small section timber from woodlands near the site. Gridshells are an innovative new way of using homegrown timber.

elements. Oak and European larch heartwood, for example, are quite durable externally and may be used without preservative treatment for decking, cladding and so on. Softwood external joinery normally needs to be treated or coated but some hardwoods do not, though bottom beads on windows are best protected, or replaced with aluminium. Cills, which are more prone to the destructive effect of UV radiation, need extra protection.

In Scandinavia, it is common to use relatively non-durable species for external cladding with no preservative treatment, but with a couple of coats of paint. If you paint external cladding, the paint is effectively stopping the timber getting wet and so it is quite possible to use non-durable timber such as spruce and pine. The important thing is to ensure that the paint is vapour permeable, will not crack and is entirely biodegradable, so that you are not creating toxic waste.

Conclusion

Perhaps the defining aspect of the environmental design movement, at present, is how it manages to remain true to its ideals whilst acknowledging the need to be mainstream and influence the majority. The use of timber in buildings, particularly the use of homegrown timber, is a useful gauge of this process, but the movement must also develop and deepen its understanding of the issues. At present there is a great deal of timber used unwisely and unsustainably. We still have a lot to learn on the subject.

One interesting development, which could have huge repercussions for the forest and timber industry in construction and elsewhere, is the idea of timber use as a carbon store. Initial work in Norway and Scotland suggests that using mass timber, and indeed timber generally, contributes more than you might imagine to storing carbon in the medium term, more even than installing PV cells on your roof, for example. This notion may have some currency in the wider carbon sequestration debate. Of course, it depends where it comes from and your views on carbon offsetting. ☯

Useful links

FSC: ***www.fsc-uk.org***

PEFC: ***www.pefc.org/internet/html***

Forestry Commission: ***www.forestry.gov.uk***

UK Forest Products Association: ***www.ukfpa.co.uk***

TRADA: ***www.trada.co.uk***

Coed Cymru for Wales: ***www.coedcymru.org.uk***

Welsh Timber Forum: ***www.welshtimberforum.co.uk***

Woodlots: ***www.woodnet.org.uk***

ASHS for Scotland: ***www.ashs.co.uk***

Further reading

'New Wood Architecture in Scandinavia' by C Affentranger.

'Out of the Woods: Ecological Designs for Timber Frame Houses ' by P Borer & C Harris from the Green Shop: 01452 770629 ***www.greenshop.co.uk***

'Timber: Its Nature and Behaviour' by J M Dinwoodie, Spon, ISBN 0 419 23580 9.

'Forests Forever Responsible Timber Purchasing', Forests Forever, (2001) 0207 839 1891.

'Forests Forever Timber in Buildings: The Environmental Choice', contact above.

'Building in Wood: Construction and Details' by G Gutdeutsch, Birkhäuser, ISBN 3 7643 5277.

'External Timber Cladding' by P J Hislop & TRADA, TRADA Technology Ltd., 2000 ISBN 1 900510 30 8.

'Timber Decay in Buildings: The Conservation Approach to Treatment' by B Rideout, E & FN Spon, ISBN 0 419 18820 7.

'The New Wood Architecture' by N Stungo, Laurence King, (1998).

'TRADA British Grown Hardwoods: The Designers' Manual', TRADA Technology Ltd., (1996) ISBN 1 900510 02 2.

TRADA Timber Frame Construction TRADA Technology, 2001 ISBN 1 900510 32 4.

'Building the Wooden House: Technique and Design' by K Wachsmann, Birkhäuser, ISBN 3 7643 5134 9.

Off-site construction

Building sites can be disorganised places and are subject to the vagaries of the weather and varying skills of a transient work-force. Some developers have found that buying pre-maunfactured buildings is the answer for speed and profitability. **Paola Sassi** reports ...

The concept of manufacturing building elements in a factory environment is not new. The prefabrication of building elements, such as doors or stairs in workshops away from the site, has a long history. In the past, prefabricated buildings known as 'prefabs' came to have a bad name. Many were used in post-war Britain in the 1950s-60s to house thousands of people following the blitz, and many of these homes are still in widespread use.

In contemporary construction the use of bathroom pods in hotels or student accommodation has become common practice. What is perhaps different about contemporary off site construction (OSC) is the potential scale of the prefabricated elements and the potential to create a better, more environmentally friendly building.

The advantages of OSC are potentially many, including minimising disruption to the locality around the building site by reducing noise, pollution emissions and traffic. Furthermore, pre-fabricated components and buildings tend to be lightweight in nature so can offer the potential for smaller foundations and therefore less groundworks, also reducing local disruption from moving spoil away from the site, and delivering concrete to use in the foundations. However, the large deliveries of volumetric or panel units and the associated cranes could be disruptive to the area and need careful management to avoid problems.

Essentially there are four types of OSC buildings and components. These range from small bolt-together sections to virtually complete buildings. Therefore OSC components and systems can be categorised as:

- sub-assemblies
- panelised (open or closed)
- volumetric
- hybrids.

Sub-assemblies

These are the most 'traditional' and widely used system of OSC prefabrication presently used. Prefabricated sub-assemblies can include elements in a variety of materials. Concrete is used for beam and block floors and foundations. Prefabricated foundation systems consist of precast, post-tensioned, concrete beams, that can be used in conjunction with geotechnical support, including piles, vibro or grouting that can result in reduced impact on the ground and reduced material use. Other sub-assembly units include glass reinforced plastic (GRP) chimneys, steel for curtain walling or simply timber stairs.

Relatively large sub-assembly units include bathroom pods, which can be made in timber, steel or concrete and have a long history of use in hotels and other repetitive serviced structures.

Panel systems

These can be open, closed, composite or solid panels made in timber, steel and concrete:

Open panels include small section timber and steel framed panels. These are connected to form a structure that is then finished in traditional manner. Open panels have been the commonest form for 'timber and brick' housing over the past 20 years or so and is commonly termed timber frame or steel frame.

Closed panels usually incorporate insulation and can include factory-applied finishes. Timber and steel versions are available. Timber versions may include service voids.

Composite panels combine two materials to form a rigid panel. These include SIPs (structural insulated panels), comprising two layers of OSB with a rigid polyurethane insulation core. Relatively new to the UK, they are extensively used in the US and Canada. Bonded polystyrene cores are also used, but produce panels of lesser strength. SIP panels are used for walls and roofs with all window and door openings pre-cut in the factory. The panels vary in thickness from 100mm to over 200mm and are glued together.

Solid panels are available in concrete and timber. Concrete wall, floor and roof panels have been used since the 1960s, but contemporary systems have overcome the structural problems previously experienced. Concrete panels can be mechanically fixed, grouted together or bonded using in-situ concrete joints. Waterproofed, prefabricated concrete basement walls are becoming increasingly popular because of renewed interest in basements, as land prices continue to rise. However, from a sustainability viewpoint, solid timber panels would constitute a more sustainable material choice, often being

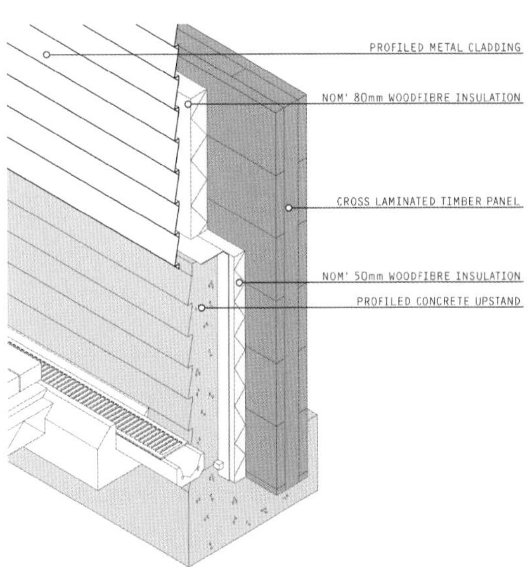

Above: cross section through a wall detail for a sports hall at Kingsdale School in London, which is built using an off-site manufactured solid panel system.

Above and below: the solid panels being erected at Kingsdale school and the roof being finally covered. The roof is actually a composite panel.

Above: photos and diagram courtesy dRMM and KLH.

The building below is a hybrid system of panallised components that are manufactured in the factory but assembled on-site. This type is most suited to smaller projects, such as housing, and there are now many 'kit' homes available in a number of styles.

Photo courtesy of URBANe.

manufactured from forestry waste material and small section timbers.

Volumetric systems

These are three-dimensional units, often framed steel structures, but can also be concrete, that can stand alone or be stacked one on top of the other to form a multi-storey structure. The interior finishes are often factory-applied and the services factory-installed. In certain cases the exterior finishes are also factory-applied. Volumetric systems are commonly used for building hospitals, schools and fast food restaurants. A stand-alone restaurant may take as little as 24 hours to assemble on site.

Hybrid systems

Hybrid OSC involves just about any combination imaginable of the previous examples. This is where we are seeing the most innovative activities at the moment with systems made from straw, eco-concrete, polystyrene and the future is likely to bring even more innovations.

Material choice and insulation

OSC systems comprise an ever-increasing range of materials and some, such as concrete or polyurethane, are associated with significant CO_2 emissions and pollution, others make use of sustainable, renewable resources. Some systems, such as SIP systems, can achieve high levels of insulation and airtightness relatively easily. Others are being used to provide nothing more than Building Regulation compliant structures. The fact that a building is constructed off-site does not automatically mean it is energy efficient or sustainable in its material makeup. It is still up to the building designer to ensure this. For many years some manufacturers have talked of foaming the insulations used in SIP systems using vegetable oils rather than mineral oil but this is still some way off in the UK, especially with the rising cost of crops.

Thermal mass

As part of a one year DTI funded project (in 2004 ARUP & Bill Dunster Architects), Chris Twinn of Arups investigated the current and future performance of lightweight and heavy-

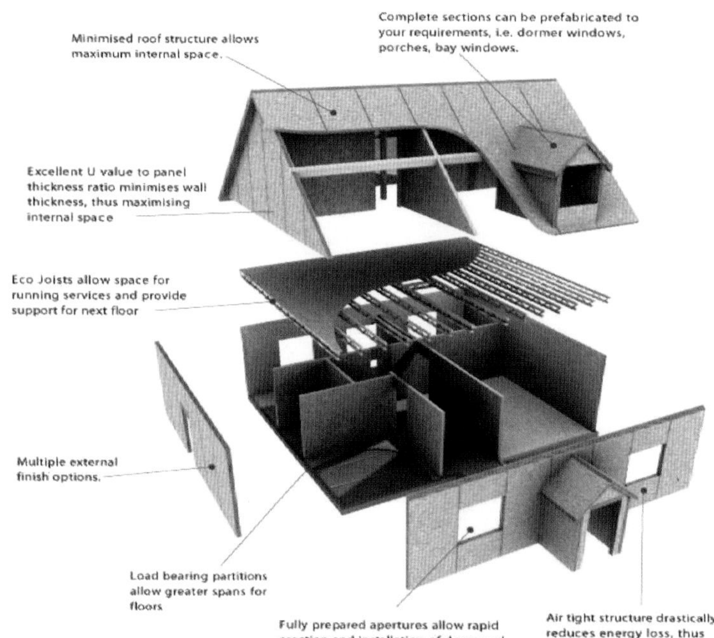
Minimised roof structure allows maximum internal space.
Complete sections can be prefabricated to your requirements, i.e. dormer windows, porches, bay windows.
Excellent U value to panel thickness ratio minimises wall thickness, thus maximising internal space
Eco Joists allow space for running services and provide support for next floor
Multiple external finish options.
Load bearing partitions allow greater spans for floors
Fully prepared apertures allow rapid erection and installation of doors and windows, thus allowing follow on trades to begin work sooner
Air tight structure drastically reduces energy loss, thus minimising running costs of completed building.

Left: this type of building is known as structurally insulated panels (SIPS) and is essentially a composite panel system. Such systems can be assembled on site very rapidly.

Image courtesy of Siptec.

weight housing constructions and concluded that, based on current global warming predictions, light weight buildings, including many of the OSC buildings, would prove uncomfortably hot in as little as 20 years time. Bill Dunster attempted to address this issue in the design of his RuralZED (bottom right), where precast eco-concrete wall panels, made of a China clay waste product, provide thermal mass. Dupont has developed a thermal mass board, less than 10mm thick, that can easily be integrated within lightweight structures and uses a phenomena called phase-change material (PCM), which was briefly mentioned on page 198. While most timber open, closed or composite panels are lightweight structures, solid timber panels, such as those shown in the Kingsdale sports hall (on page 289) still provide a good measure of thermal mass.

Above and inset: the Peabody Trust's Murray Grove in Hackney, is a housing development of 30 flats made using volumetric units - pods which were all craned into place to create the building, This demonstrated that considerable time savings are possible with the use of volumentric units. The units were assembled on site in only 10 days and saved an estimated 18 weeks in the overall construction time for the scheme.

Design for disassembly

OSC may offer opportunities for reducing waste during manufacture and the recycling of any manufacturing waste produced. However, OSC does not necessarily mean the buildings are also de-mountable, or for that matter, particularly flexible. Some volumetric systems offer the opportunity to relocate the units as required. This facility has been integrated in a number of buildings, including housing for Hyde Housing Association (see photo on page 117).

Further information.

'Prefabricated housing in the UK: a summary paper' by C Bågenholm, A Yates and I McAllister, Building Research Establishment, Watford (2001).

UK Housing and Climate Change. Heavyweight vs. Lightweight Construction. London: ARUP Research & Development and Bill Dunster Architects, (2004) can be downloaded at: ***www.zedstandards.com***

'Modern methods of house construction: a surveyors guide', Building Research Establishment, Watford: 2005.

The 'RuralZED' building (right) is a hybrid OSC system consisting of a timber, lightweight frame with pre-cast concrete sections used internally for thermal mass. The pre-cast concrete infill sections are eco-concrete, made from a mix of ground granulated blast slag, small amounts of cement, reclaimed aggregate, Cornish china clay and local sand. Even with the infill sections, the total amount of concrete used on a RuralZED home is less than that used by a conventional timber frame home with mass concrete foundations.

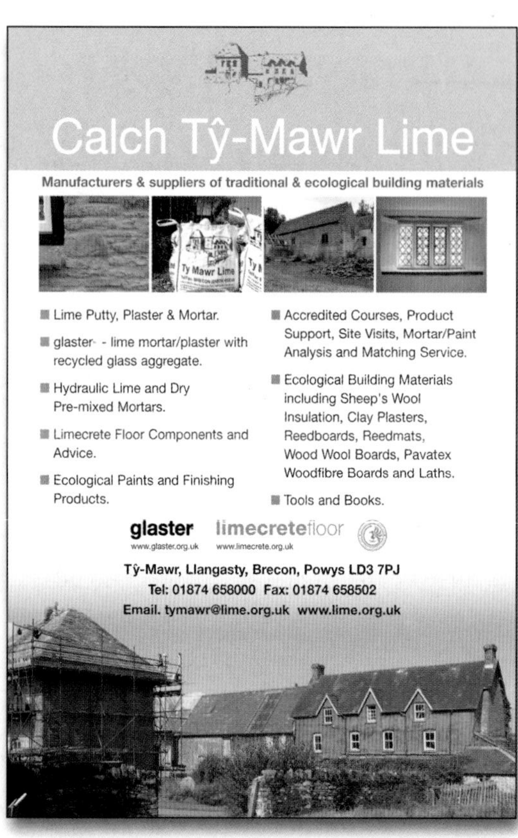
Calch Tŷ-Mawr Lime
Manufacturers & suppliers of traditional & ecological building materials
Lime Putty, Plaster & Mortar.
glaster - lime mortar/plaster with recycled glass aggregate.
Hydraulic Lime and Dry Pre-mixed Mortars.
Limecrete Floor Components and Advice.
Ecological Paints and Finishing Products.
Accredited Courses, Product Support, Site Visits, Mortar/Paint Analysis and Matching Service.
Ecological Building Materials including Sheep's Wool Insulation, Clay Plasters, Reedboards, Reedmats, Wood Wool Boards, Pavatex Woodfibre Boards and Laths.
Tools and Books.
glaster
www.glaster.org.uk
limecretefloor
www.limecrete.org.uk
Tŷ-Mawr, Llangasty, Brecon, Powys LD3 7PJ
Tel: 01874 658000 Fax: 01874 658502
Email. tymawr@lime.org.uk www.lime.org.uk

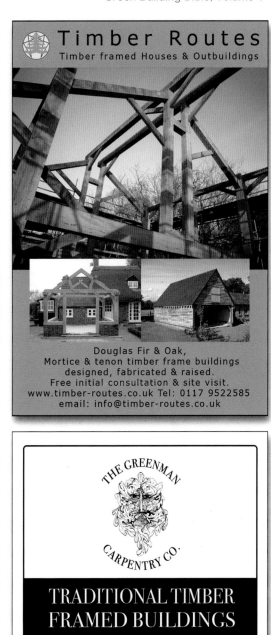

Greening the home

Saving energy and water

Domestic energy use accounts for around a quarter of the total CO_2 emissions in the UK and this is projected to rise by a further 6% by 2010. **Keith and Sally Hall** outline how we can all do something to address these issues ...

For most of us, our consumerist, cossetted lifestyles are pleasant and comfortable, but if we want to keep up such a high standard of living without robbing our children of the same opportunity, then we should all be thinking seriously about the effect that such lifestyles have on the planet. Is there anything practical that we can do to help reduce, or at-least slow-down, climate change? Yes there is. Let's first examine our every-day use of resources and look for practical compromises which will not disrupt our lives too much and could even make our lives healthier and more fulfilled.

Heating our homes uses the most energy. The best way of reducing CO_2 emissions is to use less energy. This will also save money. If you want to get a fairly accurate idea of your household's carbon footprint then visit the website of the National Energy Foundation (NEF) where you can calculate how much carbon dioxide you are producing **www.nef.org.uk/energyadvice/co2calculator.htm**

Draughts/air leakage

Next check for draughts and aim to reduce these. Try to eliminate uncontrolled draughts by adding draught proofing to doors, windows and unsealed openings, and seal all gaps around pipes and cables that pass through ceilings and walls.

Lighting

Now consider your lighting use. Turning off lights when not in use is probably something that you already do but teach others in the family the same strategy and explain why. A single 100W bulb burning all night and every night for a year is likely to create half a ton of CO_2[1]. You probably have already begun installing low energy lighting, but make sure that you buy good quality bulbs, as the cheap ones are not as good, do not last as long and can waste more resources than the old tungsten lamps. We have found that automatic sensor lights are great for lobbies and landings. These switch on and off automatically as they sense movement and can be set to suitable times, but unfortunately they should not be used with low energy bulbs which tend to blow if switched on and off repeatedly.

Appliances

What about energy and water guzzling appliances? When they next need replacement, choose only A-rated appliances. These are now available from all high street retailers and should be clearly labelled to reveal energy and water consumption. Any additional cost should be paid back quickly in energy savings so it can be false economy to opt for the cheapest appliance. Regarding their use, never leave appliances such as TV's and radios on stand-by.

'Phantom loads' as they are known, are responsible, nationally, for hundreds of thousands of tons of CO_2 per year. Turning appliances off at the wall will also help minimise any potential health risk from electro-magnetic fields and will be less of a fire hazard. Remember a lax attitude to switching things on and off leads to accidents and puts your home at risk.

Energy saving advice and green tariffs

Your local energy efficiency advice centre (0800 512012) can provide you with free advice on how to save energy and keep your house warm. There are centres throughout the UK which you can visit, or you can request free literature. Some even offer free home visits. You will be told how you can increase the insulation in your roof, walls or floors and information will be available on other related issues, including details of any grants.

Think about signing up for a green energy tariff, but this action is not sufficient in isolation as the additional premium is likely to be used to investigate future renewable development, rather than actually providing you with renewable power. Most electricity companies operate green energy tariffs. You can visit **www.green-electricity.org** for information on the companies and their performance. Green energy tariffs should support the development of energy production from renewable or sustainable sources - from wind, sun, biomass, biogas (domestic waste) and water (hydropower).

Loft insulation upgrades

Check your loft insulation. If you do change or upgrade your loft insulation investigate using natural products, such as sheep's wool or cellulose fibre (recycled newsprint) insulation as these materials have a lower environmental impact and their embodied energy in production is lower, therefore offering further CO_2 savings. But if they are too expensive then use mineral fibre or the new polyester wool that many DIY stores now stock. Don't use your loft space as a store room, especially if mineral fibre insulation is used as the dust from this material is an irritant, but more importantly, constant disturbance of insulation damages its ability to do its job properly. Find somewhere else in the house to store your junk or, better still, take it to a local charity shop or advertise it on 'freecycle' **www.freecycle.org**

Windows

Double-glazing can cut heat loss through glazed areas by up to 50%, saving around £60 per annum on heating bills and up to a quarter of a tonne of CO_2 over the heating season. If you have currently only got single glazed windows then this should be a top priority. The optimum gap between panes is 20mm and low emissivity glass (low-e) is recommended. Argon gas filled units, with rubber edged glazing bars will give even greater savings. You will also see improvements in humidity and a reduction in condensation on the glazing in the colder months, which could also help prevent moulds and fungi growing on walls near the windows. Our advice would be to use timber windows and the timber should come from a sustainable source. Standards to look out for are FSC and PEFC certified[2].

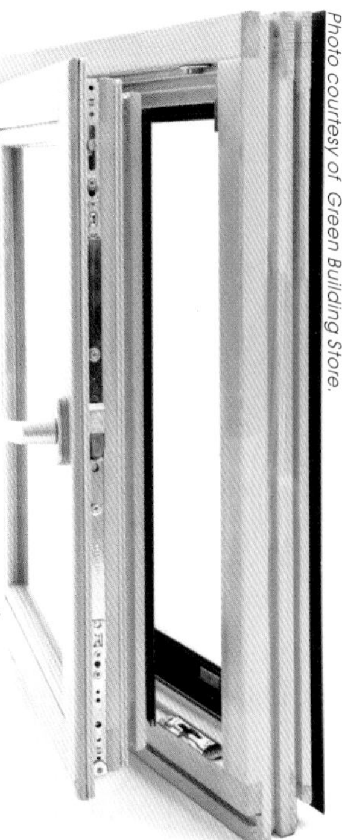

Photo courtesy of Green Building Store.

Heating and hot water

Then, take a look at your heating system. The very first question to answer is: when was the boiler last serviced? And the second one: have you got radiator thermostats fitted? If not, then get a price from a good plumber to add them when he carries out that overdue service! In the meantime experiment with turning down the main room thermostat by one or two degrees to find a lower temperature that is tolerable without being uncomfortable and, on cooler days, encourage everyone to wear warmer clothing. Don't forget to check the quality of the insulation around your hot water cylinder and pipes. If the air in the cupboard that the cylinder is in feels warm, energy is being wasted and the cylinder needs additional lagging.

Condensing boilers

Most boilers over10 years old are inefficient, some providing below 60% efficiency. New gas fired condensing boilers are very energy efficient (85-95%). These boilers recover latent heat from the combustion gases as they enter the flue. Although they are more expensive, the pay back period is just 3 years. In 2003 the Energy Saving Trust calculated that if everyone in the UK with gas central heating changed to a condensing boiler, CO_2 emissions would be cut by 18.6 million tonnes per year (3% of UK's emissions). Condensing boilers are by far the most efficient of all fossil-fuelled heating systems for running a radiator or under-floor heating system. Don't be tempted to opt for an electrical heating system as the CO_2 production would be double that of a condensing boiler. If you cannot afford to replace your boiler, upgrade and insulate your existing one and ensure it is serviced regularly.

Guide cost: £100 - £300 more than a conventional boiler

Database of gas and oil boilers, giving efficiency rating etc: ***www.boilers.org.uk***

The National Energy Foundation has a comprehensive online guide to choosing an energy efficient gas or oil boiler: ***www.nef.org.uk***

Once you have considered all the above, you could think about some of the other options listed below to reduce your CO_2 burden even further.

Renewable sources of energy and water

We can all participate in making some energy of our own now. This is a great way of getting involved in saving the planet and it is educational for us and our family at the same time. Most of us have heard of renewable technologies by now. These include wind turbines solar panels, wood burners etc. Each building and location will have good and bad aspects relating to which type of renewable energy technology could be appropriate. Most renewables qualify for a grant and some attract a reduction from the standard rate of VAT too, if fitted professionally (5% instead of 17.5%). Contact the Energy Saving Trust (EST), 0845 120 7799, **www.est.co.uk** for more information on the Low Carbon Buildings Programme, grants and other financial incentives. As a really rough guide the following should help you decide what is possible. If your home is:

in the city

- solar power - water or electricity

in a village location

- solar power
- wind power
- woodburner or boiler

in open countryside

- solar power - water or electricity
- wind power
- micro-hydro power
- woodburner or boiler

We have not included heat pumps in the list as they use electricity and so, unless this electricity is actually generated using renewables, it is debateable that they can be classed as true renewables. Therefore, for heating, unless a biomass boiler can be installed, then the next best environmental choice, in our opinion, would be a gas condensing boiler. If there is no gas in your area then you could opt for an oil condensing boiler. When considering installing renewable equipment you should contact your

Solar water heating panels and photovoltaic (electricity) panels shown combined here on the same roof of houses in Cambourne by Circle 33 Housing Association.

local planning department to check if planning consent is needed. Planning permission is still a requirement for some wind turbines and for any visual alterations or add-ons to your property, particularly if you live in a listed building or are in a conservation area or national park.

Solar water heating

Solar water heating systems use the sun's energy to heat water and can supply around 50% of a household's annual hot water requirements. Collectors, usually on the roof, absorb heat from sunlight and transfer it, by pump or gravity, to a hot water cylinder for domestic use. In summer it can provide up to 90% of the hot water demand, but less during the rest of the year. Obviously a south-facing roof is optimum but systems can be designed to suit most locations from east to west facing or even ground mounted.

Solar Trades Association: ***www.greenenergy.org.uk/sta***

Photovoltaic (PV) panels

PV's convert solar energy directly into electricity. PV cells are made up of two or more thin layers of semi-conducting material, usually silicon. When this is exposed to light, electricity is generated. PV's are available as panels, roof tiles or semi opaque glazing. Their maintenance free attributes make them the darling of the renewable's industry, although they are still expensive compared with highly subsidised grid-supplied electricity. However, as they are clean, durable and low maintenance, this technology should be given serious consideration if you have money to spend. Systems can be roof, ground or even mounted on a solar tracker.

PV UK: ***www.greenenergy.org.uk***

System design and size calculators:
www.solar-power-answers.co.uk/solar_panel.html

Woodburners and biomass boilers

If you have access to a source of logs, then a high performance wood burning stove or boiler would definitely be worth considering. Wood burning, providing that the timber comes from a supply in constant re-growth (coppice or regeneration) is CO_2 neutral because the carbon released from the burning of the wood equates to the carbon absorbed by the trees in re-growth. If you have your own woodland and are prepared to put some time and effort into felling, logging, stacking and storing timber, then here is a great opportunity to keep fit at the same time as keeping your home warm.

Timber growing and log burning can be the most satisfying and sustainable way to heat your home. If your home does not have a chimney, investigate installing one. There are many chimney kits available that do not involve major structural alterations to the building. The latest high performance, fanned flue log boilers are highly efficient (90 – 95% - providing dry wood is used) and only require a low draught chimney, so will perform adequately even in areas where conventional open fires might not work well. Most also have very low particulate emissions and can therefore be used in smokeless zones[3], but do check this with the supplier. These systems work best with accumulator tanks and have the added benefit of reducing refuelling to once per day. Another biomass fuel

Photo courtesy of Green Earth Energy.

This domestic scale wood burning boiler is as, or even more efficient than, the best condensing gas boilers and is carbon neutral if the wood is harvested and replanted locally.

resource is waste wood. Two million tonnes of waste timber is produced each year. This can and is beginning to be turned into biomass fuel (usually wood pellets). Pellet boilers and stoves are now available from many wood stove distributors. Currently most wood pellets are imported into the UK from Europe, incurring transport 'costs'. However there are now a couple of suppliers in the UK which manufacture pellets from local wood - a low CO_2 fuel and a highly automated method of heating your home.

A useful introduction to burning wood as a heating fuel can be found at: ***www.solidfuel.co.uk/main_pages/wood.htm***

Biomass Task Force report and feedback on energy from biomass: ***www.defra.gov.uk/farm/crops/industrial/energy/biomass-taskforce/index.htm***

If wind turbines are mounted on a roof then care must be taken to minimise the likelihood of turbulence.

Photo courtesy of Shore Power.

Wind turbines

There has been a lot of hype regarding small scale roof mounted wind turbines and certainly the media has had a good time promoting the idea. The entrepreneurs behind a couple of novel systems had hoped to cover our homes with as many micro wind turbines as there are satellite dishes. However, the idea and the figures promoted in the press have been criticised by many experts. There is scepticism about the predicted outputs and our own personal experience of a roof-mounted turbine is that it has needed more maintenance than anticipated due to excess wear and tear from turbulence around the building. However, when installed in a suitable location, wind turbines can be efficient and durable. If you live on an exposed, windy site and can position a turbine away from any obstructions, this is a good option to consider.

British Wind Energy Association: ***www.bwea.com/you/own.html***

Rainwater harvesting

Climate change is likely to make rainfall less predictable but it seems we will see drier summers and wetter winters. Erratic rainfall patterns make water supply management difficult, so it makes sense to save water and reuse it where possible. If you are using mains water, such measures will also save energy at the local treatment works. Simple, low cost rainwater harvesting strategies might include using water butts to collect rainwater for gardening and general outside purposes. You can save water by fitting water saving devices in existing toilets. The more adventurous water saver could investigate an automated rain harvesting system, which will give you a supply of water even during periods when hose pipe bans are in force. These systems collect rainwater that would otherwise have been lost into the drainage system. Large surfaces, such as roofs, are ideal for rainwater harvesting and can provide water for the garden, washing machine and to flush the toilet.

UK Rainwater Harvesting Association: ***www.ukrha.org***

Further information: might be obtainable from the Combined Heat and Power Association: ***www.chpa.co.uk***

References

1. Calculated by the British Astronomical Association in 1990 (concerned about lit skies spoiling the view of the night sky).

2. Forest Stewardship Council (FSC): ***www.fsc-uk.org*** *and Programme for the Endorsement of Forest Certification (PEFC):* ***www.pefc.org/internet/html***

3. The Clean Air Act and smoke control: ***www.westminster.gov.uk/environment***

Further reading

'Saving Energy in the Home' by N White. Available from the Green Shop: 01452 770629 ***www.greenshop.co.uk***

Energy and water saving assistance

We asked **Ben Bamber** to look for initiatives, grants and support that will provide opportunities to help green the homes of those on low incomes ...

Fuel poverty is on the rise and the depressed financial markets and the 'credit crunch' will continue to make things worse, not better, for thousands of families across the UK. The latest figures show that one family in six live in fuel poverty. Everything that we take for granted in our homes has a cost - electricity, gas, lighting, heating and water. Nothing is free and most of these are the basic commodities of life.

Households are said to be in fuel poverty when more than 10% of their income is needed to pay fuel bills. In 2006, one energy company said that 60,000 of its customers in the lower income brackets were benefiting from special help to pay bills. Fuel debt is proportionately more prevalent with pre-payment customers. Almost 30% of households in the UK are classified as fuel poor, that's over 7 million households. There is therefore a huge drive to motivate householders to save energy and for local councils and power companies to promote energy saving with incentives, grants and publicity campaigns.

Water supplies are also becoming a major concern as drought continues to be an issue in the south east and regular floods occur during the summer in the Midlands. Costs rise because of the aging infrastructure and the increasing cost of repairs.

As have already been discussed, there are a number of ways energy and water can be saved, and this is the best and only sure way of driving those bills down. The following is therefore a summary of the best energy and water saving devices, grants and schemes offered by a variety of different government and non-government organisations and businesses.

Grants and trusts

Firstly, if you want to search for a suitable grant to suit your particular needs, there is a grants' database and search engine available at **www.energysavingtrust.org.uk/proxy/view/full/2019/grantsandofferssearch**. If you're struggling to pay your water bills, most water companies have a charitable trust attached to the company, which in certain circumstances, may cover your bill and bring it up-to-date. This is done on a case by case basis. Internet searches can be undertaken free of charge, or for a very small cost, at just about every town library in the country.

The government is still offering a wide variety of grants for home insulation, heating and energy saving solutions.

The Low Carbon Buildings Programme, (launched 2006), still provides grants for solar PV and other renewable technologies. 0800 298 3978 **www.lowcarbonbuildings.org.uk**.

In Scotland homeowners can qualify for grants worth up to 30% of the cost of installing a renewable technology system, up to a maximum of £4,000 **www.energysavingtrust.org.uk/generate_your_own_energy/grants_for_renewables**. The Energy Saving Trust (EST) says on its website that 'a household can qualify for up to two grants'. This scheme is only available in Scotland, via the Scottish Community and Householder Renewables Initiative (SCHRI). Most micro-generation technologies are covered by the Scottish grants including: biomass, ground source heat pumps, small scale hydro turbines, solar water heating, solar space heating and wind turbines. The SCHRI also offers funding to community groups.

Eaga Partnership Charitable Trust

The Eaga Partnership Charitable Trust is running a campaign to assist people who suffer from fuel poverty, and as a key part of the campaign, along with financial help it will be providing energy saving advice and solutions. The objectives of the Trust are 'the relief of fuel poverty and the preservation and protection of health by the promotion of the efficient use of energy'. There is no minimum or maximum amount that individuals and groups can apply for, as each application is judged on its own merits. Eligibility criteria are available on its website: **www.eaga.com/charitable/charitable_trust.htm** or call 01768 210220. Eaga also offers free central heating to the over 60's.

The Carbon Trust

The Carbon Trust **www.thecarbontrust.co.uk** offers energy saving advice, and on their website there is information to help you reduce your energy bills. This includes, cleaning light fittings annually, keeping the thermostat at 19°C - costs rise by 8% for every 1°C increase, not heating unused space, storerooms, corridors and areas where there's heavy physical work. Reduce heating during holidays and weekends and keep radiators clear of furniture (can reduce efficiency and output). Check that thermostats are sited out of draughts and away from either cold or hot spots. Keep windows closed in cold weather. If you are too warm, turn the heating down instead. The Carbon Trust also says, 'If you can't measure it, you can't manage it'. Check regularly on your consumption of electricity, gas and oil, and check that your bills relate to what you actually use, rather than an estimate.

Warm Front

Defra runs a grant scheme for insulation and heating costs for people on low incomes and state benefits. It is called Warm Front and is administered by the local councils: **www.warm-front.com/warm-front-grants.** Grants for £2,700 are available to eligible applicants. Most borough councils will have a department to field enquiries for the scheme, so contact your local council for details.

The scheme provides funding for insulation measures including, loft insulation, draught proofing, cavity-wall insulation, hot-water-tank insulation, heating systems (including central heating), gas room heaters with thermostat controls, converting a solid-fuel open fire to a modern glass-fronted fire, time controls for electric space water and water heaters, heating repairs and replacements. Other measures include energy advice and free low-energy light-bulbs. This grant programme is aimed at low-income families without their own money to invest in energy saving measures. However, there are also schemes aimed at encouraging higher earners, by providing a proportion of the costs of larger installations. Again your local council will have all the details.

Loft and cavity wall insulation grants

The major power companies have been partly funded and partly compelled to offer a range of discounted and subsidised schemes to home owners and tenants. These companies offer discounts on cavity wall insulation and loft insulation. A discount of 50% or 100%, depending on whether you are in receipt of state benefits, and which type of benefit also makes a difference. People on income support will be considered for 100% grant, in most cases. Contact any of the following companies on the numbers below; although some of them are restricted to particular regions, most are nationwide:

- Npower: 0800 022 220 **www.npower.com**
- Powergen: 0500 201 000 **www.powergen.co.uk**
- Scottish Power: 0845 601 7836 **www.theenergypeople.com**
- Home energy and British Gas (Centrica): 0845 971 7731
- Scottish Hydro Electric: 0845 777 6633

The Heat Project

All households throughout Britain are entitled

to a grant for loft and cavity wall insulation through the Heat Project. In order to qualify for the free loft and cavity wall insulation, one or more individuals in the household must be in receipt of a qualifying benefit, which includes income support, housing benefit, and pension credit – for a full list of qualifying benefits go to **www.heatproject.co.uk** or call 0800 093 405. As an example of the saving you could be entitled to, based on a 3 bed semi-detached house, subject to survey and funding availability, those who do not qualify for the free cavity wall insulation can expect to receive a grant worth up to £370 based on a typical installation price of £509 without a grant. **www.heatproject.co.uk** or call free on 0800 093 405

Further energy and water saving tips

Draught excluders are a cheap and effective way of making your home more energy efficient. Much of the wasted energy is lost through gaps in doors and windows, key holes, letter boxes and gaps in loft hatches. Sometimes the most obvious things can be missed, and it is these aspects of energy saving devices which are the most available, and easiest to fix. A roll of draft proofing tape for windows will cost £6, (10m) and is available from any good DIY shop. A letter box cover can cost as little as £4, and a draft excluder for external doors, (and internal if necessary), can be picked up at about £6 each. A hot water cylinder jacket, costs about £12, depending on the size of the cylinder. It is also possible to insulate exposed hot water pipes. The basic tasks outlined above will cost about £60 in total, and could save up to £25 in fuel bills, yearly.

Secondary glazing is more expensive, and as far as I know there are no government schemes to cover the costs. A basic pack for an average sized un-openable window will cost about £65.

Radiator backing panels are also a good idea if you have central heating in your home. A good deal of the heat coming from your radiator is wasted out the back of the radiator and through the walls of your house. A radiator panel is available from **www.shopeco.co.uk/** for £25.00 for six, or £29.99 for eight. These panels can save a large proportion of the energy used to run the radiators by directing the heat back into the room. They are easy to install, and so there are no installation charges. You may also be able to get them from local healthy living shops.

If you followed all the energy saving advice above then you could expect to cut at least £165 from your yearly electric and gas bills. All of the above can be achieved within a budget of £500 - £800 and therefore it is possible to repay your investment within 3 to 5 years.

Water is often wasted in the average home. Given recent droughts, there are a number of things you can do to reduce water consumption, especially relevant if you're on a water meter. If your loo flushes 9 litres (80% of houses still use this size cistern) then fit the Interflush retrofit kit to your existing toilet siphon to save water. See **www.interflush.co.uk**. Once fitted, the average household of 2.4 people could save 27,000 litres per year. The costs of the system are £19.90 which you can buy online.

You could add a bag of water into your cistern, below the fill capacity, which could reduce the flush amount by up to 20%. You can buy manufactured clip on bags as well, from **www.h2obuildingservices.co.uk** This bag could save you up to 2 litres per flush. This company offers a service to make your property as water efficient as possible, and promise your investment will have paid for itself within 9 to 12 months. The website does not contain any price information, so ring 0113 2820 820 for details.

Finally, there is a free water usage calculator online which offers useful information to anyone who wants to make water savings in the home. See: **www.3valleys.co.uk/home/reckoner**

Further reading

'The Water Book' by J Thornton. Available from the Green Shop: ***www.greenshop.co.uk***

Tips for building your own eco-home

Doug Stewart offers a number of simple tips and sensible suggestions for anyone wishing to build a new eco-home from scratch ...

Creating a home with the correct space and specification for your requirement is like buying any bespoke, customised piece of equipment, furniture or car. Buildings can rarely be standard items and refurbishments never are. Time must be taken to get the mix right. However, where do you start? Many people dream of finding the perfect building plot and all other thoughts are blocked until that plot is found. However, idyllic building plots are in very short supply, and if they come up, literally cost the earth. The reality is that most dream homes will be built on an 'infill' plot between two other houses and this is also the best option from an environmental sense, as it can tap into nearby services, such as water gas and electricity that already supplies other homes.

Get the finances right

If you want to build a new home, then be prepared to spend at least one third of your total budget on buying a building plot. Finance is of paramount importance to any successful project and this point cannot be over emphasized. It is always worth knowing (or at least taking an educated guess) what the final value of a property might be. It will help prevent you from overspending on fancy paraphernalia that will see no return.

Builders have traditionally used a rule of thumb guide for valuing an imaginary building on a potential plot of land; it is 1+2 =3. So, basically, if the building plot costs £100,000 then the build cost and profits need to be contained within a budget of £200,000, giving a total ballpark figure of £300,000, as the final value of the property. However, with the soaring cost of land nowadays, the equation would be nearer to 1+1 so, theoretically, leaving you less spending money for the actual build before you start to waste money!

Funding for any property purchase and building works can come from many sources. The rule of thumb is the more cash you have relative to eventual cost, the better deal you will get from any funding partner. The reason for this is you are lowering the risk factor for your funding partner. Whether you use a building society, a clearing bank, or a merchant bank, any lender will evaluate its client and their project for risk. Even a joint investor, such as a wealthy friend or relative, if they have any financial sense, will need to take advice on the risk factor. For more on this read the separate 'Funding for green homes' story later in this chapter.

Losing money does happen, and when it does it can be a spiral which goes out of control. If, however, you and the funder (usually a building society) have both taken all steps possible to consolidate any risk factors, a successful project should follow. Sustainable and green projects are beginning to receive preferential treatment from some lenders, so bear this in mind. A financial ceiling should be in place from the outset identifying the total of your allocated funds for the project, and how you want to spend it. Don't forget to take account of any grants available (very few at the moment).

Choosing your building plot

The site or building you eventually acquire, to enable your vision, will form the basis of your journey into the world of construction. The impact of the choice of site should never be under-estimated, as it will have a huge influence on design requirements, eventual cost and its fitness for purpose. An evaluation, with careful consideration of all the site's downsides and potential problems, should always be carried out, working with a suitably qualified person or practice.

Remember that potential sites are in short supply. Estate agents' windows, with property photos and descriptions, often mean that the agent's close associates have already rejected the property and its possibilities. It can be a reason it is being advertised, other than achieving the best price for the seller. This may seem sceptical, but often looking outside the box or photo/description will pay dividends. The internet has many plot finder type websites, so give these a try, especially if you are looking for plots outside your home region.

Building plots usually have outline planning permission. When they do, the price reflects this. However if you can identify a 'potential' building plot before the owner has obtained outline planning permission themselves, you may be able to approach them and offer to make the application on their behalf and perhaps, if successful, get the plot at a much more reasonable price (but make sure you have first refusal in some sort of legally binding contract before you go to all that effort).

Designing and building your dream eco-home

Design and cost management should work hand-in-hand. If they do not, trouble could be on the horizon. Be sure that your designer and specifier (if you use one) is totally aware of your aims. If you want an energy saving, sustainable home, or your ambitions are for a zero carbon footprint, make it known at the beginning of the design process and contract negotiations. Also get references that will help to prove they know how to achieve your sustainability or low energy goals.

A well conceived building project can be one of the most satisfying processes a person can be involved with in his or her lifetime, but if it goes wrong it can destroy businesses, marriages, a person's financial future and the credibility of all those involved. Don't leave all the knowledge gathering to the designer. If you are well informed then you can see the process unfolding and use opportunity to be involved with the decision making. Without these skills you leave yourself open to be led by the nose. Choose your professionals carefully. There are some really good eco-architects and builders out there. If you are trying to find an architect, builder or any other professional, you can search through the membership listings of eco building organisations such as the long-established AECB (the sustainable building association), **www.aecb.net** or the more recent Green Register **www.greenregister.org.uk.** Do note, however, that being a member of either of these organisations does not include any guarantee regarding competence, quality or standard of work. You should always seek references from previous clients and ask to see completed jobs.

The skills and resources of the professionals and practices can pay for themselves many times over if chosen carefully. Egos and personalities will come into play, so you must ensure compatibility. Like marriages, there are many potential partners available, so be sure to make the right choice. Make sure any service is tailored to your needs and it will deliver what you want.

If you are reading this book carefully, you will by now know that there are many different aspects to sustainable construction, but in particular you should consider the embodied energy contained within the materials used, the energy efficiency of the fabric of the building (e.g. insulation and air permeability) and the systems utilised for power, heat and other services. A lot of emphasis is often given to the source of power and energy, be it solar, biomass or otherwise, but to make the best use of these technologies it is imperative that the design of the fabric of the building is given priority,

The various systems utilised within the home are numerous, and the interaction between the various technologies can lead to problems. As such you should always seek to ensure that you have a single point of responsibility for the design of the internal services, to ensure that the installation works properly and can be serviced effectively in the future. If you are going to embark on a new building, then you really should read Volume 2 of the Green Building Bible, the companion to this book, as it looks into the technical detailed aspects of creating low energy buildings.

Self build or contractor?

It is estimated that 20,000 'self-build' homes are constructed in the UK each year. A self-build home is generally defined as a home that is built on a single site, which is purchased and developed for occupation by the purchaser of the site. The purchaser may actually never move in, or they may move in for the rest of their life. There is no inference that the house should actually be constructed using the skills and labour of the owner!

Some self-builders may have a lead consultant, but if you have the necessary skills, knowledge, experience, nerve and confidence, then you may well play the role of lead consultant yourself. Most, however, will need to employ a construction professional, either for parts of the construction or most of it. You may need a builder, architect, project manager or designer to guide you through the maze of different materials and techniques available, and to provide the vision, expertise and solutions to ensure your project is procured and constructed successfully and the potential of your site is maximised.

Many magazines, TV shows, exhibitions, videos and books support and encourage the self-build market. Hundreds of companies have invested millions of pounds to sell to the many dreamers and potential developers and to the small percentage of people who actually own a plot with planning permission. The media is often all too quick to promote the potential profits or possible savings that can be made through building your own home. Whilst employing a professional will have a significant initial cost, it should also significantly reduce risk and, with the right choice of expert, should also bring long term savings.

Above: professionals and self-builders alike will both need to call in specialists at some time during the construction. Be sure to budget properly for this specialist input. In this case the specialist is installing cellulose fibre insulation and prices will have to be quoted by the supplier at an early a stage because work like this is unlikely to be included in most building pricing books. The same advice goes for most renewable power technologies, uncommon insulations, etc.

The multiplicity of options further exaggerate the risks and hurdles the untrained and inexperienced self-builder faces, and it is essential that all construction options are considered carefully, to ensure that right decisions are made. For major projects, a well informed, skilled working foreman, either employed by the main contractor, lead consultant or client, may pay dividends; helping to avoid delays, disputes, and ensuring attention to detail and the overall quality of the build.

A programme of works, identifying the project's critical path (and thereby areas of work which will affect the overall build-time), should be in place before the project begins, and should take into account all of the lead-times for materials and fittings. Specialist contractors should be briefed on when they will be required well in advance, to avoid any delays in the programme.

There is no point in having a programme if every effort is not made by the site operatives, sub-contractors and working foreman to keep to it. The client and lead consultant should monitor the programme weekly. It is also essential that services are ordered and in place before the building work starts. Most tradesmen will require electricity and water for welfare facilities, lighting and tools.

Unplanned changes

Wherever possible, you should avoid making major changes during the construction phase of the project, as they will almost inevitably disrupt the programme, incur (usually high) additional cost, and affect morale on site. It is essential, therefore, that there is a good degree of certainty (the reward of careful research and confident decision making) before making a start with work on site. Making it up as you go along will lead to bad tempers, disputes, and even potential disasters. Assumptions should be avoided at all cost, whether by consultants, client or tradesmen. Standards, regulations and applications are changing all the time, and details may not always be clear on drawings, if they are shown at all. If there is any doubt the team should not proceed without checking with the lead consultant or client. Well meaning decisions made by ill-informed workers to drive progress can lead to expensive alterations and remedial work later.

Remember, the site owner is responsible for site safety. Don't cut corners on scaffolding etc. if your building is unusual and regular scaffolding is inappropriate, seek advice from a scaffolding erection specialist before the sitework begins. Also ensure that you take out adequate insurance for site visitors - even unwanted ones!

Photos courtesy of selfbuilder Sarah Villers

Health and safety

Every process on a building site carries with it health and safety risks. Most of the risks require just common sense, but others, such as working from height, in the ground and with hazardous materials, plant and power tools, require more attention and care. These risks should never be underestimated, and risk assessments and method statements are now mandatory on large sites and becoming more so for small sites too, even though they do not come under the Construction Design & Management Regulations. Build safe and ignore health and safety risks at your peril.

Conclusion

Organisation, management, cost control, lead times, programme monitoring, quality control and health and safety are the essence of a successful project. ☯

Further reading

'All About Selfbuild' by B Matthews.

'The Whole House Book' by P Borer and C Harris

'Diary of an Eco-Builder' by W Anderson.

'The Green Self Build Book' by J Broome.

The above books are available from the Green Shop: 01452 770629 ***www.greenshop.co.uk***

The planning process

For many, achieving planning permission is one of the most stressful parts of the building process. If you are planning a green building, or even upgrading your property and/or integrating renewable technologies which require planning consent, then read this advice from **Gideon Richards** ...

Planners are not building regulation officers and, believe it or not, there may be little communication between the two offices. Planners have to work within a number of constraints and follow a standardised protocol that can sometimes appear barmy to the lay person. However, the rules have come from somewhere and the planner's job is to interpret them. Remember that whilst planner's have constraints, they also have a great deal of flexibility available to them in interpreting the rules and guidelines. However, in many authorities, the final decision is in the hands of elected councillors and not the planning officer. This final point can, in some cases, be the crux of the planning approval or rejection of your scheme.

The level of understanding about green building, renewable energy, environmental issues and related products varies widely among planners. Like all of us, planners have very different backgrounds and interests. What is important to you may not be of such importance to them! It isn't always about logic, unfortunately! However, there are a number of simple rules that can be adopted by anyone, which may help smooth the process of making a planning application. Some of these rules may appear obvious and straight forward, however, it is a fact that planning officers often feel that many applications submitted are missing key information.

It would be wise to try and foresee the issues and problems you are going to face with a planning application. Here is a six point plan of action:

1. Understand the planning system

A bit of research, early on, will save you a lot of stress later. Find out what the local strategy for planning is based on. A good starting point is the 'unitary development plan' (UDP) and local planning policies (LPP) or local planning frameworks (LDF) (for definitions of these please see 'glossary' on page 469). These are usually published on the internet or can be provided by your local council. Attempting to get a consent that conflicts with these policies will immediately put your application at a disadvantage and probably set you up to fail.

For applications where you wish to include some renewable energy generation, first check the 'general permitted development order' (GPDO), which, in many cases, can actually mean a planning application is not necessary! However, be careful because different councils have the right to implement the order in slightly different ways. While you may have no direct influence on the planner's or council's decisions and views on renewables and green building at local, or regional level, understanding how well the area is doing in meeting its targets, may well be a good way of highlighting the benefits of your project in demonstrating the technologies and encouraging others to be like minded. Remember, we now have mandatory national renewable energy targets, and councils should also have carbon saving targets, fuel poverty targets, etc. Ticking the council's boxes may help your cause!

In fact, in some areas, there is a requirement on the builder to incorporate a percentage of renewable energy from on-site renewables (commonly known as the 'Merton' rule). These percentages vary from council to council and region to region as 'local development documents' and 'regional spatial strategies' do not require continuity from politicians. The implication of this, is that any development put on hold for a few years may find the percentages required have changed.

Prior to completing your application form, consider the information you think will benefit your application and talk to the planners. This simple act will give you an immediate understanding of the planning officer's and the authority's standpoint and the issues that your proposal faces and has to meet. More information, when laid out well, is better than less, if it allows for better understanding of your intentions, but please keep in mind that lots of information is no guarantee of overcoming the occasional immovable obstacles that can hinder some applications. There is no doubt that well constructed information, that allows the planners to tick their appropriate boxes against relevant criteria, can help things along.

Additionally, the Building Regulations, Part L – conservation of fuel and power, is under review and will require a 25% decrease in energy in its 2010 revision, 45% by 2013 and 100% ('zero carbon homes') by 2016. Non-domestic buildings are getting a similar treatment with them becoming 'zero carbon' by 2019. It is also almost certain that this time the government will also require those extending their home by over a percentage (to be notified) to also include improved energy efficiency and energy reducing measures.

2. Research the site and location

Do your homework. A good site appraisal will show more than where your boundaries and utilities are. It will also demonstrate that you have considered any potential impacts on the site, local community and the environment.

The planners always seek comment from other parties, including neighbours, highways, parks authorities (in National Parks) and local or parish councils. There is no real order of importance in the interested parties but, suffice to say, any single one of them can be highly influential in the outcome of your application. Strategic site access and services requirements will almost certainly need to be met or addressed. Ensure that the application takes these into consideration. For instance, vehicular access to the site could be a hazard to pedestrians and other motorists. Choose your site access proposal carefully. It may be that you don't want or cannot get vehicular access. This could be a stumbling block, but some very green minded people have successfully argued for and gained planning permission for houses where vehicles cannot access.

Also for those planning on installing a biomass heating system you will undoubtedly have to overcome the ever increasing fears of air quality impacts (especially in urban areas and air quality management assessment areas). Know the type of system you plan on installing, if not the actual system, and provide good data to support your case, with emissions data wherever possible. Pictures of similar systems in similar situations would also illustrate the point well (especially of there is only a heat haze from the stack) or include a montage of how your stack might look in the existing surroundings.

3. Enquire about the opinion of neighbours and other interested parties

Remember it isn't only about planning officers approving the plan. There are many cases where planning officers have recommended approval but it has been overridden and rejected by the planning committee (elected representatives from the local council). The elected representatives have the final say, (except in an appeal against their decision, which is decided by a representative of the Home Secretary). Why might the planning committee go against the recommendations of the planning officer? Usually this happens if they have been influenced by strong local protest against the proposal.

The public, especially neighbours, can be powerful allies or enemies in a planning appli-

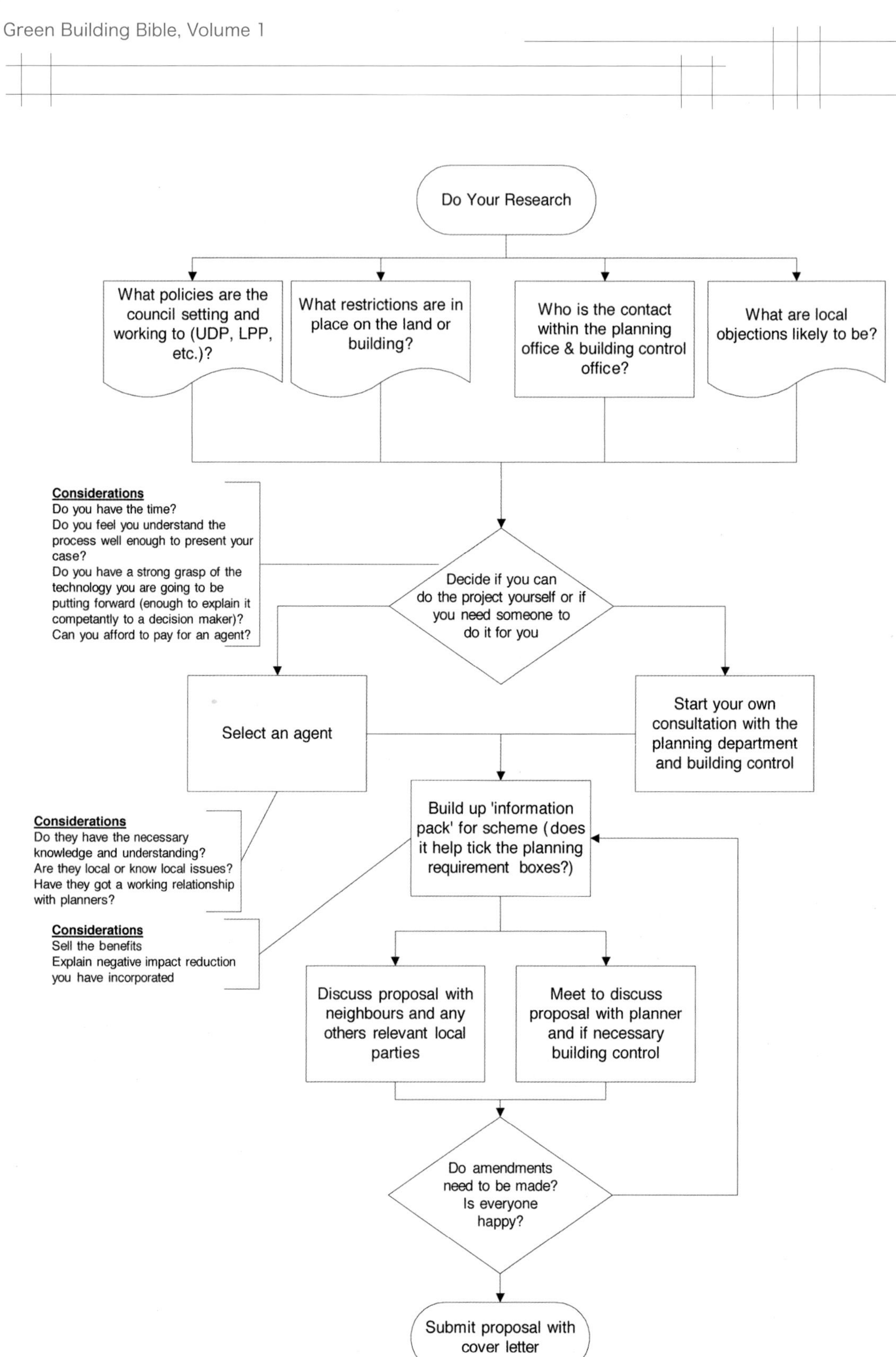
Do Your Research
What policies are the council setting and working to (UDP, LPP, etc.)?
What restrictions are in place on the land or building?
Who is the contact within the planning office & building control office?
What are local objections likely to be?
Considerations
Do you have the time?
Do you feel you understand the process well enough to present your case?
Do you have a strong grasp of the technology you are going to be putting forward (enough to explain it competantly to a decision maker)?
Can you afford to pay for an agent?
Decide if you can do the project yourself or if you need someone to do it for you
Select an agent
Start your own consultation with the planning department and building control
Considerations
Do they have the necessary knowledge and understanding?
Are they local or know local issues?
Have they got a working relationship with planners?
Build up 'information pack' for scheme (does it help tick the planning requirement boxes?)
Considerations
Sell the benefits
Explain negative impact reduction you have incorporated
Discuss proposal with neighbours and any others relevant local parties
Meet to discuss proposal with planner and if necessary building control
Do amendments need to be made? Is everyone happy?
Submit proposal with cover letter

cation. Do your utmost to get them on board with your ideas at an early stage. They have the right to inspect all applications and make observations. If they can understand what you are looking to achieve, and the efforts that have been made to reduce the impact on others, there should be less resistance. If there is strong local and neighbourly resistance to your application, then treat it seriously. Try to negotiate acceptable modifications with neighbours before you make your application. If the scheme is large enough or you are particularly concerned, there are organisations that can help develop and implement community engagement sessions and processes.

4. Prepare for strategic complications

Be prepared to accept that, in some circumstances, rigorous restrictions may be imposed on the development. There are many national, regional and local designations that can be put on land. For instance there are various planning policy guidance and statements, including the green belt (PPG2), greenfield/brownfield (PPS3), landscape designation (locally assigned – PPS7), green corridors (predominantly rural, ecology routes), listed-building, conservation areas, to name but a few. The restrictions and requirements that pertain to all of these can easily be researched on the internet .

If your project is in a restricted area, such as a national park, area of outstanding natural beauty (AONB), conservation area etc, then you will need to prove exceptional circumstances for your proposal, although the new amendment the to GPDO mentioned earlier will help if you are looking to incorporate micro-generation technologies on the building. Having established early on what the designation of the area is, or what the building's status is, a decision can be taken as to whether you give up and find somewhere else, or struggle on. If you do carry on, then building that relationship with the appropriate authorities is going to be critical. Be prepared to negotiate and adapt your proposal. If possible have the alternatives up your sleeve prior to any meeting. As a minimum, know what your bottom line is going to be.

5. Use good communication and professionals if necessary

If your proposal is complicated or very specialised and you believe that you will struggle to explain it effectively, it is worth considering hiring an architect or agent who is familiar and comfortable dealing with your type of project. Try and choose someone who already has a good relationship with the local planning department and that you can work with. Don't be bullied into decisions. Take your time to consider all the implications and if necessary do your research.

Remember good drawings, descriptions of schemes and support information may make the difference between 'high quality' applications and average ones, especially if you are looking to do something special or different.

<u>Checklist</u>

- What local restrictions are there?
  - UDP
  - LPP
  - Listed Building
  - Conservation Area
  - Green Belt
  - Green Field / Brown Field, etc.
- Who is your planning officer (PO)?
- Who is your building control officer (BCO)?
- Build a positive rapport
- How much do PO & BCO understand about renewable and sustainable buildings and energy?
- Have regular meetings to discuss your proposals
  - With PO
  - With BCO
  - With Neighbours
- Be prepared to compromise and negotiate
- If using an agent
  - Do they have knowledge and understanding of your project?
  - Are they local or have they an understanding of local planning constraints?
  - Do they have a good working relationship with the planner?
- Provide an 'information pack' to support your case
  - Explain what you have done to minimise any negative impacts
  - Demonstrate that you have ensured the planners can tick their consent requirements
- Write a cover letter that explains the project in a way that supports planning policy (i.e. This project supports the councils requirements to reduce CO_2 emissions by X through its use of Y)

Be careful, however, not to over-invest in pre-approval fees. Ask for a no-approval, no fee arrangement. You may be shown the door, but if a professional is confident and likes the look of your project, then you might get a deal.

Don't drop your own research and choose your professional carefully. For instance, when selecting an architect, ask how well does he or she know the planners/development controller for your area? A good architect will have a rapport with them. A bad architect, who fails to understand the local requirements/protocol, can be as good as pouring money, your money, down the drain. Ask for references from past clients, look at locally completed projects that they have designed and ask the opinion of the planning officer.

If you do choose a professional to represent your application, then consider going along to the first meeting between them and the planning officer to see how they get on. Look for any problems early on, before a lot of work has been put to paper. Put yourself in the planner's shoes and think through any possible objections and look at solutions or offer information in support of the benefits for your approach.

Explain why you have chosen the options you have. List the benefits that your project might have for the wider community. Remember, in the language of planning, 'cost is not a material planning consideration, however, impacts on visual amenity and the environment are'.

6. Make clear submissions

Submit a short letter outlining your proposal. This letter should help the planner tick the boxes needed to achieve the authority's objectives. Also sell the positives, but don't ignore the negatives. If there are negatives, face them head-on and explain the measures taken to mitigate and overcome them. If that's not possible, have alternative solutions up your sleeve early on. Putting the positives in a way that meets planning needs helps them to promote the project to the planning committee. Remember to always explain the benefits of your project in a way that the planning officer can understand and buy-into.

Planners are humans. They can have good and bad days. They are not infallible and they do make mistakes and unfathomable decisions. Remember, at the end of the day, if you really don't agree with the decision there is an appeal's process. Hopefully by taking the above steps you'll have come to an agreement well before that.

Conclusion

The planning process can be confusing and frustrating. It is important you do your research thoroughly. Keep smiling and develop a rapport with your local planning officer.

Most planners are looking to reach a balanced, fair outcome. Most minor developments (home extensions and improvements) are generally supported by the planning system. You may find a staged approach to a development appropriate and less fraught with difficulties. However, you would need to weigh up the benefits of doing the improvements all at once or carrying out the work piecemeal.

Help them to help you achieve your planning consent by giving them adequate information, including the benefits, for them to support your approval. Demonstrate that you have looked at all the scenarios and this is your preferred one. Explain why you consider your proposal is the best option. Remember that there are a number of boxes (policy, local strategy and technical) that need to be ticked for your plans to be approved - providing as many of those ticks as possible could give you a positive outcome.

Financial providers

Finance is a crucial part of any project. Most of us deposit our money in banks and building societies and also take out loans and mortgages from them as required. However, how many of us are aware of the ethical stance of our finance service provider? **Sally Hall** reports ...

Do we know how our deposited savings are being utilised? Should we care? Maybe we are borrowing money from an institution that also deals with businesses we would not wish to support or our savings are being used to support activities we are opposed to. You may be surprised to hear that even the most active green consumers have turned a blind eye to the activities of their banks or building societies but this situation is changing.

Ethical and green lending

The market for ethical and green mortgages is still in its infancy. This is partly because people have tended to be less concerned about who they borrow from than who they invest in, and also because the building societies have traditionally had housing only related investments. However, many of the old building societies have now de-mutualised and become much more like banks in their lending policies.

The mutual building societies are generally considered to be an appropriate choice if ethical and environmental issues are important to you. Such societies are owned by their members (not shareholders), were created in order to provide finance for building, and many have or are developing their own ethical code, guided by their customers.

The Ecology Building Society is a committed mutual society that will lend money for projects involving the renovation of empty or derelict buildings, eco new build, energy efficiency improvements, organic smallholdings, low impact building (straw bale, earth etc), and it will lend to owners/occupiers, landlords, housing cooperatives, housing associations, companies and individuals. It offers discounts off mortgage rates for those building to the AECB's silver and gold standards.

If you are borrowing money always be sure to check carefully and do the necessary research to ensure you can afford to repay any loans and that the type of mortgage chosen is suitable for your situation. You can do this yourself or employ a financial advisor but ensure they are authorised by the Financial Services Authority (FSA). There are advisors that specialise in ethical finance. To find one in your area you can use the EIRIS Financial Adviser Directory (see useful contacts).

The Ethical Investors Group can provide information and advice to people who are interested in ethical and environmental issues. The Ethical Investors Group was established in 1989 and has pioneered ethical financial advice on ethical, socially responsible and environmental investment. Never rush into any decision or sign anything unless you have read through everything in detail and understand fully your obligations. Remember that taking out a mortgage is usually a long-term commitment.

Banks and building societies

Banks and building societies are being encouraged to take environmental issues on board. Such issues range from being prepared to lend to environmentally beneficial industries, to encouraging commercial borrowers to save energy (and costs) and to reduce emissions. Many ethical issues, such as the environmental conduct of business customers, are now part of standard risk assessment and prudent banking. EIRIS, a UK based charity set up in

1983, has produced a guide to ethical and responsible banking and an equivalent guide to building societies will also be available in the future. EIRIS is reputed to be the leading global provider of independent research into the social, environmental and ethical performance of companies.

There are one building society and two banks that currently stand out from the rest; the Ecology Building Society, the Co-operative Bank and the Triodos Bank. These three are at the forefront of ethical banking and mortgage provision, and have been for many years.

Ecology Building Society

The Ecology Building Society, set up in 1981, is dedicated to improving the environment by promoting sustainable housing and communities. It uses the money deposited by savers to provide mortgages to those whose plans will be of benefit to the environment.

It is particularly interesting to note that the Ecology has a policy that is totally unique within the existing finance sector. None of its staff salaries can be more than five times the lowest full-time salary paid; a policy that is very well received by its members. The practical implication of this is to put a ceiling on the higher-end salaries (let's not forget that it is those who earn most that have the greatest impact on the environment – a fact that is rarely acknowledged, addressed or debated anywhere). This policy was introduced primarily to ensure equitable behaviour in the organization. It ensures that those who take on the responsibility of dealing with the regulators and have legal obligations do get higher salaries, whilst also recognising that they can't operate without the support of motivated colleagues. This also extends to the annual bonus system, which is currently a pool arrangement on the basis of annual profit realised and related to salary on the same basis for all, and includes part-time members of staff. Again the same percentage pension contributions also apply across the board.

This policy discourages the so-called 'fat-cat' behaviour, so prevalent in the rest of the financial sector. It's these kind of commitments that make the Ecology well worth supporting as this society has proven that being green/ethical has to extend beyond making merely statements, charity contributions etc.

Co-operative Bank

The Co-operative Bank was established way back in 1872 (as the savings and loans arm of the Co-operative Wholesale Society). A survey of customers in 1991 found that 84% wanted the bank to have a clear ethical policy and one was introduced just a year later. The ethical standards (developed and regularly reviewed in full consultation with its customers) are all based on the concerns of its customers and include such issues as ecological impact, animal welfare, genetic modification, global trade, arms trade and human rights. It will not do business with any companies involved in the arms trade, or whose conduct violates human rights. It supports enterprises with positive social and ethical intentions.

Triodos Bank

The Triodos Bank was originally set up in the Netherlands in 1980. It now has branches in the UK and Belgium. It offers the usual range of services but its business loans are only available to organisations involved in sustainable development projects - for example solar and wind energy, organic agriculture and projects in the developing world.

Building insurance

For general home and buildings' insurance there currently seems to be little choice for those who want to put their ethical principles into practice. The 'Statement of Environmental Commitment by the Insurance Industry', an initiative from the United Nations' Environment Programme (UNEP), is asking insurance companies to pledge 'to make every realistic effort towards achieving a balance between economic development, and the welfare of society, through environmentally sound management practices'. The statement calls on insurers to incorporate environmental considerations into their internal and external business activities. A number of UK insurers have signed up to this initiative so ask your insurer whether they have signed up. UNEP's website outlines the initiative in detail.

Naturesave Policies Ltd is probably the most committed and longest standing ecological insurance intermediary that offers household buildings and contents insurance, with all policies insured through Lloyd's of London. Its aim is to encourage the adoption of more environmentally aware trading practices in the business community, by using the insurance industry as a vehicle for sustainable development. Naturesave pledges that 10% of the premiums generated from the sale of all home buildings, contents and travel policies goes to benefit environmental and conservationist organisations on specific environmental projects via The Naturesave Trust.

Useful contacts

The Financial Services Authority (FSA): 0845 606 1234 ***www.fsa.gov.uk***

EIRIS: ***www.eiris.org***

The Ethical Investors Group: 01242 539848 ***www.ethicalinvestors.co.uk***

The Ecology Building Society: 0845 674 5566 ***www.ecology.co.uk***

The Co-operative Bank: 0845 7212 212 ***www.cooperativebank.co.uk***

The Triodos Bank: 0500 008 720 ***www.triodos.co.uk***

United Nations' Environment Programme (UNEP): ***www.unep.ch***

British Banking Association: (the voice of the banking industry for all UK banks) ***www.bba.org.uk***

Building Societies Association: 020 7520 5900 ***www.bsa.org.uk***

Association of British Credit Unions Ltd: ***www.abcul.org.uk***

Banking Code Standards Board: 0845 230 9694 ***www.bankingcode.org.uk***

Naturesave: 01803 864 390 ***www.naturesave.co.uk***

Below: the Ecology Building Society headquarters has been built very much with the green building philosophy in mind.

Inset: the Co-operative Bank HQ in Manchester has the largest commercial solar PV facade in the UK.

Greening a traditional property

The fabric of a building can be put at risk from replacement, alteration and adaptation, particularly where contemporary solutions are used thoughtlessly to improve thermal performance. **Richard Oxley** explains ...

In these dynamic times we must increasingly be aware of the dangers posed by trying to get traditional buildings to meet new and ever-increasing standards of energy performance. I would like to outline an introductory approach that should help to improve our understanding of older buildings and also discuss the likelihood of achieving successful improvements.

All work on traditional buildings needs to be approached in a manner that reflects their specific characteristics, (which may not match those of a modern building) if they are to benefit from appropriate improvements that are in the building's, and environment's, long-term interest.

A traditional building, therefore, should be considered as a whole and treated in a holistic way. Its structure, materials and methods of construction and patterns of air and moisture movement should be properly understood. To be in a position to make appropriate and effective improvements you have to first understand the building. This is a basic requirement within the field of historic building conservation, and one that could be applied to great effect when improvements are being planned for almost any existing buildings.

The materials and detailing of construction will influence the appropriateness and practicability of improvements that can be made. For example, if a building is constructed with soft stone or earth walls, it will be imperative to maintain, or reinstate, a good eave's overhang to protect the walls from the weather.

Understanding the building

Understanding how a building has been repaired and maintained in the past will provide an insight into problem areas and identify where inappropriate, impermeable materials have been used. An understanding of how older buildings have developed is crucial to making successful alterations, improvements and repairs. Even in a Victorian terrace, a typical dwelling can be subject to a whole range of alterations; removal of internal walls, the removal of chimney breasts, the replacement of timber floors with solid floors, the provision of a rear extension etc.

Cultural significance - it is important to understand what makes a building of interest. For instance, it could be a 19th century social housing project that forms an important part of our collective memory and culture.

Protected status - it is crucial to determine if a building is listed or in a conservation area, as protection will influence the extent and nature of work that can be carried out. It is important to appreciate that it is a criminal offence to carry out unauthorised works and, as such, works should only proceed once approval has been gained from the local planning authority.

Performance assessment methods

Once the originally intended performance is understood, it is important to assess what changes have been made from that performance and ask whether the changes are having an adverse influence on the condition of the building. Unfortunately too few older buildings have escaped the introduction of inappropriate materials. Where this is a problem for the condition of the building, the intended performance will need to be reinstated. This usually means that inappropriate materials have to be removed, where this can be achieved without causing more damage than if they are left in place. Once the inappropriate materials are removed, repairs to the exposed fabric of the building are usually required.

One of the most overlooked areas of performance is how a building performs when in use. Simple assessments can be made, but in many cases the input of a specialist is required. The methods of assessing the performance of a building include the following areas.

Data logging - a means of obtaining information on the performance of the building before, during and after improvement. The information collected typically includes the external temperature and internal temperature and relative humidity within selected rooms and roof spaces. Without this information it is not possible to assess if the improvements made have had a positive affect.

Fuel bills - a simple means of measuring the success of improvements that can be presented in monetary terms for ease of understanding by lay-people, in effect a real-life SAP calculation!

Fan pressurisation tests - these are important diagnostic tools in understanding how the building performs, they are more than just a means of providing measurements. Areas of excessive air infiltration (draughts) can be positively identified and resources targeted at actual, rather than perceived, problems.

Thermal imaging - a diagnostic tool that improves the understanding of the performance in use of the building and assists in the identification of problem areas such as cold bridges.

Dampness diagnosis - if improvements are to be made, it is important that inherent problems, such as damp, are fully understood and that remedial measures are carried out to address the causes of the damp (and this does not mean going to a specialist damp and timber contractor!). In most cases this means fixing rainwater gutters and downpipes, reducing high external ground levels and the careful removal of impermeable cement pointing and render.

Occupant feedback - the occupants and users play an important role in achieving a good understanding of the building. They usually know which rooms are coldest and where problems of condensation occur. This information is not only important before the improvements are made, but also afterwards, to ascertain if comfort levels have actually been improved.

Continued assessment - monitoring during the project, when repairs and improvements are being made, will maximise the success of the improvements and avoid progressing so far with the works that they cannot be effectively addressed before scaffold access is removed. These, and other, assessments assist in achieving a true understanding of the performance in use of a building. Only when the building is understood, can appropriate improvements be devised that are appropriate for that particular building and its individual circumstances.

Performance targets

There will be desire or pressure for existing buildings to meet targets in performance. It is important to understand what the building is

Once the original performance characteristics of a traditional building are known and adequate assessment methods have been carried out, appropriate and successful renovation to high environmental and energy standards can be implemented.

realistically capable of achieving and what is desirable for the long-term use and preservation of the building.

Targets, and how they have been calculated and set, are largely based on arbitrary assessments and assumptions that do not take into account the actual construction of the building, the real life performance and use or location. They are largely developed with the design of new build in mind. In many cases these targets cannot be met by existing buildings, or where targets are achieved. This may create problems for the building and/or the occupants. Applying targets that have been designed for new build is not guaranteed to be successful for the existing building stock.

The need to be flexible when applying targets to existing buildings is important when improving air-tightness. Ventilation rates are calculated for the general removal of odour and moisture, with 8 litres/second/person, or 0.4ach (air changes per hour) being considered what is safe for normal domestic occupancies. Typically modern airtight homes can reach 0.4ach.

In solid walled buildings an adjustment needs to be made to allow for the walls to breathe, over and above the requirement to remove odour and moisture. Adjusting the target for solid walled dwellings to 0.8ach would allow the same amount of air for the building as the occupants. This is an arbitrary figure and would need to be monitored to determine if the requirements of each building and its individual circumstances have been satisfied.

We currently do not know what the correct level of adjustment needs to be, but we can be certain that it would need to be adjusted to suit the individual circumstances of each building to reflect construction, location, exposure and intensity of use. If there is an over adjustment, where the air changes are reduced too much, this could lead to mould growth, associated health problems for the occupants and the conditions for fungal decay and insect attack of the building timbers.

As it can be seen, there are risks associated with strictly adhering to, or striving to reach, modern standards and targets as they can compromise the building's performance and create new problems.

Informed improvements

There are significant dangers in adopting standard solutions. Time invested in designing bespoke solutions, that reflect potential areas of conflict and weakness, such as wall and roof junctions, will enhance the chances of providing an appropriate and effective improvement. It is important that the materials used to improve the energy efficiency of existing buildings are selected carefully; they must have similar performance characteristics to the building fabric. In most cases this means avoiding vapour barriers and checks and looking at traditional materials and modern materials similar in character and performance, which will minimise the creation of problems. "Faulty judgements arise from ignorance of the availability of crafts and materials, the desire to find cheap and easy solutions and the belief that modern methods are, in any case, superior to traditional materials"[1].

Solutions have to be devised for each circumstance encountered, to move away from a reliance upon standard solutions and those who advocate and profit from them. This principle is reiterated, ironically, in British Standard BS 7913. British Standards and other specifications and codes of practice should not be applied unthinkingly in the context of building conservation. While the application of particular specifications, structural design codes and calculations can be appropriate in many circumstances, there can be other circumstances where it will be necessary to follow professional judgement, on the basis of what has been proved to work.

It is inevitable that modern materials will need to be used to repair or to make alterations to traditional buildings. We do not live in an ideal world where we have access to the full palette of materials or the necessary knowledge and skills, that was available when many of these buildings were being constructed, even as late as the Victorian or Edwardian period.

In building conservation there is a presumption in favour of the use of traditional materials and methods that are proven to be compatible with the performance of the building. One of the principal benefits of using proven materials and methods is that you can have confidence in the performance of the repair, whereas it is unwise to experiment with untried materials and techniques, as you can never be confident about the results.

Traditionally there was an in-depth knowledge and understanding of the characteristics and performance of the materials used to construct and repair buildings. This was primarily due to the passing down of empirical knowledge over the years, if not centuries, by the craftsman to his apprentice. The number of materials available was relatively limited, primarily masonry, mortars, plasters and timber, and would be tried and tested and used with confidence.

Today there are thousands of products on the market that can be used in the construction and repair of buildings, with new products continually coming onto the market and being actively promoted. The difficulty with using these materials in the repair and improvement of traditional buildings is that, although they most likely will meet some form of standard in their production or short-term performance, their long-term performance and compatibility is unproven.

Conclusion

The existing building stock has to make a significant contribution to the reduction of carbon emissions. We have one opportunity to get it right and it cannot be wasted. We must avoid repeating the well-intentioned, but damaging improvements of the past with a reliance on standard solutions. We cannot allow inappropriate improvements to blight these buildings that could ultimately provide justification for their demolition. This would be a case of gross mismanagement of a valuable resource.

Any improvements to the existing building stock needs to be made on an informed basis. An understanding of the building will enable targeted and effective remedial works to be implemented, rather than a best guess hit and miss approach.

The knowledge and experience gained from practical building conservation should be used to ensure that changes are well managed and truly sustainable, so that short-term solutions that pass problems on to future generations are avoided. This can be achieved by:

- maintaining and reinstating the intended breathing performance, that is proven over time to prolong the serviceable life of older buildings
- maximising the retention of existing fabric
- making improvements and alterations with reversibility in mind, so that we do not prejudice future generations with irreversible 'solutions'

Before renovating an older building it is important to stop and ask: do I understand this building? Listening to what the building has to tell us will enable appropriate and effective improvements to be made that will result in long-term solutions for this and future generations. There is a need to ensure that a significant percentage of the existing building stock is improved and repaired in a manner that is compatible, cost effective and also effective at reducing carbon emissions. This would enable these buildings to be cared for in a truly sustainable manner.

Reference

1. 'Building Conservation Philosophy' by J Earl, third edition, Donhead Publishing.

Resources

'The Survey and Repair of Traditional Buildings – a sustainable approach' by R Oxley:
www.donhead.com

'McKays Building Construction' is invaluable for tradtional building techniques. This classic (originally 3 volumes) has been re-published in one book.
www.donhead.com

Regular discussion on the appropriate maintainance and repair of old buildings goes on on the Green Building Forum which is a free internet resource:
www.greenbuildingforum.co.uk

Energy regulations

Here **Mike George** discusses the section in the Building Regulations relating to the requirements for thermal insulation in our homes - Part L ...

From April 2006 all existing houses fell under the control of the Approved Document L1b (ADL1b)[1] of the Building Regulations, 'b' being the sub-division of ADL1 which relates specifically to existing dwellings and now includes not only extensions, but newly termed 'thermal elements'. The Communities and Local Government department indicates that it is for the local authority to interpret the legislation as it sees fit. With this in mind, Barry Turner[2], a practising building control officer (BCO) was invited to comment, for the sake of preparing this article, on behalf of the local authority building control officers. These opinions are given on the understanding that they carry no legal standing.

The introduction of so called 'thermal elements' meant that any roof, wall or floor falling below given U-value thresholds, must now be thermally upgraded as part of any renovation works. These improvements are triggered by works (other than decorative finishes) to more than 25% of the thermal element. Generally, if you intend to add or renovate a 'layer', such as rendering then you must upgrade the element to the specified thermal standard. There are existing construction thresholds which trigger such improvements and these, together with the enhanced U-values, are shown in columns 1 and 2 of the table (right). Before commencing work, either a 'building notice' or a 'full plans application', outlining the nature of the work, must be submitted to the BCO. This can be retrospective in the case of emergency repairs[2]. All thermal elements in a building, subject to 'change of use', automatically attract upgrading whether renovation works are intended or not[2].

Using a cavity wall, as an example, external work results in the whole wall attracting upgrading works. Internally, if renovating a single room, less work is necessary in that the improvements are limited to the internal boundaries of the particular cavity wall. The extent of the required works is limited to that which is 'technically or functionally feasible' and where the supplementary cost of the insulation work is recoverable within 15 years. Technical difficulties vary with specific applications and BR262[3] provides general guidance on avoiding risks. Where functional difficulties exist, lesser provisions may be accepted. Examples of this, given in ADL1b, include where internal wall insulation results in the reduction of usable floor space by 5%; or where floor insulation results in difficulties with adjoining floor levels.

Although no longer exempt, special considerations apply to listed buildings and more reservedly, conservation areas. Turner[2] commented that the aim is to improve energy efficiency to an extent that is reasonable and practical. It would seem sensible, therefore, to liaise with the local conservation officer when considering the extent of energy efficiency improvements. Further guidance is available from English Heritage[4].

U-value requirements for extensions to existing buildings are more demanding and the most simple method for compliance is to meet the required U-values shown in the table, column 3. Design flexibility is permissible by a more general strategy of varying U-values and window openings, using the area weighted method, and in this case values must be no worse than those in column 4. In addition, a procedure similar to that used for new dwellings[5] may be used to demonstrate compliance via SAP 2005 software[6]. There is even further flexibility for floors, as the U-value may be calculated using the perimeter/area method for the whole enlarged dwelling. Quality control of insulation installation must now be demonstrated to the BCO. This applies to both thermal elements and works to extensions, although this falls short of pressure testing. Turner said '*Initially, a statement should be made by a suitably qualified person that appropriate construction details have been adopted. Furthermore, a system of on site inspection should be in place to ensure consistency*'. BRE IP 1/06[7] contains checklists for use in reports to confirm compliance on completion of the work and robust standard details are available for new build situations[8]. However the adaptation of such details to existing construction should be considered carefully.

DIY has become somewhat more complicated. U-values, for example must now be calculated[9] and an obvious complication is the assessment of the existing construction. For example, is the solid stone wall really solid? Is it limestone, granite? What is the thermal conductivity of the materials? How much insulation will you need? What type? This initial information must be provided by the person intending to carry out the work and subsequently verified by the BCO[2]. So what if you want to consider the effect on your fuel bills? Well, it is unclear from ADL1b how the annual energy savings should be estimated, but there is some suggestion that this could also be confirmed in a report by a 'suitably qualified' person before work commences. So do we all need to enrol on crash courses in surveying and measuring buildings? No, it is more reasonable for some generalisations, at least in the short term, to be acceptable to the BCO. Regarding this, Turner said, '*it is possible that SAP data sets and relevant tables may be adopted for use*'. With this in mind the 'Green Building Bible, Volume 2', provides a simplified tool for estimating U-values, energy savings and consequential payback periods. All building regulations provide scope for alternative methods of compliance and it is hoped that this method will simplify the compliance process and be acceptable to building control when advocated by any member of the design team, be they DIY enthusiast, builder or architect.

References

1. DCLG. (2006). 'Conservation of fuel and power', Approved Document L1b Work in existing dwellings. The Stationery Office, Norwich, UK.

2. Turner, B (2006) Response to Part L1b questionnaire. Local Authority Building Control.

3. BRE (2001), BR 262, Thermal Insulation: avoiding risks Garston, BRE publications.

4. English Heritage (2004) Building regulations and historic buildings.

5. DCLG. (2006). Conservation of fuel and power, Approved Document L1a New dwellings. The Stationery Office, Norwich.

6. Defra (2005) The government's standard assessment procedure for energy rating of dwellings, SAP 2005 edition London. HMSO.

7. BRE (2006) IP 1/06 'Assessing the effects of thermal bridging at junctions and around openings in the external elements of buildings'. Garston, BRE publications.

8. TSO (2002) Limiting thermal bridging and air leakage: Robust construction details for dwellings and similar buildings. London. HMSO.

9. BRE (2006) BR 443, Conventions for U-value calculations Garston, BRE publications.

	Threshold U-value triggering improvements to thermal elements (W/m²K)	*Requirement for thermal elements worse than column 1 (W/m²K)*	*Standard U-value requirement for extensions (W/m²K)*	*Minimum acceptable U-value for extensions *** (W/m²K)*
Cavity wall	*0.7*	*0.55 **	*0.3*	*0.7*
Other wall	*0.7*	*0.35*	*0.3*	*0.7*
Floor	*0.7*	*0.25 ***	*0.22 ***	*0.7*
Roof insulation at ceiling level	*0.35*	*0.16*	*0.16*	*0.35*
Roof insulation at rafter level	*0.35*	*0.2*	*0.2*	*0.35*
Flat roof or roof with integral insulation	*0.35*	*0.25*	*0.2*	*0.35*

U-value requirements for thermal elements and extensions.

** walls not suitable for cavity wall insulation should be treated as 'other wall'.*
*** a lesser standard may be acceptable if there are significant problems relating to existing floor levels.*
**** where alternative approaches such as SAP assessment are used.*

Does your home make you sick?

On average we spend about 85% of our time inside buildings. **Anita Bradley** frightens us with tales of things that lurk in our homes ...

Our buildings have changed over the last 30 years. We have increased their energy efficiency a little and made them warmer and less draughty, but we have also filled them with a multitude of products containing a wide cocktail of chemicals.

The way we build, the materials we use and the way we maintain our homes and offices has been proven to cause, in some people, a condition known as 'sick building syndrome' (SBS). SBS has been officially recognised as an illness by the World Health Organisation since 1986. The question we need to ask ourselves is, if we continue making our houses even more energy efficient and less 'leaky' (draughty) then will we see an ever-increasing number of people start to suffer from SBS?

'Sick building syndrome' is a general malaise of multiple symptoms of an unknown or unclearly recognised cause. It should not be confused with 'building related illnesses' (BRI) where both the disease and its cause is known – such as legionella, asbestosis, or humidifier fever. Although the two share some common features, the former is more difficult to pin down and rectify. Difficulty in identifying SBS lies in the vast array of conditions presented, the subjective nature of the complaints and the lack of solid evidence as to causes. People can react very differently to specific conditions and symptoms vary with time and location.

We let our children crawl around on the carpet but this is probably the most dangerous environment in the home as carpets act as sponges that hold chemicals, debris and millions of dustmites (inset).

Symptoms associated with SBS can include:
- headache
- loss of concentration
- nasal irritation
- dry or watery eyes
- lethargy
- skin irritation
- throat problems
- possibly more acute conditions and diseases.

SBS is a chemical, biological and mental/psychological phenomenon which, if ignored, can lead to expensive remedial action, absenteeism from work, lower productivity, and loss of well-being.

It has been estimated by the World health Organisation (WHO) that up to 30% of refurbished, and a significant number of new buildings, can cause SBS. Any type of building can house conditions that cause SBS, with several possible causes having been identified most of which will affect air quality:
- contaminated land
- radon and other gases
- asbestos and lead
- contaminated water
- volatile organic compounds (VOCs)
- electromagnetic fields
- moulds, dust and other allergens

- micro-organisms and body matter
- lighting
- heating, ventilation and air conditioning (HVAC)
- poor architectural, engineering design and specification
- inadequate facilities management
- negative ion depletion
- psycho-social factors.

Indoor air quality

The quality of the air we breathe is vital to our well-being, yet the Environmental Protection Agency found that indoor air can be as much as ten times more polluted than the outside air.

In the late 20th Century, industry and commerce has produced around 70,000 new synthetic materials and chemicals. Of these, less than 2% have been tested for safety to humans and up to 70% have not been tested at all. Around 1,000 new chemicals and materials are marketed each year, without the full cost to human or ecological wellbeing being considered. We take in this chemical cocktail via breathing, through the skin, in water and in food.

Indoor air contains microscopic particulates – perfumes, bacteria, viruses, animal dander, dust mites, respiration particles, pollen, mould; combustion products – carbon monoxide, nitrogen dioxide, sulphur dioxide, hydrocarbons; and volatile organic compounds (VOCs) – benzene, formaldehyde, chlorine, synthetic fibres, PVC and other chemical products. Pollution comes from paints, preservatives, insulation, adhesives, carpets, soft furnishings, furniture, cleaners and air fresheners. Other sources include timbers, plywood, particle board and such like, which may have been treated with preservatives, glues, paints and varnishes. Fire retardant chemicals add to this burden.

Due to increasing energy efficiency, newer construction techniques and materials have meant that buildings have become much more airtight. In such buildings the external walls have been designed to minimise leakage of air conditioned air to the outside but have also stopped fresh air permeating to the inside. Sealed windows and artificial air conditioning plant (heating, ventilation and air conditioning – HVAC) are thus needed to maintain warmth or coolness within. However, without careful consideration of all the components used, this trend seems to be allowing a build up of noxious air. HVAC plant has recently been identified as a potent cause of SBS and thus there are strict fitting and maintenance guidelines to keep such equipment working at an optimal level for efficiency and health. Microbes and bacteria were found in ducts and filters. An article in the prestigious British medical journal 'The Lancet' reported the trial of using UV light to kill bacteria within HVAC plants with a high degree of success.

Electromagnetic field pollution (EMF's)

Electromagnetic fields occur both in nature and the man-made environment. In nature these fields are very low and occur due to climate, terrestrial factors, cosmic radiation and from the body's own electrical activity. Such fields are generally very low in strength and frequency and are usually beneficial or essential to health. Man-made electrical fields (EMFs) are part of a controversy regarding their effects on the health of people exposed to

Hard floors are the darling of the anti dust mite brigade and can certainly play a role in the reduction of possible toxins from carpets in the home. There is plenty of evidence to be found that blames carpets for not only containing chemicals, but also harbouring dust etc. The British love of carpet, though, is not without reason. They make our feet feel warm and give a cosier feel to the room. So the choice is yours!

them. The fields in question are non-ionising in their action and are produced whenever there is a flow of electricity. An EMF is made up of an electric field component (measured in volts per metre – V/m) and a magnetic field component (measured in teslas – T). Electric fields form wherever there is a voltage and its strength is dependent on the magnitude of the voltage. A magnetic field arises whenever there is a current flowing. Both components reduce with distance from source. The frequency, shape and strength of these fields are important factors in determining the effect they have on health. Sources of manufactured EMFs are power lines, electrical wiring in buildings and appliances.

Studies have been carried out into EMFs since the possibility of health problems started in the 1960s. These first studies were on occupational exposure. The first study of general exposure began in the late 70s when two American researchers found a suggestive link between power line EMFs and childhood leukaemia. Since then many more and varied studies have been conducted to ascertain if there are health risks arising from exposure to a myriad of EMF sources. Studies have suggested links with cancers and leukaemia, depression and suicide, immune disorders, and allergy.

Over half the elevated levels of EMFs in buildings come from wiring configurations and appliances. The wiring regulations do not specifically concern themselves with EMFs, but, according to Powerwatch ***www.powerwatch.org.uk***, the fields produced could be minimised through careful wiring layouts. Large commercial buildings can have very low fields because the wires are housed in appropriate metal trunking, but some buildings can have high fields because currents flow along 'earthed' pipework. Electric fields can still be high if a metal conduit is not used.

Electricity can contribute to poor indoor air quality from electro-pollution. Electrical installations (the wiring layout) and appliances left plugged in on stand-by mode emits both electrical and magnetic fields.

Britain has been well behind other countries in acknowledging the risks, especially for the magnetic field component. The Radiation Protection Division of the Health Protection Agency (formerly the National Radiological Protection Board) sets maximum exposure levels as 1,600μT. For comparison, Switzerland 1μT, Sweden 0.2μT, and parts of Italy 0.2-0.5μT.

The magnetic field levels at which certain diseases have been shown to occur at are:

Miscarriage	1.6μT
Childhood leukaemia	0.3/0.4μT
Adult brain cancer	0.2-0.6μT
Depression	0.2μT
Suicide	0.2μT

(Source: 'Health effects of EMFs – evidence and mechanisms', Professor DL Henshaw. HH Wills Physics Laboratory. University of Bristol).

However, in 2004 the National Radiological Protection Board (NRPB) recommended the adoption of reduced levels of exposure to the magnetic field component of EMFs in the frequency range 0-300GHz. This is for general public exposure. The limit recommended is 100μT (down from the previous 1600μT) and is the level adopted by the International Commission on Non-Ionising Radiation Protection (ICNIRP). The frequencies covered include TV and radio broadcasting, mobile telecommunications and the electical supply. Whilst this reduction may seem large, it is not so low as to prevent illness as supported by many researchers and scientific papers. Professor Henshaw of Bristol University (an expert in this subject) states that these proposals should go much further. "The proposals to limit public exposure to magnetic fields to 100μT, 250 times higher than the 0.4μT where doubling of the risk of childhood leukaemia is acknowledged, looks ridiculous when viewed alongside the well established practice for chemical carcinogens where levels are set at least 1000 times below the level where evidence of harmful effects have been found."

According to Powerwatch the ideal magnetic field level should be less than 0.01μT and the electric field should be less than 5V/m. Levels of exposure of 0.03μT and 10V/m can be reasonably achieved. The average exposure is 0.04-0.05μT for exposure from both outdoor and indoor sources. Several organisations offer testing and advice on EMFs, including Powerwatch.

Noise

Noise is not always considered in studies of SBS, but it can contribute to the condition and cause suffering or disturbance for the building occupant. Sources of noise in buildings are air-conditioning plants, outdoor noise filtering indoors, office equipment and 'people' noise. Air conditioning systems can be disturbing if they are functioning badly, poorly maintained and ill designed. Air rushing through vents is a source of noise but the vent size can be increased for the same output, which will lessen noise levels. Ductwork can carry noise around a building, so insulation and good design are essential. However, noise control is not just about lowering levels, as a space that is too quiet can also be troublesome. Continuous soft noise is another factor to be avoided. CIBSE state an upper limit for office work of 46dBA (where decibels 'A' refers to the particular decibel scale on sound level meter). Many offices exceed this level.

Lighting

The links between lighting and sick building syndrome are well known. Glare, flicker, lack of contrast, inadequate illumination and unsuitable spot lighting can all add to a user's burden. Many offices or developments are of deep plan design and therefore are unable to be illuminated by daylight to the interior. The use of fluorescent lighting is commonplace and therefore a common problem. Their use can give rise to eye strain and headaches among other symptoms ('Fluorescent Lighting: A Health Hazard Overhead', London Hazard Centre). If these lights cannot be avoided then regular maintenance, or the use of full spectrum fluorescent, is preferable.

Another aspect of lighting design in relation to sick building syndrome is the ability of the occupant to alter their exposure to meet personal comfort. Different tasks require different lighting. CIBSE recommends 500 lux for general office work and 750 lux for deep plan offices, or where close work takes place (such as at a drawing board or reading).

Tinted glass is not recommended as we need light levels to maintain our physiology such as the endocrine system. Deprived of lighting, cues our body to change to a 25 hour cycle rather than the 24 hour cycle. Lack of light (essentially bright sunlight) can cause depression, anxiety, fatigue and the modern diagnosis of seasonal affective disorder (SAD).

Ions

Ions are essential to life and health. They are atoms that can be either negatively (-) or positively (+) charged. Negative ions are the benefices of health and are shown to reduce headache, nausea and dizziness. They also make a person more comfortable and alert. Lack of negative ions (i.e. an abundance of '+' ions), are associated with depression, lethargy and anxiety. Many buildings can give rise to a shortage of beneficial ions through materials and equipment; metal ducts for HVAC plant attracts the ions as they pass through, static electricity attracts these ions as does tobacco smoke and dust particles.

What can we do to help ourselves?

We can use plants to clean up our air. It was in 1980 that NASA's John C Stennis Space Centre first discovered that plants could remove volatile organic compounds (VOCs) from the air. The Centre was researching how to maintain the air quality within spacecrafts. NASA's studies demonstrated the ability of plants to remove formaldehyde. This led to further research to evaluate the ability of 12 common house-plants to remove such toxins from the air. The 'Plants for Clean Air Council' was established to support the cultivation of plants as a method of improving indoor air quality.

Plants emit oxygen and absorb carbon dioxide. We breathe in oxygen and emit carbon dioxide. They are also good at absorbing toxins in the air and raising humidity levels. The physical beauty of plants is also therapeutic. It is suggested that for a room that is around 12m^2, occupied by one person, would require six small table-top plants or three large, floor standing plants. Plants are proven to be nature's 'eco-friendly' living air-purifiers, with the scientific evidence to back this up.

Static can be reduced by the avoidance of synthetic materials, 'earthing' of all electrical equipment, and good building hygiene. A high density of people can also alter the ratio of negative to positive ions. There are fewer negative ions when the indoor temperature is greater than 22°C, and where there is a high relative humidity. Typical office air contains only 50 negative ions per millilitre, whereas clean outdoor air can carry as many as 1000.

Adjustable and well-designed lights with shading devices are the most desirable solution to both lighting problems and to reduce glare and heat gain.

For new buildings, techniques that allow the building fabric to 'breathe' are best. The notion of the building as a 'third skin' is ideal wherever possible. (This is an idea from the 'Building Biology' movement: the first skin is that stretchy stuff that protects the body; clothes form the second protective skin; and the building fabric is thus seen as the third protective skin. See useful contacts)

Another factor that may help reduce the effects of SBS is that of 'indoor surface pollution' (ISP). This was presented in a BRE paper addressing the importance of ISP in building management and suggests ways of reducing it. The method involves defining ISP by a 'fleece factor' (the area of carpet, curtains and other fabric, divided by the volume of the space) and the 'shelf factor' (the length of open shelving or filing space divided by the volume of the room). Above all, the recommendations in this paper stress the need for good hygiene. The need for extra, or specialist, cleaning is reduced or made easier by careful design, furniture selection and office/space layout. (*G.J.Raw: 'The Importance of Indoor Surface Pollution in Sick Building Syndrome', BRE Information Paper IP 3/94. Feb 1994.*)

The use of 'ring' circuits gives off high magnetic fields and therefore 'radial' wiring is the preferred method. Electric fields can be shielded quite cheaply, but magnetic fields are extremely difficult to eliminate, therefore they are best designed out or shielded, wherever they are generated. The page opposite offers further ideas on how we can all try to make our existing homes, or new homes that we intend to build, safer to live in.

Useful contacts

Powerwatch: **www.powerwatch.org.uk**

The Health Protection Agency: **www.hpa.org.uk**

Human Radiation Effects: **www.electric-fields.bris.ac.uk**

Women's Environmental Network: **www.wen.org.uk**

Healthy Flooring Network: **www.healthyflooring.org**

Building Research Establishment: **www.bre.co.uk**

London Hazards Centre: **www.lhc.org.uk**

Institute of Building Biology: **www.buildingbiology.net**

Further reading

'The Healthy House' by S & J Baggs

'Cross Currents: The Startling Effects of Electromagnetic Radiation on Your Health' by R Becker

'Killing Fields in the Home' A & J Philips

'Electromagnetic Man: Health Hazard in the Electrical Environment' by Smith CW & Best S. The Bath Press 1989 (a classic, which is currently out of print, but is essential reading if you can find it).

'Water, Electricity and Health -protecting yourself from electrostress at home and work' by A Hall

The Toxic Consumer; how to reduce your exposure to everyday toxic chemicals' by K Ashton & E Salter Green

Eco-Friendly Houseplants by B Wolverton ISBN 0 7538 0046 2

Most of the above books are available from the Green Shop: 01452 770629 **www.greenshop.co.uk**

Eight simple steps to reduce sick building syndrome

1. Floors

Minimise the areas of carpeting in the building. Consider other types of floor finish such as linoleum, rubber or even cork. Slate and wood floors are back in fashion but some proprietary laminated floorboard systems are not always real timber so watch out for that.

2. Ventilation

Try to design your buildings with adequate natural ventilation. This is not always easy on large commercial buildings but if considered early enough in the design stage then it may be possible to reduce the dependency on heating and ventilating plant to some degree or even eliminate its need.

3. Light and access

Make sure that your buildings are light and airy and the immediate outdoor vicinity is attractive, (fragrant flowers, grass and trees) natural and safe for children. The building user will want to open doors and windows and enjoy the fragrances of the natural environment.

4. Treatments and preservatives

Minimise or eliminate the use of preservatives on timber used within the building. This is a big problem as many builders still believe that by using treated timber they are providing their customers with a higher quality product. They are not!

5. Materials

Reduce the use of 'composite' materials in the designed fabric of the building by as much as practically possible. Remember the building user will add plenty of their own in the form of furniture, furnishings, white goods and electronics. This, of course, is out of the control of the building designer but remember, large quantities of composites can cause toxic overload in poorly ventilated user spaces.

6. Services

Minimise on excessive electrical cable provision. If necessary design in future-proofing access for adding or removing cabling as needs arise. Also keep cable runs along predetermined routes and avoid the creation of electrical 'fields' which can inadvertently be produced by poor layout design.

7. Finishes

Reduce the use of paints and other coatings to an absolute minimum. Decorating for good health means following a 'less is more' scenario. Consider specifying or using self colour materials such as clay plasters or high quality plasterboard systems that need little or no decoration. Use durable species of timbers to reduce the need for excessive painting. Even consider using unfinished (durable) timber for windows and doors.

8. Aesthetics

Avoid 'glue on' character. Use the style and structure of the building to achieve character rather than adding fake layers. Natural and minimalist is in vogue at the moment so there are few excuses.

Greening the kitchen

We may be eating organic vegetables but what about the room in which we prepare them? The most busy room in the house gets a green make-over by **Jerry Clark**. He uses his own kitchen as an example...

One of the most commonly re-arranged rooms in the home is the kitchen. Each time the house changes hands or just as a bit of a face-lift, most of us seem to like to change the decor or layout of this important room about every 5 to 10 years. This has an enormous impact on the environment because, although most kitchens are modular and could be taken out with little damage, thousands get land-filled every year.

The issues don't just stop at the units either. The kitchen contains most of the power-hungry appliances in the home, so plenty to think about in this department too. What better way to illustrate, this story, I thought, than to include all the major considerations that my family and I faced with a kitchen that we inherited when we bought our current home in 2004.

The units were a dark mahogany colour, and the walls were tiled in bottle green. The room is north facing and, even with two windows, it was dark. The layout was also so poor that the room seemed cluttered. A tall oven unit dominated one wall, there was a peninsular unit with a large built in table attached to the back, and there was a freestanding island unit in the middle of the floor - in all far too many units for the size of the room. There was not even enough free space to fit in our fridge and freezer. Also, the hot water took a long time to get to the tap for reasons which will become apparent later.

Change the kitchen or adapt it?

Our first thoughts were whether we could use the existing units and rearrange the kitchen to suit our requirements. We ruled this out for several reasons - we would have needed one or two more base units, and although the kitchen was only installed six years before, additional

units were no longer available - this is a major drawback but a sign of just how fashion orientated kitchens are! Also, this would not have addressed the darkness problem (although this could have been resolved by perhaps painting the doors a pale colour). However, we had to remove the built in table immediately in order to install our fridge and freezer – this left an unsightly mess on the back of the peninsular unit.

Another important consideration was our decision about heating the house. Although only built in 1999, and a fairly large house, it was heated entirely by electric night storage heaters. We wanted to find a way of heating with a renewable fuel - in this case wood. The solution we preferred was a wood burning Rayburn in the kitchen (top right), plumbed to heat radiators in the other rooms, and doubling up as a cooker in winter. This entailed removal and rearrangement of a considerable number of kitchen units. In the end we decided to replace the entire kitchen with something more robust and to our taste.

Make it light and bright

Having decided on a suitable layout, the next consideration was how to make it a brighter

place to work in - with the mahogany kitchen cupboards we were having to use electric lighting, even on fairly bright days. We decided to go for an off white silk eco-paint on the cupboard doors, and a matt version of the same colour on the walls. We changed the splashbacks to light cream tiles. We wanted something reflective for the worktops to bounce light back up into the room. Another consideration was a very high Cyprus hedge about 8m from the windows. After cutting over a metre off the height (it is still 2.5m high), we found that light was bounced back to us from the pale south wall of the neighbours house about 15m away. We retained the existing electric lighting configuration, but we changed

all the bulbs to low energy, reducing the power consumption to 86W from the original 700W.

Materials for the kitchen cupboards

We wanted to avoid the usual laminated chipboard carcasses, as, particularly when new, these off-gas copious quantities of formaldehyde, which is not good for the environment or your health. We decided to make the cupboards with a strong (50mm x 75mm section) FSC softwood frame with zero formaldehyde MDF for the panels. All joinery was morticed and tennoned and drawers were dovetailed for extra strength and long life.

Bespoke joinery from a kitchen specialist can be expensive. However, if you are not confident about making your own cabinets, it is still possible to save a considerable amount of money by just having the basic units made up by a joiner to your own design, rather than using a specialist kitchen company with all their overheads and profits to maintain. We deliberately placed the oven below the worktop, and kept wall units to a minimum to open out the space. The old chipboard and laminate worktops were already beginning to peel, so we decided to fit something that will last forever, solid 40mm thick granite, cut and polished at a local quarry. Again, though expensive, a lot can be saved by going direct to the quarry and using whatever material they have to offer - slate is another possibility. Worktops away from hot and/or wet areas were made of solid beech and oiled.

Alternatives to new units

If cost is a major consideration, you could just buy second hand units, (try e-bay or freecycle on the internet for instance) or put a wanted advert in your local paper. The advantage is that these will have off-gassed most of their original formaldehyde. We took out our old units as carefully as we could, and sold them quite easily through the local papers. In fact, our units found a home in two smaller kitchens, and we have heard that the new owners are delighted with them – both did have better natural light than we did!

The all important kitchen sink

The existing sink was reused, it was good quality and in good condition, but we replaced the broken mixer tap. The new one has a second spout connected to a filter for drinking water, which has saved a lot of arguments about who last used the filter jug and didn't refill it! Rearranging the kitchen gave us the opportunity to re-route the plumbing for the hot and cold water. To hide the pipes, the previous owner had routed them behind a tall oven unit, adding at least 8 feet to each pipe run.

Kitchen appliances

Our existing fridge and freezer (that we brought with us from our previous home) were very efficient 'A' rated appliances. When looking at these goods, don't just look for 'A' rating – there is a second figure which tells you which 'A' rated appliances use the least electricity – that is the kWh/year figure. Our fridge was rated at 120kWh/year, but other similar sized fridges had much higher figures and were still 'A' rated. We installed an 'A' rated oven, and the most efficient electric hob we could afford (quick reacting halogen). Apparently an induction hob would have been more efficient, but you need special pans, and there may be issues with electromagnetic fields - the fact you are advised not to use them if you have a pacemaker gives a hint!

Kitchen floors

Our existing kitchen floor is fairly dark slate patterned ceramic tiles, darker than we would have liked, but we decided to live with them to save the work and upheaval. It would be worth changing if they were in poor condition, or if underfloor heating was to be installed. If you can live with your existing floor, especially if it is cemented in place as ours is, then this will save a lot of work and resources. If you have vinyl cushion floor or similar, then changing to something like ceramic tiles or wood could be an option.

To conclude then, the remodelled and rearranged kitchen feels spacious, light, airy and much more energy efficient. ☯

Don't heat your conservatory!

Tony Cowling and **Mike George** offer us some interesting data that may challenge our perceptions and use of conservatories ...

It has become increasingly popular to add conservatories to almost any house in any location in order to increase living space. Has this been a sensible course of unchecked action to follow on such a large scale in view of the disadvantages of their heat losses? In order to get some views on this Tony Cowling started a thread on the Green Building Forum ***www. greenbuildingforum.co.uk*** entitled 'They say I like a lot of light'. Having gained the anecdotal evidence from the discussions on the forum, we decided to carry out some computer modelling to gain an idea of exactly how sustainable conservatories are.

Our investigation modelled a typical 1980's style detached house as a basis for the investigation, with typical energy use and costs from space heating being calculated. The house has a floor area of 90m^2 over two floors. The house is subsequently remodelled with a double glazed conservatory, having a floor area of 10m^2. For comparison purposes we also calculated the heat losses from an extension built to current building regulations standard as well as further conservatories with single and triple glazing. In addition, the effects of solar gain on the results are demonstrated by varying the orientation of the building. The annual cost to heat the house would be around £6.50/m^2 with the extension costing around £5.50/m^2. Tragically, the cost to heat the conservatory is around £12/m^2.

A snapshot of the initial results are illustrated below, though a more technical and comprehensive analysis can be found in Green Building Bible Volume 2.

It should be noted that in order to gain an equal comparison between results it was necessary to operate the same heating regime for both extension and conservatory. The heating is set to 21°C and is permanently on in the winter months. The spring and autumn months are heated to lower temperatures (16°C) and for shorter (morning and evening) periods. While acceptable for the house and extension, this could be considered unreasonable to assess the heating costs of a conservatory.

The Building Regulations fail miserably at preventing conservatories from being used as living rooms, such as shown here.

The costs given in Figure 1 can therefore be considered to be at the higher end of a range which will depend on many factors, not least the heating regime set by the owners. In order to get an indication of the costs at the lower end of the heating

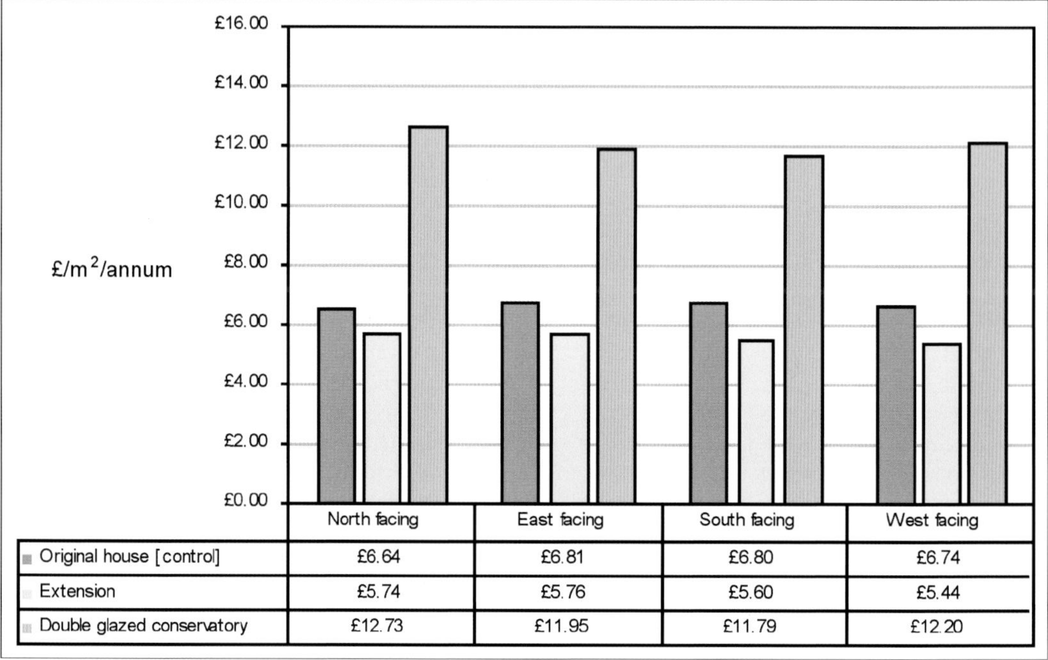

	North facing	East facing	South facing	West facing
Original house [control]	£6.64	£6.81	£6.80	£6.74
Extension	£5.74	£5.76	£5.60	£5.44
Double glazed conservatory	£12.73	£11.95	£11.79	£12.20

Figure 1. A comparison of annual energy costs for the 24 hour heating regime.

Note: House results are based on heating the original 90m² building. Extension and conservatory results are based on heating the additional 10m² in isolation.

spectrum, the same conservatories (i.e. with single, double and triple glazing) were considered with a lesser heating regime, i.e. akin to the spring and autumn scenario (Figure 2).

The results indicate a range of heating costs and demonstrate the effects of various glazing configurations, the double glazed version still costing around £7.50/m² to heat per annum, despite a drastically reduced heating requirement. So what happens if we decide not to heat a conservatory at all? Figure 3 gives an indication of the temperature in a conservatory over a typical winter week.

It can be see from Figure 3 that the difference in comfort conditions may not be as bad as some may perceive, with temperatures still able to reach around 20°C on some very cold days during daylight hours. While not shown here, the conservatory temperature is dependent on the amount of solar gain; with the middle part of this week being cloudy as well as cold.

Conclusion

Once built a conservatory has a huge heat loss potential compared to a traditionally constructed extension. It should therefore be used only as and when it is warm enough to use without artificial heating, i.e. it is a part time room. The calculated heat losses for a typical, double glazed conservatory can be as much as double that of an extension per square metre of floor area. This is exactly the opposite of what we should be trying to achieve in terms of energy use. Furthermore, for those who do not like to sit outdoors in their gardens but prefer to sit in the now all too increasingly commonly air conditioned luxury of their conservatory - there are cooling costs to consider too. Indeed it proves difficult to install enough cooling power to do so, but, nonetheless, huge amounts of energy can be expended in trying to negate the effects of solar gain (a subject also covered in detail in Volume 2). ☯

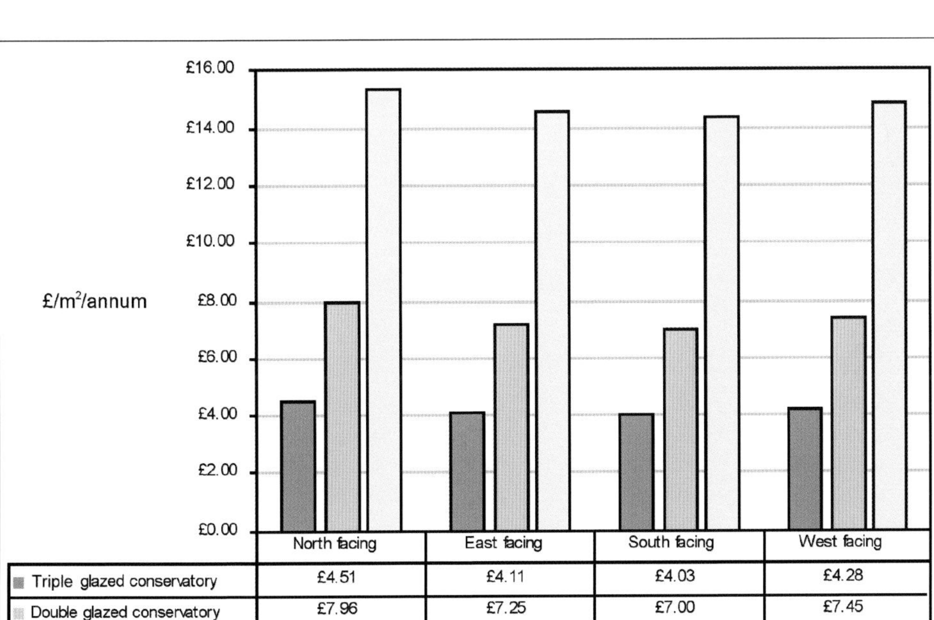

	North facing	East facing	South facing	West facing
Triple glazed conservatory	£4.51	£4.11	£4.03	£4.28
Double glazed conservatory	£7.96	£7.25	£7.00	£7.45
Single glazed conservatory	£15.40	£14.60	£14.40	£14.90

Figure 2. A comparison of annual energy costs for the reduced heating regime.

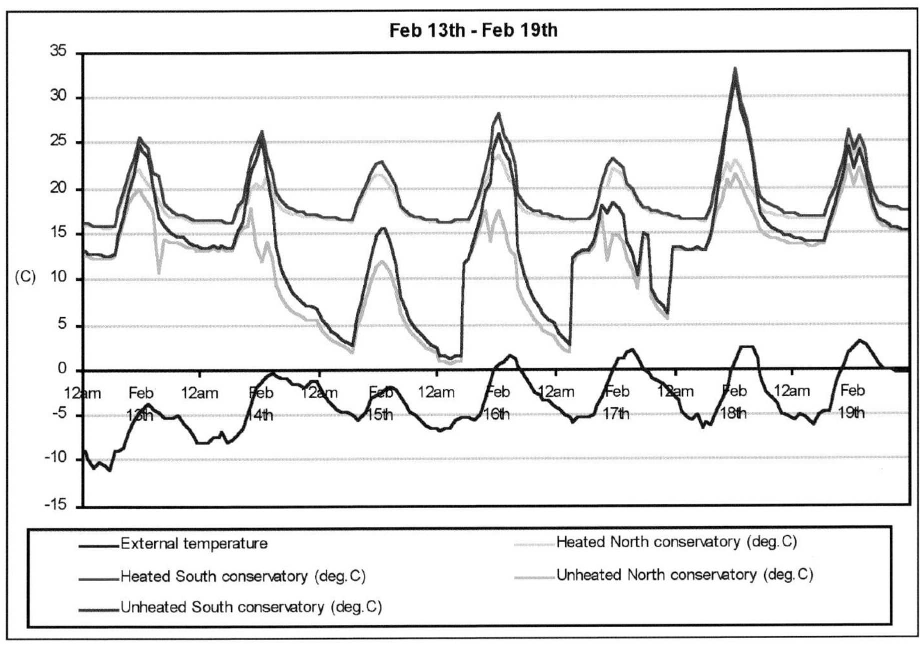

Figure 3. A comparison of heated and unheated double glazed conservatories by orientation.

Is it easy being green?

The Green Building Forum* is probably the fastest growing internet community dedicated to green building. We asked a few of its members how easy is it to be green?

www.greenbuildingforum.co.uk

First up - Mike George

Mike is a builder and here he tells us of the real challenge of becoming a green builder and some of his experiences with suppliers and customers.

The very nature of the heading suggests that this is meant to be a good old moan! Well, in terms of green building there is plenty to moan about and I have to confess to spending quite a lot of my time doing exactly this. However, there is also a lot to be positive about too, so I will try and keep the moaning to a minimum, and give some practical ideas of how to do what I think are the basics, which are often overlooked.

For more that twenty years, I have been involved in building, starting out on a government scheme learning how to plaster. Back in the early eighties, this was a wide and varied role, and seemed to involve anything from making tea, to digging holes and then actually being allowed to put some render or plaster on a wall, mostly in places like under the stairs, where no one could see it.

Most of the work back then was grant aided renovation to private housing, and I guess this is where I learned my favourite green building pastime – reusing as much as possible, though it has to be said I was brought up to the motto 'that will come in handy' (which is okay if you have a very big garage!) Anyway, re-using building materials was not practised because of any particular worries about the environment, rather that the jobbing builders I worked for were just too tight to throw things away.

Common jobs involving reuse would be clearing out and bricking up fireplaces; taking out suspended wooden floors and replacing them with solid floors – that kind of thing – all jobs which lend themselves to reuse, be it bricks for the fireplace, or general rubble used to fill floor voids, or salvageable timber floorboards and joists utilised elsewhere.

So back then small builders were practicing the three R's even before they were labelled as such; reducing and reusing, being profitable - hand in glove. The other R – recycling was most profitable for me. For as long as I can remember, there has been competition among site labourers and tradesmen to salvage anything from scrap lead and copper to moulded skirting and doors to Welsh slates off the roof. Some developed this art further, into skip diving activities, though I would never confess to stooping to this.

So why then is it hard to be green? Well it all started to get complicated for me when I decided to learn some theory by enrolling on a BSc in architectural technology at Glamorgan University. Up until then, I was blissfully unaware of energy efficiency in buildings. Insulation was just something which you were forced to put into a new building which, for me, only applied to extensions, as this by then was the type of work I was mostly involved in. During my six years of study, there were several revisions

** Membership of the Green Building Forum is free. It is open to anyone interested in green, energy efficient and healthy building. There is a simple registration process. To register go to:* ***www.greenbuildingforum.co.uk***

to Part L and this became of great interest to me, as I was also working at the sharp end, where these increases in insulation had to be implemented. My final year dissertation looked at this in great detail, being entitled 'Do small Builders Need More L?' which is the way I felt (and still feel) about this particular piece of legislation. My conclusion was no, they don't need more L, it just needs to be fine tuned.

Why? Well for me the problems we face relating to energy efficiency are not just about how much insulation is used, but about the quality of workmanship used to install it. What is the point of doubling the thickness of insulation while not having any system in place to police just how well this is done?

Furthermore, ever increasing requirements have played into the hands of the major insulation manufacturers, as it is the petrochemical derived insulations which have the most effective thickness/performance ratios. This means that it is becoming ever more difficult to consider using the more natural insulations. One very sad fact is that whilst I have offered natural insulation products, where it is technically possible, to clients for some time, I have yet to use them, or indeed see them being used, as they are simply too expensive when compared to the petrochemical alternatives.

So the main barrier to being a 'green builder' for me is cost of materials. A further example is joinery products. Back in the eighties, the cheapest windows you could buy were softwood – with uPVC double glazing being out of reach of the council grants being offered. Why now, has this reversed? It is now cost prohibitive to use softwood as uPVC can be installed far more cheaply. It seems to me that there is a green gravy train, which is lined with gold for those who care to greenwash the products being carried on it. Wading though this mire of products and solutions is ever more difficult, with legislation lending itself to their implementation.

So is there anything easy about being a green builder? Yes, reuse, reduce and recycle are the key words. Reuse is the top of my list when doing any renovation work. Just look at any rural building and it is likely that the masonry has enjoyed more than one lay of mortar. Also, take a look in any basic carpentry book and you will see that timber sections can be utilised for just about any structural purpose, though doing so may require professional advice to get through building regulations. Reusing is reducing, so that just leaves recycling. Don't just throw it on the skip! In the Vale of Glamorgan we have an online council service called 'freecycle' with automated e-mails sent to members. Posting all manner of unwanted materials rarely fails to find someone wanting – one man's rubbish and all that. Have a look to see if there is such a service in your area. Also, don't be too proud to have a go at the old skip diving!

Finally, I would like to coin a fourth 'R' but sadly such a word beginning with 'R' that means 'high quality' eludes me. Let's just describe what it is. It is first and foremost taking great care with the building process, especially where insulation is concerned. Up to 40% of heat lost from a building is lost via air circulation and draughts, so avoid just placing emphasis on reducing U-values. Instead make doubly sure that what you do use is installed in an airtight manner - all of the insulation in the world is no good if cold air is allowed to circulate around it. Also remember to research your options thoroughly before deciding which products to go for. Ah ha, looks like I may have found the fourth R after all. Do your research! The Green Building Forum is an excellent place to start.

Next - Sune Nightingale

Sune found that using natural materials was a great introduction to being green. This led on to discovering a whole host of interesting and useful eco alternatives to the normal approach.

I recently renovated an old listed building (formerly a bakery and stable), and the techniques and materials that needed to be used led to a welcome widening of my knowledge – many of the traditional ways were also surprisingly green.

My first new discovery was lime putty (Chards & sons, Bristol, 0117 977 7681) – brilliant stuff, a bit like thick yoghurt. I found it made a pliable, forgiving mortar that would stay workable for ages. Plus it has far lower CO_2 emissions than cement as it hardens by absorbing CO_2 – a clear winner. I would always go for lime over cement now, if possible – it makes sense in many ways. Wear gloves as it'll eat away at your hands and watch out for it getting under your fingernails (that hurts). It likes to dry slowly and on warmer days I covered the fresh walls with sheets which I would then hose down. To match the original wall mortar I dug clay from the ground, sieved it to a large bread crumb consistency through a big chicken wire contraption that I made from scrap wood and mixed it with the lime and a little bit of sharp sand in a cement mixer...

When one mix was done I would start the next and leave it mixing for a good 20 minutes to get the required consistency – it makes a ball in the mixer and takes a long time to properly mix. It was time consuming, but the clay was free and so was my time. This clay heavy mix was for building stone walls and would need adapting for rendering/plastering. On future projects I will try to source aggregates for mortar on site – it was much cheaper for a start.

The house is painted inside and out with limewash – an eco-friendly, breathable and ridiculously cheap paint. To make around 160lts of limewash, take 40kg of lime putty, 250ml of boiled linseed oil, pigments as necessary, and water to the approximate consistency of thin single cream. Then put it all in a big barrel and mix it up with a plaster mixing arm on a drill.

Lintels, joists and rafters needed to be replaced with oak, so I found myself at a local sawmill (Morton Timber, Thornbury, Bristol, 01454 413307) sizing up some English oak trees. Soon they were neatly cut up into a very heavy stack, which would never fit onto my poor old pick-up in one load.....she had just made it back from a trip collecting second-hand scaffolding and really deserved a break, or at least a weekend off. Erecting that scaffolding myself was a disaster – it fell down in comic book fashion with me, luckily unscathed, beneath it. A local scaffolder laughed heartily at my enthusiasm and my ignorance of his trade, and was hired. The moral: don't waste time, get professionals in for some parts of the work, such as scaffolding, 2nd fix plumbing, electrics, etc.

Cedar takes the place of pine in the house - it is about the same price and is more insect and water resistant than the pine. Back at the sawmill I discovered just how nice it is to get local, untreated wood (much nicer than 'bog standard', poor quality pine from the builders merchants), cut to the exact sizes I wanted, by someone who grew to be a friend. I ended up getting my floorboards from the same mill – cut up green and then dried out in a huge stack. If I was doing it again I'd buy the boards green right at the start and have them drying for as long as possible.

To heat the house, two wood stoves with backboilers went in (Google is a great place to search for stoves), connected to a water tank that I had made up by some metal workers. There is an LPG condensing boiler that tops up the hot water if needed. If I was doing this again I think I would invest in a larger and better heat accumulator tank so that we could eliminate the gas boiler entirely. I'd also go for some solar panels and some sort of gasification boiler that would only run occasionally on woodchip. This solution is obviously not suited for everyone – heat pumps are remarkably efficient and would be my next best choice for heating – as long as I could supply my own renewable electricity to power the pump - which probably makes the heat pump route a fair bit pricier.

We try to be efficient with our heating – we only warm rooms which we are using and wear an extra jumper in the winter, rather than turning the heat up. This makes it all the more cosy to sit around the stove in the evening.

Listed buildings are generally not allowed solar panels on the roof (which is ironic considering that extreme climate change might put the future of the buildings themselves into question), and the wind speed isn't up to it here really, but of course we are on a 100% renewable tariff with Good Energy. Switching to a green tariff is so easy and can account for a large share of your emissions. If you haven't done so, do it now and get your friends and family to do it as well,

For insulation on the roof I used a multifoil, yes, the thin space blanket stuff. I got a really good suntan putting it on the south facing side of the roof on that hot July day! The great advantage of this is that it does not raise the existing roof profile by much. However, it hasn't quite met my expectations, and I wish I had used alternative, greener insulation (like paper or sheep's wool) and gone way over spec. I am adding extra insulation at the moment by putting Kingspan between the rafters in the lofts (factory seconds are a LOT cheaper from **www.secondsandco.co.uk**).

Here are a few things I would do if I were building from scratch now:

- do a lot of research, ask a lot of questions, and seek expert advice before starting
- plan the house out on passive solar principals and get in the help of an experienced sustainable house planner from the start
- build the external walls with straw bales or lime hemp – highly insulating materials which will radically reduce heating needs to almost nothing
- build the internal walls with something with a bit of mass to it - like a stone wall or rammed earth
- look to avoiding the use of concrete if alternative foundation and floor slab constructions would be suitable
- use second hand items whenever practical from salvage yards, local free ads papers etc. second hand timber, bathroom sinks, doors, taps, radiators, the list is endless
- install grey water and rain water storage tanks because it's silly to waste good drinking water (and money) on things like flushing your toilet.

It's not easy being green, but when you are building or renovating a house it is, because for once you have the chance to do things that really will make a difference, and for many years to come.

Third up - Kate Mason

When Kate was about 15, fed up with her 'O' level choices and being bored to death in biology class, (as only a 15 year old can be bored), She suddenly realised that 'saving the planet' would be a good idea.

If only because the cure for AIDs might be in the liver of the whales we were wiping out at the time (mid eighties). Fast-forward 25 years and I still want to save the planet. I'm a middle aged, middle class mum and I'm green and proud of it, well actually sort of pale green.

- I recycle (the stuff the council will take), I freecycle stuff (even though I could sell it on eBay)
- I buy organic, free-range and local (when I can afford it)
- I renovate 'old' furniture with green paint, then clean it with eco products (and happily pay a premium to do this)
- I put shopping into a canvas shopping bag (not a poly-bag) which I occasionally wash at 30 degrees (but I rarely tumble dry)
- I use a mooncup (don't ask) and 'real' nappies, but I have baths not showers - the water is heated by my wood burning stove with a back boiler (which I buy the wood for and have it delivered)
- I drive my children to school in the people carrier (but I park 500m away so they get at least some exercise) and then I visit the farmers market on a Saturday morning (in the same people carrier) before popping into Tescos on the way home.

So when I decided to open a nursery, I needed to convert a building 'greenly'. I'd have straw bale walls with lime render, oh and a green roof with solar panels, oh and;

- grey water recycling
- rainwater harvesting
- super insulation
- reed bed
- green willow fencing
- windmill.

The research I did; straw bales and lime render, wood burning stoves, ground source heat pumps, windmills. The 'Green Building Forum' folk came to dread my questions, not only because I didn't really understand the underlying issues, but because I refused to accept the answer '*because that's the way it's done*'. I seem to have picked up a bad habit from the children I care for and can say "*Why*" over at least 3 syllables (which can be really annoying). Then they have to explain why what I wanted wouldn't work, why it was impractical, too expensive or just plain wrong. They were, and still are, very nice about this. They didn't complain (too) much.

Then of course the planning department, the building control people, the architect and other authorities got hold of the job. Lots of 'sharp intakes of breath' '*tut,tut,tut*' and a bit of '*oh..... we don't do that round here*'. But I was not discouraged, I could do this. Once the legislation was sorted (about 18 months into the project) I was left with;

- low embodied energy roofing
- lots of insulation (made of expanded polystyrene)
- water treatment plant
- ground source heat pump
- little else.

So, I pay the architect, and the structural engineer, and the traffic engineer, and the health and safety specialist, then put the whole thing out to tender. Four companies decided not to tender and the one that was left, hands me an envelope, very sheepishly, and suggests that I sit down when I read it. Needless to say I didn't. The tender was for four hundred and twenty thousand pounds - including VAT.

When I picked myself up off the floor (and stopped crying/hyperventilating), I took a very long, hard look at my need to be green. Why do I want to be green? Is it;

- to 'save the planet' - not quite sure what from - global warming; surviving after the oil runs out; the next ice age; over-population (well I only had one child)?
- reduce waste?
- use less energy and resources?
- because I hate the throw-away society that we have?
- to be ethical (whatever that is)?
- to set a good example for my daughter and the children I care for?
- prevent war over diminishing resources?
- to ensure that I don't use more than my fair share of the world's (finite) resources?
- because I am stubborn awkward and argumentative?

Upon reflection I decided on the last. So I bought a building, renovated it conventionally, only implementing the green/eco bits that will save me money in the long run and that are cost-effective. So, lots of insulation and an efficient heating system. It has been a long, frustrating and expensive exercise. But when I'm rich, things will be different - just wait until next time.

Next up James Norton

In his own work and home life James believes that practical hands-on experience is essential, but there is no replacement for practical skill and dogged research.

It seems these days that all architects seem to claim to be knowledgeable in the ways of sustainability. This is, of course, important because depending on how you crunch the numbers, buildings are, in one way or another, responsible for about half of the UK's CO_2 emissions... Great news then that we architects, particularly those of us who emerged from university during the last 10 years, are all completely prepared and able to save us all. So how come it's not actually happening then?

There are clearly many barriers in the way; a lack of commitment from clients, lack of support form government or lack of knowledge in the design team (including the architect), to name a few. Also, to assume that all practitioners are in a position to deliver true, low impact buildings is also somewhat questionable.

By way of illustration, I have read several design statements for planning applications by local architects who have proudly stated that their building will be super insulated with 100mm of mineral fibre or that the building will have solar panels. Whether these are flat panel, evacuated tube, roof integrated or PV is not mentioned, not that it would matter a great deal as they are positioned on north facing roof slopes. Perhaps more common is the pseudo-eco' specification, such as the use of imported external, timber cladding, when UK grown options exist, often tagged on to an otherwise business-as-usual building.

Whilst clearly there is still a way to go for many practitioners, knowledge, within other parts of the industry and, perhaps more critically, in those who commission buildings, is still patchy and often confused. For example only a few brief writers, critics or TV presenters have a basic grounding in terminology. Words like 'eco', 'green', 'sustainable', 'zero carbon' etc, are all prolifically vocalised with sincerity and moral grandeur but what are we actually talking about here? It might be more useful to use the term 'environmental impact in use and/or in construction' for example, but that's not very imagination grabbing is it?

The duty on the architect to educate and inform has always been there but, in my experience, that briefing stage where you try to sweep away the sound bites can be a difficult process. Often your client, whether they be corporate or domestic, has invested a lot of aspirations and hopes (and money), in those inappropriate terms and to be told that 'unfortunately the 3kW wind turbine on a £100 million development, in a poor location on the site will not really help the situation, whereas the use of cement replacement products and local sourcing of heavy weight materials throughout could actually make a real difference', is often not well received. Architects, after all, are supposed to be about delight, making dreams a reality etc, and its all too easy to find oneself in a situation where, in an attempt to bring accuracy and validity to the project, you find yourself stepping into the role of sandal wearing, puritanical, spoil sport.

Equally, despite the explicit steer in PPS1, PPS3 and the climate change supplement to the former, local planning authorities (LPA), are often less than helpful. In a recent conversation regarding sub-urban wind turbines with the local 'expert' planner on these issues, she expressed, at length, how supportive the LPA would be... ..."as long as it was sited nowhere too obvious like anywhere high or at the top of a hill..."

Conversely, in our practice, the real drive towards genuinely sustainable buildings is coming from perhaps less likely sources such as housing developers, specifically affordable housing developers. These days the Housing Corporation and LPAs are demanding the higher levels (4 and 5) of the Code for Sustainable Homes (CSH), on exceptional sites. Whilst the CSH standard is open to some quite understandable criticism, at these levels, on the budgets we have, some real design effort has to go in to achieve this goal. Naturally, of course, there is on occasion, pressure from our employer to exploit the loopholes in CSH, but largely the move towards better, more sustainable buildings, is supported by our developer clients who are often well aware of the need to avoid the 'greenwash' tag, and there are the marketing benefits.

Of course, there is always the individual client. Although the one-off eco-house commission is less common, the demand for 'eco-extensions' appears extremely strong. These can be very rewarding little jobs with great clients who have turned into partners in the design process. The challenge in practice is to provide the service at an economic level for the client. As a practice that prides itself in operating in the small domestic, as well as large commercial sectors, we have struggled to find a solution. Simply putting up the fee tends to drive away the less well-off client (and to be honest most of the more well-off ones as well), a sustainability consultation only service is difficult to manage in reality and operating on a loss leader basis obviously has a clear disadvantage.

On balance, for most practitioners, the need to put in extra time, possibly unpaid to educate oneself, to win the arguments, push the design, as well as extra costs for software systems etc to deliver genuine, low environmental impact buildings, is normally unavoidable.

I have, however, found a client who is demanding and changes his mind a lot but is sympathetic, happy for a satisfactory fee agreement, understands the potential complexity of the challenge and the time it takes... ...but is of course myself. As such, I would strongly advise any architect with the opportunity to get involved in building for themselves, whether it be true DIY self build, a garden building or even a small housing development.

My own little design project's scope has grown from a small loft conversion, to a full new storey with extension, to a new house, to a pair of decent sized semi detached houses. I dare not contemplate how many hours of research, design, redesign, etc have gone into it so far. However, owing to the fact that the architect is pretty much free, I can afford it. This experience is unbeatable for gaining that deep routed understanding of thermal design, materials, techniques etc, and the balance between these factors with cost, planning constraints, and the other pressures of you (and your family's) demanding brief.

Actually getting your hands dirty is also no substitute for practical skills. For example, only once you have tried to learn to plaster like a professional, and then compared this rather humbling experience with the all round family fun of applying clay plaster (or 'dinosaur poo' as it became known), or cleared a loft full of dusty glasswool and then installed sheep's wool, can you really start to appreciate some of the benefits.

Unlike earlier generations where the RIBA may well have stood for 'remember I'm the bloody architect' the ability to insist on one method or design approach over another is now limited, however our ability to provide informed choices to our clients and inspired solutions to their reservations requires one to work hard to gain the required knowledge, possibly by helping another architect with the clay plastering on his new house for example.

Next - John Driver

John and his wife Guilly have been diehard hippies for more years than most greenies can remember but they come from the old school where less is actually more. However, they have now treated themselves to a bit of modern green technology.

My wife and I have been doing most of the easier greenie things for many years. When we bought a fridge recently (after many years of not having one, making do with a larder), it was 'A' rated. We have never had a spin drier and we use a wind-assisted solar drier, (a washing line), but having it set up in a Dutch barn helps. We took out the open fireplaces (only 20% efficient) when we moved into our very old cottage 30 years ago and installed a wood-burning stove and a second hand Rayburn instead. We mostly burn home-grown firewood. Our loft insulation is getting thicker and thicker, and the cavity walled extension to the house has been insulated as well (there is a grant for this under the Heat Project scheme: 0870 421 5018, **www.ofgem.gov.uk**). The installers sort out the grant so we actually paid just £229. We use low energy light bulbs and, when they needed replacing, installed wooden framed, 'low e' double glazed windows and we have about 5,000 litres of rainwater storage for the garden.

So solar water heating seemed to be the next practical step to make. We are not exactly early adopters, we know, as they are almost mainstream now - reasonably priced. We initially approached a well known double glazing company who had branched out into solar water heating. A representative was invited to call and we were subjected to around four hours of hard sell techniques. The initial quoted price was a massive £14,000 but was quickly brought down to around £8,000 as a 'special' offer to us because 'they were in the area'! When we still said 'no, too expensive' a quick call to the rep's team leader brought the price down to £6,000! We were actively encouraged to sign up on the day to take advantage of this 'special' offer.

The Low Carbon Buildings' Programme (LCBP) puts the cost at between £3,200 and £4,500 and being sensible people we refused to agree the deal, preferring to get other quotes. The Office of Fair Trading has recently introduced regulations (the Consumer Protection from Unfair Trading Regulations) to clamp down on unfair sales and marketing practices so maybe we will see less of this type of extortionate price manipulation/hard selling in the future...! Our final choice of installer (Llanisolar **www.llanisolar.co.uk**) was one who offers good guarantees, is a member of various trade bodies, is experienced and fairly local. The price was £2,995 plus VAT at 5% - *"To supply and install one (2m^2) roof mounted flatbed solar collector, (10 year guarantee), all plumbing, electronic controller, pump station, electrics, expansion vessel, 140 litre insulated twin-coil hot-water cylinder (25 year guarantee), other components and installation guaranteed for two years, all to grant requirements."* This price included £50.00 to supply and fit a standard central heating pump.

Our electrician was a bit dubious about our present pump, installed in 1982. So, for an additional £60.00 we opted for the A-labelled Grundfos consuming a mere 5 watts of electricity - 'could save us up to 20% on our electricity bill'! The installation was completed in a day. Our airing cupboard has a bit less shelf room than it did before, due to the larger hot water cylinder, but our solar water system is working very well with lots of hot water, at around 60°C, in a not very sunny summer. There is currently a £400 grant from the LCBP (**www.lowcarbonbuildings.org.uk** 0800 915 0990) towards solar water heating and other small scale renewables, providing your house complies with insulation and other standards. It is estimated that solar water heating can provide around 60% of a household's hot water needs - 90% in the summer months, 50% in spring/autumn, and around 25% in winter!

Finally - Frank Brown

Frank muses on the state of the planet and his own impact. He is still looking for the perfect green route to take.

As I sit here tapping at my keyboard, thinking 'its not easy being green', I slowly turn over in my mind the concept of being green; that is consuming directly, or indirectly, no more of the earth's resources than is necessary. Seems a useful concept. I was brought up in frugal circumstances and the habits have stuck. So I ponder on the 'necessary' bit and as a Westerner I know that I consume far more resources then people in Africa, and far less then those in America.

I do not want to live in an unheated mud hut and I don't hanker after a 5 litre, gas guzzling SUV to pick my shopping up in. So perhaps I should consider my lifestyle more in relation to the average UK person. Why should I just do a comparison?, Well, I could live like the builders of my 200 year old house and consume a minimal amount, but that would be an insult to all those who have striven to make life more comfortable and last longer, both qualities I appreciate and would like to maintain. Am I greener than the next person, am I the greenest? What could I do to improve my green ranking? And perhaps the most important part - what should I be doing to improve the greenness of the UK. I could spend several thousand pounds on a solar heating array and save a few thousand kW of electricity per year, or I could spend the same time and money to get the politicians to actually legislate in a genuine green way and save millions of kW hours of electricity, but do I trust politicians? I think I had just better get on and try and sort out my own little corner. So a list of what I could do extra would be useful, so here goes.

I could use more CFLs (compact fluorescence lamps), I use many but there are problems with their size and shape, which make them incompatible with light fittings. They look ugly too and finally there is a real problem with their warm up time and disposal. I guess I could recycle more. I already take things to Hampshire (which I visit) rather than driving the 9 miles to my local town because the village recycling centre does not accept them. I could reduce my power consumption but I have no central heating (yet). I only put on a heater as and when required i.e. to warm up the bathroom prior to a shower. I wear plenty of clothing - a T shirt, lumberjack's shirt, pullover and padded shirt, and a hat when it gets really cold (< 7°C) in the house. Really not much possibility here, other than showering in a cold bathroom. I should try some heat recovery system working on the waste from the shower. When time allows, I'll get around to investigating this. I only have one TV (though I do leave it on standby). I have two electric clocks. So not much scope here!

I could increase the insulation to the house. The loft has already got 150mm of glass fibre in it and again I will boost this as soon as I think of a scheme to enable me to walk about over the added insulation but - more wood, more chipboard, more work! The walls could be usefully battened out, lined with foam plaster boarded, and plastered. New skirting boards could be installed, the old 13A sockets re-wired. Window reveals could be sorted, the radiators re-plumbed in (hung but not yet in use) and the window boards replaced. All this work is likely to cost around £2k per room - I could buy oil for years and years.

What about transport? Well, my 13 year VW Passat estate does about 36mpg on a trip and about 15,000 miles/year. I am retired so no commuting. These car is a good size for picking up building materials, so I would be very reluctant to trade down to a smaller vehicle. In my lifetime I have flown about 6 times - no long haul holiday destinations for me.

What about food? I survive on 'oven ready' meals and heat them in a microwave which saves energy. I keep on reading that we throw away 25% of our food. Not me, I throw away a bread crust twice a year and that goes to the birds. Another good point for ready meals.

So reviewing my life style, I have convinced myself that I am fairly green but could do a lot better on the comfort/heat ratio. It is too cold in the house for most people, but as it gets more comfortable the added costs and work required to keep a low energy usage would seem to rise exponentially. Trying to be green is essentially learning new habits and trying to stick to them. The green re-cycling bins, that have caused many problems to the nation according to the press, have been in full use in Hampshire for 7 years + and caused very few problems. It seems that some are not easily persuaded to learn new ways of doing things.

There is a lot of chat about 'zero carbon' housing, but a house's use of carbon is only part of one's carbon foot print. Life style choices are just as relevant and most of this can be improved with education. In closing then perhaps the important thing about being green is to learn new habits and to encourage the use of better technology.

6 Greening commercial

Green buildings pay

The green building philosophy is being adopted by businesses for a number of reasons. **Gavin Harper** explains why and how ...

When assessing whether a green building pays, you need to consider not just the financial benefits. Whilst it would be easy for me to say that green building always pays when you consider the wider benefits, it can sometimes seem hard to justify the additional up-front costs. Certainly ensuring that a building comes in on budget, and is not a financial burden, is likely to be top of the list. Payback calculations, across the whole spectrum, will be vital in proving a case for green building.

Payback periods can be long term on some renewable energy systems, and investment in such technology does not always present an instant return. However, it is important to recognise the rapidly changing environmental and economic climate, where energy prices are rapidly increasing and future supplies are uncertain. What seems uneconomical today, could well prove an attractive investment for tomorrow. Interestingly, a survey of more than 33 green building project clients in the U.S. found that the premium paid, over buildings of a traditional construction, was less than 2%[1]. This small additional cost was not borne out of additional expenditure on equipment or materials – but was mainly spent in the design stage, where additional work was put into modelling building performance. In addition, extra time was taken during projects to integrate sustainable principles into the project. This can partly be attributed to the fact that major builders are undergoing a learning curve; early adopters will pay a small premium for being 'ahead of the curve'. However, as sustainable building practise becomes more widespread throughout the professions, this cost will inevitably fall.

Green doesn't have to mean expensive. This is a common misconception. Green can also mean resource efficient; efficient in construction and efficient in use. Climate change is a reality and we now live in a society that is increasingly aware of environmental issues, so greening a building is being seen as adding real asset value and future-proofing it for the uncertain, more fuel scarce times ahead.

It is important, when designing a green building, that the design is considered holistically. With any building, it makes no sense to 'value engineer' every item against the sustainable options. For instance, a little investment in, say, better insulated and energy efficient windows, will mean a saving elsewhere. For example there could then be a reduced demand for heating plant and subsequent cheaper running and maintenance costs.

However, to keep costs down whilst making the best choices, it is important that all members of the design team are aware of a green build commitment from the earliest possible opportunity in the project. That way, together as a team, everyone should then know what is expected, efficiency should increase, ideas are pooled and costs be contained. By considering the whole building as a system and by facilitating teamwork between members of the design and build team early in the project, value can be engineered into the project as a result of the synergies that arise when all members of a team work to a common goal.

'Business continuity planning' is a tool widely used to ensure the longevity of a business. If energy prices rise significantly in the future, the businesses that will struggle the least are those that have invested in energy saving measures. However, a green building should only be one of the component parts of company-wide effort to make your whole business as sustainable as possible.

It is not enough simply to 'design green' and hope that people will use the facilities in accordance with the designer's master-plan. For a building to be truly sustainable, it needs to be used and operated as the designer intended. Post occupancy evaluation (POE) is a useful tool that can be used to assess the value of the green measures taken and give positive direction for future projects or plans (there is a POE story later in this chapter).

Another option for companies looking to reduce their impact, whilst watching their expenditure, is to refurbish an existing building, keeping the core and shell of an existing structure, but replacing and modernising fixtures and fitting throughout (refurbishment and renovation was discussed in Chapter 1 and later in this chapter).

Green buildings can save money

When looking for cost savings there are a number of tangible benefits on the services' side of things that can be done and should be a primary goal. A green building, when properly designed, should give savings in;

- energy
- plant and equipment
- maintenance.

Why would energy, plant and maintenance costs be lower? Because if you design a building that does not need to rely on air conditioning, for example, then you don't have to buy the equipment in the first place, you free up space that can be used for other purposes and you don't have to pay for ongoing maintenance and the eventual replacement in the longer term. Remember also that a business may not always have to pay the full cost of some green measures added to a building. For example, for water and energy efficiency measures, there are grants and other incentives available (including enhanced capital allowance schemes - see later in this chapter). If it is your own building then any investment in energy efficiency and green technologies should increase the value of the property and possibly even enable a premium to be charged if leasing.

Companies are fast realising that energy is not in endless supply, and in the years to come, it is wholly likely that we will be paying more for our energy than ever before. Air conditioning has become a mainstay of the commercial world, although it has been proven that mechanical cooling can be designed out of a building completely.

Greenwash - avoid at all costs

If you decide to commit to a green building then do your homework. We live in times of instant information. Most consumers are becoming more aware of the issues involved and it will be increasingly difficult to get away with greenwash, particularly if you are basing all green claims purely on carbon-offsetting measures. Businesses should ensure they are honest and up-front in all their actions (see also the story on page 120 regarding greenwash).

Promotional and public relations tool

There is great momentum in business to be

'seen as being green'; corporate social responsibility is very high on the agenda in many organisations, and increasing pressure from consumers, and legislation, is driving forward a green business agenda. However, there is a world of difference between a thin veneer of sustainability on an otherwise unsustainable company, and integrating green practise into business processes and values.

Many companies are now using tools such as 'carbon offsetting' in an attempt to be 'seen as green'. One company is stated as saying on the web ".... *is the UK's most environmentally friendly waste management company. We offset our carbon footprint 110%, so we're carbon-negative* ...." such is the view amongst many of the corporate elite, that it is easier to pay tokenistic amounts to spurious offsetting companies, than achieving real sustainability by fundamentally transforming business practises and the way that products and services are delivered.

Choosing a green building for your headquarters is a way of making positive steps towards improving the sustainability of your operations. There is a sufficient 'informed mass' of people who know that offsetting doesn't represent a viable solution. As knowledge of sustainability and the environment percolates through all levels of society, 'cheap fixes' to companies sustainability woes will cease to cut the mustard. Greenwash is futile in the age of the informed consumer. Media channels such as the internet and enhanced global communication mean that people are more informed than ever, and charlatans and mountebanks are quickly exposed.

Achieving green transformation in your business is more than just purchasing the right products or services, it is about creating an organisational culture that thinks in terms of sustainability, all the way down from the board to the shop floor. It's hard to culture a 'green mind-set' in employees and staff if the built environment in which your business carries out its affairs does not reflect this ethos.

Commerce as a catalyst for a green society

In the same way that a home reflects a person's core values and is an expression of belief structures and character, so commercial buildings should reflect the corporate missions of the business. There is no more visible a tool for a company than its premises – where the space embodies a meaning and a conveyance of the core brand values of a business that cannot be captured in anything as simplistic as a logo, a letterhead or even paper-based mission statements.

Commercial buildings are so prominent and visible, that transformations in the commercial sector have the ability to touch so many people's lives through their contact with these structures. The number of people interacting with a commercial building means that location, and sustainable transport options are key to reducing the building's environmental impact. Our built environment, in many ways, defines and shapes our patterns of consumption. If the premises of the suppliers of the products and services we use are located in an 'out of town centre' with only car access – then we are more likely to drive. However, locate that same building near good public transport facilities and reduce the size of the car park, and it can become more convenient for everyone to visit it using public transport.

Commercial buildings act as a great advert for the green building sector; if we can prove that a technology will work in a commercial setting, then it should also work in a variety of other settings where cost is less critical – commercial green buildings validate the viability of the technologies and methods.

Delivering user-friendly buildings

It is not simply enough to 'build green'. The way in which the building is designed and conceived needs to match the way in which the building will be used. The world is littered with essentially useless 'iconic' buildings that simply failed to be user-friendly. The energy savings, and hence on-going costs of a building need to be designed-in to the structure and not left to the building occupants to manage. This is not to say that the occupants should not have some control of their working environment. A green building should have opening windows, adequate daylight provision and be adaptable, but its expected performance should not rely upon the way that the occupants use the building. The correctly conceived green building will deliver many supplementary benefits, such as employee satisfaction, comfort and a reduction in absenteeism. The risks of building performance failure can be substantially reduced if a robust user-proof design is incorporated. Such techniques have been discussed elsewhere in this book but are covered in greater detail in Volume 2 of the Green Building Bible.

The Scottish Natural Heritage (SNH) office at Westercraigs in Inverness was been awarded a BREEAM environmental building rating of 84% . User-friendliness was high on the agenda, as were measures within the design to help building users participate with the philosophy of the building.

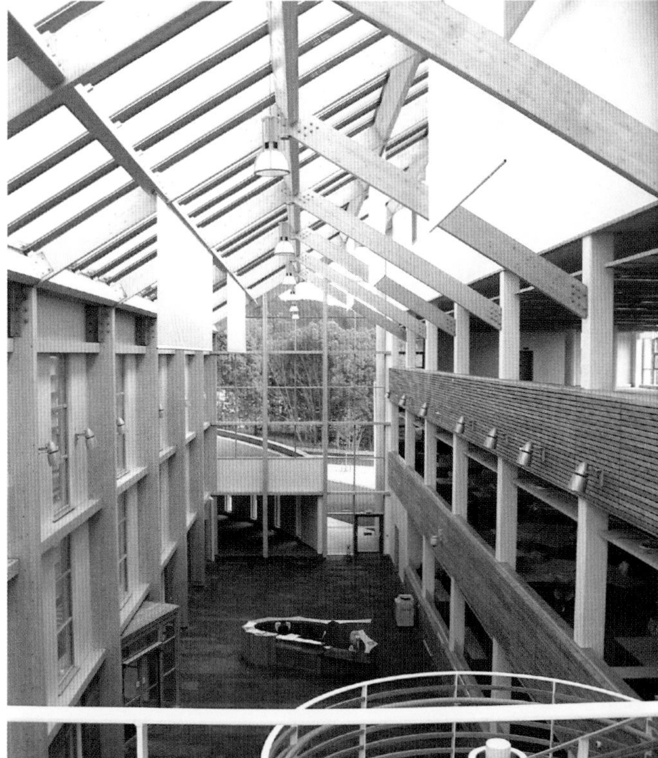

With environmental assessment methods, such as BREEAM, it has become easier than ever for developers or landlords to sell or let a building that achieves such good environmental standards. Developers who deliver commercial buildings with green credentials, and all of the benefits these entail, put themselves in a unique position, setting them above the competition.

There is an initial cost involved with getting the expertise and resources required to build green, but as you become more familiar with the process, the easier and cheaper it gets. As with anything, there are economies of scale as you increase levels of production. To sum up then, rather than relying on the cheapest options, procurement officers should look to the tangible and the supplementary cost benefits of green building. 

References

1. Kats, G.H., "Green Building Costs & Benefits", Barr Foundation, Massport, MA, U.S.

Further reading

'Green Building: Does it Pay?' Plumbing Systems and Design 2006; Vol. 5: No. 2 by Ham, Paul L. The American Society of Plumbing Engineers.

'Why Build Green?' - Rocky Mountain Institute / ENSAR built environment team.

'Great Bow Yard; anatomy of an ecobuild' by N Griffiths

'Green Building: Project Planning & Cost Estimating', edited By: R.S. Means.

'Green Buildings Pay' by E Edwards, available from: ***www.greenshop.co.uk***

Whole life costing and embodied carbon are discussed in detail on page 275 in Volume 2 of the Green Building Bible.

Green buildings pay - a case study

The NMB Bank - Amsterdam

The NMB bank building, on the outskirts of Amsterdam, was one of the first major green building projects in Europe, and was completed in 1987.

The architect was Anton Alberts – his vision was a series of 7 towers linked by walkways, each seven to eight stories high. With daylight flooding in from an atrium above, and natural ventilation accomplished with large amounts of opening windows, the building did away with energy sapping air-conditioning by using thermally massive, internal eighteen inch walls to provide night cooling of the space.

The green building theme was continued in the landscaping of the buildings – outside Alberts created a beautiful park space with formal and informal gardens, waterfalls and all manner of curiosities to delight the buildings inhabitants. Wetlands and ponds created nice spaces for employees and users of the building to seek inner calm, whilst also providing a habitat for fauna.

The NMB bank building in Amsterdam is widely praised for its natural aesthetic and green building credentials. When commissioning the building, the bank set down two objectives to be met. The first was that the design would be organic, natural and epitomise green architecture. The second mandate was that the building should cost not even a single guilder more than a similar function building constructed using traditional methods. Both objectives were met and the building exceeded first expectations.

Why in this instance did green building pay?

The project was the product of a design team that were heavily integrated from the start, it resulted in a construction that delivered massive energy savings through passive solar architecture and water savings through rainwater harvesting. The energy saving features in the building paid back within the first three months of use. The bank saw 92% energy savings, compared with a similar sized facility. Furthermore the bank made an estimated $2.9 million savings, per annum, compared with a building of conventional construction.

Turning to the supplementry benefits

mentioned earlier – absenteeism dropped by 15%, with workers reporting an increase in productivity and an increased enjoyment of their internal and external office environment. However, there is a twist in the tale – with the takeover of NMB by ING, along came a new corporate ethic. According to Coldham Architects. The new ethic meant that spending time relaxing in the grounds was an indication of a '*lack of ambition*' and was discouraged. The new politics of the new organisation meant that there was then a change in the way that the occupants interacted with their building. Coldham goes on to say "*the significant accumulation of slime on the walkways, stepping stones, pathways, etc, to the point that some are now dangerous to walk along, is evidence of their almost complete lack of use.*" This is an interesting case in point as this celebrated building demonstrates how it is not simply enough to 'design a green building', but in order to reap the rewards of good building design, you must also design a 'green ethic' for your business, that embraces the concepts embodied within the architecture and extends it to company policy and the way in which employees interact with each other and their environment. ☯

Links for further reading

www.rmi.org/sitepages/pid208.php

www.architectureweek.com/2002/1023/environment_2-2.html

www.facilitiesnet.com/bom/Nov02/Nov02environment.shtml

www.epa.gov/ne/greenbuildings/pdfs/gb_casestudies.pdf

www.rmi.org/images/other/GDS/D92-21_NMBBankHQ.pdf

Enhanced capital allowances

The enhanced capital allowance (ECA) scheme is part of the government's programme to manage climate change. It provides businesses with enhanced tax relief for investment in equipment that encourages savings in, for example, energy or water, which are the areas most relevant to the building sector. So for anyone in business this means that products purchased that are included on either the 'energy technology list' or the 'water technology list' are eligible for ECH.

The scheme allows 100% of the full cost of the investment to be written off against taxable profits for the period in which the investment is made (the general rate for plant and machinery capital allowances is just 20% per year on the reducing balance basis). Such a scheme provides a helpful cash flow boost and a shortened payback period. ECAs are claimed via income tax or corporation tax return in the same way as other capital allowances are claimed. The 'energy technology list' includes renewable energy systems, boiler equipment, combined heat and power, heat pumps, lighting equipment, pipework insulation, solar thermal systems and some heaters. The 'water technology list' includes energy efficient taps, showers, toilets, flow controllers, leakage detection equipment, meters and monitoring equipment and rainwater-harvesting equipment. Some non-listed products meet the criteria but may not appear on the list (where there are too many product variations to list, for example). Claiming for these items is more complex and the ECA website gives more details.

If you are a manufacturer of a product you can check the eligibility criteria to establish whether your product(s) is eligible for inclusion and you can apply for inclusion if appropriate. ☯

Energy technology list: ***www.eca.gov.uk/etl***
Water technology list: ***www.eca-water.gov.uk***

BREEAM

Some of us are aware of the recent changes to BREEAM yet so many more are not. **Claire Howe** reports on the changes ...

BREEAM 2008 brings the standard into closer alignment with the Code for Sustainable Homes (CSH). For example, a post construction review or assessment will become a mandatory requirement, which gives added credibility to the scheme. Some organisations, such as English Partnerships, have insisted on post construction reviews (PCR's) as they were concerned about the vulnerability of only using the 'design and procurement' assessment which is based on design stage commitments, things that we all know can get blown away when it comes to financial constraints. By insisting on the PCR they were assured of a quality construction as well as a quality design, so this is one example of how 2008 BREEAM is toughening up.

Other measures are likely to include the setting of mandatory minimum levels of performance for things like energy and water. One criticism of BREEAM is that an 'excellent' rating could be achieved without really tackling energy as an issue, on a site benefiting from good local transport links. Minimum standards, such as those that apply to the CSH, will ensure that the ratings achieved reflect the combined effort that project teams put into meeting these stringent levels.

Materials selection is another area where I anticipate minimum requirements. For example under the CSH, at least 3 of the 5 key building materials must be A+ to D rated. I believe that a similar approach will be adopted for the BREEAM version, for example, at least 4 of the 7 key building materials to be A+ to D rated in the 4th edition of the Green Guide to Materials. This in itself is quite easy to achieve as very few products are E rated. However, credits are maximised by selecting higher rated materials; A+ rated products pick up 3 points per element, on the opposite end of the scale D rated materials pick up 0.25 points and E rated materials pick up none.

Other more subtle changes include revising the weightings of categories aligned to the CSH weightings, which were the outcome of a huge consultation process conducted by the BRE, where industry representatives were asked to judge the importance of each environmental issue against others. If the categories are also aligned to the CSH, i.e. 'transport' omitted, 'surface water' added and 'materials and waste' split into 2 categories, this will mean that energy will have the highest weighting, in line with the feedback, at a massive 36.5%, water increases to 9% and materials drops to 7.2%.

My personal view is that BREEAM is an excellent tool for measuring the environmental impact of a building, yet it often comes under criticism for 'changing the goalposts' – but that's exactly what BREEAM is designed to do. Achieving any rating under BREEAM means that minimum standards have been surpassed. Over time, best practice, regulations, legislation, and codes of practice all get revised. If BREEAM stood still, carrying out an assessment would be nothing more than a paperwork exercise, instead BREEAM raises the bar and challenges project teams to meet the higher standards recognised by the BREEAM ratings. The 2008 version brings with it a new rating of 'outstanding' to recognise those buildings that exceed the requirements of the 'excellent' rating. Clearly it is these buildings that will win the BREEAM awards, as well as various other design and construction accolades.

A number of credits may be omitted from the 2008 version; for example anything which has become a legislative requirement since the 2006 version, i.e. site waste management plans, or initiatives which should be standard practice, such as designing systems to minimise the risk of legionella's disease, are likely to be omitted.

The 2008 version will see the inclusion of Innovation credits which can be achieved for implementing innovative technologies that have a real environmental benefit. These have worked well under the LEED system in the USA. Incidentally BREEAM was first, I have it on authority from Alan Yates, Technical Director at the BRE. The first version of BREEAM was launched in 1990 with LEED (Leadership in Energy and Environmental Design) following some 7 or 8 years later.

Most people are only aware of the design and procurement assessment as it forms such an important part of funding of new build and refurb schemes. However, a management and operation scheme also exists – the 2008 version brings a revamp which will be known as 'BREEAM In Use' which will be available for all existing non-domestic buildings and links up with the EPC (energy performance certificate) of the EPBD (energy performance of buildings directive).

The 2008 version should take us closer to our goals of sustainable development and those elusive government targets. However, it won't be cheap and the sooner project teams get stuck into the challenge, the better it will be for us all.

Note: The new BREEAM assessment schemes launched in the 2008 update are BREEAM Healthcare, BREEAM Education and BREEAM In Use.

SNH headquarters scored high on BREEAM

Scottish Natural Heritage (SNH) required potential developers for their new headquarters to design a building to meet the following criteria;

- a carbon output of less than 8kg/m^2/year
- BREEAM Excellent rating
- water consumption of less than 6.4m^3 per person per annum
- A' rated materials in The Green Guide to Specification (BRE) for external walls, windows, roof, internal structures, partitions, doors, carpets / floor coverings, together with all finishes, treatments, insulations both structural and services
- registration with the considerate constructors scheme
- reducing, re-using and recycling of construction materials
- airtightness to 5m^3/m^2/hr against a building regulation norm of 10m^3/m^2/hr for these type of office buildings.

Sustainability was emphasised in the specifications for the building. All goods, services, fittings and fixtures would, wherever practicable, be procured from sustainable sources and designed to reduce environmental impact. This would include consideration of sustainable development issues pertinent to the procurement, and an assessment of the extent to which goods and services could be manufactured, used and disposed of in ways which reduced resource use, energy use (including embodied energy), travel and pollution. The aim was to achieve a better than excellent BREEAM rating.

Review of commercial buildings

Gavin Harper looks at how green building techniques have been applied in the private and public sectors ...

Commercial activity takes place in many settings. We define the term loosely in this article to encompass public services and administrations, hospitals, schools, libraries, council and local authority buildings, but here we exclude heavy industry, which confronts us with a different set of energy challenges.

According to the Digest of UK Energy Statistics, published by the Department for Business, Enterprise and Regulatory Reform (BERR), the commercial sector consumed 19% of the UK's electricity in 2006 and public administration accounted for 5%[1] - combined, at 24% we can see that the sector consumption is rapidly approaching the 29% which the domestic sector consumes. Why, therefore, do we focus so slavishly on the domestic sector when so many vast strides could be made by businesses?

The challenges the commercial sector face, in terms of addressing energy usage, are distinctly different from those in the residential sector, and the drivers and motives for change commensurately differ. Where a homeowner might indulge their own 'eco-vision' for their property – with the home as an extension of self and an expression of personality - in the commercial sector, decisions are based on business practicality, profitability and utility of purpose.

Green building in the commercial sector can often make sense when assessed on just financial terms. Inefficiency and resource wastage is not only bad for the environment but a waste of money, and for a business to operate efficiently, waste must be minimised. In the new era of escalating energy prices, wasted energy is wasted profit.

One thing is evident, the cost savings for business are greatest when sustainable elements are considered from the start. Whilst some elements can be 'bolted on' or retrofitted, the biggest gains come when multiple or synergistic savings can be made – for example, saving on roof or facade materials where roof integrated solar is fitted, or reducing the amount of water to service a building's water needs by fitting waterless urinals and low-flush toilets from the start, as well as installing a greywater recycling system.

As is so often the case in architecture and the built environment, plant, equipment and services are mutually dependent – small decisions taken on one item of plant, will affect the selection decisions for other items.

Green warehouse for brewer

Set in an old gravel quarry, those looking down onto the Adnams distribution centre, would be forgiven for not noticing at first glance the 2382 square metre distribution centre. This is because Adnams brewery, in Sussex, boasts the UK's largest 'living roof'. The benefits of living roofs are many. They assist with slowing the progress of rainwater into the drains, preventing surges in a downpour. In addition, the plants are busy harnessing solar energy to convert carbon dioxide into oxygen. Furthermore, green roofs help enormously with minimising the visual intrusion of buildings.

The site also makes use of the runoff water from the roof, employing greywater recycling for flushing toilets for the workers of the site. In addition, the water is used to wash Adnams' lorries, keeping them bright and shiny without costing the earth.

Above: one of Britain's largest living roofs can be found on top of the distribution depot of Adnams brewery in Sussex.

Below: a closer view of the Adnams brewery distribution centre where it can be seen that the hemp walls look much like normal construction.

The building uses solar hot water heating to meet 80% of the site's hot water needs. Adnams also use a brewing process where steam generated during brewing is recirculated and used to pre-heat the second brew, capturing and saving 90% of the energy each time. Waste water from the site is processed using a septic tank and reed bed filtration system. The project replaced an older site Adnams occupied, in Southwold town centre; unfortunately, the previous, centrally located site meant that much traffic had to travel through the centre of town. The new brownfield location is on a disused quarry and blends in with the 85 acres of grassland in which the building stands.

In terms of the cost, Adnams estimate that

a 15% premium was paid over the cost of an equivalent 'metal box' warehouse - with the project costing £14 million in total. However, the visual improvement that such a structure has provided is immeasurable, which has led to better acceptance of the distribution centre by the local community. Andy Wood, MD of Adnams said "*We evaluate all areas of the business to find ways of lessening its impact on the environment. The environmental option came at a premium, but it makes astute business sense and is a sustainable investment for the future of this British company. As energy prices soar, this energy efficient building will make substantial savings. I believe that Adnams is shaping the path for other businesses to follow.*" The building was also well-received by local politicians, both the local councillor and mayor made positive comments about the development.

The eco-distribution centre uses a combination of lime, hemp and chalk in its construction. The walls are made from over 90,000 hemp-lime blocks that are vapour-permeable, which permits the walls to breathe, whilst also locking in carbon dioxide. The high thermal mass of the walls helps to regulate temperature inside the depot. The depot is currently the biggest building in the UK to employ this form of hemp-lime construction (see boxout right for more detail).

Adnams' green streak extends to its products – whilst many would advocate reducing consumption as a first measure, many people's emotional attachment to the beverage of choice means that reducing the impact of the product is the next best option! Adnams teamed up with university researchers from the University of East Anglia, to try and develop a carbon-neutral brew. Its 'East Green' bitter is made from locally grown barley, to minimise energy input and carbon emissions due to transportation, whilst the strain of hops 'Bodicea' has been selected to reduce the input of pesticides in production. Furthermore, the green-thinking extends to packaging, where a lightweight bottle design reduces the weight that needs to be transported onwards to the

Why hemp walls?

The Adnams brewery project saw the creation of a 4,400m^2, warehouse which trialled a new construction method utilising hemp, lime and chalk blocks to create the walls. This particular construction material uses less energy to manufacture than conventional concrete.

The 470mm thick warehouse walls have a cavity wall constructed of two skins of blocks, which are filled with a hemp-lime mix. The blocks need a high percentage of lime and a stone dust aggregate to give them the necessary strength - but this is not so effective when it comes to thermal performance. The cavity infill for this particular project will therefore have a much higher proportion of hemp to provide better insulation.

Utilising materials and concepts which have been developed and applied in Europe by Lhoist for over a decade, and its knowledge of lime based building products, Lime Technology Ltd developed Tradical Hemcrete as a sustainable alternative to traditional masonry. Lhoist and Lime Technology formally introduced it into the UK marketplace earlier this year and, working with structural Engineer Lister Beare and architects Aukett Fitzroy Robinson, designed the pioneering walls for the Adnams Brewery.

The walls are diaphragm structures, built using nearly 100,000 compressed, lime blocks and infilled with hemcrete, 150 tonnes of CO_2 has been locked up in the Tradical hemcrete infill of the walls, which is claimed to be equivalent to 1.5 million miles worth of emissions from a Ford Escort or sixty times around the Earth. Apparently the walls of a conventional building of the same size would have been responsible for up to 600 tonnes of CO_2 emissions and therefore, the Adnams warehouse has made a potential saving of up to 750 tonnes of CO_2, by using the Tradical hemp lime technology in its construction. The project also uses lime mortar from Lime Technology, plaster and render. Furthermore, the hemp construction also locks CO_2 up in the finished structure. This is due to hemp absorbing CO_2 as it grows and the lime absorbing CO_2 as it sets. Very little energy is required to produce the materials and build the walls - and now that the walls have been constructed, the hemp acts as an extremely good insulator allowing the walls to breathe', keeping damp at bay.

Sources: **www.haymills.com** and **www.limetechnology.co.uk**

point of consumption. The product used a life-cycle assessment from farm to bottle. Whilst many question the dubious nature of carbon offsetting, Adnams seem to have only committed just a tiny fraction of the whole brewing processing to this option.

Greening public buildings - York Eco Depot

The York Eco Depot presents an exciting contrast, as it shows how 'commercial space' for the public sector can also benefit from green building techniques. The recipient of a plethora of design awards, York Eco Depot was commissioned by the City of York as a replacement for one of their existing council buildings.

Most councils still haven't shaken off their brutalist, barren boxes of the Sixties, but York is determined to move forward with exciting new technologies, that show it is embracing the future rather than living in the past. The project came about as a result of collaboration between Yorkshire Forward, (the county's Regional Development Agency), the City of York council, White-Design (a Bristol based architectural practise), and Carillion (the main contractors).

The project shows how larger developers are starting to embrace green techniques and materials. The combination of technologies shows that large contractors are starting to evaluate the alternatives critically. With Carillion involved in so many government private finance innitiative (PFI) projects, it provides hope for the future of green building techniques in the public sector.

Straw bale panels and hydraulic lime is used throughout for the wall finishes and render. Council vehicles, which were previously washed using drinking water quality tap-water, are now cleaned using rainwater recovered on site, saving an estimated £25,000 a year, and cutting water use at the site by half – a lesson to be learnt here for any company or organisation that needs to maintain a fleet of vehicles as part

The York Eco-Depot has broken many moulds with its innovative design and product application on a public sector building. It was the first building in the UK to incorporate Modcell straw bale panels.

Inside the York Eco-Depot. Attention has been paid to natural materials and plenty of daylight.

of its operation.

On-site renewables also feature as a significant part of the project – the site employs both solar thermal and solar PV (which provides 25kW peak capacity). This is supplemented with on-site wind-generation capacity (which can provide 15kW in the windiest conditions). These components allow the building to meet 12% of its energy needs autonomously. Furthermore, use of underfloor heating ensures that the building is kept cosy – whilst saving 40% of the energy that would be wasted using alternative methods of heating. Real-time monitoring is being carried out to ensure that the building performs to spec and continues to meet the energy performance criteria set out at the beginning of the project.

The measures at the York Eco Depot have been calculated to save 155 tonnes of CO_2 emissions every year. Offsetting-wise, this is equivalent to planting or protecting 42 hectares of rainforest to sink the same amount. Such figures illustrate that off-setting doesn't really stack up as a sustainable solution. If the entire western world decided to improve their practise just by buying offsetting there would not be enough acreage of land to protect or plant! A far better way of achieving practical CO_2 savings is to do it locally and on-site if possible. By doing this, others are educated and the 'domino effect' will ripple through society.

The benefits of green building in other areas of the public sector can be observed in a report by the Commission for Architecture and the Built Environment, who observed that a hospital which was given an 'eco-renovation' increased its performance with a 21% improvement in discharge rates, with observed improvement in the quality of care, speed with which matters were handled, patient and employee satisfaction, reduced number of patient visits to the hospital and less drugs dispensed.

The green building society

How many financial institutions can claim to have a BREEAM 'excellent' rated headquarters? Ecology Building Society has done just that, by offering green finance solutions from a premises that captures the values of its investors and borrowers.

The fabric of the Ecology HQ building is exemplar, making use of many reclaimed materials and certified timber. Dry stone walls are constructed from local stone and insulated with Rockwool. The thermal losses through the glazing are minimised with advanced argon-filled, double glazed windows.

For internal finishes, a range of natural, non toxic paints have been selected, whilst for the floor coverings, a combination of linoleum (hessian backed and made from linseed oil), natural rubber floor finishes and wool carpets have been selected. In the wet areas, a combination of mosaic tiles, made from recycled glass, and recycled plastic finishes have been used to produce splash proof surfaces with minimum impact. The Scandinavian, ultra-low volume dual flush toilets are fed from a rainwater harvesting system, ensuring that the burden on the mains is kept to a minimum.

For the roof space, engineered joists have been used to reduce the timber burden of the building, which has the additional benefit of providing deep recesses which have been filled with cellulose fibre insulation. Additionally, the building's roof is planted with sedum which reduces run off. On one of the roof segments, aluminium has been used. Whilst having a high embodied energy content, aluminium was

The Ecology Building Society is one of the new icons of green business. Its concern for environmental care runs right through the business and covers just about every aspect of environmentalism and ethics.

selected because it can be easily recycled when the building is decommissioned.

For electricity generation, a PV array, which has generated over 3,500kWh of electricity since 2004 saves 2 tonnes of CO_2. Recap again to the earlier point on carbon offsetting, to appreciate that sustainable solutions trump cheap-fix offsets hands down.

A straw bale extension to the building provides a green meeting space, which will eventually form part of a green reference library. The flexible nature of bale-building has been taken advantage of, creating a round structure, with a conical roof that has been insulated with sheep's wool. The roof has been tiled with cedar shingles, and waste from the construction process was minimised, then sorted and reused.

Location, location, location ... and transport, transport, transport ...

It's not just about the fabric of your building and the energy performance of the structure that determines a building's impact. Siting the building with respect to the concept of sustainable transport options is also important to ensure the impact of operations are kept to a minimum.

In practise, the design of the Ecology Building Society building took these considerations on board in ensuring that, when selecting the new site, a railway station was nearby. It also took the unusual step in lobbying the local planning authority to allow it to reduce the size of its car park below that normally required by the planning system, thus dis-incentivising the business and the staff from unsustainable car-based travel patterns.

The society has made sure that provision for those wishing to travel to work by bicycle has been made by including a secure bike shed and providing shower and changing facilities. This ensures that those who travel on two wheels can arrive at their desk clean and fresh - as an un-showered cyclist could have serious impact on indoor air quality!

Cycle to work schemes and business

Under the government's cycle to work scheme, both businesses and employees benefit from creating sustainable travel plans. Employees benefit by getting a bike, paid for in advance, with the portion of the money spent being excluded from National Insurance contributions. Employers can claim the VAT back from the purchase of the bike. It means that employees can get their cycle clips on and get out on the road, without the hassle of finding a big chunk of money to buy the bike up-front - payments for the bike are then repaid over time from the salary. To take the hassle out of the process for all concerned, there are a number of third-party providers, who manage the paperwork.

In a scheme in London, employers found that improved employee retention was another corollary of the scheme, with employees feeling better about their places of work. (A Rawstron, 2008) 'Cycle to work schemes and their benefits') **www.personneltoday.com**

www.dft.gov.uk/pgr/sustainable/cycling/cycletoworkschemeimplementat5732

The Ecology Building Society's values extend beyond the business processes that are embodied within its bricks and mortar, to promoting sustainable behaviours and lifestyles to its employees. However, it's not just nice gesturing towards the environment - encouraging employees to live healthy, sustainable lifestyles also makes good business sense. According to the Health and Safety Executive, sickness and absence from work costs UK industry £12 billion every year, so integrating green travel plans into business practise benefits all concerned. It's also a win-win considering the fact that since the Finance Act 1999, (under the Green Travel Plan) employers and employees can claim tax breaks (see boxout above).

Seeing such practical action being taken by an increasing number of profitable organisations should give you some faith that a green building and a green corporate policy is the right choice for your company or organisation. The impact of the commercial sector is great, and there is an urgent need for change in many more businesses. Transforming a business has the potential to touch not only the lives of the employees, but also those of the customers and suppliers, reaffirming in their minds the notion that a green revolution is really taking place.

In an age where cynical greenwashing, and cheap fix solutions are the norm, it is easy to shine, by implementing a real green business strategy that has integrity. Selecting a sustainable premises is the first step in acheiving total transformation for your business.

Green retail

Looking now to the retail sector, This is one area that is already being forced to change, with the death-knell sounding for the free plastic bag. Sustainable consumerism is no longer the preserve of a small bunch of dedicated followers, instead it is becoming a doctrine that is spreading and rippling through society. Consumers are shoppers and they are beginning to expect the shops that they visit to reflect the ethos that they themselves hold. The Body Shop was an interesting early example of this. Also retailers are seeing true benefits in energy savings and increased store visits. User-friendly and well daylit stores have been found to appeal to their targeted customer ethos. In a report by Heschong Mahone Group (1999), it was found that adding skylighting to a retail store increased productivity of staff by 40%[2]. Staff are also more content. Happy staff are friendly staff and this increases customer satisfaction.

Tesco's 50,000 square foot store at Wick near John O'Groats was purpose built to have a carbon footprint 50% smaller than stores of a similar size. You can't miss it – it has 5 wind turbines on the roof! The store is also pioneering the use of other green technologies, such as water cooled refrigeration units with energy-saving LED lighting, 50% more energy efficient bakery ovens, roof top rainwater collection for use in toilets and car washes that save an estimated 1 million litres a year. And those five wind turbines, together with photovoltaic roof cells, generate enough electricity to power the tills and reduce overall energy consumption by 10%.

On another store in Swansea, Tesco has installed a CHP system. This is a 210kW(e) and 317kW heat output unit. Tesco's claim that this store is 34% more energy efficient than a typical, similar sized store. The other food retail giants are all posturing similarly with plans in the pipeline or already in progress. All in all, it seems that the major food retailers are feeling the pressure of consumer demand to clean up their act. An overall footprint reduction is, of course, something to celebrate but the death of shopping in town centres and the homogenisation of our communities will probably continue unabated. As new, green technology gets adopted by the large retailers, the performance feedback and extra investment should help contribute to better technology at cheaper prices for the consumer.

However it is the new wave of green retailers that could make the best difference. Whilst the Ecology Building Society has carved its way up the building society popularity stakes, few ethical retailers have done similarly well. Most green retailers seem to be locked up in the retailing of so-called eco-gadgets (stuff that we could probably do without) rather than bringing greener choices of the everyday items that we need. However, on the plus front the human scale eco-retailer is finding an ever-greater presence in the high street which is good news if the consumer can somehow be tempted to keep visiting it!

Greening the business meeting

Corporate conferences and exhibitions often generate masses of waste. A new corporate venue in Dover, Pines Calyx, wanted to make a difference by offering businesses an alternative by creating a commercial ecological conference venue where businesses could take employees out of the normal, every day setting, and focus on positive change in a pleasant environment with carbon neutral credentials.

The building's construction is unusual, being of 'rammed chalk' – a natural, local material which is readily available in that corner of Kent. The walls are 650mm thick and the rammed chalk provides a breathable, load-bearing construction, which helps to moderate humidity in the building. The roofs are constructed using a technique known as catalan/timbrel vaulting. The gently doming ceilings create a large, clear space for holding events, without pillars, supports or other visual intrusions – whilst at the same time eliminating the use of concrete and its carbon intensive connotations in construction. The project shows us how avant-garde architecture can acquire and appreciate ideas from ancient approaches, in reviving the vaulting technique which is centuries-old, and applying it in a modern setting.

The building compares favourably with traditional constructions, both in terms of embodied energy, and embodied carbon, with the estimated energy embodied in the building being 299MJ/m², compared to 1393MJ/m² for an equivalent concrete construction. The figures for embodied carbon are 33kg CO_2/m² as opposed to 147kg CO_2/m².

The thermal mass of the chalk and ground-sheltering afford good thermal properties to the building, with additional heat being provided courtesy of a biomass boiler. The garden waste collected from the tranquil setting of the six acre organic 'Pines Garden' of St Margaret's Bay, Kent provides a sustainable biomass feed-stock for the boiler, meeting most of its fuel needs.

The building sets an exciting precedent for earth-sheltered buildings, which commonly employ large amounts of concrete in constructing retaining walls. The building's energy in use is kept to a minimum. Natural ventilation ensures a good internal environment, with the

Below: Pines Calyx under construction, showing the rammed chalk walls (a variant on rammed earth, see page 253).

Above: the finished Pines Calyx building with the roof ready for seeding, and inset: interior view of one of the conference rooms showing the vaulted ceiling/roof.

breathable walls and high thermal mass of the construction providing a high level of indoor air-quality and a stable indoor temperature. Waste from the building and its environs is kept to a minimum, with the organic waste from the site's gardens being used to keep the building warm, and the waste water from the building going to a reed bed filtration system. Hot water for the building is solar-heated.

The CIS Tower in Manchester

Whilst building new tall buildings from scratch is arguably not a sound move towards sustainability, refurbishing an existing building makes some sense – the carbon for concrete production has already been expended – and demolition would result in more waste ending

Right: the CIS Tower in Manchester, boasting over 7,000 solar panels.

High rise high impact?

Around the world there are a large number of commercial tall buildings that are starting to integrate renewable energy technologies into their fabric. Architects around the world are starting to explore how sustainable architecture could work in the context of tall buildings. Interesting structures, such as the new Bahrain World Trade Centre, where utility-scale wind turbines are built into a series of interconnections between the BWTC's two sail-like towers, is one example.

However, despite these very public, perhaps flamboyant, gestures towards embracing renewables, there are still fundamental questions surrounding the nature of tall buildings and whether some key questions remain unanswered about their green credentials.

In a number of articles published in Green Building magazine, Professor Sue Roaf, argued that, judged against so many different criteria, tall buildings cannot be considered sustainable at all. Whether it is the energy investment in their structure; the energy in use to power plant, such as lifts, which are necessitated by their very form; or the fact that beyond the 11th floor fire protection becomes nigh on impossible.

As buildings tower ever higher, it becomes increasingly hard to achieve, for example, passive heating and cooling. Windows tend to be sealed for safety reasons, and so the last resort is generally air-conditioning - an energy vampire. The worrying thing is, despite enthusiastically embracing a range of new (and hitherto sometimes untested technologies), no attempt seems to be made to conserve energy in these lavish structures. The argument that the cheapest watts to generate are 'negawatts' does not seem to carry much currency in the petroleum-rich Middle East or Russia, where many of these buildings are proposed.

Furthermore, the materials' properties, demanded by such challenging structures, mean that there is less room for creative experimentation with natural building materials; demanding the use of carbon intensive concrete and steel which, with global demand and resource shortages, continues to rally in price. Until some of these interesting yet dubious visions prove themselves, the jury is still out on whether they can be considered sustainable, or whether their innovative technologies are just a token gesture to the trends of the moment movement.

For business owners, the moral of this story is to think very carefully before moving into a tall building. Whilst the carbon costs of concrete production have already been spent, with rising energy prices, can you afford to meet the ongoing energy costs for services that a low-rise structure would make irrelevant.

up in landfill. The CIS tower is home to the Co-operative group and has been given an eco-refurb with building integrated renewables. As one of the best examples standing of renewables integrated into tall buildings in the UK, the 7,244 solar PV panels in a 400ft high array, create 180,000kWhs of renewable electricity each year, alongside 24 wind turbines on the roof. However, combined, these will only meet 10% of the building's total energy requirements.

However, the CIS Tower (previously called Beetham) has come in for particular criticism as a 25 storey tower block was built to the south of it, thus blocking out sun for some periods of the year. However, if we do accept tall buildings as being a feature of our future urban landscape, there is surely a case for a greater degree of 'master-planning' and consideration of solar access for other nearby buildings that can contribute to the 'energy balance' of a city, and protecting those that make a positive impact.

Regional development agencies

Regional development agencies (RDA) have been very pro-active in promoting alternative technologies in the localities that they manage. Whilst many would criticise central government for its relatively slow movements on sustainable construction and next generation energy technologies, this trend is bucked by the regions who want to ensure a sustainable future for the people in the area they are responsible for.

The website for RDA's resonates with positive messages of sustainability. The visual cues, such as the wind turbine in the site design, and the references to being '...guided by the principles of sustainability...', are not just rhetoric; as we are seeing in concrete action, regional development agencies are being innovative in helping organisations make positive contributions to the built environment in a way that is sustainable.

If your business is looking for premises that don't cost the earth, both literally and metaphorically, then some of the green business units being developed by the RDA's serve as an ideal springboard to a green building of your own.

Furthermore, through their economic savvy, and knowledge of funding structures, RDA's are often able to assist with developing your business along lines that will strengthen your local region in a manner that is long lasting and sustainable. Contact your local RDA before you proceed with your plans to see what local help or innitiatives there may be to help you along with your plans to green your business. **www.englandsrdas.com**

Conclusion

In all the examples that we have featured in this article, there is an overwhelming feeling of client and user satisfaction with their new green buildings. Careful thought given to design and selection of materials can result in exciting spaces, which serve as interesting talking points, generating word-of-mouth advertising for your building.

At the moment, green buildings are still in the minority – and there remains a learning curve for the mainstream building establishment to overcome before green building starts to become the norm – this results in a carefully calculated trade-off. Early adoption of new technologies creates novelty and interest – but the price paid by early adopters is absorbing some of the 'learning curve' in terms of time and costs as part of their project. However, there is an alternative way to look at this dilemma. It has been shown consistently that the additional costs for a green building can be modest, or even result in a saving due to plant and equipment that is not installed. This goes hand in hand with savings over the lifetime of the building due to reduced operations and maintenance costs. With the competitive advantage that a green building affords your business as a result of increased custom, productivity and association of your brand with green ideals... ask yourself the question – can your business really afford not to build green? ☯

Coping in a post oil society

Any disruption to business function results in lost productivity, down time and consequently affects the bottom line. All the time an external influence disrupts your business, you are busy paying the wages whilst no profit is being made.

Integrating sustainability into business practise can be used to help mitigate against the threat of disasters. For example, for some sensitive business applications, an uninterruptible power supply is considered a must. Imagine a small business that is trading in a commodity whose price rapidly fluctuates – a power cut could isolate that business from the ability to buy and sell on the open market, preventing that business from responding to, for example, a fall in price of that commodity.

As an example, the hydrogen office, by storing excess renewable energy that has been produced on-site, has the ability to provide its own uninterruptible power supply, which allows business to carry on as usual even when the public grid may be suffering from a black out.

Businesses are becoming increasingly aware of the long-term impact of resource shortages and how escalating energy prices will affect their operations. Big logistics and transport companies, like TNT for example, are already starting to invest in electric trucks to counterbalance the impacts that soaring oil prices are having on their business.

Generating on-site energy is a way of giving a business a lasting measure of security against voatile energy markets impacting on the bottom line. Investing in energy conservation and renewables for your business now, protects against long term energy price rises and helps to ensure the continuity of your business.

References

1. The Digest was published by BERR. However, it should be noted that public administration also accounts for street lighting and civic electricity provision.

2. Heschong Mahone Group (1999). Skylighting and Retail Sales. An investigation into the relationship between daylight and human performance. Detailed Report for Pacific Gas and Electric Company. Fair Oaks, CA .

Sherwood Energy Village - a case study by Sally Hall

Sherwood Energy Village (SEV) is a unique development in the heart of Robin Hood country. SEV is the trading name of Sherwood Environmental Village Ltd, an organisation founded in 1996 when it purchased a former colliery site from British Coal. The organisation is an Industrial and Provident Society; a full trading company, with its profits ploughed back into the project. It now has a subsidiary consultancy company, SEV Solutions, which offers advice on setting up similar projects across the UK and abroad. The profits from this company go to SEV.

The SEV project is unique as it evolved from direct action by the local community who, back in the '90s, were concerned about the future of the two main industries (mining and hosiery) that provided the bulk of employment in the small village. A group of determined members of the community took the SEV project forward when the decision to close the colliery was made, and the group managed to do this with no direct involvement from any local authority or government agencies. The colliery site was purchased; 36 hectares (91 acres). The local people wanted jobs with good housing and leisure facilities.

From the outset the main aim was to create a mix of industry (38 acres), housing (11 acreas) and leisure/amenity space (42 acres). Strong eco-credentials, including energy efficiency, renewables and biodiversity were introduced into the proposals early on. SEV is now in year twelve of the regeneration of this former mining community, with the wider surrounding area also benefiting from the project. Unlike other similar regeneration projects that have failed, SEV's voluntary directors have worked hard to ensure the project has stayed true to its original aims and objectives and not merely been used by short term profiteers.

All buildings are constructed to a high environmental standard. The E-Centre, completed in 2006, is also the new headquarters for the SEV, which occupies the top floor. It is an unusual crescent-shaped building with green roofs, rainwater harvesting and renewables. Ground source heat pumps provide heating in the winter and cooling in the summer. There is also a full height winter garden acting as the 'lungs' of the building, capturing light, heat and passive ventilation. It includes 'transitional work points' for small businesses/self employed that need minimal office space and can benefit from the shared office facilities (photocopying, telephone services etc). Other industrial units and offices completed to date have been rented out to different businesses, which benefit greatly from the low energy builds.

Images courtesy of Sherwood Energy Village Ltd.

In addition to the commercial area, the 11 acres allocated to housing are being developed by the SEV. The building work commenced August 2006. A total of 196 dwellings are planned, ranging from single dwelling bungalows and apartments through to terraced, semi detached and detached houses. There are even 4 earth-sheltered houses proposed. All will be sold freehold and designed to achieve a minimum EcoHomes 'excellent' rating. SEV believes the challenge for Britain is to provide housing types that people want, and which perform well in environmental terms, including:

- reduced energy costs
- water efficiency
- well-built, architect-designed dwellings
- sense of space, community spirit
- safe, secure environment
- walking distance from shops and services
- a nice place to live, work and play, in which people can buy to occupy.

Much of the external works are now complete. Off-grid renewable powered lamp-posts illuminate the landscaped grounds. Water conservation and management is an important integral part of the village and it has the UK's largest application of engineered SUDs (sustainable urban drainage), with all surface water being managed on site. To help alleviate flooding, swales have been installed. The successful scheme adds to the biodiversity of the site, mitigates flooding and looks attractive. SUDs deals with surface water run off from the roads and other hard paved areas. The water gently permeates or evaporates creating green corridors through the site and stopping any risk of flash flooding.

The colliery tips are now restored and provide local amenity space with community woodlands, golf course, heathland habitats, lakes and nature trails. There is an arena of 6.46 hectares (16 acres) forming a natural amphitheatre, with mature trees bounding the area. The clay-lined swales have formed a wetlands area with the arena designated for the development of sporting and recreational pursuits.

Post occupancy evaluation

Here, **Isabel Carmona**, with help from Bill Bordass and Adrian Leaman, outlines a few techniques that were used for measuring the delivered achievements of a range of commercial buildings ...

If we claim that our buildings are green, ecological, sustainable, carbon neutral, or energy efficient, we need to ensure (more than ever!) that we know how well they perform once they are in use, and how closely this relates to our design intentions.

There continues to be a discrepancy between design input and outcome in the construction industry as whole. Examples of buildings that have been monitored, green or not, show that, normally, the results are not as good as the design expectations (Ni Riain et al, 2000; PROBE team, 1995-2002). But knowing what caused the problems and why can be a positive thing, if you learn and share your findings with others. The aim is to create virtuous circles of continuous improvement (Bordass et al 2001).

Buildings are active systems, with users and owners in constant interaction. Occupants just use the building features to suit their needs – and their behaviour may not accord with the design intentions – which may not be clear to them intuitively, and about which they may never have been told. We have to decide what we would like to know about our buildings in use and find out the best way of obtaining that information.

Collecting feedback

As part of a partners in innovation project, the Usable Buildings Trust (UBT) collected available feedback techniques into a multi-dimensional matrix. The matrix can be viewed by sector, the stage of development of the technique (e.g. is it new or well-established), and where to use in the life cycle of a building or a construction project[1]. The portfolio was expanded from ten general-purpose techniques, to include a number which are specific to a particular sector (e.g. schools).

Feedback collection techniques

Techniques currently fall into six main groups, as outlined below:

Facilitated discussions: where team members discuss and share their experiences in a positive non confrontational manner.

Packages of techniques: where more than one technique is used as a set to provide an all around POE assessment. PROBE (post-occupancy review of buildings and their engineering), for instance, includes a preliminary questionnaire, a building use studies' occupant survey, CIBSE TM22 energy assessment and reporting methodology, and sometimes, a building envelope pressure test to CIBSE TM23. This combination of soft and hard issues was used for the PROBE studies series, published in the Building Services Journal between 1995 and 2002[2].

Process improvement: where special arrangements improve the design and construction process, in particular to learn more from existing buildings and the experiences of the client, project and management teams, to facilitate a smooth transition between handover and occupation, and to improve performance in use.

Questionnaires and interviews: these include paper and web administered questionnaires, and one to one interviews. For example, the building use studies (BUS) occupant survey and benchmarking method covers 44 variables, including a self-assessment of health and productivity. Design quality Indicators (DQI) has 100 questions organised on three sections: functionality, build quality and impact.

Technical assessments: these methods help define how well design requirements match achieved outcomes with regards function and performance. For instance, medical architecture research unit (MARU) evaluation studies provides a range of techniques for health buildings.

Sustainability: these techniques look at the impact of the buildings in their surroundings. Of these, BREEAM stands amongst the best known in the UK, but at present it is mostly design-focused and provides an overall rating with little information on specific achievements. CIBSE TM22 focuses on energy use; it can be used to report design expectations, actual energy use and predicted savings from changes (see diagram).

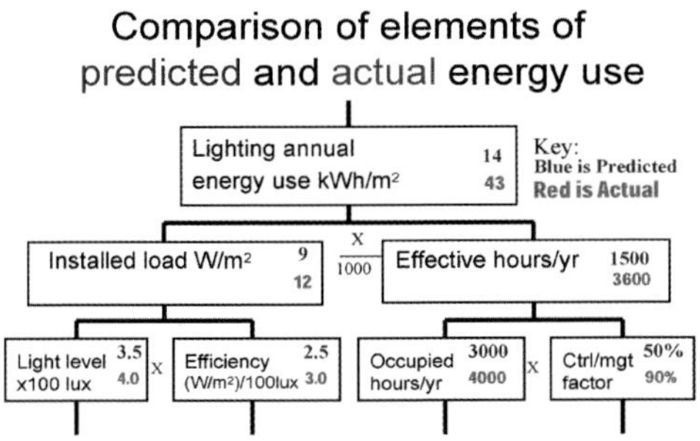

Comparison of elements of predicted and actual energy use

Flow chart comparisons of elements of predicted and actual energy use.

Type of buildings: The PROBE portfolio includes techniques suitable for defence, education, health, office, leisure, housing and other buildings. Some other techniques such as BREEAM, BUS occupant survey, CIBSE TM22 and 'learning from experience' are suitable for most building types. Others, like AMA Toolkit (offices and similar workspaces), NEAT (health), MARU (health), DEEP (defence), are suitable for specific building types.

A user group of designers and clients tested some of these techniques on case studies of their choice, in the course of a UK research project that ran between 2001 and 2004 (Bordass, Leaman, 2005).

What to test for?

We are getting used to claims that buildings (or whole developments) are green, energy efficient, or even carbon neutral. Those claims need to be substantiated by some independent assessment in order to prove their success. POE has shown that expectations tend to be more optimistic than the results.

There are often valid reasons for some of the differences, but they need to be understood if we are to produce better designs in the future, which take proper account of what really happens. As a minimum we suggest that you aim to go back and check two things.

1. Natural resource use (energy and water)

Energy use, where it is not provided by renewable sources, is the main source of CO_2 emissions. We suggest you collect data on a monthly basis and analyse usage on a yearly basis, keeping electricity separate from other fuels. Translate energy use into CO_2 emissions.

Benchmark your emissions against similar buildings, if data exists, or collect your own to compare your year on year progress. If you use renewable sources of energy, measure their contribution and establish how much you are reducing emissions. You can analyse the data further to know which uses are the greatest (e.g. lighting, office equipment, catering...).

More data on truly green buildings should encourage improvements beyond the current good practice standards, which sadly are often not reached. Useful techniques available include:

- National Energy Foundation CO_2 calculator[3]
- CIBSE TM22 energy assessment and reporting methodology.

Water is, increasingly, a scarce resource. Meter and monitor your water use, analyse what it is used for, and communicate results.

Benchmark your water use against similar buildings. Useful techniques available include the Envirowise water account tool[4].

2. Occupant satisfaction

To be successful, 'green' buildings must provide a comfortable environment for occupants. Sadly, this is not always so. Designers normally do not occupy the buildings they design, their clients or tenants do! The challenge is to make buildings easy to operate and live with, not over complicated, with effective controls (that give feedback of what they do!), and have sensible default conditions, which provide safe conditions with minimum energy use[5].

Occupant satisfaction is often considered a 'soft' issue, supposedly difficult to measure and quantify. However, there are well-established ways of recording and evaluating occupants' opinions and needs, such as questionnaire surveys, formal discussion groups and accompanied building visits and interviews.

As a minimum, return to the building once it has been occupied for a while, after all the initial tuning faults have been resolved, and have a frank discussion with the users. Match your methods to the building type – a bulky questionnaire might not be appropriate for a single dwelling. Record the responses to provide a reference if you decide to go back further down the line. Ideally, share your findings so that others may benefit from the lessons learnt.

Important questions are:

- are basic needs, like space and comfort requirements, being properly met?
- do people feel healthy?
- does the building affect productivity?
- what are the good features?
- what are the annoying features?
- what can be improved tomorrow?

Useful techniques available include the Building Use Studies (BUS) occupant survey (widely used in the UK and internationally, with benchmarks available).

Conclusion

POE studies provide lessons that we can learn from - some general, some specific[6]. For major effect, those lessons from case studies need to be communicated to a wide audience. Public exposure of green buildings will help promote their features, intelligent critiques will facilitate their acceptance and greater realism about their intended and achieved performance will improve future implementations.

References

1. You can access the UBT Feedback Portfolio at ***www.usablebuildings.co.uk/fp/index.html***

2. The full list of the 23 Probe studies is available from UBT's website: ***www.usablebuildings.co.uk*** *under PROBE.*

3. ***www.nef.org.uk/energyadvice/co2calculator.htm***

4. You can find information on monitoring and submit your data for benchmarking on Envirowise's website: ***www.envirowise.gov.uk/page.aspx?o=wateraccount***

5. Read more on usability in the Quick Intro section of UBT's website, see 1, above.

6. Building Research and Information, Vol. 29, No2, March-April 2001 gives a strategic review of POE.

Further reading

'Assessing building performance in use 5: conclusions and implications' by W Bordass, A Leaman and P Ruyssevelt (2001), Building Research and Information, 2001, vol 29, no 2, 144-157.

'Making feedback and post-occupancy evaluation routine 3: Case studies of the use of techniques in the feedback portfolio' by W Bordass, A Leaman, (2005), Building Research and Information, 2005, vol 33, no 4, 361-375.

'BRE's Environmental Building: Energy Performance in Use' by C Ni Riain, J Fisher, F MacKenzie, J Littler, (2000), CIBSE Conference papers.

'When Rivers Run Dry: Water: the defining crisis of the twenty-first century' (2006), Eden Project Books.

PROBE team, 1995-2002, Post-Occupancy Review of Buildings and their Engineering, PROBE 1- 23, Building Services Journal, 1995-2002.

'Closing the Loop: Benchmark for sustainable buildings' by S Roaf (2004) RIBA.

There is a further POE article on page 280 of Volume 2 of the Green Building Bible which investigates post occupancy evaluation for housing.

Sustainability appraisal

A number of tools are available for carrying out sustainability appraisal (SA) which can help guide businesses towards sustainability. We asked **Nick Gardner** to examine the use of one such tool - SPeAR.

There are a number of tools available in the marketplace today for assessing the sustainability of commercial buildings and their use. Perhaps the most frequently referenced in this book and elsewhere are those developed by the Building Research Establishment (BRE) whose Environmental Assessment Method (BREEAM), launched in 1990, was one of the first to attempt to standardise the assessment of a commercial building's environmental performance. Other tools include CEEQUAL (the civil engineering equivalent of BREEAM), NEAT (NHS environmental assessment tool), EARM-OAM (energy assessment and reporting method's office assessment method; which analyses the energy performance of a building) and SPeAR (sustainable project appraisal routine).

Use of such sustainability appraisals is currently, for the most part, voluntary. However, with an ever-increasing level of environmental awareness in the industry, coupled with growing public concern about their own impacts, sustainability appraisals/assessments for buildings are in growing demand. Particular standards are starting to be demanded by planning authorities and building procurers and these minimum standards are being pushed upwards.

The Housing Corporation, for example, now requires all new homes they fund to achieve an EcoHomes 'very good' rating at a minimum (over the last two years alone this has advanced from a requirement of 'pass' and then 'good'); English Partnerships requires a minimum BREEAM or Code for Sustainable Homes 'level 3' (Previously EcoHomes 'very good') rating for all developments on its land, and for millennium communities has set targets of 'Excellent'. What's more, in broader development terms, sustainability appraisal (SA) now forms an integral part of the statutory planning framework, under the Planning and Compulsory Purchase Act 2004[1] (see Building for a Future, Spring 04).

There is also a growing demand, emanating from the private sector, for sustainability appraisals as part of a business case. They provide a good way for a construction company or developer to show they are engaged with the sustainability agenda, and to set themselves apart from their competitors, both in tendering for projects and in selling buildings. In addition, today's consumer tends increasingly to think past standard economic reasoning when buying products, consciously incorporating environmental and social decisions, as can be witnessed in the Fairtrade movement and the growth in eco-labelling (e.g. Forest Stewardship Council for wood). A recent WWF report concluded that "Clear and open corporate disclosure that spans environmental, social and financial issues, and makes a public commitment to CSR through a published report, offers strong reputational benefits if done sincerely"[2].

In this article I do not propose to compare and contrast the various SA tools for the construction industry. Others have explored the key differences between some of these[3], and have argued that the range of tools reflects the difficulties of applying a standard methodology to an industry which is inherently varied. Instead, I use the example of one particular assessment to explore a range of lessons learnt for businesses and organisations considering using a sustainability assessment tool.

Sustainable project appraisal routine (SPeAR)

Launched in 2000, SPeAR was developed by Arup as a 'response to the challenge of moving sustainability from theory into practice'. It is based on the UK government's set of sustainability indicators (DETR 1999), and is organised under the four broad headings of environment, societal, economic and natural resources. This model allows for these 'fields' of sustainability to be illustrated graphically (see below) and to be treated equally; as such it is not simply an 'environmental appraisal'. The diagram is also useful for showing conflicts between indicators, particularly those in different 'fields'.

The graphical display of the results enables easy demonstration of negative as well as positive situations (moving towards the centre represents an increasingly sustainable position), but does not offer a 'pass/fail' mark, as it believes in working with organisations in a non-confrontational way. Indeed, Arup discusses sensible benchmarks to use with the client as a part of the process. This lack of a single scoring system sets it apart from other indicator-led approaches. Peter Braithwaite, director and head of environmental and sustainability services at Arup, explains: "Many organisations would like to improve the way they are doing things, but don't want an assessment system that tells them that their performance is 'poor'!".

Crucially, the SPeAR tool recognises that sustainability is not static: a sustainability assessment is inherently time limited, as regulations and fashions change, technologies develop and we achieve a growing understanding of sustainability. Organisations can request a regular review, and with it compa-

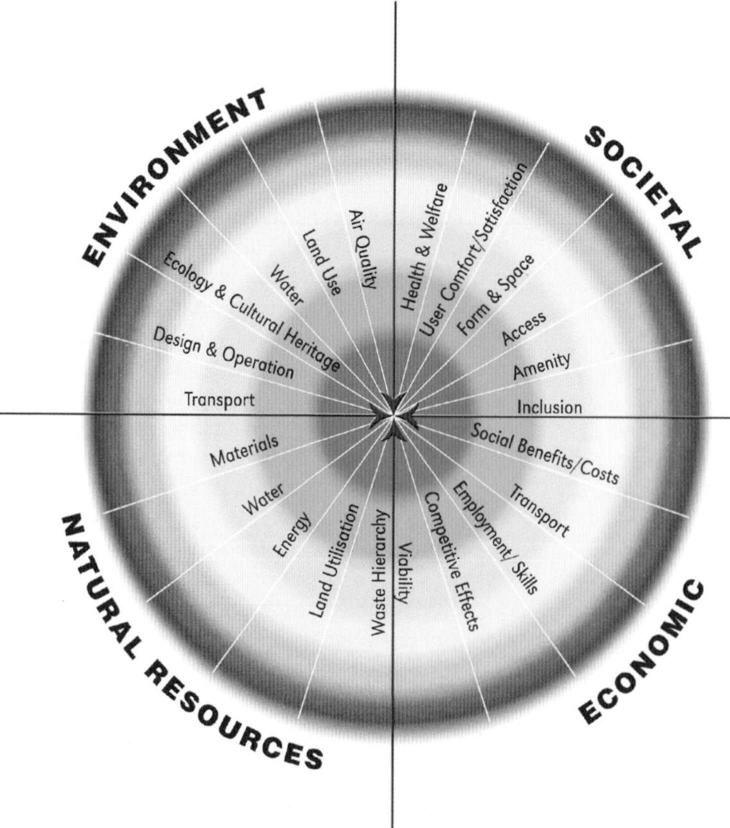

Arup based its SPeAR® tool on the UK government's set of sustainability indicators (DETR 1999), and is organised under the four broad headings indicated. This model allows for these 'fields' of sustainability to be illustrated graphically. Behind the diagram is a series of detailed worksheets, with over 120 sub-indicators.

Key aspects of SPeAR

As a tool, SPeAR demonstrates a number of facets which make it successful, and give it the potential to be transferred to a number of situations

External	An independent assessment, with impartial results.
Robust	Capable of being repeated annually.
Flexible	Ability to identify information of direct relevance to the organisation, allowing individually tailored, practical, recommendations for management.
Neutral	Not just an environmental assessment; SPeAR embraces the full gamut of sustainability. Each of the four fields is treated equally, and no single indicator has a preference over others. In providing an objective assessment of the baseline situation, all sides can accept the outcome. If the client wishes to attribute prominence to one factor over another, then they are able to.
Current	Keeps pace with best practice within the industry.
Simple	Graphical output, rather than a dry list of performance indicators or complicated matrix; supporting easy dissemination to a wide range of audiences and a clear set of suggestions on moving forward.
Useful	Provides managers with a management/assessment tool, without an onerous input of management time. The pragmatic approach to setting individualised, realistic targets for companies and organisations encourages organisations to take sustainability seriously.

rable diagrams as a visual check of progress from year to year. This enables an organisation to continue with their journey towards sustainability without themselves having to keep up with every latest development of policy, technology, etc. Performance and policies are measured against 'best practice' criteria, and to this end the tool is continually reviewed in the light of new standards, best practice and legislation. Updated on an annual basis, the tool can continue to push standards from the front. A client explains: "If we continue with the same practices in any one area, our position in that part of the diagram is likely to slip in next year's appraisal, as the rest of the industry moves forward".

One of the key benefits of the SPeAR tool is its flexibility. Originally a tool for assessing building design/structure, it has developed to cover projects, processes or products. SPeAR has now been used to assess regeneration schemes, economic and planning policies and strategies, manufacturing processes, and even products such as cars.

Case study - Kingspan Insulation plant

In 2004, the SPeAR tool was employed to provide a process-based application in order to evaluate the production process at Kingspan Insulation's Pembridge plant in Herefordshire[4]. The tool examined the manufacture of products, but also included, for example, how the company looks after its staff and the firm's relationship with the local community. This holistic approach to sustainability is an important next step for a firm which already promotes the environmental benefits of its products.

Peter Wilson, Managing Director of Kingspan, believes that specifiers will increasingly request details of economic and social sustainability statements, as well as environmental statements, from manufacturers of building products. Whilst reporting on aspects of sustainability is likely to be a requirement in the future, the company has proactively committed to year-on-year reports on social and environmental sustainability – as part of the SPeAR review – and intend to continue to make the results publicly available.

Key findings

As 2004 was the first year of assessment, the tool has produced a baseline for comparison with future assessments; the summary position is given in the diagram (below). The appraisal found that Kingspan is already meeting legislation or best practice in the majority of areas, and in some cases moving beyond best practice. However, several opportunities for further improvement were also highlighted – some of which were potentially 'quick wins', whilst others posed a challenge over a longer timescale.

Environment

The plant scored relatively well on ***design and operation***. "Although the new warehouse extensions on the site did not strictly use BREEAM criteria, Kingspan did use some aspects, e.g. reuse of demolition materials on site and rainwater soakaways. Buildings have in-built flexibility to extend life, especially the high-bay warehouse... and buildings have been refurbished rather than replaced wherever possible" (old aircraft hangers were re-clad for use as warehouses).

The maintenance and protection of ***water quality*** was most positively assessed. Additional soakaways have been provided, the site has a strong history of compliance with regulatory water quality requirements, and septic tanks and a reedbed are used for waste water in place of foul drainage. The least positive assessment was associated with ***transport***. The rural location of the site contributed significantly to a poor assessment: all freight traffic is by road as there is no other viable option, and there are few alternatives to the private car for employees (itself a barrier to recruitment). A lack of footways to the site limits opportunities to encourage cycling or

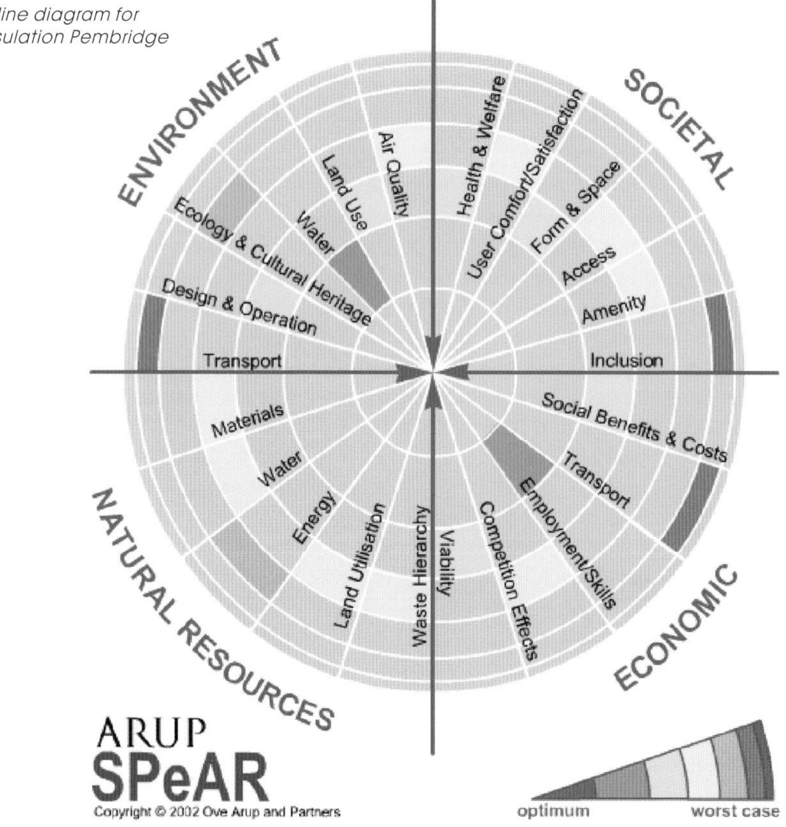

SPeAR baseline diagram for Kingspan Insulation Pembridge plant.

walking. However, short of moving location, it is unclear how this could be improved.

Societal

The plant scored relatively well on ***health and welfare***, with a low rate of absenteeism and hourly wages benchmarked against the area. With regard to ***access***, few facilities were found to be available locally although key facilities such as a canteen and company doctor are available on site. Free computer, literacy and language training is available at a nearby college for employees.

Despite regular noise monitoring (with no issue of statutory nuisance) and a traffic survey revealing that the site had no substantial impact on local roads, the plant did not perform well on ***amenity***. The report states that there was minimal green space on site, and that the design of the buildings was not appropriate for the surrounding farmland (although green cladding does help them blend in). The plant scored lowest on ***inclusion***, with a maximum of 0.1% of pre-tax profit allocated to community projects, limited reporting of environmental or

Kingspan are keen to emphasise that their plant blends into the surroundings even though it is in open countryside (above and below) and it was one aspect in which the Pembridge plant scored rather well. It also scored quite well as the site was previously industrial and therefore classed as brownfield.

social performance in the public domain and little consultation with the local community. In addition, the company had no policy on ethical trading or code of conduct or business principles, and there was no knowledge of company involvement in Agenda 21. The sustainability of the sources of certified timber was not audited (and some timber was not certificated).

Economic

The plant scored well on ***viability***; "At least 10% of CAPEX is allocated to investing in improving environmental performance and process changes tend to be driven by environmental considerations... Information about the impacts of manufacture and COSHH sheets are available to customers on request. The product has a long life cycle and is 'A' rated according to the green guide to specificiation. Although the product tends to be landfilled, Kingspan can advise the customer on alternative methods of disposal or on reuse". As a major employer for local people and high use of local contractors, the site also scores well on ***employment/skills*** and ***social benefits*** & ***costs***.

In this category again, ***transport*** is rated poorly. While public transport does exist, bus services are limited and employees largely depend on the car. There is no alternative to road haulage as the nearest rail station does not take freight.

Natural resources

Most of the components of this field had an average score. With regard to ***materials***, around 5% of raw materials are currently from recycled sources. Whilst life-cycle analysis has been utilised, this has not resulted in the 'greening' of the site's purchasing policy. Analysis of the ***waste hierarchy*** found that trials are being undertaken to reduce production waste. Factory seconds are sold on to recover costs, leaving only 1.5% of total production as waste. Minimum packaging materials are used on site and packaging waste is segregated for recycling. However, as waste disposal is subcontracted, Kingspan are not aware of the destination of all waste streams.

The lowest rating is for the site's ***energy use***. Whilst there is some specification of low energy consumption equipment, energy supply was from 100% non-renewable sources, as there was no direct payback from using a green energy supplier. On the other hand, the production process generates a lot of heat which is not currently utilised.

Response

Kingspan responded with an action plan on the basis of the assessment, outlining some quite significant proposed changes, described by Braithwaite as indicative of a "sea change in attitude". These include some 'quick win' solutions such as the recycling of all office paper, and changing the specification of plastic cups. However, the biggest changes six months after the report was published, have been ones of policy and attitude.

Plans for various studies have been set out, for example a feasibility study into the use of rain and grey-water and a full viability study for a biomass-fuelled CHP plant. Various policies have also been implemented as a result of the SPeAR process, including a corporate governance policy and a new green transport plan. Internal policies have also been developed stating that any further development work or major refurbishment will be subject to a BREEAM assessment, and that new vans purchased will run off LPG fuel. However, given the short timescale since these were introduced, they have not yet been implemented.

Braithwaite believes the most significant response so far has been "a real commitment (by Kingspan) not only to improve their own performance but also to positively influence their suppliers". The company came to the conclusion that it needed to improve on the performance of its product range against likely future legislation and regulation. In particular, the company is aware that it will have to look more closely at the 'embodied' environmental impacts of its products.

Peter Wilson is clear that, as Building Regulations progressively tighten the environmental impacts of buildings in use, "the construction industry will be forced to look at the environmental impacts of the materials from which buildings are constructed". Following the SPeAR report, a purchasing policy to include ethical trading, timber product certification and the use of local sourcing is being created. Kingspan are also requesting that their supply chain provide information on their environmental performance and detail how they intend to improve. John Garbutt, head of marketing at Kingspan, explains that they have already written to a number of their main suppliers, although "it is a hard job to get them to change!".

Conclusions

This article has highlighted some transferable lessons for businesses thinking about undergoing a sustainability appraisal (SA), as well as some useful aspects to consider when selecting a SA tool.

Undergoing a SA can make good sense for any business, particularly those in the construction sector. Taking a holistic view of sustainability, a SA can help with market differentiation on the one hand, and operational efficiency (and hence competitiveness) on the other. It could also suggest ways to achieve compliance with increasingly stringent building legislation concerning environmental and social issues[5]. Additionally, firms incorporating the recommendations from a SA could also encourage indirect benefits, such as higher staff retention and finding new ways to save money (both in the short and long term).

It is only really recently that sustainability has been seen as a mainstream business issue, rather than an add-on. Arup's Peter Braithwaite thinks that perhaps the SPeAR product was even launched too soon, "The market was not really ready; it is really only recently that clients' views have been changing, and there is more acceptance now that this kind of process is necessary".

From Arup's point of view, several factors enable a smooth appraisal process. These include: forward-thinking individuals within a company/organisation who are willing to take a proactive view on 'what if' scenarios a number of years into the future; a good level of 'buy-in' from the management team; and openness and honesty throughout the assessment process. In Kingspan's case, there was a rapid take-up of the issues raised in the report, including the production of an Action Plan. This was not considered by the company as another burden, rather as a tool to help drive the company forward.

So, which sectors have shown the most interest in SA to date? Evidence from demand for the SPeAR tool suggests that first-tier suppliers were interested from an early stage, mostly from larger organisations, and – at the other end of the construction spectrum – appraisals have been carried out of planning policies and masterplans. At the moment however, there does not appear to be much interest in the middle. Once contractors value this process, it is likely to "cascade down the supply chain", as has happened in the automotive industry with environmental management systems. However, the SA process will fail to reach its full potential in driving forward sustainability in the construction industry if gaps in uptake persist.

Arup and SPeAR : **http://www.arup.com/environment**

References

1. ***http://www.odpm.gov.uk/stellent/groups/odpm_planning/documents/downloadable/odpm_plan_034816.pdf*** *(paras 8 and 9).*

2. 'Building Towards Sustainability: Performance and Progress Among the UK's Leading Housebuilders', WWF, January 2004.

3. 'Selecting the right (sustainability) tool for the job', Christopher Harris and Mike Priaulx in 'eg magazine', May 2003.

4. The report of the first year's (baseline) assessment was produced in October 2004, and is available from info.uk@insulation.kingspan.com .

5. 'With fiscal incentives such as the Landfill Tax and Climate Change Levy increasing, there are substantial cost savings to be made' (WWF, see ref. 2 above).

Note

Kingspan also subjected its insulation products to the BRE's Environmental Profile scrutiny, see:
http://cig.bre.co.uk/envprofiles

Eco-renovation

Before looking in detail at renovation strategies it may be helpful to consider the market for new and renovated commercial buildings and the context in which decisions are made. **Adrian Birch** explores the concept...

The last 30 years has seen the ongoing decline of manufacturing and a move to service industries, with the workforce becoming more office-bound. Coupled with this has been the IT revolution, the desktop computer at every workspace, and the consequential development of the out of town business park near to motorway connections. The growth of car ownership, lack of investment in infrastructure and public transport and inner-city congestion has fuelled this migration of offices from the traditional business districts to the suburbs. This has left a residue of unloved crumbling concrete monuments to the first post-war office boom becoming hard-to-let and neglected, and thus offering potential for those developers and others, with the requisite nerve and funds, to renovate or redevelop.Because of the buoyancy of the housing market many obsolescent city-centre office buildings have often been converted to residential use, student accommodation or budget hotel use. Local authorities have generally welcomed this, as it can serve to revitalise city centres, which in turn increases demand for leisure and other facilities, gyms, restaurants etc.

Many industrial estates, established in the post–war period, are in inner city and inner suburban areas. Most buildings are of steel or concrete portal-frame construction and many are clad with asbestos cement or steel profiled sheet claddings, with minimal insulation. There was little provision made for offices, car parks and landscaping and many estates are looking run-down by comparison with more recent developments nearer to motorway junctions. Industrial buildings are less reliant on location than offices but easy access to the motorway network and to the available labour force is desirable. Inner city industrial sites may be incompatible with the residential use surrounding them. Because industrial buildings were often constructed as short-life buildings, there is less incentive to renovate them, and redevelopment may be more attractive. Planners have to strike a balance between retaining manufacturing employment and improvement of the environment.

The participants

The commercial property market in the UK is one of the most sophisticated in the developed world, with battalions of pinstripe-suited property professionals offering a wide range of property investment advice to the unwary, for a fee. Commercial and industrial property, more than any other, is treated as a commodity to be traded in a market where the property agent sets the ground rules.

Major commercial and industrial developments are normally owned by pension funds and other financial institutions, which expect property they invest in to meet certain 'institutionally-acceptable' criteria. These organisations are generally risk-averse and will normally only purchase a completed development from a developer when it is fully-tenanted and is providing a regular flow of income in the form of rents and service charges. The 'risk' is taken by the property development companies who purchase sites for redevelopment in locations they think will maximise their returns in the relatively short term. They will normally manage the development process from inception through to the final sale to the financial institution, and may engage external project managers, architects, surveyors and engineers to provide advice and to share the design risk.

The commercial and industrial agent is the professional go-between providing market sector advice to developers and investors and procuring tenants for projected or completed developments. Developers will try and manage their risk by ensuring that a suitable tenant or tenants are signed up in a 'pre-let', and that the pension fund or other institution is willing to take on the completed development, before the developer commits funds to the development. In order to appeal to the widest range of tenants, the property has to be 'lettable'. Most office agents will say that for the building to be lettable it needs to be sufficiently flexible to accommodate different space-plan configurations, and air-conditioned to accommodate variable occupational densities. They can also charge a higher rent if the building is air-conditioned, as this 'adds value' in their terms. This of course 'adds value' to their fees, which are based on the rent achieved. They don't add that air-conditioning adds significantly to operating and maintenance costs, as well as consuming substantial amounts of electricity, and if poorly maintained can lead to humidifier fever and other respiratory infections, such as legionella.

Tenants will normally base their property decisions on a number of different criteria, with location, parking provision and space flexibility being high on their list. Operating and maintenance costs are of less consequence, as they will argue that these form a minimal part of their overhead, maybe as little as 5%, and any reduction will have minimal effect on the bottom line. It is perhaps not surprising, therefore, that there is little incentive for tenants to save energy, and property agents will argue that the market is tenant-driven. The government has set an ambitious energy-reduction target and has introduced the Climate Change Levy in an attempt to raise awareness of the issues by hitting the bottom line. Responses to this have been mixed. Forthcoming EC legislation will require commercial buildings offered for sale or lease to have an 'energy label' to inform prospective tenants of the building's energy consumption, in an attempt to encourage developers and agents to improve energy efficiency.

Approaching the renovation

For environmental design an holistic approach is essential, whether for a new-build or renovation. The external fabric of the building acts as a climatic filter, allowing light, air and solar gain in, and allowing polluted air out. Openings, such as windows and vents, provide fine control of the airflow. When assessing an existing building, various strategies need to be considered both individually and collectively in order to reach an optimum environmental solution. This then, has to be tested alongside other criteria such as initial and lifecycle costs, time, buildability, risk etc.

BRE's sustainable refurbishment/redevelopment decision support tool, Office Scorer, enables users to systematically compare and test the environmental and economic impacts of different office design concepts, using BRE's Ecopoints system: ***http://projects.bre.co.uk/envdiv/sustainable_refurb***

'Low Carbon Refurbishment of Buildings; a guide to achieving carbon savings from refurbishment of non-domestic buildings.' Conventional refurbishment projects often lead to unnecessary increases in energy use. This interesting report from the Carbon Trust is aimed at those who wish to ensure a planned refurbishment delivers carbon savings. ***www.carbontrust.co.uk/publications (ref: CTV038)***

7 Outdoors

Sustainable garden design

Whatever the size of your outdoor space, there is much you can do to help save energy, conserve water and encourage wildlife and biodiversity. **Louise Zass-Bangham** introduces us to some sustainable garden and landscaping ideas ...

The outdoor environment that surrounds our buildings is a vital part of our eco-system. It is our direct link to the natural environment, a place where you can relax and enjoy nature. There are many ways to reduce environmental impact by using sustainable materials and avoiding chemicals. This will ensure that your efforts to create a green building are not undone the minute you step outside the door.

Shelter from weather extremes

A combination of shelterbelts, shade trees/ shrubs, foundation planting and climbers can modify the micro-climate around your home and even help reduce the heating needs of a house. A shelterbelt or windbreak is made up of rows of trees, planted to deflect wind. A mixture of evergreen and deciduous gives fast growth, winter protection and longevity. A row of shrubs

Is your house exposed to the weather or sheltered by planting?

on the windward side filters wind at ground level, where trunks are often bare. A shelterbelt needs to be much longer than it is high because otherwise wind deflects around it and actually increases wind speed in places. In a small urban garden, filtering the wind with a mixture of smaller deciduous trees and large shrubs will be a more realistic option than a complete shelterbelt. Careful positioning of the plants will balance the need for shelter, sunshine and root space. Remember that if you try to block wind completely with a solid fence or wall, it creates intense eddies on both sides of the fence.

Planting evergreen trees/shrubs around a house can also help reduce energy costs. Foundation planting filters wind nearer the building and creates a dead airspace between shrubs and the building. When the shrubs are mature there should be a 30cm gap between them and the structure. Refer to page 421 regarding planting trees near buildings.

Climbing plants, providing support where necessary and choosing species carefully so the building fabric is not damaged, can act as an additional layer of insulation, trapping a thin layer of air against the building. The soil layer in a green roof (decribed in more detail in Chapter 4), will also provide thermal insulation in winter.

Cooling the house in summer

To help reduce problems associated with overheating in summer, deciduous trees can block 60-90% of the sun. Bare winter branches will still block around 30-50% of sunlight so there has to be careful planting to avoid shading solar collectors. A pergola, arbour or awning-frame alongside the house, clothed with a deciduous climber, gives shade to the building and windows during the summer, while allowing more sun through in winter months.

Air is also cooled by transpiration from the plant's leaves - like sweating - so plenty of plants will create a cooler summer garden. Climbers and green roofs will take heat out of the air right by the building, whilst providing shade.

Hard paving if left un-pointed will become colonised by species such as black medick, hawkweed and clover, providing sources of nectar for bees and other insects.

Hard landscaping materials

Hard landscaping means all the built garden structures, e.g. paving, paths, fencing, shed, and pergola. In a new garden, install these first. It's really tempting to plant immediately but restrain yourself until the basic structure of your garden is ready, as the plants may not

Top 10 sustainable garden tips

Ten, at a glance tips for caring for your garden and the wildlife that lives in it and the wider environment. Further information relating to all of the tips can be found throughout this chapter.

1. Plan a new garden to scale before you buy anything
2. Use the garden to help conserve heat and reduce overheating in the house.
3. Choose sustainable and preferably local or recycled/reclaimed materials.
4. Look after your top-soil during building works.
5. Avoid using any chemicals, use natural controls instead.
6. Plant for your local climate conditions and soil type.
7. Take every opportunity to save water and use it wisely.
8. Mulch.
9. Encourage bio-diversity with your planting choices.
10. Start a compost heap.

survive being trampled during construction.

Environmentally friendly surfaces

Firstly, consider minimising hard surfaces - for several reasons. If an area is paved then it isn't growing plants, so it isn't cleaning the air or supporting wildlife. Rainwater runs off down the drain rather than gradually returning to the water table through the soil. Sustainable drainage systems (SUDS), which are discussed in detail later in this chapter, are an essential part of our contribution to the environment and ensure our access to clean drinking water.

Some areas of hard surface are usually needed for easy access to the house and garden. There are a number of different options, which reduce environmental impact. These include reclaimed paving and brick stocks, which are widely available via paving and architectural salvage merchants. Don't use stone obtained from the natural rock formations known as limestone pavements. Such areas are scarce and declining habitats that support a unique range of flora and fauna.

Cement is frequently used in laying paving and can be substituted with lime mortar. Paving can be laid so that it is permeable, by using sand in the joints and bedding it down in a very weak mortar. Make sure water that runs off will go into a flowerbed or soak away, rather than to the drains.

If you really want new stone, despite the environmental consequences of extraction, at least choose local stone that has not been transported around the world to reach you. Stone from overseas may seem cheap but ask yourself why - the environmental and human costs are often hidden. Investigations into quarrying practices in developing countries have uncovered child labour, bonded (slave) labour and a scant regard for workers' health and safety.

A loose surface, such as gravel, has the advantage that it can become a diverse wildlife

Dry stone walls are great for attracting beneficial invertebrates, lizards and newts.

habitat if planted into. If you have off-street parking, you can plant low-growing plants between the tyre tracks and to the sides. The plants will be kept in check automatically by occasionally being driven over. However, bear in mind that gravel is extracted from land or sea. Millions of tonnes are effectively strip-mined from the seabed, destroying marine life in the process. The UK even exports 30% of its marine aggregate production to other European countries. More sustainable alternatives to gravel include recycled glass chips. These are available in a more natural look as well as a range of colours. Some companies now sell recycled gravel, if you look hard enough. Also consider organic materials, such as bark chips or shells - which are more sustainable and a waste by-product.

Outdoor structures

Reclaimed materials are gaining in popularity for garden structures and can be integrated if chosen carefully. If you need a solid wall, consider reclaimed bricks and lime mortar. It is possible to do away with mortar altogether and build a dry stone wall, an excellent habitat for insects and other wild creatures. However, there is the issue of sourcing the stone for the wall as this has got to come from somewhere, unless it is reclaimed too. Alternative sustainable building techniques would be equally suitable for use in the garden – from rammed earth to cob. If you want an individual and obviously recycled look, old tyres or other discarded items can be used as experimental bed edgings. Mesh gabions filled with old terracotta or other materials are also popular choices at the moment.

Homegrown cedar is now easily available. It tends to be paler than the imported cedar but very nearly as durable. Most of the imported cedar is still harvested from old growth forests and is therefore not a sustainable option.

Recycled aggregate tends to be more colourful than virgin stone aggregate and is just as durable.

Timber is a great material to use in the garden, providing it is certified sustainable and preferably locally sourced. Destruction of the world's rainforests is sadly a continuing problem, devastating local habitats and the global environment. Always check that timber is from a well-managed, sustainable source - look for the trademark of the Forest Stewardship Council (FSC) or the Programme for the Endorsement of Forest Certification (PEFC) and choose wood that is certified by these bodies. This includes bark chips too.

Oak and sweet chestnut should not need treatment and will age to a beautiful silver. If you do want to preserve the original colour, however, you will need to put on some sort of coating. Linseed oil can make oak go black so do test samples to ensure you will be happy with the finished result. Be sure to only use natural finishes that are harmless to humans and wildlife.

Other hardwoods are available, but mainly imported. One popular choice is western red cedar (a durable softwood) but whilst it is possible to obtain some local supplies, most is imported. Timber structures that will be bearing a lot of weight and are in contact with the ground, such as fencing or a pergola, should have an appropriate footing that keeps them off damp soil.

Coppicing is still practiced in a few managed woods in the UK, usually for sweet chestnut, hazel and willow. This is highly sustainable because the trees are not felled but instead rods or poles are cut off at the base. The tree re-grows new stems, which can be coppiced a few years later. Coppiced hazel and willow rods are used to make wattle hurdles, a very traditional form of fencing. Sweet chestnut poles are used for a wide range of garden features, including fences, arches and arbours.

Be aware that timber and fencing materials for outdoor use may already have been treated with preservative (pressure treated) but not labelled, so you should always ask for details. If you do decide to buy treated timber, make sure the chemicals used are non-hazardous.

Reclaimed wood, including oak and other hardwoods, is available from architectural salvage specialists. Old railway sleepers are banned because of the creosote content. If you see wood for sale advertised as railway sleepers, ask for more information because it probably isn't recycled. You can always ask for sustainably sourced wood to be supplied to the same chunky dimensions.

Care during building work

Topsoil is the upper layer of soil, where most soil-life and nutrients are found. It is usually 15-60cm deep and darker in colour than the stony sub-soil underneath. If the topsoil becomes

Sustainable gardens are not new. Here is a living willow fedge, low hurdles, shady pergola and a permeable surface in a restored Medieval garden.

heavily compacted - by machinery, building materials or heavy boots - plants struggle to grow. Contamination with building products and construction waste needs to be avoided too. Trees are particularly vulnerable around the root collar at the base of the trunk: an inch or two of extra soil built up around it can be all it takes to let in infection. It will take up to 7 years for damage caused during building work to finally kill a tree, so it is difficult to diagnose or remedy later. Damage to roots must therefore be avoided, to give trees and shrubs the best chance of survival.

During any construction works remember:

- make clear paths to prevent the whole site being trampled
- fence-off whole areas or individual trees
- lay boards or a very thick mulch to spread the weight of heavy machinery
- don't mix-up turf, topsoil and sub soil - make separate heaps and cover them
- keep soil heaps to a maximum of 1-2m high to avoid compaction
- never move or work soil when it is wet
- don't move extra soil onto the area under a tree canopy
- avoid digging a trench through tree roots - dig a tunnel or work by hand around tree roots.

Hedges and fedges (living fences)

Even more sustainable than wood that has been harvested, is wood that is living. A good old-fashioned hedge absorbs carbon dioxide, helps recycle your compost, filters the wind and could outlast your house. A mixed hedge is excellent for providing food and shelter for wildlife. Some of the most effective intruder- and livestock-proof boundaries include spiky firethorn or blackthorn, but consider how you will tackle them yourself if they need trimming.

A fedge, or living fence, is commonly made of willow rods or whips (see left). These are traditionally woven or tied into open diamond patterns, in a technique that has been used for centuries. Many different willow species are available for different uses, several with brightly coloured stems. A fedge is easily trimmed each year, like a hedge. The main advantage is that a willow fedge takes up much less room than a hedge, being about as slim as an average fence. The principles of weaving living willow can be applied to garden structures too, such as arches, arbours, a summerhouse, seating or sculpture - there is plenty of scope to be imaginative. Turf banks also have good design potential, but are more time consuming to maintain.

Ecological planting

This is not about bio-diversity or saving plants; this is about growing plants that are in tune with your local environment or ecology. You wouldn't expect a penguin to survive in the desert or a camel to enjoy the South Pole. Plants are equally adapted to their native climate. If you get the planting right, once garden plants are established, you shouldn't have to water them. This is particularly important now we are seeing many areas of the UK hit by drought and hosepipe bans.

Many of the plants available to buy today are descendents of plants brought back to this country by the Victorian plant hunters from expeditions overseas. Certain species have become popular over the years - particularly those that continue to be used in the showy annual bedding schemes that the Victorians so adored. The wild parents of many garden plants come from habitats as diverse as tropical rainforests and mountain ranges. We have been conditioned to believe that we need to water our gardens constantly, raise plants from seed in heated greenhouses and buy special growing mediums. However, if we focus on plants that suit our climate and our soil type, our garden will be naturally low-maintenance, with strong, healthy plants that can fend for themselves.

Such plants are usually our native species, or ones that originated in a climate similar to ours. If your soil is sandy and free-draining, plant things that like it dry. If the soil is naturally boggy, grow things that love the wet. Whatever your situation - chalky soil or heavy clay, salt spray or blazing sunshine - there are beautiful plants adapted to cope. Find out what your soil conditions are. Do a really simple pH test (available from your garden centre) and find out the sunny areas of your garden. You can then choose from a wide range of beautiful plants that will thrive in your garden. Remember though that hybrid species do not tend to be so rich in nectar so are not as desirable to insects.

Using water wisely

New plants will all benefit from some watering during their first year. This is because a pot has restricted their root systems. They need time to reach out to obtain the best water supplies. If you are going to water, do it thoroughly. Water sprayed lightly around the plant encourages the roots to come to the surface, exactly where you don't want them to be. Water should be directed at the base of the plant to reach the roots easily, not splashed around the foliage. Make sure the plant receives a thorough soaking once a week for the first few weeks, and that should be enough. Try to always water in the early morning or evening. Don't water in hot midday sun because most of what you apply will soon evaporate or little droplets of water will act like magnifying glasses, scorching the leaves.

Keeping water in the soil

Mulching is essential to retain moisture. A thick mulch layer, 5-7 cm deep, is one of the best methods of water conservation. The most sustainable materials to use are organic, such as cocoa shells, bark chips, well-rotted stable manure, compost or grass clippings. Mulch after heavy rain or thorough watering. The mulch also keeps weeds down, reducing competition for water. Avoid mulching right up to plant stems, so rot is not encouraged. When planting, mix a handful or two of compost or other well-rotted organic material into the planting hole. This will help the soil hold moisture around the roots, assisting with nutrient uptake and improving soil structure.

Avoid planting too close to the base of walls or fences, in the rain shadow. Plant climbers about 40cm away from the wall, tilting the stems back in. A shelterbelt helps prevents soil evaporation and protects plants from the drying effects of the wind.

If you must water...

In an ideal world, you've planted a garden full of things that do not need watering, and it's all got a nice deep mulch. However, there may still be times you might need to water, such as helping to establish new planting or a thirsty food crop. Consider using wastewater from other household uses. For more information on this please refer to the rain harvesting section that follows this article.

You could also install water butts, an economical option for storing rainwater for garden use. Some local authorities can offer special deals on water butts so contact your local council for details. Water butts fill very quickly when attached to the down-pipe from the main roof, or even just from a shed or greenhouse roof. Always ensure water butts have tight fitting lids. Remember young children can easily drown in exposed water - so can birds and other creatures.

Improving the soil generally

One of the most sustainable things you can do is to start a compost heap for your kitchen and garden waste. Add compost to the soil when planting, or use it as mulch. Urine is an excellent activator when added to compost heaps. For more information on this subject most good gardening books and websites will cover composting. Many local authorities can provide compost bins at much reduced prices so contact your local council to see if you are eligible for any such offers.

The use of peat in your garden is unnecessary. The Royal Horticultural Society (RHS) considers the use of peat to be unacceptable for soil incorporation and mulching. Peatlands are an important carbon sink - removal of this sink exacerbates climate change. The UK's peatlands are globally important and the effects of extraction are irreparable. Due to increasing government restrictions on peat extraction, the majority of peat used in the UK is imported, simply shifting the problem to countries with weaker legislation.

Prior to the 1960s gardeners used soil conditioners from a whole range of sources. Sadly, despite long-running media coverage of peat bog destruction, peat products remain on sale. If you don't make your own compost, choose local, non-peat-based products, such as well-rotted stable manure – available at most garden centres. Check labels carefully before buying.

Biodiversity

There are many reasons for supporting diversity of plant and animal species. Man has yet to understand a fraction of the relationships that make our eco-system work. There are things that nature could provide for us that are currently undiscovered so it's important to help a wide variety of species survive – remember that the raw material for aspirin was discovered in willow bark and new drugs continue to be found in plant material. Try to support your local wildlife, even if in a small way. There are hundreds of beautiful native plants that make great garden plants.

Some garden-escapees (alien species) have caused big problems in the countryside, such as Japanese knotweed and Indian balsam. Such plants provide little value to native wildlife and can quickly colonise vast areas, crowding out beneficial native species. However, other non-natives, such as buddleia much favoured by many of our butterfly species, are suitable to include in your planting. Many common plants arrived here relatively recently – for example sycamore and horse chestnut – so check what is actually native to your area. The Natural History Museum website will give you a long list appropriate to your postcode, covering everything from annuals and perennials to shrubs and trees.

If you are going to be developing land consider a wildlife survey before building work starts. Your local wildlife trust should be able to offer advice on this. This will reveal any rare species and enable you to take appropriate action if there are any species of interest.

With grateful thanks to Sally Hall for providing some of the text and pictures for this article.

Further information

Sustainable Housing Design Guide for Scotland: ***www.archive2.official-documents.co.uk/document/deps/cs/shdg/index.html***

Planting for shelter and shade, University of Minnesota: ***www.sustland.umn.edu/design/index.html***

Preventing construction damage to trees, University of Missouri: ***http://muextension.missouri.edu/xplor/agguides/hort/g06885.htm***

Conserving water in the garden, Thames Water & Gardening Which?: ***http://news.bbc.co.uk/1/hi/world/2945018.stm***

Encouraging wildlife - English Nature: ***www.english-nature.org.uk/Nature_In_The_Garden***

Natural History Museum: ***www.nhm.ac.uk/nature-online/life/plants-fungi/postcode-plants/index.html***

Royal Horticultural Society: ***www.rhs.org.uk***

The general website for the UK wildlife trusts: ***www.wildlifetrusts.org***

For an international directory of UK suppliers of architectural salvage, including used timber, bricks, stone and cast iron: ***www.salvo.co.uk***

'Peat and the Gardener', Royal Horticultural Society Conservation & Environment Guidelines: ***www.rhs.org.uk/Learning/research/documents/c_and_e_peat.pdf***

'Briefing: Lowland Raised Bog', Friends of the Earth: ***www.foe.co.uk/resource/briefings/lowland_raised_bog.html***

'Peat Alert!', Do or Die Issue 10, Eco-action, 2003: ***www.eco-action.org/dod/no10/peat.htm***

The Ethical Trading Initiative is an alliance of retailers, NGOs and others working collectively to tackle ethical issues: ***www.ethicaltrade.org***

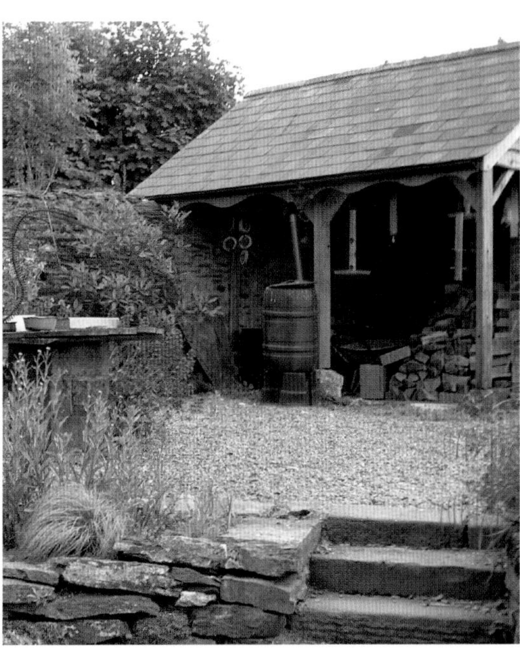

Rainwater harvesting

Forget the rising cost of mains water. Collecting rainwater from our own roofs may soon be the only way of ensuring an adequate water supply for our buildings during a drought. **Keith Hall** explains how the systems work.

It is likely that rainfall patterns will continue to fluctuate and most predictions suggest we will need to get used to short sharp bursts of rain which will cause more flooding and soil erosion than we have been accustomed to in the past. Such rainfall patterns do little to top up the underground aquifers that most of us currently rely upon. Add to this the fact that household water consumption is increasing per capita and, as the climate warms, natural evapo-transpiration will increase, so we will have to find ways to reduce, retain and even reuse water.

Firstly we should look to reduce the amount of water we use. This we can do by installing water efficient appliances; air entraining taps, shower heads and low flush toilets should be installed. Alternatively install water reduction devices[1]. Next we should find alternatives to the high quality drinking water that we use for low grade uses, such as toilet flushing and watering the garden. There is no longer any justification in cleaning and purifying water to 'drinking' standards when most of it is used where lower quality would suffice.

Water should also be 'kept in play' for as long as possible; in other words, not flushed down the drain so quickly but retained for reuse (if it is not too dirty) wherever possible. Water from bathing and washing (commonly referred to as greywater) can be collected and essentially

Jo Burt

reused for toilet flushing or car cleaning etc.

As water becomes more scarce we will all learn to improvise, but we should start to think ahead now. We are all used to the idea of water butts in the garden, but at a more serious level, underground water storage tanks can be installed as part of a rainwater harvesting system which collects rainwater, usually from the roofs of the buildings. The advantages of rainwater collection and storage are twofold - not only will the system collect and store rainwater for reuse, but, if enough systems were to be installed, it will also assist in preventing flash flooding of rivers and streams.

If flooding is a problem in your region then a sustainable urban drainage systems (SUDs) might also be appropriate, and on new developments may even be required as a condition of planning permission. These can also be used as giant reservoirs below car parks or grass verges on larger developments or housing estates. SUDs can include features such as swales (shallow, wide ditches channelling surface water overland from the drained area to a storage discharge) and basins (designed to hold back storm runoff, reducing peak flows to rivers and reducing flood risk). Existing or new ponds can also be designed to accommodate peak variations in water levels to provide flood-storage capacity, but a risk analysis should be carried out by qualified ecologists before natural, established ponds are filled with water run-off from roofs and roads.

At the present level of water rates (metered), the pay back time on a full domestic rain harvesting system is typically 10-20 years. For commercial properties with high water consumption needs and large roofs, the pay back can be very much shorter, sometimes only months. The benefits however, are much greater than just financial. The environmental aspect of capturing and retaining water provides some security against water shortages and saves energy in the movement of water to and from the water treatment works. It should also be remembered that because water is becoming a highly precious commodity, with demand beginning to outstrip supply, water authorities are now seeking permission from the government to apply considerable price increases. As this continues the pay back period will become shorter.

The principles of rainharvesting

Note: the numbers in brackets refer to diagram on page 402.

The principles of collecting and storing rainwater are fairly simple and easy to follow. The water must be stored in the dark below 18°C, then the system will supply clean, perfectly usable water for most purposes other than drinking. The water is collected by normal roof gutters and is directed to the rainwater filter (1) where the water is separated from leaves and other debris at the bottom of the rainwater downpipes. As much debris as possible must be removed from the water before storage, as any decaying material in the tank will consume oxygen (from microbial action) that is in the water. The result would be smelly, putrid water - the stored water must be oxygen rich.

The filtered water is then transferred to the storage tank via a water smoothing inlet (2) so as not to disturb the sediments on the bottom. The filter will have screened out all but the smallest of particles. The choice of mesh size of the pre-filter system has to be a compromise between maintenance intervals and water quality. The finer the filter screen, the more regularly it will have to be cleaned, if the collecting efficiency is to be maintained, because the filter is so designed that water which cannot pass through it is sent off down the normal stormwater sewer.

The floating particles will be organic material such as pollens, which must be flushed out as, if they were left in, they would cause the water to become stagnant. This is done by designing the tank overflow so it has a skimming effect on the surface of the water when it overflows. The system should be sized to overflow quite regularly but at least twice a year, and in doing so it keeps itself clean. The heavy particles that sink to the bottom of the tank (usually sand or grit in nature) accumulate at about 1-2mm/yr, a negligible amount - 50 years will result in 50-100mm. The overflow pipe to a soakaway will help recharge underground aquifers, or the system may be connected to the main's storm water system. If the latter, then an anti-vermin trap and an anti-backflow device need to be included if there is any risk of flooding and backing up.

The water thus stored can be delivered anywhere in the property on demand, using a submersible pump (3). The pump will be drawing water via a floating filter (4), ensuring the water is taken from just below the surface which will be the cleanest water in the tank. The pump is controlled by the flow control/pressure switch (5). The pump supplies the building directly on demand. This gives enough pressure and flow rate to feed commonly encountered appliances, including washing machines and garden hoses. Mains water is also connected to the underground storage tank via a solenoid, which includes a WRC statutory air gap to ensure that the rainwater in the tank cannot back up into the mains water system (6a and 6b). This connection will supply any small amounts of top-up from the mains to fulfil the requirement until the next rainfall replenishes the system.

The rainwater tank should never be allowed to become empty as this would have a detrimental effect on beneficial bacteria that have established in the tank, which will be keeping the water clean. Dry running protection for the pump should be built into the control system in case the water runs out and then an emergency switchover mechanism will revert to using mains

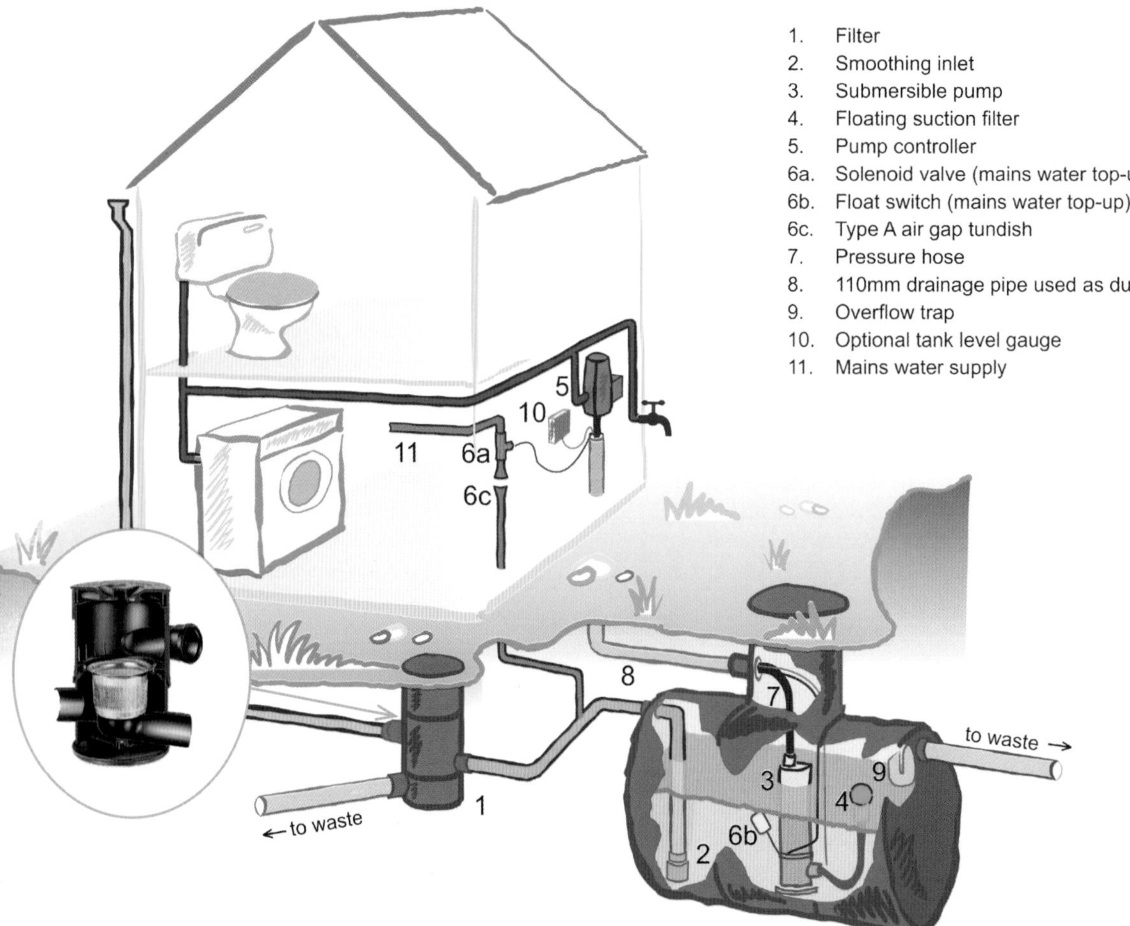

water. Further incoming rainwater brings oxygen with it, keeping the system working. Simple monitoring equipment and system overrides can be conveniently located in a utility room or workshop (10).

The water collected has many uses, without any need for further treatment. It will be particle free, so uses that do not involve human consumption or skin contact, such as toilet flush, garden irrigation, and washing machine use, are ideal. If a wider range of uses are required, such as drinking or bathing, or the application is more sensitive, such as a hospital, then a risk assessment should be carried out to assess what further purification might be required. Further particle filtration, pH correction and UV sterilisation can be employed in such circumstances. This extra filtration/treatment costs more and uses more energy, so an evaluation of operational cost/benefit, also needs to be undertaken.

A well designed system will need no maintenance other than cleaning the rainwater collector filter four to six times a year; about 10 minutes work each time. Systems with extra particle and UV sterilisation will require maintenance as scheduled for these components, i.e. changing of lamps etc. Commercial systems can be more sophisticated with double pump, duty-standby, or multi-pump systems, all sized for the specific application and often linked into a building management system.

If large enough, the tank itself could be designed to perform more than one function, i.e. it could act as stormwater retention and rain harvesting system combined. A double sized tank could be employed, where the top half could have porous sides to allow slow water release, or alternatively, a floating overflow in a solid tank. This would slowly release excess storm water into the sewer or soak-away, the lower half would fulfil the rainwater harvesting function. Or, for other applications, perhaps where no mains water is available, the bottom half could be an emergency service reserve water supply, so the normal, 'usable' water from the tank would be from 50% to full but the remainder below could be called upon in times of severe drought.

Rainharvesting - case studies

Domestic

Private home, Gloucestershire

One of the earliest domestic rainwater harvesting systems installed in the UK used a modern German technology from Wisy. The system was installed in 1998 in a house that, whilst fairly conventional in its construction, incorporated several ecological features. The rainwater system used downpipe type filter-collectors, which collect and filter water from the roof directly into a 1500 litre holding tank in the basement. The tank contains a submersible pump, which delivers water directly to the WC's and the cold-fill on the washing machine. A low-level switch activates a top-up feed from the mains water supply should the tank run low on rainwater. The system saves approximately 38,000 litres per year.

Private home, Wales

Undoubtedly the easiest method of rainwater harvesting is the simple positioning of a water butt below a rainwater downpipe. However, you can't do a great deal with the few gallons that the common sized water butt will hold, so the owner installed two huge ones. They are about 2 metres tall, 1.1 metres in diameter and are black, ex industrial fruit juice containers. They hold 400 gallons (1500 litres) of water each, ideal for use in the garden or for car washing. These two water butts collect the water from the rear slope of the roof. They fill up after just 3 inches of rain has landed on the roof, which, over a year, equates to about 15 refills, given the rainfall in Wales. The water is primarily used for irrigation in a nearby polytunnel. The owner paid, in 2000, about £90 for each of the 1500 litre butts from the Tank Exchange:
www.thetankexchange.com/home.htm

Commercial

Market Bosworth Country Park WC block, Leicestershire

The block replaces a temporary toilet at the 87-acre park and its environmental features include:

- rainwater collection and use to flush the toilets which are low volume flush
- the gents' urinals are waterless
- meters record how much water is used
- the performance of the sewage treatment plant is monitored monthly.

The system uses the Wisy WFF vortex filter, which is wall-mounted within the building and picks up all the water from the shingle-clad roof. The filtered water is then directed to a small tank (1000 litres) at low level, and from here the water is then pumped using a 12V pump up to a break tank, at high level, to supply the WC's. The break tank also has an automatic back-up from the mains cold water supply. Despite this being a relatively small building, with a high water demand, the system saved over 4000 litres during the first six months of use. This is equal to about 900 flushes of the low water use WC units.

Industrial

Tolvaddon Energy Park, Cornwall

Built in 2001, the Tovaddon Energy Park in Camborne, Cornwall was designed to provide low cost, comfortable and work-inspiring business units that demonstrate a commitment to renewable resources and protection of the environment. The 17 industrial units include green building features, such as solar heated hot water, heavily insulated floors walls and roofs, underfloor heating and rainwater harvesting. Eight of the units have rainwater harvesting systems for supplying water to WCs. Rainwater is collected and filtered using Wisy WFF vortex type filters.

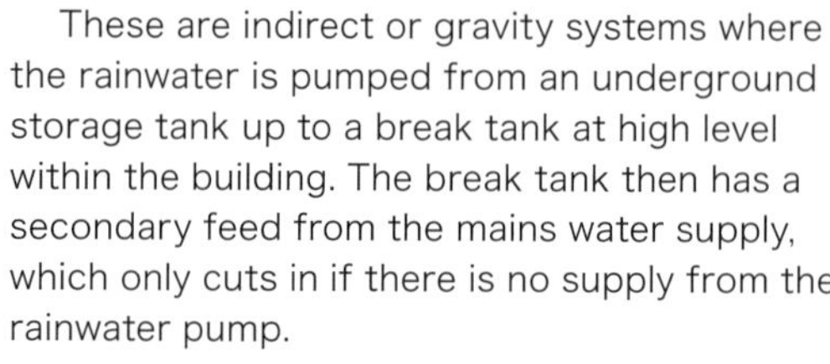

These are indirect or gravity systems where the rainwater is pumped from an underground storage tank up to a break tank at high level within the building. The break tank then has a secondary feed from the mains water supply, which only cuts in if there is no supply from the rainwater pump.

This development has several units close together, so it was decided to use shared rainwater storage in order to save cost and ground works. The tank in this case is the only shared item, with each unit having its own pump and controls. Each system is therefore independent and can be isolated should one of the units remain empty for any significant time.

With grateful thanks to Roger Budgeon of the Green Shop Group and Derek Hunt of Rainharvesting Systems Ltd for providing data for this article.

Reference

1. One example would be from a company called Interflush who make a Water Council approved product (also on Water Technolgy List for Enhanced Capital Allowance) that can be simply installed in most common WC's: ***www.interflush.co.uk***

Further information

General design calculations for rainwater harvesting systems have been included in Volume 2 of the Green Building Bible: ***www.greenbuildingbible.co.uk***

The UK Rainwater Harvesting Association (UK-RHA) was formed in 2004 to serve as a focal point for organisations with business interests in the rainwater harvesting industry. ***www.ukrha.org***

If you plan to install a commercial system and the components are on the Water Technology List, then the installation may qualify for enhanced capitol allowance. This means that you could claim tax relief on the whole rainwater harvesting system expenditure during the first year after installation: ***www.eca.gov.uk***

Waste water management

Every litre of water piped into our homes has to leave again one way or another, mostly carrying away with it contaminants of waste and washing. Wiser management of our effluent, before it leaves our buildings, could help reduce our environmental impact. But how easy would this really be? **Keith Hall** introduces the options ...

In cities and large towns a network of sewer systems take away our effluent to municipal sewage farms, but more remote properties have to fend for themselves. The common answer has been to use a septic tank with a soakaway field but it is widely acknowledged (especially by those living downstream of such installations) that they don't work! Percolation alone, on anything but the most suitable of soil and subsoil conditions, is doomed to failure and localised contamination.

A newer solution to this age-old problem is an on-site sewage treatment system. These work on the same principles as the municipal sewage farms but are now available sized for even single homes. The drawback with these systems is that they need power (electricity) to run air pumps to oxygenate the waste water within a plastic or concrete tank. This simple process stops the waste from becoming anaerobic which would suffocate microbial action that helps break down the solid matter into harmless water and sediment.

While the treatment afforded to the waste water by these package systems is quite acceptable, especially in situations where land is at a premium, if sustainability is your aim, both the long-term energy consumption (of the pumps) and the high embedded-energy of such systems are a downside, especially in times of power outages or pump failures.

These systems have actually been designed to exploit natural biological processes in a confined space, i.e. natural organisms to do the work of breaking down the sewage into water and solids. Without the natural microbial activity the faeces would become a putrid, sticky and toxic mess.

More natural solutions

Useful systems then, especially in restricted space but if you wanted to avoid the use of electricity or power, achieve similar or even better results and have some space, then consider installing a constructed wetland or a reed bed system.

Constructed wetlands (or horizontal flow reed beds) are designed and built in a similar way to natural wetlands; some are used to treat waste water. Constructed wetlands for waste water treatment consist of one or more shallow depressions, or cells, built into the ground with level bottoms, so that the flow of water can be controlled within the cells, and from cell to cell. Roots and stems of the wetland plants form a dense mat where biological and physical processes occur to treat the waste water. These work particularly well for low strength effluents, or effluents that have undergone some form of pre-treatment.

Vertical flow reed-bed systems can be more effective in reducing contaminant levels and eliminating smells than horizontal flow reed-beds. By their design they occupy a smaller space and can also cope with much stronger effluents. Single stage vertical flow reed-beds, when properly designed, can be used for the full treatment of domestic sewage - black and grey water. There are also combination systems available. These incorporate one or two stages of vertical flow, followed by one or more stages of horizontal flow.

Such systems use living plants and microbes to perform the same function that pumps and forced air do in a sewage treatment plant, but, as stated earlier, without the need for any power supply. Nature provides this with sunshine which makes the plants grow. The plants use nutrients from the sludge and water. They are also very beneficial for wildlife, attracting a host of wetland flora and fauna, such as dragonflies, butterflies and birds. In such systems, the reed beds would replace the soakaway field that would normally be used in conjunction with a septic tank system. Therefore, anyone with such a system already installed, could trace and intercept the outflow pipes and install a reedbed in-line to carry out further treatment to the outflow. This will greatly improve the underground water quality near the property. The septic tank will continue to perform the first settlement stage.

Separating waste - the options

The following solutions could be used with any system mentioned above, even standard septic tank systems or municipal mains sewage systems!

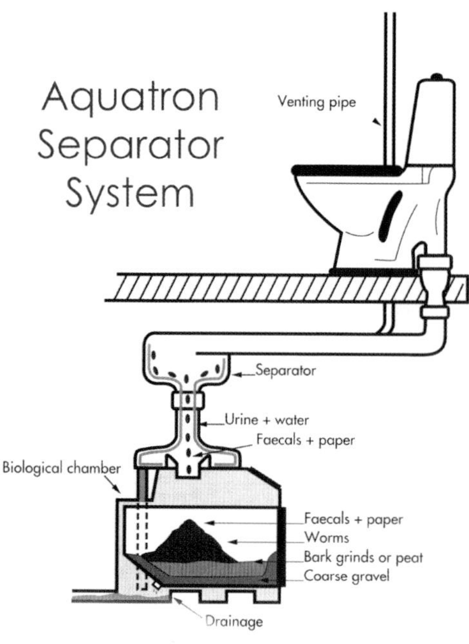

www.solutionelements.co.uk/atron.htm

Black water

If you want to separate faeces from the sewer water, then a vortex separator unit, such as shown in the diagram below left (Aquatron), could be used. This does not require any electricity to operate. It will collect the faecal matter for composting in a chamber beneath the separator, while the flush water and urine continue to the septic tank or reed bed. The cleaner waste water results in improved discharge quality or smaller treatment area. This type of system is very handy where you want to recoup the nutrients in the faecal matter but still wish to use a flush toilet in your home. Another way to minimise the impact on the environment, and maximise the recovery of nutrients, is to use a urine separating toilet to take out nitrogen-rich urine before discharging the waste to the system. The urine can then be used as a liquid fertiliser. Used in combination, a urine separating toilet and a vortex separator unit can remove the vast majority of polluting matter from black water and save it in the form of re-useable nutrients. The final waste water is thus much cleaner, entering the local environment of the treatment system for final cleaning.

Another approach might be to consider a dry (composting) toilet. This would also cut down your water consumption, as there is no flushing needed with such systems. There are many ways of achieving a composting toilet, with a number of off-the-shelf loos already available in the UK, or you could build your own. Organisations like the Centre for Alternative Energy (CAT)[1] or Intermediate Technology (IT)[2] and others produce easy to follow guides on constructing compost toilets.

Grey water

A reed-bed, or constructed wetland, can also be used on just grey water systems, i.e. outflow from a kitchen sink or bathroom. You need to be fairly careful with your choice of cleaning products, and try to avoid harmful ingredients. You could even set up a simple irrigation system where the greywater flows down through pipes

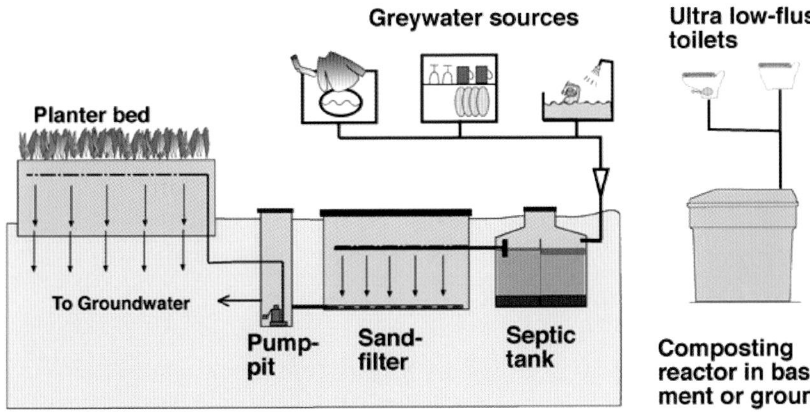

*Above and right: diagram of a separated greywater and blackwater treatment system. This bespoke greywater treatment system from Clivus (**www.multrum.com/uk/**) may not be available in the UK but does show the principle workings and layout.*

*Images courtesy of Greywater Irrigation: **www.greywater.com***

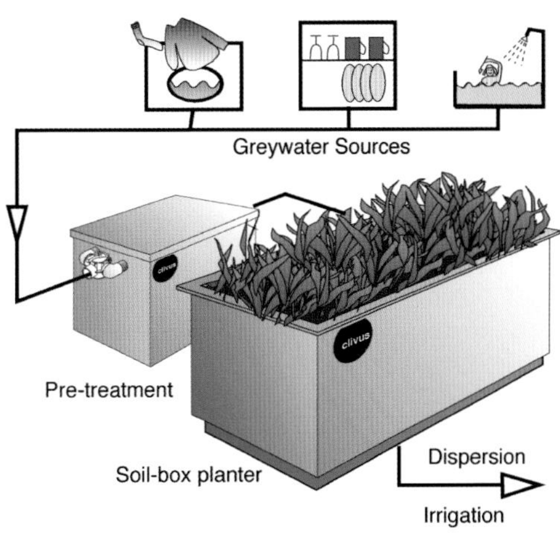

buried just below the surface in a vegetable plot in the garden. There are a number of resources on the internet that can provide more details of establishing simple greywater recycling systems. Ecosans Res, for instance, offers a free to download pdf document on the subject[3].

With a little bit of filtration and storage in a cool tank, it could also be used for toilet flushing (though this might entail some serious re-plumbing), and car washing as well as uses in the garden. With a little imaginative plumbing you might be able to plumb the waste outlet from the wash hand basin to the toilet cistern to cut down on clean water use where it is not necessary, but be careful to ensure that the overflow is working properly or you could get a flood!. Even though the water from grey water systems is not used for drinking, bacteria should be removed and this is usually done with an ultra violet (UV) light filter. Although reported water savings within the range of 30% are potentially possible, installation and equipment costs, reliability and maintainability issues have all meant that the overall cost effectiveness of such systems has usually limited them to large scale projects, rather than domestic applications.

With thanks to Féidhlim Harty for providing the original article upon which this article is based.

References

1. *Centre for Alternative Technology:* ***www.cat.org.uk***
2. *Intermediate Technology:* ***www.itdg.org***
3. *EcoSanRes (Ecological Sanitation) Useful report on greywater management:* ***www.ecosanres.org***

Further reading

'The Humanure Handbook - a guide to composting human manure' by J Jenkins available from Green Shop: ***www.greenshop.co.uk***

Constructed wetlands

Constructed wetlands are a cost-effective, low energy and robust way of treating industrial, agricultural and domestic waste water - sewage and greywater. They have been used successfully to purify domestic sewage in the UK since 1903. **Jay Abrahams** explains the latest thinking.

Constructed wetlands are suitable for the treatment of sewage from single households, or from small communities, and are currently being used to treat sewage from populations of up to 10,000. There are at least 500 constructed wetlands currently in the UK, treating a variety of waste water, and there is substantial experience and expertise available for the design, construction and operation of such systems to allow confidence in their widespread application.

These systems use little or no electricity or fossil fuels in their operation, and rather than emit the greenhouse gas, CO_2, such systems absorb this gas and store it - as plant biomass and soil. As well as purifying waste water, these plant based systems purify the air and produce oxygen through the photosynthetic process. These systems are also visually very attractive and offer a haven for wildlife. The basis of the purification process is, as with conventional mechanical treatment processes, microbiological; it relies on the biochemical transformations provided by the plethora of micro-organisms found in the gravel, sand or soil, which are used as the purification and growth media within the constructed wetland system. The bacteria and fungi which transform the waste are in a symbiotic, mutually beneficial, relationship with the roots of the wetland plants. The plant roots provide oxygen, sugars (an energy source) and attachment points for the microbes, whilst the microbes mineralise the organic matter found in the waste water making this available to the growing plants.

Types of constructed wetland

There are several types of constructed wetland in use, ranging from simple un-planted pond systems, planted lagoons and reedbed treatment systems (both horizontal and vertical flow), as well as high-rate planted sand filters and soil based multi-species wetlands called wetland ecosystem treatment (WET) systems. There are also the greenhouse-enclosed, hydroponic tank-based systems - developed by John Todd at Ocean Arks International and called 'living machines' which I have not discussed. Here I will concentrate on conventional reedbed treatment and WET systems, in particular the latter.

Reedbed treatment systems

Both horizontal and verticalflow reedbeds, are the types most familiar to people in the UK, whilst on the continent 'facultative pond' and 'lagoon systems' are often used for the purification of sewage from small towns, villages and hamlets. In both the horizontal and the vertical flow reedbed systems gravel is used as the purification and growth medium and these systems are generally planted with only the common or Norfolk reed (*Phragmites communis*).

A reedbed treatment system comprises one or more lined lagoons filled with gravel. They usually have a relatively high aspect ratio (they are longer than they are wide) and the depth of the reedbeds is usually no more than 1 metre, as the roots of the reeds rarely grow deeper than 600mm. There are often horizontally placed plastic pipes located below the gravel matrix (to ensure that the waste water flows throughout the whole volume of the lagoon to avoid 'dead spaces') and also vertical pipes to bring air to the lower reaches of the gravel bed.

Horizontal flow reedbed systems have the waste water entering at the surface of the gravel on one side of the lagoon and flowing through it to the other side, the outlet being at approximately the same height as the inlet. The waste water flows horizontally through the lagoon. This type of reedbed has only a limited surface area for aeration to occur - between the water surface and the atmosphere - and so the horizontal flow type functions mainly anaerobically. Thus, this type of reedbed is usually used for the 'polishing' of low strength wastewater, and can be found at the out-fall of many conventional sewage works to keep the final effluent within the consented limits.

Vertical flow reedbed systems address the limited area for gaseous exchange in horizontal flow systems, because, in these systems, the inlet is at the surface of the gravel layer, whilst the outlet is located at the bottom of the gravel layer at the other end of the lagoon. The floor level of the lagoon is constructed so that the outlet end is lower than the inlet end and this defines the direction of flow. Thus the waste water has to flow 'vertically' downwards through the gravel and also from one end of the lagoon to the other. The gravel matrix is therefore sometimes totally submerged with the liquid, but is periodically flushed through with air as the water passes through and the water level varies from full to empty. This type of reedbed is able to function aerobically for more of the time and is therefore able to handle higher strength wastes, such as settled sewage, more effectively. This being the case it is usual to have a vertical and a horizontal type working together 'in-line', the vertical bed being dosed so that it fills and empties alternately and feeds a horizontal type for 'polishing'. It is also quite usual to have two parallel vertical flow systems working sequentially, with each taking its turn to be 'flushed' through with the waste water, whilst the other is periodically 'rested'.

Although less energy intensive than conventional mechanical/electrical sewage systems, conventional reedbed treatment systems have a high embodied energy content due to the sand/gravel which is used as the purification and growth medium, the requirement for plastic distribution and aeration pipes and the concrete/brickwork that is used to create the lagoons for the reedbeds.

The high embodied energy of reedbed treatment systems has led some practitioners and designers of sustainable waste water purification systems to develop soil based wetlands. These systems do not use imported gravel or cement; only topsoil found on site is used as the purification medium and where possible the clay subsoil is compacted to form an impermeable base to the system. Some designers also prefer to plant their constructed wetlands with more than just one species of reed, using reeds, rushes and sedges to create a range of root depths and a more varied habitat for wildlife. Some also advocate the use of wetland trees, such as willow, within the systems they create.

Wetland ecosystem treatment (WET) systems mimic the microbiological and geochemical transformations found in nature; these naturally occurring processes purify water in the global hydrological cycle. A WET system, is the next stage in the evolution of constructed wetlands for waste water purification. Such a system is based on permaculture design principles and good ecological practice. Its aims are to mimic nature to a greater degree, to purify water with little or no use of non-renewable energy, to have a lower embodied energy content and to thus be a more sustainable form of waste purification system than simple reedbed treatment systems.

A WET system has a much lower embodied energy than a reedbed system because it uses topsoil (found on the site) and not imported gravel as the purification medium. The major energy input of a WET System is the fuel used by the earth-moving equipment during its creation. A series of swales are created to form a water reticulation system through which the wastewater flows. This enables the waste water to soak into and through the planted soil banks. It can therefore be created on slopes ranging from 1:500 to 1:25. This is in distinct contrast to conventional reedbed treatment systems which need relatively large areas of flat ground to be present, or to be created on site, for their installation. A WET system, therefore, reflects and responds to the landscape and looks far more natural than a rectilinear reedbed. This becomes more apparent and therefore important the larger the constructed wetland needs to be to service the design loading.

WET systems are planted with several reed species, as well as a range of aquatic and marginal plants (up to 30 species) and a variety of willow types and wetland tree species. As the waste water flows through the root systems of the densely planted wetland trees and marginal plants, it is both purified by microbiological action and transpired by growing plants.

The systems generate a biomass resource; willow wands can be harvested from the coppiced willow each year. These are used for a range of traditional and contemporary crafts. The biomass yield from a well managed system can include one-year old coppiced willow wands for basketry, two-year old wands for hurdle making or living willow domes and tunnels, as well as binders - used for hedge-laying, and three-year old wands which are used for the construction of living willow structures and garden furniture.

Rapidly growing, large, biomass willow types can also be planted and, when harvested and seasoned, these can be used to fuel simple woodstoves, ceramic stoves or combined heat and power (CHP) boilers and so contribute to the energy needs of the site. A WET system, being designed with soil and not gravel and having a 'plug-flow regime, can withstand both intermittent and shock loading without failing, whereas should the input to a conventional gravel based reedbed treatment system be cut off for any length of time and the bed dry out, the purification processes often fail or are severely curtailed as the gravel dries out and the reeds die back.

WET system - case studies

Over 50 systems have now been created for a wide range of domestic sewage and other applications; these include systems for full time populations of one person up to 380 people. Here are three studies;

The Hunters Inn Pub, Gloucestershire - this was the first system (established in 1994), to be created by Biologic Design, when the pub's new conventional soakaway system (a conventional perforated pipe laid in a gravel/) failed within a month of being installed, due to the local heavy clay. The system here is a total absorption system with no outfall. The situation we found when we initially visited the site in 1994 was that the Environment Agency were about close the Pub down. The sewage, after passing through a holding tank fitted with a macerator pump, was being pumped up to the top of the hill behind the pub. From here it was 'fed' into the new soakaway, but it was actually bubbling out of the ground above the soakaway, flowing down the hill, across a cricket pitch and into the next door farmer's grazing land, where it crossed a public footpath, as well as then crossing the pub's car park to end up in a road drain.

The system was created and planted in under a month, and, as the original owner of the pub wanted it to become a 'wildlife haven', it has had no maintenance at all for over 12 years. It has of course become very overgrown and due to the large brambles growing into it from the surrounding hedges, it is now virtually impossible to walk around it easily, but it is still effectively purifying the sewage.

Ivycroft Plant Nursery, Herefordshire - this system, established in 1996, purifies the settled sewage from a plant nursery which is open to the public on a limited scale. It thus has a base load of two people who live there, plus the two or three people who work there seasonally, and customers, as well as groups of up to 20 people who visit for tea and a tour of the garden. This system is an integral part of a beautiful garden. In winter, after exceptionally heavy rainfall, there is, very occasionally, an overflow of purified water from the final polishing pond into the local brook.

Westons Cider Mill, Herefordshire - this 5 acre site, established in 1994, was initially designed as a total absorption system with no outfall required. The original volume of waste water from the cider mill was around 17,500m^3/year with 80% entering the system during the 3 month cider making season. The waste water has an average Biological Oxygen Demand (BOD) of around 6,000mg/litre (sewage is around 350) although there can be 'slugs' of up to 40,000.

The waste water has a pH of about 3.5 but, fortuitously, whilst carrying out trial-pits to assess the topsoil profile and to see what the local geology could offer us for our design, we discovered a 1.5 metre deep limestone gravel layer just below ground level over around one third of the site. This was integrated into the design to give us the pH modification we required with no chemical dosing system needing to be installed, as the acidic waste water, when channelled through the limestone gravel, has its pH increased from 3.5 to 7.5, or around neutrality. Due to the 6-fold increase in cider production since the creation of the system over 14 years ago, and the building of additional processing facilities at the factory, such as a new kegging plant and the 2.5 miles of new pipework linking the new juice storage tanks with the production areas, the wastewater input has grown to around 120,000m^3/year. To accommodate this increased input, the system at Westons has had two additional swales added, as well as the final ponds being enlarged and deepened - all within the original footprint of the site. It is no longer a total absorption system per-se, but the purified water in the polishing ponds is now pumped up to a trickle irrigation system, which feeds around 150 acres of orchard, thus making the orchards 'drought-proof' as well as increasing the apple yield of the orchards by about 2.5 tonnes per hectare. Now over 50,000 trees, mainly willow (50 varieties), as well as 35 species of wetland marginals have been planted. The site (see photo below) is a wildlife haven and 60 species of bird have been recorded there by the British Trust for Ornithology. ☯

This 5 acre wetland treatment system at Westons Cider Mill was established in 1994. It was initially designed as a total absorption system, with no outfall required. The original volume of wastewater from the cider mill was around 17,500m^3/year with 80% entering the system during the 3 month cider making season.

Sustainable urban drainage systems (SUDS)

Rainwater that falls on urban areas needs to be controlled and drained to avoid inconvenience, damage, flooding and health risks. Imaginative use of this water could provide habitat and amenity and prevent some of the problems that

To understand the best approach to dealing with the rainwater that falls on a site, compare the two scenarios in Figure 1 of what happens to water when it lands on an undeveloped and a developed site before and after development.

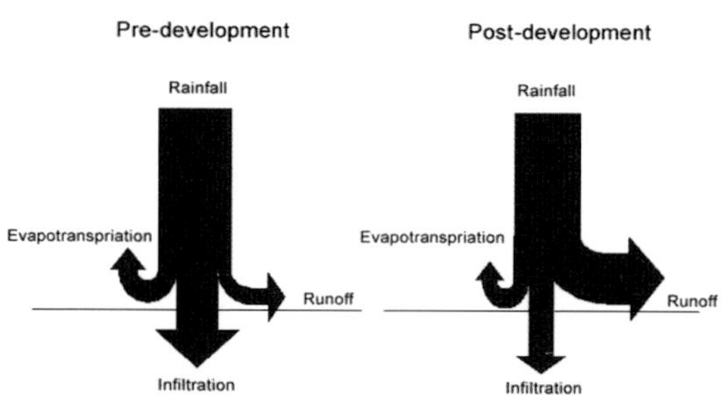

Figure 1. The fate of rainfall pre and post development.

Before development of the site, when rain hits the ground, some of the water evaporates (or is transpired by plants 'breathing'), and some of the rain infiltrates into the ground. This infiltration is important to maintain groundwater supplies. A proportion of water will also run off the ground surface and become streams or rivers. If we cover the ground surface with something that's largely impervious, like a house with a tarmac drive, the rate of infiltration is drastically reduced, and the run off is increased (Figure 2).

Graphs of surface water run off over time are shown in Figure 3. Pre-development, run off is prolonged but is never very great. After development, however, the peak flow is much higher and occurs sooner than in the pre-development state. The end result of covering the UK in impervious surfaces is therefore an increase in the amount of surface water run off, and the tendency of this flow to peak much more suddenly. This leads to flash flooding, and with a conventional approach to drainage requires pipes to be sized to cope with these big peaks in flow. But flow is only half the problem. Impervious surfaces also result in impaired water quality, since pollutants and sediments on the ground surface in urban areas, such as heavy metals, fuel and tyre rubber, will get washed straight into water courses, rather than infiltrating into the ground where they are naturally treated.

In much of the UK, this bad situation is made worse by connecting these stormwater drains into the foul sewer system, resulting in huge variations in the amount of sewage flowing to sewage treatment works, sewage being discharged untreated into rivers via combined sewer overflows and impaired sewage treatment owing to the effects of the pollutants on the microbiology of the sewage works.

Solutions for large scale developments

Enough of the problems, what about the solutions? In many instances, planning permission for new development will stipulate a maximum rate of surface water run off from the site that goes to storm drains after rainfall of given intensities, which in turn is based on a probability of that rainfall event occurring. In order to meet these requirements, the conventional solution is to install attenuation tanks with

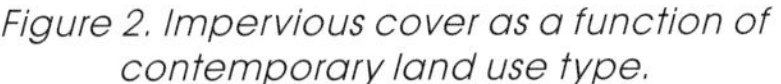

Figure 2. Impervious cover as a function of contemporary land use type.

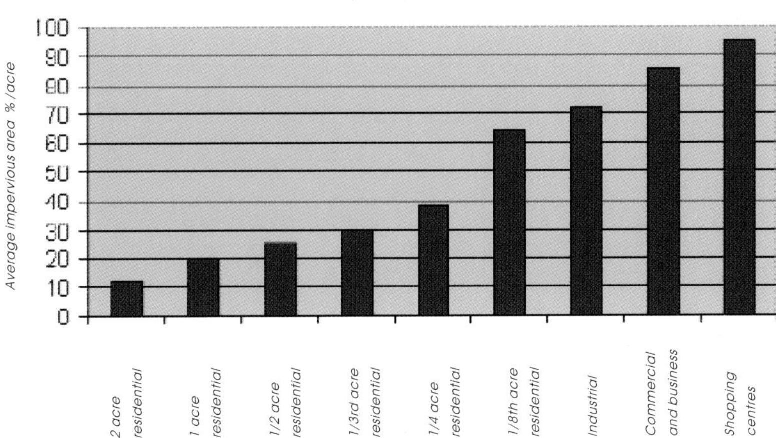

'throttles' controlling the outflow, or tank sewers. Both solutions are basically large underground voids, which store peak flows and discharge them more slowly into the mains drainage system. These have a lot to recommend them. They are a 'hard' engineering solution, with recognised design standards, and critically for small sites and commercial developments, the ground above the tanks is still useable. The provision of this type of temporary storage often makes little difference to the flood impact on the local river (since the events that cause river flooding are often low rainfall intensities over long durations), but does serve to prevent flooding of the drainage network itself.

Increasing emphasis on environmental water quality, flood prevention and amenity provision, as opposed to simply the hydraulic capacity of piped drainage systems is leading to increased uptake of (SUDS). SUDS techniques are designed to mimic natural systems and allow treatment of pollutants to occur at the same time as preventing flooding. There are a number of types of SUDS that can be installed in large scale developments, but central to the approach is the idea that stormwater should be dealt with on site wherever possible.

Figure 3. Surface water run off after rainfall events for a typical developed catchment.

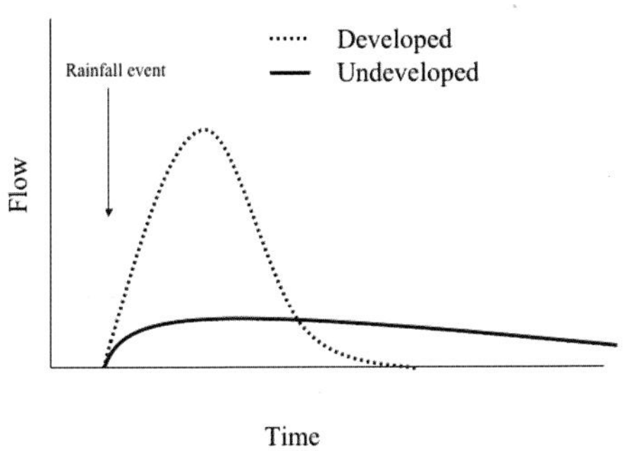

The first priority is preventing run off and pollution, wherever possible. This means minimising the use of impervious surfaces and preventing build up of pollutants on surfaces by regular housekeeping and spill prevention. The next step is to optimise infiltration where ground conditions are suitable. Permeable pavements may be an option; these are porous paved areas with a sub base that acts as a storage reservoir for gradual infiltration. Any flow remaining after the above measures is then dealt with by a large scale solution, such as a detention basin or retention pond. These are large ponds that fill during storm flows and hence buffer flow rates (see case studies later). They can also be designed to promote settlement of the particles in stormwater, for example by using forebay areas or wetlands at their entrance. Since the heavy metals in stormwater are usually bound to solid particles like grit, this sedimentation provides significant water treatment.

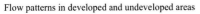

Small is beautiful

When looked at on the scale of large housing developments, many storm drainage installations (including some SUDS), look distinctly over engineered; unsurprising given the massive buffering capacity that may be required of them. But where does this leave the person looking for a pragmatic but ecological drainage system for their single eco build house?

The first point is to ensure that you are maximising your use of surfaces that allow infiltration, so consider your ground coverings carefully. Grass is the obvious choice, but if you need a more hardwearing surface for part of your property, a range of materials are available, such as block paving with gaps in between, porous blocks and reinforced grass. Unfortunately, most of these products are based on concretes or virgin aggregates. Even in areas where you are using an impermeable surface, paved areas such as paths and driveways should be profiled to shed water onto adjacent permeable areas such as lawns and flower beds.

You may be considering a green roof, and these are promoted from a wide range of angles such as biodiversity, aesthetics, reduction of airborne pollution as well as reduction of stormwater run off. However the limited storage capacity of a green roof means they are unlikely to help flood control during prolonged rainfall, so you will want to make sure that you have other justifications for wanting one. It's also worth pointing out that green roofs are generally incompatible with rainwater harvesting systems where the water is to be used in the house (the water will contain a lot of solids and may well be discoloured).

We should all store as much rainwater as we can for garden use, rather than the token water butts normally installed. However this is more for reasons of water efficiency than SUDS. Standard water butts are of little value as part of a SUDS solution since they are generally small (less than $0.5m^3$) and you won't be using the water in the garden during rainy periods, which is precisely when the flow buffering would be useful. In the future, widespread use of rainwater butts with throttled overflows might provide worthwhile stormwater attenuation, but at present, use of water butts in a development does not allow for any reduction in other drainage measures required.

Test your soil porosity (details in Part H of the Building Regulations), and see how much water you will be able to infiltrate into the ground. If your calculations suggest that infiltration can only ever be a partial solution, you can look at SUDS as part of your overall landscaping scheme for your property. You might be able to incorporate a wetland and a pond into your garden, with only the overflow from your pond being discharged into a local watercourse, or failing that, local storm drains. Anything that slows the flow of water off your property, and provides some filtration and treatment will be of benefit.

Sewers for adoption?

In the UK, developers pass on the long term responsibility for various aspects of their site to other organisations. These are known as 'adoption agreements'. In the case of piped drainage systems, this agreement is generally with the local water company, who take future responsibility for the drainage system from the point it leaves your property, provided that the developer builds it to recognised standards. These standards are set out in the delightfully named book 'Sewers for Adoption'. This system works pretty well for conventional piped drainage systems, but less well for SUDS, which water companies are reluctant to take on. So who else may adopt the system? In larger scale developments, planning permission is often dependent on provision of public outdoor space, and this space is 'adopted' by the local authority (LA). In some instances, LA's have adopted SUDS as part of this open space since the ponds, wetlands and swales created are of habitat and amenity value. The alternative is for the SUDS to be adopted by a housing association, formed by the local residents who then organise any maintenance necessary; an option worth considering on eco-housing developments. The National SUDS Working Group developed an Interim Code of Practice and a set of model agreements, which will go some way to making larger scale SUDS a realistic proposition for developers.

Conclusion

Inevitably, some green builders will be disappointed by the lack of detailed guidance available on SUDS installation at the household level. However, when looked at from the point of view of your entire ecological footprint, your water use, sewage disposal and drainage systems are a very small part of your overall environmental impact (less than 5% in most cases). Consequently, if you have a limited amount of eco-enthusiasm, or a limited budget to dedicate to environmental aspects of your house design, you should not be concentrating on green drainage solutions. In most instances you would be better off focussing your eco-enthusiasm on energy or heating issues. With that proviso aside, you may be able to incorporate the basic principles of SUDS design into small scale building projects with little cost; store as much rainwater as you can use for garden watering, minimise your use of impermeable surfaces and infiltrate stormwater to ground via a soakaway wherever possible. If your property is large enough, consider using ponds to buffer any residual flow. ☯

Further reading

SUDS. Interim Code of Practice, model maintenance agreements, publications and further information: ***www.ciria.org.uk***

Sustainable drainage systems – hydraulic, structural and water quality advice. CIRIA publication C609.

Infiltration Drainage – Manual of Good Practice. CIRIA publication R156.

Drainage of Development Sites – A Guide. CIRIA publication X108.

Post-project monitoring of BMPs/SUDS to determine performance and whole life costs; phase 2. WERF, AWWA, UKWIR. – a detailed report into the long term effectiveness of SUDS and their costs.

A database of SUDS installations in the UK, with comments on performance, maintenance and monitoring: ***www.suds-sites.net***

SUDS for schools - case studies

Two school sites required rainwater runoff attenuation and management solutions and the decision was taken to adopt an approach that combined these needs with an approach to SUDS, which enhanced the sites, providing habitats, opportunities for study and visual interest. **Robert Lewin-Jones**, principal architect for the schemes reports.

Matchborough First School - Redditch

The site for this new school was a relatively low-lying flat greenfield site close to the Ipsley Brook. However, initial investigations through the Environment Agency confirmed that the floodplain does not extend a significant distance from the brook and that a flood risk assessment was unnecessary. There is a distinct low area associated with the brook and this was identified as the land that floods during heavy rainfall.

The site was drained in the past by a hedge and ditch to the west and another to the east. Nonetheless, the site was generally very flat which caused water to lie on all surfaces for a time following rain.

The SUDS scheme for the site addresses the immediate issues of site drainage as well as modifying ground form to encourage surface draining of hard and soft play surfaces.

Assuming a 1 in 100 year return period and a requirement to achieve a 'greenfield runoff rate', the sustainable drainage plan is designed to collect water where it leaves hard surfaces, trap sediments, control pollution (e.g. oils from parked cars) and store runoff before discharge to the Ipsley Brook. The design seeks to establish a natural drainage pattern, following existing contours and landscape features.

The existing hedgerow ditch was re-profiled as a narrow swale to intercept overland flows from adjacent higher land and create a level access path along the eastern boundary. The swale protects the east elevation of the school from sheet runoff during heavy rainfall, when channel drains at entrances may surcharge, and prevents constant saturation of the playing field. An existing land drain was routed under the new playground into a swale collecting surface runoff from the hard play surface.

Downpipes and channel drains on the eastern part of the school building also feed into the manhole. Runoff from the remainder of the roof collects in a pipe which discharges directly to the swale. The playground is profiled to collect runoff and deliver it as sheet flow into the collector swale. Water collected in the swale flows quickly to a detention area wetland along the western boundary to avoid standing water next to the playground.

As the school car park may generate modest hydrocarbon (petrol) pollution, runoff is therefore collected and stored in a small detention basin where silt is trapped and pollution broken down naturally in wetland vegetation. Water flows slowly through a controlled outlet, under the access road, into the next collector basin and then to the boundary storage swale. Water from the school's main drive is treated in a similar way, flowing into a collector basin, and any light pollution which passes through the first basin is trapped in the storage swale.

Rainwater from the western side of the building is collected for use in toilet flushing. Surplus roof water overflows into the swale, and runoff from adjacent hard surfaces flows across the grass lawn to be stored in the swale. The swale meets storage requirements for the main drive, roof and adjacent paving, and discharges through a controlled outlet under the lower access footpath to the detention area wetland.

When rainfall is heavy or prolonged, then water is stored in a shallow detention area wetland along the western boundary to help prevent flooding downstream. The basin normally drains down in 48 hours and leaves a marsh habitat which is used for education purposes. Changes in level create temporary pools and an interesting mosaic of wetland vegetation.

Water is released from each storage basin in a controlled way to prevent flooding downstream, reduce damage to the stream bed and generally mimic the natural pattern of drainage for the site. The drainage for the site is largely accommodated by shallow ground modelling, usually no deeper than 450mm, with water levels 300mm or less. Water levels will normally

Above: simple swales shown here at one of the schools, are able to cope well with flash floods and add natural interest to the learning environment.

be no more than 150mm deep.

Maintenance of the SUDS drainage is undertaken as part of normal grass mowing together with checking inlets and outlets. These can easily be cleared by site staff, although overland flood routes will be present in case of any blockage. Capital and maintenance costs on the site are less than conventional drainage without a requirement to pay charges to the Water Company for storm sewer management.

Redhill Primary School - Worcester
This school is situated on a site of approaching 2 hectares, with the new school and surrounding hard areas comprising over 5000m^2. The previous school, which was demolished to make way for the replacement, drained directly to the combined sewer with no on-site attenuation.

Discussions with the Severn Trent Water Company confirmed the requirement to discharge stormwater separately to the storm sewer at a controlled rate of 10 litres per second for the whole site. It was acknowledged that due to historical development there was no access to a watercourse nor an overland flood route from the site. Therefore flows in excess of the 30 year flood will discharge to the sewer directly as they have done in the past. The SUDS design endeavours to maximise storage of runoff wherever possible.

The site falls from higher ground to the east, where the sports pitch is, down to the new school, where runoff is directed around both sides of the building. The southern route flows from the play area, along a sett channel, into a short collector swale before entering a pipe taking water below the access road into the woodland basin. The sett channel also collects water from an outdoor terrace related to the new classrooms. The water is cleaned and stored in the basin before it flows slowly to the sewer or overflows, in extreme events, directly to the site outfall.

The northern route flows from the lower play area to the car park, where water with possible pollution from cars is cleaned, before collection, into below-ground storage using geo-cellular boxes where water is stored before it again flows to the outfall. An overflow grating allows extreme events to flow directly to the outfall. The SUDS scheme can therefore provide the storage to meet the 1 in 30 year attenuation required by Severn Trent, a minimum of one treatment stage for all runoff required by SUDS guidance and various amenity opportunities for the school.

The woodland basin forms the main landscape feature on the site. Close to the caretaker's house, and unsuitable for building on or for sports, with help from Bishop's Wood Environmental Centre, this area was identified early on in the design process for its potential as a urban wildlife and outdoor teaching area. A series of shallow turf-lined swales now curve around the existing mature lime trees that once formed part of an avenue. This area has been dubbed 'the swale maze' as it criss-crossed by sleeper bridges and will form the major habitat area on the site, planted with wetland species and including a permanent pond, giving many study opportunities. The woodland area will be bounded by an earth berm (allowing the water collection facility to temporarily rise to a higher level in extreme rain), as well as newly planted hedges and fences. The school has been carefully involved in developing the ideas for this spot and anticipate using it for activities related to Forest Schools, pond dipping, investigating mini-beasts and the identification of wild flower species. Bat and bird boxes will also be erected. Smooth newts, which had to be translocated from the old school pond, to a new pond adjacent to the school field, have already returned to the woodland basin area.

The use of a sustainable drainage system is seen as an environmentally-friendly complement to the new primary school itself, which is designed with ground source heat pump heating, timber framing, rainwater harvesting, and an emphasis on the use of recycled products in construction. ☯

Space to grow!

Our outdoor space should have provision for growing at least some of the food we need. **Keith Hall**, a recent convert to self sufficiency in food, reports ...

There are troubled times ahead, with fuel shortages likely to be just the start. Recently there have been concerns regarding crop failures and food shortages in some countries. This means we could see increasing problems with food supplies in the future. In fact in parts of the world there are even riots taking place because of the shortages and constantly rising prices of food. People in the main food producing countries can no longer afford to eat, because we in the west are seemingly happy to keep paying higher prices in order to obtain continued supplies.

Food prices are intrinsically linked to oil prices and as the latter gets scarcer, and hence more expensive, then so food will follow. The underlying problem is the intensive and chemical-led nature of food production that has become the norm. Nitrogen and other fertilisers have, for many years now, been produced in a totally unnatural, energy intensive way. In the 1980s this led to over-production in Europe and 'food mountains'. Those food mountains have now gone but there is a new pressure on food - fuel crops. Farmers are turning their food producing land into fuel producing land and can no longer be relied upon to 'feed the world'.

Modern farmers have lost the knowledge and ability to grow food in a sustainable manner and as the prices of chemical fertilisers rocket they find themselves at a loss for what to do. Organic farming has become more established recently, but it is currently just a drop in the ocean and is not ready to sustain all our needs. Therefore, anyone with a garden or some space where some food plants can be grown should now be pulling those gardening books off the shelves and working out a planting and harvesting regime to supplement their weekly food plans. Schools should introduce gardening as a major curriculum subject. Dr Susan Kay-Williams, former Chief Executive of Garden Organic, said: "Concerns about child nutrition are constantly hitting the headlines. But youngsters really need to develop their own interest in what they eat if they are going to keep up healthy diets as adults. There is no better way to encourage a child to enjoy their vegetables than helping them to grow their own!"

If reading this book has inspired you to find ways to save energy in your buildings, my hope is that it will also inspire you to grow at least some of your own food. Buildings, people, food - they are all intrinsically linked. The permaculture concept is not far off from where we need our society to be heading.

Further information and useful contacts

Garden Organic: ***www.gardenorganic.org.uk***

'The Organic Gardener's Handbook' by M. Littlewood. ***www.crowood.com***

'Food from your Garden' - Readers Digest

'Organic Gardening' by R Lacey

Be sure to plant at least part of your garden as an area for growing some food. Tending a vegetable plot is one of the most rewarding and health promoting exercises that we can perform and in these times of spiralling food prices, will also offer some food security.

Encouraging wildlife

As the UK's natural habitats become degraded from the pressures of development and intensive agricultural practices, gardens become increasingly important survival grounds for many of our native species. **Sally Hall** encourages us to make our outdoor spaces more wildlife friendly ...

Residential areas, including gardens of all sizes, can be excellent and popular habitats for native flora and fauna, even acting as wildlife corridors to other, less built-up areas. Witness the silence and lack of life when walking over land that is intensively farmed and compare this to a vibrant, living garden managed for nature, which is full of bird song and activity from a diverse range of creatures.

In our increasingly 'busy' society people are becoming more and more detached from the natural environment. Children spend much of their time indoors. Obesity and health problems are rife across all age ranges. However, encouraging an interest in our natural environment can be totally absorbing, stimulating all our senses and encouraging an interest in a healthy, active, outdoor life. The popularity of TV programmes, such as the BBC's Springwatch and Autumn watch series, prove that many of us already have an interest in wildlife. We now need to do more to safeguard our precious flora and fauna. Many species are declining and even species that used to be so common, such as the house sparrow and song thrush, are now absent from many areas. Our native species are at risk from pollution, chemicals in the environment, habitat destruction and introduced predators, such as cats. We can all do our bit to help safeguard our precious flora and fauna.

Attracting wildlife

A garden that consists mainly of tarmac, concrete, showy borders and close-cropped lawns will support little wildlife. So how do you attract more insect and animal life? All species need the same things we do – water, food and shelter. The size of a garden and its location will dictate the diversity and number of species you will be able to attract. If you are creating a new garden you can build the concept of biodiversity into the design right from the start. For example, if you are considering a hedge, plant some prickly species to keep predators away from nests and include species that produce berries that birds can eat. Choose native plants and shrubs that encourage benefi-

A lawn left to grow longer will enable species, such as clover, to flower and attract bees, hoverflies and butterflies. The dry stone walling will attract invertebrates. The valerian in the foreground and marjoram in the background will also attract beneficial insects. The mullein is the food source for the striking mullein moth caterpillars.

cial insects, such as bees, butterflies, moths etc, and a good selection of species, so you will have flowers for most of the year. Consider too planting fruit trees, which will provide a crop for you and wildlife. There are many different species and sizes available to suit most gardens.

Leave as much as possible of your garden to go wild. A wild garden needs less management and will help save resources, as you will rarely need to mow. Wildflower seeds or plug plants of many different species are widely available but make sure they come from a reputable, cultivated source. An area of wildflower meadow is a popular and attractive garden feature, but cutting your lawn less is an alternative option and will allow many wildflowers to flourish.

Even in areas left wild you may want to control dominant species if they start to stifle other plants but remember clumps of nettles are the larval foodplant for butterfly species, such as the small tortoiseshell, red admiral, peacock and comma. A wild flower only becomes a weed when it is in a place where it is not wanted.

If you do have to clear areas, for example for growing food crops, refrain from using weed killers which can be hazardous to wildlife. Instead use discarded black plastic or cardboard, anchored down with heavy objects. This method clears most growth in a few months, although for areas of persistent perennial plants, it can take a year.

Any wetland area, from a tiny pond to a large lake, attracts a great diversity of life. Always make sure the sides are gently sloping to allow access for frogs, hedgehogs, birds etc. Even small areas of water will quickly attract species of dragonfly, damselflies, hawkers and their larva, all completely harmless and wonderful to watch, particularly if you are fortunate enough to witness the metamorphosis of larva to adult.

Most of us keep our gardens too tidy; removing plants that have died back, sweeping up leaves and clearing away grass clippings, bits of bark, logs etc. However, an overly tidy garden has very few hiding places for beneficial insects and mammals, so leave piles of leaves, prunings and logs around as habitat piles. They will be quickly colonised by a diverse range of creatures and fungi. A pile of logs or large stones left in a corner makes an ideal habitat for many species. Lizards, who like the warm sun on their bodies at certain times of the year, will be attracted to slates, logs or even old tyres left in sunny areas. Species like hedgehogs need somewhere to hibernate. Such mammals may use bonfire piles, so these must be checked thoroughly or preferably re-stacked, just before lighting. Similarly, hedgehogs and slow worms may inhabitant your compost heap so always take care when using spades and forks.

The ideal place to conserve and encourage species is in our garden. However, we may not be so happy to encourage wildlife into our buildings, so you should ensure that all buildings you wish to keep free of uninvited inhabitants are insect proofed, using good detailing and mesh over vents. Don't forget that for some species, for example swallows, owls and bats, buildings are important roosting and breeding areas. You can therefore leave appropriate openings in sheds and outbuildings, but ensure these are small enough to exclude cats. Small rodents will move into buildings and greenhouses during the cold months if they can. They will usually depart in the spring. If they cause a problem you can live trap them and release them elsewhere – do bear in mind that rodents are an important food source for species such as owls and other birds of prey.

Trees

If you have the space, consider planting trees and shrubs. We all know that trees grow, increasing in height and spread over a number of years and many will last for hundreds of years, so bear these points in mind before selecting where to plant. Many people take trees for granted, yet they are vital habitats with many benefits:

- trees absorb carbon dioxide
- timber is used for many purposes, including building, furniture, firewood and charcoal
- trees are an excellent food source (leaves,

sap, bark, fruit and nuts)
- trees improve the landscape, they screen and improve the appearance of buildings
- trees provide shelter and wildlife habitats
- trees help stabilise easily eroded soils and spoil tips
- trees form hedgerows.

Trees near buildings

Not all trees growing close to buildings will affect the structure. Many other factors can be responsible for structural damage and so if you suspect any problems with existing trees, or you wish to plant close to a building, detailed site assessments by qualified professionals should be undertaken. Structural damage is generally limited to shrinkable clay soils. Trees, particularly species such as ash, take moisture out of these soils, thereby exaggerating soil shrinkage. This results in shifting foundations, which cause structural cracking. Conversely removing large trees from clay soils can cause the ground to swell, again leading to structural displacement.

Remember that roots, particularly species such as willow, may block drains, causing cracking and leaking problems. Branches can cause damage to roofs and guttering, suckers can disturb paving and stems can rub against walls. Many factors can affect root spread and roots often extend for a radius wider than the tree height. If unsure always seek professional advice before planting. A tree is the property and responsibility of the landowner, who may be liable for any damage caused. Always check with the local planning authority whether a tree preservation order is in place before working on a tree.

Birds

It is interesting to note that the government uses wild bird statistics as one of its 'quality of life indicators'. Birds are very important. They devour huge numbers of pest species, are visually appealing, wonderful to listen to, and many different species can be attracted to gardens of all sizes and locations. They need all the help they can get, as many species, even those common up until recent years, are now in decline. Most people enjoy looking at birds in their gardens. Feeding birds will definitely encourage them and studies have shown that supplementary feeding is important for winter survival and breeding success. The bird feed industry is booming (now worth around £200 million annually) and we must bear in mind that most of the feed sold is imported from abroad, so has mileage and resource implications. Suppliers which do grow much of their own seed and grain include Vine House Farm (**www.vinehousefarm.co.uk**) and WigglyWigglers (**www.wigglywigglers.co.uk**). Grow plants that provide a food source for birds (berries, fruits, seeds, etc) and also plants that attract insects, which will encourage insect eating birds (the book 'Gardening for Birdwatchers' is an excellent source of information on this). A birdbath is essential, particularly in hot dry weather but again, you must keep it filled and it should be positioned away from cats.

To discourage rats ensure you do not overfeed. All food on the ground should be consumed before nightfall or fit trays to feeders to limit the amount of food falling on the floor. If on the rare occasions we see rats, we never resort to poisoning, but discourage

What about cats?

Cats are the number one predator of our wildlife, killing and injuring millions of species each year. There are over 7.5 million cats now kept as pets in the UK with a further 1 million plus feral cats and the population is still growing. The RSPCA urges people to neuter their cats and this is vital to help reduce numbers, as well as dealing with feral populations.

For their size, domestic cats are very effective predators. They do not respect boundaries and have extensive territories, being difficult to keep out of any area. The domestic cat can hunt and eat about one thousand species. Many pet cats successfully hunt and kill rabbits, rodents, birds, lizards, frogs, fish, and large insects by instinct, but many do not eat their prey. It is estimated that domestic cats in Britain kill around 250 million items of prey each year. If you have a cat, a correctly fitted collar and bell can help reduce predation. So can piles of bramble or other prickly plants around a bird feeding area or a scattering of chilli powder at building entrances. If you don't have a cat, think twice before you get one!

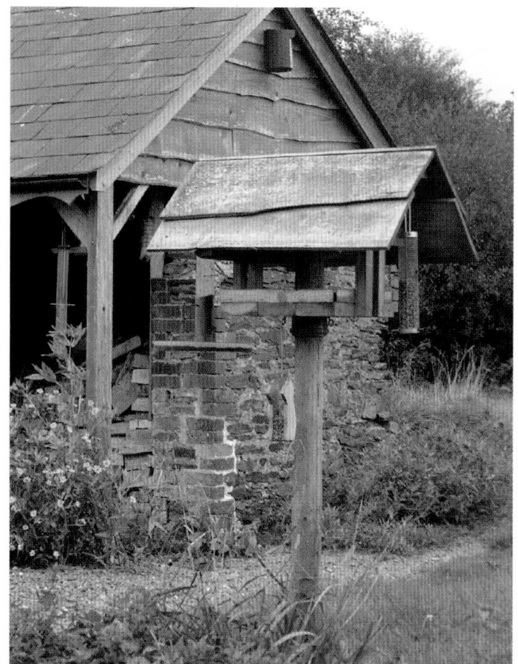

Birds will benefit from feeding help all the year round. Feeding can be from bird tables or feeders, home-made or purchased. A diverse range of species use this station.

Sadly barn owls have declined significantly, due to the conversion of many old farm barns over the past few decades, decreasing habitat and road kills. If you have this species in your area you can take steps to encourage them by providing the appropriate habitat and buildings. Contact the Hawk and Owl Trust for more information.

them by locating and blocking up their runs. We also keep all food out of their reach and the rats disappear quickly, probably falling prey to the larger mammal species frequenting our garden.

Nest boxes will encourage birds to breed in your garden and can be installed where natural potential breeding sites, such as holes in trees, dense hedges etc, are scarce. Nest boxes are available for a diverse range of bird species and can also be made easily from timber off cuts. Boxes must be designed correctly and hole size is important for many species. Advice on making boxes for different species and siting instructions are available from organisations such as the RSPB, BTO or your local wildlife trust, (see end of article for contact details). Ensure you site nest boxes well away from cats. Open-fronted ones need to be camouflaged and well hidden by vegetation. We have had great success with the Woodcrete boxes, which are made from sawdust and concrete and come with a 25-year guarantee. However, the spotted woodpecker can predate even these boxes, both eggs and young. The problem with nest boxes is that they tend to be visible and it does not take long for a predator species to recognise them as a potential food source during the nesting season.

Thousands of birds are killed or injured each year from flying into glass, particularly young birds in their first year or ones fleeing predators. Birds are attracted to the bright reflections of sky and vegetation seen in the glass. Site feeding areas and nest boxes well away from glazed areas. If you have a problem you can brush a soda crystal solution on to the glass surface (internally will last longer) to make it opaque during the times of highest risk (summer and autumn).

Do bear in mind that if you have a healthy population of birds, they will attract natural predators, such as the sparrow hawk. While some may be distressed to see birds killed by hawks, remember that it is a native species, high in the food chain, that must eat to survive. The species is only just starting to recover from its previous decline due to widespread pesticide use. We have a resident pair but they take fewer birds than the feral and neighbouring cats.

Bats

There are seventeen species of bat in the UK but many are now rare. Development of all kinds destroys roosting sites and feeding grounds. Gardens are therefore becoming vital for these useful species. They cause no harm to people or buildings. You are most likely to see the pipistrelle (our smallest species) in your garden at dawn or dusk and it will eat, on average, 3,000 midges per night during the summer! Bats will use bat boxes and may even breed in them. Many shelter and breed in buildings, behind hanging tiles and boarding and in roof spaces.

Bats and buildings

In the UK, law protects bats and their roosts. A roost is defined as 'any place that a wild bat uses for shelter or protection', and the roost is protected, whether bats are present in it or not. If the roost is in a dwelling house and any works require planning permission then you should inform the local planning authority about the bats during the period of public consultation. The local Statutory Nature Conservation Organisation (SNCO) office will advise on the best way to carry out the work, causing minimal disturbance to the bats. If planning permission is not required (e.g. a re-roofing), then you need to contact the Bat Conservation Trust for advice. Always avoid using chemical treatments in a roof that is used by bats.

If the roost is in a structure that is not a dwelling, such as a church or a barn or a tree, then the developers will need to obtain a Habitats Regulations license in order to carry out any work. Someone with experience of bats must apply for the licence. In this situation you should write to the planning office to alert them to the presence of a bat roost, and to advise them that a Habitats Regulations licence is needed before any work goes ahead. They should then ensure the developer proceeds with the proposal only if a licence is obtained.

Bees

Bees are essential for pollinating a wide variety of plant and tree species. The decline in bumblebee populations has been receiving increasing news coverage over the last few

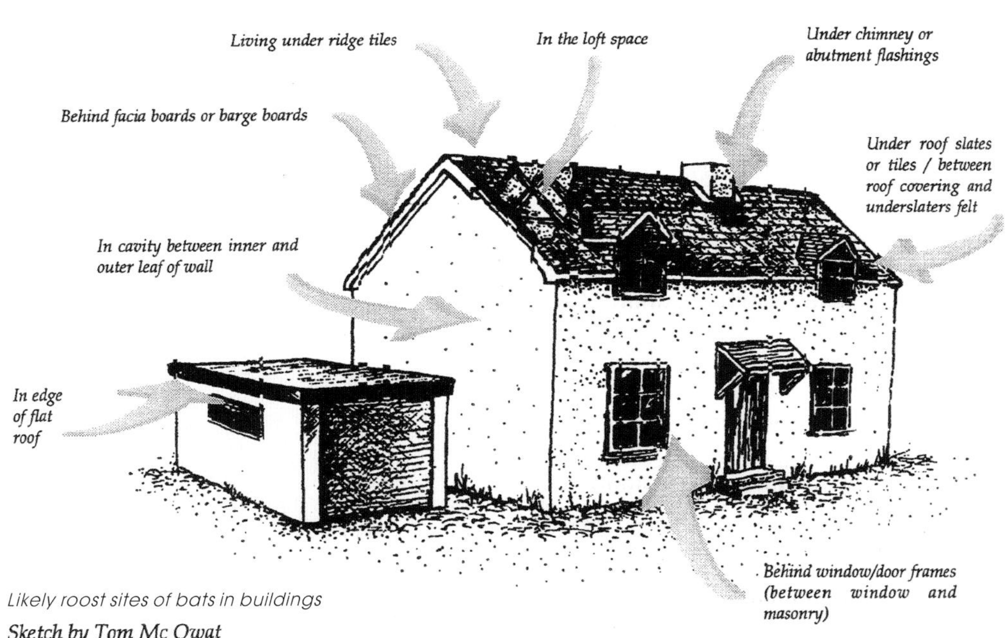

Likely roost sites of bats in buildings
Sketch by Tom Mc Owat

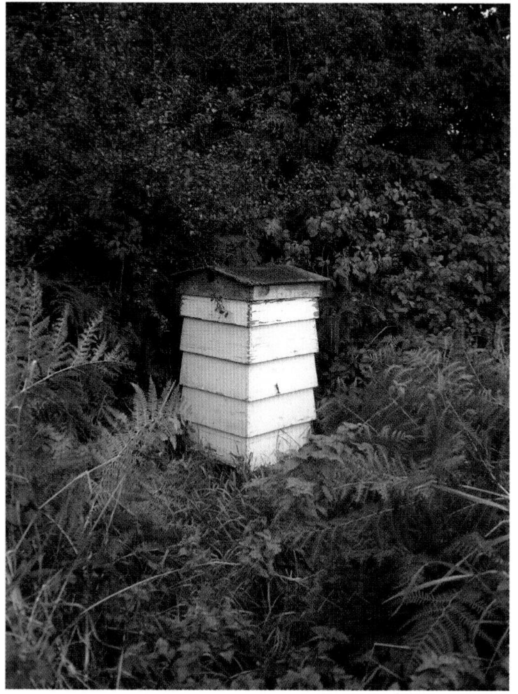

As well as supplying us with honey, the honey bees pollinate a wide range of plants and trees, including fruit species. This hive is tucked away in the corner of a fruit orchard.

years. Three of the UK's twenty bee species are already extinct. Agriculture depends on bees for pollination of crops. Certain species of bees and the plants they pollinate, are declining together in numbers. This is because insects can develop specialised tongues for reaching the nectar in particular plants and therefore effectively specialise in pollinating only these plants. The Bumblebee Conservation Trust aims to help prevent bee numbers from falling further.

Unfortunately even the honeybee is declining and now almost all UK apiaries are infected with varroa, a parasitic mite which weakens the bees. Many hives are collapsing, unless managed carefully. However, if you have a large garden with plenty of space around, you could consider getting some bee hives and start bee-keeping. If you decide to keep bees, locate hives behind fences or hedges to ensure the bees are encouraged to fly high and away from people. You should also consult your local bee keeping organsation for more advice.

Natural pest control

The practical benefit of a bio-diverse garden is that it will attract more garden predators, such as birds, hover flies and ladybirds. The better the eco-system you create, the fewer pests you will have to worry about. Ponds are excellent for encouraging beneficial predators such as frogs, toads, newts etc, but remember the sloping sides so creatures can get out easily. If your garden has a healthy population of insects it will attract predators, such as birds, bats and hedgehogs. A hedgehog can eat its own bodyweight in insects in one night, naturally helping keep insects down to manageable levels. Hedgehogs will also help by eating slugs and snails. If you want to attract hedgehogs, create access under a gate or via a hole in a fence and do not use slug pellets.

Moles eat many pest species but many people are not happy with the molehills they produce. If you have a wilder garden you should hardly notice the earth mounds or you can easily clear these away - the soil makes an excellent, free potting compost.

Sadly many people still use slug pellets. These certainly kill slugs but the poisoned carcasses are eaten by creatures higher up the food chain, such as birds and hedgehogs, with disastrous results. You should not need to control slugs where garden plants and wildflowers are established. You may need to control them if you have young seedlings. Nematodes are the latest environmental control. This is a natural slug parasite which is watered into the soil. They are slug-specific, so can't harm other animals in the food web. Avoid using them close to ponds, however, as they will also affect water snails. The most environmentally benign method though is hand-picking slugs from areas of young plants at dusk or dawn.

In general, choose plant varieties that have natural resistance to pests and diseases and are useful for attracting and encouraging wildlife. A healthy soil will help build strong plants to help resist attack and companion planting can help. This is where research and experience has shown that certain species grow well together. You should not need to use any chemicals in your garden if you get the natural balance right. You may find that on occasions you get an explosion of pest species but it shouldn't take long for predators to bring them under control.

Surveying the natural environment

With the current concerns about climate change, on-going surveys of our natural species are becoming increasingly important for monitoring purposes. For example, the index of wild bird populations is one of the government's key indicators for sustainable development in the UK. Bird populations are considered as a good indicator of the broad state of wildlife and countryside because they occupy a wide range of habitats, they tend to be near or at the top of the food chain, and considerable long-term data on bird populations is available. Birds are placed on the red (globally threatened), amber (moderate declines) or green lists (stable). A total of 247 species have been assessed.

You can get involved with the four year BTO Bird Atlas Project, which commenced winter 2007/8 and aims to record birds across the UK, including those seen/breeding in gardens. You can also help with other surveys by reporting what you see in your garden and the surrounding area. See the contacts below for some of the on-going ones, (free unless stated otherwise).

With grateful thanks to Louise Zass-Bangham for providing some of the information for this article and Keith Hall jnr for the photos.

Surveying opportunities

British Trust for Ornithology (BTO), different surveys, including Bird Atlas (free) and Garden BirdWatch (£12 per annum): 01842 750050 **www.bto.org**

Royal Society for the Protection of Birds (RSPB), Big Garden Birdwatch: 01767 680551 **www.rspb.org.uk**

UK Phenology Network, Spring Watch and Autumn Watch: 0800 77 1234 **www.naturescalendar.org.uk**

PlantLife's annual Common Plants Survey: 01722 342730 **www.plantlife.org.uk**

Further information and useful contacts

For advice on trees and buildings, and contacts for professionals who can help in the case of problems with trees and buildings: **www.rhs.org.uk/advice/profiles0101/trees_buildings.asp**

Information on planting, care, species: **www.treecouncil.org.uk**

Courses for builders regarding building near trees: **www.nhbcbuilder.co.uk/Consultancyservices/Training/BuildingnearTrees**

The place to visit for information, news and discussion on Britain's wild predators: **www.toothandclaw.org.uk**

Further reading

'Gardening for Birdwatchers' by M Toms, I & B Wilson.

'Guide to Garden Wildlife' by R Lewington.

'Bringing a Garden to Life' by J Steel.

'Wildlife Gardening for Everyone' by M Tait.

'How to Make a Wildlife Garden' by C Baines.

A Year in the Life of an English Meadow' by P Devlin.

The above books are availabe from the Green Shop: 01452 770629 **www.greenshop.co.uk**

Useful organisations

Bat Conservation Trust: 0845 1300 228 **www.bats.org.uk**

The Bumblebee Conservation Trust: **www.bumblebeeconservationtrust.co.uk**

Garden Organic (HDRA), national charity for organic growing: 024 7630 3517 **www.gardenorganic.org.uk**

Hawk & Owl Trust: 0870 990 3889 **www.hawkandowl.org**

Royal Society for the Protection of Birds (RSPB): 01767 680551 **www.rspb.org.uk**

Royal Society for the Prevention of Cruelty to Animals (RSPCA): 0870 33 35 999 **www.rspca.org.uk**

The Mammal Society: 020 7350 2200 **www.abdn.ac.uk/mammal**

The Wildlife Trusts: 0870 036 7711 **www.wildlifetrusts.org**

The British Dragonfly Society: **www.dragonflysoc.org.uk**

Butterfly Conservation: 0870 7744309 **www.butterfly-conservation.org/index.php**

British Hedgehog Preservation Society: **www.britishhedgehogs.org.uk**

Natural swimming pools

The two most important benefits of a natural swimming pool are the absence of chemicals and the provision of habitats for wildlife. **Michael Littlewood** brought the concept to the UK ...

Many people can still remember the joy of bathing and swimming in natural waters in the countryside, whether it was a lake, river or a pond, in sunshine or moonlight, whatever the weather, with or without clothes, in groups or as a solitary soul, planned or spontaneous. Alas this has all changed and most children today are unlikely to experience such natural bathing due to numerous reasons, such as health and safety, trespass and land ownership, litigation and polluted waters. However, not all is lost as there are now natural systems for private and public swimming that can be built for the enjoyment of everyone. Natural swimming pools are based on ponds and pools that were once found so abundantly in the landscape.

The comparison to a landscape pool is deliberate because that is what a natural swimming pool is – a large pond with special provision for people to enjoy the water, as well as the various creatures that are attracted to it. Nature offers the best examples.

With natural ponds and lakes, these are cleaned and purified by the combination of plants and micro-organisms, including beneficial bacteria. These micro-organisms break down organic wastes into substances which plants can use directly as nutrients. This is very different from the conventional public and private pools that use chlorine to 'purify' the water. Chlorine is a poisonous gas that can irritate the skin and cause eczema and even more serious

Children playing in a safe, chemical-free natural swimming pool. *Photo courtesy Richard Weisler.*

diseases. Chlorine reverts easily to its natural gaseous state and so has to be topped up regularly, which is an on-going cost avoided with natural pools.

The pleasure of using natural, chemical-free water once again for bathing and swimming is now available to many people, whether it is in the privacy of their own home or publicly at a hotel, a park, or any recreational centre in the mountains or at the seaside! They are sheer bliss in which to swim and a joy to see. The original concept was developed in Austria by a number of people, who were very conscious of the health benefits of bathing in natural waters found at spas and hydro places. It was not until 1985 that the idea was commercially developed by an Austrian based company, called Biotop, by the founder Peter Petrich who conceived the idea of a self cleaning biosystem for swimming ponds.

These have been favoured by many European homeowners and have also become very popular in hotels and resorts. Biotop was followed by Bionova of Germany, who planned and executed the first public pool in 1998, with considerable success. Biotop and Bionova were followed by Bioteich of Switzerland, and during this period there were several other companies who undertook the building of natural swimming pools. More than 1000 pools have now been built in Austria, Germany and Switzerland by many contractors. Each one has something unique to offer with their individual systems but all are variations on the same theme.

As part of my philosophy of ecological design I had, for some time, been looking for an alternative to chemical swimming pools. A visit to a Biotop in Vienna early in 2000, where I studied their system, resulted in bringing the concept back to this country. The first natural swimming pool was built in September 2001 for a client in Gloucestershire.

How they work

Natural swimming pools, are a chemical free combination of swimming area and aquatic plant garden. The swimming area merges with the planted area, creating an environment that is intertwined and mutually dependent on one another. These ecologically balanced, self cleaning swimming pools combine the natural cleaning properties of plants with filtration and skimming systems, so that there is no need for harmful chemicals or intensive sand filtration.

Pond or swimming pool?

What is the difference between a natural pond and natural swimming pool? The former is just an ordinary pond that you can swim in if you wish (see below). The latter is a pool created specifically for swimming in. Natural ponds are balanced ecosystems, which achieve water clarity from natural cycles. A natural swimming pool, on the other hand, uses a more sophisticated filtration system that carefully controls water quality.

The result is a biologically clean, chemical free swimming environment. The water is clear but not sterilised, as in the traditional swimming pool, and it is able to sustain the normal range of pond life, microscopic organisms, invertebrates and even frogs and toads. The aquatic flora and fauna are indicators of the state of the environment and at present their loss in the landscape is very worrying.

While designs of the natural swimming pools may vary, all consist of a swimming area and a regeneration (plants) zone. The swimming area can range between 1.2m and 2.2m deep and this area is kept plant free. It is usually lined with a rubber liner or foil to prevent water leakage and it is separated from the regeneration zone by a barrier wall. This prevents the invasion of plants and soil leakage from

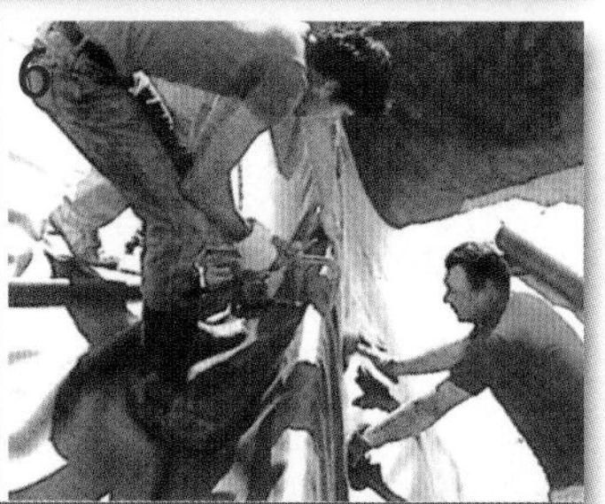

the regeneration zone into the swimming area. It also makes it much easier to service and drain each separately. The wall top will actually be approximately 100mm below the surface of the pool in order to allow free transfer of water between each area.

Within the regeneration zone the water is cleansed biologically by the roots of the aquatic plants and micro-organisms. The plants act as living filters and provide a very important function in the whole system by absorbing decomposing materials and bacteria, as well as pollutants, from the water and converting it into biomass (plant tissue), thereby cleaning water. Water plants rely on these nutrients for their growth.

Zooplankton is important for the natural swimming pool as they feed on single-celled algae and filter them out of the water. Through this natural self-cleaning process the use of harsh chemicals is unnecessary to keep the pool free from algae and safe. There is very little need for maintenance.

Plants

A range of aquatic plants are used covering submerged (oxygenators), floating, shallow marginals, deep marginals, bog/marsh and waterside species. Wherever possible indigenous plants are used but a definitive plant list is not always possible as each region should have plants from its own locality, if they exist, as this will provide for more interest. All aquatic plants grow far more quickly than soil based species and there is always the necessity of thinning and pruning.

Construction

A swimming pool requires a deep area of at least 1.5m to 2.2m, with near vertical walls, which needs to be constructed for the swimming area and waterproofed by means of a rubber liner with an underliner. The swimming area should be a minimum of 25m^2 (50m^2 is the minimum for the total area). The internal walls should be constructed from sustainable materials wherever possible such as recycled plastic, stone, timber or geotextile bags. As they will be acting as a retaining structure for the material and plants in the regeneration zone, they should be carefully engineered. The walls usually have a capping. They should finish 100mm below the water surface to maintain the visual effect of one pool. Ideally the liner should be placed behind the wall (but in some cases it goes over the wall) to ensure that it is both hidden and protected.

The water is drawn down through the substrate in the regeneration zone and through

The construction sequence of a natural swimming pool is similar to that of an elaborate garden pond. The important notes to remember are that the swim area walls are kept 100mm below the finished surface water height to allow water to mix between the swim zone and the plant zones.
Photos courtesy Biotop, Austria.

perforated pipework to the pump. The water is also taken via the surface skimmer to the pump where it is again filtered before returning to the bottom of the swimming area. The regeneration zone must be of the same size as the swimming area and have an average depth of 300mm of aggregate, usually graded from 50 to 450mm approximately.

In some pools the plants would surround the swimming area, giving a soft planted margin to the pool. In small pools it is better to plant on one side only so as to avoid a tight enclosed effect. Where space is at a premium, an alternative is to create a second pool, perhaps uphill, to allow the water to flow between the bodies of water, probably using a pump and waterfall.

The regeneration zone utilises a course inert substrate, such as shingle/gravel and not topsoil or any other growing medium as this would bring high levels of nutrients to the water and would counteract the cleaning effects of the plants, while contributing to the silting process. By planting the aquatic plants in shingle they must draw their nutrients from the water itself and so clean the pool. Also by cutting and removing the plant mass each autumn, the impurities held in the plants are physically removed from the water, allowing the cycle to begin again in the following spring. A surface leaf skimmer is also used to help remove floating debris from the water.

Silt, a combination of decaying vegetation, dust and other detritus, will always form in any body of water, and depending upon the size and location of the pool, it can easily be removed by either a vacuum or bottom purge system. A drainage ditch is constructed completely around the pool to ensure that no water runoff enters the pool thereby causing any differences in the pH and the water quality.

It has been assumed by many people that the cost of building a natural swimming pool should be considerably cheaper than the conventional ones. Sadly, this is not the case, due to the many complexities with the biological, as well as the construction, processes. Currently the average cost is £450/500 per square metre with a minimum size of 50m^2.

Water quality

The quality of the water is of special significance. The layout of the pool with its natural regeneration zone promotes the self-cleaning forces of the water and the mechanisms provide a long term stable and hygienic quality. The use of chemicals would only lead to the destruction of the biological balance in the water. The shallow warmer water of the regeneration zone circulates with the cooler deeper water of the swimming area and increases its temperature much more quickly. Solar methods can be used providing care is exercised and it is not used until the plants have grown to combat the algae. Fish are not allowed in the

Recreational exercise can be in harmony with the environment and not at its expense. Swimming pools that integrate with the garden are easier to maintain and visually more stimulating.

Photo courtesy of Biotop, Austria.

pool as they cause damage to the water quality and also encourage birds, such as herons, who could also damage the liner. Ducks, geese and any other waterfowl, are also discouraged plus any pets, such as dogs.

Wildlife

The natural swimming pool provides an attractive biosphere for various kinds of animals and is quickly inhabited after its creation. They stay mostly in the regeneration zone that serves them well with food and shelter. There are many predatory insects that feed on mosquito larvae. Amphibians use the regeneration zone as a breeding ground too. They appear in early spring to lay their eggs. The amphibians usually migrate from the pool before the swimming season commences.

Health aspects

Numerous users state that the joy of using water free from chemicals is profound. As previously mentioned chlorine is a skin irritant and been implicated in other, more serious diseases. It is also thought to aggravate asthma, especially in those children who make frequent use of chlorinated swimming pools. Chlorinated water contains chemical compounds called trihalomethanes which are suspected carcinogens resulting from the combination of chlorine with organic compounds in water. They do not degrade very well and are stored in the fatty tissues of the body.

What about converting an existing swimming pool?

While the majority of natural pools built in this country over the last seven years have been new ones there is no reason why existing conventional swimming pools cannot be converted, changing them into a natural, chemical-free pools. Many people are unaware that this conversion can easily be undertaken provided that there is sufficient space around it for the aquatic plants in the regeneration zone. It is even sometimes possible to locate the regeneration zone away from the swimming pool if there is insufficient room adjoining the existing pool.

The conversion task is not difficult and there are a number of advantages;

- thousands of litres of water could be saved by not having to empty the pool every autumn. If the average swimming pool is approximately 100 cubic metres capacity, then that equates to 100,000 litres of water! Even taking a very small number of 200,000 swimming pools in the country, that adds up to 200 million litres of water
- by not emptying the natural swimming pool there is always a supply of water for use in the case of emergencies
- there are less maintenance costs as no chemical top-ups are needed and the natural pool should be healthier for the user
- less energy is used as the water warms up much more quickly due to the black liner and the shallow water in the regeneration zone. The circulating pump can be operated quite easily by a photovoltaic cell - free energy from the sun
- there are no unsightly views of an empty pool in the winter, which collects leaves and debris and has to be cleaned out every spring before water filling can commence. In addition, when viewed from the air those unsightly turquoise blots on the landscape can be removed
- existing landscape materials surrounding the conventional pools, such as paving slabs, edges, trims, copings etc, can all be reused and thereby save energy, money, time and filling up more rubbish dumps!
- no major upheavals in the garden need to occur by the use of large machinery and equipment as the main structure – the swimming pool –has been built.

Conversion process

A large part of the construction - namely the excavations, the removal of all the surplus soil and debris and underground drainage has already been undertaken and this should be in good working order. The pool has probably been built with either concrete or concrete blocks and rendered or in some cases tiled. It will probably have copings around the edge of

Before and after pictures of the conversion of a regular chlorine treated swimming pool into being a natural swimming pool that does not need chemicals to keep it clean.

Photos courtesy of GartenArt, London.

the pool and paving slabs forming the terrace or patio. These can be removed completely to a safe place or reused or recycled.

If it has been decided to keep to the size of the existing pool for swimming then the regeneration zone must be made to approximately the same area. If not then the pool area can be sub-divided by building new internal walls, either of concrete block and covered with the liner, or of natural stone on top of the liner. The whole of both areas are covered with the protective under-liner and black top liner to make them waterproof.

The area surrounding the pool will need to be excavated to the correct profile and size for the creation of the regeneration zone. It will also have to allow for the special substrate material in which the plants are grown.

There is usually a bottom drain in most conventional swimming pools for emptying the pool and this can also be used to ensure that no water collects under the liner. One will need to be installed if a drain is not already in place as it is a vital component necessary for emptying and cleaning. The majority of the plumbing and electrical work will be in place but different skimmers, filters, pipe work, etc, will need to be installed. It may even be possible to use any existing underwater lights.

A perimeter wall will be necessary to hold the liners in place and to define the edge. An underground drain next to the wall will also be necessary to ensure that no surface water run-off goes into the pool as it is very important to control the water quality. The substrate is then placed in position followed by the planting of the aquatic plants and, finally, the whole area is filled with water.

Conclusions

There is no doubt that our landscape is in severe distress and the loss of wetlands, especially ponds and pools has now reached a critical stage. Natural swimming pools can, therefore, make a very important contribution to the restoration of aquatic flora and fauna. We must make every effort to design in harmony with nature. For, as many owners of natural swimming pools commented, 'it is that harmony, a seamless blending of environments that is the major advantage and it has enriched our lives. While you are separated from the plants you still feel surrounded by them when you swim, which creates a very special kind of mood.' The colour of the flowers from spring throughout the summer and into the autumn, along with the chorus of the birds and the frogs, make people feel far closer to nature. It provides them with a very special place to be at any time of the day or night, throughout the whole year. It is their very own natural oasis.

Further reading

'Natural Swimming Pools; an inspiration for harmony with nature' by M Littlewood .

'Natural Swimming Pools; a guide for building' by M Littlewood .

Both books available from the author: 01460 75515.

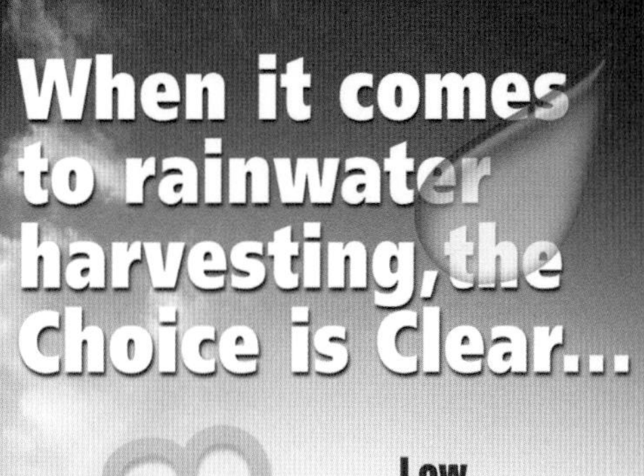
When it comes to rainwater harvesting, the Choice is Clear...

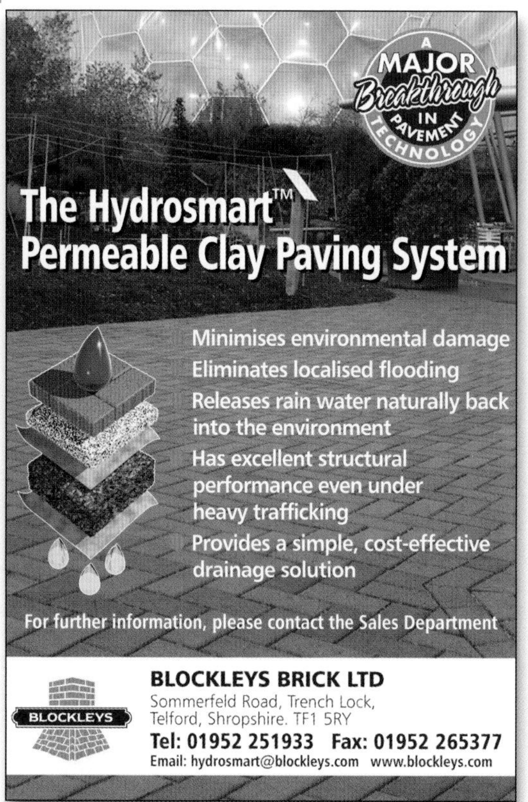
A MAJOR Breakthrough IN PAVEMENT TECHNOLOGY
The Hydrosmart™ Permeable Clay Paving System
Minimises environmental damage
Eliminates localised flooding
Releases rain water naturally back into the environment
Has excellent structural performance even under heavy trafficking
Provides a simple, cost-effective drainage solution
For further information, please contact the Sales Department
BLOCKLEYS
BLOCKLEYS BRICK LTD
Sommerfeld Road, Trench Lock, Telford, Shropshire. TF1 5RY
Tel: 01952 251933 Fax: 01952 265377
Email: hydrosmart@blockleys.com www.blockleys.com

BioTecture Ltd
Modular Green Walling Systems
01243 782121
3 Chapel Street
Chichester
PO19 1BU
info@biotecture.uk.com
www.biotecture.uk.com
The Award Winning BioWall™

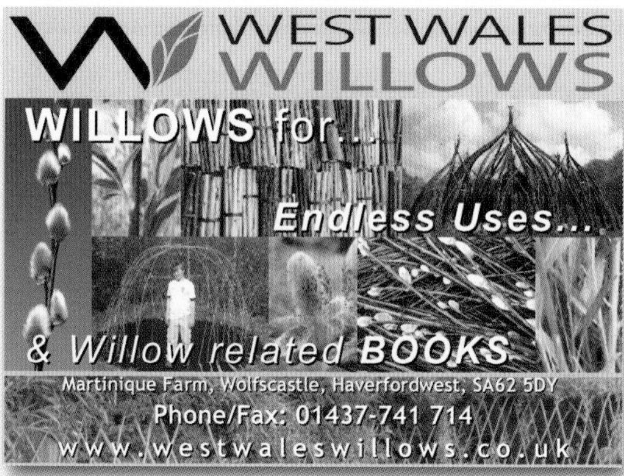
WEST WALES WILLOWS
WILLOWS for...
Endless Uses...
& Willow related BOOKS
Martinique Farm, Wolfscastle, Haverfordwest, SA62 5DY
Phone/Fax: 01437-741 714
www.westwaleswillows.co.uk

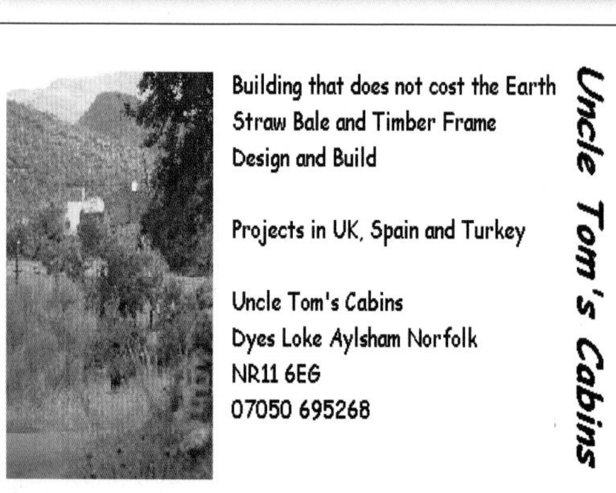
Building that does not cost the Earth
Straw Bale and Timber Frame
Design and Build
Projects in UK, Spain and Turkey
Uncle Tom's Cabins
Dyes Loke Aylsham Norfolk
NR11 6EG
07050 695268
Uncle Tom's Cabins

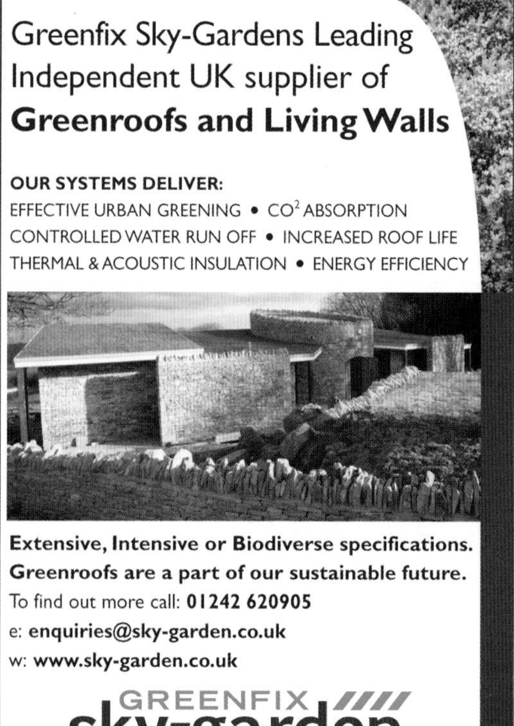
Greenfix Sky-Gardens Leading Independent UK supplier of
Greenroofs and Living Walls
OUR SYSTEMS DELIVER:
EFFECTIVE URBAN GREENING • CO2 ABSORPTION
CONTROLLED WATER RUN OFF • INCREASED ROOF LIFE
THERMAL & ACOUSTIC INSULATION • ENERGY EFFICIENCY
Extensive, Intensive or Biodiverse specifications.
Greenroofs are a part of our sustainable future.
To find out more call: 01242 620905
e: enquiries@sky-garden.co.uk
w: www.sky-garden.co.uk
GREENFIX sky-garden

8 Inspiration and help

Organisations

There are now many organisations in and around the building industry that offer membership, advice, training and support on any aspect of the green building arena. Here are some of the long-standing and significant players.

AECB

The AECB, (Association for Environment Conscious Building), the sustainable building association, was founded in 1989 to facilitate environmentally responsible practices within building. Its members are committed to reducing the environmental impact of buildings and there is a vast range of knowledge and expertise within the organisation. If you are looking for a builder, architect or other building professional with experience of sustainable building, many of its members are at the forefront of sustainable design and construction. Details of its members can be found at **www.aecb.net** where members can be searched by county or trade. The AECB's annual ecobuilding conference is held at different venues across the UK where workshops and debates run in tandem with networking. There are also local groups in many areas. The organisation is currently focusing much of its resources on measures to tackle climate change and, in particular, is concentrating on reducing energy consumption in buildings as a vital step forward. The AECB's CarbonLite programme is being developed to refine and enhance sustainable design skills in the area in which they are currently the weakest, i.e. energy performance. The programme is based on the German passivhaus standard and, is a complete 'carbon literate' design and construction programme based around passivhaus, silver and gold standards. The AECB runs one and two days training under the programme, which is aimed at those working in all areas of the building industry. The current courses reflect the AECB's current focus on energy efficient construction. The AECB can also design and run customised courses and CPD training for companies, local authorities, voluntary groups, colleges etc. Its vision is to act as a key player in the sustainable construction arena for government, the construction industry and its members. It aims to inspire, debate, raise awareness of the problems, assist with policy guidance, disseminate knowledge and produce appropriate guidance and tools. It is now a key player in lobbying and advising government and other key institutions, responding to all relevant consultations. 0845 456 9773
www.aecb.net and **www.carbonlite.org.uk**

BioRegional Development Group

BioRegional Development Group is an entrepreneurial, independent environmental organisation. It develops commercially viable products and services which meet more of our everyday needs from local renewable and waste resources, to help enable 'one planet living' – living within our fair share of the Earth's resources. Its initiative, One Planet Products, is a not-for-profit service developed by the group, which has recruited some of the UK's leading developers, housing associations and architects to drive a green supply chain and help reduce the environmental impact of housing developments. Membership is open to developers, including housing associations, local authorities and contractors, with associate membership for non developers, including architects, quantity surveyors and consultants. 020 8404 6982 **www.bioregional.com** and **www.oneplanetproducts.com**

Centre for Alternative Technology (CAT)

CAT takes a refreshingly positive look at environmental issues and, through a variety of services and experiences, offers practical solutions to all aspects of sustainable living. Its areas of expertise are renewable energy, environmental building, energy efficiency, organic growing and alternative sewage systems. Visitors to the site (open 7 days a week) can see different building techniques, gardens, interactive displays, and take-home examples of sustainable living. CAT also publishes and sells a range of books, offers a free information service and, for bigger projects, provides a consultancy service. It offers a diverse range of inspiring courses with introductory day classes, long running short residential courses and accredited specialist courses for professionals in renewable energy and sustainable water management. The Graduate School of the Environment (GSE) offers a range of postgraduate programmes in renewable energy and environmental architecture which, from 2009, will be held in the new, purpose built Wales Institute for Sustainable Education (WISE). 01654 705950 **www.cat.org.uk**

Cornwall Sustainable Building Trust (CSBT)

CSBT is a charitable company committed to making building design and construction as sustainable as possible, with minimal negative impact on the environment, both locally and globally. This is achieved through the promotion of design that minimises energy consumption, and sources local and renewable materials. Wherever possible, CSBT aims to highlight the social, environmental and economic benefits from the provision of affordable, well-designed, healthy homes and business accommodation with low running costs, throughout Cornwall. Working closely with small and medium sized businesses within the construction sector in Cornwall, CSBT assists them in developing their capability to understand and respond to the expanding traditional and sustainable construction market, helping them to increase their market potential.
01872 277000 **www.csbt.org.uk**

Ecos Trust

Ecos, a charity based in Somerset (previously called the Somerset Trust for Sustainable Building) and aims to make sustainable building the norm. It lobbies for sustainable building in the south west, offers a consultancy service, organises training courses, conferences and seminars (including working with the Genesis centre), has an online directory of eco businesses and contacts for the south west and holds the popular Homes for Good annual sustainable home and garden exhibition. Its development arm is Ecos Homes (the new name for South West Eco-Homes Ltd). Eco-Homes has already built the pioneering eco development at Great Bow Yard, Langport (the excellent book; Anatomy of an eco build' gives full details of the project). Other sustainable builds are planned for Stawell in Somerset and Bridport in Devon. 01458 259400 **www.ecostrust.org.uk**

Ethical Junction (EJ)

The EJ network was originally established in 1999 as a networking website for environmental groups and individuals and its remit has expanded considerably since then. Its constitution as a not-for-profit community interest company, ensures 100% of any profit is donated annually to causes that promote sustainable living. EJ members are asked to test themselves annually against six fundamental ethical principles relating to business and lifestyle. As well as a directory of members, its website now includes 'ethical pulse' (an on-line news and information forum), and an ethical advertising network which is exclusive to ethical companies in the network. EJ is building a solid and dependable network brand. It has assisted hundreds of ethical businesses gain a higher profile since it began. EJ is teaming up with a number of partners to create resilient communities. The term resilience will be well known to those familiar with the 'transition town' concept. It borrows from ecology the ability of something that can withstand systemic shocks without dying. And there is no doubt that with the age of cheap energy now over, there will be many severe shocks to our lifestyles and communities. **www.ethical-junction.org**

Good Homes Alliance (GHA)

GHA is a group of housing developers, building professionals and other industry supporters whose aim is to close the gap between aspiration and reality by showing how to build and monitor good homes which are sustainable in the broadest sense. All GHA developer members have signed up to meet GHA Code requirements, which are Code for Sustainable Homes level 3++, or approximately EcoHomes 'excellent'. All members must also sign up to the GHA charter, which covers other aspects of social and community-scale performance. The GHA helps to deliver real improvement through education, research, guidance and technical support. It also engages in active policy and promotion activities to ensure that market conditions encourage and incentivise developers to take a more sustainable approach.
020 7841 8909 **www.goodhomes.org.uk**

Hockerton Housing Project (HHP)

This organisation, a practical example, acts as a catalyst for change towards ecologically sound and sustainable ways of living. The last couple of years has seen a significant increase in interest in sustainable design and construction as evidence of climate change becomes ever more apparent. This has been fuelled by rising energy prices and growing water shortages. HHP is no longer seen as a curious oddity, but as an inspiration for others to develop solutions to these growing problems. It has seen a change in the attitude of visiting building professionals, from early scepticism to a desire to learn and integrate sustainable design principles into their building projects. HHP offers both full day technical workshops and consultancy services to assist building professionals, housing providers, government officers, students and self-builders. Over the next couple of years there are plans to develop these further to meet skills' gaps in delivering low carbon buildings. The HHP's community building, the Sustainable Resource Centre, can be hired as an inspirational venue for meetings, seminars or team-building activities. 01636 816902 **www.hockertonhousingproject.org.uk**

Low Impact Living Initiative (LILI)

LILI runs courses in the south-east, south-west and the north. Courses include building with straw-bales, cob, rammed earth, timber and hemp, plus making biodiesel, wind and solar electricity, self-build solar hot water and many more, with an eco-advisor's scheme and online courses planned for the future. It also has a huge online bookshop, free factsheets, a forum, and probably the best value solar hot water system you can buy (and LILI will teach you how to install it).
01296 714184 **www.lowimpact.org**

Scottish Ecological Design Association (SEDA)

SEDA is a member-run organisation which is open to anyone who is interested in ecological design. No qualifications are required, although many members are from professions in the built environment. The membership includes individuals, students, families, self-builders, charities, companies of all sizes and government organizations. With this considerable body of knowledge, SEDA provides a network and source of information, with particular reference to Scotland, for people who are interested in the principles of ecological design and how they may best be applied to buildings, communities, products and environments in the hope that we can swiftly develop a civilization which is founded on mature stewardship of the planet and planetary ecosystems. A magazine is published three times a year, and e-mail bulletins are circulated roughly once a month. There are also regular talks, site visits and other activi-

ties, which gives an opportunity for members to meet one-another informally and exchange ideas and experiences. The Association has recently produced three design guides which are available on the web site: 'design for deconstruction', 'design for airtightness' and 'design for chemical reduction' in buildings.
01361 840 230 **www.seda2.org**

Sponge

Sponge is a network of individuals who share a particular interest in sustainable development. They generally work in, or are associated with, the development of the built environment; from bricks and mortar through design, engineering and planning to communities and regeneration. Sponge provides a focus for fresh ideas in building; demonstrating how sustainable development can improve the quality of the built and natural environment. The group is aimed at young professionals and participation is open and encouraged to all. As an independent network Sponge gathers, debates, clarifies and promotes new ideas and successful initiatives relating to sustainable development and the built environment.
www.spongenet.org

The Green Register (TGR)

The Green Register is an independent, self-funded organisation whose central goal is to promote sustainable building practices across all disciplines of the construction industry. This is achieved through the three main activities:

- raising awareness of sustainable building practices by running training events across the UK. These events range from in-house CPD seminars, half-day practical workshops such as 'integrated design - the way forward' and 'lightweight versus heavyweight construction - which works best for the environment?', through to the two-day introductory 'sustainable building and services' course that all Green Register members have attended
- networking – Green Register events provide an opportunity to exchange ideas, provide mutual support and make professional connections with other like-minded individuals
- the register itself – full details of all members are listed on the website. This database is fully searchable and freely available to potential clients who are looking for construction professionals with a demonstrated commitment to sustainable building practices.

One of the Green Register's core principles is to encourage cross-disciplinary debate, so Green Register events and membership are open to everyone with an interest in sustainable construction. A course which ran in October 2007 attracted over 70 delegates, signalling the groundswell of interest and concern about the health of the planet. The Green Register will continue to address this critical problem in the future by attracting more members who will, in turn, work together to reduce the impact the construction industry has on the environment in which we live.
0117 377 3490 **www.greenregister.org.uk**

The Land is Ours (TLIO) and Chapter 7

TLIO campaigns peacefully for access to the land, its resources, and the decision-making processes affecting them, for everyone, irrespective of race, gender or age. Chapter 7, the planning office of TLIO, campaigns for a planning system which actively encourages sustainable, low impact and affordable homes, and, drawing on experience from Tinker's Bubble, published the report 'Defining Rural Sustainability: 15 Criteria for Sustainable Developments in the Countryside'.
01460 249 204 **www.tlio.org.uk** and **www.thelandisours/chapter7**

The Permaculture Association

This association is an educational charity run by its members, which helps people use permaculture in their everyday lives to improve the quality of life and the environment. It

- provides information on all aspects of permaculture and runs a national office providing information and support from 10.00 am to 4.00 pm, Monday to Thursday
- runs a membership scheme
- supports the development of permaculture education and training
- organises national and local events

Costs and membership benefits of the main existing UK green building trade organisations.

Organisation	Date established	Current number of members	Joining rates / fees / per annum, excl. VAT	Magazine or newsletter
AECB (the sustainable building association) *www.aecb.net*	*1989*	*1500+*	*£25 - £250 based on turnover*	✔✔
Scottish Ecological Design Association (SEDA) *www.seda2.org*	*1991*	*250*	*£22 (student) - £100 (corporations)*	✔
The Green Register (TGR) *www.greenregister.org*	*2000*	*500+*	*£45 (student) - £85 depending on size of business*	✔
Ecos Trust (formerly Somerset Trust for Sustainable Development) *www.ecostruct.org.uk*	*2000*	*150+*	*£12 (student) - £300 based on turnover*	✔
Cornwall Sustainable Building Trust (CSBT) *www.csbt.org.uk*	*2002*	*300+*	*£15 - £500 based on company size*	✔
Good Homes Alliance (GHA) *www.goodhomes.org.uk*	*2006*	*11 developers 55 supporters*	*£1250 - £10,000 based project value*	✔
UK Green Building Council (UK-GBC) *www.ukgbc.org.uk*	*2006*	*300+*	*£100 - £12,000 based on turnover*	✔

*For additional fee **   *Corporate only ***

- networks nationally and internationally.

0113 2307461 **www.permaculture.org.uk**

UK Green Building Council (UK-GBC)

The UK-GBC aims to bring cohesion to the green building movement and was launched in early 2007. It is a campaign for a sustainable built environment with a membership consisting of businesses from across the industry. In addition to industry, its members include NGOs, academic institutions and government agencies. The UK-GBC is part of the World Green Building Council federation, membership of which is growing as new national green building councils are established across the globe. For its members it provides information, opportunities to take action, and a vehicle for influence. Its main programme of work is based around the interactive UK-GBC 'Roadmap to Sustainability' and associated 'task groups'. The roadmap is designed to provide a shared vision of a sustainable built environment and provides a path for the industry, its clients and policy makers to follow to achieve that vision. The task groups bring together stakeholders to tackle particular policy issues for time-limited periods. The first task group report in December 2007 led to the Chancellor's announcement that all new non-domestic buildings would be zero carbon by 2019. The future will see further work on the zero carbon agenda in domestic and non-domestic sectors, as well as an increasing amount of work on reducing emissions from the existing housing stock. Task groups such as measurement and reporting, biodiversity and skills, will continue to develop their reports and members will propose further pieces of work to contribute towards the development of its web-based roadmap. The website will continue to be developed as a place where the industry can go for guidance and clarity on a range of issues, as well as a place where members share information through dedicated forums. UK-GBC runs a very active events programme.

0207 580 0623 **www.ukgbc.org**

Due to space restrictions, in this section we have not included the established professional associations, trade federations and those groups that may deal with specific areas of building or renewable energy. However, many of them can be found elsewhere in this book - see the Index.

Yearbook / online listings	Local groups and networking	Events and conferences	Training and workshops	In-house standards	Use of logo	Members' area or website forum	Online member profiling	Lobbying	Information and advice	Criteria for joining or membership
✓✓	✓	✓	✓	✓	✓	✓	✓	✓	✓	*Must acknowledge agreement with charter*
✗	✓	✓	✓	✗	✓**	✗	✗	✓	✓	✗
✓	✓	✓	✓	✗	✓*	✓	✗	✗	✓	*Compulsory attendance of 2 day course*
✗	✗	✓	✓	✗	✗	✓	✗	✓	✓	✗
✓	✓	✓	✓	✗	✓	✗	✗	✓	✓	✗
✓	✓	✓	✓	✓	✓	✓	✗	✓	✓	*Must adhere to standards*
✓	✓	✓	✓	✗	✓	✓	✗	✓	✓	*Must acknowledge agreement with its principles*

Others groups, bodies promoting green building

Walter Segal Self Build Trust:
www.segalselfbuild.co.uk
Building Research Establishment -
(a government dept. until late 1990s):
www.bre.co.uk
Green Building Press
(established 1990):
www.greenbuildingpress.co.uk
National Green Specification:
www.greenspec.co.uk
Devon Sustainable Building Initiative
(established 2006):
www.sustainablebuild.org
The Eco-Renovation Network
(established 2006):
www.eco-renovation.org
The Existing Homes Alliance (established 2008)
01225 816848:
www.existinghomesalliance.org

Looking for building professionals for your project?

Sustainable building is now moving ever-closer to being mainstream and if you do plenty of pre-contract research on the subjects that concern you the most then it should be possible to achieve a successful green building project using competent construction industry professionals or businesses. However, not all professionals are yet sufficiently knowledgeable or interested in the subject, so you should first ascertain their willingness to come on-board with your ideas and aspirations. There is still much merit in the idea of seeking out professionals that are already on the same wavelength and thankfully this is a growing group. Many of the organisations listed here will have professional members among their ranks but you will be hard pushed to find a better group than the AECB's membership. The AECB was established in 1989 and its members (around 1500) are renowned for being at the forefront of sustainable design and construction. Details of its members, searchable by country, trade etc, can be found at **www.aecb.net**. Many members even have extended listing profiles which tell you more about the work they do.

Do remember that whoever you choose to contact, always obtain references and details of past projects prior to making any decision to employ. Non of the organisations listed offer any guarantees regarding employment and workmanship.

Inspirational places

A guide map for the inspirational places

Putting all the theory into practice, there are an increasing number of energy efficient and low impact projects completed in the UK. The majority use reclaimed and sustainable materials with high levels of insulation. Some have already been mentioned in previous chapters, but here **Sally Hall** has compiled a selection from across the UK, with very brief notes on some of the main features only, as more details can be found on the websites. Many welcome visitors, but ensure you telephone or check the website before calling in. We have not had the space to list every scheme and some of the websites listed also include details of other interesting eco projects not included in this list.

London

London Boroughs, *various projects by Architype, architects specialising in eco design. Projects include eco houses, commercial, new build, refurbishment, extensions, new build: 020 7403 2889* ***www.architype.co.uk***

The Calthorpe Community Centre*, Kings Cross, is an early example built in 1992, using natural materials with a green roof: 020 7403 2889* ***www.architype.co.uk***

The Tree House*, Clapham, completed 2006, on a tiny infill plot with a mature sycamore tree which influenced the design. Full story in the book, Diary of an EcoBuilder by Will Anderson:* ***www.treehouseclapham.org.uk***

The Millennium Centre*, The Chase Nature Reserve, Barking and Dagenham, completed 1997, uses a number of large 'helical screws', which anchor the building to the site, acting as foundations, so if the building were removed it would not leave a mark on the landscape: 020 8595 4155* ***www.barking-dagenham.gov.uk/8-leisure-envir/park-country/millennium/millen-c-menu.html***

The CUE *(Centre for Understanding the Environment) building, (completed 1995) using sustainable materials with a grass roof. It now houses the Horniman Library: 020 7403 2889* ***www.architype.co.uk/cue.html***

Angell Town Estate*, Brixton is a regeneration and refurbishment project. From 1998 refurbished and partly rebuilt in a series of separate packages designed by different architects. The London Borough of Lambeth Policies for Sustainable Housing has provided a policy basis for green construction and its translation into practice in this project: 020 7704 1391* ***www.ecoconstruction.org/c_study_angell2.html***

Greenwich Millennium Village*, eco 'village' in London; residential development from one-bedroom apartments to penthouses:* ***www.englishpartnerships.co.uk/gmv.htm***

Mile End Park*, East End, an ecology park with lakes, themed areas and grass-covered buildings. Used for art, sport, play and the study of ecology. A 'green bridge' of shrubs and trees spans a busy road, linking the two main areas of the park:* ***www.cabe.org.uk/default.aspx?contentitemid=201***

Gherkin *office building, (Swiss Re skyscraper) opened 2004, an innovative design (hence its name), which uses half the energy typically required by an office block:* ***www.fosterandpartners.com/Projects/1004/Default.aspx***

Bow, *East London. Small block of four flats on a tiny urban infill site, It has a communal clean burn wood pellet boiler, a micro wind turbine, and wind driven heat recovery: 020 8404 1380:* ***www.zedfactory.com/bowzed/bowzed.html***

South Harrow, *low carbon homes and office block conversion to ZED homes, high density flats:* ***www.zedhomes.com/html/developments/edf***

Stansted, *UK's largest straw bale office/auction rooms building completed 2007, incorporating glulam frame,* *cedar shingles, biofuels, renewables:* ***www.ukauction.info/2007/09/29/straw-bale-auction-rooms-nearing-completion***

Hackney, *Murray Grove Tower, nine-storey aprtment block, tallest timber recreational building in the world using cross-laminated timber panel construction. Completed 2007:* ***www.treehugger.com/files/2007/06/waugh_thistleto.php***

Emily House, *Kensington (Octavia's HQ), largest PV system of any housing association in UK, CHP system: 020 8354 5500* ***www.sterling-sustain.com/case-studies.html***

The Saville Gardens Gridhsell, *Windsor Great Park, visitor centre. Roof is a timber gridshell using Eurpean larch. The largest gridshell structure in the UK, completed 2006:* ***www.greenoakcarpentry.co.uk/g-body-savill-garden-gridshell.htm***

The Creative Media Training Centre*, Southwark Bridge Road, (opened 2006) is a refurbishment and extension of a disused Victorian library. Features include wind turbine, wood pellet heating system, passive ventilation, full building energy monitoring: 020 7403 2889* ***www.architype.co.uk/southwark.html***

South East

Braziers Park*, Oxfordshire features an eco-renovation, and low impact, community housing: 01491 680221* ***www.braziers.org.uk***

Oxford Eco House*, domestic dwelling and one of the most high profile low energy houses in the country, as featured in EcoHouse 2: 01865 484075* ***www.tve.org/ho/doc.cfm?aid=224***

Sutton Courtenay*, Oxfordshire (completed 2002) environmental education centre, sewage treatment system filtering liquids through an underground leachfield. Composted solids are used as fertiliser for tree planting. Mini reedbeds treat grey water. Set in a 13 acre nature reserve: 01235 862024* ***www.bbowt.org.uk/content.asp?did=23503***

Integer House*, House of the Future, Hertfordshire, built by BRE, hight tec, recycled materials, sedum roof, reedbed:* ***www.integerproject.co.uk***

BRE Innovation Park*, Watford, Hertfordshire, showcase of low energy, low carbon, low cost building prototypes. These including the Kingspan Lighthouse, the Barratt Green House, EcoTech's Organic House, the Hanson EcoHouse, the Osborne House, the Stewart Milne Sigma Home, a sustainable learning environment for schools and sustaiable community landscaping: 0845 2232966* ***www.bre.co.uk/page.jsp?id=634***

Redfield Community, *Buckinghamshire, sustainable community living, eco renovation of large house with workshops and training areas, regular courses: 01296 713661* ***www.redfieldcommunity.org.uk***

Holywell Mead *Environment Centre, High Wycombe, Buckinghamshire, opened 2002, utilises a redundant building refurbished using sustainable and natural materials. Heated using a biomass boiler: 01494 511585* ***www.ecobuzz.org.uk***

The Living Rainforest*, near Newbury, Berkshire is an educational centre, jungle (in greenhouses) with the Human Impact timber educational centre, opened 2006: 01635 202444* ***www.livingrainforest.org***

Taplow Court Estate*, Berkshire, UK headquarters of SGI-UK, eco-build completed 2001: 01628 773163* ***www.sgi-uk.org/index.php/centres/Taplow_Court***

Reading International Solidarity Centre*, Berkshire. Forest garden containing over 160 types of edible and medicinal plants, including trees. Temperate agroforestry is possible, productive and attractive. Established 2001:* ***www.gardenvisit.com/garden/risc_roof_garden***

Kent Wildlife Trust's Romney Marsh visitor centre*, opened in 2004, has rendered straw bale walls, a green roof, rainwater conservation system and sustainable woodchip heating: 01797 369487* ***www.kentwildlifetrust.org.uk/reserves/romney-marsh***

Visitor Centre at Shorne Wood Park*, Gravesend, Kent built from locally sourced sweet chestnut. Demonstrating sustainable building techniques and technologies with a wind turbine and solar panels, rainwater harvesting, a woodchip boiler: 01474 823800* ***www.kentdowns.org.uk/map_details.asp?siteID=53***

Pines Calyx*, Kent, an eco conference centre using rammed earth (chalk) walls, completed 2006 (story on page 371): 01304 851737* ***www.pinescalyx.co.uk***

Bedzed*, Surrey is the UK's largest eco village of around 100 homes with community facilities and workplaces, exhibition centre and shop. Residents have been living in the homes since 2002: 020 8404 4880* ***www.bioregional.com***

Carshalton Grove, *Sutton, Surrey, renovated victorian semi by Parity Homes, a ground breaking project to demonstrate what can be achieved in existing homes regarding energy efficiency: 07904 224410* ***www.parity-projects.com/july2006.pdf***

Pestalozzi Childrens Village Trust*, Hastings, East Sussex is an education centre with some eco buildings, including straw bale, ancient woodland: 01424 870444* ***www.pestalozzi.org.uk***

Flimwell Woodland Enterprise Centre*, East Sussex is a Gridshell building using chestnut with an automated wood-fired heating system, designed to be low-energy consuming, and recyclable at the end of its life, plus a new woodland training centre: 01580 879552* ***www.woodnet.org.uk***

Stanmoor Park Earthship Building*, Brighton, Sussex, built from recycled materials, including tyres plus renewables: 07974 122770* ***www.lowcarbon.co.uk***

Diggers Self Build and Hedgehog Self Build*, Brighton, Sussex are timber frame (Segal) builds using natural materials: 01892 511652* ***www.forevergreen.org.uk***

The Milliners*, Forest Row, Sussex, four sustainably built, low energy maisonettes, built on difficult infill plot:* ***www.douchpartners.co.uk/millinersgallery/index.html***

Woking*, West Sussex, Green Oak housing association, 14 low energy homes, first sustainable project by this housing association:* ***www.greenoakha.org/sustainability/developments.php***

Ben Law's house*, Prickly Wood, Wessex was completed 2002, using sweet chestnut cruck timber frame with straw bale walls and sweet chestnut wood shingles:* ***www.ben-law.co.uk***

Weald and Downland Open Air Museum *of historical buildings, Chichester, Wessex, plus the Downland Gridshell timber (oak) building constructed in 2002: 0845 121 0170* ***www.wealddown.co.uk***

South West

St Werburgh's self build*, Bristol was built in 2004, by the Ashley Vale Action group, a group of self builders on a 2 acre former scaffolding site, using sustainable materials and renewable energy:* ***www.ashleyvale.org.uk***

Bordeaux Quay*, Waterfront, Bristol City Centre, local timber, recycling, heat pump, solar hot water, rainharvesting: 0117 954 7333* ***www.white-design.co.uk***

Hanham Hall, *Bristol, proposed first eco town of allegedly zero carbon homes built to CSH level 6. Site identified by government's Carbon Challenge, run by English Partnerships:* ***www.hanhamhall.co.uk/home/***

Heeley City Farm*, Bristol is a community based and led training, employment and youth project employing over 30 people, on a range of environmentally based enterprises. Includes high thermal mass, passive solar design, powered by renewable energy from photovoltaics and a wind turbine. Living green sedum roof: 01904 468752* ***www.ecoarc.co.uk***

Cherry Orchard*, Bristol, is a market garden and educational building, Camphill Community, low impact materials: 01952 433252* ***www.simmondsmills.com***

Create Centre*, Bristol, is an environment centre which features a purpose-built eco home and also hosts a range of events and exhibitions: 0117 922 2000* ***www.bristol-city.gov.uk/create***

The Congresbury Home*, Bristol, is a new fast track erection house, shell completed in 24 hours, using sustainable materials: 0117 955 7224* ***www.urban-e.com***

Barton Hill*, Bristol, school, eco-build, exciting glazing installations, sound responsive light features, children involved in whole process:* ***www.shedsite.wordpress.com***

The Glebe, *Blisland, Cornwall, new centre, local wood/slate, shop, PO, geothermal, renewables, rainwater harvesting: 01208 851730* ***www.blisland.com***

The Eden Project*, St Austell, Cornwall features the renowned 'Biomes', which represent three of the* *world's climate zones in domes, a visitors' centre and education facility with earth and timber buildings: 01726 811911* ***www.edenproject.com***

Trelissick Gardens*, Cornwall, energy efficient restaurant, local materials, micro-generation, National Trust: 01872 862090* ***www.nationaltrust.org.uk/main/w-vh/w-visits/w-findaplace/w-trelissickgarden***

St Mellion*, Nr Callington, Cornwall, new eco housing by Living Village: 020 7937 7537* ***www.livingvillageatstmellion.com***

Prince Charles' new village at Poundbury, Cornwall, *mixed urban development of town houses, cottages, shops and light industry:* ***www.planning.org/thecommissioner/fall98.htm***

Timber Cabin*, Redruth, Cornwall, timber cabin building with grass roof, classroom facility for horticultural students: 01209 891500* ***www.pioneerebc.co.uk***

Cob buildings*, Cob in Cornwall, involved in a number of mainly cob buildings in the Cornwall area but also other low impact projects that include straw, lime, turf roofs etc: 01326 231773* ***www.cobincornwall.com***

Mount Pleasant Eco Park*, Porthtowan, Cornwall is a 42 acre site with eco workshops for artists and crafts people. Also permaculture, training courses and eco holidays: 01209 891500* ***www.mpecopark.co.uk***

Lanlivery CP School*, Cornwall in 2003, added an 88m² super-insulated, low-energy construction built from local/recycled materials with a green roof planted with sedum: 01208 72100* ***www.arco2.co.uk***

Lyon House, Dittisham*, cob house built by long-established Kevin McCabe Cob Building Specialists:* ***www.buildsomethingbeautiful.com***

Oak Meadow*, South Molton, Devon is 35 affordable eco houses for rent, built in 2005. Also features wildlife corridors and habitats. Every home has a garden, fruit trees and Devon hedge banks:* ***www.dcha.co.uk/sustain***

Straw bale house, *Totnes by Jim Carffrae:* ***www.sustainablebuild.org/documents/jim_carfrae.pdf***

Neal's Yard Remedies*, (retailer of natural toiletries and medicinal products), Gillingham, Dorset, new industrial building for manufacturing, office and associated facilities, surrounded by productive landscape:01225 852545* ***www.feildenclegg.com***

The Genesis Centre*, sited at Somerset College in Taunton, is a living exhibition of sustainable building materials and techniques promoting energy efficiency and sustainable courses: 01823 366743* ***www.genesisproject.com***

Tinkers Bubble*, Somerset is a community of low impact dwellings and sustainable living: 01460 249204* ***www.tlio.org.uk/chapter7/photos.html***

Stawell, *Bridport, Merriott Carhampton, Dorset, new eco homes: 01458 259400* ***www.ecoshomes.co.uk***

Foundry House, *Yeovil, eco-refurbishment of a listed industrial buiilding plus 32 low energy homes.* ***www.southsomerset.gov.uk/index.jsp?articleid=17335***

Lower Coxbridge House*, Baltonsborough, Somerset, private dwelling, with renewables, water recycling: 01458 445100* ***www.markormearchitects.co.uk***

Polbury Mill*, Bruton, Somerset, community centre and nursery, cedar clad timber frame and recycled materials, an examplar building for the local authority: 01458 445100* ***www.markormearchitects.co.uk***

Great Bow Yard*, Langport, Somerset, 12 new timber frame houses, using natural and locally sourced materials and a variety of energy saving features built 2006: 01458 259400* ***www.swecohomes.co.uk***

Heelis Centre*, Wiltshire, HQ of National Trust built in 2006, natural ventilation, passive solar, renewables, thermal mass, sustainable materials, visitors welcome, free tours: 01793 817400* ***www.nationaltrust.org.uk/main/w-trust/w-thecharity/w-new_central_office.htm***

Wiltshire Wildlife Trust Visitor Centre*, Lower Moor Farm Reserve, Nr Oaksey, prefabricated off site, flowering meadow on roof, cladding leaving spaces for bats, wildlife habitat, renewables, natural finishes: 01380 725670* ***www.wiltshirewildlife.org***

Kindersley Centre*, Lambourne, Wiltshire is an eco conference centre built in 2005 on an organic farm: 01488 674737* ***www.sheepdrove.com***

Stroud Co-housing*, Gloucestershire was first new build co-housing scheme in the UK, built in 2004. Based on the Danish model, co-housing is a form of collaborative housing that aims to create a real sense of community. 35 private houses and flats with a shared common house at the heart. Timber frame construction from renewable sources, photovoltaic roof tiles:* ***www.springhillcohousing.com***

Green Shop, Gloucestershire is a builders' merchant, eco buildings, shop, renewables, rainwater harvesting, demonstration centre, new eco headquarters opened 2008: 01452 770629 **www.greenshop.co.uk**

Oxstalls Campus, Gloucestershire, university buildings, renovation, sustainability as a key component with low energy consumption and environmental control as major objectives: 01225 852545 **www.feildenclegg.com**

HQ of Wildfowl and Wetland Trust, Slimbridge, Gloucestershire, with visitors'centre built in 2000 includes reed beds for recycling grey water: 01453 891900 **www.ecda.co.uk/pdfs/slimbridge.PDF**

Living Green Centre, Bourton-on-the Water, Gloucestershire, green choices in real home setting. Shop, garden, eco-trail, grass roof, renewables and rain-harvesting: 01451 820942 **www.living-green.co.uk**

Green and Away, Gloucestershire, tented conference centre with innovative and eco-friendly, low-impact structures, including straw bale building: 0870 460 1198 **www.greenandaway.org.uk**

Tranquility, Gloucestershire, new house built 2008: **www.tranquilityhouses.com**

Sustainability Centre, East Meon, Hampshire, eco renovations, visitor centre, woodlands and hostel: **www.earthworks-trust.com/html/about_the_centre.html**

Anderwood End Cottages, Anderswood, Burley, near Ringwood, Hampshire, two new timber homes (semi detached) in New Forest, commoners cottages: 0845 367 3787 **www.forestry.gov.uk/newforest-ruralhomes**

West Midlands

Humber Marsh, Herefordshire is a renewables demonstration centre and timber building on nature reserve: 01568 760671 **www.windandsun.co.uk**

The Straw House, Putley, Herefordshire is made from straw bales: 01531 670934 **www.thestrawhouse.co.uk**

Self build, Herefordshire, energy efficient, externally insulated new house and converted stone barn: 01531 670934 **www.oxlet.co.uk**

The Wintles, Living Village Trust, Shropshire, new development of eco houses at Bishops Castle: 01588 630475 **www.livingvillage.com**

The Woodland College, Shropshire, study and conference building (built 1999) for Green Wood Centre, innovative pole framed structure building, low impact: 01952 433252 **www.simmondsmills.com**

Fordhall Farm, Shropshire, community land initiative bought in 2006, organic community farm with eco buildings planned: 01630 638696 **www.fordhallfarm.com**

Bishopswood Environmental Centre, Stourport, Worcestershire, timber educational building, wildlife landscaping, ancient woodland, green roof: 01299 250513 **www.bishopswoodcentre.org.uk**

The Cropthorne Autonomous House new super insulated house at planning stage: **www.cropthornehouse.co.uk**

Willans Green, Rugby, Warwickshire (completed 2005) new development of affordable homes built to BREEAM EcoHomes excellent: 01827 260600 **www.debutbyredrow.co.uk**

Wolseley Sustainable Building Centre, Leamington Spa, Warwickshire, interactive showcase used to demonstrate sustainable building: 01926 705000: **www.wolseleysbc.co.uk**

HQ of Organic Gardening (HDRA), Coventry, with a range of eco buildings together with demonstration areas relating to many aspects of organic gardening: 024 7630 3517 **www.gardenorganic.org.uk**

Bourneville Village Trust, Borunville, Birmingham, trial eco-refurbishment of a 1929 house, completed 2007 and being monitored: 0121 472 3831 **www.bvt.org.uk/ecohome/index.html**

Centre of the Earth, Birmingham headquarters of Urban Wildlife Trust, built 1992, innovative timber structure, low impact wildlife gardens: 0121 515 1702 **www.wildlifetrust.org.uk/urbanwt/education/coe/introduction.htmprimaryprospectus.htm**

St Luke's Church of England Primary School and The Willows, 2008, Wolverhampton: 01981 542111 **www.architype.co.uk/education2.html**

North West

The Footprint, Cumbria, the first straw bale building in Cumbria for the National Trust: **www.strawfootprint.org/galleries/movies/index.html**

Tullie House, Appleby, Cumbria, earth sheltered house started in 2002: **www.greenbuildingstore.co.uk/case-ecoplus7.php**

Solaris, Lancashire, demonstration centre for energy efficient systems, renewables and wildlife habitat, eco renovation, rainwater harvesting, CHP: 01253 478020 **www.solariscentre.org**

The Maharishi School Woodley Park Sports and Arts Centre, Lancashire, is the first public building in the UK that has been designed and constructed according to principles of an ancient and comprehensive system of architecture from India. Natural and non-toxic building materials including timber and clay, rammed earth for the external walls (story on page 253): 01695 729603 or 0207 241 4684 **www.rammed-earth.info**

Preston headquarters of the Wildlife Trust for Lancashire, Manchester and Merseyside uses recycled and local materials , woodchip-fuelled heating and renewables: 01772 750001 **www.lancswt.org.uk**

North Manchester 6th form college and North City public library, innovative low carbon building: **www.solarcentury.com/news/solarcentury_news/solarcentury_project_wins_top_architecture_award_for_design_excellence**

Dunham Massey and the Stamford Brook Sustainable Housing Development, Cheshire, new eco housing estate on former National Trust land: 08459 335577 **www.stamfordbrook.co.uk**

BDP HQ Piccadilly Basin**, Manchester, 2007 allegedly first naturally ventilated office building in Manchester, BREEAM 'excellent', green roof: **www.constructionmall.com/press/article/18780

Trafford Hall**, Cheshire, (opened 2005) eco friendly training unit, timber frame, renewables, biofuels, biodiversity: 01244 300246 **www.traffordhall.com

North East

Alnwick Gardens**, Northumberland includes one of the biggest tree houses in the world, using redwood and cedar: 01665 511350 **www.alnwickgarden.com

Nature's World**, Middlesborough, high tech eco structure with geothermal bore holes, earth sheltered design, renewables, waste minimisation: 01642 594895 **www.naturesworld.org.uk

Rivergreen Centre**, Aykley Heads, Durham, low impact office buildings and conference centre, awarded BREEAM for offices 'excellent' : **www.rivergreen.co.uk

Yorkshire and Humber

Heeley City Farm** is a farm and environmental centre in Sheffield. The training and resource centre building is an innovative design linked with brown field urban regeneration utilising a local employment construction scheme. The building is high thermal mass, powered by renewable energy. It has a living green sedum roof: 0114 258 0482 **www.ecoarc.co.uk/case-study5_Heeley.html

Anns Grove Primary School**, Sheffield has a new building using glue laminated timber frame with load bearing masonry and natural materials: 01179 547333 **www.white-design.co.uk

Earth Centre**, Doncaster, the infamous eco demonstration centre and Landmark Millennium Project which sadly closed to the public in 2004. It was used during the floods of 2007 as temporary accommodation for those whose homes had been damaged : **en.wikipedia.org/wiki/Earth_Centre

Lockton Youth Hostel**, West Yorkshire, eco renovation, one of first UK winners of European Eco Label: 01904 46875 **www.ecoarc.co.uk

Ecology Building Society**, new eco headquarters building at Silsden, West Yorkshire, plus straw bale meeting room building: 01535 650780 **www.ecology.co.uk

York Zero CO_2 Environmental Centre**, is a centre to promote sustainability. The building is high thermal mass with passive solar design powered by renewable energy from photovoltaics and a wind turbine: 01904 411821 **www.ecoarc.co.uk

Meanwood Valley Urban Farm**, Leeds Epi Centre, timber visitors' centre with turf roof, solar heating, composting toilets, reed beds, farmland: 0113 262 9759 **www.mvuf.org.uk

Skelton Grange**, Leeds, environmental education centre for British Trust for Conservation Volunteers (BTCV): 0113 200 9380 **www.leda.org.uk/sg.htm

Gibson Mill**, Hebden Bridge, eco-renovation of an old mill (National Trust), relying solely on renewable power and natural resources: 01422 844518 **www.ecoarc.co.uk/index.html

Dalby Forest Visitor Centre, North Yorkshire**, energy efficient, natural materials, renewables, natural ventilation, biomass, rainwater harvesting, clad in local larch: 01751 472771 **www.forestry.gov.uk/dalbyforest

East Riding**, Yorkshire, holiday cabin built from straw bales, natural materials, low energy: 01430 410662 **www.homegrownhome.co.uk/02_cabin.htm

Primrose Hill, Huddersfield**, solar energy project by Kirklees Council: **www.wates.co.uk/living_space/living_space_projects/primrose_hill

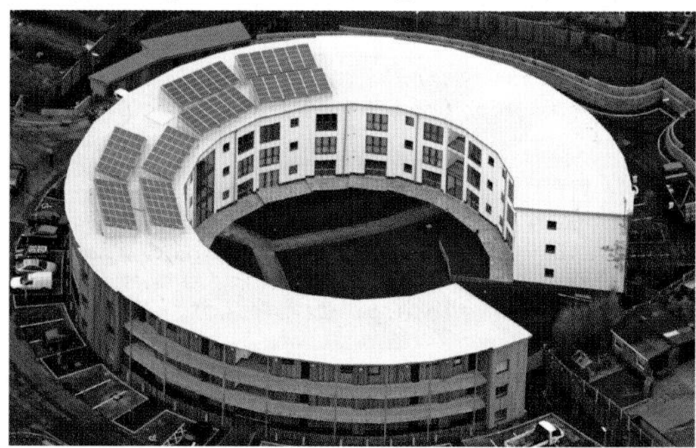

City of York Council's EcoDepot**, exemplar of sustainable design, passive design, local materials, new system super insulated straw bale cladding (see story on page 367): 01904 613161 **www.york.gov.uk/council/Council_departments/buildings/ecodepot

Beacon Youth Hostel**, North York National Park, eco renovation of dilapidated school building to the YHA's first 'green beacon' youth hostel: 01904 468752 **www.ecoarc.co.uk/case-study6_Locton_YHA.html

East Midlands

West Beacon Farm and Whittle Hill Farm buildings**, Leicestershire, renewable energy demonstration centre, biodiversity, biomass: 01509 610033 **www.beaconenergy.co.uk

Brocks Hill Country Park**, Leicestershire, environment/ecology centre, demonstrations and exhibitions: 0116 257 2888 **www.oadby-wigston.gov.uk/Home/Brocks%20Hill/Home%20Page.aspx

Leicester EcoHouse, *converted 1920's house demonstrating eco features and ideas, internationally renowned environmental show home: 0116 222 0222* ***www.environ.org.uk***

Hill Holt Wood, *Lincolnshire, thirty-five acre woodland with straw bale buildings and other low impact initiatives: 01636 892836* ***www.hillholtwood.com***

Sutton Work Life Project, *Lincolnshire, earth sheltered house and office: 01406 364646* ***www.searcharchitects.co.uk***

Northampton Academy *independent secondary school building with south facing solar atrium, PVs, rainwater harvesting: 01225 852545* ***www.fcbstudios.com***

Attenborough Nature Centre *of the Nottingham Wildlife Trust, new building for visitors, mainly timber framed. Heat exchange system which transforms low level heat recovered from the lagoon, within which the building sits, into usable heat for the under floor heating system. Reed bed system. Rewewables: 0115 772 1777* ***www.attenboroughnaturecentre.co.uk***

Nottingham Eco House, *a complete eco renovation: 0115 914 3893* ***www.msarch.co.uk/ecohome***

BASF House, *Nottingham University, energy efficient and affordable housing project demonstrating passive heating and ventilation: 0118 978 1238* ***www2.basf.de/en/uk/house/new***

The David Wilson Millennium Eco Energy House, *test and demonstration house for energy systems: 0115 951 3157* ***http://www.nottingham.ac.uk/sbe/research/projects/tour/eh/eh_01.html***

Hockerton Housing Project (HHP), *Nottinghamshire, earth sheltered, self sufficient and ecologically sustainable housing project. Regular tours and events: 01636 816902* ***www.hockertonhousingproject.org.uk***

Millennium Green, *Collingham, Nottinghamshire, 24 conventionally styled homes for the mass market: 01636 894900* ***www.sdg-nottinghamshire.org.uk/index/appendix_i.htm***

Sherwood Energy Village, *Nottingham, office units, industrial, new housing on former colliery site (see case study on page 376) : 01623 860222* ***www.sev.org.uk***

Ashbourne, *Derbyshire, proposed rotating house built using tyres: 01949 851815* ***www.fishergerman.co.uk***

East

University of East Anglia, *Essex, Elizabeth Fry Building, low energy teaching building built in the 1990s:* ***www.johnmillerandpartners.co.uk/fry.htm***

Chilterns Gateway Visitor Centre, *Dunstable Downs, Bedforshire, (built 2006) community and education facilities; woodchip heating system, rainwater harvesting, timber frame with lime render finish to the external solid walls: 08444 121800* ***www.chilternsgateway.org.uk***

Guilden Gate, *Cambridgeshire, organic smallholding, new timber-framed cottage, rainwater harvesting, straw and bark filters vertical and horizontal flow reed beds, solar pond, willow trench soakaway, dry twin vault compost toilet, renewable power: 01763 243960* ***www.guildengate.co.uk***

Purfleet Environment and Education Centre, *Rainham Marshes, Essex. New building, built to BREEAM 'excellent' rating on the RSPB nature reserve: 01708 892900* ***www.birdsofbritain.co.uk/features/rainham-marshes.asp*** *and* ***www.rspb.org.uk***

EcoTech Centre, *Swatham, Norfolk, eco centre in large timber framed building with wind turbine which visitors can climb up: 01760 726100* ***www.ecotech.org.uk***

Welney Visitor Centre, *Norfolk Fens, timber skin of larch, sustainably sourced, nature reserve: 01353 860711,* ***www.wwt.org.uk/visit/welney***

Honingham Earth Sheltered scheme, *Norfolk, the UK's first earth sheltered social housing scheme of four bungalows: 01406 364646* ***www.searcharchitects.co.uk***

Norfolk Wildlife Trust *visitor centre, Cley Marshes completed 2008:* ***www.norfolkwildlifetrust.org.uk/nature%20reserves/map-links/cley.htm***

The Greenhouse, *Norwich, Norfolk, environmental centre which promotes sustainbility. The eco renovation of the listed building was undertaken in the 1990's: 01603 631007* ***www.greenhousetrust.co.uk***

Suffolk Hemp Houses, *Suffolk Housing Society. 2 houses built using hemp as an experiment to compare their performance to 2 adjoining brick and block built houses: 01284 767224* ***www.suffolkhousing.org/pages/hempage.html***

Adnams brewery, *Southwold, Suffolk, new warehouse, lime, energy efficient, renewables with largest sedum roof in UK, rainwater harvesting (see story on page 364): 01502 727200* ***www.adnams.co.uk***

Elmswell, *Suffolk, sustainable and affordable housing project, 26-home scheme. Timber frame and using hemcrete (hemp and lime mix):* ***www.burohappold.com/BH/NWS_2008_Elmswell_ecodesign.aspx***

March, *Cambridge, Tommy Walsh's eco house as featured on TV series. Built in 60 days at cost of £60,000:* ***www.newbuilder.co.uk/news/NewsFullStory.asp?ID=1923***

Scotland

Craigholme School, Mintlow, *Aberdeenshire, passivhaus, triple glazed timber sport's pavillion, SMC Davis Duncan architects: 01463 729307* ***www.davisduncan.co.uk/educational.htm***

Canmore Place, *Kincardine O'Neil, Aberdeenshire, flexible, lifetime homes, considering the social, life-*

cycle of housing: 01224 263700 **www.rgu.ac.uk/sss/research/page.cfm?pge=32988**

The Van Midden House, *Bridge of Muchalls, Stonehaven, Aberdeenshire, a six-bedroom, affordable eco timber house created as part of an iterative design process at the Robert Gordon University: 01224 263700* **www.rgu.ac.uk/sss/research/page.cfm?pge=32981**

Findhorn eco-village project, *Inverness, many buildings using diverse range of sustainable, natural materials and methods: 01309 690311* **www.ecovillagefindhorn.com**

Inchdryne Lodge, *Nethy Bridge, Inverness, building constructed from Scottish timber, passive solar gain, built 2001: 01854 613040* **www.northwoodsdesign.co.uk/galleries/nw_houses_gallery2.htm**

Inverlae, *Lochbroom, Inverness, building constructed from Scottish timber (European larch and Doulas fir), built 2005: 01854 613040* **www.northwoodsdesign.co.uk/galleries/nw_houses_gallery3.htm**

The Rochester Eco House, *Ullapool, Inverness, autonomous eco house completed 2002: 01904 468752* **www.ecoarc.co.uk/case-study8_Rochester.html**

Highland Eco Centre, *Spinningdale, Inverness, an exemplar of autonomous technology and sustainable building as a demonstration of ecological best practice in the Highlands: 01862 881259* **www.highlandeco.org.uk**

Great Glen, *Scottish Natural Heritage Office HQ, Westercraig, Inverness, sustainable office building (see story on page 363):* **www.scotland.gov.uk/News/Releases/2006/10/03102007**

Larick House, *Argyll (2008), new house designed using the passive house approach, space heating using wood, innovative waste treatment methods: 01786 825111* **rps.gn.apc.org/la/glenreasdale.htm**

The Lotte Glob House, *Loch Eriboll, Durness, Sutherland (2004), low energy, passive solar building:* **www.rgu.ac.uk/sss/research/page.cfm?pge=32983**

Lothian Gridshell, *Pishwanton, low impact, gridshell building:* **www.buildingforafuture.co.uk/winter02/gridshell_building.pdf**

McLaren Leisure Centre, *Callander (built 1998), the largest dynamically insulated building in the world and the first to use the technique in a pool: 0131 557 9191* **www.gaiagroup.org/Architects/sport/mclaren/index.html**

Sports and Environmental Interpretation Centre, *Drumchapel, Glasgow (1999), a reflection and deomonstration of the Gaia approach to earth, air, fire and water: 0131 557 9191* **www.gaiagroup.org/Architects/sport/drumchapel/index.html**

Community and Sports Centre, *Kinlochleven, (2001) community sports centre with dynamic insulation, healthy internal fit-out and woodchip heating: 0131 557 9191* **www.gaiagroup.org/Architects/sport/kinlochleven/index.html**

Balgowan House, *Methven, idiosyncratic design is a modern interpretation of the vernacular, including reclaimed materials, home grown timber: 0131 557 9191* **www.gaiagroup.org/Architects/individual-houses/balgowan/index.html**

Glencoe Visitors' Centre, *built from locally sourced timber, woodchip heating and low impact:* **www.naturalspace.com/naturalworld_broadband/glencoetext.htm**

Peterculter, *Aberdeen, the zero heat house built and monitored in collaboration with Robert Gordon University and Aberdeen Council: 01224 262000* **www.rgu.ac.uk/sss/research/page.cfm?pge=32982**

Low impact building, *Aberdeen, visitors welcome, larch building, post and beam, raw sheep's wool (waste from local mills), deconstruction, passive solar, renewables: 01330 830057*

Fairfield *Perth (1997) healthy, low allergy, energy efficient housing scheme for the Fairfield Housing Co-operative, sun scoop form, breathing walls and natural finishes: 0131 557 9191* **www.gaiagroup.org/Architects/housing/fairfield-leslie/index.html**

Dumfries, *£4000 straw, turf and reclaimed wood house built by Steve James, Dumfries:* **www.devicepedia.com/eco-friendly/building-the-4000-eco-home-step-by-step-guide.html**

Wales

St Fagans, *Cardiff, a museum of buildings, including the House of the Future with its sedum roof and high tech interior: 029 2057 3500* **www.museumwales.ac.uk/en/197/**

Assembly Building, *Cardiff, Sustainability is at the heart of this new building for the Welsh Assembly Government: 0845 010 5678* **www.assemblywales.org**

Cwmbran, Torfaen, *demonstration eco building, renewables, first building in world to use a barrel-vaulted prefabricated, straw bale roof cladding system: 01179 547333* **www.white-design.co.uk/WhiteDesign/Torfaen_Eco_Building.html**

West Wales Eco Centre, *Pembrokeshire, eco renovation, renewable power, pellet heating: 01239 820235* **www.ecocentre.org.uk**

Scolton Manor, visitors' centre**, Pembrokeshire, timber building, renewables, ancient woodland: 01437 731328 **www.pembrokeshire.gov.uk/content.asp?id=5910&d1=0

Brithdir Mawr**, Newport, Pembrokeshire, a community of people living and working together in a sustainable way, eco refurbishments, new builds (round houses) low impact, organic farming, wildlife landscaping, visitors welcome, eco tourism. Includes the world famous round house by Tony Wrench: 01239 820164 **www.brithdirmawr.co.uk

Nant-y-Cwm Kindergarten**, Pembrokeshire, green roof, natural materials: 01437 563640 **www.nant-y-cwm.co.uk/kindergarten.htm

The National Botanical Gardens for Wales**, Carmarthenshire, various buildings, including the largest single span glasshouse in the world and restored double walled (brick) garden: 01558 668768 **www.gardenofwales.org.uk

New Art Centre**, Cardigan for Small World Theatre, eco building: 01239 615952 **www.smallworld.org.uk

***Penwhilwr (Rachels house)**, Cardigan, first 2 storey straw bale house in UK (see story on page 277).*

*): **www.gwaliaessences.co.uk/sustainablelivin.html***

Centre for Alternative Technology** (CAT), Powys, visitor's centre with inspirational and diverse range of eco buildings, alternative technologies, demonstration centre, courses. The AtEIC building (rammed earth) and the WISE (hempcrete/lime) building are the most recent projects: 01654 705950 **www.cat.org.uk

Ty-Mawr**, the Welsh Centre for Traditional and Ecological Building; products, courses, eco renovation: 01874 658249 **www.lime.org.uk

David's House**, Monmouth, low embodied energy, super insulated, timber frame construction: 01904 46875 **www.ecoarc.co.uk

Northern Ireland

Conversion of Old Mill** into two adjoining dwellings Crossgar, County Down, eco renovation, low impact: 028 4483 0988 **www.bevanarchitects.com

Cedar Primary School**, Crossgar, County Down, load bearing straw bale building: **www.buildingforafuture.co.uk/winter97/straw bale.php

Southern Ireland

Ireland's first hemp building**, Co Monahham: **www.oldbuilders.com/indexmainpage.htm

The Hollies**, Enniskeane, Co. Cork, creating a model of permaculture and rural sustainability in practice, cob, straw bale: 00 353 23 47981 **http://thehollies online.com

The Spiral House**, Co Mayo, built in 2001, Europe's first 2 storey, load bearing straw building: **www.straw balefutures.org.uk

*For a range of eco buildings in Ireland, using hemp, lime and timber frame, visit: **www.oldbuilders.com***

Other sources of information

'Sustainable Housing Schemes in the UK'.** available from Green Shop 01452 770629 **www.greenshop.co.uk

Sustainable Homes Eco Database**, listing 173 projects around the UK: **www.sustainablehomes.co.uk

Chapter 7** – list of low impact dev in UK: 01460 249204 **www.sustainablehomes.co.uk/EcoDatabase.aspx

Straw bale projects** in UK and Irealnd: **www.straw bale-building.co.uk/index.php?page=projects

Sustainable Habitat Design Advisor**, a new website with several project case studies: **www.sustainable-buildings.org/casestudies.php

Low energy and passive house buildings**, a new database of case studies: **www.carbonlite.org.uk

Training and education

This feature aims to provide an overview of what training and education is available in the UK for those interested in green building. There is something here for everyone, whether you are planning your career, or just looking for an informative diversion.The internet offers a great low-impact way of finding out about courses **www.hotcourses.com** allows you to search for courses - from evening classes to postgraduate study.

For those solely interested in university education **www.ucas.co.uk** is a good place to start, and for post-graduate study **www.findamasters.com**

For a list of UK permaculture related courses visit **www.permaculture.org.uk**

Training

Training courses are ideal for those wishing to learn a specific skill or facet of the subject, without comprehensively covering a wide subject matter in all of its detail. Training courses fall into one of two kinds, accredited and non-accredited. An accredited course might be a prerequisite if, for example, you wish to install solar panels for a living, - accredited courses give some guarantee of quality and might be validated by an organisation such as City and Guilds, or a trade association. However, if you simply want to pursue a skill for your own development, then a non-accredited course might suffice and be cheaper.

The CarbonLite programme being developed by the AECB, concentrates on reducing energy performance in buildings **www.carbonlite.org.uk** The programme, which is based on the German passivhaus standard, is a complete carbon literate design and construction programme based around passivhaus, silver and gold standards. The courses and workshops are one or two days and the training is aimed at those working in all areas of the building industry. **www.aecb.net**

The Centre for Alternative Technology **www.cat.org.uk** is one of the longest standing providers of sustainable construction courses in the UK. It has an established reputation and a body of core experts in their field providing training, in such diverse fields as heating with wood, to alternative heating systems.

The Dorset Centre for Rural Skills offers a variety of courses in skills suitable for green building. Courses include cob building, working with dry stone walling, timber framing, lime and straw bale construction. **www.dorsetruralskills.co.uk**

LILI, the low impact living initiative, offers a variety of practical courses suited to home owners and builders that are interested in a low impact way of life , further details can be accessed at their website. **www.lowimpact.org**

The Cornwall Sustainable Building Trust has burst onto the scene with a wide range of courses focused on the theme of sustainable building and construction. It offers BREEAM Code for Sustainable Homes assessor rating training, straw bale construction workshops, courses on cob and hemp-lime, as well as occasional free seminars throughout the year. **www.csbt.org.uk**

The Genesis Project, a fairly new eco building and education centre opened by Somerset College of Arts and Technology offers a range of short CPD courses. **www.genesisproject.com** **www.somerset.ac.uk**

Sustainable Homes is a leading training and advisory consultancy operating in the field of sustainable housing. Established in 1997 it has particular expertise in providing training on environmental standards, such as the Code for Sustainable Homes and EcoHomes for new build and existing buildings (XB), mainly for housing associations. **www.sustainablehomes.co.uk**

The Weald and Downland Open Air Museum, a centre of excellence in building conservation, provides a range of learning programmes from the academic to the practical and recreational. A wide range of practical workshops and seminars are held for surveyors, architects, craftsmen and anyone else with a keen interest in building conservation. **www.wealddown.co.uk/courses**

For those in north Devon, the Yarner Trust offers a range of courses on subjects as diverse as reed-bed filtration systems, green oak construction, yurt building and getting 'off grid.' **www.yarnertrust.org**

Amazonails runs a variety of courses focused on straw bale building and working with lime. **www.straw balefutures.org.uk**

Green Dragon Energy runs a variety of courses in

renewable energy technologies.
http://greendragonenergy.co.uk/courses.htm

There are a number of providers of courses for working with lime. These include Mike Wye Associates **www.mikewye.co.uk** Ty-Mawr Lime **www.lime.org.uk** the Lime Centre in Hampshire **www.thelimecentre.co.uk** and Cornish Lime **www.cornishlime.co.uk** Abey Smallcombe does a range of courses on cob lime and earth building. **www.abeysmallcombe.com**

Eco-Consulting offers a course delivered at a location of your convenience on eco-building and training **http://ecoconsulting.net/www/training_ecobuilding_04.htm**

For those in South Wales, Rounded Developments Enterprises Limited offers general training in sustainable building. **www.rounded-developments.org.uk/training/1372**

If you're interested in making furniture for your green-build from natural materials, Sylvantutch will teach you how to craft beautiful rustic furniture from wood from the forest.
www.sylvantutch.co.uk/courses.htm

Green Building Solutions and Rippledown Environmental Education Centre offers straw bale build training days. The one day course, covers the basics of straw-bale construction, and participants will construct a section of straw bale wall. **www.greenbuildingsolutions.co.uk** and **www.rippledown.com/training**

If you want to know about renewables Consulting with Purpose offer regular courses. **www.cwp-ltd.com**

Higher nationals / foundation degree

For those wishing to pursue a vocationally relevant education, higher nationals and foundation degrees present an attractive alternative to a degree programme. Generally these programs will have flexible study arrangements which permit work at the same time as study. Many employers will support learners on an HNC or foundation degree whilst working.
Blackburn College East Lancashire Institute of Higher Education offers an HNC in sustainable construction. It also offers a foundation degree in sustainable construction. **www.elihe.ac.uk**

Dewsbury College offers a Foundation Degree (FdA) in Sustainable Design. **www.dewsbury.ac.uk**

Accrington and Rosendale College offers a Foundation Degree in Sustainable Construction. **www.accross.ac.uk**

For those interested in building renovation, Cornwall College **www.cornwall.ac.uk** has a foundation degree programme in building renovation and design.

Weymouth College offers an applied architectural stonework and conservation FdSc.
www.weymouth.ac.uk

Undergraduate level

At undergraduate level, the focus tends to be on a breadth of education in a certain subject area, for that reason, you are unlikely to find a bachelors' degree that is specifically targeted at green architects, as a bachelors' in architecture will cover fundamental knowledge about a diverse range of architecture rather than honing in on one specific angle. The UCAS website provides listings for all of the university level courses in the UK. You might find that an institution offers a green building option as a module of a degree.
www.ucas.com

The University of the Highlands and the Islands offers undergraduate courses in sustainable construction management through its partner colleges in Inverness, Moray and Perth, leading to a full BSc. (Hons.) in sustainable construction management. **www.uhi.ac.uk**

The University of Plymouth now offers a BSc (Hons) architecture, design and structures as well as a BA (Hons) in architectural technology and the environment. **www.plymouth.ac.uk**

Nottingham University offers a BA (Hons) in sustainable built environment, which encompasses a range of energy and environmental themes, married with a knowledge of construction and architecture. **www.nottingham.ac.uk**

Blackburn College East Lancashire Institute Of Higher Education are the exception from the rule in that it offers a BSc. sustainable construction award. **www.blackburn.ac.uk**

If you are balancing study with other commitments, distance learning is a good way to extend your knowledge and work towards a qualification whilst being able to maintain other commitments. The Open University has an established reputation for the provision of distance learning degree programs in the UK. Its course T172: working with our environment: technology for a sustainable future, provides an introduction to carbon footprinting and making an assessment of the ecological footprint of your home. **www3.open.ac.uk**

Postgraduate level

At postgraduate level, courses become more specialised and narrow. For this reason, there are a much greater number of courses that offer green building and allied subjects as a whole option. Although it would be assumed that you need a degree to start a masters' programme, many courses offer flexible entry routes - such as an option for mature candidates.

The University of Hudderfield runs an MSc. sustainable architecture available over a year full time or two years part time. **www.hud.ac.uk**

The Martin Centre at Cambridge University, offers an MPhil course in Environmental Design. Teaching at the University of Cambridge has ranked consistently in the top two of the broadsheet league tables for several years. **www.cam.ac.uk**

The Architectural Association School of Architecture now offers an MSc. and an MArch in sustainable environmental design. The MSc runs over 12 months and is suited to both architects and engineers, whilst the MArch is geared towards those with existing architectural qualifications. **www.aaschool.ac.uk**

The University of Strathclyde offers a masters degree in environmentally sustainable building design and management. **www.strath.ac.uk**

The University of Nottingham offers an MSc. course in renewable energy and architecture. **www.nottingham.ac.uk**

CAT offers an MSc. in renewable energy in the built environment, in addition to the MSc. architecture: advanced environmental and energy studies. The course is now run by the Graduate School of the Environment, based at the Centre for Alternative Technology, with the degree being validated by the University of East London. The course is delivered either on-site at CAT, or via distance learning. In addition, for those wishing to pursue careers in architecture, CAT now offers a part II professional diploma. **http://www2.cat.org.uk/graduateschool**

For those interested in timber constructions, Napier University offers a range of postgraduate courses designed for those who are interested in building with wood. **www.napier.ac.uk**

London Metropolitan University runs an MA in the architecture of scarce resources which includes a single, week-long residential week at CAT. **www.londonmet.ac.uk**

Oxford Brookes has a good reputation for postgraduate education in sustainable building. It also runs an MSc in energy efficient and sustainable building as well as a number of research programmes. **www.brookes.ac.uk**

DeMontfort University runs an MSc. energy and sustainable building design, which is recognised by CIBSE as counting towards the requirements of chartered engineer status. **www.dmu.ac.uk**

The University of Plymouth runs an MSc/MRes programme in sustainable construction. **www.plymouth.ac.uk**

For those in Ireland, Queens University Belfast offers an MSc. in integrated sustainable design. **www.qub.ac.uk**

Useful contacts

ASSOCIATIONS AND NETWORKING

Specific trade associations are under their relevant category.

AECB *(the sustainable building association).* ***www.aecb.net***

Architects and Engineers for Social Responsibility *Working for peace, ethical values and a better environment.* ***www.sgr.org.uk***

Beacon Energy *Increasing public awareness about climate change.* ***www.beaconenergy.co.uk***

BioRegional Development Group *Independent environmental organization that develops commercially viable products and services.* ***www.bioregional.com***

Building Research Establishment Ltd. (BRE) *01923 664100 - centre of expertise on buildings, construction, energy, environment, fire and risk.* ***www.bre.co.uk***

Business in the Community (BITC) *0870 600 2482 - UK companies committed to improving their positive impact on society.* ***www.bitc.org.uk***

Centre for Alternative Technology *01654 705950 - environmental charity offering practical solutions to environmental problems.* ***www.cat.org.uk***

Centre for Earthen Architecture *01752 233608 - focus for UK earth building activity with links to similar centres across the world.* ***www.buildingconservation.com/directory/ad392.htm***

Constructing Excellence *0845 605 5556 The organisation influences the government in the formulation of construction policies.* ***www.constructingexcellence.org.uk***

Construction Industry Council (CIC) *020 7399 7400 the CIC is the representative forum for the industry's professional bodies, research organisations and specialist trade associations.* ***www.cic.org.uk***

Construction Skills *01485 577577 CITB-Construction Skills provides assistance in all aspects of recruiting and training the construction workforce.* ***www.citb.org.uk***

Cornwall Sustainable Building Trust *01872 277000 CSBT exists to raise awareness and so minimise the impacts of construction on the Cornish and Global environments.* ***www.csbt.org.uk***

Department for Business Enterprise and Regulatory Reform (BERR) *Helps to ensure businesses are successful.* ***www.dti.gov.uk***

Devon Sustainable Building Initiative *Promoting sustainable consctruction in Devon.* ***www.sustainablebuild.org***

Ecos Trust *01458 259400 To make sustainable building the norm by 2010. Organise the popular Homes for Good event each year.* ***www.ecostrust.org.uk***

Engineering for a Sustainable Future (IEE) *020 7240 1871 Group of engineers, aiming at developing a sustainable society.* ***www.iee.org/OnComms/pn/sustainability***

Environmental Investigations Agency (EIA) *020 7354 7960 Detailed investigation and lobbying to highlight international concerns, eg tropical timber issues.* ***www.eia-international.org***

Ethical Junction *Ethical business networking.* ***ethical-junction.org***

Ethiscore *0161 227 9099 Ethical Consumer magazine's online shopping guide to a wide range of products and services.* ***www.ethiscore.org***

Existing Homes Alliance *A partnership of organisations formed to cut CO_2 emissions in the UK's existing housing stock.* ***www.existinghomesalliance.co.uk***

Good Homes Alliance *(GHA) A group of housing developers, building professionals and sustainability experts whose aim is to build and promote sustainable-homes and communities in the UK.* ***www.goodhomes.org.uk***

Green Building (formerly Building For a Future) magazine *An excellent, quarterly magazine giving an overview of the green construction industry in the UK, with articles describing experiences and case studies, technical information on building materials and technologies, as well as green building news. Free downloads of BFF recent and back issues are also available .* ***www.greenbuildingmagazine.co.uk***

Green Building Press *An online resource built up over the last 16 years and the main website of the Green Building Press. Freely downloadable back issues of Building for a Future magazine. GreenPro, the on-line green building products database. Regular news and artices from leading experts in the field of sustainable building. Forum for discussions and questions.* ***www.greenbuildingpress.co.uk***

Green Street. *Information and advice on improving energy efficiency; water efficiency; material use; waste reduction; and health and wellbeing in the home.* ***www.greenstreet.org.uk***

Higher Education Environmental Performance Improvement (HEEPI) *Aiming to improve the environmental performance of universities and colleges, including improving building standards.* ***www.heepi.org.uk***

Hockerton Housing Project *01636 816902 The UK's first earth sheltered, self-sufficient ecological housing development. Tours and workshops.* ***www.hockertonhousingproject.org.uk***

International Ecological Engineering Society *A forum for anyone involved in ecological engineering projects.* ***www.iees.ch***

Low Impact Living Initiative (LILI) *Sustainable building information and courses for the south west.* ***www.lowimpact.org***

NBS Green Construction *Keeping you up to date with green building developments.* ***www.greenconstruction.co.uk***

One Planet Products *Bulk buying of eco building products and servoces. A BioRegional inititaive..* ***www.oneplanetproducts.com***

Renewable Energy Association *(with* ***British BioGen)*** *The voice of the renewables' industry in the UK.* ***www.r-p-a.org.uk***

Rounded Developments *029 2040 3399 Centre that encourages sustainable development.* ***www.rounded-developments.org.uk***

Scottish Ecological Design Association *SEDA promotes ecological building design and construction in Scotland.* ***www.seda2.org***

Square One *Information on energy efficient and sustainable design.* ***www.squ1.com***

Sponge *Sponge is a network for young professionals who share an interest in sustainable construction.* ***www.spongenet.org***

Straw bale Building Association *An informal, grassroots association for those who have an interest in straw bale building.* ***www.straw bale-building.co.uk/***

Sustainable Homes *020 8973 0429 A project for housing asociations and their partners. It provides training and advice.* ***www.sustainablehomes.co.uk***

The Eco-Renovation Network *A network launched in 2006 to encourage householders to take action to increase the sustainability of their homes.* ***www.eco-renovation.org.uk***

The Green Register (TGR) *0117 377 3490 Providing training and registration for professionals who are interested in sustainable building.* ***www.greenregister.org***

UK Rainwater Harvesting Association *01865 285717 Representing the rainwater harvesting industry in the UK.* ***www.ukrha.org***

Walter Segal Self Build Trust *A newtwork promoting the benefits of community self build using the Segal method of construction.* ***www.segalselfbuild.co.uk***

WWF Reports *variety of downloadable reports and studies related to sustainable construction, including information on the 'one million sustainable homes' project.* ***www.wwf.org.uk/sustainable-homes/reports.asp***

ASSESSMENT TOOLS

BREEAM *(BRE Environmental Assessment Method) - sustainability evaluation method for offices, retail, and industrial buildings.* ***www.breeam.org***

BRE Sustainable Construction *BRE offers many tools to help assessing and reducing the environmental impacts of the built environment.* ***www.bre.co.uk***

Civil Estate Benchmarking Tool *Energy managers can calculate the energy performance of a building periodically, and compare it against benchmarks for similar public buildings.* ***http://projects.bre.co.uk/gpg286***

Envest 2 *Software tool assesses the environmental impacts of a building at its early design stage.* ***www.bre.co.uk/service.jsp?id=52***

Standard Assessment Procedure (SAP) *The SAP specification may be downloaded free of charge, in PDF format. The SAP is the Government's recommended procedure for an energy rating of dwellings, with a final rating ranging between 1 to 120 - from worst to best - based on the annual energy costs for space and water heating. SAP also calculates the Carbon Index, on a scale of 0 to 10, based on the annual CO_2 emissions associated with space and water heating. A SAP rating for every new dwelling has become compulsory to fulfil the Building Regulations requirements of notifying and displaying an energy rating in new dwellings.* ***http://projects.bre.co.uk/sap2005***

Sustainability Works 2005 *Specifically designed to help housing professionals and their partners deliver sustainable development efficiently, from policy level to project delivery.* ***www.sustainabilityworks.org.uk***

AWARDS

For a full list of awards ***www.environmentawards.net***

Ashden Awards *open to schemes within the UK that can boast significant CO_2 savings through the provision of renewable energy technologies or energy efficiency measures.* ***www.ashdenawards.org***

BUILDING - GENERAL

Key Performance Indicators *Department of Trade & Industry Construction Industry Key Performance Indicators (KPIs). KPIs are national data sets against which a project or a company can benchmark its performance.* ***www.berr.gov.uk/sectors/construction/ConstructionStatistics/KPIs/page16440.html***

Considerate Constructors Scheme *The Considerate Constructors Scheme is a code of practice for improved construction sites.* ***www.ccscheme.org.uk***

Construction Industry Council *Sustainability studies, including 'Constructing for Sustainability'; 'Brownfields - building on previously developed land'; and 'Water Conservation in Business'.* ***www.cic.org.uk***

Managing Sustainable Companies *MaSC facilitates the introduction and development of more sustainable business practices.The site includes guides and site visits.* ***http://projects.bre.co.uk/masc***

Women and Manual Trades *020 7251 9192 Women and Manual Trades is the national organisation for tradeswomen and women training in the trades.* ***www.wamt.org***

BUSINESS & ETHICS

Carbon Trust *Helping business cut carbon emissions through carbon trading.* ***www.carbontrust.co.uk***

Green Futures magazine *Green Futures provides a lively snapshot of the latest news and opinion.* ***www.greenfutures.org.uk***

One Planet Living UK *020 8404 4880 A bulk-buying initiative working with partners within the construction and refurbishment industries to increase the supply of sustainable building products and services.* ***www.bioregional.com/oneplanetliving/products***

COMMUNITY PROJECTS

Findhorn Foundation Ecovillage Project *01309 690311 The ecovillage model is a conscious response to the extremely complex problem of how to transform our human settlements.* ***www.ecovillagefindhorn.com***

Sherwood Energy Village *01623 860222 A 91-acre former colliery site being transformed into an environmental enterprise; industry, commerce, housing, education, recreation, tourism and leisure.* ***www.sev.org.uk***

The Eco House/Groundwork Leicester *0116 254 5489 Britain's original showhome open to the public.* ***www.gwll.org.uk/ecohouse***

COURSES

See Training and Education on page 452.

ENERGY SAVING ADVICE

National Home Energy Rating (NHER) *Energy rating scheme and energy efficiency advice.* ***www.nher.co.uk***

Office benchmarking tool *Assessing the energy consumption of an office building, by comparing an office consumption with national benchmark levels for UK office buildings.* ***http://217.10.129.104/Energy_Benchmarking/Offices/default.asp***

Save energy *0845 120 7799 How much money and energy is your home consuming and how can you make reductions?* ***www.saveenergy.co.uk***

ENVIRONMENTAL ORGANISATIONS

Council for the Protection of Rural England *020 7981 2800 CPRE campaigns for the protection of the countryside. Magazine is Coutryside Voice.* ***www.cpre.org.uk***

Energy 21 *Now run as part of CAT.* ***www.energy21.org.uk***

Environ *0116 222 0222 Leicester charity working to improve the environment and the communities we live in.* ***www.environ.org.uk***

Environment Agency *Leading public body for protecting and improving the environment in England and Wales.* ***www.environment-agency.gov.uk***

Envirowise *0800 585794 Government-funded programme that offers UK businesses free, independent, confidential advice to reduce environmental impact.* ***www.envirowise.gov.uk***

Friends of the Earth *020 7490 1555 Friends of the Earth aims to provide solutions to environmental problems which make life better for people.* ***www.foe.co.uk***

Greenpeace UK *020 7865 8100 Greenpeace is an independent non-profit global campaigning organization that uses non-violent, creative confrontation to expose global environmental problems and their causes.* ***www.greenpeace.org.uk***

National Energy Foundation *020 7820 6300 Promoting renewable energy and sustainable lifestyles.* ***www.nef.org.uk***

National Trust *01793 817400 Protecting historical buildings and gardens.* ***www.nationaltrust.org.uk***

New Economics Foundation (NEF) *01908 665555 Promotes innovative solutions that challenge mainstream thinking on economic, environment and social issues.* ***www.neweconomics.org***

Reforesting Scotland *0131 554 4321 A network group of those active in the ecological and social regeneration of Scotland.* ***www.reforestingscotland.org***

Wildlife Trusts *There are 47 local Trusts in the UK, working to improve wildlife. Several examples of sustainable buildings on Trust land. Its magazine is Natural World.* ***www.wildlifetrusts.org***

Women's Environmental Network *020 7481 9004 Campaigning organisation, which represents women and campaigns on issues, which link women, environment and health.* ***www.wen.org.uk***

World Land Trust (WLT) *0845 054 4422 International conservation charity that purchases and protects threatened areas.* ***www.worldlandtrust.org***

World Wildlife Fund (WWF) *01483 426444 In 2002, WWF launched its One Million Sustainable Homes (OMSH) campaign to bring sustainable homes from the fringes of the housing sector to the mainstream by 2012 (refurbished as well as new homes).* ***www.wwf.org.uk***

EVENTS

Events tend to have a significant carbon footprint because of their temporary nature. Resource use, waste and travelling can be considerable. Ensure events you attend have or are working towards BS 8901. www.bsi-global.com/bs8901

Ecobuild *020 7153 4569 Comprehensive conference and seminar programmes and exhibition.* ***www.ecobuild.co.uk***

Greener Homes and Buildings *0845 602 4087 Encouraging greener building in Wales.* ***www.ghb.org.uk***

Homes for Good exhibition *01458 259400 Exhibits, talks and demos on ecological building and lifestyle.* ***www.ecostrust.org.uk/h4g***

SALVO Fair *01225 422300 Annual fair exhibiting architectural salvage and reclaimed building materials.* ***www.salvo-fair.com***

GRANT SCHEMES

BRE/Big Lottery Fund *Capital and project grants to not-for-profit, community-based organisations to reduce energy and environmental impact.* ***www.communitysustainable.org.uk***

Eaga Partnership Charitable Trust *0800 316 2808 Grants for heating and energy saving measures for those on low incomes.* ***www.eaga.co.uk***

Heat Project UK *0800 093 4050 Grants for all home owners and private tenants for discounted loft and cavity wall insulation.* ***www.heatproject.co.uk***

Local authorities *Check with your local authority as some now offer grants and incentives for reducing energy and environmental impact.*

Low Carbon Buildings Programme *0800 298 3978 Government programme launched April 2006, providing grants for solar PV and other renewable technologies.* ***www.lowcarbonbuildings.org.uk***

The Carbon Trust *Finance for emerging, clean energy companies that demonstrate commercial potential.* ***www.carbontrust.co.uk/technology***

Warm Front *Contact your local council for details of grants under this government funded scheme for insulation and heating for those on low incomes*

HEALTH CONCERNS

London Hazards Centre *020 7794 5999 Resource centre dedicated to fighting health and safety hazards in the workplace and community.* ***www.lhc.org.uk***

Pesticide Action Network UK (PAN UK) *020 7065 0905 Support group for anyone whose health has been affected by exposure to pesticides.* ***www.pan-uk.org***

Powerwatch *emf's etc.* ***www.powerwatch.org.uk***

LIFESTYLE

Clean Slate magazine *01654 705950 The magazine for members of the Centre for Alternative Technology (CAT).* ***www.cat.org.uk***

Ethical Consumer *0161 226 2929 Leading alternative consumer association, reserachiong the social and environmental records of companies, Excellent magazine.* ***www.ethicalconsumer.org***

Green Guide Online *Directories on sustainable living and Pure magazine.* ***www.greenguide.co.uk***

Greenhouse Trust *01603 631007 A key aim of this Trust was the renovation and conversion of the building as a DIY model of what can be done to improve old and listed housing stock. Lots of information on environmental issues.* ***www.greenhousetrust.co.uk***

Garden Organic (HDRA) *024 7630 3517 The national charity for organic growing.* ***www.gardenorganic.org.uk***

Green Parent magazine *Green lifestyle magazine for the whole family.* ***www.thegreenparent.co.uk***

Grown up Green*, on-line resource Encouraging people to protect and improve the natural environment.* ***www.grownupgreen.org.uk***

Juno magazine *A natural approach to family life.* ***www.junomagazine.com***

New Consumer *Ethical lifestyle magazine.****www.newconsumer.com***

New Internationalist magazine *Reporting on issues of world poverty and equality. Debates and campaigns for radical change.* ***www.newint.org***

Organic Way *024 7630 3517 The magazine of the Garden Organic organisation (HDRA).* ***www.gardenorganic.org***

Permaculture magazine *01730 823311 Solutions for sustainable living.* ***www.permaculture.co.uk***

Positive News and Living Lightly magazines *01588 640022 Two publications that report on events and influences around the world that are positive in terms of encouraging a sustainable future.* ***www.positivenews.org.uk***

The Positive Network *an on-line resource 01460 249 204 Information exchange network promoting sustainable living.* ***www.thepositivenetwork.co.uk***

Resurgence magazine *01237 441293 dedicated to the service of the soil, soul and society; helping to create a world based on justice, equity and respect for all beings.* ***www.resurgence.org***

Soil Association *0117 314 5000 promoting organic gardening and farming.* ***www.soilassociation.org***

The Greenhouse *01603 631007 Environmental centre which promotes sustainbility.* ***www.greenhousetrust.co.uk***

The Living Green Centre *01451 820942 Show home in Cotswolds for green products and solutions.* ***www.living-green.co.uk***

PLANNING

Chapter 7 *01460 249204 campaigns for a planning system which actively encourages sustainable, low impact and affordable homes.* ***www.tlio.org.uk***

The Land magazine *01460 249204 Campaigning for access to land. Supporting low impact development.* ***www.tlio.org.uk/TheLand/index.html***

PRODUCT DIRECTORIES

GreenPro *Online resource of over 1000 green building products plus case studies, articles and research information.* ***www.newbuilder.co.uk/greenpro***

GreenSpec *GreenSpec is a website allowing constructors to design using greener materials specifications for their developments.* ***www.greenspec.co.uk***

Materials Information Exchange (MIE) *Free materials 'dating agency' for the construction and landscaping sectors; especially for waste materials.* ***www.salvomie.co.uk***

REGULATORY AND ADVISORY

Energy Saving Trust (EST) *Free guides to help produce energy efficient homes.* ***www.est.org.uk***

Sustainable Development Commission *020 7238 4995 The government's independent advisory body on sustainable development.* ***www.sd-commission.org.uk***

UK Climate Impacts Programme *01865 285717 Scenarios that show how climate change will affect our future.* ***www.ukcip.org.uk***

RENEWABLE ENERGY

British Hydropower Association *Information on site suitablilty for water power, and energy potentials.* ***www.british-hydro.org/***

Heat pumps *Useful basic information about heating-only applications with heat pumps.* ***www.heatpumps.co.uk***

Home Power magazine*. Input data for your electricity loads, and helps determine what PV panels, batteries, and other equipment are needed. The same information can be used for wind or water generators. The site is that of the Home Power magazine, with US expertise.* ***www.homepower.com/resources/energy_master.cfm***

Other power*. Lots of practical information about renewable energy sources from alternative energy enthusiasts.* ***www.otherpower.com***

Renew *Information and comment regarding UK energy supplies and the renewable sector.* ***http://eeru.open.ac.uk/natta/rol.html***

SOLAR ENERGY

Degree Days *How much solar energy falls in different regions across the UK throughout the year.* ***www.vesma.com/ddd***

Insolation tables *Solar calculators for electric and thermal (water) panels.* ***www.powertech-solar.com***

Loads calculator*, an array size calculator, a battery calculator to help design a basic solar electric system.* ***www.solar-power-answers.co.uk/solar_panel.html***

National Energy Foundation *Solar energy.* ***www.nef.org.uk/renewableenergy/solar.htm***

Soltherm Europe *Stimulating market growth of solar thermal products. Tools and calculators for small and large scale solar water heating projects. Registration is required, but it is free and quick.* ***www.soltherm.org/tools_guidelines.asp***

The Solar Trade Association *07760 163559 Promoting solar hot water in the UK.* ***www.solar-trade.org.uk***

TIMBER FORESTS AND WOODLAND

BRE - Timber *A variety of links to best practice projects. involving timber constructions.*

http://projects.bre.co.uk/default.htm#Anchor-Timber-47857

Eco Lots *A free web-based centre for buying, selling and exchanging any service or product relating to timber, land management and wildlife.* ***www.ecolots.co.uk***

Forest Stewardship Council (FSC) *01686 413916 International organisation dedicated to promoting responsible management of the world's forests.* ***www.fsc-uk.org***

Living Woods, magazine *01285 850481 new magazine focusing on trees, use of woods, sustainable management of forestry and woodland crafts.* ***www.britishwoodworking.com***

Soil Association (Woodmark) *0117 314 5000 The Woodmark programme (FSC accredited since 1996) is concerned with responsible forest management and the labelling and promotion of forest products. Woodmark provides a full FSC-accredited certification service.* ***www.soilassociation.org***

Timber Research and Development Association (TRADA) *01494 569600 Centre of excellence for the specificartion of timber and wood products.* ***www.trada.co.uk***

Welsh Timber Forum *0845 456 0342 For those working in wood-based industries in Wales.* ***www.welshtimberforum.co.uk***

Woodland Trust *National charity protecting our native woodland heritage.* ***www.woodland-trust.org.uk***

WASTE & RECYCLING

BREWEB *BRE's Waste & Environmental Body facilitates ongoing environmental improvement in the waste and construction industries by the use of landfill tax sponsorship in high-profile demonstration and research projects.* ***www.breweb.org.uk***

Centre for Resource Management *01923 664100 - disseminating information on reclaimed/recycled construction materials.* ***www.bre.co.uk***

DEFRA – recycling & waste *Information about UK regulations with regards to waste.* ***www.defra.gov.uk/environment/waste/index.htm***

Design quality indicators (DQI) *DQI online, an interactive tool for designing buildings.* ***www.dqi.org.uk***

EcoConstruction *Information and case studies of recycled & reclaimed material use.* ***www.ecoconstruction.org***

Scope *020 7619 7100 Recycling schemes for printer/toner cartridges, phones, IT equipment, CDs and books, across England and Wales, to raise funds for charity* ***www.scope.org.uk/recycling***

Recycle more *Hints and tips for managing household rubbish.* ***www.recycle-more.co.uk***

Resource magazine *0117 907 7245 Providing a new perspective on waste.* ***www.resourcepublishing.co.uk***

Salvo *Online directory for antique, reclaimed, salvaged, and green building materials for gardens and homes.* ***www.salvo.co.uk***

SMARTWaste System *Set of tools to help sustainable waste management.* ***www.smartwaste.co.uk***

Warmer Bulletin *01756 709800 international journal of sustainable waste management and resource recovery.* ***www.residua.com***

Waste Watch *020 7549 0300 National organisation promoting and encouraging action on the 3Rs - waste reduction, reuse and recycling.* ***www.wastewatch.org.uk***

WIND POWER

Database of wind characteristics. *Categories of wind data for wind turbine design purposes and site analysis.* ***www.winddata.com***

Windpower website *Hugh Pigott is a guru of the small scale wind power world. His website contains numerous links summarizing all of his knowledge.* ***www.scoraigwind.com***

Windpower *This Danish Wind Industry Association's website is excellent for understanding wind power.* ***www.windpower.org/en/stat/units.htm***

Appendix A

John Willoughby's 'Domestic fuel price guide No 33' April 2008

FUEL	PRICE	p/kWh	£/GJ	Quarterly Stand. Chg	Relative to Gas	Rank	kg CO2 / kWh
GAS	6.46 p/kWh $ 2.71 p/kWh $$	6.46 2.71	17.96 7.53	£ 25.13++	1.00	4	0.19
ELECTRICITY (on-peak)	14.70 p/kWh** 13.64 p/kWh***	14.70 13.64	40.87 37.92	£ 1.93++	5.42 5.03	11	0.42
ELECTRICITY (Economy 7) night rate	22.26 p/kWh** 14.69 p/kWh*** 4.79 p/kWh	22.26 14.69 4.79	61.88 40.84 13.32	£ 13.78++	8.21 5.42 1.77	12 7	0.42 0.42
OIL (35 sec)	59.27 p/litre*	5.63	15.65		2.08	10	0.27
OIL (28 sec)	53.50 p/litre*	5.56	15.47		2.05	9	0.27
COAL	£ 175.00 /tonne +	2.10	5.84		0.77	1	0.29
ANTHRACITE	£ 201.00 /tonne +	2.21	6.15		0.82	3	0.32
LPG	38.90 p/litre*	5.45	15.14	£ 14.69	2.01	8	0.23
Wood Pellets Wood Pellets	£ 235.00 /tonne@ £ 148.09 /tonne	4.45 2.80	12.37 7.79		1.64 1.03	6 5	0.03 0.03
Logs (B'leaf)	£ 70.00 /load@@	2.12	5.90		0.78	2	0.03

$ based on British Gas direct debit price for first 7.3kWh/day

$$ based on British Gas direct debit price for over 7.3kWh/day

*** based on nPower first 182kWh/q*

**** based on nPower for over 182kWh/q*

** based on 1000 litre delivery*

+ based on 1 tonne delivery

@ 15 kg bags. 1 tonne + delivery (£49+VAT) bulk delivery (10 tonne 80 miles)

@@ cost in Lydney. Stacking ratio 0.56, 9GJ/m³

All prices include VAT at 5%

CO_2 figures from SAP 2005

Prices obtained from nPower, B Gas, Welsh Biofuels, Brookridge and 'best price' from local suppliers.

Price relative to gas now distorted by new two tier tariffs and no standing charges. Second tier used for relative prices.

++ If consumption over first tier you can use 2nd tier price plus equivalent standing charge.

Thanks to Alan Clarke for logs' cost

Updates at August 2008 since April 2008

$ Gas prices up to 7.29p/kWh for first 670kW per quarter.

*$$ Gas prices up to 3.68p/kWh for subseguent consumption. (**www.britishgas.co.uk/products-and-services/energy/gas/standard-gas/rates.html**)*

**Oil 35 sec up to 61.95 p/litre*

**Oil 28 sec up to 55.45 p/litre*

*The above data supplied courtesy of John Willoughby: **www.johnwilloughby.co.uk***

Appendix B
Circuit diagram of the solar and biomass heating system at the Greenshop Group HQ

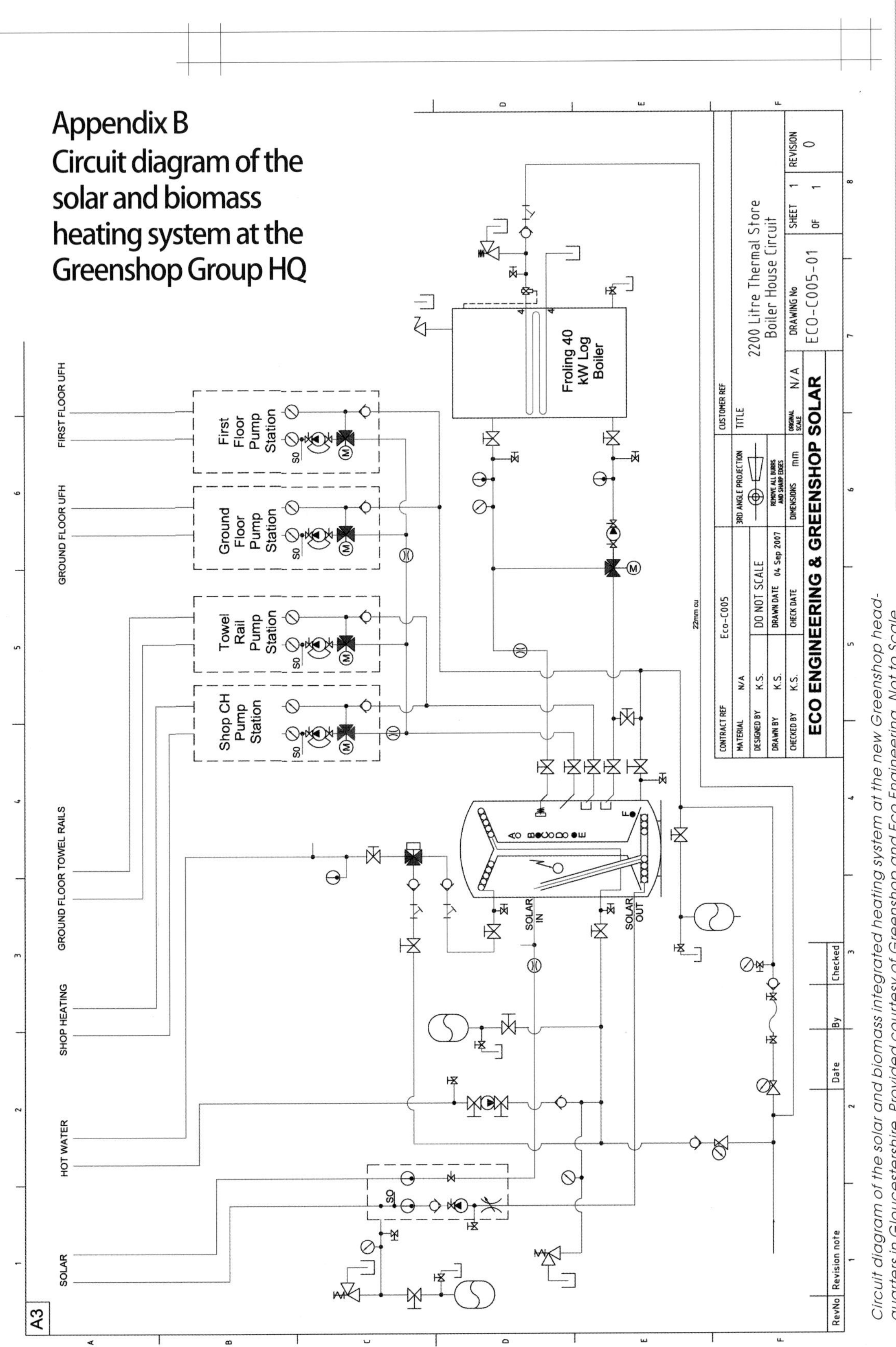

Circuit diagram of the solar and biomass integrated heating system at the new Greenshop headquarters in Gloucestershire. Provided courtesy of Greenshop and Eco Engineering. Not to Scale.

Appendix C
Author profiles

About the publisher

The Green Building Press is an independent publishing business run by people who are committed to sustainable living. It was established in 1990 to encourage and promote sustainable and environmentally responsible construction with the aim of delivering this information to as wide an audience as possible. Its website (which includes masses of free information) and publications help people create healthy and ecological homes and buildings. Its publications include the quarterly magazine, 'Green Building' (formerly Building for a Future), the 'Green Building Bible' and 'GreenPro', the online eco building database. At the free web forum anyone can ask questions about any aspect of eco building. The information is presented in a user-friendly manner to appeal to both professionals and the general public. The business model also follows the same philosophy and all work is to a strict environmental policy. The offices are in a building renovated to high environmental standards on a farm managed for timber and wildlife. All in-house energy requirements are provided from renewables (wind, sun and water).
www.greenbuildingpress.co.uk

Adam Wiseman & Katy Bryce

Adam and Katy completed an apprenticeship in natural building with the Cob Cottage Company, Oregon, USA. Adam is from the US and Katy from the UK. On returning to the UK they started their company, Cob in Cornwall, specialising in the new build and restoration of earth structures in the south-west of England. In 2003 they won a 'Pioneers to the Nation' award for their work with cob. They are authors of 'Building with Cob' and 'Using Natural Finishes'
adamweismann@hotmail.com

Adrian Birch

Adrian originally trained as a chartered building surveyor and for over 15 years worked in various architect and building surveying firms in London and Bristol, managing new-build and refurbishment projects in all property sectors. He now heads the Building Surveying courses at the University of the West of England. In addition to teaching and research in the field of sustainable design and construction, he also provides consultancy advice to individuals and organisations seeking to design, construct or refurbish buildings in a sustainable way. Current projects include a village shop/cafe/business centre in Brockweir, Glos and a nursery school in Llandogo, Monmouthshire.
Adrian.Birch@uwe.ac.uk

Anita Bradley

Anita has an architecture degree from Liverpool University. She regularly reviews books for 'Green Building' magazine. Her particular interests are electro-pollution and geopathic stress. She is currently investigating sustainability issues regarding the built environment.
miltunes@blackpool28.wanadoo.co.uk

Ben Bamber

Ben is an author who specialises in both clinical psychology and architectural literature, which reflect his interests in a wide variety of other subjects, including politics and religion, as well as works of fiction. He also has an interest in graphic design and computer generated art.
dedicate@blueyonder.co.uk

Cameron Scott

After graduating from a degree in architecture he took some time to find out how buildings are put together. Working for the National Trust, John Makepeace's Hooke Park College and the Centre for Alternative Technology inspired a specific interest in timber architecture. He studied timber structures with 'Les Compagnons du Tour de France' for a year in Toulouse. On returning to the UK he worked for Carpenter Oak & Roderick James Architects for a decade, allowing him to pursue his interest in timber architecture at both a practical and design level. In 2002 he formed Timber Design Limited to specialise in the design of contemporary, sustainable timber architecture. Projects to date include an all-timber restaurant (including foundations) in the centre of London, a new passively ventilated office building for The Northmoor Trust and a studio, along with domestic projects ranging from extensions to large new homes.
cameron@timberdesign.com

Cath Hassell

Cath is an expert in sustainable water strategies formed from a background of 14 years experience in the conventional plumbing industry and 10 years in environmental building. She uses her extensive experience of conventional and sustainable building services to successfully incorporate both water efficient and carbon efficient systems into the built environment, working with councils, developers, housing associations, architects and engineers. She lectures extensively on the sustainable use of water and carbon efficient energy systems, both in the UK and abroad.
cath.hassell@ech2o.co.uk

Chris Laughton

Chris is one of the leading solar engineers in the UK. With a wide experience in all aspects of the building trade and a variety of environmental and ecological projects, Chris is a fellow of the Institute of Domestic Heating and Environmental Engineers (Chair of renewable group), CORGI/HETAS registered installer, SHINE21 trained solar installer and active in the National Standards' committees. His articles are regularly published in technical and environmental publications and he is experienced in the media of television & radio. He also writes regularly for Green Building magazine.
chrisl@effco.co.uk

Chris Morgan

Chris gained 2 first class degrees in architecture at Newcastle University before working both as a builder and architect. He gained experience with Christopher Day in Wales, Malcolm Newton in Northumberland, working on the Earth Balance project, across New Zealand and, from 1997 to 2004, with Gaia Architects in Edinburgh. At Gaia, Chris was responsible for a number

of projects, including the Glencoe Visitor Centre. In 2004, Chris set up Locate Architects to continue work on ecological design projects and sustainable development related consultancy, research and teaching. The practice aims always for innovative and contemporary design, with particular expertise in healthy specification, timber and other low impact material based construction, low energy solutions and a desire to 'locate' buildings more fully into their surroundings. Chris has qualifications in permaculture and building biology and is accredited by the RIAS to a 3 level in sustainable design.*
mail@chrismorgan.fsnet.co.uk

Clare Howe
Clare is a chartered environmentalist with a background in construction. She founded Corporation Green Ltd to help the industry meet its obligations and move towards a more sustainable future. Corporation Green is an environmental consultancy formed to help raise awareness and understanding and offers practical advice and solutions for the construction industry. It provides the full range of BREEAM assessments, auditing and management systems, training, help with legalisation, EPC's and more.
cg@corporationgreen.co.uk

Dave Barton
Dave has worked in sustainable energy for over 12 years, and is an expert on product marketing, project management and policy development with recent experience on utility, local authority and fuel poverty programmes. Dave's interests include building and transport technologies, sustainable communities, natural systems, zero emissions research and Initiatives (ZERI) principles, creative problem solving and helping people and organisations reduce their environmental impact whilst addressing core values. Prior to setting up his own consulting company, Impetus, Dave worked as an associate for the Energy Saving Trust, where he helped to manage the HEC Action programme as well as assisting EST in fuel poverty and other policy areas. Before this, He worked at BRE for nearly 5 years on the Energy Efficiency Best Practice Programme. He has worked in marketing and business development for four private companies, developing existing markets and moving into other markets. He has also managed a number of public and private sector research and development projects.
dave@impetusconsult.co.uk

Dave Elliott
Dave has written extensively on renewable energy issues over the years. His book, 'Energy, Society and Environment', now in its second edition, combines an analytical overview of the policy issues, with assessments of the practical deployment opportunities and problems. In his regular contributions to Green Building magazine he has focused on the latter, looking at examples of successful initiatives and programmes in the domestic housing and built environment field. He is director of the Open University Energy and Environment Research Unit and editor of Renew, the journal on renewable energy policy and developments.
D.A.Elliott@open.ac.uk

David Olivier
David is principal of Energy Advisory Associates. He is an energy consultant specialising in the efficient use of energy in buildings. He has helped to design many energy-efficient buildings, including several with record low energy bills for the UK. He is also the author of numerous reports and papers on the subject and gives regular lectures to seminars and conferences.
dolivier@energyadvisoryassociates.co.uk

Doug Stewart
Doug started his own construction company 40 years ago and has a BSc in building processes. He is very interested in environmental issues and as Director of DGS Construction, has been pioneering the construction of genuinely sustainable buildings. DGS Construction was shortlisted for the Building magazine Sustainability Award and in 2005 and was awarded a Caradon Council Design Award for the construction of an energy efficient and environmentally friendly super–e home in Cornwall. Another recent project was the extensive rebuilding of a 16th century timber frame cottage in Buckinghamshire.
doug@dgsconstruction.co.uk

Gavin Harper
Gavin holds a diploma in design and innovation, a BSc. (Hons) Technology from the Open University and an MSc. in sustainable architecture. He is currently reading for his Ph.D at Cardiff University and is in the process of completing an MSc. in social science research methods (business track). He has also undertaken additional study with both the OU and Loughborough University. He is author of several books, including 'Fuel Cell Projects for the Evil Genius' and 'Solar Energy Projects for the Evil Genius' he is awaiting publication of 'Domestic Solar Energy - A Guide For The Homeowner'. He is a regular contributor to 'Green Building' magazine. He has had work featured in the journal 'Science' and worked with a number of NGO's.
gavindavidjamesharper@gmail.com

Gideon Richards
Gideon has, over the past ten plus years, advised companies, organisations and individuals on ways to maximise their resources and profits as a management consultant. With a diploma in management studies and an HND in electrical and electronic engineering, Gideon started his career as a project manager in the passenger lift industry. He moved on to have successful posts as a regional sales manager and business development manager, before starting Consulting With Purpose in 1996. Gideon currently sits on a number of European Standards' working groups for TC335 Solid Biofuels and TC343 Solid Recovered Fuels and is the chair of the British Standards' Institute's PTI/17 mirror committee for TC335 and TC343. He is on the executive board of The British Pellet Club and a trustee of the charity CREATE (Create for Research Education and Training in Energy). He also writes regularly for 'Green Building' magazine.
gideon.richards@btinternet.com

Howard Liddell

Howard is principal in the Scottish/Norwegian Ecological Design practice, Gaia Architects, and visiting Professor at Oslo University. He is the RIAS Sustainability spokesman and a principal adviser to the Scottish Executive on sustainability. Primarily he is a practising architect with many international award winning projects to his name, but he is also an author of original think-piece articles, runs CPD courses throughout the UK for the RIBA and lectures and acts as a consultant on eco-building and urban ecology worldwide. His new book ''Eco-minimalism – the antidote to eco-bling' was published in 2008.
howard@gaiagroup.org

Iain Calderwood

Iain is a City & Guilds qualified heating and ventilation engineer with 28 years experience in the solar thermal industry. He is a director of Secon Solar Limited, which imports and distributes a range of solar thermal products. He has extensive knowledge of both sealed and pressurised and drainback systems, mostly with flat plate collectors, but also experience of heat pipe and direct flow vacuum tube collectors. He is a director of the Solar Trade Association and, with fellow directors, has represented the association on various technical issues.
iainc@seconsolar.com

Isabel Carmona

Isabel is a fully qualified architect, EcoHomes assessor and accredited to provide SAP ratings. She holds an MSc in environmental design and engineering. She runs CA Sustainable Architecture, an architecture practice combining architecture, sustainability consultancy and research. Isabel is interested in the real outcome of architecture, both in terms of energy performance in use, and the user's appreciation of the building, including comfort. She is convinced of the need for more and better feedback on buildings, and published in Building Research and Information the article 'Architects need Feedback'. Her research in sustainability includes an 'Environmental Management System for Designers' for an architect's firm, and 'A scoping study for developing the criteria for sustainability in commercial buildings' for the DTI in collaboration with the Usable Building Trust and British Property Federation.
isabel@ca-sa.co.uk

Jay Abrahams

Jay was introduced to sustainable technologies (photovoltaics, windmills and anaerobic digestion) as a member of his university's 'alternative research group'. His interest in 'waste to energy' technology was furthered by postgraduate work on anaerobic digestion. He gained experience of a wide range of conventional 'energy-intensive' treatment processes within the wastewater treatment industry. Following a permaculture design course he established his company, 'Biologic Design' to create WET systems; multi-species constructed wetlands for sustainable wastewater purification. His company views wastewater not as a problem to be disposed of, but as an unused resource, purifying wastewater with minimal non-renewable energy use, creating a species-rich wildlife habitat and biomass resource (the coppiced willow can be used in both traditional and contemporary crafts and as a fuel for ceramic and other types of stoves. Biologic Design is a home-based business, which, having no mains services, is run on renewable systems - a windmill, photovoltaics, wood burner and WET system.
01886 884721 ***postmaster@biologicdesign.co.uk***

Jerry Clark

Jerry has had a long interest in matters environmental, developing a concern for endangered wildlife as a child during the sixties. He spent many years as a cabinet-maker, and injected his environmental concerns into which timbers and finishes were used, often turning down commissions where the customer insisted on the use of an inappropriate timber. In the late 1990s Jerry gained a first class honours degree in environmental sciences and put a lot of his new-found knowledge into practise while creating a super-insulated, eco-home on a smallholding in Wales. He also has a permaculture design qualification and a diploma in pollution control. He works on a freelance basis, that includes work for the Green Building Press. He is now in Cornwall where he lives in a multi-generation, eco-retrofitted house with his wife, daughter and father (his son has long since flown the nest). Other interests include listening to music (mostly loud), and kayaking around the estuaries and coasts of Cornwall.
jerry@newbuilder.co.uk

John Garbutt

John has been in the insulation manufacturing industry for almost twenty years and is currently marketing director at Kingspan Insulation Ltd. He has worked for manufacturers of mineral wool, extruded polystyrene, rigid urethane and phenolic insulation. He is widely respected in the field for his technical expertise and has played a major role in the UK government's consultation process for the next revision to Approved Document L of Building Regulations for England & Wales. In his role at Kingspan Insulation, John has been responsible for steering the business into carrying out the first independently certified 'ecoprofile' for any insulation material (via BRE) and the first independent three pillar sustainability appraisal for the manufacture of a building material to be published (using Arup's SPeAR tool). John was also instrumental in the publishing of the ground breaking work 'Insulation for Sustainability' by sustainability consultants, XCO2. With a BA Hons in natural science from Cambridge University, and a masters in earth sciences from the University of Minnesota, John is an avid environmentalist in his private life and has family membership of Friends of the Earth. He is professionally and personally interested in the topic of sustainability and believes with a passion that manufacturers need to be open and honest about what they do, and that they should be responsible about what they make and how they make it.
john.garbutt@insulation.kingspan.com

John Renwick

A civil engineer, John Renwick of Beacon Construction, designed the Maharishi Sthapatya Veda rammed earth walled sports centre in Skelmersdale, supervising its construction. He is confident that interest in the principles of Maharishi Sthapatya Veda will increase. 'These principles can be applied to the planning of towns, regions, even countries as a whole,' he says. 'They offer a reliable way to improve public health, reduce crime, boost the economy, and create a better quality of life.' Maharishi Sthapatya Veda design and planning is being used worldwide for private homes, corporate headquarters, and even whole communities. This summer, Maharishi Vedic City - the USA's newest city - was incorporated in Iowa and is using this system for town planning and construction throughout.

John Sauven

John has been executive director of Greenpeace UK since September 2007. Before that he was the director responsible for greenpeace communications and working on solutions with business. With a background in forests he was instrumental in getting protection for the Great Bear temperate rainforest on the west coast of Canada. It was an epic battle, mostly fought in the market place between logging companies, timber traders and their retail customers in Europe and North America. It also involved pushing the industry as a whole to accept Forest Stewardship Council (FSC) certification that guaranteed legal and sustainable products, now widely recognised in both the timber and paper sectors as the mark of sustainability. It was from the lessons learnt in the Great Bear campaign that similar tactics were used elsewhere, including in Indonesia, the Congo in central Africa and the Amazon. John co-ordinated the international campaign to secure a moratoria on further destruction of the Amazon by soya producers. It involved eventually bringing together a huge alliance of US and European mulitinationals along with Brazilian counterparts involved in the soya producing, commodity trading and food retailing sectors. It was one of Greenpeace's most successful campaigns to protect large areas of the world's last intact rainforests, providing both climate and biodiversity protection. ***info@uk.greenpeace.org***

John Shore

John graduated from the Architectural Association, specialising in ecological design and renewable energy. He was responsible for designing, building and monitoring the 'integrated solar dwelling' at Brighton in the 1970's – the UK's first self-sufficient, zero-heat house. He has been involved with pioneering research, development and demonstration with sustainable buildings and energy systems since the l960's. As well as writing extensively on self-building and sustainable design and running the wind and solar energy company Aerodyn-Shorepower, he has lectured at schools of architecture and worked at Croydon College of Art, Brighton Polytechnic and Somerset College of Arts and Technology. Current projects include designing low-cost, zero-heat sustainable housing and workspace schemes.
sustainablebuildingandenergy@talktalk.net

Judith Thornton

Judith worked at the Centre for Alternative Technology for 5 years, focusing largely on water and sewage systems. She now works part time as a lecturer on CAT's MSc in Architecture and part time as a water and waste management consultant. She is author of 'The Water Book', a guide to small scale water supply systems and has worked on a wide range of small scale water and sewage treatment systems.
info@water-works.org.uk

Keith Hall

Keith completed a three year City & Guilds apprenticeship in carpentry and joinery way back in 1974. In the early 1980s he formed his own building business that included general building, renovation and new housing. In 1988 he became concerned about environmental issues, particularly the use of unsustainable tropical timber. From that concern he launched a magazine called Building for a Future (now Green Building magazine) and co-founded (with his partner Sally) the Association for Environment Conscious Building (AECB) in an effort to promote the concept of green and sustainable building. In 1990 he established the Green Building Press, a business dedicated to promoting and providing information about eco and healthy building. He is now editor of both 'Green Building' magazine and the 'Green Building Bible'. He has been involved in designing, building and renovating numerous sustainable building projects.
keith@newbuilder.co.uk

Kevin Boniface

Kevin has worked at a company called Sustain, an energy and environmental consultancy in Bristol since January 2006, in the role of Senior Technical Consultant. He is involved primarily in carrying out detailed design as well as sustainable energy feasibility and scoping studies for clients in the social housing sector and commercial sectors. Kevin is degree qualified in Mechanical Engineering and worked previously as a Senior Consultant at BRE, managing projects for the Governments Energy Efficiency Best Practice Programme. He has written and project managed publications on sustainable energy, and was instrumental in developing new Best Practice Standards for new housing in the light of tighter Building Regulations.
kevin.boniface@sustain.co.uk

Leonie Greene

Leonie Greene is now head of external affairs at the Renewable Energy Association. Previously she was political adviser at Greenpeace UK where she wrote the report 'Decentralising Power'. Before that she worked at the GLA for the deputy mayor of London.
LGreene@r-e-a.net

Louise Zass-Bangham

Louise specialises in sustainable garden design, particularly integrating house with garden, sustainable materials and ecological planting. Work includes complete design services, rejuvenation and consultancy. Louise is an experienced writer and lecturer. Changing career after 10 years in fashion design and marketing, Louise brings her eye for colour, texture and form to garden design. Louise and her husband live in Twickenham. ***louise@zass-bangham.com***

Lynn Edwards

For four years, from early 2000 to early 2004, Lynn was employed at the Green Shop, Bisley, where she was responsible for the day-to-day running, promotion and development of its natural paint department. During this time she co-wrote 'The Natural Paint Book' (re-released as 'The Natural Paint Decorator' in 2007), and ran some weekend workshops for LILI (Low Impact Living Initiative) on the use of natural paints. In the past couple of years she has increased her practical experience of eco-paints by working as a self employed painter and decorator. In 2007 she wrote 'The Eco Paint Handbook'. ***edwardslynn@talk21.com***

Mark Gorgolewski

Mark is an associate professor at the School of Architectural Science at Ryerson University in Toronto, Canada, where he recently moved from the UK. Mark is a fully qualified architect who has worked for many years as an environmental consultant in the UK construction industry. He has worked on a wide variety of research projects for government, local authorities, housing associations, private developers, materials producers and others, focusing on sustainable construction issues and new technologies and processes. He has published widely on construction technology and environmental issues. Mark is a past chair of the AECB.
mgorgo@ryerson.ca

Michael Littlewood

Michael is a natural landscape architect and environmental planner with extensive experience of successfully designing and implementing sustainable land use projects. His mission has been the introduction of ecological design and planning into the mainstream and is founded on years of practice in a wide variety of situations, landscapes, climates and uses of land for public and private amenities on scales ranging from the residential garden to a village or town. His outstanding international reputation derives from work over many years. His clients have included national, regional and local governments, landowners, developers, schools, colleges and universities, farms and estates. Michael is the author of several publications, including a series of technical books on landscape detailing, covering all aspects of construction, also a Guide to the Maintenance and Management of School Grounds. He has also produced several posters and calendars on organic gardening and a series of brochures covering his concepts of the forest village, forest farm, forest school and forest home/garden to promote sustainable self sufficiency by communities and individuals.
michael@ecodesignscape.co.uk

Michael Smith

Michael is a mechanical engineer and chartered information professional, working for NBS as an information specialist on the information services team. His responsibilities include: an editorial role on the Construction Information Service (CIS) and the RIBA Office Library Service products. Michael also edits and maintains the information content of Green Construction (a stand alone green building website) and Green Construction Round-Up (a twice monthly newsletter). He also writes regularly for Green Building magazine.
Michael.Smith@theNBS.com

Mike George

Mike George has more than twenty years experience in the construction industry, having trained as a plasterer and progressing to building maintenance and small building works. In 2004 he obtained a first class honours degree in Architectural Technology from Glamorgan University, where he is now a part time lecturer in the thermal analysis of buildings. He also runs a small environmental consultancy and is actively involved with research into thermal upgrades of existing buildings.
mike.george6@btinternet.com

Mischa Hewitt

Mischa has always had a passion for the environment. For the last 3 years he has been working on the Earthship Brighton project, a pioneering 'green' development in Brighton to build a sustainable community centre. Prior to this he worked in finance. In his spare time he enjoys playing the piano and composing classical music. He is co-author of 'Earthships; building a zero carbon future for homes'.
mischahewitt@hotmail.com

Neil May

Neil May is the Chairman of the Good Homes Alliance, an association of sustainable housing developers, building professionals and environmental charities and action groups. He founded this group to bring about a step change in the way that house building is undertaken in the UK through the promotion and delivery of very high standards of sustainable housing developments. He also established Natural Building Technologies (NBT), suppliers of ecological building materials and systems.
neil@natural-building.co.uk

Nick Gardner

Nick previously worked as a researcher with Ecos Trust and now works for SQW Consulting as an environmental economist. His work focuses on two areas - evaluations of community development and regeneration projects, and policy/strategy development relating to reducing carbon emissions in business. He has a masters degree in environment and development, and is currently developing a website networking local and community-based environmental groups, called ProjectDirt.com
nickgards@yahoo.co.uk

Oliver Lowenstein

Oliver runs the green cultural review, Fourth Door Review, the annual cross-disciplinary art, architecture, design and craft, new music and new media journal. He co-ordinates the Cycle Station Project, as part of Fourth Door Research. He writes regularly for Green Building magazine, as well as many other magazines. He edits The Fourth Door web-magazine, 'Unstructured' and is working on a book on twenty first century timber-build. ***fourthdoor@pavilion.co.uk***

Olwyn Pritchard

Olwyn is on-line news editor for the Green Building Press, and a regular contributor to Green Building magazine as its 'newshound', summarising eco-building news from around the UK. She has a varied background including some time spent experiencing social housing, community living, low impact living and a long standing interest in green issues. She is interested in buildings and architecture generally, is a competent handywoman and dreams of one day building the ultimate low impact, energy efficient and funky home for herself.
olwyn@newbuilder.co.uk

Pam MacDonald

Pam has been a decorator, designer and lecturer for twenty years. In 2000, she set up The Natural Decorating Company, a company using only environmentally friendly paints and materials and also helped establish The Natural Paint Store in Bath. Her aim has always been to promote awareness of healthy, sustainable products used in decorating and interior design and she has lectured and taught courses in natural paints and finishes, as well as eco interiors. Her current interest is in developing and using low-impact finishes, sourced from local materials such as clay, lime and milk etc. ***naturaldecorating@phonecoop.coop***

Paola Sassi

Paola is a partner of Sassi Chamberlain Architects and a lecturer at the department of architecture at Oxford Brookes University. She is the author of 'Strategies for Sustainable Architecture' published by Taylor & Francis Group, an illustrated overview of sustainable design approaches and technologies exemplified through 60 case study buildings in UK, US, Australia, Germany and Austria. ***psassi@brookes.ac.uk***

Paul Jaquin

Paul is a civil engineer has completed a PhD at the University of Durham looking at historic rammed earth structures. His research looks at rammed earth as a geotechnical material, and the analysis and conservation of historic structures. Paul has studied rammed earth in Europe and India and hopes that historic earthen architecture can inform modern sustainable building practices. ***p.a.jaquin@dur.ac.uk***

Paul Jennings

Paul studied engineering design and appropriate technology at Warwick where he developed an interest in energy and sustainability. He went on to do a masters in energy resources management at South Bank. He has been air pressure testing buildings ever since and has carried out over 10,000 tests upon buildings and parts thereof for a wide range of applications, particularly energy efficiency (both Building Regulations Part L and the more demanding green and eco standards, such as Canadian Super-E housing), checking advanced ventilation systems, testing for fire separation and containment. Paul has tested across the UK and overseas, including Europe, Africa and the Middle and Far East for a vast range of clients. He has also delivered numerous presentations to builders, architects, local authorities and insurance bodies. Specific buildings that he has tested include the AtEIC building at CAT, Sue Roaf's Oxford Solar House and the Nottingham Eco-house.
paul.jennings@retroteceurope.co.uk

Peter Acteson-Rook

Peter developed a keen interest in the environment over many years. After completing two house renovations this naturally moved into the area of renovation and self build. A high interest in green roofs grew after completing the MSc in architecture, advanced environmental and energy studies at the Centre for Alternative Technology with UEL. He has also conducted experiments on green roof run off and is a qualified EcoHomes assessor.
peter@acteson-rook.com

Rachel Shiamh

Rachel lives in a straw bale home called Penwhilwr after self building it with Amazonails and a team of about 200 workers and volunteers. She has been living in the woodland for ten years, growing herbs, making flower essences, jewellery and exploring natural healing. Since self building and project managing her house, she has set up the 'Quiet Earth Project' and started to give tours, consultations and courses in straw bale and natural building, yoga and meditation. She is presently joining Amazonails' straw bale ambassador team and supporting local 'green living groups' towards living more sustainably locally.
www.quietearth.org.uk

Richard Nicholls

Richard is an applied physicist who began his career in buildings as a research assistant engaged in field trials of low energy houses and condensing boiler heating systems. He then spent time in industry as an energy manager with the role of reducing the energy and water consumption of a large group of local authority buildings. He is currently a senior lecturer in the department of architecture, Huddersfield University, where he teaches environment and services to all undergraduate and postgraduate pathways and is course leader for the MSc. in sustainable architecture. Writing credits include the book 'Heating, Ventilation and Air-Conditioning' and editor of the website
www.info4study.co.uk

Richard Oxley

Richard is a chartered surveyor and an independent historic building's consultant with RICs diploma in building conservation. He is RICs accredited in building conservation. He has an active interest in developing the link between sustainability and historic buildings. He lectures widely on this subject and is author of the book, 'Survey and Repair of Traditional Buildings'.
oxleyconservation@btinternet.com

Rob Scot McLeod

Rob studied as a student on the UEL/CAT MSc architecture: advanced environmental energy studies course. He wrote a paper titled 'Ordinary Portland Cement-Extraordinarily high CO_2 Emissions' which assessed the cumulative effects of growing CO_2 emissions from the cement industry and practical alternatives that might help this sector maintain Kyoto targets.
rob_scot@hotmail.com

Sally Hall

In 1989 Sally co-founded the AECB and still works for this organisation on a part-time and voluntary basis. She also works for the Green Building Press. She has many years experience of practical eco-building and renovating, and regularly researches and writes articles on this subject. She worked full time in finance and personnel management until 1996 when she downshifted to live a more sustainable life on a 140 acre farm in West Wales . Here she helps run the farm, which is managed mainly for wildlife using organic principles. She helps care for a diverse range of habitats, including ancient woodland, marshland, traditional hay meadows, orchard and ponds. Her passion is wildlife and conservation and she undertakes regular surveying work for the British Trust for Ornithology. ***sally@aecb.net***

Stephen Letch

Stephen Letch is an experienced full time thatcher and grower with over 33 years' experience. He has extensive knowledge of the four main types of thatch used in the British Isles. He has served as a member/ technical advisor for long straw thatching/growing for the Conservation of Historic Thatch committee. He has undertaken regular thatch consultancy work for English Heritage. In the 1990s he trained a group of thatchers in Eire under a government scheme to improve standards and skills lost and he is currently Chairman of the East Anglia Master Thatchers Association.
letch@masterthatcher.net

Stephen Lowndes

Stephen is a Chartered Engineer with over 20 years experience working as a Building Services Engineer. During this time he has worked for some of the UK's top services design and energy consultancy organisations and has been involved in a variety of projects in both the private and public sectors in the UK and Europe. Stephen has extensive experience in undertaking designs for low energy buildings that optimise the utilisation of natural ventilation and passive solar heating, as well as engineered schemes encompassing biofueled community heating systems, small-scale combined heat and power (CHP) and solar/wind powered rain water harvesting systems.
s.lowndes@ntlworld.com

Steve Allin

Steve runs a successful hemp building consultancy in Kerry, Ireland. He has enthusiastically pioneered the use of hemp in building for the last 10 years & is the author of 'Building with Hemp' 2005. He was a director of Hemp Ireland Ltd. (1998-2003) which was set up to research and develop a hemp processing facility in Ireland. ***steveallin@eircom.net***

Sue Roaf

Sue is currently working as a private consultant with the Green Consultancy and the Carbon Trust, and in research and teaching with Arizona State University and in association with the Open University. She is an author, an Oxford City Councillor for Wolvercote ward, holds a number of honorary positions for a range of organisations and charities, and is occasionally engaged to design eco-buildings. She is Chair of the 2008 Oxford Conference on Resetting the Agenda for Architectural Education and in 2006 chaired the 2nd International Conference on Solar Cites. She also writes regularly for Green Building magazine.
s.roaf@btopenworld.com

Thornton Kay

Thornton is senior partner in Salvo LLP, established in 1991, which networks information about the trade in architectural salvage, an area in which he has been involved since the 1970s. Over the years he has designed and built using salvage and has been a dealer in reclaimed building materials. Salvo has a very active web site with around 15,000 visitors a day. Salvo is occasionally consulted by government, has undertaken several key research projects in the past fifteen years and sits on a few sustainable building products committees. Salvo is a lean, but well-connected outfit of three people, which is currently keen to work with government agencies, large businesses, corporate builders and disaster relief agencies interested in expanding their levels of reuse.
thornton2@salvoweb.com

Tom MacKeown

Tom has spent many years in the construction industry, from design to completion; working as a contractor in UK, Turkey, Switzerland, Russia, Azerbaijan and Ireland. Projects have included restoration of a Welsh long-house, sustainable tourism resorts, dry stone walling, design of a straw-bale school and restoration of a Spanish village house. All of these projects involved the use of natural, local materials and processes learned from local craftsmen, which have been adapted for modern applications and needs. In recent years, Tom has specialized in straw bale and timber-frame construction, developing a system of straw panels to enable precision engineering of straw and widening its potential as a construction material in larger projects. Recent projects include the design of an eco-village in Bulgaria, sustainable tourism accommodation in Norfolk, as well as several residential projects..
tom_mackeown@yahoo.co.uk

Tony Cowling

Tony has run a successful building business for the past thirty years and is now planning on early retirement. He has two science degrees and takes a practical and down to earth approach to problem solving, often thinking 'outside the box' to do this. He has always been keen to reduce both energy consumption and waste of all kinds. His future activities may very well include some consultancy work.
antonycowling@gmail.com

Appendix D Glossary of terms

Absorb: the ability to soak up by chemical or physical action - usually slowly.

ACH: air changes per hour, stated as the volume of air changed per hour/volume of room.

Airtightness: of increasing importance within the building regulations, energy efficient building design should ensure that ventilation only occurs as desired by the occupants, and not through unwanted draughts and air leakage through or around the building elements.

Alternative energy: the use of energy produced using non-carbon resources, e.g. solar, wind, water, thermal etc.

Biomass: this is the organic materials produced by plants and trees. The term 'biomass' is intended to refer to materials that do not go directly into foods or consumer products, but may have alternative industrial uses. Common sources of biomass are; (1)agricultural wastes, e.g. straw and manure from cattle, poultry, etc, (2) wood materials, e.g. wood or bark, sawdust, mill scrap; (3) municipal waste, such as waste paper and (4) energy crops, such as poplar and willow. In some cases, microbial and animal metabolic wastes are also considered biomass.

Biofuel: this is any fuel that is derived from biomass. It is a renewable energy source, unlike petroleum, coal and nuclear fuels. Like coal and petroleum, biomass is a form of stored solar energy. The energy of the sun, during the growth of the plants, is 'captured' through the process of photosynthesis. A common biofuel is commonly known as biodiesel which is used in vehicles. Biofuels can be made from oil rich crops such as rapeseed, linseed etc. Some companies also make biodiesel from waste vegetable oil from restaurants and chip shops. In South America biofuel (ethanol has been made for many years from the distilation of sugar cane.

Biological oxygen demand (BOD): the amount of oxygen required by aerobic microorganisms to decompose the organic matter in a sample of water and used as a measure of the degree of water pollution. (Also called biochemical oxygen demand).

Borax/boron/borates: a family of natural mineral based products which have the ability to protect timber and natural insulation from rot, insect attack and fire (spread of flame) if applied and used correctly. Harmless to humans at normal concentrations.

Breathable sheathing: many boards are now available which are sufficiently vapour permeable to allow them to be used externally on a timber frame and allow vapour generated within the building to pass through to the outside without risk of condensation within the fabric.

Breather membrane: usually paper or a woven membrane which is used to prevent water entry to the construction, whilst allowing vapour to escape.

Breathing construction: a term used to describe vapour resistant layers within a wall or roof construction to ensure that moisture is allowed to pass safely (e.g. without condensing) from the interior to the exterior of a building.

Brown roof: a roof covering comprising rubble and earth which is designed to be wildlife friendly in urban environments where certain species have adapted to inner city living.

Capilliary action/attraction: the tendancy of liquid to rise as a result of surface forces.

Carbon dioxide $C0_2$: this is a colourless, odorless, tasteless gas, about 1.5 times as heavy as air. Under normal conditions it is stable, inert, and nontoxic. The decay (slow oxidation) of all organic materials produces CO_2. Fresh air contains approximately 0.038% CO_2 by volume and rising. In the respiratory action (breathing) of all animals and humans, CO_2 is exhaled.

Carbon index: an addendum to the SAP rating (see later in glossary) which measures the CO_2 'created' in use, expressed as a measure of the CO_2 / m^2 of floor area. One method of satisfying the building regulations re thermal properties.

Carbon neutral: a term used to describe a building design that consumes no fuels that will release carbon dioxide or that uses renewable fuels as energy sources to ensure that the total production of CO_2 related to a building or project is zero.

Cellulose insulation: can be manufactured from recycled newspapers (pre or post consumer waste), cellulose is shredded and treated with borax against insect and rot attack. Can be installed as loose fill, damp spray, or dry-blown to a specified density.

Chlorofluorocarbons (CFCs) are compounds containing chlorine, fluorine and carbon only, that is they contain no hydrogen. They were formerly used widely in industry, for example as refrigerants, propellants, and cleaning solvents.

Closed panel construction: panels built on site with sheathing to both sides (internal and exernal) usually with insulated cavity - often using breathing wall technology and materials. Differs from panels used in typical timber frame construction which are sheathed to one side only.

Coefficient of performance (CoP): an example of CoP; a geothermal heat pump, operating at CoP 3.5 is able to move 3.5kWh (11,946BTUh) of heat for every 1kWh it consumes. This can also be viewed as an efficiency of 350%, which, on the face of it, compares very favourably to high efficiency (condensing) gas burning furnaces (90-99% efficient), and electric heating (100%). The CoP of an air source heat pump may be 2.0 (200% efficiency) at low outdoor air temperatures before its backup electric resistance heating coils are turned on.

***Cold bridge**: a building term used to describe a heat loss path through a material which has a much lower thermal resistance than the surrounding material and is placed so as to create a 'bridge' from the inner (warm space) to the outer (cold space) of a structure.*

***Desorb**: to cause the release of an absorbed substance.*

***District heating**: heat which is generated at a central source and stored either as steam or hot water. then delivered on demand to a group of buildings. Most district heating systems in Europe distribute hot water from 'energy centres', where combined heat and power generation (CHP) equipment make heat and electricity at the same time.*

***Embodied energy**: the energy required to produce a material, through extraction, manufacture, transport or installation.*

***Facade**: the face of a building, especially the principal face.*

***Facultative**: capable of functioning under varying environmental conditions. Used by certain organisms, such as bacteria that can live with or without oxygen.*

***Future proofing**: to design-in an ability to adapt to future trends. this may be in the form of lifestyle trends or the availablility of resources such as fuel.*

***Greenhouse effect**: a term used to describe the heating up of the earth by radiation from the sun being trapped with the atmosphere by atmospheric gases. These gases act as insulators preventing radiated heat from the warming of the earth from escaping to space. The gases are found naturally in the atmosphere but in recent decades, levels of some (carbon dioxide and methene in particular) have been bolstered by human activity.*

***Green roof**: a description of a 'living' roof finish of some kind, usually grasses or sedum.*

***Heat recovery**: the use of heat exchangers to extract heat from waste air or water, and transfer it into an incoming air supply.*

***Hempcrete:** a mixture of hemp and lime to form a composition for laying between shuttering to build walls.*

***Humidity:** see relative humidity*

***Hygroscopic**: a feature of natural insulants such as wool or cellulose, it allows vapour to be 'held' within the material without condensing, and later to release it into the atmosphere. A key principle of a breathing wall specification.*

***Interstitial condensation**: created where warm moisture laden air migrates through the building fabric and condenses onto a cold surface within the fabric, potentially leading to both damage to the fabric, and to an unhealthy internal environment.*

***Life cycle analysis (LCA)**: this is a methodology that identifies the environmental impacts associated with the life cycle of a material or product in a specific application, thus identifying opportunities for improvement in environmental performance.*

***Lignin**: naturally occurring 'adhesive' in wood. High levels of lignin in woods used for some compressed wood fibre boards reduces the need to use synthetic adhesives.*

***Limecrete**: is a mixture of lime with normal aggregate to make a concrete replacement.*

***Local planning policy** – these are also being incorporated into other framework documents, so ensure you identify what the policies are.*

***Low-e glazing**: low-e (low emittance) refers to a metallic oxide coating applied to the inner face of a double or triple glazed unit, and which reduces heat loss through the glass, thereby improving the thermal perfomance of the unit. Can also reduce solar overheating and light levels.*

***Microporous finishes**: usually attributed to paints, stains and waxes, which may be naturally produced or petrochemical based, which allow vapour to be released from the material they cover, whilst remaining impermeable to water.*

***Moisture content**: most natural materials will contain moisture to some extent - for example seasoned timber can still contain between 8 and 18% moisture in use, but at these levels will not rot or suffer insect or mould attack.*

***Natural**: a very imprecise term which is used to describe a variety of products, some of which may have a petro-chemical base, but which would on the whole be manufactured from non-petrochemical ingredients.*

***Organic**: an often misleading term which has come to be a little abused in recent years. Two descriptions follow: 1. chemical term relating to or defining material that contains carbon, chiefly of biological origin. For instance coal and oil are organic compounds as are humans. Organic compounds are often not safe or toxin free as the term has come to suggest. 2. used to describe food or farming methods where chemicals are avoided in the production of food and even non-food crops such as cotton, wood and other fibres.*

***Ozone (O_3)**: a colourless, toxic, unstable gas formed from oxygen and electrical discharge or ultraviolet light. It differs from oxygen by having three atoms rather than two. Ozone is a pollutant when it occours at ground level usually as a result of high traffic concentrations. However, natural ozone at high levels in the atmosphere prevents harmful ultraviolet rays from reaching the surface of the earth. (see ODP below).*

***Ozone depletion potential (ODP)**: the potential for the manufacturing process of a material (usually the 'blowing' of foam based insulants) to release chemicals that are known to destroy the ozone layer around the earth. CFCs and HCFCs are the most common, and have largely been replaced by air.*

***Pascal:** the SI unit of pressure, equal to one newton per square metre.*

***Passive**: a building term describing a structure or component that needs no mechanical assistance to operate. For instance: passive solar design uses the structure of the building and it's solar orientation to collect energy from the sun. A further example would be a thermostatic radiator valve where the air temperature in a room will cause a wax capsule to expand or* *contract, thus allowing hot water to flow or not.*

***Passive stack ventilation**: the use of building shape and design to produce sufficient natural ventilation without the use of electrically powered fans. Stack ventilation uses vertical ducts to stimulate natural airflow due to the 'flue' effect.*

***PPG** – these are the government's **planning policy guidelines**, which give guidance to planning departments and the public on how the government's planning and development policies are interpreted. The revised equivalents to these are PPS planning policy statements.*

***Recycling**: the reprocessing (breaking down and reforming) of an existing material to manufacture a new material for a new use.*

***Reuse or reclaimed**: the reuse of whole and intact building materials in their originally produced form. Often refered to as architectural salvage.*

***Relative humidity**: this is the amount of moisture within the atmosphere, or a material, expressed as a % of the total saturation moisture content that could be contained.*

***Renewable resources**: materials or energy sources which can be replaced, hopefully within the lifetime of the product e.g. timber can be re-grown.*

***Renewables/non-renewables**: material from a source that is renewable (e.g. wood) versus that which is not or which has a finite non-renewable supply (e.g. fossil fuels).*

***Resource depletion**: the specification of certain materials, products or processes can lead to habitat damage, environmental degredation, and rarity, e.g. fossil fuels, peat and Welsh slates.*

***SAP rating**: an energy rating system for housing which measures the enegy cost in £/m² floor area. Now a pre-requisite for calculating the carbon index which is one method of satisfying the building regulations re thermal performance of housing.*

***SIPs**: structurally Insulated Panels, or prefabricated wall or roof elements produced from petro-chemical based insulation boards bonded to timber based boards.*

***SUDS**: sustainable urban drainage system. Aims to reduce the water load on the man-made drainage systems, and to reduce flood risk, by designing the external environment to redistribute rainwater falling onto a site via porous surfaces, etc.*

***Thermal conductivity**: Is a measure of the rate of energy or heat flow through a material, stated as W/mK.*

***Thermal properties**: the characteristics of a building material which define how heat, or energy, passes through the material, e.g. thermal resistance and density.*

***Thermal resistance**: this is a measure of resistance to heat flow given a specified thickness of a material and a temperature difference each side.*

***Unitary Development Plan** – sets out a statutory framework for land-use, to ensure consistent decision making. It aims to secure the most efficient and effective use of land in the public interest.*

***Urban heat island effect (UHI)**: an urban heat island is an urban area which is significantly warmer than its surroundings. As population centres grow in size from village to town to city, they tend to have a corresponding increase in average air temperature, due to the mass of the buildings.*

***U-value**: a measure of heat transmission through a building part or a given thickness of insulating material, expressed as (W/m²K) that will flow in 1 hour through 1 square metre of the structure or material from air to air with a temperature differential of 1°C.*

***Vapour barrier**: usually in sheet or brush-on form, used in 'non-breathing' construction to prevent water vapour from entering the construction. Unreliable due to difficulties in effecting a seal.*

***Vapour permeability**: vapour permeable materials allow moisture to migrate from inside to outside of building fabric in a controlled manner. BS5250 suggests that vapour should permeate through external sheathing materials at a rate 5 times that of the internal sheathing or lining material so as to reduce the risk of interstitial condensation.*

***Volatile organic compounds (VOCs)**: These are organic chemical compounds that have high enough vapour pressures under normal conditions to significantly vaporize and enter the atmosphere during use, application or drying out of a paint or other coating.*

***Water conservation**: the design of water useage and waste systems to minimise wasteage, reduce flooding and un-necessary re-processing to ensure that an essential primary resource remains readily available.*

To advertise in our publications contact:
Jerry Clark on 01208 895103
jerry@greenbuildingpress.co.uk

Appendix E List of advertisers

Advertising policy of the Green Building Press

Advertising space will only be offered to companies whose products or services (in our opinion) offer clear environmental advantages over similarly available products for the same purpose. In particular we will not accept adverts for products that:

- *include ozone destroying gasses*
- *are wasteful of energy or are high energy consumers*
- *contain components that are considered harmful to human health, either by passive or active exposure*
- *are racist or sexist in nature*
- *are misleading or promote/rely on carbon offsetting.*

The product selection criteria used for our GreenPro database forms the basis of our advertiser selection process.
www.newbuilder.co.uk/greenpro

Appendix F List of tables and diagrams

Index

R

S

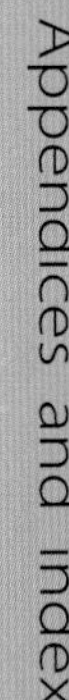